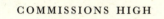

COMMISSIONS HIGH

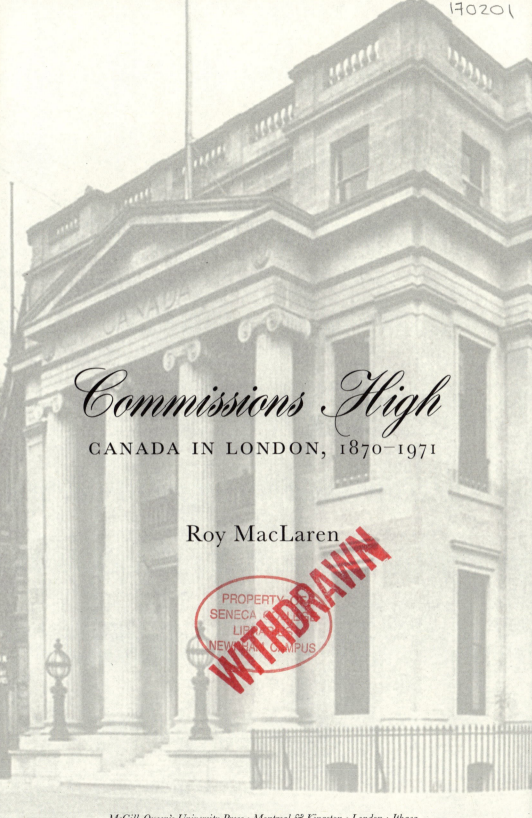

Commissions High

CANADA IN LONDON, 1870–1971

Roy MacLaren

McGill-Queen's University Press · Montreal & Kingston · London · Ithaca

for Alethea

© McGill-Queen's University Press 2006
ISBN-13: 978-0-7735-3036-2; ISBN-10: 0-7735-3036-3

Legal deposit 3rd quarter 2006
Bibliothèque nationale du Quebec

Printed in Canada on acid-free paper that is 100% ancient forest free
(100% post-consumer recycled), processed chlorine free

This book has been published with the help of grants
from the Henry N.R. Jackman Foundation and the
Centre for International Governance Innovation.

McGill-Queen's University Press acknowledges the support of the
Canada Council for the Arts for our publishing program. We also
acknowledge the financial support of the Government of Canada
through the Book Publishing Industry Development Program
(BPIDP) for our publishing activities.

Library and Archives Canada Cataloguing in Publication

MacLaren, Roy, 1934–
Commissions high : Canada in London, 1870–1971 / Roy MacLaren.

Includes bibliographical references and index.
ISBN-13: 978-0-7735-3036-2; ISBN-10: 0-7735-3036-3

1. Canada – Foreign relations – Great Britain.   2. Great Britain – Foreign
relations – Canada.   3. Canada. Canadian High Commission (Great Britain)
– History.   4. Ambassadors – Canada.   5. Diplomatic and consular service,
Canadian – Great Britain – History.   6. Nationalism – Canada – History.
7. Commonwealth of Nations.   I. Title.

FC245.M33 2006   327.71041   C2005-907126-5

Set in 11/13.2 Monotype Baskerville with Hogarth Script
Book design & typesetting by zijn digital

CONTENTS

PREFACE

This book is ostensibly about the high commissioners for Canada in the United Kingdom of Great Britain and Northern Ireland between the informal establishment of that office in 1870 and the entry of Britain into the European Economic Community a full century later. The book soon became more than that. To discuss the office of the high commission makes little sense without reference to the broader political history of Britain and Canada and, to a degree, of the Empire and Commonwealth. Further, the involvement of the high commissioner in domestic politics before his appointment abroad, joined with other more personal factors, helped to determine his individual role and contribution.

The terms of the first representatives, Rose, Galt and Tupper, for example, would be largely meaningless abstractions without reference to a host of post-Confederation projects, especially the contentious financing of the Pacific Railway. The South African War and Joseph Chamberlain's fervent imperial commitment in all their ramifications informed Lord Strathcona's record term of office. Issues arising from Canada's role in the First World War, especially the conscription crisis of 1917, defined not only Borden's premiership but Perley's high commissionership. Mackenzie King's long-held if largely unjustified conviction that imperial "centralists" determined British policy towards the dominions and were a fundamental threat to Canadian unity cribbed and complicated the London years of his benefactor, Larkin.

The economic depression of the 1930s had determined R.B. Bennett on an imperial economic crusade that in the end led nowhere, leaving Ferguson frustrated in his ambitions to place Canada at the heart of the Empire. No high commissioner could have played a more pivotal role in Anglo-Canadian relations than Massey during the Second World War, but King's suspicions of centralists extended even to his own high commissioner. As a result, Massey was able to do much less than he might otherwise have achieved and Canada played a lesser role than it might have done. Even during the immediate postwar years, Robertson was not immune from the anachronistic imperial obsessions of King. Later still, Wilgress, Drew, Chevrier, and Ritchie were all, to a greater or lesser extent, caught up in the convoluted efforts to define Britain's place in the newly minted united Europe, a vexed venture that was to cause controversy into the twenty-first century, and to alter the very nature of the Commonwealth. An account of the High Commission and, more generally, Anglo-Canadian relations should accordingly help us to understand better how we arrived at where we are and where we can choose to go from here.

Under the direction of Ottawa, the High Commission was long at the centre of the kaleidoscope of options. Choices were made, prejudices expressed, and opportunities exploited – or missed. The High Commission at birth was unique, born of the singular status of Canada within the Empire in the immediate post-Confederation period. Given Canada's evolving imperial place, it could not be an orthodox diplomatic mission; it was neither legation nor embassy. During the last decades of the nineteenth century, Canada quite contentedly left foreign relations (although not foreign commercial relations) to the Foreign Office in London. It was not until 1909 that an embryonic Department of External Affairs was created in Ottawa. Further, in diplomatic practice a representative of a sovereign nation (and Canada only gradually became that) was accredited from one head of state to another. Since Britain and Canada had – and still have – the same head of state, it was a logical absurdity for Queen Victoria to accredit a representative of herself to herself. Hence the novel international nomenclature of high commissioner reflected a basic reality: the high commissioner, sent from one government to another within the Empire, was more and not less than an ambassador. He was more in the sense that, by virtue of representing a self-governing entity within the Empire, he had ready access to every level of Whitehall and Westminster that no foreign representative could hope to achieve. The degree of consultation and information on offer was unique to high commissioners, especially during those many decades when the incumbent was a former politician rather than a career civil servant, an advantage that several incumbents believed would have been enhanced by requiring that the high commissioner be concurrently a cabinet minister, as Tupper and Perley were. Borden's thinking about the nature of the Empire might well have included such status; King, in appointing a high commissioner who was neither a former nor active politician, departed from the tradition and ended any possibility that a cabinet minister would fill the office and give thereby particular expression to Canada's participation in the Commonwealth. Nevertheless, the mission retained its preeminence after Britain itself had lost its capacity during the Second World War to play a central role in international political and economic affairs. Something of the intimacy of the traditional relationship remains to this day.

The bulk of the material about the High Commission is in the National Archives in Ottawa where files and related material of the Department of External Affairs as well as of individual high commissioners have long resided. Not surprisingly, there is limited material about the London years of Rose and Galt, everything being handwritten and necessarily despatched by surface mail, and not much more about Tupper. During later decades, however, a range of memoirs matched the growing volume of official records (the bibliography lists most).

To a very limited extent I have also been able to draw upon my own recollections of several high commissioners. The earliest whom I knew was Vincent Massey. My few encounters with him were only brief formalities and certainly did not include any prolonged conversation. So it was with Lionel Chevrier. But with Norman Robertson, Dana Wilgress, and Charles Ritchie, the opposite is true. Both Robertson and I attended – decades apart – the imperialist-sounding General Gordon school in Vancouver. Following our discovery of that link when we first met at a reception for graduates of the University of British Columbia at British Columbia House in London in 1955, we talked later of many things during his occasional visits to the Canadian students at Cambridge University (where I then was) or on my visits to London. He spoke candidly of his days with King (as Pearson also did when we were together from time to time in Ottawa or Barbados).

In my final year at Cambridge, Robertson chaired at Canada House the "oral board" for would-be foreign service officers of the then Department of External Affairs who had passed the written examinations. As one such candidate, I crossed the seemingly endless carpet of what Charles Ritchie once rightly described as the Mussoliniesque office of the high commissioner to sit in front of the panel where Robertson was joined by several other senior officers, including a second Oxonian, Arnold Smith, the future secretary-general of the Commonwealth. At the conclusion of their hour-long oral assessment, Smith, perhaps noting my covert scrutiny of that splendid room, observed with mock solemnity, "Mr MacLaren, if you are so fortunate as to be appointed a probationary foreign service officer, you should know that you will never sit in this room, since it is by tradition reserved for superannuated political pooh-bahs." In the event, it took me almost forty years to contradict his first proposition by becoming an embodiment of the second.

My last conversations with an ailing Norman Robertson were in 1964 in Geneva when my wife and I arranged for him and his wife to have our leased *hôtel particulier en vielle ville*. It was also in Geneva that same summer that I first met Dana Wilgress. For almost four months we sat together, day after day, at the first United Nations Conference of Trade and Development. With great good humour, Wilgress described vividly life in Omsk and Vladivostok in 1916–18, Geneva and Ottawa in the inter-war years, the Soviet Union in wartime, and London in the 1950s, as we whiled away the seemingly endless hours of largely identical speeches of other equally bored delegates.

Charles Ritchie I first came to know when we were colleagues in the Department of External Affairs. Later in London and later still in his unwelcomed retirement in his native Nova Scotia I rejoiced in his inexhaustible instances of the drolleries of the world. But beyond his wry wit was an incisive mind that could skewer the densest pomposity, bluff, or hypocrisy. His urbane diaries reflect wonderfully well the man. I regret only that he died some years before I became high commissioner, so that we never had the occasion to compare our thoughts as we each had stood, so many years apart, in the same place in the high commissioner's room, gazing out on Trafalgar Square. As the Second World War became imminent, Ritchie had "stared gloomily, nervously, out at Trafalgar Square ... St Martin-in-the-Fields and the National Gallery were grey too, so was the water in the fountains – so were the pigeons ... A wet wind blew the water in the fountains in fine showers over the passers-by. A man and a woman with their arms around each other stood near one of the fountains. He bent his head to her with some lover's joke which made them laugh a little. Her arm tightened around him. Scarlet buses supplied the invariable London colour combination and the note was carried out by the red letters of the posters telling Londoners that Civil Defence is the business of every citizen." Ritchie survived the Blitz, as did Canada House, despite several near misses, enabling me in time also to watch a wet wind blow the water in the fountains on Trafalgar Square in fine showers.

Finally, George Drew I hardly knew. In late 1960, at that time a mere second secretary, I was declared *persona non grata* by the Czechoslovak government in retaliation for Ottawa's expulsion of a wayward Czechoslovak diplomat. Following our hurried departure from the legation in Prague, my wife and I passed briefly through London. Learning that we were there en route to Ottawa, the high commissioner's assistant invited me to call upon Drew. In that same great room which I had first known as a candidate, Drew, upon receiving me, launched into a half-hour tirade about the base treachery and various other deep iniquities of communists everywhere. When he finally wound down, he rose to indicate that I should depart, but he did pause long enough to inquire what I had said my name was.

ACKNOWLEDGMENTS

I thank Marilyn Myers and my son Ian for their indispensible help in the preparation of this book. The intrepid Diane Mew was, as always, both an inventive and patient editor. My friend Hal Jackman provided help in a variety of welcome ways during the necessarily long gestation of this book, especially in offering the tranquility of Overdown farm. My wife, Alethea, was again in every way supportive.

COMMISSIONS HIGH

CHAPTER ONE

Sir John Rose, 1869–1880

Although Sir Alexander Galt was in 1880 the first formally appointed high commissioner, it was Sir John Rose who, in everything but title, filled the role from 1869. The devising of the title of high commissioner did not prove easy, since behind the debate of how exactly Canada's representative should be designated lay the larger question of what he should be asked to do. Upon removing himself to London from Canada's rudimentary capital, Rose's personal priority was to make money and only coincidentally to be Canada's representative, but acting informally for the government could be useful to him in advancing his banking interests. For his part, Sir John A. Macdonald regarded Rose's informal appointment as a handy stopgap until he could no longer put off the question of how Canada should be best represented in Britain.

Rose assured Macdonald that he could carry out his official "duties in a way in which his other work would in no way interfere with ... I think I have some claims to consideration ... especially as any other appointment at the moment I went there would certainly be calculated to place me in a false position."[1] During the summer of 1869, when Macdonald and Rose had discussed the latter's intention to resign as finance minister to become a banker in London, then the financial centre of the world, they had agreed that he would also unofficially represent Canada. Conflict of interest rules, to the degree that they existed at all, were rudimentary. Macdonald (who had combined business and political interests) and Rose saw nothing to be gained by forcing a discussion of what title the Canadian representative might best carry, since such a discussion might be misinterpreted by some as a step toward eventual separation of Canada from Britain. The new Dominion of Canada did not seek independence, although at least some in Gladstone's first two governments would have welcomed such a step. It remained legally a colony, whose representative could not be a diplomatic minister or an ambassador. Yet the title of agent or even agent general, which had long been in use, might be interpreted as relegating the Dominion to the status of a minor colony. There being quite enough to do in post-Confederation Canada without worrying about quasi-diplomatic titles, Macdonald was content to leave the question to settle itself in due course. The order-in-council of 2 October 1869 appointing Rose was accordingly vague on the point. He was simply "accredited to Her Majesty's Government as a Gentleman possessing the confidence of the Canadian Government with whom Her Majesty's Government may properly communicate on Canadian affairs." This was the broad mandate without a title that Rose himself had sought.* In fact, the absence of a formal title proved for a few years to be no real detriment in representing Canada's interests. Macdonald knew the designation of "Gentleman" could only be an interim arrangement that flowed from past practices and at the same time pointed to a more formal status for Rose's successor.

Before Confederation, governors and governors general in North America had provided the formal nexus between colonial governments and London. Following Confederation, it had gradually become clear that the evolving relationship of the Dominion with both Whitehall and Westminster required an active advocate of Canadian interests. The governor general would find it awkward, for example, to encourage British emigration, a priority for Canada, when Whitehall continued to exhibit little enthusiasm for official emigration schemes. Further, although the financing of Canadian railways and canals was done largely from British savings, few thought that this was something that a governor general should promote. Military cooperation was regarded as more of a two-way street, but even here the demands of Empire, the price of admiralty, were set by London and not by the colony, however self-governing. On the diplomatic front, many in Ottawa (including the prime minister) were convinced that Canada's interests in Washington would be better heeded if the full diplomatic weight of Britain were to be added to whatever voice Canada could informally muster there. As Sir Charles Tupper, a Father of Confederation and later high commissioner, concluded, "nothing would be more detrimental or suicidal to the best interests of Canada than to divest ourselves of the potent assistance of standing under the aegis of the mightiest Empire in the world."

That standing soon required something more than the office of governor general to act as an interlocutor. Lord Dufferin was to describe him-

---

* A title of a different sort soon came to Rose: he was knighted in the New Year's honours list of 1870.

self in 1877 as someone "[who] merely walks about with a little tin vessel of oil in his hand and [who] pours a drop here and a drop there, as occasion or the creaking of a joint may require." Other governors general would bring various understandings to Rideau Hall, but they all had to adapt to more assertive parliaments and governments as well as the presence of a high commissioner in London. Increasingly they had to attempt to reconcile their "ambiguous role of the Governor General ... [as] a surrogate headship of state with an incompatible role as representative of the Government in Westminster."

The office of high commissioner did not suddenly emerge full-blown: it had longstanding and diverse antecedents. For mundane rather than constitutional reasons, colonial agents had long been resident in London, in the case of the colony of Virginia as early as 1642, but later centred mainly on the demands of Caribbean planters to have their problems more fully aired. It was the British West Indian colonies that had first developed the practice of commissioning an agent by an act of the local assembly from which he received instructions and payment and to whom he reported: in short, the same process that was later followed by British North America, Australasia, and the Cape of Good Hope. Prior to Confederation, the several colonies of British North America had attempted to devise for themselves representation that would meet their individual needs. In 1762 the Nova Scotia Assembly, four years after its formation, had designated an agent. Three years later, merchants in Lower Canada had retained the services of a London lawyer "to solicit at the public offices such business relative to that Province as may be recommended." New Brunswick had followed in 1786. The lieutenant-governor of Upper Canada, John Graves Simcoe, had informed the secretary of state for the colonies in 1794 of the legislature's prudent decision "to appoint an agent for purchasing such provisions as the Province affords." The Duke of Kent, Queen Victoria's father, who knew Quebec and the Atlantic colonies well, had urged the merits of a suitor who hoped to be appointed agent of both Lower Canada and of Nova Scotia. In 1872 it promptly designated an emigration agent. Prince Edward Island formally named an agent in 1902 and Ontario and Quebec in 1908.

The results of these appointments proved to be many and varied, but few in Britain took much interest, some wishing that the colonies would simply go away. In 1849, eighteen years before Confederation, Lord Grey had noted a changing mood at Westminster: "There begins to prevail in the House of Commons ... an opinion ... that we have no interest in preserving our colonies and ought therefore to make no sacrifice for that purpose. Peel, Graham and Gladstone, if they do not avow this opinion as openly as Cobden and his friends, yet betray very clearly that they entertain it."[2] Carlyle satirized the attitude: "If you want to go from us, go: we by no means want you to stay; you cost us money yearly, which is scarce; desperate quantities of trouble too; why not go, if you wish it?" More prosaically, John Bright added, "If they are to be constantly applying to us for guarantees of railways, and for grants for fortresses, and for works of defence ... then I think it would be far better for them and for us – cheaper for us and less demoralizing for them – that they should become an independent State."

The great free trader Richard Cobden interpreted Confederation as "a step in the direction of an amicable separation." On the eve of Confederation, Lord Stanley, the foreign secretary, declared that if the colonies "choose to separate, we on this side shall not object: it is they who protest against the idea. In England separation would be generally popular." With mounting costs in India, Benjamin Disraeli, as chancellor of the exchequer, was even more succinct: "leave the Canadians to defend themselves." *The Times* agreed: "We look to Confederation as the means of relieving this country from much expense and much embarrassment ... a people of four million ought to be able to keep up their own defences." Forty years later, Sir Charles Tupper could recall that "While the Confederation of British North America in 1867 was sustained by both parties in England many public men in both parties regarded it as a stepping-stone in getting rid of responsibility connected with Canada."[3] If any further confirmation were needed of the eagerness of some in London to sever remaining ties it had been reflected in the indifference with which Westminster had dealt with the passage of the British North America Act. "The great body of the House was utterly indifferent ... The House got livelier and better filled when a dog tax bill came up ... It showed that they [the members] considered colonists being so little related to them as the inhabitants of some nameless Chinese mud village."

Given the indifference in Westminster and Whitehall to the settlement colonies, Macdonald knew that the only real threat to Canada was the United States. Ties with Britain were the sole counter to continentalism. Britain was the leading world power; association with it might occasionally cause commercial or other friction, but the benefits were incomparably greater. Sentiment aside, Macdonald understood that early creation of a stand-alone, fully independent nation was a pipe-dream; absorption into the American union would soon follow. The nature of the link with Britain would no doubt evolve, but in the meantime it remained essential.

Always wary of the expansionist nationalism of the United States, Macdonald carefully avoided giving any reason to anti-imperialists to interpret the appointment of a London agent with prominent status as a step towards full Canadian independence. He steered a careful compromise between the advocates of formal representation and those who rejected it altogether on the grounds that the governor general remained an adequate link between the imperial metropolis, with its reserved powers in foreign and military affairs, and a colonial government which had since 1848 been responsible for domestic matters. A more practical consideration was the recognition that access to London's money markets would continue to be more readily available to a colony than to others. At first, Macdonald embraced the suggestion that the proposed federation of British North America would be of such consequence that no less than a viceroy should be appointed to Ottawa (as in Dublin and Calcutta) instead of the lesser-sounding governor general. In the event, however, no such grandiose title was instituted, the last governor of the Province of Canada, Lord Monck, simply becoming the first governor general of the new confederation. As the suggestion of a viceroy was not adopted, the second part of the proposal that a Canadian representative in London should join in the councils of the Empire as a member of the British cabinet was never addressed.* Eventually a more gradualist approach to the question of representation emerged, in part because of the eager if somewhat chaotic solicitation of immigrants by the colonies.

The hostility of some British parliamentarians and officials to emigration and the appeal of the United States combined to place the onus for promotion upon colonial governments. Before Confederation, haphazard efforts had been made by the Province of Canada to distribute promotional pamphlets, setting forth the various reasons why it was a superior destination to that of either the United States or the Australian colonies. Temporary promotional agents had also been appointed in Scandinavia and France, but it was eventually concluded that such efforts had produced little in relation to costs. The several colonies in Australia had been early in their efforts to seek immigrants; during the 1850s and 1860s most of them had emigration offices in Britain. They had gradually evolved into representative agencies in a broader sense, pursuing and reporting matters of interest to their governments. Accordingly, British North

---

* The advocates of this radical approach to the question of Canadian representation were silent on the point of whether, to open his way into the cabinet, the "Secretary of State for Canada" should first seek election to the British House of Commons or be made a peer to sit in the House of Lords.

America had found itself lagging in the competition for emigrants with Australian colonies, as well as with the United States. The challenge was the greater, since many emigrants, particularly Irish, were unaware that British North America existed at all; they were under the impression that the whole continent was the United States. It did not take long for those labouring under such a fundamental misapprehension to drift southward in search of work.

A few years before Confederation, the Province of Canada had realized that something had to be done to win a steady flow of immigrants. A committee of the Legislative Assembly organized hearings on how immigration from Britain might best be promoted. Its recommendations contributed to the province's decision in 1859 to appoint an agent in Liverpool, the principal embarkation port. The agent soon reported that the Colonial Office had made it clear that it would make no effort to encourage prospective emigrants to select Canada as their destination. The Foreign Office, however, would at least facilitate the accreditation of Canadian agents in Europe, instructing embassies, legations, and consulates to assist them in their local endeavours. Agents were so designated in Norway, Germany, and France, all to be somehow coordinated by the modest Liverpool office, and all to attempt to counter the skullduggery of unscrupulous ticket agents.

As 1 July 1867 approached, the conviction had grown that Confederation would be something more politically important than the dismissive description of one Colonial Office official: "half a dozen colonies were but a federated colony after all." In a sense, the official was right, but in practice it was recognized that Canada was not simply the equivalent of any other colony. Another Colonial Office official wrote judiciously, "we now treat [the] Dominion pretty nearly as an independent Country. It consists of nearly four million inhabitants and we have to leave them the whole responsibility and power of managing their own affairs."[4] Whatever the theory, circumstances were moving the new Dominion in the direction of assuming increasing responsibilities. Uncertainties about the policies that a post-Civil War United States might seek to pursue, including that tiresomely self-righteous doctrine of "manifest destiny," made it that much more important that Canada's voice be heard in the Foreign Office and beyond at the international negotiating table itself. On the other hand, minority opinion persisted that no substantial increase in representation was required; the combination of the office of governor general, frequent ministerial visits, and two London banks remained all that even a self-governing Dominion could possibly require. In fact that debate was all but over; Canada was already edging towards more formal representation.

Ottawa soon undertook to "establish and maintain at its expense an efficient Emigration Office at London, and in such other places in the United Kingdom as the Government may from time to time think proper." William Dixon of the Department of Agriculture was appointed Dominion agent for emigration from "abroad" (i.e., from Europe). "It is not an exaggeration to describe Mr. Dixon, with his two small rooms in Adams Street, with two clerks and a messenger as his staff, and with subordinate agents in other port cities of the British Isles, as Canada's first resident agent abroad and as the predecessor of the high commissioner in London."[5] His role was not an easy one, as several levels of government in Canada still had reservations about promoting "promiscuous" migration of frequently indigent, sickly, and illiterate immigrants. Further, the British North America Act had given Ottawa and the provinces concurrent jurisdiction over immigration, resulting in duplication and even competition in immigration promotion. Although each province remained free to appoint its own agents if it so chose, Ottawa decided to place agents in Paris, Antwerp, Dublin, and Glasgow, to be coordinated by Dixon from London. With varying degrees of vigour and cooperation, they attempted to bring greater order to the chaotic emigrant scene by distributing pamphlets, placing advertisements and posters, organizing lectures, and retaining "special agents." Dixon's ability to review their work being limited by the willingness of the agents themselves to cooperate with him, Ottawa eventually decided to establish a higher level of representation in London in the person of an agent general.

Progress towards the appointment of more comprehensive representation, however, proved to be as crab-like in the area of finance as it was in emigration promotion. The pressing need for investment, especially in railways, had long been seen as requiring the expertise of London financial houses, even if their fees were substantially higher than those of a financial agent sent from Canada. Baring Brothers, already active in the United States, had been appointed agent for Upper Canada as early as 1837 in partnership with the bank Glyn, Halifax and Mills (later Glyn, Mills). Both banks were to be closely associated with financial requirements for the next six decades, beginning with the financing of canals and railways in Nova Scotia and New Brunswick and later in the Province of Canada.*

* Eventually a Canadian headed Barings. Sir Edward Peacock (1871–1963), a former master at Upper Canada College, joined Barings in London in 1907. He later became a director of the CPR, the Hudson's Bay Company and the Bank of England and, like Rose before him, a financial advisor to the royal family.

The banks also provided valuable ancillary services: they advised upon a wide range of financial policy questions and arranged ministerial visits, and most of all strove to secure a more favoured status in the metropolitan money market for the new Dominion.

As always, "Old Tomorrow" took his time, but Macdonald knew that a more substantial appointment would sooner or later be needed. He was fortunate to have at hand a cabinet colleague who could fill the bill, but who would not himself raise questions of his exact status which Macdonald had no desire to provoke. The happy medium could be struck by Sir John Rose, his second finance minister and long-time colleague and associate of two other finance ministers, Sir Alexander Galt and Sir Charles Tupper. Rose was well qualified to undertake informal representation in Britain, particularly in the area of finance, central as that was to Anglo-Canadian relations during the post-Confederation decades. As a young man, the Scottish-born Rose had soon become a leading lawyer in Montreal and a Conservative member of the legislature of the Province of Canada. He had accompanied his close friend Macdonald to London in 1857 in a vain attempt to help raise funds for the completion of the Intercolonial Railway from Montreal to Halifax.* Rose was solicitor general and later commissioner of public works of Canada East and a delegate to the Confederation discussions in London. In November 1867 he became minister of finance, at the same time continuing to build his large and remunerative law practice in Montreal. Since his days as a rising young lawyer, Rose had been involved in a range of banking activities. In 1859, at the age of thirty-nine, he had been elected a director of the Bank of Montreal. Within two years, Rose, Galt, and the two London merchant banks, Barings and Glyns, were all involved in the negotiations over the insolvency of the Bank of Upper Canada and the related financial difficulties of the faltering Grand Trunk Railway. By 1866 the Bank of Upper Canada was gone, but the Grand Trunk had managed to sustain its fragile existence partly as a result of government favour. Canadian railway securities, however, never fully regained their appeal on the highly competitive London money market. As minister of finance, Rose became deeply involved in the design of a banking system for Canada, but in the face of parliamen-

---

* Rose was among thirty government members who were reported to a legislative committee as having been elected fraudulently: allegedly "hundreds of Grand Trunk workers, who were not entitled to the franchise, were brought to vote in his constituency in his interest; and $6,000 were spent in bribery in that riding alone." The attorney general did not act upon the committee's recommendations (Preston, *My Generation*, 17).

Sir John Rose was not formally appointed high commissioner by Sir John A. Macdonald, but he was in other respects the first Canadian representative in London to cover the full spectrum of subjects that were to be the mandate of his successors, Galt and Tupper. Upon moving to London in 1870 as a private banker, Rose was introduced to the British goverment simply as "a Gentleman enjoying the confidence of the Canadian Government." Later, as a reflection of his earlier role as Canada's second finance minister, he was designated "Financial Commissioner" until the formal appointment of Galt as high commissioner in 1880.

tary opposition, the government decided to withdraw his controversial bank act.

The frustrated Rose, eager now to be gone to more lucrative activities, discussed with Macdonald during the summer of 1869 how Canada could best be represented in London. In September he resigned after less than two years as minister of finance to pursue his personal financial interests, this time on a transatlantic basis.* He moved with his wife to join their three married children in London and to take up a promising invitation to be affiliated with a New York bank, Morton, Bliss and Co., headed by his American friend, Levi Parsons Morton. With Rose's arrival, Morton's London office was made a separate bank, Morton, Rose and Company, which remained in close cooperation with the New York bank, although it was formally independent.† Thereafter, Rose's private and more official activities became so intertwined as to be largely indistinguishable, making it difficult to disentangle his financial dealings, complex and obscure as they frequently were, from his role as informal representative for Canada. Their complexities were only increased by the fact that he was a close friend of Thomas Baring, a Conservative MP and a principal in Barings which, with Glyns, remained the virtual central bank of Canada. Rose took with him Joseph Colmer, his highly able assistant who was in time to achieve a role in the London bond market.‡

Once settled with his family and moving easily through the City as well as the broader British establishment, including Victoria's elaborate court, Rose set about, with his habitual vigour and affability, the simultaneous advancement of his personal interests and those of Canada. Macdonald's

* Upon Rose's resignation, Macdonald in vain invited Galt to return to the government as minister of finance.

† Rose managed the London bank for seven years, from 1869 to 1876, when his second son, Charles, succeeded him.

‡ Joseph Colmer (1857–1937) was secretary of the High Commission from 1880 to 1893. Born in London, he emigrated to Canada where he first entered the nascent public service before joining a bank. He returned to Britain with Galt and continued as secretary under Tupper. Following his resignation in 1893, he worked closely with Lord Strathcona when high commissioner, as well as pursuing his merchant bank ambitions, serving on Joseph Chamberlain's tariff commission when Strathcona prudently decided that he had to put some limits on his public interventions in what was essentially a domestic debate. Colmer flourished in the City, especially in the difficult placement of Canadian railway bonds through his Western Canadian Investment Trust, but when Agnes Macdonald, Sir John A. Macdonald's impecunious widow, applied to Strathcona for financial help, she found Colmer "priggish and rather vulgar."

secretary later described his "singularly happy disposition and affection-
ate nature" and his "courteous and pleasant manner" which carried him
far in Ottawa, London, Washington, and New York.[6] His interests and
activities ranged widely, well beyond the Colonial Office, although the
order-in-council had made no reference to the existence in Britain of both
Dominion and provincial emigration representatives nor to the longstanding arrangements with Barings and Glyns, no duplication evidently
being anticipated. Rose's vague mandate was given a little more precision by the subsequent enumeration of matters which he should address.
They involved the broadening and deepening of Confederation (including
the discussion of entry conditions for Newfoundland and Prince Edward
Island); terms for the transfer to Canada of the vast territories of the Hudson's Bay Company; promotion of emigration; revision of the banking
arrangements for the financing of the Intercolonial Railway in the maritime provinces; British legislation that would give greater recognition to
Canadian needs in copyright law; transatlantic steamship subsidies; and
relations with the United States as they affected Canadian interests in
fisheries, law of the sea, and trade. He would deal directly with the War
Office and the Admiralty on questions of British garrisons. He would
inform Ottawa at length about Whitehall's attempts to reduce government expenditure; how the Royal Irish Constabulary could be the model
for the proposed North West Mounted Police; how Macdonald might
employ British precedents to defend his use of secret service funds; and
how United States fishermen might be excluded from Canadian waters.

The highest priority for Rose following his arrival was the increasingly
worrisome question of the future governance of Assiniboia or the Red
River Settlement in what was to become Manitoba. French-speaking
Métis were in the vanguard of those settlers who were deeply uneasy when
Rupert's Land, or some part of it, was transferred from the Hudson's Bay
Company to Canada by the British government. Louis Riel, their leader,
demanded and, in Macdonald's view, deserved answers. But before they
were addressed, a lieutenant-governor, William McDougall, minister of
public works, was dispatched to the Red River. Riel's opposition hardened
against McDougall's assumption of office, pending arrival from Ottawa
of the assurances that the Métis sought.

Macdonald, when informed that McDougall was held at the US-Canada
border, telegraphed Rose to ascertain whether the nominal payment that
Canada was to make for the vast Rupert's Land had in fact been paid to
the Hudson's Bay Company. Upon receiving Rose's confirmation that it

had not, Macdonald bought time by taking the position that the British government must recognize its responsibility to transfer the territory in "peaceable possession." In an attempt to understand what was happening on the distant Red River, he despatched seriatim three commissioners, the third being Donald Smith, a senior officer of the Hudson's Bay Company, Rose having determined from the company's headquarters in London that Smith could be made available.

Macdonald was not entirely convinced that Smith was the right man for a complex and even hazardous job. Accordingly, he sent with him Dr Charles Tupper, a voluble and dynamic Nova Scotian MP, to report on conditions while Smith attempted to negotiate an agreement with the Métis and other settlers. Macdonald wrote to Rose that "Dr. Tupper who accompanied him [Smith] from Ottawa ... says he seems to be a very good man but exceedingly timid ... the doctor has told me that he is incapacitated from usefulness by the most wretched physical cowardice." In the event, reconciliation between the Métis, the local "Canadian" party, and American annexationists proved impossible. Although Smith did eventually turn over the governance of the Red River to McDougall's successor, it was only after an Anglo-Canadian force had imposed Ottawa's authority.

For his part, McDougall "returned a broken and discounted figure." He accused everyone in Ottawa of hopeless stupidity. Rightly sensing no future for himself there, he directed his abundant energies overseas. Following an extensive European tour, he attempted to define for Macdonald what an agent general could do in Britain and, more widely, in Europe, especially in the promotion of emigration to the North West. In stressing that "United States consuls and Ministers in Europe are little more than emigration agents and never lose an opportunity to extol the advantages of the United States," he urged that "the Government of Canada establish an office ... in London which, so far as constitutional and political [factors] will warrant, shall also be the official agency of the Government in Britain." Everything should be under the direction of a single agent general. Not surprisingly, McDougall indicated that he himself would be available for the post. The transatlantic ambitions of "Wandering Willy" were, however, never fulfilled. In October 1873 the Pacific Scandal suddenly brought down the government of Macdonald before he could appoint McDougall to London, if indeed such was ever his real intention.

Meanwhile, Rose's continuing mandate was to assist in the consolidation of Confederation, which included the settlement of financial terms for the entry of Newfoundland and Prince Edward Island. The Newfoundland agreement was quickly concluded by Rose, only for its pro-Confederation government to be defeated upon the return of its delegates to St John's. The terms for Prince Edward Island took longer to negotiate, given the complexities of longstanding land ownership disputes and the troubled financing of its rail line. One railway historian has alleged that Rose virtually forced Prince Edward Island into Confederation: he "is said to have undertaken to spoil the London market for the Prince Edward Island Railway debentures," thereby panicking Charlottetown to sue Ottawa for entry.[7] In the case of Nova Scotia, Rose had in 1867 been fully aware of the unhappiness among some Haligonians at the prospect of Confederation. Now he had to work from London to help counter the machinations of those who would take Nova Scotia out of Confederation before it was barely in.

As a former minister of finance, Rose was closely associated with British-guaranteed loans which helped to consolidate Confederation. Well before his arrival in London in the autumn of 1869, he had been involved in their negotiation. Accordingly, he was fully aware of increasing British scepticism about such lending in general, especially when low-interest funds were employed by colonies for purposes other than those for which Westminster believed that it had granted them. In London the urbane Rose continued to employ every device at hand, including his friendship with John Delane, the long-serving and influential editor of *The Times*, to win parliamentary approval for a total of four additional guaranteed loans. He was fully aware of the widespread conviction in Ottawa that perfidious Albion had sacrificed the interests of Canada, especially in fisheries, in the ill-negotiated Washington Treaty of 1871. Exploiting that conviction, Rose managed to extract compensation from Britain in the way of a guaranteed loan for the Fenian Raids made on Canada largely by discharged Irish soldiers of the Union army. He even secured Whitehall's support for the fourth guaranteed loan on the grounds that, as Gladstone explained to an unenthusiastic Parliament, it was the price that Britain had to pay "to be extricated from a false and mischievous colonial policy" that had earlier been foisted upon the unsuspecting British people by the unscrupulous Tories.

Canada's efforts in 1868 to secure guaranteed loans coincided with Gladstone's first term of office, the high watermark of anti-imperialism during Victoria's long reign. Gladstone's Liberal government was supported by the recently enfranchised middle classes, including those who were disparagingly called "Little Englanders" for their enthusiasm for colonial autonomy and free trade, the reduction of military spending (especially in the colonies) and the rejection of additional colonial territories. The chancellor of the exchequer, the foreign secretary, and even the colonial secretary and the president of the board of trade joined in urging the early independence of the major dependencies. Even Disraeli, against the background of the perennial fisheries disputes between Canada and the United States, proclaimed, "These wretched colonies will all be independent too in a few years and are millstones around our necks," asking "what is the use of these Colonial deadweights which we do not govern?"

Parliamentary opposition to guaranteed loans was a manifestation of mounting scepticism about the value of colonies. Delane of *The Times* published a blunt leader on 30 October 1872 addressed to Canadians: "Take up your freedom, your days of apprenticeship are over ... From this time forth, look after your own business yourselves; you are big enough."* *The Times* was not a voice in the wilderness. To many in government the benefits that the settlement colonies offered the British taxpayer remained unclear. Partly in an effort to limit such unproductive government spending, if not to escape it altogether, the termination of imperial garrisons (except in India) was increasingly advocated. Plans were made for the withdrawal of troops from Canada (slowed only by the Red River events). Even a Maori uprising in New Zealand did not deter the British government in its intention to bring home the distant garrisons.

There was no particular theory of colonialism in mid-Victorian Britain. The rebellion in thirteen of the North American colonies had left Westminster wary of traditional mercantilist theories. A century after the American War of Independence, there had developed a widespread acceptance of the contention of the Manchester School that a tariff-free Britain would be better off without its overseas appendages. The colonies, however, showed no signs of going. Their reluctance met with a flexible response from the Colonial Office, a willingness simply to roll with the times, not to impose a rigid concept of empire while colonial thinking evolved. The patient Gladstone contented himself with the definition of

---

* Lord Tennyson, the imperialist-minded poet laureate, denounced this advice as "villainous." He fulminated against it in the epilogue to the 1873 edition of his *Idylls of the King* and received in return the fulsome thanks of the governor general, Lord Dufferin. On the other hand, Anthony Trollope, following a visit to Canada, had Phineas Finn proclaim, "Not one Englishman in a thousand cares whether Canadians prosper or fail to prosper."

colonial autonomy as everything which did not affect broad imperial needs: "Every quest in which you cannot show an imperial interest shall be left to be dealt with and managed by the colonies themselves."

Discussion in Britain about the desirability of early or at least eventual independence for the self-governing colonies found some expression in a parliamentary debate instigated in part by the Liberal member for Cambridge University, R.R. Torrens (later premier of South Australia) who was convinced that the channels for communication between the self-governing colonies and London were no longer adequate. The governor or governor general had become an imperfect agent for the representation of the views of the colonial government. If the colonies did not send envoys to London, decisions would be made by the Colonial Office without full knowledge of colonial wishes. Torrens contended that "The alternative lay between ultimate separation [or] the recognition of those colonies on the same footing as foreign states in alliance as far as regards this matter of diplomatic relations."[8] The debate was not much welcomed by the British government, convinced as it was that time alone would best show the way forward. Lord Dufferin, the governor general of Canada, later summarized the basic Colonial Office approach: "Under any circumstances a discussion on the limits of Colonial autonomy is a very thorny and barren topic."[9]

In the background to the parliamentary debate, Rose, as both the unofficial representative of the largest self-governing colony and a person in whom both the British and Canadian governments had confidence, played a pivotal part. He was asked by the Colonial Office for his advice about Torrens's advocacy of envoys. In three letters from a "Colonist" to *The Times* on 18, 19, and 20 January 1870, Rose argued strenuously for the status quo, aware that there were several in Gladstone's government who looked upon the colonies as having the potential of involving Britain in costly foreign entanglements. On the other hand, in Canada, the Australian colonies, and New Zealand, most opposed full independence. In these circumstances, Rose saw no need for envoys, reflecting Macdonald's thinking as well as his own self-interest. Two months before, the prime minister had written to him, "we have no wrongs to complain of; we are quite satisfied with our position and relations with the mother country."[10] Rose did, however, advance the argument indirectly that self-governing colonies should have the right either to negotiate or at least to veto any commercial agreements directly affecting them. Fully aware of Canadian efforts which had begun even before Confederation to assert a more active role in trade negotiations, he cited several examples to bolster his arguments. These the Colonial Office did not explicitly endorse, but it continued to display empiricism in selecting those of Rose's arguments that suggested flexibility in the status quo: "No British statesman desires the continuance of the connection on any terms but those of goodwill."[11] In his intervention in the debate, Gladstone was notably circumlocutional. It was not his government's policy to bring "about a separation, but of providing a guarantee that, if a separation should occur, it should be in a friendly way ... [This policy,] while securing the greatest likelihood of a perfectly peaceable separation, whenever separation may arrive, gives the best chance of an indefinitely long continuance of a free and voluntary connection." As he often did, the Grand Old Man had it about right.

Gladstone accepted that, sooner or later, the separation of Canada from Britain would come, but it must come as a result of evolution; it should not be forced. The prime minister's statement echoed that of Lord Granville, the colonial secretary, to Lord Russell a year earlier: "Our relations with North America are of a very delicate character. The best solution of them would probably be that in the course of time and in the most friendly spirit the Dominion should find itself strong enough to proclaim her independence."[12] As Granville had done, Rose had foreseen that part of that friendly evolution would involve the colonies assuming increasing responsibilities for their commercial relations with countries beyond Britain. Looking back three years later, Lord Kimberley concluded to Rose's gratification, "As we had given the ... colonies self-government, it was perhaps better that ... we should assume that the colonies knew their own business better than we knew it."[13]

From a personal point of view, Rose was pleased that the parliamentary debate had been concluded without any change in his comfortable informal status. That would only have focused attention on the dual nature of his activities, possibly forcing him to chose between banking and government. He had reinforced his affiliation with Glyns and Barings in his guise as managing director of Morton and Rose and as a member of the London committee of the Bank of Montreal. He was also a director of the London and Westminster Bank and of the new Bank of British Columbia, as well as the London solicitor of Sir Hugh Allan's Mercantile Bank of Canada. Given these and other interests, including insurance, there was never a clear distinction between Rose's private role as a banker and his public role as representative of Canada. His years in Britain remain a notable instance of how public and private interests were frequently indistinguishable in the boisterous financial world of the City. He was careful not to venture directly into activities which Barings and Glyns had long undertaken on behalf of the Canadian government, but there remained ample, even increasing, work for all. Additionally, Morton, a prominent politician in the United States, helped to ensure that Morton and Rose was appointed a fiscal agent in London for the United States from 1873 to 1884, particularly in the highly profitable refinancing of government debt following the end of the Civil War.

Nowhere was the blurring of the distinction between Rose's private and public interests more marked than in the financing of the rail line to be built from Ontario to the Pacific Ocean within ten years, a commitment that Macdonald had somewhat rashly made to British Columbia in return for its entry into Confederation in 1871. That Rose played a role, sometimes directly, sometimes indirectly, in the long conundrum of the Pacific rail financing is evident. What is less evident is the exact nature of his role at any given time. That Rose was a close friend of Macdonald is everywhere acknowledged. Further, George Stephen, the driving force behind the CPR, declared that he "was almost my oldest intimate friend." But Rose had also been vice-president of the Grand Trunk, long involved in its own troubled financing. Not surprisingly, from the day in 1872 that the Canadian Pacific legislation had been adopted, the Grand Trunk saw its eastern operations threatened. It was theoretically a candidate to build the new line to the Pacific, but it was itself frequently near bankruptcy. It had been financed by British investors, constructed largely by British contractors, and managed by a board in London, many of whom had become disillusioned with Canadian railways. The Grand Trunk was clearly in no financial condition to contemplate the additional massive costs and managerial challenges involved in building a line through what was considered the impossible terrain north of Lake Superior and eventually through the even greater barrier of the Rockies.

Hugh Allan, the Scottish-born Montreal shipowner and railway entrepreneur, had offered to build the Pacific line, but in Macdonald's views his consortium was seriously flawed by the participation of several influential American railwaymen, including Jay Cooke and his partners in the Northern Pacific. Their presence in the consortium called into question Macdonald's pledge to build an all-Canadian line, both in terms of ownership and route. For his part, Macdonald's friend Charles Brydges of the struggling Grand Trunk strongly opposed an all-Canadian route, threatening as it might its traffic from Montreal to Chicago. The GTR could, if suitably encouraged, extend its line across the Canadian prairies and to the Pacific, bypassing the rocky wilderness north of Superior by cobbling together a western network of river boats and rail lines based on Chicago.

With Macdonald's opposition to any part of the line passing through the United States in mind, Rose began to work against Allan. He wrote to Macdonald that, although he had supported Jay Cooke's Northern Pacific in the past, he "understood" that its financial position was now no longer sound, hence for it to be included in the consortium would be decidedly damaging to the government's reputation. One historian of the period has concluded that Rose even resorted to spreading false rumours about Allan's consortium "which effectively undermined ... [its] attempt to raise international capital," while at the same time reporting to Macdonald that City interest in the project was minimal: "the difficulty of getting responsible parties willing to undertake so large a responsibility ... [is] nearly insurmountable."[14] Macdonald had to recognize, however, that Allan was the only real contender for the Pacific contract. Hoping still to see, somehow, participation of London money, he wired Rose in January 1872, "Take steps to make known that Dominion is about to construct railway through British Territory," rejecting any line through any part of the United States.[15]

Not surprisingly, Allan found himself unable to sell his railway bonds in London during the few months that remained before the Pacific Scandal suddenly erupted in Parliament in April 1873 and destroyed his project and Macdonald's government with it. Liberal revelations of Allan's freely bestowed gifts – or bribes – amongst government members meant that, dodge as Tupper and Macdonald might, the government had no real option but to resign on 5 November 1873. Its final condemnation was delivered by Donald Smith, the member for Selkirk and resident governor of the Hudson's Bay Company. "For the honour of the country, no government should exist that has a shadow of suspicion resting upon it, and for that reason I cannot give it my support." Others more cynically said that Smith's action arose from his festering discontent that Macdonald had repeatedly failed to reimburse him for his expenses as commissioner during his conciliatary efforts on the Red River.

With the collapse of the Conservatives, the Liberal leader, Alexander Mackenzie, was invited by the governor general to form a government. In the ensuing mid-winter election of 1874, the Conservatives, in Charles Tupper's phrase, "returned a corporal's guard." The arrival in office of the Liberals suspended temporarily any role for Rose in the financing of a Pacific railway. Mackenzie first commissioned Alexander Galt to attempt to negotiate a financial release with British Columbia, but he declined. The new government then sought Canadian investors to participate, but when there were no takers, it proceeded reluctantly to attempt to finance the construction as a public project, concentrating upon the preliminary surveys of possible routes north of Superior and through the Rockies and the linking elsewhere of waterways and a few short lines. Useful work was done, but with the return of the Conservatives in October 1878, the Pacific railway was only a little farther along than when the Liberals had entered office five years before.

On the question of Canada's representation in London, the Liberals demonstrated more initiative, but with no greater results. Without terminating the informal arrangement with Rose, Mackenzie decided to appoint an agent general, Edward Jenkins, a member of Parliament at Westminster, who had family and other ties with Canada.* With Jenkins's appointment, Rose had reason to expect to be cast aside by the new Liberal government, although he had never been notably partisan. His conviction that the formulation of sound public policy was not assisted by excesses of partisanship was evident throughout his legislative career. In addition, he was well known to members of the incoming Liberal government, particularly the new finance minister, Richard Cartwright, who had earlier been a pronounced Tory. To Cartwright's chagrin, Macdonald had appointed Sir Francis Hincks, the former premier of the Province of Canada, to succeed Rose as minister of finance.† Upon being passed over, Cartwright had crossed the floor to the Liberals, retaining thereafter a consuming hatred of his once close friend, Macdonald. Later, with the defeat of the Conservatives, the caustic Cartwright found his reward as Mackenzie's minister of finance. If Cartwright needed any evidence of the useful role

---

* Edward Jenkins was born in Bangalore, India, the son of a Presbyterian missionary who later had a parish in Montreal. A graduate of the universities of McGill and Pennsylvania, he succeeded in 1874 in being elected the member of Parliament for Dundee on his third attempt. Jenkins learned of his election when he was in Canada accepting Mackenzie's offer of appointment as agent general in London. He was more successful as a novelist than as a politician. In addition to his several imperialist tracts and newspaper articles, he wrote a popular satire, *Ginx's Baby, His Birth and other Misfortunes*, and such lurid (for their day) novels as *A Week of Passion* and *A Secret of Two Lives*.

† The Irish-born Sir Francis Hincks (1807–85) was something of a surprise appointment; he had, as premier of the Province of Canada accepted shares of the Grand Trunk while at the same time promoting the railway. Hincks had intended to accept its presidency upon the defeat of his ministry in 1854, but he instead accepted the offer of a colonial governorship, seeing it as vindication of his controversial conduct. For the following fifteen years, he was a governor first of Barbados and the Windward Islands (1855–60) and subsequently of British Guiana (1860–69). Hincks resigned as minister of finance in 1873.

that his old colleague Rose could play for the Liberal government, he soon had it during a successful visit to London in 1874 to negotiate yet another British loan.

The result was Rose's appointment in March 1875 as "Financial Commissioner of the Dominion of Canada," one year after Edward Jenkins had been appointed "General Resident Agent for the Dominion," two appointments that, oddly enough, appear to have been regarded as unrelated. Rose's title reflected the emphasis placed by the new government on his continuing and now enhanced role as Canada's representative in the world's greatest financial market. The future need for additional railway and other loans were foreseen and, in any event, good fiscal management required, if possible, the consolidation of the Canadian public debt into a single instrument with a single rate of interest. Cartwright understood well what an asset the experienced and affable Rose could be; if anyone could reduce Canada's borrowing expenses in London it was he. As part of his now more formal duties as financial commissioner, Rose was "to have the market well watched so as to effect one or two considerable loans on favourable terms," to convert existing bonds to a new series, and "to sell (if we can) a fair proportion of new bonds by private sales of say £200,000 or £300,000 a year ... I should think a person of good standing conversant with the City ... might easily work off a few hundred thousands a year by actual sales of this kind." His mandate was, however, more extensive: he was "to communicate with Treasury and all other Departments of Her Majesty's Government ... in relation to financial or any other matters that may be entrusted to you ... [and] other matters ... which the Government may desire to avail themselves of your services."[16]

Rose was also expected to sell Canadian bonds, a duplication of the role of Glyns and Barings that might have caused friction. He was, however, too agile to allow a conflict with bankers with whom he himself had so long been associated. They had played a valuable part in bond placements by taking substantial amounts themselves; there were currently few if any other banks in London willing to do that for a Canada plagued by economic depression and excessive railway construction. Against this background, Rose, in his capacity as the London partner of Morton and Rose, pursued quietly his own financial interests, floating two smaller loans, earning commissions on them as well as on orders for coinage.

Although Rose's activities mounted, Edward Jenkins was nevertheless made agent general in February 1874. Mackenzie, soon after becoming prime minister, appointed the member of Parliament for Dundee on the basis of little more than a brief meeting in Montreal when Jenkins was visiting his parents. Dufferin wrote to the colonial secretary of his surprise at Mackenzie's decision:

The circumstances connected with Mr. Jenkins' appointment are by no means satisfactory. It seems to have been a sudden freak of Mackenzie's who made him an offhand offer across the dinner table or in some such unpremeditated manner. The Order in Council which was submitted to me merely designated Mr. Jenkins as "Emigration Agent", and for such a post he was of course as well suited as another. It was in this apprehension that the rest of Mackenzie's colleagues acquiesced in his nomination. It appears, however, that after he reached England he telegraphed to Mackenzie asking for the title of "Agent General", and that Mackenzie, not at all comprehending what he was doing and without consulting his cabinet, granted him permission to adopt it ... it is certainly a pity that the institution of a quasi-ambassador from Canada to London should have been set on foot with such little consideration.[17]

From the beginning, Jenkins's two years as agent general were decidedly less than happy for the Canadian government, the British government, and even for himself. A Radical Liberal MP, an ardent imperial federalist, and secretary of the National Emigration League, he had written for the *Contemporary Review* two influential articles extolling imperial federation. As he had already done in various public speeches, he had taken the occasion of his victory speech in Dundee and in subsequent articles to attack the Disraeli government. Thereafter, Jenkins was regarded in Whitehall as untrustworthy, suspected of using information that he had obtained as a representative of Canada for his own partisan political ends in Britain. Being unwelcome at the Colonial Office as a result, he could not adequately fulfil his new role, giving rise in turn to questions in the Canadian Parliament about what exactly his status was. The Conservative senator and professor of law at Queen's University, Alexander Campbell, went to the heart of the matter:

Was he [Jenkins] simply appointed as the Emigration Agent ... or had he a right to represent this country almost in the same way as an ambassador from Portugal or Belgium ... if they were to take the gentleman's own words and conduct, he was far more than an Emigration Agent ... It might be very right and proper to have somebody in England like an ambassador at St. James's from Canada in the same way there was an ambassador from the United States. It would be of advantage in a social point of view, and they would then have a representative to whom Canadians could appeal, who would be a sort of warranty that they would be able to get into official circles, or be able to obtain access to high officials ... Such a representative ought to be a man well acquainted with all the wants of Canada, and whose knowledge on all matters would be accurate ... But such he did not consider the gentleman who was sent to England as Emigration Agent or whatever else he was, for he took it upon himself to lampoon in a very coarse sort of way the Prime Minister of the mother country. He could not think that the present Government of England would think much of the person sent to represent this country in England.[18]

Despite this broadside, Jenkins seemed at first to get almost everything he wanted from the Mackenzie government. During a visit to Canada in late 1874, he induced both Ottawa and the provinces to recognize that his London office would henceforth coordinate all immigration promotion in Europe. He even succeeded in convincing Mackenzie to instruct his ministers that all "communications that your Departments may ... have occasion to have with any of the Departments of the Imperial Government should be through the Agent General." In correspondence with Ottawa, he spoke consistently of "the general purposes ... [of] a general agency, serving several departments." The governor general was far from convinced that this was wise, not because he feared for his own prerogatives but rather out of conviction that Rose was a decidedly superior representative to Jenkins.

Jenkins, as Dufferin feared, was a failure as Canada's first and only agent general. His status vis-à-vis Rose was never clearly set forth and, wisely, Rose appears to have steered well clear of Jenkins, whose problems arose largely from his own inflated idea of his status. Combative by nature, he was soon embroiled in continuing disputes with the Department of Agriculture about his immigration initiatives across Europe. Following a visit to Berlin in 1875, he reported that British consuls were "generally ignorant or indifferent" regarding emigration promotion – not surprisingly, given German government hostility to all emigration. His proposed promotional responses were costly, much beyond the intentions of Mackenzie's government, beset as it was at home by severe economic depression. That depression was taken as the occasion by the Department of Agriculture to reduce its representation in Europe; henceforth the head of the office in London would be no more than an immigration agent, acting under the department's close control. Not surprisingly, given his several ambitions, Jenkins soon thereafter resigned. The superintendent of immigration in Ottawa was delighted: "We have done with all the mock ambassadorial functions of an Agent General. We are going to have [instead] a simple Canadian [immigration] agent under the direction of this Department." The resolution of how Canada might best be represented was not, however, that easy. Whatever Jenkins's several failings, the need for a single representative drawing together all the increasingly varied interests of Canada was becoming evident. And that comprehensive role would also need to incorporate the more specialized services provided by Rose, the financial commissioner.

Jenkins was in any case an unlikely figure to become involved in the arcane world of Canadian railway financing. For a brief moment he did so both publicly and uselessly. When Hugh Allan resurfaced after the Pacific Scandal, he began to promote several shorter rail lines. His proposals for financing were received in London with general disdain, *The Times* condemning any such proposals with the flat statement that, "No amount of argument can ... lead sensible people in this country to put more money into railway projects in the Canadian Dominion."[19] A week later Jenkins waded in with the curious reply that the problems of British financiers arose from them not having sought sufficient Canadian financial participation. The head of the Grand Trunk matched Jenkins's allegations with a claim of his own: the railway, although having been assured of immunity from competition for all through-traffic on its lines, was now threatened with just such competition. Jenkins having in the meantime resigned, Mackenzie asked Rose to concert with Barings and Glyns about inducing the Grand Trunk to stop its public outbursts which had such an adverse impact on Canada's standing in the London money market. Rose smoothed things over temporarily, but the question of railway financing was to remain a bugbear throughout much of the subsequent tenure as high commissioner of both Galt and Tupper.

Rose's skills as a conciliator – and he was a master at the amiable reconciliation of conflicting views – were frequently called upon during the term of Mackenzie's faltering government. He was, however, uneasy about the Liberals' nationalist inclinations, especially those of that pronounced "Canada Firster," Edward Blake, the minister of justice. Blake's ally, George Brown of the Toronto *Globe*, would, Rose feared, attempt to discriminate against Britain in negotiating free trade with the United States.* The establishment by Mackenzie of the Supreme Court of Canada

---

* Edward Blake (1833–1912) resigned as leader of the Liberal party and as a member of the Canadian Parliament in 1891 and sat as a member of the British Parliament from 1892 to 1906. George Brown (1818–80) was the Scottish-born editor of the Toronto *Globe*, a major Liberal journal. Although in the end the US Senate simply did not consider the

and the vain attempt to abolish appeals to the Judicial Committee of the British Privy Council also left Rose uneasy. Another cause for concern was that, beginning in 1875, Galt, nominally as a British representative, presented the Canadian case to a commission on fisheries with the United States without much reference to London.*

Although Rose retired from active participation in his bank in 1876, he continued to serve as financial commissioner upon Macdonald's return to office in the landslide election of September 1878. The economic depression that had plagued Mackenzie's one-term government had lessened support for Canadian bonds on the London market, but Rose nevertheless was soon active in the City on behalf of the new railway syndicate which, following Allan's débâcle, had taken up the challenge of completing the transcontinental line. Rose's other activities continued to range over a remarkable spectrum, from obtaining club membership for Macdonald in the Athenaeum to ensuring that British health regulations were not employed to exclude the import of Canadian cattle. Later, his ability to move easily through the City was reflected in his valued participation in the preparatory committee for the Colonial and Indian Exhibitions and on royal commissions on copyright and on extradition.

During the eleven years between his informal designation in 1869 and Ottawa's decision to appoint a full-time, salaried high commissioner, Rose had amply demonstrated to both the British and Canadian governments the value of a representative performing duties well beyond the scope of those once performed by the governor general, yet not in conflict with his prerogatives. His success in bridging a change of government in Ottawa was in part the result of his personal qualities, experience and skills, qualities which the agent for the Australian colony of Victoria had observed closely. In writing to his premier, he noted that "Half the secret of the

---

draft trade agreement before its adjournment, Mackenzie could at least console himself with the thought that, "Whether we obtain the Treaty or not, we have gained this great advantage that the Yankees know now the Canadians are able to do their negotiating effectively, and that the days of English poltroonery and blundering is [sic] over on this continent" (Mackenzie to Mrs. George Brown, 29 June 1874, quoted in Waite, *Thompson*, 207).

* Alexander Mackenzie was determined that Galt should have a free hand in the fisheries negotiations: "I told them frankly [the British ministers whom he had seen in London during the summer of 1875] we were all but ruined from first to last by English diplomacy and treaty making, and we would have no more of it at any price" (Mackenzie to Galt, 15 July 1875, quoted in Skelton, *Galt*, 502–3).

good understanding with the Dominion [of Canada] is the admirable manner in which they [*sic*] are represented here by Sir John Rose, who is treated with as much confidence both by the Colonial Government and the Colonial Office as if he were a formally accredited Minister." Lord Granville, the secretary of state for the colonies, so regarded him: "the presence of Sir John Rose has been of great use and comfort to me. It is impossible to have an abler or more pleasant man with whom to transact business." The need, however, was increasingly clear that such a pivotal role in Anglo-Canadian relations must be played by someone who was unambiguously and comprehensively designated as representative of Canada.

Jenkins as agent general had clearly not filled the bill, partly as a result of his awkward efforts to advance his own political and other interests. William Annand, a former premier of Nova Scotia, had succeeded Jenkins as agent, but he was eminently unsuitable, given his conviction that Confederation was "hateful and obnoxious." The Quebec agent was astonished: "I was disgusted with his conduct and regarded him as a useless, meddlesome man who was dangerous to Canada. I could not believe that such a man would be named agent. He spoke in the rudest manner of the Government at Ottawa, Confederation and everything Canadian. He should not be allowed to represent the people whom he despises publicly." Not surprisingly, when Macdonald returned to office in 1878, Annand's services – whatever they were – were promptly terminated. The way was now clear for the appointment of a comprehensive and full-time Canadian representative of eminent status. Rose had acted as *de facto* but not *de jure* high commissioner. The devious McDougall had never even made it to London. Jenkins's judgment had been spectacularly weak. Annand was quite hopeless. It was clearly time for major change. The convergence of various government interests in Britain led inescapably to the conclusion that a single representative of enhanced status must be appointed. A year after regaining government, Macdonald finally acted.

CHAPTER TWO

Sir Alexander Galt, 1880–1883

Upon returning to office in October 1878, Macdonald led a government pledged to development through economic nationalism, an ambitious programme that at every major point directly or indirectly involved Britain. For the first year of the new government, Sir John Rose continued to fill the representational gap in London. He again performed a variety of services for his former colleagues, including financial and emigration, but he realized that the informal representation of the past could not continue indefinitely. In several speeches in 1875, Macdonald had underlined his conviction that the ties between Britain and the settlement colonies were no longer those between a metropolitan power and dependencies but rather between a central power and associate (or "auxiliary") nations. For him, the evolving nature of the Empire made impracticable an imperial parliament. Canada and the other "auxiliary kingdoms" would instead be separate nations ranged about the mother country with a monarch in common. The link with Britain would remain essential, in part as a counter to territorial ambitions from south of the long and porous border.

At the centre of Macdonald's "National Policy" were tariff increases intended to shelter manufacturing as well as to raise revenue – a policy fully familiar to finance minister Galt from pre-Confederation days, but seen by Gladstone's Liberals as a betrayal of an Empire mainly defined by free trade. Canada's protective tariffs were one more reason why several among them wanted to be rid of the trouble and expense of colonies. Although some at Westminster talked of attempting to override the protectionist tariff policies of the colonies, Gladstone wrote to the new governor general, the young Lord Lorne,* that nothing but the "gentlest

---

* Lord Lorne (1845–1914), the future Duke of Argyll, was governor general from 1878 to 1883 and was, in Macdonald's view, "a right good fellow and a good Canadian." His marriage to Princess Louise, Queen Victoria's fretful daughter, was an uneasy one, perhaps in part the result of Lorne's eccentric character. Queen Victoria recorded sadly that her

advice" could be offered by Britain if its self-governing colony chose to stray into the morass of protectionism. "Every one here I think feels that it is a hard case on this Mother Country, poor old lady, to have her products taxed by her offspring ... I do not see what we, or you, can do except by the gentlest advice, and watchfulness for opportunities to give it."[1]

By 1878 the recognition had deepened in Ottawa that Canadian ambitions required something more than the informal or limited representation of Rose in London if the North West was to be settled and industry promoted with British assistance (in part by an imperial tariff preference if Westminster would ever agree to one). The requirement for a formal representative was also prompted by the need to ensure that in treaty-making full recognition was given by the Foreign Office to the interests of Canada.

Galt discussed with Macdonald his conviction that a resident representative, with quasi-diplomatic status, should represent all interests in London – financial, immigration, military, trade or whatever – and thereby assert a status that would in turn ensure a freer hand in commercial negotiations. Macdonald was receptive both to Galt's arguments and to his growing ambition to have the appointment. Since Galt's condemnations during the Pacific Scandal, it was hardly surprising that their friendship had so cooled that Macdonald was pleased at the prospect of seeing him somewhere other than in Canada. A delegation of the prime minister, the minister of finance, Leonard Tilley, the minister of railways and canals, Charles Tupper, and Galt sailed for Britain in June 1879 to attempt to raise loans to retire debt and simultaneously to explore the complex question of how a transcontinental railway might be financed by private capital and an imperial tariff preference created, but the delegation also carried with it Galt's proposals for representation of a more exalted status – what he named a "legation" – headed by a person capable of conducting continuing consultation.

In August, after exploring the matter with his acquiescent friend Rose, Macdonald presented to the colonial secretary a memorandum signed by himself, Tilley and Tupper, but prepared by Galt. In making the case for "an extension of more formal relations," the memorandum argued that Canada was a trustee in North America for the whole Empire, thereby

childless daughter had "a perfect aversion" to her husband. Princess Louise – "Her Canadian Majesty" – spent only limited periods in Canada. In later years, the then Duke of Argyll and the princess were in effect separated (even the proposals to make the Duke the King of Romania or, later, governor general of Australia did not bring them together).

countering in advance the response that a more formal relationship should only be a step in the direction of independence, a step that would have recommended itself to Gladstone's government. The memorandum listed several instances of direct Canadian interest in international negotiations, especially with the United States, as illustrative of the need for daily contact in London by a representative whose exalted standing would be reflected in his title and the recognition accorded him. Galt was clear about what "the dignity of the office" needed: the representative must be a member of the Privy Council for Canada and carry a "more expressive title than that of Agent General"; he should be Resident Minister. Such a title would give "the Canadian representative a quasi-diplomatic position at the Court of St. James's, with the social advantages of such a rank and position."[2] Macdonald soon added that the mission must be seen as something more than an emigration and financial agency. "The Minister" must have primarily a political role, to be confirmed by participation in commercial treaty negotiations.[3]

Galt's memorandum opened a lively discussion between the Foreign and Colonial Offices about the pretensions of the new Dominion, but after a further exchange with the Canadian government, it was finally agreed that the diplomatic title of minister should be foregone in favour of "High Commissioner" ("High" to distinguish the office from a mere commissioner of whatever sort).* On the question of title, Macdonald was much more relaxed than Galt. He had written to the governor general, Lorne: "It seems to me that it is a matter of no importance to the Imperial Government what title we may give our Agent. We might call him Nuncio or Legate or Latere Gubernatoris if we pleased ... Why not give at once what some day must be conceded, the name of Resident [cabinet] Minister?"[4] As "a good Canadian" – Macdonald's phrase – Lorne in turn waded in on behalf of Ottawa, triggering an exchange of letters with Lord Salisbury, the formidable foreign secretary, who was sceptical about the constitutional proprieties of such an appointment. In late September 1879, upon the return of Macdonald and his colleagues to Ottawa, Lorne wrote to Salisbury that Galt's appointment had been hailed by opposition as well as by government, "a concurrence of opinion very rare in Canadian

* The title of high commissioner was not novel to the Foreign Office; for example, it had itself in 1877 so designated the British representative in the western Pacific and in 1878 the representative in Cyprus. New Zealand appointed a high commissioner in Britain in 1905, Australia in 1910, and South Africa in 1911.

politics." As resident minister (sitting in either the House of Commons or the Senate), Galt should be included "in treaty arrangements ... in all matters concerning Canadian Trade and Commerce ... Among sensible men here there is no wish to conduct negotiations separately, but only that the interests of what Sir J. Macdonald calls this 'Auxiliary Kingdom of the British Empire' be pushed as an integral part of the whole."[5] Salisbury was not at all convinced. He replied austerely to Lorne in terms which in part recalled Disraeli's description of him as "a great master of jibes and flaunts and jeers":

[Britain's] connection with them in respect to internal affairs is so faint that it has almost disappeared. In respect to external affairs it is kept alive by the one solid and palpable fact that if they are attacked England must defend them. A necessary corollary of this liability is that England must decide what their foreign policy shall be. It would not therefore be possible to concur in any formal act recognizing that they have a foreign policy of their own. If a foreign state makes a treaty with England affecting Canada, England is bound to see that the treaty is executed; but if the foreign state makes a treaty with Canada direct, independently of England, it is obvious that no such liability can attach to the English Government.

Of course we shall be very glad to see Sir Alexander Galt at the Foreign Office, and to extract from him all the information he is able to give us, and to consult him on all suitable occasions.[6]

The governor general, however, would not capitulate to the foreign secretary's relentless logic. He offered instead compromise language that eventually carried the day.

The Canadian Ministers quite acknowledge the force of the remark that no foreign power can deal with a hydra-headed Foreign Office, and are quite ready to acknowledge the advantage of working through trained Diplomats representing the power of a great Empire, but they want assurance that these men shall work for their interests as they do for those of their own British Isles. The desire for rank comes from a fear that unless recognized position be given to their man he may not only not be respected by foreigners, but may also be slighted by Britishers, and the interests he represents be not strongly backed.

If the favours given to Canada and to Britain by foreign nations be different on account of the difference in Tariffs, the same treaty may surely settle the terms accorded to Mother Country and Colony, a schedule giving the differing Tariff rates accorded by foreigners to each.

Sir J. Macdonald professes himself satisfied and so do the others, if the Commissionership carry with it the power to know what is going on. If these essentials, proper backing and equal opportunities be given, we may hope to keep public men here content with the present system.[7]

Both the Colonial and the Foreign Offices finally agreed in late November to the title of high commissioner to act "as Resident Canadian Minister."

The office of high commissioner was launched on its uncertain course by the speech from the throne of 12 February 1880, read by Lord Lorne. The following day, when Alexander Mackenzie, leader of the opposition, welcomed the appointment "of an agent residing in the vicinity of Her Majesty's Government," he recalled Macdonald's opposition to his own efforts when prime minister to appoint an agent general. Other Liberals, however, ridiculed the appointment of what they called "a quasi-ambassador to Europe," susceptible to the wiles of the Colonial Office. His presence might even confirm an unduly subordinate role for Canada in the Empire. "It is nonetheless ironic that the Liberals, advocates at that time of commercial autonomy and of permanent, independent representation, should have been so utterly opposed to the creation of the post that was to advance both causes considerably."[8]

Rose had already been told by Macdonald that a more comprehensive representation was now required. His response was equitable: "I have thought a good deal as to how the object you desire is to be attained, namely preserving my status with regard to Canadian affairs without rendering Galt powerless in public estimation and ... without impairing his usefulness ... I can only assure you that wherever the government may indicate a desire for my cooperation it will be given loyally and cordially."[9] He had reservations, however, about the qualifications of his outspoken former colleague Galt to be the incumbent: "confidence and the willingness to participate in financial operations are here so much matters of personal relation and of such slow growth that it is not easy to estimate the effect." Rose agreed to continue as financial commissioner until the government believed that it could dispense with his services altogether. The reason why he took such a detached view was that he had retired from his bank two years before. There was no longer much personal benefit to be gained from continuing as financial commissioner.*

---

* From 1883 until his death on 24 August 1888, Rose was a principal financial advisor to the Prince of Wales, in his capacity as receiver general of the Duchy of Lancaster. He died while deer stalking in Scotland. Of his three Eton-educated sons, one succeeded

Before the new post of high commissioner could be formally launched with a parliamentary debate and a vote, Galt had not only told Macdonald that he fully expected to be the first appointee, but had made his wishes known publicly in an effort to ensure greater certainty. Even a farewell dinner had been held for him in Montreal before the formal announcement was made.* Without waiting for parliamentary approval, Galt and his family sailed from Halifax on 29 March 1880. Three days later, the debate began in the Canadian House of Commons. It was largely perfunctory, Macdonald recommending the value of having "a resident Minister" with a status "among the corps diplomatique which has not ... been accorded to any portion of Her Majesty's Empire."[10] The Liberals for the most part contented themselves with asking such rhetorical questions as why the appointment was required when Rose could continue to provide the necessary representation. The debate lasted less than a day, the bill being approved on 29 April by a substantial majority and receiving royal assent on 7 May 1880. Meanwhile, Galt, being a man of energy and determination, was already at work in London, his place of birth.

When Alexander Galt, the youngest of three sons, was born in London in 1817, his father, the writer John Galt, was already thirty-eight years old, prospering erratically in his London business ventures but noted more for his lives of Wolsey and Byron (with whom he had travelled in Asia Minor) and such novels as *The Entail*, *The Ayrshire Legatees*, and pre-eminently *Annals of the Parish*. When Alexander was eleven years old, John Galt had taken his family to Montreal and later to York where he played a leading role in the Canada Land Company. The family remained for not much more than two years in the Canadas, but Alexander Galt returned in 1835 to work as a junior clerk for the British American Land Company, organized to develop lands in the eastern townships of Lower Canada. Galt soon rose to be commissioner of the company at the age of twenty-seven. He helped to promote the St Lawrence and Atlantic Railway from Montreal to ice-free Portland, Maine, but the difficulties of railway financing and construction contributed to his understandable conviction that Britain was fundamentally uninterested in its overseas settlements. The

him at the bank and a second became a prominent Liberal member of Parliament (until his death in 1913 "from the effects of an aeroplane flight"). Two grandsons died within six weeks of each other in the South African War.

* Sir John A. Macdonald himself had intended to attend the dinner as an additional indication of the importance that he attached to the new office, but illness or some other indisposition forced his cancellation.

repeal of the Corn Laws in 1846 had phased out the tariff preference for agricultural products from British North America. Worse, the granting of responsible government in Lower Canada was seen as another transfer of power to French Canadians, leaving some Anglo-Montreal merchants feeling abandoned by their mother country. Further, if Britain remained unwilling to forego free trade to make an imperial tariff preference possible, Galt was willing to contemplate annexation by the United States. He accordingly joined John Rose and the future prime minister John Abbott in signing the 1849 manifesto recommending annexation (paradoxically the same year that he first took the oath of allegiance to the Queen as a member in the Lower Canada Assembly). Abbott later dismissed the annexation manifesto as the protest of those who had no "more serious idea of seeking annexation than a petulant child who strikes his nurse has of deliberately murdering her." But Galt never quite shook off the stigma of his youthful exasperation.

From the penumbra of Galt's various financial and political manoeuvrings (the political often intended to support the financial), two additional facts eventually emerged. First, Galt, already knowledgeable regarding emigration promotion, became even more committed as a consequence of his railway enterprises. Without railways there would be little settlement, but without settlement there would be little need for railways. Second, with railway investment coming largely, if sporadically, from London, he had from 1845 became something of a transatlantic commuter, developing a close association with Barings and Glyns who were to remain involved in the financing of the Grand Trunk and other rail lines over the next several decades.

Galt was elected to the Assembly of the Province of Canada in 1849, an assembly that embodied Britain's grant of self-government to the former colonies of Upper and Lower Canada, but in which relations between French and English had remained difficult. After nine years of observation and reflection in the uneasy single legislature, Galt delivered himself of his solution: a federation of all the colonies of British North America and its subsequent incorporation of the vast lands of the North West. His advocacy became even more vocal upon the formation of the Cartier-Macdonald government of 1857 in which he was inspector general (minister of finance). For the next decade, Galt would be an imaginative, forceful, and persistent advocate of Confederation.

In his ministerial capacity, Galt affirmed the right of the Province of Canada to decide "the mode and extent to which taxation will be imposed" and by his tariff increases implicitly rejected Empire-wide free trade,

The notably intelligent and experienced but prickly Sir Alexander Galt was Canada's first minister of finance as well as first high commissioner. He was restless and impatient in London and ambiguous in his support for the railway to be built to the Pacific by George Stephen and his cousin Donald Smith (later Lord Strathcona), but he did place the office of high commissioner on a firm basis.

creating a precedent that would complicate imperial relations in the decades ahead. His tariff policy he described as "properly known as incidental protection though it might [have] more appropriately been termed modified free trade," but free-trade Britain regarded it as additional evidence of the uselessness of colonies. In a lively pamphlet, *Canada; 1849–1859*, Galt took the high road, "The future may change our political relations, but I feel sure [that] the day will never arise when Canada will withhold her support, however feeble it may be, from Great Britain, in any contest for the maintenance of her own position as the foremost champion of civil and religious liberty." More tangibly, with his eye on additional market access to the south, Galt visited Washington in 1861 to explore closer economic ties with the United States. Against the background of the *Trent* affair, the first year of the US Civil War was not a propitious moment. Instead of engaging in detailed trade discussions, President Lincoln took Galt to see "the lines of the army across the Potomac," an experience that gave him much to reflect upon.

As an ardent advocate of Confederation, Galt's transatlantic crossings became yet more frequent. In 1858 he was in London for three months with George-Etienne Cartier to discuss the terms of the withdrawal of the Hudson's Bay Company from the North West and the further financing of the Grand Trunk. He stayed twice with the colonial secretary and his frequent correspondent, Sir Edward Bulwer-Lytton, was received at court by Queen Victoria, and met both Gladstone and Disraeli.* In 1865 and again in 1867, when he was with Macdonald in London for the final discussions about Confederation, Galt was again received by the Queen and Gladstone and called upon Palmerston, everywhere expounding his conviction that "the question is simply one of Confederation ... or of ultimate absorption into the United States."

No one, not even Rose, knew better than Galt the scope and nature of British investment and loans in Canada. Widely regarded as the financial Father of Confederation, Galt was invited by Macdonald to become Canada's first minister of finance. The fiscal problems of the new Dominion were, after all, somewhat the same as those of the Province of Canada, if a little larger. Although Galt moved decisively to establish fiscal autonomy, including the introduction of an industrial tariff, the Liberal *Globe* was not impressed: "He has not the courage of a mouse, nor has he the sense of

---

* Sir Edward Bulwer-Lytton (1803–73) was colonial secretary, 1858–9. He was better known as the author of popular romances and periodical articles.

right and desire for the people's good ... He is a jobber at heart; the benefit of the people is his last thought in considering a public question."[11]

Galt was knighted in 1869 for services to Canada and, more broadly, to the Empire as author of the financial texts of Confederation. Before receiving the honour, however, he had acknowledged to the governor general, "I regard the Confederation of the British North American provinces as a measure which must ultimately lead to their separation from Great Britain."[12] That separation must, however, be at Canada's timing. It was not for Britain to decide. He wrote to his wife from London while attending the Confederation discussions, "I am more than ever disappointed at the tone of feeling here as to the Colonies. I cannot shut my eyes to the fact that they want to get rid of us."[13] Lord Granville, the colonial secretary was infinitely flexible. He confirmed that "Her Majesty's Government value the existing relationship ... while it is valued by the Canadians, and while it is useful to the Canadians. They have no desire to maintain it for a single year after it has become injurious or distasteful to them."[14] The governor general was guided by the accommodating attitude of the colonial secretary, proclaiming in turn to the Canadian people that they were "in reality independent," leaving them to decide whether they wished to retain the connection with Britain "or in due time in the maturity of the Dominion to change it for some other form of alliance."

Galt did not last long as Canada's first finance minister. He resigned after only four months. A journalist later wrote about his resignation, "there has always been an air of mystery as to the cause. Sir John Rose, who succeeded him, told friends that he found the business of the Department [of Finance] in ragged shape, a fact which might indicate irresolution for some time. The correspondence subsequently made public shows that he resented the refusal of his colleagues to go to the rescue of the Commercial Bank, in which he was heavily interested."[15] After a few uneasy years on the backbenches, Galt left politics in Ottawa to pursue from Montreal his increasingly lucrative if uneven business interests, including advocacy of the Grand Trunk constructing a rail line to the Pacific partly through the United States. Having declined Macdonald's offer of reappointment as minister of finance upon Rose's departure for London, Galt's relations with Macdonald, never entirely happy, deteriorated to the point that the prime minister wrote in relief to Rose, "Galt came out ... formally in opposition, and relieved me of the difficulty connected with him ... he is now finally dead as a Canadian politician."[16]

Macdonald was correct in his forecast: Galt never returned to Parliament, refusing a nomination to a safe Conservative seat in the election

of 1873, following the Pacific Scandal. He continued, however, to undertake specific tasks for the governments of both Mackenzie and Macdonald, including complex trade negotiations with Spain regarding Cuba
and Puerto Rico and with France over a tariff dispute. He went again to
Washington to explore the possibilities of the renewal of tariff reciprocity. In his quasi-diplomatic role, Galt continued to see Confederation as a
way station en route to full independence within the Empire, an attitude
which led Tupper to denounce him in the House of Commons for his "disloyalty." Macdonald himself had misgivings about Galt's enthusiasms and
his shrewd but impulsive and volatile nature. On learning of Galt's ambition to be head of a Grand Trunk line to the Pacific, he described him as
"unstable as water, and no one can depend upon continuous exertion in
one direction with him for 48 hours." Further, "He was not a man who
could easily unbend in public life ... of the handshaking arts of the lesser
politician he had few."[17] On the other hand, Dufferin, Lorne's predecessor
as governor general, had found Galt "very clever, very genial and agreeable," given his energy, experience and successes in finance, emigration
promotion and international negotiations.

Galt, with his wife, Amy, eight daughters and one son (from a total of
eleven children), took up residence at 66 Lancaster Gate in May 1880,
only to be soon disappointed in his eagerly-sought appointment. On the
question of precedence, Galt had assumed that he would be ranked with
foreign representatives, with entrée to the court. The Foreign Office was
equally clear that he would not. There were representatives of foreign governments and there were representatives of colonies; Galt was among the
latter. To the Foreign Office it did not matter whether he was called high
commissioner or agent general or whatever. If he were to be accorded
a status beyond that of other colonial representatives, resentment would
result. Eventually Galt was ranked immediately after British privy councillors, but even that reduced standing arose not from his role but rather
from his recently-achieved status as a Knight of the Grand Cross of the
Order of St Michael and St George.

Donald Creighton, Macdonald's biographer, describes well the new
high commissioner's first days in London. "Galt was always writing letters. He was the highly articulate romantic who is always pouring forth
his soul on paper. From the moment he landed in England he had experienced the most intoxicating succession of hopes, doubts, slights, encour-
agements, anxieties and mental excitements generally. He worried about
his house, his family, his expenses, his 'status' in the 'corps diplomatique'

and the delicate problems of his introduction into the society of official London."[18] Galt's preoccupation with his social position centred on his second wife, Amy. Her sister, his first wife, had died in childbirth two years after their marriage. The following year, Galt had married Amy (who became the mother of their eleven children), a marriage that in England was excluded by the Deceased Wife's Sister's Act. Accordingly, Lady Galt could not be presented at court, prompting Galt to threaten to return to Canada. The combined efforts of Lorne and his brother-in-law, the Prince of Wales, eventually overcame the court's objections on the grounds that Galt's second marriage had been valid where it had been performed (in the United States). Galt was gratified: "I have never felt more relieved in my life as the notoriety of the affair would have been perfectly frightful." Sadly, when Lady Galt was finally received, she did not make much of an impression. Lorne's sister wrote to him,

we have had Sir Alexander and Lady Galt to dinner. I think she is quite the most formidable lady I have ever seen. It is a weighty matter to extract a smile from her. She thinks London a sort of whirlpool and is much astonished at the custom of leaving cards without asking for the people at whose door they are left. "We should consider that quite an affront" she said with a look of just self-respect and she added that she had been told that there was no time for visiting in London, and this seemed to her to add insult to injury.[19]

A problem that was to plague Galt throughout the three years of his high commissionership was his salary. He had been allocated an annual salary of $10,000 (that of a lieutenant governor) and $4,000 for expenses. Galt regarded this as about half of what was required to ensure adequate representation: "This cannot be done by staying at home." After the Galts had moved into their house at Lancaster Gate, it soon became evident that their expenses would considerably exceed his income, both public and private. Despite having sent several of his daughters to school in France as an economy measure and sailing, as he put it, "close-reefed topsails," he soon concluded that he must again resign, being convinced that Ottawa would never give him sufficient resources to do the job, a persistent lament that was not to be unique to the first high commissioner. He was right; Macdonald again refused both an increase and his resignation: "let the dignity of the office as far as hospitalities etc. are concerned go to the devil."

Before sailing for Britain, Galt had assumed that Canada would more likely attain quasi-diplomatic and commercial negotiating capacity from Disraeli's Conservatives than from Gladstone's free-trade Liberals. He had, during his earlier negotiating excursions with France and Spain, come to know both the foreign secretary, Lord Salisbury, and the colonial secretary, Sir Michael Hincks-Beach. On that acquaintance and on the basis of Disraeli's positive if decidedly vague reaction to Macdonald's plans for the settlement of the North West, Galt had optimistically concluded that the Conservatives would be more receptive to his major preoccupations. Some Tories had begun to show interest in an imperial tariff preference, reflecting thereby their growing recognition that a united Empire had something to be said for it in an increasingly uncertain world.* Prudence should have suggested to Galt a more bipartisan approach, but prudence was not prominent among his several virtues. All his imaginings had come to naught when he was on the high seas. Disraeli had been resoundingly defeated by Gladstone, partly on a wave of anti-imperial rhetoric. And Galt was soon convinced that Gladstone's new government was, like his previous one, indifferent to the colonies and wholly committed to free trade: "With a new Liberal Government, we must anticipate much more opposition to our new [protectionist] fiscal policy." Following the change of government at Westminster, he added to Tilley, "we can scarcely hope to have as friendly a government to deal with as that which is about to pass away," adding more optimistically to Macdonald, "Our card was the Conservative Party and I still think will be again."[20]

How Lord Kimberley, Gladstone's new colonial secretary, regarded Galt is unrecorded, but Galt himself was decidedly unhappy at his initial interview. "It could not be worse," he reported despondently to Macdonald. Once a proponent of merger with the United States, he had long since changed his mind. Now to his consternation, Kimberley and several of his colleagues "would be quite happy to see Canada join the Yankees tomorrow."[21] Galt was also uneasy about his personal reception: "the Members of the Ministry unmistakably ignore me, from Gladstone downwards I have never seen the inside of one of their houses."[22] Alexander Mackenzie, the leader of the opposition, was not surprised. As early as the debate on the legislation creating the office, Mackenzie had urged Macdonald "not to send an ambassador ... to Great Britain, whose last act on leaving Canada was to administer a feeble kick to them, and characterise them in terms [that] we have no right to use to any friendly people, this seems the very height of diplomatic folly." For his part, Macdonald was sceptical

---

* Galt's status among free traders in Whitehall was presumably not enhanced by the fact that the Australian colonies, in imposing duty on British products, cited his 1859 tariff measures as a colonial precedent.

about Galt's reaction: "Lord Kimberley is not celebrated for cordiality of manner and Galt jumped at once to the conclusion that the Government were unfriendly. He is, I suppose, reassured by Mr. Gladstone's remark that he was glad Canada had taken the step of creating the office."[23] At an initial dinner with Gladstone at the residence of the Prince of Wales, the prime minister had cryptically told Galt that he welcomed his appointment "as a step in the right direction." At least the influential Canada Club, London's oldest dining club, had warmly welcomed him within a month of his arrival.

Galt was also less than happy about what he came to regard as major limitations on his freedom of action. His instructions had been considerably watered down by Macdonald from those that he had originally drafted for himself:

It is not desirable at present to ... make any specific propositions with respect to pecuniary assistance to the construction of the Pacific Railway or with respect to a British *Zollverein* [an imperial commercial union] but you are desired from time to time to suggest for the consideration of Her Majesty's Government such reasons as may occur to you on these various subjects, with a view of preparing the way to ultimately submitting definite proposals.[24]

Imperial defence had not been foreseen as among the subjects for Galt's immediate concern but it was the first to come before him. Two months after his arrival, testifying in confidence before the Carnarvon commission during a visit to London, Macdonald had contended that it was better to settle military arrangements between Britain and a colony on an individual basis rather than attempting to establish an Empire-wide system of defence.* No commitments should be sought from the colonies when the Empire as a whole was not threatened: "a permanent overseas obligation would seriously divide Canadians." On the other hand, he added presciently, "I have no doubt, from my intimate knowledge of the feelings of the people of Canada, their strong affection for the mother-country, and their desire to maintain the connection, that they would, on the spur

---

* Lord Carnarvon (1831–90), as secretary of state for the colonies (1866–7), had sponsored the British North America Act of 1867; he was colonial secretary again from 1874 to 1878. A friend of Macdonald, he had invited him to discuss in camera his understanding of imperial defence. An early member of the Imperial Federation League, he was an advocate of federation as a means of accommodating Home Rule for Ireland in a wider context.

of the moment, in a spirit of patriotic enthusiasm ... aid substantially in the furnishing of men ... [and] money, in aid of the Empire."[25] Two years before, he had raised with Dufferin the idea that "a fleet of fast cruisers" be provided by Britain for the defence of Canada's Atlantic seaboard. Not surprisingly, the hard-pressed Admiralty queried why Canadians did not "avail themselves of their own resources for the protection of Canadian ports and shipping." Macdonald did not respond.

Defence questions being more or less out of the way for the moment, Galt was clear about what his priorities should be: emigration; guarantees for the financing of a railway to the Pacific; the right to negotiate commercial treaties; and the creation of an imperial tariff preference (plus a host of lesser issues such as the export of cattle). He assured Macdonald that in accordance with his instructions, "I have absolutely avoided raising any question about aid to the C.P.R., or, in fact, any doubtful question, with the new men [of Gladstone's government]. And, of course, I shall not suggest a *Zollverein for the present*! If I can get them committed to aid Emigration, it will be the thin edge of the wedge."[26] He soon added, "My intention was to get the [British] government committed to Emigration, as it must involve the Railway and administrative questions afterward."[27] In seeking emigration assistance, Galt was following his instructions: "The most important subject which can engage the attention of the High Commissioner in England [*sic*] is the development of the North-West Territory." Since Galt largely drafted his own instructions, he presumably found little difficulty in recognizing this priority, knowing that if he could once get the British government to pledge itself to large-scale assisted emigration, it would also need to commit itself to some form of assistance for railway construction if the North West were to be opened to "surplus populations."

Galt was responsible for all emigration work across Europe, drawing upon the resources, however limited, of offices now in Liverpool, Glasgow, and Bristol, but his preferred source was Ireland. The prairies were a vast fertile area under the British crown, capable of absorbing almost any amount of "the suffering people of Great Britain and Ireland." Such settlers could in turn provide business for the Pacific railway by growing the grain for Britain to replace imports from beyond the Empire. This mutual interest seemed self-evident to Galt and to Ottawa; it was not, however, equally evident to Whitehall, at least in any practical sense. In an effort to devise a common approach, Galt urged that Canada assume all the costs of administering the territories vacated by the Hudson's Bay Company and that free homesteads be offered to the "surplus populations," but Britain should meet the specific costs of travel and initial settlement. The British government, however, showed no sign of abandoning its longstanding indifference to the destination of its emigrants, a laissez-faire policy which had the practical result that most – certainly most Irish – chose the more dynamic United States. If people wanted to emigrate that was their affair; the government would take no part in their decision.

This policy cul-de-sac offered little hope to Galt of any early contribution by Britain to the settlement of the North West, but somehow large-scale emigration from Ireland might still be possible, offering some relief to its endemic rural poverty. The Canadian Parliament had voted substantial sums for famine relief in Ireland; it would presumably be no less ready to provide assistance to would-be emigrants to what Macdonald called "the new Ireland." Galt was clear that "There is no other way of making the west of Ireland support its 600,000 souls than to take half of them away." He had also in mind that if he could somehow induce the British government to support emigration from an increasingly unruly Ireland, "it will then be a comparatively easy task to make them apply the same principles to emigration from England and Scotland [and even] ... German emigration." Kimberley was generally supportive, but W.E. Forster, the chief secretary for Ireland, was doubtful, finally informing Galt that Gladstone would not countenance the cost. In any event, employers in Ireland opposed the loss of their cheap labour and advocates of Irish Home Rule as well as the Roman Catholic hierarchy opposed emigration, seeing it as a subterfuge to avoid the central question of how Ireland should be governed, attacking only the symptoms of the malady, not the disease itself.

During his three years in London, Galt was indefatigable in promoting Irish emigration, attempting to stimulate private support in Toronto and Winnipeg. He worked in particular with Roman Catholic bishops, seeking their help in inducing parish clergy in Ireland to drop their opposition. Macdonald himself in 1882 intervened directly. Following encouraging discussions in London with Cardinal Manning, he arranged the visit of Archbishop Lynch of Toronto to promote assisted emigration to "New Ireland." Kimberley, however, was not enthusiastic, making clear to him the British government's anger at the meddling of the Canadian Parliament in the internal affairs of the United Kingdom by calling for the full restoration of civil liberties and by endorsing early Home Rule. If that were not enough, the murder of the viceroy in Dublin by Fenians put an abrupt end to consideration of assisted Irish emigration. Four years later, the advocacy of Galt and others of emigration to Canada as a cure for Ireland's woes was briefly echoed by Salisbury in the 1886 election campaign. If the British government "could emigrate another million of the Irish people ... to Manitoba, the result would be magical upon the social conditions of the Irish people."[28] Once in office, however, Salisbury, adamantly opposed to Home Rule, lost his enthusiasm, leaving Galt's successor, Tupper, with no new opportunities to pursue.

Galt's ambitions for the settlement of the North West were not limited to the Irish. From January 1882 he worked with Lord Rothschild to facilitate the migration to the North West of "agricultural Jews" from Russia. At a supportive meeting organized by the lord mayor at Mansion House, attended by the Archbishop of Canterbury and Cardinal Manning, he joined an organizing committee. Macdonald responded promptly, informing Lorne that Galt "has been attending to the Jews ... I hope something will come of this. He will be instructed to act for the Immigration Department, and we are quite ready to assign the Jews lands."[29] To Galt, who had recently sent him one of his several resignations, he wrote, " After years of ill-concealed hostility of the Rothschilds against Canada, you have made a great strike by taking up the old clo' [clothes] cry, and going in for a Jew immigration into the Northwest. By following up this subject, and establishing a Jew colony here, whether ultimately successful or not, a link – a missing link – will be established between Canada and Sidonia [the Phoenician city]. I should prefer *you* [to remain in London] to write another epistle to the Hebrews, rather than a newcomer."[30] The first of fifteen hundred Jewish immigrants from Russia arrived in Moosomin in late 1882, many soon moving to the boom town of Winnipeg.

Fundamentally, the success of any schemes to people the North West, whether public or private, turned on the early completion of the transcontinental railway. Macdonald was at first willing to explore the possibilities of constructing the line to the Pacific as a public project, as Mackenzie had earlier envisaged, but he had soon concluded that public enterprise was likely to be more costly and even more susceptible to delay than private. The British-owned Grand Trunk was chronically in a fragile financial state, unable to attract additional capital. For a while Sir Henry Tyler, its managing director, hoped that a new line might somehow be restricted to the North West, limited to the "desolation" from Lake Nipissing, the westernmost point of the GTR, to the far Pacific. With the gradual realization that the Pacific syndicate had in mind a line that would begin at least as far east as Montreal, Charles Brydges, the general manager, was determined to do what he could to discredit the project on the London money markets.

At this distance it is impossible to be certain what Galt and Rose did to counter the machinations of their old friend Brydges, but the opposition of the Grand Trunk did not deter the ambitions of George Stephen, the most remarkable Canadian financier of the nineteenth century, whose peerage in 1891 as Lord Mount Stephen recognized his unique achievements both as railway man and as banker. In Macdonald's first foray into transcontinental railway construction, he had had little choice but to select Allan and his motley consortium. But in 1880, Macdonald had that rarest of political opportunities, a second chance. And the second time he got it right. However difficult and demanding Stephen was, only he had the push to get the hazardous, complex and immensely expensive job done. The Pacific Railway Act of 1879 set the wheels, as it were, in motion, with Tupper enthusiastically picturing for the House of Commons "an Imperial Highway across the continent of America entirely on British soil ... a new and important route from England to Australia, to India and to all the dependencies of Great Britain in the Pacific and also to China and Japan."

For the hapless Galt in London, Stephen was, however, an unwelcome choice. Galt and Stephen knew each other at the entrepreneurial apex of a country of only four million. But Stephen mistrusted Galt as a long-time director and advocate of the Grand Trunk and as a controversial railway entrepreneur in his own right. He may have also had lingering misgivings about Galt's kinship, however distant, with Hugh Allan, his long friendship with Brydges and especially his involvement with Glyns and Barings who had urged that while the Grand Trunk remained a good thing, the projected Pacific line attracted little support.

The highly controversial bill authorizing construction of the Pacific railway received royal assent in February 1881. Four months later, Macdonald and Tupper were again in London to find, as they already knew from Rose and Galt, that the financing of the line remained anything but an easy sell. Stephen, long active in railway projects with his cousin Donald Smith, was a director of the Bank of Montreal from 1871 to 1881 and president from 1876 to 1881. He had become the indispensable man. With some difficulty, he put together a consortium with, among others, Smith and Rose. In the documents, however, the name of Smith was intentionally omitted, although he was in fact a major participant. Both Macdonald and Tupper, now minister of railways, had remained deeply resentful about Smith's role in bringing down their government seven years before. Stephen acknowledged to Rose in December 1880 that he was having a "terrible bother with Don Smith because his name is not printed in the papers submitted to the House ... He was like a baby over the thing."[31] Nevertheless, named or not, Smith, soon "excited almost to a craze," came to play a major part following the signature of the railway contract in October 1880. Tupper, at Macdonald's behest, confirmed again with the Grand Trunk that it would not undertake construction of a line north of Lake Superior (i.e., an all-Canadian route).

Stephen, like Macdonald, blamed the fact that the London money markets were practically shut against the Canadian Pacific "largely on the machinations of the Grand Trunk and its paid ink-slingers in London [who] are doing their best to damage their bonds and the whole enterprise." *The Economist* could "see no reason why the British investor would want to risk his money" on a Pacific line, since it could anticipate only "a long and dreary season of unprofitableness." *The Times* recommended would-be emigrants to go to Australia. In September 1881, Henry Labouchère, MP, in an article in *Truth* entitled "The Canadian Dominion Bubble," launched a full broadside. Many newspapers across Britain picked up his comment that the line was "never likely to pay a single red cent of interest on the money that may be sunk into it." Stephen, increasingly anxious about whether the consortium could raise funds on the London market, was convinced that Galt was continuing to work behind the scenes. He complained to the prime minister in January 1882 that both the Grand Trunk and the high commissioner were working against the construction of the Pacific line, despite the commitment that Macdonald had made to British Columbia. Rose wrote optimistically to Macdonald that "I think Stephen is wrong in attributing to Galt intentional or malevolent misrepresentation ... He may have been indiscreet his opinions ... I am trying to bring them together – but how it may result I know not." Macdonald, however, remained distrustful of his own appointee. It was to Rose, not Galt, that he consistently wrote about the Canadian Pacific.

Stephen was so suspicious of Galt and his tiresome connection with the Grand Trunk that he himself financed the publication of the *Canadian Gazette*, a London periodical ostensibly reporting on Canadian affairs but in reality a puff sheet for the Canadian Pacific. The temperamental Galt, however, remained sceptical. In January 1883 he wrote to Macdonald, "the Canadian Pacific will never be finished without coming to London for money, and that it is bumptious folly for Stephen to neglect – as he has done – every means of conciliating this market."[32] Stephen's basic problem was not, however, his neglect of the London market but rather the continuing wariness of Canadian railway bonds by City banks and investors: "No one in England would take a shilling in the company ... No one in London believed in [its] success." The prime minister had, however, the final word:

Canada has the power not only to see through its Government that her interests are not imperilled by the ambition or jealousy of any railway company, but has also a *locus standi* as a creditor. The G.T.R. owes her [i.e., the government] 32 millions sterling with thirty years' interest ... It has now become an American line with its terminus [termini] at Chicago and Portland. The Canadian local transport business has been made secondary ... and Canada must legislate so as to put a stop to that or enforce its debt. A threat of that kind, judiciously used at the right time, would soon bring those people to their bearings.[33]

Although Morton and Rose were represented in the Pacific consortium, Rose advised Stephen not even to attempt an offering on the London market. Some part of the reason for his attitude may have arisen from the animosity that he felt toward Donald Smith. A deputy governor and influential director of the Hudson's Bay Company, Rose was Smith's main opponent when Smith had in effect taken over the company. Rose in turn was no more enthusiastic about Smith as a principal player in the Pacific railway.* Smith eventually lost all faith in Rose, convinced as he was that Rose's son Charles (who had assumed the management of the bank) was in the pocket of the Grand Trunk. Rose was no longer a problem in the way of Canadian Pacific financing; it was Galt who remained the proverbial thorn in Stephen's side until the coal requirements of the rail line gave Stephen the opening to force the high commissioner away from his troublesome and covert support for the Grand Trunk and its British shareholders.

At the age of sixty-six, the high commissioner embarked upon a major new commercial venture. His older son Elliott, who had already made substantial profits for his father and himself in Winnipeg land speculation,

---

* From 1879 Donald Smith and John Rose had been at loggerheads over the appointment of Charles Brydges, the former head of the Grand Trunk, as land commissioner of the Hudson's Bay Company. Irregularities in his land dealings and statements against the CPR led Smith to attempt to oust Brydges, but from London Rose kept defending him. Brydges managed to hang on, even asking Macdonald to intervene with Smith, to leave him alone. Macdonald did request Tupper (then high commissioner in London) to discuss the matter with Smith, but Brydges himself conveniently died before Tupper could do so.

had been appointed by Macdonald an assistant Indian commissioner in the North West. From that vantage point, in 1879 Elliott had identified promising coal deposits in what would in time become southern Alberta. During the late summer of 1881, Galt had himself travelled by rail, water, and wagon to the North West to see with his son how the deposits might be exploited to supply the railway to the Pacific. Following his return to London, he began the difficult task of shopping the coal project around the City, undeterred by the fact that he was concurrently high commissioner. In April 1882, after finally attracting several partners (including Charles Brydges, W.H. Smith, the son of the bookseller and former Conservative minister, and his business colleague, William Lethbridge), he incorporated the North Western Coal and Navigation Company. From Ottawa, he wrote in June to his wife in London that Macdonald had assured him that he would receive the additional land that he sought for his colonization activities in the North West (which included renaming the town of Coalbanks after his colleague, Lethbridge). This gave Macdonald and Stephen an unparalleled opportunity to curb the wayward high commissioner. There could only be one customer for his coal: the Canadian Pacific. Stephen wrote triumphantly to Macdonald that Galt had reversed himself, "now wanting to see the C.P.R. a success for the sake of the venture he has embarked in." As one railway historian has noted,

Galt's position and attitude toward the Canadian Pacific were changing. In August 1883, the first coal from the Lethbridge mine came down the Oldman River by boat to Medicine Hat and was given a triumphant test run on the C.P.R. In 1884 Stephen placed a five-year contract for coal with Galt's company. Almost certainly its duration was designed to win Galt's goodwill. A railway was built from Lethbridge to Medicine Hat and Galt was, so to speak, in clover. By 1890 they were mining five hundred tons a day, all of it taken by the C.P.R.[34]

Now with a direct stake in the success of the Canadian Pacific, Galt became more assiduous in attempting to counter the indifferent London press in its analyses of Canada's economic prospects by extolling the manifold benefits that a transcontinental rail line would bring.

The negotiation of commercial agreements, a major ambition of Galt, remained both challenging and troublesome. From the first, he was unrelenting in his pursuit of the right of Canada to negotiate its own commercial treaty obligations. As he had told the enthusiastic Montreal audience who had gathered to salute his appointment, the British North America Act had placed Canada in the same position as far as commercial questions were concerned "as we stood toward any foreign government ... it is clearly a negotiation to which we must be an assenting party as well as the imperial government." Even before Galt's arrival in Britain, the secretary of state for the colonies had informed Lorne that "it is not thought desirable to appoint a Canadian commissioner to take part in the negotiation of any treaty, but if your government desire to send a person enjoying their confidence to advise with Her Majesty's Government, or with the British ambassador on any questions that may arise during the negotiations, Her Majesty's Government will be happy to give attention to his representations."[35] Galt had sought this opening more than all others, having contended as early as 1859 that a colony was not truly self-governing if it enjoyed fiscal responsibility but not the concomitant right to set its own tariffs. Not surprisingly, this claim aroused misgivings in the Foreign Office (although not, to any comparable degree, in the more flexible Colonial Office). In the end, a compromise was reached. After several false starts, it was agreed that the self-governing colonies would be excluded from commercial treaties unless they explicitly asked to be included (hitherto colonies had been automatically included). Opting-out became a way station en route to full commercial negotiating independence, sought by Galt and endorsed during the office of his successor, Charles Tupper.

The perennial concern of Canada to maximize its exports re-emerged when Canada sought to negotiate preferred access to the markets of South America and the Caribbean. When Macdonald had returned to office in 1878, he had wanted to expand transatlantic trade and to assert a more active role for Canada in international negotiations by commissioning Galt – for whom by then something had to be found – to negotiate trade treaties with European countries, first with Spain, including the Spanish Antilles. The Foreign Office, however, had regarded Galt as an advisor to the British minister at Madrid, who would negotiate upon Canada's behalf. Even less fortunate was Galt's experience in Paris when he had attempted to resolve a trade dispute directly with the French authorities. Only an appeal to the foreign secretary had induced the British ambassador to abandon his "marked discourtesy," to receive him at the embassy, and to introduce him to the French authorities. In the cases of both Spain and France, Galt had been obstructed in his ambitions to conclude separate commercial agreements as much by domestic events in the two countries as by misgivings in the Foreign Office. In time, it became evident that whatever the particular mode of negotiation with France, its invariably protectionist-minded government would not reduce tariffs on terms acceptable to Ottawa. In Spain, negotiations were delayed by renewed internal turmoil, but the Foreign Office had acknowledged Canada's right to conclude its own commercial treaty, asking only that it be given the opportunity to examine the final text of whatever was agreed between Galt and the Spanish minister in London so that it could endorse it to the government of Spain. Practical diplomacy had overcome the niceties of theoretical diplomacy. Galt had, in fact, achieved something of the independent commercial negotiating status for Canada which he had long sought.

Even in terms of Canadian representation at international conferences, Galt had also managed to move forward his agenda. Both Tupper (then minister of railways) and Galt attended the International Monetary Conference in Paris in 1881. Its subject, bi-metallism, was of limited interest to Canada (and none at all to Britain, which was not even represented), but by its participation Canada advanced its claims to its own negotiating status. In any case, as Galt wrote to Macdonald, the conference in Paris would give Tupper and him the opportunity "to have a good time for a week or two." But Galt remained dissatisfied with his progress in achieving full negotiating authority. He privately agreed with Edward Blake, the leader of the opposition, that Canada should assume full responsibility under the crown for all commercial negotiations affecting it. "We ... must act on our own behalf if we are ever to promote our own commercial relations, or to secure to ourselves that share of the commerce of the world which our population and our wealth entitle us to expect." Blake was, however, more outspoken in his criticism of British representation of Canadian interests than Galt: "The history of the diplomatic service of England as far as Canada is concerned, has been a history of error, blunder, wrong and concession."[36]

Having been the principal instigator of Canada's tariffs, Galt urged the British government to address seriously colonial advocacy of an imperial customs union. The basic problem, in Galt's view, was that Gladstone's government, committed to free trade, would not contemplate either itself or a colony adopting a preferential tariff for the Empire. In his new-found enthusiasm for an imperial *Zollverein*, Galt was entering a debate that was to inform Anglo-Canadian relations for almost a century. The profound influence of that debate over time could not be foreseen, but he must have known that he was entering upon a contentious issue with Gladstone's government. Certainly Macdonald did. Accordingly he was more cautious than his enthusiastic high commissioner. Briefly, the issue was whether a way might be devised to give products from the Empire, especially food, a preferred place (i.e., at a cheaper price) in the British market. A later and even less feasible variation of imperial tariff preference was Empire free trade: no tariffs whatever among the colonies and mother country.

Imperial preferential trade would never prove to be the glue that many hoped would bind the Empire together. The problem was basically that the British poor would be denied the cheapest food available from world markets, being limited instead to the frequently more expensive produce of the Empire. During the 1840s, when Galt was embarking upon his land settlement activities in Upper Canada, Richard Cobden and the radicals of the Manchester School, on one of those rare occasions when political scientists have had an effect on government, had convinced Sir Robert Peel to repeal the Corn Laws and to adopt free trade by abandoning agricultural protection and phasing out imperial preferences in food grains. They would henceforth be purchased from the lowest cost source. Since they would encounter no tariff upon entering Britain, bread would not be taxed, directly or indirectly. If the price of imperial unity was higher bread prices, that price should not be paid. No government that permitted more expensive staples could hope to survive.

Such a policy was, of course, the opposite of what many in the colonies sought: Canadians continued to hope that their wheat and Australians their beef and grains would sooner or later be given a preferred place in the British market. Lorne found Galt "firmly convinced that England will go in for modified Protection before long – yet I can't convince myself that such a miracle can be accomplished. Sir A. Galt of course thinks that this will be the beginning of exceptionally favourable arrangements between the Old Country and the big children."[37] Galt was undeterred. In 1881 he delivered two speeches on the future of the Empire which were later reprinted in pamphlet form: *The Relations of the Colonies to the Empire: Present and Future*. It was the future which engaged his capacious mind, believing as he did that intelligent young people in the settlement colonies would not for long be content with a subsidiary position in the Empire. The Empire had to go forward or separation would spawn several small and ineffective independent states. The better option was some form of imperial federation, embracing Ireland (which would then indirectly achieve Home Rule) as well as England, the Australian colonies, Wales, Scotland, New Zealand, Canada, and the Cape of Good Hope. When Macdonald became aware of the erratic Galt's conversations with the opposition as well as the Colonial Office about the role that an imperial tariff preference might play in fostering imperial unity and more especially of his speeches and pamphlets about an imperial federation based upon a tariff preference, he cautioned him that the free trader Gladstone might well resent any such advocacy by a quasi-diplomat: "Keep quiet and friendly with the powers that be and pray every night that they may soon be exchanged for better men ... Gladstone, if I read him aright, is a man governed by his hates, and is spiteful as a monkey. In a fit of rage he might denounce Canada and its future ... In fact there is no knowing what he might do."*[38] Publicly Macdonald could hardly have been clearer about Canada's intention to make its own decisions. Speaking in Toronto in November 1881, he had himself declared, "We will govern our own country, we will put on the taxes ourselves. If we choose to misgovern ourselves we will do so, and we do not desire England, Ireland or Scotland to tell us we are fools."

Galt was undeterred by Macdonald's colourfully expressed but deeply felt caution. Ignoring his admonitions, he plunged boldly into the debate about imperial federation and Home Rule for Ireland. During the following year – his third in London – he spoke in Liverpool, Edinburgh, and Glasgow, defending indirectly controversial resolutions of the Canadian House of Commons in favour of Irish Home Rule. With its own local assembly, Ireland would be both self-governing and yet an integral part of a federated empire, with the economic underpinning of a tariff preference. Galt, who was always in a hurry, summarized his views to Macdonald, "My opinion is that the present system of government here is on its last legs, that Irish Home Rule must be conceded and that it can only be safely done through the confederation of the United Kingdom and the self-governing colonies."[39] The unheralded and repeated excursions by Galt into what some regarded as the internal affairs of Britain was received by an irritated Macdonald with renewed unease. On 2 February 1883 he wrote: "I hope that you have not committed yourself too much to the project of Imperial Federation, which, in my humble opinion, can never be worked out."[40] A fortnight later, Macdonald cautioned him in terms similar to his advice of a year before that in his advocacy of imperial federation he was undermining his own office. "The Canadian High Commissioner is now acknowledged to be an Ambassador, and as such it is his duty to be *persona grata* to the Government to which he is accredited. Now the [British] Government may resent or feel irritated at your stirring the question. An Ambassador *can't* speak his private sentiments on the political questions arising in the country to which he is sent."[41]

---

* That Macdonald held Gladstone in low regard was noted by a public servant in Ottawa who recorded in his diary that "Sir John talked of Gladstone, Lord Russell and Palmerston. He said he thought the former two were among the greatest scandals [scoundrels?] of the century and that the only excuse for Gladstone was that he was mad" (NA, MG29E, vol. 15).

The London-born Galt (here wearing decorations, including the Grand
Cross of the Order of St Michael and St George), was the son of John
Galt, the Scottish author who played a key part in the Canada Company and the British America Land Company. Following his three years
as high commissioner, Galt became involved in the development of coal
mining in the North West in collaboration with his son.

Within months, when Galt's coal mines in the North West were in place, he resigned, effective 1 June 1883. He had resigned before, but this time Macdonald accepted his resignation, promptly cabling him that his successor was to be the minister of railways and canals, Sir Charles Tupper. Galt cannot have been surprised; as early as March 1881 Tupper, on a visit to Britain, had told him that he would like to be high commissioner.* Additionally, he knew that Tupper, on yet another visit ten months after his own arrival, had reported to Macdonald that "Sir A.T. Galt has fully decided to leave ... If I become able to stand the strain of the Commons again [Tupper's health was uncertain] I am at your disposal; if not, I would like you to send me here where I think [that] I could do some good work for Canada."[42] In February 1882 Galt, who had come to regard his acceptance of the post as "a most serious error," wrote to Tupper, "You mentioned while you were here that you would yourself rather like this English [sic] mission. I confess I am heartily tired of it, and the post is quite at your service."[43] Macdonald was reluctant to lose Tupper, his principal lieutenant, but being greatly indebted to him, he presumably wanted to meet his repeated wishes to absent himself from the hurly burly of the House of Commons and place himself under the care of a leading London physician. In any event, Macdonald needed a high commissioner with more evident enthusiasm for the Canadian Pacific than Galt ever displayed.

Galt, brilliant but impulsive, had been frustrated in London by his apparent failure to move forward significantly his various initiatives in finance, emigration, and commercial treaty-making, which he blamed largely upon lack of support from Ottawa and the Liberals in London. He had plunged into the questions of Home Rule for Ireland, an imperial tariff preference, and an imperial federation without much care for the sensibilities of the governments of the day in either Ottawa or London. But on one point at least there could be no doubt: he had established the office of the high commissioner on a permanent basis, with a status, as Macdonald had noted, "acknowledged to be [that of] an Ambassador."[44]

---

* Galt considered standing as a Conservative in the British general election of 1886, but eventually decided against doing so. During the years following his resignation as high commissioner, he was frequently in London, raising funds for his several coal mining and land ventures. He died in Montreal on 19 September 1893, age seventy-six. In addition to memorials in Canada, a small plaque in the Chapel of the Order of St Michael and St George in St Paul's Cathedral records his knighthood.

Sir Charles Tupper, 1883–1896

The appointment of Galt had lent distinction to the new office of high commissioner. His successor, Sir Charles Tupper, like Galt a Father of Confederation worthy of that rare accolade of statesman, further enhanced its status. Yet Tupper during his thirteen years as high commissioner mixed partisan politics in Canada and diplomacy in Britain to a unique degree. Rose had dextrously combined representation with private banking. Galt had nimbly pursued his personal interests in parallel with his public office. It was Tupper, however, who demonstrated the greatest agility, combining both private and parliamentary interests with his beloved London appointment.

When Tupper's appointment was gazetted on 30 May 1883, he was sixty-two years old, four years younger than Galt, but diagnosed as being of uncertain health. Being an Edinburgh-trained physician himself, he was eager to consult specialists in the British Isles who assured him that he would soon regain his habitual rude health (they were correct; he lived to be ninety-four). Despite his medical misgivings, Tupper had agreed at Macdonald's express urging to retain his seat in Parliament and to continue as minister of railways and canals. Although the demands of this onerous dual role would be many, his debut in London was easy, unlike Galt's. "Nothing could exceed that cordiality of my reception," he wrote upon his arrival, "I find the interest taken in Canada is immense."[1] From Ottawa, Lord Lorne kindly made certain that Tupper was everywhere received as the leading Canadian statesman that he was, including the honour of a private audience at Windsor with Queen Victoria shortly after his arrival. Tupper himself did not make Galt's elementary error of appearing to take sides in British partisan debate. He soon became a friend of Kimberley, Galt's Liberal nemesis. He was equally even-handed in his attitude to visiting Liberals (Alexander Mackenzie, Edward Blake, and Oliver Mowat, the premier of Ontario, were all in London within months of his arrival). Yet some part of Tupper's initial success was the indirect result of Galt's efforts. To a degree, it was Galt who had planted the seeds for the crop which the more dynamic Tupper soon began to harvest. His arrival was timely. The virtues of an ever-expanding British Empire in Asia and Africa, as well as in the Americas and the Antipodes, were being extolled by, among others, Rudyard Kipling in print and by Charles Dilke in Parliament. In the ferment of public debate about the Empire, Tupper would be in his element.

Born in Amherst, Nova Scotia, in 1821, Tupper, twelve years after completion of his medical studies at the University of Edinburgh, had done the unexpected: he had vanquished the seemingly unbeatable Liberal Joseph Howe in the 1855 elections to the Nova Scotia Assembly. As premier from 1864 to 1867, Tupper was deeply committed to Confederation, soon becoming Macdonald's indispensable ally. Probably the only person who could have induced Nova Scotia to join Confederation against the opposition of Howe and Annand, he had every claim to be a Father of Confederation, urging the case in London, Quebec City, and Charlottetown as well as in Halifax. Tupper's progress from provincial to Dominion politics was not, however, unblemished. Even in the then easy world of government finance, the involvement by the premier of Nova Scotia in the construction of the Truro-Pictou rail line had raised questions in the minds of more than his political opponents. Always eager to advance in whatever fashion he could his family's interests, the premier's controversial collaboration with Macdonald's friend Charles Brydges, the general manager of the Grand Trunk, and especially with the Scottish-born engineer Sandford Fleming, paid off handsomely, but left behind a taint of corruption that would follow them for the rest of their lives.

Known familiarly as the "Ram of Cumberland" (his Nova Scotia constituency), Tupper, fortified by a formidable memory, was a determined and persistent advocate of whatever cause he embraced. Upon his death, Laurier was to recall that his chief characteristic was his force and audacity. Some found him pompous and unduly aggressive, occasionally aloof and distant, but there was never any doubt where he stood on any particular public issue, giving rise to the observation that the only person who could answer a Tupper speech was Tupper himself. Half-measures were never to his liking. Upon Tupper's appointment, Lorne had alerted Lord Derby, the new colonial secretary, to his vigorous and abrasive nature, including his "strong temper and character ... in debate here [he] has always been a violent and voluble speaker."[2] It was an accurate description, particularly of Tupper's years in opposition when the ailing Macdonald had been uncertain whether he could continue as leader. In the words of an admiring Ottawa journalist: "no matter how threatening the gale, he braced his feet, like a fisherman bound for the Grand Banks, and faced the danger without flinching."[3]

Tupper was a principal driving force in the 1878 Conservative election victory. His immediate reward was to be promoted from inland revenue to public works and railways. Thereafter, as Macdonald's chief lieutenant, he travelled with him to London in 1879, seeking financing guarantees.* In late 1880 and again in early 1881 he guided the highly contentious Pacific Railway legislation through the House of Commons as part of the projected "Imperial Highway across the Continent entirely on British soil." Railway building had, however, proven a major drain on his health. When in Britain in both 1881 and 1882, he became convinced that he could contribute more from there than he could by remaining in Canada itself. Upon his return home in March 1881, he informed both Macdonald and Galt of his ambition to become the second high commissioner.

Tupper was at least as experienced as Galt in dealing with major problems in London. His central role in railway financing and construction dated as far back as 1858 when, as provincial secretary of Nova Scotia, he had crossed the Atlantic with Galt to seek British guarantees for loans to the Intercolonial line. Frequent contact with Westminster, and to a lesser extent, with Washington, meant that Tupper was far from a neophyte in diplomacy, demonstrating greater tact and sensitivity than had his predecessor, despite his forceful reputation. Always sanguine, he was certain

---

* The collaboration of Macdonald and Tupper in railway matters did not, however, extend as far as Tupper would have liked, if the memory of Sir Joseph Pope is reliable. "Shortly after the return to power [of the Conservatives in 1878], Sir Charles Tupper wished the Government's legal work to be given to their sons, Hugh Macdonald and Stewart Tupper, who were in partnership at that time in Winnipeg. Sir John would not agree ... Sir Charles Tupper told me in London after Macdonald's death in the year 1893 that for at least two years and I think somewhat longer, they never exchanged one word in private" (Pope to Willison, 4 May 1922). Earlier in 1879, Tupper had readily accepted Macdonald's nomination for a knighthood. However, "the open and voluble scoffing of the more intemperate Liberals made it very difficult to have honours regarded as such. As a way out of the trouble Lorne advocated a distinct Canadian order ... to be called the Order of the Canadian Union which would be divided into four classes. Kimberley facetiously dismissed the proposal. 'The local order would have to be given locally and would be certain to be jobbed.' He remarked upon his difficulty in comprehending why anyone who had done nothing discreditable should fail to have an honour. In Russia this was virtually the rule concerning official people, and in Prussia there was the old saying that there were only two things a man could not escape, death and the third class of the Red Eagle. A Canadian order ... would soon fall into disrepute" (MacNutt, *Days of Lorne*, 136).

that he could handle whatever came along (there was no lack of robust self-confidence in his complex character) and that he could, concurrently if necessary, fill the several roles of member of Parliament, minister of railways and canals, and high commissioner. Among his several roles, if Tupper had had to state a preference, he evidently would have chosen high commissioner, but the choice did not need to be made. He readily agreed with the grateful Macdonald to be simultaneously minister of railways and high commissioner (he could not receive two salaries; his solution was to accept no salary as "acting" high commissioner). All in all, he was highly gratified to be back at the centre of the Empire, pledging to do all that he could for Canada as well as "the advancement of British civilization and the progress of the world," the two being largely identical in his mind.

From the day that Tupper and his family arrived in Britain in June 1883, he continued to live up to his sobriquet of the "Ram." During the voyage, his normally vigorous health had begun to return so that he had barely disembarked in Liverpool before undertaking speeches at the Royal Colonial Institute, at City guilds, and at chambers of commerce across the British Isles, distributing promotional materials, including lantern slides and the texts of lectures, and in negotiating agreements with steamship companies to provide subsidized passages. Lorne's wife, Princess Louise, supported Tupper in his advocacy of the emigration of women at a meeting organized by the redoubtable Lady Salisbury, the spouse of the prime minister. Tupper was similarly active in the Netherlands and Switzerland, in an unenthusiastic France, and even in Prussia where Princess Louise's sister, the crown princess, was especially welcoming, although the government itself was decidedly not.

As had Galt, Tupper was soon confronted with the general prohibition imposed on the import of cattle, including Canadian. Characteristically, he acted decisively:

a consignment of [Canadian cattle] was condemned at the landing-wharves in Liverpool on the ground that some were affected with pleuro-pneumonia. The agent in Liverpool, to whom the condemned cattle had been consigned, reported by cable to the shipper in Canada that the whole of the shipment would have to be slaughtered, because some of the steers were tainted with the dreaded disease. The shipper at once cabled to Sir Charles Tupper for advice.

Sir Charles was busy in his office shortly after the opening hours on the Thursday on which the cablegram was received. It was handed to him by his Secretary, Mr. Colmer. The usual course in such a case would have involved a certain amount of red tape and circumlocution. But Sir Charles disregarded precedents and procedure. He inquired from his secretary as to where were the nearest surgical instrument shops, and the nearest booksellers who supplied medical books. He told him to reserve him a compartment on the first train to Liverpool. At the bookseller's Sir Charles got the latest works on the diseases of cattle, put them in his hansom cab, and was driven rapidly to the surgical instrument maker's. He emerged with a big case of instruments, and when he reached Euston Station dashed along the platform with the books under one arm and the surgical instruments under the other. Colmer was in readiness for him, handed him his ticket, and saw him safe into his compartment. On the way down Sir Charles, so to speak, tore the heart out of the books so far as they related to the disease in question. By the time he reached Liverpool he was well up in the knowledge of pleuro-pneumonia.

Arrived there he drove immediately to the cattle yards and asked to see the condemned cattle that had recently arrived from Canada. Then he called for the inspectors who had condemned them. Sir Charles put each of them through a sharp examination. He made each one define his reasons for his action. Going again to the yards the inspectors were requested to point out an animal which they considered was affected. Each was asked to state what would be found, on dissection, to be the condition of the lungs and other organs of the body. Each man was pinned down to exact details. Then Sir Charles ordered that the condemned animal should be slaughtered. He then rolled up his sleeves and dissected the various parts – doing this with a thoroughness that left no opening for uncertainty. Another and yet another animal were brought in and subjected to the same operations. No symptom whatever of disease was found, and by the evening he had proved that the inspectors had been quite erroneous in their conjectures. Sir Charles left the cattle yard in triumph, and had the pleasure of writing to the Canadian shipper that his cattle were all right. "As for the Liverpool inspectors, ... they made no more condemnation of Canadian cattle lest," as they said, "that old devil from London should blow down here again."[4]

Nevertheless, the 1882 prohibition of live cattle remained in place. Tupper's vigorous and public protests did not sit well with the British government. During a by-election in Scotland, Tupper again employed direct methods in his attempts to counter what he was convinced was disguised protectionism instigated by officials of the Board of Agriculture. Lords Rosebery and Ripon knew that the Liberals would lose votes in Scotland if Tupper continued to broadcast Whitehall's exclusion of Canadian cattle which were popular for breeding. The prime minister wrote to his foreign secretary, "Could you not talk to Sir John Thompson [the Canadian justice minister then in London] and point out that Tupper's action is an actual impediment to our doing anything [to permit Canadian imports], besides its gross indecorum?"[5] For all Tupper's vigour, the protectionist prohibition on cattle would not go away; it was to cause recurring difficulties for every high commissioner until the Second World War.

Tupper was no less prompt than Galt in advancing the claim of Canada to participate in international negotiations which touched directly upon its commercial interests. From a submarine cable conference in Paris, the bilingual Tupper happily reported to Macdonald, "Canada took her place in an International Conference on an equal footing with all the other powers." In turn, Macdonald used Tupper's role at the conference to inspire a laudatory editorial in the Toronto *Globe* setting out his moderate claim for Canada to negotiate for itself on commercial issues of first importance to it. He wrote to Tupper, "You have made a good start and I have no doubt your intercourse with the Government will be both agreeable and useful. I cannot help but think that your practical successes will be greater than Galt's. He was always thinking of posing as an English statesman and trying to impose his own views on the English public for self-glorification."[6]

More intractable than problems of emigration promotion, cattle exports, or commercial treaty negotiation were those of railway financing. Concurrently minister of railways and acting high commissioner, Tupper was acutely aware of the fact that the rapid construction of a line to the Pacific would require financing far beyond that which had been foreseen when he was still in Ottawa. There was much advocacy to do, given the success of the Grand Trunk in helping to close the London money market to Canadian Pacific borrowing. In late October 1883 a determined but increasingly apprehensive George Stephen had appealed yet again to Macdonald who agreed to guarantee the Canadian Pacific dividend for ten years. But even that did not bolster the shares on the London market, where investors were intimidated by stories of unrest in the North West as well as by the apparent financial fragility of the line itself. Macdonald wired Tupper to gather additional evidence that the Grand Trunk was still undermining the CPR. "The attempts to ruin that enterprise ... are most atrocious. Can you and Rose get us reliable evidence of the unfavourable action of the G.T.R. – Sir H. Tyler and Abbott [its Montreal lawyer and future prime minister] and Co.?"[7] By 1 December it had become imperative that additional government financing must somehow be arranged. Tupper cannot have been surprised when, during a banquet in Birmingham three days later, he was handed a telegram from Macdonald, "Pacific in trouble. You should be here ... Important for Pacific you sail next steamer."[8] Still minister of railways, Tupper did so. Upon his arrival in Ottawa, he launched an immediate investigation into the financial affairs of the CPR, satisfied himself of its probity and helped to arrange yet another and final advance from the Bank of Montreal. Having partly covered the bank loan by personal collateral, Stephen took the occasion to attempt a reconciliation between Macdonald and his cousin by writing to the prime minister on 10 February 1884, "The pluck with which he [Donald Smith] has stood by me in my efforts to sustain the credit of the C.P.R. made it almost duty on my part to try and restore friendly relations between one who has stood so courageously by the company in its time of trouble and you to whom alone the C.P.R. owes its existence as a real Canadian Railway."[9] During the debate in the House of Commons, Tupper took the lead from an exhausted Macdonald and, despite the opposition of the Grand Trunk, successfully steered the long acrimonious debate to a conclusion: a total government loan of $30 million at four percent (with a mortgage on the rail line itself and adjoining land). With the vote on 28 February 1884, another financial crisis had been resolved for the moment, but the Liberal opposition also attacked the expense of the railway when sluggish emigration from Britain suggested that the line alone was not proving to be the catalyst that would finally trigger the substantial flow to the North West that had been long sought.

Tupper's transatlantic success in wearing two hats was not to be permanent, the Liberals attacking the duality of his role. Despite his frequent Atlantic crossings, Tupper himself knew that he could not indefinitely fill both roles effectively. There was no doubt which job he wanted if he had to choose. To be high commissioner was a more glorious thing than to be a minister in Ottawa – and more rewarding in what he could achieve for Canada. With financing for the Canadian Pacific finally in place, or so it seemed, in May 1884 he resigned both as minister of railways and canals and as member of Parliament. Upon his departure for London, he had been drawn by his colleagues in a carriage from the Parliament Buildings to the nearby rail station. A fortnight later, Tupper was contentedly back in London, moving into a larger leased residence on the Cromwell Road and resuming from there his always voluminous correspondence with Macdonald.

Upon his welcome return to London, Tupper's immediate priority, as had been Galt's, was the promotion of emigration, with trade a close second.

Under Galt, the agents in Glasgow, Bristol, Liverpool, and Ireland had begun to work together in a more coordinated way; under Tupper, they became yet more of a team, even supporting Stephen's ultimately vain efforts to induce the British government to help finance large-scale emigration. At Tupper's direction, the emigration agents also assumed commercial promotion, although funds from Ottawa were limited. The agent in Liverpool in particular became something of a trade promotion enthusiast across Europe, he and Tupper making at least one tour together, visiting continental agents. With good reason, Tupper could report that his London staff and agents were "keenly alive to the necessity of doing everything in their power to create new markets for Canadian produce of various kinds."[10]

In British markets, food was Canada's prime opportunity, but despite Tupper's best efforts, obstacles in the form of phytosanitary and animal health regulations kept getting in the way, occasionally it seemed for the sole purpose of discouraging imports. Canadian exports of cattle, butter, seafood, pork, and condensed milk all encountered difficulties sooner or later in both British and continental markets. A more fundamental problem was the indifference of Canadian exporters to the European market when the United States market was so close at hand. However, a combination of higher us tariffs on imports and a determined campaign by Tupper to inform prospective Canadian exporters of European packaging, pricing, and labelling requirements combined to increase by more than one-half the exports of foodstuffs, especially following the creation of the Department of Trade and Commerce in December 1892.

Tupper also showed notable energy in furthering Canadian participation in various exhibitions, primarily the great Colonial and Indian Exhibition of 1886. From his vantage point as a member of the Prince of Wales's commission for the exhibition, he obtained additional display space for Canadian products. He had returned home the year before, travelling across the country to identify the most promising products. At the Colonial Exhibition itself, he helped to organize more than eighty lectures and other meetings, all intended to draw additional attention to the excellence of Canadian products and to the burgeoning opportunities for emigrants and investors. In his promotional efforts, the high commissioner had two British clerks who did little else but handle correspondence and distribute pamphlets and lantern slides. But as subsequent high commissioners would experience, they were also frequently called upon to arrange theatre tickets, letters of introduction, passports, and even hotel reservations for the growing numbers of visitors. Lacrosse teams, Indian chiefs, businessmen, and a motley collection of politicians all presented their peculiar demands. Among the seemingly endless stream was the young Robert Borden, the Halifax law partner of Tupper's son, Charles Hibbert Tupper. Borden called upon Tupper several times to learn more about evolving imperial relations as well as to discuss politics in Nova Scotia.

In trade and emigration promotion, despite the limited funds available, Tupper had something of a free hand, and he used it. Decidedly less free was his hand in all matters financial. Although Tupper himself acknowledged that Barings and Glyns, had performed well, their several banking charges remained high. Barings had collaborated with Tupper first when he was premier of Nova Scotia in the crucial pre-Confederation year of 1865, but fifteen years later he was not so certain that the services of the two banks were still required. Contracts with them would of course be observed, but the high commissioner should henceforth be involved in every financial transaction, in part to ensure that the best possible terms were obtained. Tupper was on good terms with Rose, but suspected that the self-interest of his old friend intruded occasionally upon his objective financial acumen. He was doubtful whether Rose should be involved in projects in which he had a pecuniary interest, a practice that hitherto had apparently bothered no one.

Tupper realized, as Galt had done before him, that the high commissioner could not assume complete financial control from the two banks, given their contractual rights over existing loans. However, he took the first occasion available to demonstrate that Canadian credit was such that the two banks need be no longer involved in placements and that he could obtain better terms for new loans than Rose could in the renewal of existing loans (on which Rose was paid a commission). On the first occasion of a new borrowing, Tupper took it upon himself to shop it around the City (Leonard Tilley, the finance minister, and his deputy minister were in London, but both were ill). Having successfully pressed the Bank of Montreal to take part of the loan on terms more favourable to the government, Tupper felt able to reject Rose's offer on behalf of a British bank syndicate (which not surprisingly included the London and Westminster Bank, of which Rose was a director). Instead, he skilfully raised the balance elsewhere in the City, including from two Australian banks. The evidence was now ample, Tupper wrote to Macdonald, that "the best interests of the country require that the High Commissioner should represent here the Dominion financially to the fullest extent and should under advice from Ottawa be charged with negotiations of all loans."[11]

Tupper was prompt in accepting a leadership role among the agents general for Canadian provinces and for New Zealand, the Cape of Good Hope, and several Australian colonies. Upon Lord Derby's appointment as colonial secretary in 1882, Galt had begun the practice of occasional meetings with him to discuss the evolving place of the self-governing colonies of the Empire. In reaping the benefit of Galt's initiative, Tupper became in effect the dean of the colonial representatives, leading the successful charge, for example, against the imposition on colonial loans of the substantial stamp duty on foreign securities. He also became something of a spokesman on Pacific affairs, associating himself fully with his Antipodean colleagues in the desirability of Britain occupying the New Hebrides and of laying a Pacific cable. Canada, he explained succinctly, would become even more of a Pacific nation with the completion of the rail line to Vancouver.

Canada would also have become a Caribbean nation if the colonial authorities in both Jamaica and Barbados had succeeded in their ambitions. In June 1884, when Canada was seeking more liberal access for its products in the British West Indies, Macdonald informed Tupper that Jamaican representatives would call upon him to discuss that troubled colony's entry into Confederation, a subject of interest to the prime minister since his second wife, Agnes Bernard, was the daughter of a former Jamaican privy councillor (twenty years Macdonald's junior, she had once described herself as a "poor Creole without a shilling"). The entry of Jamaica into Confederation "cannot come to anything, but still we should hear what they have to say, as it is a high compliment to Canada to have such a desire to join her political system coming from other colonies ... through Sir F. Hincks, enquiries were made last week from Barbadoes [sic] as to whether or not we would take them in."[12] Tupper gave no encouragement, but it was not the last time that inquiries, if not entreaties, from the British West Indies were to be made.

Imperial affairs were of growing interest to Tupper, but even in London he could not escape the demands of domestic politics. In 1885 the completion of the Canadian Pacific was once again in doubt. Although Tupper had resigned as minister of railways the year before, he remained deeply involved in the final stage of the long financing saga. In late 1884 Macdonald and Stephen had crossed to Britain where Tupper reviewed with them the unfriendliness of the London money markets to CPR financing. A plea from Macdonald to Tupper in early 1885 to return yet again to Ottawa arose largely from discontent in the cabinet at the prospect of yet another government loan. Tupper stalled for time, replying to Macdonald in late

February that "I like the position here very much. It suits me. My health is much better and I am vain enough to believe that I am fairly well qualified for the position and able to do important work for Canada, but I look upon the success of the C.P.R. as so vital to the progress and greatness of Canada, that I have no hesitation in placing myself unreservedly in your hands."[13] For the moment, however, Tupper escaped return to Ottawa, the fortunes of the CPR gradually recovering, thanks in part to his success in inducing Barings to participate in a mortgage offering by the railway.

Galt had been high commissioner when the first urgings of imperial defence cooperation were heard. The Carnarvon commission of 1883, with which Macdonald had met, had accepted Britain's prime responsibility for imperial defence, so its allusion to colonial contributions could be ignored by Macdonald, following his one statement on the subject. But even he was unable to escape entirely. Tupper in 1884 pressed upon him the dispatch to the Sudan of volunteers from the Canadian Permanent Force to join Australian colonial units in the effort to rescue General Gordon, besieged in Khartoum. Macdonald was having none of it, and did not share Tupper's hope that the contribution of a few Canadian soldiers in the Sudan might make a British railway loan more likely. He wired Tupper, flatly rejecting the idea: "Our men and money would be ... sacrificed to get Gladstone and Co. out of the hole they have plunged themselves into by their own imbecility."[14] He argued that only the office of the governor general could supervise the recruitment of volunteers by the War Office, adding that "the reciprocal aid to be given by the Colonies and England should be a matter of treaty, deliberately entered into and settled on a permanent basis."

The romantic notions of Canadian military participation to help relieve Khartoum were soon forgotten in the face of a domestic imbroglio: the Riel Rebellion, or what Tupper described as that "disagreeable little outbreak among the half-breeds in the North-West." The fact that in March 1885 Ottawa was able to place troops on the Red River within eleven days was promptly cited as evidence of the central role of the Canadian Pacific in binding the country together, physically if not spiritually. In light of that success, Parliament approved in June 1885 yet another railway loan, however reluctantly. In London, Stephen arrived with the reassuring news that the government had agreed to take up $20 million of the total CPR first mortgage bonds of $35 million in replacement of the stock that it had held in the company. On that basis, the Bank of Montreal would be willing to extend yet again its loans. The covert campaign of the Grand

Trunk had not prevented the financing of the Pacific line, although its adverse propaganda would hinder even Canadian government borrowing for some years to come. Once in London, Stephen was highly gratified by confirmation that Barings, having swallowed its basic unhappiness over the fact that the Grand Trunk had not been chosen, would assume the balance of the $15 million CPR bond issue. It was largely Tupper's persistence that had convinced the bank to participate in the final stage of the financing, although Morton, Rose and Company declined, despite Rose's assurances to Macdonald that Stephen "may depend on my doing all I can for the enterprise and I am putting all the friends I can influence with the stock."[15] Stephen was sceptical, remaining convinced that Charles Rose, Sir John's son, was in the pocket of the Grand Trunk.

The completion of the line to the Pacific was a close-run thing. By 5 November 1885 Stephen was able to reassure Macdonald that the line was "out of danger." Two days later, Donald Smith drove the last spike at the suitably Scottish-sounding Craigellachie, about twenty miles west of Revelstoke. By the end of 1886, government loans had been rapidly repaid, either by the return of grant land or by cash, and George Stephen was created Lord Mount Stephen. In another few years Smith was made Canada's second railway baron, Lord Strathcona. Tupper's rewards were more immediate. When he had returned to Canada in August 1885 to promote the Colonial and Indian Exhibition to be held in London the following year, the directors of the CPR gave him $100,000 in shares. Lady Tupper received a jewelled brooch fashioned from the last spike. Tupper in turn promised the two cousins that he would now press the British government for a Pacific steamer subsidy, ensuring thereby an all-red route from Britain across the Atlantic, Canada, and the Pacific to Asia. Memories of past parliamentary animosities had faded in the bright light of success.

Despite the completion of the Pacific line, Macdonald's government continued to show increasing infirmities as the 1887 election approached. Neither Macdonald personally nor his government were in sound health: the execution of Louis Riel for murder had handed Quebec to the Liberals. In Nova Scotia the separatists were again rampant. Macdonald well knew that he needed all the help that he could get. "Come out," he had again cabled to Tupper in late July 1886, but Tupper, loath to leave London, had managed to put off the inevitable for six months. By January 1887, however, he was in New York en route to Ottawa. From there he wrote to Macdonald, "As I have not been able to convince you that it was best for me to remain in England ... as a good party man I am entirely

The "Ram of Cumberland," Sir Charles Tupper, in full court kit as concurrently minister of finance and acting high commissioner, embodied what he long advocated: that the high commissioner be a member of the Canadian cabinet. Mackenzie King later rejected the idea out of hand, although in Vincent Massey he did eventually appoint a former minister.

at your disposal ... I will go to N.S. and make the best fight I can in sup-port of our party [against the Liberal secessionists] and then return to England, or I will resign my office and contest my old constituency as a private member or as a member of the Government, as you may decide."[16] Tupper and Macdonald promptly agreed that he would immediately re-join the government as minister of finance and subsequently contest his old Cumberland seat in a by-election, all the while continuing as high commissioner, again in an "acting" (i.e., unpaid) capacity. On 27 Janu-ary 1887, two days after his arrival in Ottawa, Tupper was sworn in as minister of finance. During the next sixteen months, he first won the by-election and then plunged into the subsequent general election, winning Nova Scotia (and rendering himself thereby even more clearly Mac-donald's successor), brought down a budget, and presided with his usual vigour over Canada's finances. As acting high commissioner, he returned to London in late July 1887, only to cross again to Ottawa in October to deliver his first budget as minister of finance.

In June 1887 Queen Victoria's fifty years on the throne were marked, in Lord Salisbury's words, by "black Queens, Indian feudatories, and gen-eral royal festivities" – and the first in a series of colonial conferences. Rec-ommended to Salisbury by the Imperial Federation League, the colonial conference was a loosely organized meeting, a sort of family gathering, the invitation to the settlement colonies stating casually that "any leading public man who may be at liberty to come to England next year would be welcome." The agenda was brief, giving primacy of place to defence, although imperial post and telegraph were included. Salisbury himself, however, was not amused by either royal festivities or by the conference. In his view, an imperial federation or customs union remained "distant and shadowy." In any case, British fiscal policy needed no change. What might be more feasible was "neither a general union nor a *Zollverein*, but a *Kriegsverein* – a combination for purposes of self-defence."[17] Land defences were to a limited degree accepted as the responsibility of the self-governing colony. In the case of the navy, Salisbury, having recently lost the erratic Randolph Churchill from his cabinet ostensibly over high tax-ation arising from military spending, was presumably gratified when the otherwise tiresome Australian colonies agreed among themselves to put up annually £126,000 (and New Zealand £20,000) to help keep a Royal Naval squadron in their waters. But he remained sceptical about the value of additional or even existing colonies.

Adamantly opposed to Home Rule in Ireland, Salisbury had no inter-est in colonies, however large or distant, that had ambitions to a voice in imperial policy at Westminster. If the self-governing colonies could not accept that policy-making was the exclusive prerogative of Britain, they were free to leave the Empire. All in all, Salisbury found the 1887 colo-nial conference such a bore that he contrived to ensure that another was not held in London for another seven years. The celebrations neverthe-less unleashed yet more territorial acquisitions, especially in the scramble for Africa. Bechuanaland, Burma, and Nigeria had been acquired during the preceding two years; Somaliland and Zululand in 1887; Kenya and Sarawak in 1888; Rhodesia in 1889 and Zanzibar in 1890.

At the conference (which Macdonald and Tupper could not attend, Parliament sitting), the Canadian representative was Alexander Camp-bell, the recently appointed lieutenant-governor of Ontario, and Sand-ford Fleming. Campbell ignored the proposal of the Cape of Good Hope that all colonies place a tariff on non-imperial goods to pay for imperial defence. Blake, the Liberal leader of the opposition, agreed: "We should not be called upon to expend our blood and treasure in carrying out Jingo schemes ... on the other side of the water." In supporting Campbell's rejec-tion of Admiralty proposals for imperial naval cooperation, Fleming con-tended that the completion of the transcontinental railway would make a major contribution to imperial defence by its ability to convey rapidly troops from Britain to the Pacific, by-passing the Suez Canal. In May 1886 the CPR had applied for a subsidy for a fortnightly mail service to China and Japan "at 14 knots." Tupper enlisted the assistance of leading Tories, basing his request on the precedent of the subsidy to the P&O for its Suez service to the East, drawing in part on a strongly supportive despatch from the British minister in Tokyo (which Tupper may well have prompted). By the end of 1887, his campaign had proven successful, confirmed by a CPR contract "for conveyance of H.M. mails, troops and stores between Hali-fax or Quebec and Hong Kong" (upon which the trans-Pacific "White Empress" service of the next fifty years was to be based). The chancellor of the exchequer conceded ruefully to Tupper that it was he himself and not the high commissioner who had made all the concessions in the nego-tiation of the subsidy. Less successful was Sandford Fleming's advocacy of a trans-Pacific cable. British financing was not forthcoming.

Even on his occasional visits to Ottawa as minister of finance, Tupper became further engaged in international affairs. He was soon embroiled in a different kind of free trade debate: in 1886 he had been called upon by Macdonald to travel to Washington to review Canadian relations with the United States, including in particular commercial ties in the wake of a persistent sealing dispute in the Behring Sea. The area was in international waters, but Washington, ostensibly acting in the name of conservation, applied its own regulations extraterritorially and excluded Canadian vessels. In both the Behring Sea case and the almost concurrent dispute about inshore fishing violations by Americans off both Canada and Newfoundland, the United States acted "contrary to the established principles of international law" by attempting to extend its national law beyond its borders. In the House of Commons, Tupper stressed that only the British government could act in a dispute involving international waters. Later, from London, partly through direct correspondence with his son, Charles Hibbert Tupper, since 1882 a member of Parliament, he played a significant role in ensuring that the British legation in Washington followed a stiff line, despite Salisbury's detached attitude.

Recurrent problems with the United States in the inshore fisheries resulted in the setting up of a joint high commission, consisting of Tupper; the Birmingham industrialist and member of Parliament, Joseph Chamberlain; and Sir Lionel Sackville West, the British minister in the United States. The minister of justice of Canada, John Thompson, served as counsel. From his place on the commission, Tupper pressed repeatedly on a somewhat sceptical Foreign Office the merits of a tough line against US fishing and dominated the British side of the negotiation, including keeping Chamberlain "up to the mark" to the point that the US secretary of state observed that "Mr. Chamberlain has yielded control of the negotiations over to Sir Charles Tupper."[18] Thompson was less impressed. He wrote to his wife that Tupper had said that he and Chamberlain "had differed as to the point and the English Law Officers had sustained *his* opinion! We should be humble in the presence of such gifts."[19]

Back in Ottawa in April 1888, Tupper saw through the House of Commons a bill approving a draft treaty with the United States. However, the US Senate rejected it in August. For the next decade a *modus vivendi* largely recognized Canadian fishing interests and the seal dispute in the Behring Sea entered a period of dormancy, despite Tupper's efforts in London to stir both the British and his colleagues in Ottawa to take decisive action by seeking the protection of the Royal Navy for Canadian seal hunters. Ottawa's perception that the Foreign Office under Salisbury was less than resolute on Canadian questions, seeking instead to placate the United States, added to the growing conviction not that a Canadian navy was needed but that better ways must be devised for Canada's voice to be heard in international affairs, especially in Washington, whenever its own interests were directly involved. Precedents were being established.

When the Behring Sea negotiations in Washington concluded, the parliamentary session in Ottawa had already begun. Tupper could not hope to return at an early date to London; his parliamentary duties as finance minister for the time being were inescapable. By May 1888 when the session ended, George Stephen organized something of a campaign to keep Tupper at home. More importantly, Macdonald himself informed him that "If you will only consent to remain, I will publicly recognise you as my successor."[20] But Tupper would heed no entreaties to remain as the ailing premier's favoured successor. On 22 May 1888, following sixteen months in his dual role as minister of finance and acting high commissioner, he resigned from Parliament and embarked for Britain. Tupper could now undertake, unfettered, the more challenging and rewarding single role of Canada's representative in London. His son, Charles Hibbert Tupper, whose interests his father constantly strove to advance, was soon appointed minister of marine and fisheries.

Some of the tasks awaiting Tupper were as familiar to him as they had been to Galt; others were more novel and controversial. The familiar were those relating to financial needs; the promotion of emigration and trade; and the negotiation of commercial treaties. Again like Galt, Tupper could barely restrain his desire to enter into the debates over Ireland that convulsed Westminster, with Gladstone pledged to Home Rule and Salisbury opposing it. In Ottawa, Edward Blake was so certain that Tupper would involve himself in the Irish question that he forecast that the high commissioner would soon stand for election to the British Parliament.

Upon his return to London, Tupper plunged into the task of floating a $25 million government loan on the London markets, the approval for which, as minister of finance, he had pushed through Parliament not six months before. Rose obtained offers from the Bank of Montreal and the Bank of British Columbia (not surprisingly, since he was a director of both), as well as from the ubiquitous Barings and Glyns. But Tupper, with the assistance of Thomas Skinner, a London director of the Bank of Montreal, successfully pressed the two banks to do better, in part a reflection of the increasing creditworthiness of Canada. "We stand nearly on a par with India [in creditworthiness] and in less than a year I hope to lead India," Tupper wrote proudly to his son.[21] With that particular triumph behind him, Tupper was ready to take on responsibility for all future borrowings.

With the loan of 1888, the days of Rose as financial commissioner ended, at least as far as new placements were concerned. His dealings came briefly under the scrutiny of Parliament, the result of Tupper's success in obtaining better terms. In a debate in the House of Commons on 27 May 1887, the erratic and eccentric Peter Mitchell, former premier of New Brunswick and once a cabinet colleague of Rose, Galt, and Tupper, had dismissed Rose's informal representation of Canada's interests as little more than "obtaining titles for gentlemen in this country" (Mitchell himself being desperately disappointed at not having been knighted). Perhaps, Mitchell mused, Rose had in turn instructed Tupper in "how to perform these little duties ... by bowing and scraping." The rough and blunt Mitchell concluded his sarcastic review by urging that "we shall hear no more of Sir John Rose receiving commissions."*[22] Thus warned, Tupper rejected the commission fees on several small borrowings.

There remained, however, the contracts with Barings and Glyns, valid for another five years. Tupper, fully backed by Ottawa, worked to extricate Canada from the increasingly anachronistic and costly agreements. In light of the fact that Barings, following bankruptcy in 1890, had been reorganized and Glyns had been reincorporated as Glyn, Mills and Currie, the Department of Justice conveniently found that there was now no longer reason why Ottawa should not appoint a new agent. Not surprisingly, the Bank of Montreal, the largest of the Canadian banks, was eventually designated by an order-in-council of 3 February 1893 (when in any event the ten-year agreement with the two London banks would expire). Finally, thirteen years after the office of high commissioner had been formally established, and twenty-three years after the arrival of Rose, the leading role of the High Commission in matters financial had been affirmed. When the Bank of Montreal became the government's sole financial advisor, the role of the High Commission in financial matters became yet more direct. Correspondence from the High Commission soon reflected its increased responsibilities in all matters financial. Of the total of ten thousand letters prepared by the office in 1895, no less than fifteen hundred related in some way to accounting or fiscal management, ranging from placement of government securities to subsidies for transat-

* Max Aitken, the future Lord Beaverbrook, greatly admired his fellow New Brunswicker, Peter Mitchell (1824–99). Aitken's clergyman father had buried Mitchell with honour (despite the dislike that his Presbyterian soul must have felt at Mitchell's habitual philandering). Aitken, undeterred by such foibles (which he himself subsequently greatly exceeded), later erected a monument to Mitchell in Newcastle, New Brunswick.

lantic and trans-Pacific carriage of mail and migrants, the best arrangement for recovering from the royal privy purse the cost of the Queen's
Plate for the annual flat race in Toronto, and the acquisition of small arms
for the Canadian militia.

It had taken patience and perseverance by both Galt and Tupper for
the High Commission to gain control of Canada's many financial requirements; decidedly less amenable to patience and perseverance were the yet
more intractable problems of emigration. Here the difficulty was basically
the continuing unwillingness of the British government to offer assistance
in the absence of guarantees from Ottawa to repay advances proposed
for would-be emigrants. Without assistance, the poor could not migrate,
however eager they might be to leave urban squalor or rural poverty for
the new world.

A more fundamental deterrent to emigration was the lingering economic depression in both Britain and Canada. News of the sluggish
Canadian economy discouraged some, but the decade-long economic
depression of 1886–96 had a further adverse effect; it reduced even the
limited amount of Canadian government revenue available for emigration promotion. In 1891 Tupper proposed to Ottawa a package of additional measures to promote Canada throughout Europe as the land of
infinite promise, but the package was rejected. The subsequent transfer of
immigration responsibilities from the Department of Agriculture to the
Department of the Interior meant eventually the adoption of several of
Tupper's proposals, but the United States remained the preferred destination for most European emigrants until the turn of the century.

Tupper, however, was not easily discouraged, convinced as he was that
much more could be done if additional funds became available. Even limited promotion would in time pay dividends. With his old friend Sandford Fleming, he travelled through Scandinavia in 1892, surveying the
prospects. In Liverpool in 1893 he brought together all those who were
involved in Canadian emigration promotion in Europe: Dominion and
provincial agents and representatives of shipping companies and railways.
As Galt had soon recognized, part of what was needed was more favourable news about Canada in the British press. Canadian exports to Britain
on the one hand and Canada as a place for investment and settlers on the
other should be emphasized, especially in the uncertainties following the
Riel Rebellion. Longer-term objectives could also be advanced: an imperial tariff preference; improved imperial communications and transport;
and Canadian autonomy within the Empire. However, the several efforts
of Rose, Galt, and Tupper to place favourable stories in a reluctant or

indifferent British press or even to publish journals themselves seldom succeeded, partly as a result of the erratic and tardy flow of reliable Canadian news to the High Commission. By 1884 Joseph Colmer, the secretary of the High Commission, was in near despair: "people say that the Government office is the last place to go in London for information of anything that is going on in Canada."[23]

Although the British press remained indifferent to stories supplied by the High Commission or its agents, *The Times* finally appointed a correspondent in Canada in 1896, as Rose had proposed more than two decades before. Since that appointment could not itself guarantee favourable coverage, Tupper increased the annual distribution of leaflets to a remarkable one and a half million, bought advertising space, and cooperated in the launch of the *Colonial Register*. Beginning in 1883, the ubiquitous Thomas Skinner had published the more ambitious *Canadian Gazette*, an avowedly promotional paper (not surprisingly its bias was toward the Canadian Pacific over the Grand Trunk since it was largely financed by George Stephen).* Tupper also supported the new paper, but it soon proved to be of only short-lived assistance to broader promotional efforts, suffering as it did from the suspicions that it was pro-Liberal. With the completion of the CPR finally in prospect, the *Canadian Gazette* also expired. With its demise, the emigration field was, despite the torrent of Canadian leaflets and advertising, still handicapped in its competition with the yet more energetic agents of the Australian colonies.

Less prompt in results were Tupper's efforts to carry forward Galt's campaign to negotiate commercial treaties that directly affected Canadian interests. In 1884 Tupper had taken satisfaction in obtaining from the British government designation as a full plenipotentiary, in tandem with the British ambassador, in commercial negotiations with Spain, again mainly about the Spanish Antilles. As Galt had found, continuing Spanish domestic uncertainties limited the negotiations, but Macdonald was nevertheless pleased with the important precedent that Tupper had established. "You certainly have scored a great point in securing your being united with the British Ambassador, not only in the negotiation but the completion of the Treaty."[24] That agreement had ensured that Canada received most-favoured-nation treatment, but Tupper's participation in subsequent

---

* Sir Thomas Skinner (1840–1920), founder of various business publications, was a director of the CPR, the Bank of Montreal, and the North West Land Company, in which Stephen's cousin, Donald Smith, was principal shareholder.

negotiations with Spain was less successful. Spain would not extend the treaty to its Antilles, its market of prime interest to Canada, and it proved uninterested in additional mutual concessions, having recently secured reciprocal access to the much larger United States market.*

More successful in the longer term was Tupper's single-handed negotiation in Paris in 1893 of minimal tariff access to France for a range of products (the British ambassador, Lord Dufferin, the former governor general, limiting himself to a formal role). It took two years, however, for the treaty to be ratified by the Canadian Parliament, a source of consternation to Tupper. The lassitude displayed by Mackenzie Bowell, the minister of trade and commerce and soon to be prime minister, caused both Tupper and his son, by then minister of justice, to threaten resignation. Eventually the delay was overcome, thereby confirming Tupper in his success in negotiating a commercial agreement as a plenipotentiary. From 1893 onwards, Canada itself would negotiate the substance of all its commercial agreements.

The negotiations with Spain and France paralleled discussions with far-reaching political implications: the creation of an imperial tariff preference. In June 1885 Tupper was the principal speaker at the inaugural meeting of the new Canadian trade section of the London Chamber of Commerce, proclaiming that "The old story of the Colonies being a burden has passed away." A circular sent to prospective members before the meeting had identified imperial federation as agenda item one. Probably Tupper put it there. Aware, however, that Macdonald viewed with caution proposals for imperial federation, he approached the subject gingerly. Nevertheless, he shared with the meeting his conviction that there could be no question that proposals for greater imperial collaboration were timely for Canada: "We were lapsing into a state of complete dependence on the United States."[25] Although he avoided endorsing outright an imperial tariff preference, he came close to extolling the *Zollverein* approach to imperial unity. "The Government of this country and the Government of Canada," the minutes of the London Chamber of Commerce record Tupper as stating, should "draw up such a tariff as between themselves ... to bind together the great outlying dependencies of the Empire itself to

* Lord Granville, the friend of Sir John Rose and several times colonial secretary and secretary of state for foreign affairs, had endorsed in mid-1884 the role of the Canadian plenipotentiary: "the actual negotiations would probably be conducted by Sir Charles Tupper, but the convention, if concluded, must be signed by both [British and Canadian] plenipotentiaries."

these British Isles by ties not only of sentimental loyalty but of the closest and most intimate commercial relations, which would be found to be of the greatest possible advantage to all (applause)." In short, why not create "one tariff within the Empire and another without?"[26] An immediate challenge was Britain's commercial treaties with Germany and Belgium, which contained most-favoured-nation clauses by which any tariff preference between colonies and Britain would be extended to them as well. Both countries declined to forego the MFN clause, leading the Canadian Parliament to urge Britain to renounce the two treaties altogether.

In launching himself into the growing debate about the merits of free trade versus an imperial tariff, Tupper was not only undertaking a challenge that had been troublesome to his predecessor; he was also assuming an advocacy role that would prove contentious for his successors, in greater or lesser degree, for decades to come. Other issues would come and go, but the question of an imperial tariff preference versus free trade would remain something of a leit-motif in Anglo-Canadian relations until almost a century later.

During the summer of 1884 an Imperial Federation League emerged from a meeting in London attended by Lord Carnarvon, the sometime colonial secretary; Galt's friend, W.H. Smith; Oliver Mowat, the Liberal premier of Ontario; and Tupper. Although supportive of a "Greater Britain" based upon a willing partnership of Dominions and the United Kingdom, it was unclear where the League would stand in the still inchoate imperial debate. A journal was published from 1886 and Toronto and Montreal branches were soon formed. Opposed as the two branches were to commercial union with the United States, they strongly favoured an imperial tariff preference. The first chairman of the Imperial Federation League, W.E. Forster,* the recent chief secretary for Ireland, invited Tupper to join the council, but he declined on the grounds that to attempt the political federation of the Empire was a longer route to imperial unity than "fiscal arrangements by which the outlying portions of the Empire would be treated ... on a different footing from foreign countries." He was fully aware that in Canada the league's goals included a trade policy "between Great Britain and her colonies by means of which a discrimination in the exchange of natural and manufactured products will be made in favour of one another and against foreign nations." Macdonald had

---

* W.E. Forster (1818–86), under-secretary for the colonies at the time of the British North America Act, had been chief secretary for Ireland from 1880 to 1882. He was a collaborator of Lord Carnarvon on both colonial and Irish questions.

no difficulty with such ideas, declaring in a speech in London in 1885, "if you will give colonial produce [a preference], I will commit myself ... [to] give British goods, and only British goods, preferential treatment." He did, however, have reservations about his ministers joining the league and implying thereby acceptance of military or other imperial expenditures. George Stephen added his similar advice: "we out here will have enough to do if we take good care of the Empire *here* without attempting to extend our efforts to the management of affairs in England or in other [*sic*] outlying parts of the Empire."[27] Tupper had readily agreed: "we will for many years find ample work in consolidating our existing constitution and developing our material resources." Macdonald, however, continued to doubt Tupper's real convictions, carefully cautioning him again not to become ensnared in projects for imperial political federation. "I don't believe that a practical scheme can ever be worked out for a *legislative* Confederation of the Empire, but, as you say, it would have been highly impolitic of you to throw cold water on any attempt at a greater consolidation or drawing together of the different parts of the Empire."[28] No imperial tariff preference emerged, but the league could claim some of the credit for the pioneering Colonial and Indian Exhibition, the foundation of the Imperial Institute, and the first colonial conference.

Five years after the founding of the league, Tupper accepted the renewed invitation of its second president, the Liberal imperialist Lord Rosebery (who was to become prime minister four years later), to join its council, its focus having shifted from political to economic questions. As guest speaker at the league's annual dinner in 1889, Tupper contended that

you will not be able to maintain public interest in the League much longer unless you propound some practical policy for promoting the union of the Empire ... I therefore venture to suggest that a conference may be called by the Imperial Government of representatives of the self-governing colonies to consider the best means of promoting the object ... when a conference takes place it will be found that the adoption of a policy of mutual preferential trade ... will provide the tie of mutual self-interest in addition to the purely sentimental bond which now exists.[29]

Tupper also advocated the inclusion of ministers from the self-governing colonies in the British cabinet when foreign policy was to be discussed. Only then might one contemplate colonial contributions to imperial defence. Macdonald was displeased at Tupper's speech to the league, concerned as he was about its effect among French-speaking Canadians, including Hector Langevin, his chief Quebec lieutenant. "It would be well, I think, for you to let it be known as widely as possible that you spoke your own opinions, and not in any way as High Commissioner ... The Quebecers here have got it into their heads that your proposal that a general conference should be held involved the discussion of the expediency of altering the British North America Act."[30] Tupper was unimpressed with Macdonald's misgivings, especially since they came from someone who had himself been a member of the league.

I have been much surprised to learn that my action in regards to Imperial Federation has excited a good deal of dissatisfaction in Quebec ... although you and two other members of the Government are on the council of the Imperial Federation League, I have stood somewhat aloof. I have not disguised the opinion that the difficulties in the way of a parliamentary federation were insuperable.

When I proposed that a conference should be invited to consider the practicability of adopting a fiscal policy by which Colonial products would be protected here against those coming from foreign countries, I only propounded a policy which I had avowed as the policy of our party when in opposition ... I said, "I do not in any way represent the Government of Canada, but simply express my own views and opinions with regard to this question." ... When I made this bold proposal to strengthen the tie that connects Canada with the crown by taxing corn [wheat] and cattle from the United States of America and all other foreign countries – for such in effect it was – I had little idea that it would be received with such favour here and be so completely misunderstood in Canada.[31]

With that, Macdonald let the matter drop, probably concluding that nothing was to be gained by stirring up further the Ram of Cumberland (to whom in any event he remained indebted for his readiness to rejoin the political fray in Canada).

Tupper, however, was intrigued by the idea, earlier advanced by Galt among others, that representatives of the major colonies should sit in the British cabinet. He joined a committee of the league in calling for "a Council of the Empire," underpinned, as the Canadian branches urged, by an imperial *Zollverein*. Publicly he expounded the idea in the *Nineteenth Century* in both October 1891 and April 1892:

We shall stand in the position of having three great dominions [Canada, the Australian colonies, southern Africa] ... When that is accomplished, the measure which the Marquis of Lorne has suggested, of having the representatives of these colonies during their term of office here in London, practically cabinet ministers [could be instituted, giving] the government of England an opportunity of learning in the most direct and complete manner the views and sentiments of each of those great British communities in regard to all questions of foreign policy affecting the colonies.

The representatives of those three great British communities here in London should be leading members of the cabinet of the day of the country they represent, going out of office when their government is changed ... whoever represented those dominions in London should have a seat in their own parliament, and be a member of the administration ... when a member of the cabinet of Australasia, of South Africa or of Canada represented it in London, he should ex-officio be sworn a member of the Privy Council in England and practically become a cabinet minister here ... they would have the opportunity of addressing to the whole cabinet the views that animated the governments of their colonies, and they would have the advantage of learning fully the views of the government of this country, and in that way be able to communicate its sentiments more perfectly to their respective colonies.

Macdonald did not take up directly Tupper's proposal, but the possibilities of an imperial preferential tariff continued to attract him. Following the Conservative election victory of 1891, an address to the crown was formulated by Galt at Macdonald's request, pressing for the preference. Later in the year, Macdonald wrote to W.H. Smith, Salisbury's leader in the House of Commons, that if the Conservative government won re-election at Westminster, "some imperial [tariff] policy can be formed and carried out." Only months before his death, Macdonald wrote to Galt in terms that left little doubt that he had come to agree with him that an imperial preference of 25 per cent would serve as a counter to the Liberals' flirtation with tariff reciprocity and even commercial union with the United States. That there was something useful in domestic partisan terms in Tupper's enthusiasm – and to a degree the Conservative party's – for an imperial tariff preference is incontrovertible: it was a useful stick with which to beat the Liberals who were portrayed as hell-bent upon annexation to the United States through progressive tariff reciprocity, leading to full free trade and eventually commercial union. The fact that the Conservatives, including Tupper himself, had sought more trade with the United States did not deter their support for an imperial *Zollverein*. Paradoxically, Lord Lansdowne, the governor general, waded into the debate, reviewing the advantages of some form of commercial union with the United States as a desirable alternative to what he saw as the unpopularity of Macdonald's

National Policy, especially in rural Canada. Lansdowne was a last gasp of Gladstone's anti-imperialists and the prime minister was not unduly concerned about his opinion. "Commercial union is a dead duck," Macdonald wrote to Tupper in his sprightly way: "Lansdowne sees now that my policy ... of allowing the cry of commercial union to blaze, crackle, and go out with a stink, without giving it undue importance, was a wise one."[32] Commercial union, Macdonald was confident, had finally been seen for what it was: an irreversible step toward annexation by the United States.

Support for an imperial tariff preference was not, however, to be found among all members of the league. Some knew very well that any increase in British tariffs (especially the introduction of a tariff on food) to make a reality of a preference was politically infeasible. Nonetheless, Tupper, in his two articles in *Nineteenth Century*, had repeated his earlier advocacy that Britain and all the colonies might have "one rate of duties for all British countries and another for foreign countries." In a letter to the editor of the *Imperial Federation*, he continued to advocate the economic route to greater imperial unity: "it might be arranged to have in this country, and in all the colonies, a double column tariff, one rate of duties for all British countries and another for foreign countries. These tariffs would not necessarily be the same in different colonies."

The league eventually split on the question of both a tariff preference and a common defence policy and, having "reached the limits of its effective action," dissolved itself in November 1893. Many members blamed Tupper for forcing the issue of a preference and thereby undermining the league's unity, but he was unrepentant. He subsequently sought more unified advocates for a preference in the successor British Empire League, founded in July 1894. Additionally, support for enhanced imperial ties appeared to be in the offing in the more tangible form of subsidies by both Canada and Britain for a fast steamship service between Liverpool and Montreal and between Vancouver and Japan and Hong Kong. A trans-Pacific cable, again to be subsidized by Britain, also seemed in prospect, following repeated urgings by Tupper, the agents general of the Antipodean colonies, and the first colonial conference.

Canada took an imperial initiative of sorts in convening what has come to be counted as the second colonial conference. In 1889 Parliament had offered a subsidy for a steamer service between Canada and Australia, but not until four years later was the initial sailing made from Sydney to Vancouver. In June 1894 Prime Minister Sir John Thompson, to the displeasure of the Colonial Office, invited representatives of the Australian colonies, Fiji, New Zealand, the Cape of Good Hope, and Hawaii to meet in

Ottawa. Britain was free to participate as it saw fit. Defence cooperation, to the Colonial Office's subsequent regret, was not mentioned, beyond the re-emergence of the proposal by the Cape of Good Hope for an empire-wide tariff to pay for imperial defence expenditure. The feasibility of a telegraphic cable linking Canada and Australia was eventually assigned to a committee that included Donald Smith of the CPR. Although five of the eight colonies represented pledged their broad support for "a customs arrangement between Great Britain and her colonies by which trade within the Empire may be placed on a more favourable footing than that which is carried on with foreign countries," unanimity was impossible in the face of the opposition of Queensland and New South Wales to what they regarded as an attempt to undermine with low-cost Canadian as well as British manufactures their own fledgling domestic industries.

All colonies could, however, agree in their opposition to Britain having most-favoured-nation treaties with foreign countries which left "the self-governing dependencies of the Empire" with no option but to offer countries outside the Empire the same tariff rates they offered to Britain. At a meeting in London of agents of Australian colonies, New Zealand and the Cape of Good Hope in November 1890, Tupper was requested to write to the colonial secretary suggesting that no British commercial treaty should in the future be binding upon the colonies without their assent, "but that every such treaty should contain a clause enabling the colonies to participate in its provisions, or not, as they may devise."

The doctrine of colonial commercial responsibility had come a long way since Galt had first expounded it. So had Anglo-Canadian relations: the anti-imperialist sentiments of Gladstone's first government had been transformed in a surprisingly short time into a debate throughout the Empire over the best framework to sustain the links between the imperial centre and distant colonies, as the post-Waterloo primacy of Britain in world affairs began to be questioned.

Given the fact that Canadian diplomacy continued to be conducted largely through London, Tupper came to regard himself implicitly, if not explicitly, as the Canadian foreign minister. That the role of the governor general was thereby diminished did not bother him; he would himself be the principal route for communication with the Foreign Office. As interlocutor he would necessarily, at least in his view, be consulted by Ottawa at every step in the formulation of external policy. On the other hand, the governor general was eager to ensure that protocol be followed by insisting upon the observance of the well-established precedent that all formal communications to London from "his Government" should pass through his office. Macdonald agreed, but clearly regarded the procedure as merely an initial formality, informing Tupper that the governor general "quite understands ... that the communication once opened, it is your business as our ambassador to urge the adoption of our views on the Home Government [*sic*] with all your power."[33]

Tupper's peripatetic diplomacy at international conferences in Paris, Vienna, and St Petersburg as well as in London was suspended when Macdonald urgently requested him to return home to campaign in the 1891 election. He was not surprised. Macdonald was again sickly, public policy increasingly uncertain, and relations with the United States endlessly troublesome. Tupper suggested that Macdonald accept a peerage and become British minister in Washington but he declined; he would not give up the premiership; he would fight yet one more election and Tupper must return to help him. By February 1891 Tupper was back in the familiar fray, although not this time seeking a seat himself.

The Liberals were not amused by Tupper's return to the electoral scene. Having become high commissioner, he should not simultaneously campaign at home in an election. That he, as high commissioner, was engaged in an overtly partisan way was blandly explained away by Tupper himself as an overriding duty at a time of national crisis. Canada's whole future would be at stake if a Liberal government pursued its policy of "unrestricted reciprocity" with the United States. Such a policy would result severing of ties with Britain and annexation by the United States. Macdonald himself left no doubt where he stood. "Under the broad folds of the Union Jack, we enjoy the most ample liberty to govern ourselves as we please, and at the same time we participate in the advantages which flow from association with the mightiest empire that the world has ever seen. Not only are we free to arrange our domestic concerns, but practically we possess the privilege of making our own [commercial] treaties with the outside world."

The Conservatives were re-elected, but only just. The CPR had again proven helpful to them, but it was Tupper who was the main target of Liberal complaint. Following the election, the resurgent opposition, led by Wilfrid Laurier, expressed outrage at the shameless role of "the sneak" in the election and urged that his unprincipled behaviour was "calculated to destroy the efficiency of the said office [of high commissioner]." Tupper paid no heed to the Liberals' lamentations before promptly departing for Washington to do just what he had so vigorously denounced the Liberals for proposing to do wholesale: to test the waters for some form of tariff reciprocity. From the spring of 1891 to mid-1893, Tupper, Foster, and Thompson attempted repeatedly to interest the United States in something less than full reciprocity only to be told that it must be a commercial union or nothing. Tupper explored the question both in Washington and with the United States ambassador in London, but to no avail. Macdonald in the meantime had died on 6 June 1891, two months after his election victory. With him expired the impetus behind the parliamentary address to the Queen on imperial economic relations, drafted by Galt. It was so watered down by Macdonald's successor, Sir John Abbott, that it came to nothing. And in Britain the defeat of Salisbury's Conservatives by Gladstone's Liberals meant that free traders were back in office.

If Tupper had remained in Ottawa for two more months before returning to London, he might have become at once prime minister. Three years before, when George Stephen had urged him to continue as minister of finance, Macdonald himself had spoken to Tupper in terms of holding himself in readiness for the premiership. Now Lady Macdonald urged the governor general, Lord Stanley, to send for Tupper – to the consternation of the Liberals. If Tupper had heeded his supporters, he might have become the Conservative leader, five years before he finally did so. However, while acting as a British delegate to an international postal conference in Vienna, Tupper received a telegram from his son pressing him to return at once to succeed the dying Macdonald, but he declined: "nothing could induce me to accept the position" (including even the likely offer of Macdonald's safe seat in Kingston). Instead, he recommended to his son that, Hector Langevin having been tarnished by scandal, he support John Thompson, the minister of justice. But Thompson in turn declined, believing that more time had to elapse until his conversion of twenty years before from Methodism to Roman Catholicism would be more widely accepted. Instead, John Abbott, the former Grand Trunk solicitor and veteran of the Pacific Scandal who, in an earlier observation of Macdonald, "had not a single qualification for the office," became prime minister. It was widely assumed, however, that he would in turn stand down when the next general election approached. Tupper's son, Thompson noted, was "as mad as he can be at the cold shoulder which the old tramp has got in many quarters," but the fact remained that while Tupper had enthusiastic advocates within the Conservative party, he also had implacable foes.[34] He was himself fully aware that it was not clear that he could win the leadership.

Between 1891 and 1896, given the domestic preoccupations of the government in Ottawa, Tupper had largely a free hand as high commissioner, working from 17 Victoria Street (near the agents general of four Australian colonies and the United States embassy). During those five years, three short-term prime ministers succeeded each other: Abbott attempted for seventeen months to govern from the Senate; Thompson* died after two years in office; the British-born senator, Mackenzie Bowell, the first minister of trade and commerce, lasted only sixteen months. Speculation had centred on Tupper to succeed Thompson, Macdonald's former secretary recording that "Sir Charles Tupper, who on Thompson's death should have been summoned without delay ... for some inexplicable reason was passed over by Lord Aberdeen in favour of Mr. Mackenzie Bowell, a worthy, loyal man, but one as little qualified to be Prime Minister of Canada as Lord Aberdeen was to be Governor General."[35] There had been an expectation that the indecisive Aberdeen would, despite his wife's well-known penchant for Liberals, finally send for Tupper, but the "war horse of Cumberland" did not appeal to the "weak and incapable governor under [the] control of an ambitious and meddlesome woman" (possibly Tupper had tactlessly let it be known that "the Governess General" did not appeal to him).

During this period of political confusion, Tupper was generally able to pursue policies that appeared best to him, but his informal mandate no longer embraced Canada–United States relations, although the Colonial Office continued to consult him on the subject and he exerted considerable indirect influence through his son, the minister of marine and fisheries, in the seemingly endless dispute in the Behring Sea. Charles Hibbert Tupper spent the summer of 1892 in London working with his father,

* Sir John Thompson, Tupper's fellow Nova Scotian whom he had encouraged to leave provincial politics for national, died on 12 December 1894, age fifty, while staying overnight at Windsor Castle upon being sworn to the Imperial Privy Council. Queen Victoria was shocked at his death: "I placed 2 wreaths on the coffin and turned to Sir C. Tupper, who was quite overcome, kissed my hand and said 'Canada will never forget this.' Sir J. Thompson was only 48, a very clever, able man, most loyal and excellent, and his loss a very great one to Canada" (Queen Victoria's journal entry for 13 December 1894, Royal Archives, Windsor). Tupper arranged for the prime minister's remains to be transported to Halifax by a fast cruiser, but was himself unable to accompany it, as had been his intention, due to a sudden illness. Possibly the illness was diplomatic; there had never been much love lost between the Tuppers and the Thompsons. Lady Aberdeen recorded complacently that Lady Thompson was privately pleased that "the old wretch Sir Charles Tupper" had been ordered by his physician to remain in Britain.

attempting to stiffen British resolve, having already concluded "that in future negotiations with the United States no British Minister at Washington should act for us." Despite the fact that the arbitration award of 1893 was largely in Canada's interests, Ottawa was determined to engage itself directly in future negotiations that affected Canada's fundamental interests, downplaying the intermediary role of British diplomats. In the perennial question of Newfoundland's entry into Confederation, both Galt and Tupper had been involved in discussions among St John's, London, and Ottawa, but Bowell finally decided that such discussions should henceforth be conducted primarily between Ottawa and St John's.

Tupper was convinced that he had helped to reverse the attitude of indifference of Britain to its colonies: that attitude had "induced me to accept the position of High Commissioner for Canada and during the thirteen years that I controlled that office all that was changed."[36] His reports on the activities of the High Commission during the year 1895 – his thirteenth and final year in London – reflected the greatly increased volume of work. Cabinet documents, despatches and other correspondence received from Ottawa had grown from an initial thirty-two pieces in 1880 to fifteen hundred in 1895, relating to the Departments of Agriculture, Finance, Public Works, Militia, Marine and Fisheries, Customs, Post Office, Interior, and Justice. The role of the High Commission under Tupper's sure direction had grown enormously as Canada's status within the total Empire continued to evolve. The office had, in several respects, become a full-blown legation in all but name. That a senior cabinet minister filled the office added, of course, to its status. Whatever the constitutional niceties, by the time that Tupper had completed his long and certainly varied term as high commissioner, the governor general had become more a ceremonial head of state than an active agent of the British government or the exclusive medium for communication between Ottawa and London. In practice, if not always in theory, it was generally held that Britain's relations with Canada had become increasingly political rather than colonial; diplomatic rather than administrative. The high commissioner did not seek colonial privileges; rather he advocated policies of mutual benefit – or at least so they were regarded by the Canadian government.

Tupper was happy in London, but his personal preference could not in the end prevail against the barrage of appeals from Canada to lead the faltering Conservative party into the approaching election. Sooner or later Tupper must be prime minister. The only surprise was that it took so long and that the route had proven so circuitous. A delegation, chiefly from the

CPR, this time led by its most eminent director, Sir Donald Smith, and its president, William Van Horne, visited the high commissioner in January 1895 to urge him to return, but to no avail. He said that only two considerations would induce him to return: the opportunity to further the policies of a fast Atlantic steamship service and the commercial union of the British Empire. Tupper did later admit to his son that if pressed he would have considered simply switching places with Bowell, even contemplating that he would go to the Senate as prime minister while his son would be government leader in the House of Commons. He added, however, that "nothing could induce me to make the slightest bid in any way for the position."[37]

In February 1896 Tupper was again in Ottawa, this time ostensibly to promote the fast transatlantic service and the Pacific cable. Before his departure from London, he had discussed the proposals with the new colonial secretary, Joseph Chamberlain, and in a speech at the Royal Colonial Institute had recommended both policies as additional ways, in Chamberlain's words, "to think imperially." His success in obtaining in principle British concurrence in enhancing imperial communications was his last official act. To the regret of the London press, he did not return as high commissioner, having left the office temporarily in the hands of Colmer. That Tupper remained in Ottawa was the result of seven ministers – half the cabinet – threatening to resign if the procrastinating Bowell did not make way for him. Lady Aberdeen, working tirelessly both through her supine husband and directly, attempted to prop up the dithering prime minister. She even induced "His Excellency" her husband to encourage an acquiescent Bowell to sound out Sir Donald Smith on his availability to lead the Conservative party.

While the final weeks of Bowell's government were played out, Lady Aberdeen embarked upon various stratagems, all intended to place Wilfrid Laurier in office. Knowing that Tupper would be a more difficult opponent for Laurier to defeat than Bowell, she plotted to have her husband call upon Laurier to form a government upon acceptance of one of Bowell's repeated offers to resign. Many years later, Tupper recalled

When a majority of the members of the Bowell cabinet had resigned and the party had been broken into pieces, I was reluctantly induced to come to the rescue on the meeting of Parliament in December 1895. Asked by the recalcitrant members of the cabinet to assume the leadership I refused, declaring that I would not do so except at the request of the premier, Sir Mackenzie Bowell. It

Sir Charles Tupper, photographed at the time of his final departure from London to seek, reluctantly, the leadership of the Conservative party. He succeeded the hapless Mackenzie Bowell to become prime minister in May 1896, but the victory of Laurier's Liberals the following month meant that he had given up his beloved high commissionership only to become Canada's shortest-term prime minister.

was not until all efforts on his part at reconstruction had failed that he requested me to become leader of the party. I told him that I would do so if he were prepared to receive back all of his colleagues, to which he assented.

The government was then reconstructed by my appointment as Secretary of State and leader of the party in the House of Commons until after the session was over, when by arrangement, I was to succeed him as prime minister. Sir Mackenzie proposed that my son, Sir Charles Hibbert Tupper, should succeed me in the office of Canadian High Commissioner in England. I told him that in view of the vitally important question of the establishment of a fast Atlantic steamship service, for which I had previously made arrangements with Right Hon. Joseph Chamberlain, and the impending Pacific cable conference, I thought it desirable that the position should be tendered to Lord Strathcona [i.e., Donald Smith] in view of his prominent financial standing. One of my first official acts on assuming the premiership was to appoint Lord Strathcona High Commissioner.[38]

Only on 1 May 1896, upon becoming prime minister following Bowell's resignation did Tupper finally, formally, and reluctantly resign as high commissioner.*

During the general election that followed, the party remained split over tariff protection. The Liberals readily exploited Tory divisions and advocated what was in effect an imperial tariff preference by the reduction in the general tariff. They also happily seized upon the supposed extravagances of both the governor general and of the high commissioner as another stick with which to belabour the Conservatives. Sir Robert Borden later recalled (and Lester Pearson repeated) that during the rough and tumble campaign it was the custom to read a list of articles provided for furnishing the high commissioner's house. One Liberal campaigner, in reading the list, came across an item "dinner-wagon."

Someone in the audience asked what a dinner-wagon was. The orator had not the slightest idea of its purpose but this did not deter him from the following vivid explanation: I am glad that question was asked. This man, Tupper, gives great dinner parties, paid for by your money and mine, to which he invites the swells of London. At these dinners every kind of wine is served, paid for by your

---

* Tupper had the doubtful distinction of being prime minister for only ten weeks, the shortest term of any. Having resigned on 8 July 1896, he became leader of the opposition until at age seventy-nine he was defeated in the election of 1900. He resided in Vancouver before returning to Britain in 1913 to live with his daughter (married to Major-General D.R. Cameron).

money and mine. In great flowing goblets, it is passed around and the toffs whom Tupper invites to his dinners drink it until they can drink no more. Finally one of them slips off his chair and falls under the table. Then two of Tupper's flunkeys, paid for by your money and mine, haul the guest from under the table, place him on the dinner-wagon, take him to the front door, call a cab, and send him home. Then another goes under the table and the flunkeys bring the dinner-wagon again and so on until all the guests are disposed of. That, ladies and gentlemen, is the purpose and use of this dinner-wagon, paid for by your money and mine." The audience marvellously enlightened, went home full of indignation at this scandalous and iniquitous misuse of public funds.[39]

On election day, 23 June 1896, an elated Lady Aberdeen rejoiced in Laurier's twenty-eight seat majority. She cheerfully took credit for Tupper's exclusion: "Never if H.E. [her husband] could help it should Sir Charles be again in Canadian politics." Joseph Pope, the former secretary to Macdonald and successive Tory prime ministers, recalled that during the two month campaign, Tupper had been

fighting like a lion ... against tremendous odds. Through no fault of his, he had no chance. Had he been called upon when Thompson died, the outcome might have been, and would probably have been, different, but the late Government had made such a mess of everything they had touched that nothing could have saved their successors ... Sir Charles Tupper, then verging on his seventy-fifth year, whose courage and amazing vitality evoked the strongest admiration alike from friend and foe, the Conservative Party made a tremendous fight, but in vain. I shall never forget the jaunty air with which the intrepid old man came down to his office the morning after the battle, nor the brave and resolute manner in which he faced the reverse which he must have realized at his age meant the death-knell of his ambitions and hopes.[40]

Laurier himself later said of the 1896 election, "it has always been a mystery to me ... that Sir Charles Tupper was not sent for when the old chieftain died [in 1891]. He was sent for at last, but then it was too late. The battle was already lost, and notwithstanding the vigour and brilliancy with which he threw himself into the battle, he could not redeem the fortunes of his party."[41] Tupper resigned office on 8 July 1896, marking the end of eighteen years of Conservative government. Laurier appointed his ministers on 13 July, Lady Aberdeen congratulating herself on what she complacently regarded as her pivotal role in the defeat of the detestable Tupper and the victory of Laurier and her beloved Liberal party.

CHAPTER FOUR

Lord Strathcona, 1896–1914

Upon becoming prime minister, Tupper did not appoint his son high commissioner. Instead he offered the coveted post to Sir Donald Smith, MP, who it was rumoured had already declined successively the governor generalship and a senior portfolio in Tupper's proposed cabinet. Tupper, supposedly convinced that the post would best be filled by a wealthy businessman who supported the Conservative party financially, moved quickly to respond to Smith's lobbying for London. Upon appointing him on 24 April 1896, Tupper also arranged for him to be suitably adorned with the GCMG (his KCMG was a decade before) and a privy councillorship.

Tupper must have decided upon Smith's appointment early in the new year 1896, if the decision of Smith and his wife to marry formally was related. Aware of the protocol for presentation at court, Smith arranged a private wedding ceremony in New York City in March. He was aged seventy-five and Bella seventy, but they had never been married according to the rites of the Church of England. The Scottish-born Smith had arrived in Montreal in 1838. Fifteen years later in Labrador, his daughter was born to Bella Hardisty, the granddaughter of a Cree. Bella, however, was already "married" to one of Smith's fellow Scots, also of the Hudson's Bay Company. Neither that first marriage nor her subsequent marriage to Smith had been orthodox: her father had performed her first wedding ceremony "without jurisdiction" and the second "was performed by Donald Smith himself by virtue of powers held as an officer of the Hudson's Bay Company."[1] Since there were few clergy in the whole of Labrador in the mid-nineteenth century and only limited registration of marriages, such informal arrangements were common enough. But Smith was well aware of the ostracism that had awaited Galt in London. The New York wedding of the Smiths, forty-three years after the birth of their only child, not only resolved the question of acceptance at court but helped to open the way for him to be made a peer.

Why Tupper decided to offer the high commissionership to Smith and not designate his son may have been due to his misgivings about Conservative chances in the imminent general election, which in turn would raise the question of how long his son might expect to retain the London post if the Liberals formed the next government. Tupper had in any event political ambitions for his son in any government that he might form. Over the longer term, several years overseas would do little to advance his political prospects. But why Donald Smith? The secretive Smith destroyed most of his papers, leaving his biographers to speculate about his motives and goals during his long career. Tupper himself offered the briefest of explanations: an affluent businessman of experience – and clearly Smith was that – was required to conclude the prolonged discussion of a fast transatlantic steamship service which would incidentally benefit the CPR and of a Pacific cable which would benefit the Empire. By 1896 Tupper needed Smith, knowing very well that he effectively directed the political influence of the CPR, the Hudson's Bay Company, and the Bank of Montreal.

If Tupper's motives for appointing his erstwhile antagonist remain unclear, so do Smith's reasons for seeking the post. Smith's daughter, son-in-law, and their three children lived in England. In his native Scotland, he was building a large house at Glencoe where, at the age of seventy-five, he was said to be looking forward to spending more leisure time. Certainly he had no wish to continue in Parliament: eighteen years had not enamoured him of it. Quick to take offence, he had seldom participated in the frequently extravagant and raucous exchanges that pass for parliamentary debate, speaking on few matters other than those that might affect his own interests or those of the Hudson's Bay Company. He saw himself, or at least attempted to present himself, as neither an overt nor a consistent partisan (Lady Macdonald once described him as "never a party man"). He had first been elected to the House of Commons as the member for Selkirk in a by-election in March 1871, assisting his new friend, Sandford Fleming, the following year in his transcontinental survey of the most promising rail route to the Pacific.* Upon being re-elected in 1873,

---

* After being the first member of Parliament for Selkirk from 1871 to 1880, Smith was the member for Montreal West from 1887 to 1896. Accordingly, he sat in Parliament with Edward Blake, including the years when Blake was a minister in Alexander Mackenzie's Liberal government, but later when Blake was for fifteen years in the British House of Commons and Smith was in the House of Lords, there is no evidence that they saw each other.

Smith had told his electors, "As he has no favour to ask and nothing personal to desire from any government he will support only such measures as are conducive to the advancement of Manitoba in the Northwest ... and the general prosperity of the Dominion."[2] In a bitter exchange with Tupper in May 1878, Smith had declared to the House of Commons, "I always desired to keep myself entirely free and independent." Macdonald was unconvinced. Contemptuous of Smith's sanctimonious manoeuvrings, he proclaimed, "I could lick him quicker than hell could scorch a feather." Later, in the election of 1887, Smith piously described himself to the electors of Montreal West as one who was "disposed to judge of measures more than of men ... I come forward as an independent candidate, prepared to give my support to what I believe is in the interests of my constituents and of vital interest to the Dominion."[3] Much later, in 1900, six years into Smith's appointment in London, his partisan flexibility was again noted. Frederick Borden, the Liberal minister of militia, wrote to Laurier, following a visit to Smith in Scotland, that he was convinced of his friendship for Laurier and his government. "Equally there is no doubt of his personal dislike of Tupper [then leader of the opposition] and contempt for many of those who surround him."*

At the time of the Pacific Scandal, Macdonald was joined by Tupper – who likely recalled his days on the Red River with Smith four years before – in describing his one-time friend as a "mean, treacherous coward" and "the biggest liar I ever met!" Twenty-five years later, upon appointing Smith to London, Tupper had completely reversed himself, transforming his denunciations into praise. "The Canadian Pacific Railway would have no existence to-day, notwithstanding all that the Government did to support that undertaking, had it not been for the indomitable pluck and energy and determination, both financially and in every other respect, of Sir Donald Smith." Smith's parliamentary career had temporarily ended in a Supreme Court appeal finding against him when two local Conservatives charged him with corrupt practices in the election of 1878. Despite the court's verdict, Sam Hughes, the excitable and staunchly imperialist member for Victoria North in rural Ontario, was not alone in proclaiming in vain, "There is one man, and one man alone, who can save the ...

---

* Tupper and Frederick Borden (1847–1917) had long been political antagonists, especially since Borden, as minister of militia from 1896 to 1911, had, as one of his first acts, dismissed Tupper's son-in-law, the Red River veteran Major-General Donald Roderick Cameron, as commandant of the Royal Military College of Canada. Borden's only son, a medical student at McGill University, was killed in the South African War.

Conservative Party from falling to pieces, and also who can command the respect and confidence of the whole country, and that is Sir Donald A. Smith."

Smith had been born the year George III had died, but lived to see the development of the aeroplane. That long span of years was in itself unusual, but then Smith was a unique Canadian, certainly a unique high commissioner. In Labrador with the Hudson's Bay Company until almost the age of fifty, he rapidly became thereafter a leading businessman in Canada. By the time of his death in 1914, he had been associated with the Hudson's Bay Company for seventy-five years. He had been a director of the Bank of Montreal for forty-two years, during eighteen of which he was its president as well as for fifteen years president of the Royal Trust Company; thirty-two years a director of the Canadian Pacific Railway (which enabled him to acquire land to be sold through the North West Land Company, which he also headed); and six years chairman of both the Burmah and Anglo-Persian oil companies (later to become British Petroleum). These interlocking corporate activities coincided variously with his four years in the Manitoba legislature, eighteen years in the House of Commons, and eighteen years as high commissioner.

When Smith was appointed to London in 1896, the Hudson's Bay Company required urgent attention·if it were to make the transition from primarily a fur-trading company to a more general merchandiser, active across Canada. Smith's long-time associate in the CPR, William Van Horne, was in no doubt of the necessity for his old colleague to be at the head office of the company: "The London board is a collection of pernickety and narrow-minded men who don't know enough about business to manage a peanut stand ... the Hudson's Bay Company is going to pot in consequence ... Sir Donald is the only one in the lot who wears a hat a man's size."[4]

Smith began his eighteen years as high commissioner with a staff of a secretary, two first-class clerks, one second and two third-class clerks, two messengers, and an office boy. The month following his arrival, he was visited by an aspiring Canadian journalist, later to become his biographer: "[I]n his gloomy office in Victoria Street ... He is not an imposing figure, nor in spite of his great age and white beard, patriarchal. My impression is of just a shrewd, quiet, rather 'pawky' Scotch businessman. Talks with great deliberation and almost with humility. Odd contrast to Tupper, with his aggressiveness, his loud voice and physical vigour."[5] The journalist might also have added that it was evident that Smith was

Lord Strathcona, the high commissioner for a record eighteen years, as seen by a cartoonist: a fast transatlantic steamer is in his right hand, the symbol of a service that was not only to bind the Empire together, but to benefit the CPR. In his left arm is his horse, the metaphor for the regiment that he raised for the South African War and paid for himself.

much enamoured of the *grande monde*. In his final years in Montreal, he had recorded with quiet satisfaction that he had entertained there a future king and queen, a royal prince and princess, eight dukes, seven marquises, twenty-one earls, and six viscounts.*

Odd contrast with the ebullient Tupper as he undoubtedly was, the secretive and solemn Smith found some of the same challenges awaiting him in London that had confronted his predecessors: the promotion of emigration continued to be pre-eminent; the Pacific cable still wanted attention; the question of subsidies for fast trans-oceanic ships to make a reality of the global "all-red" route; the efforts to match Canada's fiscal responsibilities with the right to negotiate commercial treaties (which had gradually been condoned from Galt onwards by a generally helpful Colonial Office). That right, however, was increasingly recognized as part of a continuing task of defining the place of the settlement colonies in the larger Empire, including their possible provision of coordinated if not unified military forces.

There was never any question in Smith's mind that Canada's interests were best served by close collaboration with Britain in its imperial ventures. When he arrived in London, the "Little Englanders" of Gladstone had been replaced by the imperialists of Disraeli and later Salisbury and Balfour. The content and the context of the imperial debate had decidedly altered. By 1871 British troops had been withdrawn from Canada (except for small garrisons at Halifax and Esquimalt), the Australian colonies and New Zealand. All would henceforth assume prime responsibility for their own defence, relieving the British taxpayer of a small part of that particular imperial burden. During the following thirty years, British military support was happily not required by the self-governing colonies, but paradoxically colonial military support began to be sought by Britain. Imperialism and militarism had become so entwined that, try as he might, even Laurier was to find that he could not disentangle the two in the deft way that Macdonald had done fifteen years before.

Upon the defeat in June 1896 of Tupper's short-lived government, Smith returned promptly to Ottawa, embarking in Liverpool amidst persistent rumours that he would succeed Aberdeen as governor general. One of Smith's biographers later observed, "It was a great advantage to have

* Later, the governor general, the Earl of Minto, displayed no gratitude for Strathcona's hospitality: "Lord Strathcona's house, which he has let us have – the taste of the house appalling. Maple furniture, plush, and fine pictures hopelessly jumbled" (Journal, 14 November 1902; Stevens and Saywell, eds., *Lord Minto's Canadian Papers*, II, 222).

a rich man in the post, and the new Liberal Government at Ottawa evidently thought so too, for, in spite of Smith's politics, they besought him to remain. But Sir Donald considered it prudent to have a personal interview with Premier Laurier, and accordingly took a hurried trip to Canada."[6] Laurier knew Smith well. As a so-called independent member of Parliament, Smith had been in correspondence with the Liberal leader even after Tupper had appointed him to London. That correspondence has not been recovered, nor is there any record of financial contributions by Smith – through the CPR or otherwise – to either the Conservative or Liberal parties. Macdonald had confidently expected that the CPR, in return for the crucial support that it had received from the government, would in turn support the Conservative party financially. Laurier would have expected, and received, hardly less for the Liberal party once in office. No stranger to the ways of patronage, Laurier had himself a trust fund for his own support financed by favour-seekers and admirers, prominent among the latter being the affluent Toronto tea merchant, Peter Larkin. If Smith, a director of the CPR, the Hudson's Bay Company, the Royal Trust, and the Bank of Montreal, wanted to continue in London, the new prime minister would see that he did so. One of Smith's detractors later wrote, "For sixteen long years Laurier complied with his every wish."[7]

On what were becoming the perennial questions of an imperial tariff preference and an imperial federation, Laurier and Smith basically differed, but on those two fundamental questions the prime minister was probably content that English-Canadians would see that in London there was an imperial Canadian. He could offset suspicions that the government was not as sound as it might be regarding the place of Canada in the Empire. For Canadians sceptical of the imperial loyalty of their first francophone prime minister, Smith was a reassurance, as Laurier knew full well. If he had been perceived as easing him out of office, the imperialists – and there were many – would have been increasingly doubtful of his real allegiance.

Immediately following his arrival in London, Smith was happily in collaboration with the new colonial secretary, Joseph Chamberlain (whom he had first met in Canada in 1886). In June 1895 Chamberlain had asked Salisbury to appoint him secretary of state for the colonies in his new government, a surprisingly secondary post for the ambitious turncoat Liberal to seek, but indicative of his commitment to the Empire – at least the white Empire. Earlier in Toronto, Chamberlain, who had resigned from Gladstone's government over Home Rule for Ireland, had declared, "the federation of Canada may be the lamp lighting our path to the federation of the British Empire. If it is a dream – it may only be the imagination

of an enthusiast – it is a grand idea ... Let us do all in our power to promote it and enlarge the relations and goodwill which ought always to exist
between the sons of England throughout the world and the old folks at
home." He had coupled his advocacy of closer imperial ties with his conviction in "the greatness and importance of the destiny which is reserved
for the Anglo-Saxon race ... infallibly predestined to be the predominat-
ing force in the future history and civilization of the world."[8]

Chamberlain made his first major speech advocating the greater economic unity of the Empire when he addressed the Canada Club in London in March 1896, one month before the arrival of Smith.* In his speech
which *The Times* described "as a bolt from the blue," the new colonial secretary asked: "What is the greatest of our common obligations? It is imperial defence. What is the greatest of our common interests? It is imperial
trade. And those two are very closely connected." Imperial trade, however, remained trammelled by the fact that "We have a proposal by
British free traders which is rejected by the British colonies. We have a
proposal by colonial protectionists which is rejected by Great Britain."[9]
Tupper, from the opposition front bench in Ottawa, welcomed Chamberlain's declaration as "manly, straightforward and plucky." Tupper's views,
however, had no immediate import: he was only leader of the opposition.
What mattered was Laurier's reaction. The prime minister was wary. He
declared to the Canada Club,

That practical statesman, Mr. Joseph Chamberlain, has come to the conclusion
that the time has come when it is possible to have within the bonds of Empire a
new step taken, which will give to the colonies, in England, a preference for their
products over the products of other nations ... The possibilities are immense ...
Mr. Joseph Chamberlain, the new and progressive Secretary of State for the
Colonies, has declared that the time has come when it is possible to discuss the
question. But, sir, if England is going to give us that preference, England would
expect something from us in return ... that we would come as closely to her own
system of free trade ... as it is possible for us to come.[10]

Smith was fully aware of Laurier's studied caution. He recognized that
the moment had not yet arrived to join overtly in an attempt to force
the consolidation of the Empire, including through a tariff preference,

* Joseph Chamberlain (1836–1914), having been the popular mayor of Birmingham, was
elected to the House of Commons as a Liberal in 1876. However, he subsequently split
with Gladstone over Home Rule for Ireland in 1886 and joined Salisbury's third government as colonial secretary in 1895.

knowing that before the election Laurier had been exploring privately the possibilities of tariff reciprocity with the United States. Nevertheless, following his hurried visit to Ottawa in July 1896, he spoke in support of Chamberlain: "We want to bring the Colonies into closer relations with the Mother Country. We wish to develop trade between the different parts of the Empire, as well as with other countries, and we must appreciate the great services of Mr. Chamberlain in directing public attention prominently to the matter."[11] Not surprisingly, the developing friendship between the colonial secretary and the high commissioner soon led to collaboration in Chamberlain's campaign for an imperial tariff preference and ultimately an imperial federation.

Manufactured imports from Britain already enjoyed a modest preference in Canada, but in return Canada could not expect any early preferential access for its foodstuffs in Britain. The colonies would first need to demonstrate their ability to supply the British market on terms competitive with the lowest-cost sources. Until that happy day, imperial tariff preferences held no appeal for the increasing numbers of newly enfranchised voters, despite the lively advocacy of the new colonial secretary. Bread in Britain was cheap. Real wages were growing. Despite an expanding population, standards of living were increasing, however unevenly. "Hands off the people's food" found a ready response among an electorate more satisfied with its lot. For his part, however, Smith remained unconvinced by the cry, "Your food will cost you more." In his understanding, free trade with anyone, including the United States, would be bad for Canada: he, the CPR, the Bank of Montreal, and the manufacturers had supported the increased tariffs of Macdonald's National Policy. "While they [the United States] maintain high protective tariffs, if we allow everything to come in here just as they should like, we all know what would very soon become of Canada ... while free trade may be very good for England and while I might support it there with certain modifications, I should be very sorry to see it introduced in this country and would oppose its adoption." In short, Smith knew that Britain would never accept an imperial preference if it meant higher food costs, but equally he knew that for Canada the absence of an imperial preference would mean that free trade with the United States would merely increase the already proliferating north-south ties.

Speaking of the summer of 1896, one of Smith's early biographers contended that "Sir Donald ardently hoped for preferential trade within the Empire, but political considerations soon made his championship of the proposal incompatible with his tenure of a non-political office."[12] That was publicly; privately Chamberlain turned frequently to him for support. Neville Chamberlain acted for his father in other fundraising initiatives, but it was Chamberlain himself who dealt with Smith: he was too important a source and symbol of imperial support to be left even to the care of Neville. Smith in turn explained to Chamberlain his true feelings: "[Although] I cannot, from my position, publicly support you, nor even hint in public here at my sentiments, you know what those sentiments are."[13] Throughout his term in Britain, Smith may have convinced himself that he was not acting publicly, but his speeches never left any doubt about his "sentiments" and he conveyed them privately to another of Chamberlain's sons, Austen, who had become chancellor of the exchequer on his father's resignation from Balfour's government. In constant touch with the Chamberlains, *père et fils*, he had ready at hand a way of supporting covertly imperial federation.

Smith was early in boarding Chamberlain's imperial bandwagon, undeterred by Laurier's misgivings and the concurrent Liberal preoccupation with markets in the United States. To the Congress of the Chambers of Commerce of the British Empire in 1896 he proclaimed to the gratification of Chamberlain, "The Secretary of State for the Colonies has said that there is on one side free trade and protection on the other, but he has pointed out another way, either the Colonies should approach the Home Government or that the Mother Country should approach the Colonies, to ascertain how far each is willing and prepared to go in the way of a *Zollverein*." Smith was instrumental in engineering an unanimous if somewhat anaemic resolution which urged that "the union of various parts of His Majesty's Dominions [could be] greatly consolidated by the adoption of a commercial policy based upon the principle of mutual benefit."[14] This was widely understood to be an endorsement of Chamberlain's policy but had been watered down to win the support of Canadian manufacturers fearful of British competition.

Smith and all who urged an imperial tariff preference were gratified by the Liberals' fulfilment of their election pledges of June 1896. Both parties had advocated imperial tariff preferences, the Conservatives by raising tariffs on extra-Empire imports and the Liberals by reducing them on imports from within the Empire. In the April 1897 budget, Laurier's finance minister, W.S. Fielding,* introduced unilaterally a two-tier tariff.

* W.S. Fielding (1849–1929) was minister of finance from 1896 to 1911 and from 1921 to 1925; a biographer of Strathcona, Beckles Willson, described him as "a brisk, amiable, matter-of-fact Nova Scotian, without a trace of genius or erudition" (*From Quebec*, 149).

The existing rate would continue to apply against countries with a tariff against Canada (for example, the United States), but an immediate preference of 12.5 per cent (to increase to 25 per cent in July 1898) would henceforth apply to any country such as Britain which admitted Canadian goods at a rate equivalent to or less than the minimal Canadian tariff. At a stroke, Fielding had in effect created a tariff preference for Britain. *The Times* reported that "Conservatives and Liberals alike have hardly yet recovered from the astonishment with which the new tariff has affected them." The astonishment rose in part from the apparent reversal by the Liberals of their decade-long policy of free trade or even commercial union with the United States, a policy which had contributed to Laurier's electoral defeat in 1891. Although remaining committed to tariff reciprocity with the United States, rebuffs from Washington had led Fielding to declare that Ottawa would "find other markets to build up the prosperity of Canada independent of the American people."

However, the Fielding tariff was not the direct step toward an imperial preference that some, including Chamberlain, hoped – and which inspired Kipling's eulogistic "Our Lady of the Snows." Fielding asked, "Why should we wait for England to take action? England has dealt generously with us in the past. England has given us a larger degree of liberty perhaps than is possessed by any country on the face of the earth. She has given us liberty to tax her wares even when she admits our goods free, and we have taxed them to an enormous degree. Why should we wait for England to do more? Somebody must make a move in this matter, and we propose that Canada shall lead the way." Fielding's budget triggered a lively debate over tariff policy generally: whether Canada should have a protective tariff for its infant manufacturing industry or a revenue tariff to contribute more to the national coffers. In the end, governments, whether Liberal or Conservative, faced with a stark choice between the immediate interests of Canadian manufacturers and a comprehensive imperial preference, would invariably sacrifice the latter.

Sir Donald Smith was introduced into the House of Lords as Lord Strathcona in February 1898, more than a year after Tupper had recommended his peerage and a full six months after it had been gazetted. He made his maiden speech that summer (on the need to reform matrimonial law, partly perhaps with Galt if not himself in mind), but during the following sixteen years he seldom spoke. Consistent with his earlier practice in the Canadian House of Commons, he limited himself in the House of Lords

to interventions on a few social questions, keeping well clear of imperial or foreign policy debates where any overt contribution by him might
be interpreted as Canadian participation in the councils of the Empire,
something that Smith himself would have welcomed, but Laurier would
not. In his public restraint, he also expressed his own instincts: he always
worked most happily behind the scenes.

Strathcona's barony helped to open additional doors. He made the most
of his personal wealth by entertaining lavishly, primarily at his residence
at 28 Grosvenor Square. His notable generosity was also reflected in his
gifts to hospitals in both Britain and Canada and to the new University
of Birmingham (at the request of his friend "Birmingham Joe" Chamberlain); to the University of Aberdeen where he was made rector; and to St
John's College, Cambridge, which elected him an honorary fellow. The
scale of his entertainment became widely noted, including at his leased
house, Knebworth, in Hertfordshire – to which he arranged for special
trains to convey his guests – and subsequently to his house at Debden in
Essex and his new houses at Glencoe in the Highlands and later on the
islands of Oronsay and Colonsay in the Hebrides.* Perhaps his single most
spectacular entertainment was his reception for four thousand and dinner
for twenty-five hundred to mark the quatrocentenary of the University of
Aberdeen in September 1906: for that occasion he had a temporary building erected in which he proclaimed the virtues of the British Empire and,
inter alia, "such allies as young Japan. We know that they are not the less
proud of having Britain always at their right hand."

During his years as high commissioner, the commitment of "the representative Canadian," as he was sometimes called, to the Empire was to
take a variety of forms, one of the most romantic being his enthusiastic support for full Canadian military participation in the colourful celebrations
of Queen Victoria's diamond jubilee in June 1897. Canadian dragoons
and hussars rode alongside a total of forty-six thousand men from across
the Empire in the great jubilee parade. A concurrent colonial conference
had touched on imperial unity, but not to the degree that Chamberlain
now intended. In accepting the invitation, Laurier had responded that
the pageantry "would tend powerfully to cement the union between the

---

* Strathcona leased Knebworth from the family of Edward Bulwer-Lytton, secretary
of state for the colonies, 1858–59, when Cartier, Rose, and Galt had been entertained
there.

Wilfrid Laurier participated with other premiers from the settlement colonies in the great imperial spectacle of the diamond jubilee of Queen Victoria in June 1897. The British prime minister, Lord Salisbury, remained sceptical about the value of the colonies, but his colonial secretary, Joseph Chamberlain, sought at the concurrent colonial conference the creation of a council of the Empire. Laurier joined Strathcona in greeting the Canadian contingent (Strathcona is third from left, Laurier fourth to his left), declaring that "the Canadian soldiers who made such a good appearance on parade would give just as good account of themselves on the battlefield."

Mother Country and her colonies, both socially and politically." Having crossed the Atlantic for the first time, he participated in all major events, surprisingly declaring before his departure that he would welcome the offer of a seat in the British House of Commons. "It would be the proudest moment of my life if I could see a Canadian of French descent affirming the principles of freedom in the Parliament of Great Britain."[15] In addition to such pre-conference imperial rhetoric, his enthusiastic welcome to

Britain had been in part assured by Fielding's tariff preference.* Privately, however, he was disconcerted by the sudden bestowal of a knighthood.†

At the colonial conference itself, Joseph Chamberlain, undeterred by constitutional niceties, contended that the "closer union" and "true partnership" of the burgeoning Empire, in a world of increasing economic and political rivalry, gave Britain an unique advantage. He fervently hoped that "the Colonies will desire to substitute for the slight relationship which at present exists for a true partnership ... This could take the form of a great council of the Empire to which the Colonies would send representative plenipotentiaries" to evolve in time into "that Federal Council to which we must always look forward as our ultimate goal."[16] The colonial conference fostered a sense of imperial kinship, but Chamberlain mismanaged the question of colonial contributions to an imperial navy by raising it prematurely and starkly, including citing the Royal Navy as the only sure bastion against United States imperialism. When forced to it, the several Australian colonies, followed by the Cape Colony, again confirmed contributions to the costs of stationing warships in their waters, but Laurier's response was a clear if courteous negative: Canada had no significant naval needs since it was, quite simply, "an inaccessible country." Evidently regarding Britain as in some way obliged to provide Canada with free maritime protection, Laurier was, however, careful to balance his opposition to an imperial navy with a statement to the Canada Club in July 1897 that "the soldiers of Canada" in the jubilee parade had made him proud. "As a Canadian and as a British subject ... he believed that those men might hold their own with the well-tried veterans of England ... if it should be the misfortune of England or the Empire to be engaged in war, no matter with what country, the Canadian soldiers who had made such a good appearance on parade would give just as good an account of themselves on the battlefield."

---

* To entertain his guests at a large reception in honour of the Lauriers, the new Lord Strathcona had employed a favourite singer of Queen Victoria, the Canadian Marie Louise Cecile Emma Lajeunesse, whose stage name was Emma Albani. In London Laurier was awarded the Cobden Club's gold medal for services to free trade (i.e., Fielding's budget).

† Laurier later stated that he had accepted the knighthood "for political reasons [but] I have not changed my own view that the acceptance of honours by a public man in the active and daily struggles of political life is a mistake. I further believe that we have enough titles in the Cabinet already" (Laurier to Mulock, 21 August 1901; *Minto's Canadian Papers*, II: 67).

Joesph Chamberlain, the dapper former Liberal who became colonial secretary in the Conservative government of Lord Salisbury in 1895, convened the first colonial conference in June 1897. Despite the support of Tupper and Strathcona, the imperial federation ideal came to naught following Chamberlain's withdrawal from active political life in 1906. Chamberlain (seated) has Sir Wilfrid Laurier on his right. Directly behind Laurier is Strathcona. Chamberlain's imperial unity campaign, allegedly financed in part by the affluent high commissioner, seriously divided the Conservative party under prime minister Arthur Balfour.

Lord Salisbury, the sardonic prime minister, was deeply sceptical of, but nevertheless remained largely passive towards, the imperial enthusiasms of his own colonial secretary. By his inactivity Salisbury helped to ensure that the conference did little more than establish a precedent of sorts for another such gathering of premiers seven years later. The colonial representatives, participating in Chamberlain's "informal discussion of many questions of greatest imperial interest", had nevertheless made clear that for a variety of reasons there was no ready support for his proposal for a great council of Empire or for an imperial *Zollverein*. The urbane Laurier contented himself with simply endorsing the existing relations between the self-governing colonies and the metropolitan power. He declined to commit to naval cooperation. He did, however, ask Strathcona to seek from the War Office and the Admiralty advance notice of tenders for matériel that Canada could supply, particularly forage contracts which might help to secure for the Liberals several uncertain Quebec constituencies.

Although chagrined that the conference took no decisions on Sandford Fleming's proposal for a trans-Pacific cable despite enthusiastic support from Tupper on the opposition benches in Ottawa, Strathcona did see the colourful pageantry of the jubilee partly as an opportunity for renewed emigration promotion, an opportunity, in the words of Robert Service, for "building Britain's greatness o'er the foam." Laurier, however, while understandably ambivalent about Canada's place within a dynamic Empire, was certain that any sharing in the decision-making at the centre could involve unwelcome obligations. Ideas of Canadians participating in an imperial parliament or council or even the suggestion that the Canadian high commissioner and the various colonial agents should form some sort of imperial advisory group did not win his direct support, conscious as he was of likely domestic divisions if Canada became entangled in British ventures "o'er the foam." Nevertheless, Strathcona's support for imperial federation could be turned to good account by the prime minister. Having him in London expounding the supposed virtues of imperial federation would do no harm to the fortunes of the Liberal party in Ontario, even if Laurier, with Quebec in mind, had on occasion gently to rein him in.

John Hay, the imperialist-minded United States ambassador in 1897–8, contended that modern British imperialism, "as a popular force, was largely the joint production of four men": Joseph Chamberlain, Alfred Harmsworth, Rudyard Kipling, and Donald Smith. Harmsworth (later Lord Northcliffe) had founded the *Daily Mail* in the spring of 1896, precisely when Smith was embarking for Britain. Soon he was cooperating with the new high commissioner in attempting to provide more news about "Our Western Empire," but the efforts of a single newspaper owner could not offset the longstanding indifference of many. Smith had lamented to Laurier in August 1896 that

Canadians who visit England are struck by the lack of Canadian news To have Canada and Canadian news of a desirable nature appearing frequently in the English papers would be of great use to us. It would help emigration, it would help the extension of trade and would be beneficial from every point of view ... It would be most useful ... to receive from you once or twice a week, or even a little more frequently, telegrams informing me of anything that may be happening in the Dominion of an interesting nature and illustrating the progress of the country.[17]

Although in response Ottawa did provide more information, it remained meagre. *The Times* continued to have a correspondent in Canada, but the high commissioner was never content with the role of British newspapers in promoting either Canada or enhanced imperial ties, doing himself whatever he could by letters to the editor to fill some of the gap. A speech to the Royal Colonial Institute in April 1898 well summarized his thinking about Canada's continuing need for British emigrants, linking the promotion of settlers to the promotion of trade and investment. "It is by ... thus adding to the population of the Colonies that we shall increase their wealth and strength, and be enabled to maintain with their help the position of being the greatest Empire the world has ever seen. What we want in Canada are more people and more capital."

Urged on by Clifford Sifton, Laurier's dynamic minister of the interior, the High Commission expanded its emigration promotion, producing lantern slide shows, school packs, lectures and articles and advertising for newspapers, all intended to stimulate interest in the North West in particular. Initiatives of Dr Barnardo and several church groups to send orphan or destitute children were financially and otherwise supported (an estimated seventy-three thousand were despatched to Canada between 1869 and 1919). Less successful, however, was Strathcona's effort to resolve the perennial problem of who should supervise emigration promotion agents throughout the United Kingdom and across northern Europe. Since Alexander Mackenzie's ill-advised appointment of Edward Jenkins as agent general, it had been more or less understood that all agents were to be under the supervision of the high commission, working in close conjunction with the CPR as they had under Galt. Sifton regarded British immigrants as not only desirable in themselves but essential to deflect criticism from his "open door" policy, which was seen by some as introducing the "scum and dregs" of central and eastern Europe. Emigration from Britain was, however, slowing as its economy recovered. Further, as Sifton told the *Winnipeg Tribune* on 25 June 1897, "Owing to the persistent representation in Britain of Canada as a land of ice and snow, emigration has been chiefly going to Australasia and South Africa, and it is now the endeavour of the Department to counteract the effect." Despite the frustrated Sifton's best efforts, however, the annual total of British emigrants to Canada between 1897 and 1900 stubbornly hovered around ten thousand.

At home, Sifton, not for nothing known as "the young Napoleon," criticized his own department as the "Department of Delay." In Europe, part of the problem in his view was an aging and unreliable Strathcona. Far from satisfied that the high commissioner and his small staff were sufficiently energetic, he also suspected that the long-serving secretary, Joseph Colmer, was an incorrigible Tory, an affiliation, real or otherwise, that was anathema to the highly partisan minister. Sifton soon convinced himself that the emigration flow would increase if promotion were largely taken out of the hands of Strathcona and Colmer and responsibility for the supervision of all agents across Europe be his alone. Strathcona, sensing what was coming, urged upon Sifton that the agents should continue to "receive their instructions and make their reports through this office. If this is not done, no supervision can be effectual." Sifton's curt reply nodded in the high commissioner's direction, but it really left no doubt what he intended. "Although a general supervision of the Agents should be exercised by your office, [it would be] quite impossible to make any fixed rule which would preclude me from having direct communication with an Agent when I consider it advisable."[18] Sifton had obvious misgivings about whether the seventy-seven-year-old high commissioner could provide the desirable leadership, not only in Britain but across Europe. In 1899 Sifton appointed an emigration commissioner who effectively assumed responsibility for promotion in Europe.

In France, Scandinavia, and especially in the German Empire, governments either informally or officially discouraged emigration. As Tupper had done before him, Strathcona attempted to understand better the nature of the various restrictions and even to consider clandestine possibilities by visiting in 1898 the major source countries and their steamship agents, but he was not welcomed. His presence in Hamburg, for example, was castigated in a local newspaper: "Apart from the weakening the Fatherland which the success of such propaganda entails, the attempt to lure our fellow-countrymen to this desolate, sub-arctic region is, upon humane grounds alone, to be denounced as criminal."[19] The German ambassador warned Salisbury that Strathcona, having acted contrary to German law, would be arrested if he returned. A Canadian government and a CPR agent having both been expelled, Strathcona added ruefully to Ottawa that given the hostility of the German and Austro-Hungarian governments, the British ambassadors in Berlin and Vienna were understandably wary of involving themselves directly in emigration promotion. Sifton decided that the new emigration commissioner would accordingly work independently of them, as well as of the high commission. Two decades later, Sifton recorded with satisfaction that at his initiative, "In Great Britain we confined our efforts very largely to the north of England and Scotland ... The result was that we got a fairly steady stream ... [of] the very best settlers in the world."

Canada in 1899 was a prosperous country and rapidly becoming more so. Immigrants began finally to pour into Canada, prompted in part by leaflets and posters in Slavic and Scandanavian languages, as well as in English and French. British purchases of Canadian bonds (but generally not of equity, that being left largely to American investors) fuelled greater confidence in an affluent future. That sense of well-being helped in turn to generate an incipient nationalism and a growing interest in Canada's evolving place in a wider Empire. Newspapers debated the advantages of an imperial federation, while explorers were opening new and exotic lands for the delectation of avid readers. During the final decades of the nineteenth century, an imperial fervour swept through much of the world, English-speaking Canada included. The sense of imperial mission was not limited to European powers; the United States, that emerging focus of envy and hence of resentment, had, within thirty years of almost tearing itself apart in a bloody civil war, become itself an imperial power, seizing islands in the Caribbean and the Pacific from Spain and engaging in a near-clash with Britain over the border – of all places – between British Guiana and Venezuela. The United States, Germany and Russia were all surging ahead in industrial production and in world trade, each contributing to a mounting apprehension in Canada as well as in Britain that the mother country was perhaps not quite so omnipotent as it had so long seemed.

For Strathcona, as for Macdonald and Tupper, that same mother country remained the best guarantee of immunity from the manifest destiny of the United States to rule the whole of North America. The continuing need for imperial underpinning for a still fragile Canada had been to the fore in Macdonald's thinking. Later, however, as imperial attitudes in Britain had changed from indifference to enthusiasm, attitudes in Ottawa had also evolved. Imperial ties were not a priority for Laurier. In a variety of ways, his government was preoccupied with the contemporary manifestations of that perennial Canadian challenge: national unity. That other, related, perennial challenge, the implications of sharing a continent with the United States, also preoccupied him and his cabinet as the differences over the Alaska boundary dragged on and relations between Britain and the United States soured over the Venezuela border dispute. And underlying those basic and omnipresent questions were the challenges of settling a vast and still largely unknown territory, into which land-hungry Americans were now beginning to pour.

Whatever the interest in imperial questions was among English-Canadians, there was no unanimity. Among imperialists themselves there had emerged two main camps. Some contended that "the Old Country" was not merely *primus inter pares*, but incontestably the heart and soul of the Empire. Others, who advocated an imperial federation, sought a place for Canada in a voluntary mutual-help society. Beyond them, at one end of the spectrum of public opinion, there was the "ready-aye-ready" school, especially in Ontario. At the other end, there were those who, to the contrary, could not see why distant imperial ventures should be of concern. The sceptics lived mainly in Quebec (although in Toronto, Goldwin Smith, the tedious and frequently maddening Oxonian arch-continentalist, sometimes sounded remarkably like them).* Those were the poles of the imperialist spectrum. Somewhere in between resided the great majority of Canadians. When war came to southern Africa in 1899, it was Laurier's unenviable and unavoidable task to attempt to maintain a rough equilibrium among them, giving enough support to Britain to satisfy at least moderate Canadian imperialists but not so much as to alienate the more temperate nationalists.

Writing forty years later, Donald Creighton, Macdonald's biographer, reflected the misgivings many Conservatives had about Laurier's policies:

Laurier, we are told, foiled the conspiracy of the British imperialists, though it could be argued that the conspiracy was nothing more sinister than an attempt to fit the British Empire, as it then was, for the terrible times which in fact overtook it in the second decade of the century. Laurier was largely responsible for the defeat of these attempts. But for what purpose? What part did he want Canada to play in the Empire, or in the world as a whole? He is admiringly called a nationalist; yet he seems to have feared the maturity and to have avoided the responsibilities of nationalism ... If this is Canadian nationalism, it is an extremely negative kind ... a nationalism which, in its casual acceptance of imperial forms and benefits and its determined rejection of imperial duties, is not very far away from the dependent colonialism of [Henri] Bourassa.[20]

---

* From before Confederation, the prolific controversialist Goldwin Smith (1823–1910) had been expounding his doubts about the Empire and had been advocating Canadian union with the United States. (See, for example, *The Empire* [London, 1863].)

Certainly Laurier offered little creative thinking about the evolving Empire (even Fielding's tariff was crafted with Canadian rather than broader imperial interests in mind). By contrast, Australians, New Zealanders, and South Africans in varying degrees and in various ways did. Laurier proposed no role for Canada in a collaborative Empire nor in the yet greater world beyond, content as he was to shelter behind "those far distant, storm-beaten ships" of the Royal Navy as well as the Monroe Doctrine which it had enforced before the United States Navy became capable of doing so. For Laurier, national unity had to be constantly monitored and fostered until eventual full independence would somehow arrive. In the meantime, do-nothing passivity was the best policy for a Canada subject to deep racial and religious differences. The octogenarian high commissioner could be counted upon to do or say nothing that would be disruptive in domestic terms. He was sent little information and fewer instructions. Accordingly, his opinions and activities could be more readily denied, as happened once or twice. Better that way than to have a high commissioner who might involve Canada in imperial controversy.

In Britain, the South African War of 1899–1902 marked the apogee of imperial sentiment. During the twenty years embracing Gladstone and Salisbury, the British government had moved from contemplating the casting adrift of its colonies to fostering such imperial unity that the world would be forced to recognize in the British Empire a vast, unique and cohesive power. The Nile expedition of 1884–5 had been seen by some Canadians, including Tupper, as a welcome occasion to join with Australian colonies in contributing to that cohesive power. The War Office had taken the short-term view that it did not need help, but in Canada and the Australian colonies the presence of their soldiers on the Nile had been urged by some as demonstrating imperial unity that could have benefits internationally and would, in any event, underpin the greater economic cohesion of the Empire. Fifteen years later, Whitehall itself, uneasy at unexpected military reverses in South Africa and mounting hostility in Europe, began to perceive benefits in imperial cooperation.

By 1899, however, only the most unreconstructed imperialist believed that Canada or the Australian colonies could be coerced into an imperial venture that did not recommend itself to them. Coaxed or cajoled, perhaps, but certainly not coerced. Canadian volunteers did embark for war in southern Africa – eventually more than seven thousand – but they went for what in the end were at least partly Canadian rather than exclusively imperial reasons. In Britain, justifications for the war were hotly debated.

In Canada, the strains were to remain containable, thanks largely to Laurier's remarkable balancing act and to the fact that the enemy was never so formidable as to be able to mount more than what a later generation would call a limited war. Even so, Tupper, as leader of the opposition, was convinced that "the peculiar circumstances under which the decision to send the first Canadian contingent [to South Africa] was arrived at constituted one of the most acute political risks through which the Canadian Confederation has passed."

The problem for Strathcona, as high commissioner, remained that his prime minister did not share his imperial enthusiasms. They politely and tacitly disagreed on almost all matters imperial. Accordingly, Laurier seldom sought his high commissioner's opinion. Undeterred, Strathcona publicly set out his thinking about "the growth of Imperialism, and to the efforts that are being made to bring about the consolidation of the Empire." In his inaugural address to the University of Aberdeen as its rector, Strathcona recalled that during the 1850s and 1860s "the Colonies were not popular." Since then, all had changed. The federation of Canada and, three decades later, of Australia were steps toward imperial federation, closely associated with the grant of responsible government. For Strathcona the Empire at the beginning of the new century was standing at the crossroads, faced with the choice of attempting to prolong the status quo or to winning

a closer unity for Imperial purposes and for defence. The general feeling in favour of the latter will assume the different parts of the Empire full liberty of self-government, while giving them a voice in Imperial policy ... There are some who think that the solution of the problem is to be found in the representation of Canada and the Colonies in the Imperial Parliament ... In time to come ... there may be local parliaments to deal with local affairs in England, Scotland and Ireland; ... Parliament with representatives from different parts of the Empire ... But, in the meantime, the formation of an Imperial Council, in conjunction with the Colonial Office, consisting of representatives of Her Majesty's Government, and of Canada and the Colonies [may serve].[21]

In 1899 the population of Canada was 5.5 million. Public servants were few, the militia headquarters minute. Only a handful of men played a role in deciding whether Canadians might serve in a war in southern Africa. Those directly involved were aware of the deteriorating relations between British and Boer, the Colonial Office keeping the governor general informed of Chamberlain's commitment to the preservation of what he saw as imperial interests in southern Africa. Chamberlain wrote to Lord Minto, the governor general:

If ... an ultimatum is sent the only chance of its acceptance will lie in the support of a great demonstration of material force ... here is an opportunity of showing the solidarity of the Empire, and if a really spontaneous request were made from any Canadian force to serve with H.M. troops on such an expedition, it would be welcomed ... Such a proof of the unity of the Empire would have a great moral effect and might go far to secure a pacific settlement. Is such an offer probable? If so it should be made soon, but I do not desire that it should be the result of external pressure or suggestion.

Then Chamberlain proceeded to make the very suggestion that he had just denied having any intention of making: "please cable your reply after ascertaining the views of those concerned ... I am communicating with New South Wales and Victoria in the same sense." The colonial secretary knew that his mere query would be a form of pressure on the colonies. His goal in applying such pressure was a "spontaneous response" that could be acclaimed as clear evidence of the Empire working together, united in a common cause. He had first sought Strathcona's advice, writing to him twice in July 1899 that "a resolution of sympathy and support in the Canadian House of Commons would be most cordially welcomed."[22]

Sam Hughes, opposition member of Parliament, outspoken militia officer, and one-time advocate of Donald Smith for Conservative leader and prime minister, was clear about what Canada's response must be. A few years before, he had urged that Canadian volunteers should be sent to help relieve Khartoum. When in London for the diamond jubilee, he had pressed upon both Strathcona and Chamberlain, of all people, the merits of imperial cooperation. At Strathcona's expense, he undertook a lecture tour of the Antipodes, advocating imperial federation. As early as May 1899, he had moved a resolution in the House of Commons calling for Britain to enrol a Canadian brigade of volunteers for imperial service abroad, "to perfect the union of Britain and her colonies."

Hughes's resolution was soon set aside, but the ominous noises coming from southern Africa might nevertheless afford an early opportunity to give it effect. Among the Australian colonies, the unease arising from any threat to the Cape route had led to an offer of 250 troops by Queensland in mid-July. In response, the excitable Hughes was again on his feet, urging the government to enlist a brigade of five thousand to help "vindicate the honour of the old flag" since Canada was the "senior colony of all the British colonies." From the opposition benches, Tupper joined Laurier in hoping that push would not come to shove, but urged "that the outlying portions of the Empire would be ready, in case of necessity, to strengthen the arms of the mother country." Hughes himself was certainly ready. He made his proposal to raise troops through official channels, but he also wrote direct to Chamberlain to renew his offer "thrice previously made" to head a regiment "or if necessary a brigade" that he himself would recruit on a voluntary or even pay-your-own-way basis. Hughes could thereby give substance both to his Canadian nationalism and to his imperial commitment, an entwined concept that defied close analysis.

Laurier concluded reluctantly that the least that he must do to meet the wishes of the imperial-minded in Ontario would be to move a resolution affirming support for the Uitlanders (foreign residents) in the Transvaal if that was what the colonial secretary sought. Not surprisingly, Chamberlain replied that such a resolution would indeed be of great significance in maintaining peace. Tupper having offered to second it, Laurier knew that if he did not himself move the resolution, the leader of the opposition would do so to embarrass the government in English-speaking Canada. In any event, a government resolution might do something to satisfy the more ardent Canadian imperialists, while being sufficiently innocuous not to alienate those opposing the recruitment of volunteers. Like most prime ministers, Laurier moved only when absolutely necessary. As Macdonald had demonstrated so adroitly, inaction was always the best course, except on those rare occasions when inaction caused more offence than action.

In his moderately-worded resolution of 31 July, sandwiched between a question about the infrequent mail service between Ottawa and Cyrville and a leisurely debate about the appointment of a judge in Queen's County, PEI, Laurier described the harmony in which "two distinct races" live in Canada as a model for the Transvaal, expressed support for the position of the Uitlanders and the imperial authorities and hoped that "this mark of universal sympathy might cause wiser and more humane councils to prevail in the Transvaal and possibly avert the awful arbitrament of war." The resolution was adopted unanimously by both Houses of Parliament, members and senators rising to sing "God Save the Queen." Chamberlain was gratified, writing hyperbolically to Strathcona, "the action of the Dominion marks a distinct stage in the history of Imperial relations."[23] And there for the remainder of the summer of 1899 the matter rested.

Chamberlain may have been momentarily gratified by Laurier's resolution, but it did not satisfy the growing numbers of English-speaking Canadians who throughout the summer continued to press for a specific commitment to send soldiers if, as seemed increasingly likely, war did come. A postwar memorandum by Tupper observed piously, "Enjoying perfect freedom themselves, Canadians could not regard unmoved the disabilities suffered by men of their own race [sic] in the Transvaal." British citizens there were deprived of civil rights, despite being a majority of the population and the principal entrepreneurs who had generated unprecedented wealth for the Republic. Further, Tupper noted, "as a strenuous and progressive people themselves, engaged in the active development of rich but long latent natural resources, Canadians had little respect for the commercial inertia of the Boers ... They looked to South Africa as a market for many of their own products, and they were naturally anxious to see that market developed by the influx of an element that would be open to trade with them."[24] Added to that thinly based commercial enthusiasm was the mounting military ardour that seemed inseparable from imperial commitment.

More than six weeks passed between the introduction of Laurier's carefully worded resolution and when his hand was finally forced. During that time, Salisbury's government had successfully sought a war loan of £5 million and had despatched ten thousand soldiers to the Cape to join those already there. But war itself had still not been declared. Laurier shared the waning hope of the governor general that the Boers would not be so rash as to take on the British Empire, a contest that could only be ludicrously uneven. In any event, Laurier believed that if war did come, it would be nothing more than a "petty tribal conflict." For his part, Sam Hughes was certain that ample volunteers would be forthcoming once they were invited. As if to prove his point, several leading Canadian newspapers gave prominence to an appeal that he had made for volunteers. In little more than a fortnight, twenty-three thousand had sent Hughes their names – or so he later claimed.

In late September, following his return from Britain where he had spent hours with Chamberlain and Strathcona discussing imperial relations, Tupper announced publicly that he had telegraphed Laurier urging the immediate offer of a contingent. On one level he was not far wrong when he said that the temper of English Canada was approaching "fever heat," particularly in Ontario. Laurier now had to recognize the inevitable. As the editor of the Liberal *Globe* (and *The Times* correspondent) John Willison had observed, Laurier had either to accept participation or to resign.* Faced with that stark choice, he decided to attempt to placate English-speaking Canada by enabling volunteers to go, while attempting to mollify French-speaking Canada by contending that his decision, taken when Parliament was not sitting, established no precedent for any future employment of Canadians in imperial wars. Many years later, Tupper described his own role in the debate as central to the prime minister's reluctant decision. "When the South Africa war broke out, Sir Wilfrid Laurier declared his inability to do anything to aid the British Government. I pressed him in the strongest possible manner and pledged him the support of my party to the policy of sending a Canadian contingent and was fortunately able to induce him to change his attitude."[25]

For Strathcona, "the momentary indecision about sending troops made him secretly indignant." On 11 October he sent a long telegram to Laurier listing the contingents being readied by New Zealand and the Australian colonies. He concluded with a quotation from *The Times*, contending that if Canada had not yet designated a contingent, it was not the result of lack of enthusiasm among the people "but solely on account of hesitation on the part of the Government which, though its reasons may be legitimate, already excites considerable impatience throughout the Dominion."[26] An order-in-council of 14 October made it clear that the government itself and not individuals would organize a volunteer contingent, but such a procedure should not be regarded "as a departure from the well known principles of constitutional Government and colonial practice, nor construed as a precedent for future action." Not surprisingly, Chamberlain took a different view of the decision. Having taken the war as an occasion to press imperial unity yet more actively, he wrote to Minto hailing "his government's decision as an expression of that growing feeling of the unity and solidarity of the Empire."

One thousand volunteers were approved, preferably to be "kept together as a Canadian contingent." In accordance with a War Office decision, the Canadian government would equip and transport the unit to Cape Town, but thereafter Britain would pay all expenses, including those of the return voyage. No sooner was the contingent sanctioned than it began to be urged in English Canada that its expenses should be met by the Canadian government throughout the campaign and not just until it

---

* Sir John Willison (1856–1927) was editor of the Liberal Toronto *Globe* from 1890 to 1902 and of the Conservative *Toronto News* from 1903 to 1917. He was Canadian correspondent of *The Times* from 1909 to 1927, an ardent member of the Round Table and an advisor in turn to Laurier and Borden.

arrived at Cape Town (some critics derisorily called it the "C.O.D. contingent": Cash on Delivery). It struck in the craw of all good Canadian imperialists, including Strathcona, that Britain would pay for the Canadian "mercenaries" once they had arrived in South Africa. Laurier strove to make clear the voluntary status of the contingent by confirming to Minto "that the force thus raised is for a special purpose, and the nature of the purpose pretty clearly laid before the public. Otherwise the public would not understand why the men are given a special rate of pay, and why the British Authorities undertake to pay the whole expenditure."[27]

Always quick to exploit an opening, Chamberlain, upon the despatch of the first and second Canadian contingents in March 1900, had proposed to the governor general that he explore with the prime minister and the leader of the opposition the creation of an imperial council. He recalled his proposal to the colonial conference of 1897 of "a great Council of the Empire to which the Colonies would send representative plenipotentiaries." He left Minto in no doubt about what he had in mind:

Two questions arise ... First, would the Colonies like to be consulted in connection with the ultimate settlement after the war? ... The second question is of still greater importance. It is whether the time has not now come for the creation of something in the nature of an Imperial Council, sitting permanently in London and acting as permanent advisers to the Secretary of State for the Colonies ... Probably in the first instance questions concerning Imperial Defence would be those which would be chiefly considered by the Council.[28]

Strathcona was enthusiastic in his support at meetings of the Empire League, but Laurier, echoing Macdonald, remained opposed: "I do not think it would be a sound policy ... to ask Canada to apply a larger portion of her revenue to a definite plan of Imperial Military organization."[29] Minto understood well his premier's thinking: "He recognizes the fact that his French Canadian fellow countrymen must follow the Anglo-Saxon lead and will do his best to educate then up to it ... but I believe it to be much more with the idea of the welding together of a Canadian nation, than of forming part of the great Empire."[30]

Strathcona's imperial initiative paradoxically helped Laurier. The creation of Lord Strathcona's Horse was a major, if personal, imperial statement made in the face of the prime minister's distinct lack of enthusiasm for Canadian participation in "Joe's War." Yet Strathcona's decision to finance a mounted regiment was welcome since it helped to answer the continuing demands of many English-speaking Canadians for yet more volunteers. The despatch of two contingents had been difficult enough. The immediate despatch of a third would have refuelled the now receding, but far from forgotten, initial controversy. Strathcona's imperial gesture relieved indirectly some of the pressure, making Laurier's life a little easier outside Quebec – and even in Montreal where Hugh Graham's jingoistic *Montreal Star* led the penny press in calling for full Canadian participation.*

It does not seem that Strathcona sought Laurier's reaction before he offered a mounted regiment to the British government, but he had invited Chamberlain's support at the end of November 1899. Perhaps inspired by the example of several of his fellow peers and the City of London Corporation who were financing specific units, Strathcona recalled his own offer to raise troops during the Riel Rebellion of fifteen years before. Having received a warm endorsement from the colonial secretary for such an offer, Strathcona simply informed Laurier a month or so later of his decision. He would raise and pay (through the Bank of Montreal) for a completely equipped regiment of 540 men already "accustomed to life in the saddle" (many were former North West Mounted Police). Strathcona did, however, ask Laurier to authorize the Department of Militia to undertake on his behalf the recruitment and outfitting of his regiment (he had in mind specifically Major-General E.H.T. Hutton, the British officer commanding the Canadian militia).† Three days later, the prime minister agreed without comment or congratulation, noting only that preparations would be undertaken immediately, following the despatch of the second contingent of infantry volunteers.

The high commissioner wisely absented himself from decisions about the selection of officers, the militia being shot through with political patronage, resulting in continual friction between the British officers who commanded the small Canadian force and politicians who saw the militia as one more opportunity for pork-barrel politics. Strathcona had origi-

---

* Hugh Graham (1848–1938), publisher of the *Montreal Star*, Canada's largest and most profitable daily newspaper, was created Lord Athelston in 1917 on the recommendation of Borden in recognition of the newspaper's strong pro-conscriptionist stance. Nevertheless Borden regarded Graham as "a singular mixture of cunning and stupidity. His great weakness lies in his belief that he can hoodwink others ... Evidently he is consumed with an immense desire for a peerage."

† Major-General Sir Edward Hutton (1848–1923), a veteran of service in Egypt in 1882 and commandant in New South Wales (1893–6), was appointed in 1898 general officer commanding the Canadian militia.

nally hoped that General Hutton and his "non-political" staff would be involved, but Frederick Borden and other Liberal politicians inevitably took a direct interest in Strathcona's remarkable gift. Hutton recorded that "Strathcona is extremely indignant at the Canadian Government for having taken the organization of his Corps out of my hands, and at their having made much party political capital out of it all. He told me that if he had known the result he would never have made the offer."[31]

In the event, Hutton could do the high commissioner no service. Arrogant and insensitive in his single-minded pursuit of his own status and of Canadian participation in the war, Hutton soon ran afoul of Laurier and Frederick Borden (whom he regarded as a drunken buffoon). In their eyes, Hutton had mixed unforgivably in domestic politics. By February 1900 Laurier had concluded that the general had to go. He wired Strathcona that Hutton had proven himself "meddlesome, ignores the authority of the Minister, and constantly acts as one who holds himself independent of civil authority."[32] Knowing that the governor general and the major-general were close friends and collaborators, Laurier employed both Strathcona and Minto to arrange for Hutton's immediate recall, the high commissioner confirming to Laurier on 3 February that Chamberlain would ask the War Office to recall him. Chamberlain recorded in a minute, "I informed Lord Strathcona of what I am doing to get a settlement. I told him that in the present circumstances and having regard to the possible actions of [Canadian] Ministers in connection with the Colonial contingent, I thought that I was bound to avoid doing anything to embarrass them and should therefore endeavour to get matters settled as they wished without raising any public controversy." Face was saved by the War Office appointing Hutton to a command in South Africa.

Laurier wanted the high commissioner left in no doubt at what was at the root of the matter. Towards the end of February, he wired Strathacona, "It is impossible to understand the conduct of General Hutton except by the assumption that being an Officer of the Imperial Army he was superior to the Minister of Militia," a contradiction of the fundamental principle of responsible government.[33] This exchange of telegrams, brief in itself, was part of a process of fundamental change, leading in time to the appointment of a Canadian rather than a British general officer to command the militia. More importantly, it marked a major step in the evolution of the office of the governor general from being the representative of the British government to being the representative of the monarch in Canada. The high commissioner in London, and eventually a British high commissioner in Ottawa, would become the preferred channels for communication between the two governments, with the governor general assuming an increasingly ceremonial role.

After a farewell parade on Parliament Hill in Ottawa (attended by both Minto and Tupper), Lord Strathcona's Horse entrained for Halifax from where they sailed for South Africa on 17 March 1900. The accompanying tributes to Strathcona were many and varied, both in Britain and in Canada.* The reaction of *The Times* was predictable ("It is proof how this war ... [is] in truth knitting us together as we never were before"), but what Strathcona made of an unique suggestion from Tupper is unrecorded. The leader of the opposition, who believed that he would be returned to power in the pending election, informed Strathcona that he would "be the successor" to the governor general and that "on no condition [should he] vacate the High Commissionership before a general election takes place," thereby preventing a Liberal appointment[34] However, with the Conservative defeat on 7 November 1900, Tupper was never able to deliver upon his proposal. In any event, if there was ever any question of Strathcona leaving his post before he himself wanted, it was ended with his extraordinary imperial gesture of raising a regiment at his own expense.

Strathcona had indirectly helped Laurier through a particularly difficult period. And he had supplied a regiment of light horse especially adept at the peculiar warfare of the veldt so unfamiliar to the long-suffering British Tommy. He had also bought himself an indefinite extension to his term as high commissioner. No prime minister – and certainly not Laurier – could afford to be seen as terminating the appointment of such an eminent and influential Canadian who had, in the eyes of many, responded so magnificently to the imperial need. Whatever else Lord Strathcona's Horse did, it helped to ensure that the high commissioner could remain in London as long as he wanted.

From London, Strathcona followed the adventures of his regiment with the closest attention. And after its year of service in South Africa, he arranged for it to return to Canada via London, where he pulled out all stops to give it a resounding imperial welcome, including an inspection by King Edward VII and a reception with Joseph Chamberlain present. Its embarkation for Halifax after ten days of revelry did not, however,

* The popular impact of Lord Strathcona's imperial gesture lingered on in Sellars and Yeatman's comic *1066 and All That*: "Numerous battles were fought against the Bore leaders (such as Bother, Kopje, and Stellenbosch) at Nek's Creek, Creek's Nek, Knock's Knee, etc., and much assistance was given to the British cause by Strathcoma's memorable horse (patriotically lent by Lord Strathcoma for the occasion)."

In snow in February 1901, the men of Lord Strathcona's Horse, in their stetsons and greatcoats, were addressed on the parade square of a London barracks by the former governor general, Lord Aberdeen, on their return from their year's service in the South African War. The hatless Strathcona, who arranged an elaborate series of entertainments for the troopers in London, is visible at the centre, his long white beard being especially evident.

mark the end of Canada's involvement in the dreary, disease-ridden conflict between Briton and Boer, although Strathcona continued to portray it as a splendid manifestation of imperial unity.* He assured Laurier that the British people "were so favourably impressed with the unmistakable

---

* The South African War had an impact upon prime ministers beyond Tupper, Laurier and Borden. Mackenzie King was "greatly moved" as he watched the Coldstream and Grenadier Guards march through London before embarking for Cape Town. R.B. Bennett berated the Mormon settlers in the North West for their alleged pro-Boer sympathies. Lester Pearson recalled the boisterous celebration in Aurora, Ontario, when Mafeking was relieved. John Diefenbaker had the misfortune to fall into a wagon of slops on his way to a parade in Toronto to welcome home the volunteers of the first Canadian contingent.

and enthusiastic loyalty of the people of the Dominion as a whole that the strictures of one or two Quebec newspapers were hardly noticed," adding that "Canada has gained greatly by her action in sending out the contingents."

The war finally dragged to its disreputable end in May 1902, South Africa eventually becoming an uneasy partner in the Empire. Two months later, Arthur Balfour succeeded his uncle, Lord Salisbury, as prime minister. In October Strathcona and the lieutenant-governor of New South Wales joined a royal commission appointed the month before to report on the "Military Preparations and Other Matters connected with the War in South Africa," but also reflecting the unspoken sense of insecurity arising from the hostility of the rest of the world to the war. Presumably someone in Whitehall had recognized that if the participation of self-governing colonies was to be sought in future conflicts, it would be advisable to include a Canadian and an Australian as commissioners into any inquiry how small Boer commandos had continually harassed or even defeated much larger regular British armies in the field. In the event, their belated appointment added little to the commission's meagre findings. Under the chairmanship of the Earl of Elgin (the Canadian-born son of the former governor general), the hearings were frequently banal; discussions of faulty harness were undeniably important, but they were only one of many instances where the commission allowed the trees to obscure the woods. And as in the case of Strathcona (as well as his Australian colleague) the members refrained from discussing imperial relations, especially naval, in time of war as well as military cooperation in time of peace.

The commission's report of July 1903 was something of a whitewash – in which Strathcona joined. He was not going to do anything on the one hand that would rock the imperial boat nor, on the other, to allow his status as an imperialist to be doubted. In any event, whatever his personal inclinations, the high commissioner knew very well that Laurier was a decided agnostic when it came to prior imperial commitments (although he had continued to press Chamberlain for military contracts for Canadian suppliers).

Not surprisingly, the bland report was given only passing scrutiny by the London press. Its lasting impact was indirect, resulting from one of its members, Lord Esher, seizing upon it to force reforms upon that quintessentially reactionary institution, the War Office. Since 1885 there had been a largely ineffective Colonial Defence Committee chaired by the secretary of state for the colonies. From late in 1892 the new Committee for Imperial Defence (CID) was to have long-term implications for Canada, although Strathcona played no direct role in shaping it. In sanctioning the creation of the committee, Balfour had hoped that the colonies would thereby learn more about and possibly contribute voluntarily to imperial defence, but he wisely recognized that "the self-governing Colonies will never allow ... any representative of theirs to come to the Defence Committee if [it] had the smallest authority to impose obligations, financial, political, military, or naval on the Colonies ... the only thing the Defence Committee may give ... is advice." The presence in London in 1903 of Frederick Borden to discuss details of Canada's militia bill gave immediate, if slight, imperial substance to the CID (despite the fact that Balfour dismissed him to Edward VII as a "gentleman ... of rather inferior quality"). Eventually, the committee would become a chosen vehicle for the efforts of Frederick's cousin, Robert Borden, when prime minister, to cooperate in imperial defence and foreign policy.

It would have been unrealistic to expect Strathcona at the end of 1903 to grasp the profound military implications of the Wright brothers' recent flight – few people did – but the high commissioner might have been expected to place before Laurier the more immediate questions of imperial military organization and collaboration that needed to be answered.* No such decisions having been made, Laurier and Strathcona were soon faced with a replay of Hutton's dismissal. In June 1904 the general officer commanding the militia, Lord Dundonald (a South African war veteran whom Minto described as having "a brain about the size of a pin's head"), "publicly accused the Government of jobbery in militia matters."[35] Laurier immediately instructed Strathcona to inform the colonial secretary that Dundonald had been relieved of his duties (no one having taken seriously his counter threat to seek a seat in the Canadian House of Commons). The following year Frederick Borden, the nemesis of Hutton and Dundonald, affirmed with Laurier's concurrence civil governance of the military by creating a Militia Council (along the lines of the recently minted Army Council in London), appointing a Canadian to command, and replacing the British garrisons at Esquimalt and Halifax with Canadian regulars. Strathcona advocated yet another royal commission, this time to inquire

---

* The report did not anticipate Winston Churchill's later speculation that Chamberlain's war in South Africa had led to the eventual end of the British Empire: put simply, Germany, having been shown as impotent to do anything about the South African War without a first-class navy, set about building a fleet that could challenge the Royal Navy (D.C. Gordon, *The Dominion Partnership in Imperial Defense* [Baltimore, 1965]).

"into the security of our [i.e., British] food supply in time of war." He hoped in vain that an answer might thereby be found to those who had opposed an imperial tariff preference if it included food: foodstuffs, he contended, would be more dependable if they came from Canada or Australia than if they came from the United States or Argentina or Russia – and if the routes to the British Isles were guarded by imperial forces.

Queen Victoria died in January 1901. The events of August 1902 surrounding the coronation of Edward VII, conducted in the full imperial afterglow of the South African War, were another occasion for Strathcona to affirm his loyalty to the Empire. When the Queen's grandson and his wife, the future King George V and Queen Mary, visited Canada, he was prompt to offer his house and hospitality in Montreal, only to earn from the governor general the private and convoluted comment, "poor old Strathcona attempting to head society the ways of which he is ignorant of, with a squaw wife who is absolutely hopeless, what could one expect?"*36 Although not noted for his contribution to public policy, the high commissioner did strive to project Canada both on the British and on the broader imperial scene. As on the occasion of the diamond jubilee, Laurier was on hand, both for the coronation and a fourth colonial conference, as were Canadian troops in a second great imperial parade, this time including veterans of Strathcona's Horse. A peerage for Laurier was privately canvassed, but the prime minister declined. Large garden parties and a dinner for visiting colonial leaders both in London and at Knebworth represented only a fraction of the high commissioner's efforts. Apparently at the suggestion of one of his small staff, W.T.R. Preston, the high commissioner took the occasion to erect a massive arch on Whitehall ostensibly marking the coronation but in fact promoting emigration to Canada: "Britain's granary" offered "free homes."

For the agenda of the June 1902 colonial conference the Antipodean premiers suggested items arising partly from the military collaboration

---

* The "squaw" appellation persisted beyond Strathcona's lifetime. For example, Lord Lonsdale, recalling a meeting with him during a visit to Canada in 1888, later recorded imaginatively that "one night in the middle of a fierce storm an Indian girl, on her way south to join her husband, sought refuge in his [Smith's] log cabin. She stayed with him for the rest of her life ... Every year he gave a great reunion party for all her relations who would come to her house in Montreal and sit on the floor of her drawing-room to smoke the traditional pipe of peace" (D. Sutherland, *The Yellow Earl: The Fifth Earl of Lonsdale* [London, 1965]).

of the Empire in the South African War. Laurier, however, had already made clear his opposition to any broad-ranging discussions, military or otherwise. He knew well that one agenda item would be "in the direction of organizing a general plan of defence of the Empire," a reasonable assumption which determined his characteristically cautious reply to Chamberlain's invitation: "The political relations now existing between the mother country and the great self-governing Colonies ... are regarded by my ministers as entirely satisfactory ... and they do not anticipate that in the varying conditions of the Colonies there can be any scheme of defence applicable to all," naval service included. With the difficult parliamentary debate about the war in South Africa in mind, he flatly refused a War Office proposal that "a certain force should be set apart by each one of the Dominions and earmarked ... for foreign service."[37] Australia, New Zealand, the Cape Colony and Natal, all conscious of the protection offered them by the Royal Navy, announced at the conference expansion of their financial support for either the maintenance of an Australasian squadron or of the Royal Navy generally. Despite having a large merchant fleet, Canada would make no such contribution, Laurier contenting himself with vague references to the possibility of creating a small Canadian navy (which he repeated when the first Australian prime minister, Sir Edmund Barton, briefly visited Canada en route home from the coronation).

With regard to imperial trade, the leader of the opposition, Robert Borden, inquired whether the government recognized that Britain had "adopted a policy with regard to duties on breadstuffs." The immediate background to Borden's question was the bothersome intention of the British government to help defray the unexpected costs of the war in South Africa by reimposing the old "registration duty" on imported wheat. If it did so, a tariff preference for Canadian grain would become possible. In April 1902 Laurier requested Strathcona to ascertain whether such a preference would be considered. During the subsequent months, the Conservative government of Balfour vacillated, but both the vexatious question of the "registration duty" and the consequent Canadian demand for a preference was resolved within a year by the tax itself being withdrawn. Instead of instituting a tariff preference for grain from the Empire, the British government abolished its short-lived and highly unpopular tax on imported wheat. What Borden was also saying by his question to Laurier was that the Canadian Conservative party, despite its oft-professed devotion to British institutions and traditions, regarded the new Canadian tariff as "a useless preference to the motherland and yet injurious to

Canadian [manufacturing] interests," having been unilaterally bestowed, without any reciprocity being asked. At the end of the day, if a choice had to be made between a tariff preference for British goods or protection for Canadian manufacturers, protection would win every time. Equally, in Britain the cost of food would be placed before any imperial sentiment.*

Before leaving Ottawa, Laurier had said that the only question worthy of discussion at the conference was not imperial defence but imperial commercial relations. He was being pressed by the Conservative opposition and even some of his own supporters to seek from Britain reciprocity for the unilateral tariff preferences that his finance minister, W.S. Fielding, had concocted (the Canadian Manufacturers' Association limited itself to advocating preferences on War Office and Admiralty contracts). At the gathering itself, Laurier repeated his offer to extend Canada's tariff preference for British goods on a reciprocal basis to Australia, New Zealand, and South Africa. He had already suggested to New Zealand and Australia that the three colonies meet in London during the coronation of Edward VII in the hope of securing a preferred place for their products (in Canada's case especially wheat) in the British market. The Colonial Office was not much pleased with Laurier's unexpected trade initiative – even Strathcona had not been forewarned – and in the event little came of it.

Little also emerged from the 1902 colonial conference. Chamberlain had been eloquent in his plea for military help:

We do require your assistance in the administration of the vast Empire which is yours as well as ours ... If you are prepared at any time to take any share ... in the burdens of the Empire, we are prepared to meet you ... [by] giving to you a corresponding voice in the policy of the Empire. Suggestions have been made that representation should be given to colonies in either or both Houses of Parliament ... but ... the most practical forum ... would be the establishment ... of a real Council of the Empire.[38]

In face of Laurier's rejection of a standing imperial force and his reluctant commitment to reduce the cost to the British taxpayer of the maritime defence of Canada's vast coastline, the only agreement was to convene an

---

* Strathcona was supportive from its inception in 1905 of the Free Importation of Canadian Cattle Association of Great Britain which attempted to win the removal of the continuing obstacles, but to no avail. He did not himself raise the issue in the House of Lords.

imperial conference at least once every four years. Back in Ottawa, the prime minister made clear his conviction that at most the periodic conferences would act as an advisory body with all decisions being left to "the free nations" of the Empire, "owing the same allegiance to the same sovereign, but all owing paramount allegiance to their respective peoples."

This may have been how Laurier regarded the Empire, but it was certainly not Strathcona's idea of what it could become. Possibly the high commissioner privately shared some of the frustration, if not the lively language, of that arch-imperialist and premier of the Cape Colony, Dr Starr Jameson, who had described Laurier to Kipling as "That dam' dancing-master who had bitched the whole show." In fact, the failure of the colonial conference of 1902 to move in the direction of Chamberlain's coordinated empire was not primarily the result of Laurier's passive resistance. More fundamentally, as one imperial historian has noted,

It was caused by the difficulties obviously inherent in co-operative control of defense without complete centralization in every other related sphere, where such a development was utterly impracticable. Defense centralization would have removed control of a large block of expenditures from the colonial legislatures. It would have done so without any real concession of a voice in the policy for which the contributions had been made. Colonial legislatures were no more willing than the British Parliament to accept any reduction of their status.[39]

Despite that, Strathcona continued to speak publicly in favour of closer imperial cooperation. At the Colonial Club in February 1903 he put as much distance between himself and Laurier as he prudently could when he recognized that Canadians "were not quite ready yet to tax themselves heavily for the Imperial forces," but perhaps recalling Sir John A. Macdonald's statement to the Carnarvon commission, he added, "when there was a necessity for it and when a practical proposition was put forward, Canada would not be backward in doing her duty."[40] The Ontario-born member of Parliament and novelist, Sir Gilbert Parker, added his support. Britain "could make no demand upon the Colonies for the Navy, but ... a moral obligation on the part of the colonies existed which could not be overestimated."*

* Gilbert Parker (1862–1932), the Ontario-born member of Parliament for Gravesend (1900–18), was a popular novelist and a staunch supporter of imperial unity; somewhat incongruously, he was also a close friend of the free-trade prime minister, Henry Campbell-Bannerman.

Amidst his several imperial activities, Strathcona never neglected his business interests. In 1901 the shah of Persia granted to the Anglo-Persian Oil Company, controlled by William Knox d'Arcy, Strathcona's Australian neighbour on Grosvenor Square, an exclusive sixty-year concession for petroleum exploration and exploitation (except for the region bordering on a suspicious Russia). D'Arcy, made rich from gold digging in Queensland, despatched a drilling crew of Canadians and Poles to Abadan. Oil fields in abundance were anticipated, but before any major strikes were made, even the wealthy d'Arcy began to run low on funds. He scouted all possibilities – the Admiralty, Royal Dutch Shell, Standard Oil – before the Admiralty and he together struck upon the happy combination of Burmah Oil and Lord Strathcona. Without reference to Ottawa, but apparently with the encouragement of the First Sea Lord, the high commissioner plunged into the petroleum business in 1905. When oil was struck in commercial quantities three years later, the Anglo-Persian Oil Company (eventually to evolve into British Petroleum), had Strathcona as a principal investor and chairman. Rapid expansion followed, but so did financial demands, leaving the new company still vulnerable.

Salvation lay with the Admiralty. Fortuitously, the First Sea Lord, the redoubtable Admiral Lord Fisher, had long been an advocate of propulsion by oil rather than by coal in His Majesty's warships. Equally fortuitously, a new First Lord of the Admiralty had recently been appointed. Fisher had little difficulty in convincing Winston Churchill that oil was the fuel of the future. Strathcona, when he appeared in December 1911 before a commission considering "whether or not it would be practical to largely or entirely replace Coal by Fuel Oil," testified that oil was indeed the answer to the Royal Navy's prayers. British-controlled, high-quality petroleum from Persia was "practically inexhaustible." He added piously that his commitment to the company was based upon public policy rather than commercial considerations: "it was not as a mercantile company that I looked upon it, but really from an Imperial point of view." In 1913 the British government took formal control of the company and the depleted coffers of Anglo-Persian were soon restored by Admiralty contracts, literally weeks before the outbreak of the First World War.

Throughout Chamberlain's controversial eight years as colonial secretary, Strathcona supported him at every turn, whether in his folly in sanctioning a war in southern Africa or in his ultimately futile advocacy of an imperial tariff preference as the copestone of imperial federation. From the opposition benches in Ottawa, Tupper also lent support. To the *Daily Mail* of 12 September 1901 he wrote, "Preferential tariffs are bound to come. You will soon have a federated South Africa, the Commonwealth of Australia and the Dominion of Canada all pressing you for preferential tariffs on a reciprocal basis: you will have to give way. Look after yourselves and your own Empire." In Chamberlain's Birmingham constituency, Strathcona urged that the colonial secretary had it all exactly right: "The public mind is beginning to see the advantage, to put it mildly, of the relations between the different parts of the Empire being so arranged as to place Imperial trade on a friendly or, should I say, on a family footing."

Laurier, however, remained sceptical about Chamberlain's altruism: his own convening of a meeting with the prime ministers of Australia and New Zealand at the conference in 1902 had not been well received by the colonial secretary, although there was nothing that he could do about it. Further, at home there was no enthusiasm amongst manufacturers for anything but a protective tariff. Following a speech by Strathcona in Toronto extolling a "united Empire," the *Globe* editor, John Willison, who helped to keep Laurier informed of thinking in Ontario, reported that Canadian manufacturers wanted neither Empire free trade nor even an imperial preference, unless it resulted from Britain imposing duties on imports from all countries other than the Empire, thereby creating an imperial preference. "The Canadian manufacturers who profess to want preferential trade with the Mother Country are not very frank. They are really hostile to the existing British preference and look for a movement toward protection in Great Britain rather than to further advance toward free trade in Canada. Both parties here fear the manufacturers, and properly so, for they have been the controlling factor in every election since 1878."

Never one for half-measures, Chamberlain plunged into the debate on an imperial federation underpinned by a preferential tariff. By the autumn of 1902, undeterred by the meagre results of the recent colonial conference, he was again in full flight, deeply dividing the Conservative party. Despite his tireless advocacy, and even the resignation of several junior ministers in his support, an uneasy Balfour prevaricated as long as he could. The centrality of free trade in Whitehall economic thinking, reflecting popular and deep-seated opposition to any tax on food, again prevailed, but the debate left his government in terminal turmoil. Striving to hold it together, Balfour finally challenged his own minister: "You will never have a tax on the food of the people in this country except as part of a big policy which they heartily and conscientiously accept." Chamberlain took up the challenge. Despite the opposition of much commercial opinion, he resigned from Balfour's government in September 1903 to launch a well-funded Tariff Reform League with the broad purpose of "booming the Empire" in the words of George Bernard Shaw. What the leader of the opposition, Campbell-Bannerman, described as a "rash and fantastic scheme of so-called fiscal reform" was to divide and doom the Conservatives in the pending election, but at Chamberlain's farewell reception, Strathcona "delivered a sympathetic and regretful address on behalf of the other Colonial representatives."

Two months after his resignation, Chamberlain wrote to Minto, "the movement is making extraordinary progress here ... Lord Strathcona was to have communicated with Sir Wilfrid on the subject."[41] Strathcona did in fact continue to urge upon Laurier imperial unity, although the baffled Chamberlain eventually gave up on the elusive and intentionally ambiguous Canadian premier: "I would rather do business with a cad who knows his own mind." As Chamberlain's campaign for an imperial tariff preference faltered, the prospects for imperial federation waned in the face of Balfour's continuing scepticism. In no way deterred, Strathcona redoubled his adulation of the former colonial secretary. For his trouble, Strathcona's advocacy of Chamberlain's ideas became at least briefly a contentious issue in the House of Commons in Ottawa. For Henri Bourassa, an imperial tariff preference would reduce Canada's fiscal freedom. Did Strathcona's speeches in favour of Chamberlain's thinking represent government policy? In reply, Laurier came close to disowning the high commissioner's imperial enthusiasms with a paradox: "He simply expressed his views and, of course, he has a right to his own opinions but in doing so he does not in any way bind the Government of which he is an official."[42]

Strathcona was not the only Canadian exponent of Chamberlain's imperial policies. Two days before Chamberlain's resignation from Balfour's government, Sir Gilbert Parker had again attempted to stir the imperial pot, this time by appealing to Sir George Foster, temporarily out of Parliament, to come to England "to speak for us." A graduate, like Tupper, of the University of Edinburgh, a formidable and frequently vitriolic orator and advocate of reciprocal tariff preferences within the Empire, Foster spent a month during the autumn of 1903, addressing public meetings across Wales, England and Scotland. Chamberlain was grateful, writing to him, "Let us get mutual trade relations and trust that our successors may find a way to bind the Empire closer together in other directions." Tupper, now retired from active politics but always ready to offer an opinion on public policy, proclaimed himself convinced that Chamberlain's policy was "certain of ultimate success."

Not content with extolling publicly Chamberlain's person and policies in Britain, Strathcona in August 1903 again carried his advocacy across the Atlantic to Montreal where the Congress of the Chambers of Commerce of the British Empire was meeting for a second time. He proposed a resolution, unanimously adopted, stating that "the bonds of the British Empire could be materially strengthened and the union of the various parts ... greatly consolidated by the adoption of a commercial policy based upon the principle of mutual benefit." In March and April of 1905 Strathcona, again on a visit to Montreal, assured his audiences that "the great bulk of the people of Canada are in favour of preferential treatment in favour of the Mother Country."* Possibly they were, if the proposition was put simply enough, but the British voter remained decidedly unenthusiastic. All the lively words of Sir George Foster and all the abundant money of Strathcona, even when joined with the ardent advocacy of Chamberlain and his many acolytes, were insufficient to overcome the hostility of the increasingly sophisticated British voter to anything that looked like a tax on food. The British election of January 1906 ended any doubts where majority opinion lay. The Liberal free traders of the benevolent Henry Campbell-Bannerman, with Herbert Asquith leading the fight against "tariff reform," routed Balfour's ambiguous Conservatives with a majority greater than any since the first Reform Bill.† Any early possibility of an imperial tariff preference was gone with them.

Chamberlain confirmed for Robert Borden, the Conservative leader of the opposition in Canada, that tariff reform, despite the election results, was "not indefinitely postponed." In seeking in turn to back Chamberlain in his undiminished commitment, Borden wrote to the *Daily Mail* that the support shown for Chamberlain "has its significance not only for the mother country but for all the dependencies of the Empire." For his part, Strathcona was again active behind the scenes at Congress of Chambers of Commerce of the Empire, this time in London in July 1906. A resolution explicitly favouring an imperial preference was adopted (although not without opposition from protectionists). Tupper, also at the congress, was among those who moved another resolution congratulating Chamberlain

* In return, the irrepressible Sam Hughes described Strathcona in the Toronto *Mail* of 10 January 1906 as "the greatest advantage and best advertisement" that Canada had in Britain.

† However benign and measured, Sir Henry Campbell-Bannerman (1836–1908) was not widely recognized by his countrymen: "When attending a dinner for colonial premiers ... Lady Derby asked her neighbour who the man was next to his wife. 'That,' replied Sir Wilfrid Laurier, 'is your prime minister'" (Wilson, *C.B.*, 595). Lady Derby's husband, the sixteenth Earl of Derby (as Lord Stanley), had been governor general of Canada from 1888 to 1893, when Laurier was leader of the opposition.

on his seventieth birthday. Unknown to the delegates, however, on the day following his birthday, Chamberlain had suffered a severe stroke. With his permanent incapacity, the advocacy of an imperial tariff preference lost much of its steam. For Strathcona, the absence of his hero from the public scene meant a more muted tone after 1906. He remained, however, unfailing in his praise of him: "Mr. Chamberlain ... has, perhaps, done more than any other man in bringing closer the Mother Country and the Colonies and strengthening the ties of friendship which happily exist throughout the Empire."[43]

By 1907, imperial terminology was altered to match altered circumstances: colonial conferences became imperial conferences; colonies became dominions; and the British prime minister replaced the colonial secretary as chairman. Ideas about imperial councils and various schemes for greater military and economic cooperation had proliferated in London, Toronto, Sydney, and elsewhere in the evolving Empire. Some envisaged a council of high commissioners, presided over by the secretary of state for the colonies and supported by a secretariat, which would provide continuity between imperial conferences. To that end, in an article entitled "The Problem of Empire" in the May 1907 issue of *Nineteenth Century*, almost two decades after his imperial unity advocacy in the same periodical, Tupper urged again that the high commissioner be also a cabinet minister at home. "Having during four years represented Canada while I at the same time held a seat in the Canadian Cabinet, I found in discussing matters with the Imperial Government the additional weight given to my representations from the fact that I was not only a representative of the Canadian Government but also a member of it." Tupper sent a copy of his article to Laurier, who responded enigmatically that "my views coincide exactly with yours."

Such ideas were, however, unwelcome in Whitehall, wary as they were of any erosion of Britain's capacity to decide for itself. Nor were such ideas, for quite different reasons, any more welcome to the free-trade Liberal government of Campbell-Bannerman. Having in effect defeated Chamberlain's ideas, the new prime minister was not about to embrace tariff reciprocity and instead proposed in vain free trade throughout the Empire. The new president of the board of trade, David Lloyd George, attempted to offer an alternative when he imaginatively called for faster and less expensive shipping (in part to make imperial foodstuffs fully competitive in British markets). For his part, Laurier remained wary of all ideas of imperial unity. Those who sought a centralized Empire or a federation underpinned by an imperial tariff preference rightly placed little hope in the conference taking early decisions. Before Laurier arrived in London, Tupper spoke at the Canada Club in an attempt to help point him in the right direction of closer Empire unity. Laurier, however, at his third imperial conference, continued to follow the line that he had first pursued ten years before: Canada was satisfied with existing imperial arrangements and institutions which recognized that each Dominion had the absolute right to manage its own affairs, including fiscal.

As for naval cooperation, Laurier drew upon a resolution of the House of Commons to state that Canada would "proceed as we have done with our Militia. We should consult with the Naval authorities of the British Government ... and after having organized a plan, we should carry it out in Canada with our own resources and out of our own money." The Admiralty would needs content itself with a small Canadian navy associated with the Royal Navy rather than a cash contribution to it. In light of all this, the 1907 conference was no more dramatic in its results than its predecessors. Suggestions by Australia and New Zealand for an imperial council, supported by a secretariat, to oversee foreign and defence policy wilted in the face of continuing Canadian opposition. An historian of colonial and imperial conferences has contrasted the approach of the Australian prime minister, Alfred Deakin, with that of Laurier:

Both were ardent nationalists concerned with the enhancement of Dominion autonomy but Laurier, shielded somewhat by the North American continent and with a complex racial-religious problem to keep in balance, tended to be conservative, fearful of commitments and of added responsibilities, while Deakin, more exposed in the South Pacific to the vagaries of international friction and faced with the necessity of enlarging Australian prosperity, was that much more inclined to see parochial needs in an imperial setting ... Deakin's flexibility certainly enabled him to view imperial organization with more critical imagination than Laurier and to realize its inadequacies both of form and substance. Sir Wilfrid, on the other hand, "a master in the art of procrastination", never took a fence until he could help it, often marking time and postponing decisions about the imperial relationship for months and years if necessary. He was far more the dextrous party manager than a statesman.[44]

The musings of the Earl of Elgin, the colonial secretary, that the high commissioners for Canada, Australia, New Zealand, and South Africa should all be made peers (or at least imperial privy councillors), meeting periodically under his chairmanship, did not recommend itself to Lau-

rier. The prime minister of Australia recorded that the Dominion premiers, with the exception of New Zealand's, had opposed any transfer of
authority to high commissioners meeting in a representative council; ministers only should meet in council. The imperial conference did, however,
welcome the creation of a small secretariat within the Colonial Office
(a Dominions Section was duly instituted) to assist in preparations and
other more ill-defined duties, but it could not be the fully fledged coordination agency that some had sought. There is no record that Strathcona,
despite his enthusiasm for imperial federation and his wide commercial
experience, participated in the implementation of even the lesser, more
mundane steps toward imperial cooperation. Laurier had made it clear
that he sought no such initiatives, large or small, the only exception to his
otherwise passive imperial policy being a continuing invitation to Newfoundland to join Confederation, but not to the British West Indies: "we
are not prepared ... to invite or encourage political union" with them.

Following a year of attempting to deal directly with his motley of immigration agents across Europe, Sifton, bypassing Strathcona, had moved
yet more decisively to transfer promotion away from the high commission and to place it, at least indirectly, under his own control. In January 1899 he had appointed W.T.R. Preston, a Liberal party organizer in
Ontario, to be housed on Charing Cross Road to supervise the European
agents and eventually the North Atlantic Trading Company and, later
still, the Canadian Labour Bureau. These two shell organizations were
to help divert continental migration towards Canada, including the payment of bonuses to agents, frequently against the express wish of local
governments. For eight years Preston and Strathcona nominally worked
together, but rarely in real unison. That the ambitious Preston brought a
new energy to promotion was undeniable. For example, he ordered that
all lantern slides used in schools and at lectures, showing ice palaces, snow
slides, and Indians, be replaced by those showing farming success and
industrial growth, since "many of the schoolmasters also act as unofficial emigration agents and distribute pamphlets to intending emigrants."
Gradually there was a gratifying increase, but in injecting his new dyna-
mism into promotion, Preston, ever wilful and prickly, ignored Strathcona
to the degree that in 1906, the year following Sifton's resignation, Laurier
gently chided him about his cavalier attitude toward the high commissioner: "You always expressed yourself as gratified at his uniform kindness
and courtesy. I certainly shared then and still share now this opinion. I
told you before and I beg to repeat that Lord Strathcona spoke in the most

complimentary terms of yourself and the manner in which you discharge your work."[45]

The following year the controversial Preston was gone, transferred to trade promotion, first in South Africa and later in Asia. He had accepted the advice of Sir Thomas Skinner, deputy governor of the Hudson's Bay Company, who knew Strathcona well, "that I was wasting my time in the immigration work in London as the High Commissioner was bitterly opposed to me personally, and jealous of the success of my efforts, and above all, most deeply chagrined that this work had been taken from under his immediate jurisdiction."[46] But for more than a decade he had successfully resisted all efforts of Strathcona to assert his overall authority for emigration promotion in Europe, convinced as he was that the nonagenarian high commissioner was beyond providing the leadership that was required in the relentless international competition for immigrants. For his part, Strathcona had encountered difficulties in attempting to ensure that Preston, in his bull-headed enthusiasm, did not violate local practices on the continent. Only in 1907, when the high commissioner was finally rid of the troublesome Preston, was his own office able to resume its more customary if decidedly less dynamic supervisory role.

In the autumn of 1906 William Lyon Mackenzie King, Laurier's young deputy minister of labour, made his second crossing to Britain, this time on an official visit broadly concerned with fraudulent emigration schemes. Following his arrival, he saw Strathcona several times before he met with Elgin and Winston Churchill, Elgin's notably articulate parliamentary under-secretary and spokesman on colonial matters in the House of Commons. With regard to Strathcona, King recorded in his omnipresent diary that "one of [my] major tasks was to soothe the old man and avoid any suggestion that [he] was being superseded," while at the same time retaining his assistance in approaching British ministers and officials. "I also wished to frame the letter [to Elgin] in such a way that Lord Strathcona would be drawn into the matter of the negotiations, though, at the same time, keeping their control in my own hands. I thought I would read the letter over to him, and appear to consult him as to the advisability of proceeding in that way, although I was quite determined to see that the above purposes should all be secured."[47] King, it seems, was as adept at manipulating Strathcona as was Laurier. As part of his manoeuvrings, he adroitly bypassed the high commissioner in his dealings with the British government. Even in matters of immigration, the high commissioner was not to be regarded as the preferred route of communication between the two governments.

In 1907, following race riots in Vancouver, a "gentlemen's agreement" was concluded with Japan to restrict emigration to Canada. In early 1909 King was himself in Calcutta attempting similarly to restrict the emigration of "British Indians" to Canada, a "grave question" in the view of Minto, now the reforming Viceroy of India. Upon his return to Ottawa, King was clear in his recommendation to Laurier: "Canada should be kept for the white races and India for the black."[48] In separate negotiations with the mandarins of Peking, he placed Canada for the first time in direct official communication with China. For his trouble, King was gratified upon his return to be made a Companion of St Michael and St George, recognition for his services in ensuring the exclusion of Chinese, "a race unfitted alike by their constitution, temperament and habits for permanent residence."

In Tokyo and Peking agreements or procedures were now in place to limit severely Asian immigration. In the case of India, the Dominion had for a decade "been ready to acknowledge the Imperial importance of the question." In the end, however, Ottawa disregarded the fact that India was the brightest jewel in the imperial crown and all but closed the door. Given Britain's valued alliance with Japan, Strathcona endorsed to Laurier a friend's recommendation that Japanese immigrants should be directed towards "manufactures" while "the white man should alone own and work the soil, unless in the course of time the Canadian Government is willing conditionally to permit the Japanese to become British subjects and make their allegiance to the British Empire." Laurier did not respond, leaving the difficulties and rancour, including the race riots in Vancouver, focused in the statement of the British Columbia Trades and Labour Congress in 1906: "We have no need of cheap peoples." The Conservative member for Calgary, R.B. Bennett, agreed (probably the only occasion that he agreed with both organized labour and Mackenzie King). The following year he proclaimed, "We must not allow our shores to be overrun by Asiatics and become dominated by an alien race. British Columbia must remain a white man's country." Premier Richard McBride and the great majority of the people of the province agreed. King predicted that the province would secede from Confederation if Asians were not excluded. Following the death of Strathcona in early 1914, the acting high commissioner was instructed by the Conservative government of Borden, sounding like Laurier, to inform both the foreign and colonial secretaries "that public opinion in this country will not tolerate immigration in any considerable number from Asiatic countries and that even more drastic measures and regulations will if necessary be provided in order to prevent an influx."[49] Imperial considerations were not to take precedence over local prejudices.

Strathcona's relations with Canadian commercial agents – the Department of Trade and Commerce had been created in 1892 – were hardly happier than his relations with emigration agents, some of whom had doubled as commercial representatives. As early as October 1897 and again in February 1898, the Toronto *Globe* gave as its firm opinion that the Canadian offices on Victoria Street were not worth their salt, being the "least useful of colonial offices" and should be moved to the City. The appointment of Harrison Watson as the first full-time commercial agent was to have the effect of placing in the City a senior representative who would work "in conjunction with the office of the High Commissioner for Canada and with the Canadian section of the Imperial Institute, and will also co-operate with the Commercial Intelligence Branch of the [British] Board of Trade."[50] However much Watson's appointment was welcomed by the Canadian Manufacturers' Association, which had first urged it, Strathcona remained sceptical, still labouring under his discontents with Sifton's emigration arrangements. The deputy minister of trade and commerce recorded his several misgivings to Cartwright about disharmony in London:

Frequent commercial enquiries [including tariff schedules] ... were received from him until recently, when under orders from the High Commissioner's Office, no direct correspondence was allowed to pass between this Department and Mr. Harrison Watson. Thus Mr. Watson's energies were stifled to his own chagrin and regret ... I would therefore recommend that as soon as any change be contemplated, a Commercial Agent should be appointed in London distinct from the High Commissioner's Office and under the direction of the Department of Trade and Commerce at Ottawa.[51]

Cartwright sent the deputy minister's memorandum on to Laurier, but in return he "was given to understand that as long as Lord Strathcona was High Commissioner, no change was possible."[52] Cartwright thereupon dropped the matter; possibly he personally welcomed Laurier's negative reaction, being himself in debt to Strathcona for a substantial sum of money.

During the British election of 1908, a press report appeared alleging that Strathcona was continuing to support imperial Conservatives against free-trade Liberals, even being rumoured as a possible purchaser of *The*

Times. A later hagiographic biographer recorded that Strathcona's "allegiance to Mr. Joseph Chamberlain was matter of commontalk, and, at times, of partisan complaint."[53] Strathcona himself felt it necessary to protest his innocence to Laurier: "I would consider it absolutely out of place for me to say or do anything which might be considered ever so remotely as an interference in any party contest."[54] Redolent as this was of his statement of innocence a decade before, the high commissioner appeared to the chief Canadian immigration commissioner as protesting too much. What Strathcona did covertly was to continue to employ his ever-ready tool – money – to support the imperial crusade of the invalid Chamberlain. As Preston noted, "All his influence was exerted in the background" in the continuing debate over the nature of the Empire.

Among Balfour's bickering Conservatives, the divisions were many and deep (with the future prime minister, Bonar Law, emerging as one of the more ardent advocates of an imperial tariff preference). The internecine dispute between the advocates of free trade and those urging an imperial tariff preference became even more sharply defined with the creation of two opposing organizations: the Free Food League and the Tariff Reform League. The latter, urging an imperial tariff preference, was better disciplined and financed. Money poured in from industry and the aristocracy, especially Tory landlords eager to see their farms protected from cheap extra-Empire imports. Prominent amongst the donors to the Tariff Reform League, Preston was convinced, was Strathcona. In the year of the high commissioner's death and ten years after the events which he described, the bilious Preston published in his memoirs that

Lord Strathcona experienced not a little uneasiness at the persistent efforts of several members of the British House of Commons in a certain direction, during the early session of Sir Henry Campbell-Bannerman's administration, to trace a persistent rumour to the effect that the High Commissioner for Canada had contributed, 150,000 to the funds of a political organization [the Tariff Reform League] that was then carrying on a very costly and extensive propaganda throughout Great Britain. For three or four weeks repeated notices of inquiry to the Government were given to the officials of the House on the subject, but these never appeared on the official records ... It was believed by those high in authority that it was not in the public interest that Lord Strathcona's practical sympathy with this question, in view of his official position, should be generally known. The fear of having his association with a political policy that was opposed by the Government to which he was accredited announced to the public, to say nothing about his oft-repeated assurance to friends that he took no interest in British party politics, disturbed Lord Strathcona's equanimity sadly. It was obviously a case where it was advisable that the right hand should not know what the left was doing.[55]

If Strathcona did in fact have any such compunctions, at least in the *British Empire Review* of January 1909 he did not hesitate to support other imperial initiatives, such as the "all-red route" around the globe, penny postage, cheaper books in English, and lower cable rates.

A much younger Canadian was beginning to emerge as a yet more controversial advocate. Max Aitken, the future Lord Beaverbrook, paid his first visit to Britain in 1908. When he arrived from Saint John enthusiastically in favour of an imperial tariff preference, he called upon the affluent Bonar Law (first elected eight years before as a Conservative member of Parliament from Glasgow), partly to recommend to him some highly productive Canadian bonds. When in 1910 Aitken was again in London – purchasing the Rolls Royce motor car company in an idle moment – "to take part in the Empire plan was a controlling desire ... My success in making mergers in Canada had turned out so wonderfully well. Why not exercise the same talent in making a worthy contribution to the effort of bringing all the Empire units into one commercial combine?" Chamberlain "was not unwilling to encourage a young supporter from abroad but a stroke had put an end to his political career, though the fiction of his leadership was still maintained."[56] Having called upon Strathcona and Tupper, Aitken soon sought a safe parliamentary seat for himself. With Law's indispensable help, he was duly elected the Conservative member for Ashton-under-Lyne in December 1910.

From 1908 there had arisen in Britain growing misgivings and an unwonted sense of maritime insecurity resulting in large part from the proliferation of new and powerful navies based upon technological change. Germany had embarked upon warship construction that could threaten the supremacy of the Royal Navy, a rude awakening for Britain from a century-long complacency. HMS *Dreadnought*, laid down in December 1905, had set a radically new standard in battleships which the German imperial navy had been quick to emulate. Asquith's government responded with its controversial and expensive Naval Bill of March 1909, increasing the number of dreadnoughts to be constructed. The strain on the exchequer might be partially offset by contributions from the Dominions, preferably in the form of money, but failing that even in some form of local naval forces, however modest.

Laurier knew full well that the deepening public concern in English Canada over the German maritime challenge could not be ignored, especially following a memorable speech from the opposition benches by Sir George Foster in which he contended that although Canada had so developed that it "cannot escape the common burden ... the common duty ... the common responsibility ... as to naval defence." To continue to rely wholly upon Britain was the essence of colonialism. Again the differing attitudes of English and French-speaking Canadians to "imperial defence" were surfacing, as in the South African War a decade before. Both the Conservative and Liberal parties continued to avoid too precise a definition of their policies, knowing that the naval controversy had the potential to recreate major differences. Both parties being divided, the initial Canadian response to the naval crisis of 1909 was broadly bipartisan, although that initial concord did not last long. Seeking compromise between the support in English Canada and the opposition in French Canada, Laurier proposed in vague terms the creation of a Canadian navy on both coasts, leaving aside the question of an early contribution to the Royal Navy. Mackenzie King, now minister of labour, defended the policy when he wrote to Lord Stanhope, a long-time friend and an ardent imperial federalist, "You do Sir Wilfrid Laurier an injustice in regarding him as an opportunist ... He understands the problem of self-government within the Empire as few men before him or living to-day have done ... [He] believes that a united progressive Canada is a more valuable asset to the Empire ... than a Canada divided in opinion, or professing an obligation it is not in a position to meet."[57]

Robert Borden, faced with the necessity of responding as leader of the opposition, was unhappy at the dilemma in which he found himself, both nationally and within his own party, during the increasingly emotional debate. If he supported unequivocally an immediate financial contribution to the Royal Navy, the prospects for his party and for national unity could be threatened by discontent among Quebec Conservatives. On the other hand, if he simply supported Laurier's compromise of a small Canadian navy, he would be seen by many in his party as procrastinating, as failing in the promotion of Empire unity. Tupper, somewhat surprisingly, recommended the policy of Laurier: "The construction of local navies ... to act as effective units with the British Navy." It was that course that Borden followed. He told the House of Commons that he was "entirely at one [with the prime minister in] having a Canadian naval force of our own." He assured French-speaking supporters that neither he "nor any member of the [Conservative] Party proposes that we should spend money in building Dreadnoughts."[58] But this was precisely what many of his English-Canadian supporters wanted him to do. Internal party fissures began to appear publicly, plaguing him until the outbreak of the First World War subsumed the question in yet broader, more momentous issues.

Following unanimous passage of the apparently bipartisan resolution on the creation of a Canadian navy, Borden visited Britain during June and July 1909, immediately before the imperial conference of that year, assuring everyone that Conservative naval policy, "while its terms might not upon their surface seem as significant at the moment as the offer of one or two Dreadnoughts would have been, [it] laid down a permanent policy for the Dominion of Canada upon which both parties united and which would serve a more practical purpose than any such offer of Dreadnoughts."[59] Tupper had continued to correspond with Borden, helping to shape his naval policy and set the stage for his visit to Britain, but there is no evidence that Strathcona ever discussed the naval question with Borden. Winston Churchill knew Strathcona, even later lauding his imperial commercial enterprise in his *History of the English-Speaking Peoples*, but from his office in the Admiralty he dealt direct with Ottawa, utilizing all his Canadian contacts, including the governor general, to press for a contribution to accelerated and enlarged dreadnought construction.

In this great and continuing controversy, which masked the fundamental question of what a polycentric Empire should be, Strathcona was well aware that active advocacy on his part of a cash contribution to the Royal Navy could bring him into direct conflict with his prime minister. Equally, the Liberal ministers Sir Frederick Borden and Louis Brodeur, representatives at the 1909 imperial conference on the naval and military defence of the Empire preparatory to the imperial conference itself, were unlikely to have shared their thinking with the high commissioner. They were to state clearly their government's intention to have a national navy, however small it might necessarily be. For the longer term, Frederick Borden's additional statement that imperial unity and local autonomy must go hand-in-hand, that Canada could make no prior commitments, that Parliament alone would decide, would be heard frequently from Laurier's successor in the years ahead, but the prime minister's immediate focus was on a separate naval service.

Third reading of the Naval Service Act was concluded in April 1910. Between then and the election call in July 1911, the Laurier government did take a few steps in the direction of creating a minuscule navy, but certainly nothing remotely resembling an effective force. Mackenzie King, minister of labour, was unrepentant. He wrote to his friend, Lord Stanhope, "If we wish the Empire to endure, it will not be by increased centralization ... Had Sir Wilfrid sought separation from Britain as some of his opponents most unfairly insinuate, he could not have helped to secure this more surely than by advocating a direct contribution to Britain for the building of Dreadnoughts."[60]

Naval questions dominated the imperial conference of 1911 and three concurrent meetings of the Committee of Imperial Defence. Australia, increasingly uneasy at the pace of Japan's naval construction as well as Germany's growing presence in the Pacific, committed itself to more units of its own. Laurier reaffirmed Canada's pledge to create its own navy (under its own control in peacetime), rather than an immediate cash contribution to the Royal Navy. The effect of the Anglo-Japanese treaty on naval dispositions was considered and the nature of the command of Dominion forces in war was reviewed, finally culminating in a unanimous resolution: "In time of war, when the Dominion Fleets ... have been placed under the control of the Imperial Government, the ships are to form part of the Imperial Fleet and to remain under the control of the Admiralty ... and be liable to be sent anywhere during the continuance of the war."[61] Following the conference, Canada did purchase two aging Royal Navy cruisers, neither of which, Frederick Borden lamented, was "a very large one."

The conference was also divided over the question of a permanent committee of high commissioners. Some premiers were convinced that if the high commissioners were cabinet ministers they could provide the ideal forum for consultation, but Laurier led the way in endorsing the current system of quadrennial conferences of prime ministers, again shying away from any intra-conference mechanism. The conference did, however, confirm Dominion representation in the hitherto British-only Committee of Imperial Defence. Either a cabinet minister visiting London or the high commissioner could sit on the CID. The rationale was evident. "The [Imperial] Conferences were too infrequent and lacked the machinery through which representatives of the Dominions could be consulted on matters of high urgency to the Empire. On the other hand, the CID could meet whenever the situation dictated, was adequately equipped with subsidiary organs, and had power to create more if need be." A parallel committee should be established in each Dominion. Laurier's response to the invitation was cautious. In his statement to the conference, he did not reject the invitation to the CID out of hand, but emphasized the more traditional role of high commissioners.

They are not only ambassadors, their position in one respect is far larger; but in a technical sense, with regard to the Imperial Government, they are in the position of ambassadors ... the Governor-General communicates direct with the Imperial Government, but ... there are constantly occasions when a despatch is sent to the High Commissioner asking him to press the matter on and to see the Secretary of State for the Colonies and represent to him the views of the particular Dominion Government. We know that besides the official despatch there is the confidential talk, in which more meaning is conveyed than in a despatch. The High Commissioners are expected to come ... to the Secretary of State for the Colonies to represent that the Dominion Government has sent a despatch to him on some particular question, but he wishes to press forward this or that consideration which is not included in the despatch.[62]

New Zealand proposed instead an elaborate if vague federal system of governance for the Empire, including the creation of an Imperial Council of State and an enhanced role for high commissioners in formulating foreign policy. Laurier rejected such ideas as "absolutely impracticable." Asquith had already given the New Zealand proposals the coup de grâce, not because of their impracticability but because all proposals could curtail Britain's own freedom of action in both political and military spheres.

It would impair if not altogether destroy the authority of the government of the United Kingdom in such grave matters as the conduct of foreign policy, the conclusion of treaties, the declaration and maintenance of peace, or the declaration of war and, indeed, all those relations with Foreign Powers, necessarily of the most delicate character, which are now in the hands of the government, subject to its responsibility to the Imperial Parliament. That authority cannot be shared, and the co-existence side by side with the Cabinet of the United Kingdom of this proposed body ... would, in our judgment, be absolutely fatal to our present system of responsible government.[63]

This was acceptable to Laurier who, consistently and courteously negative, had again expressed his conviction that well enough be left alone. Having proposed nothing himself, he had stated yet again that he had "the happy privilege of representing here a country which has no grievance to set forth and very few suggestions to make. We are quite satisfied with our lot." With his eye firmly on his recent agreement on tariff reciprocity with the United States, Laurier offered no support for an imperial tariff preference but only most-favoured-nation treatment for other members of the Empire (by 1911 Canada had negotiated trade agreements with Japan, the Austro-Hungarian Empire, Belgium, the Netherlands, Switzerland, Germany, Italy, and France). He did, however, agree that a commission of Britain and the Dominions might usefully examine the prospects for greater intra-Empire trade, in the secure knowledge that the free-trading British would oppose an imperial preference. Laurier nominated as Canada's representative his financial benefactor, Peter Larkin, who could be counted upon to say little and do nothing. He was suitably modest in his acceptance: "Lacking as I do, experience in public life, I was most reluctant to allow my name to go forward ... and it was due to Sir Wilfrid Laurier's personally expressed desire that I permitted it."[64]

In January 1910 the governor general, Lord Grey, had vainly suggested that Laurier take the lead in proposing the creation of a Dominions Office, as distinct from the Colonial Office. Grey, the brother-in-law of his predecessor, Lord Minto, was a popular, no-nonsense imperialist. A former Liberal member of Parliament, he had distinguished himself as the impresario of the highly successful visit of the Prince of Wales to the Quebec tricentenary celebrations of 1908. A tireless advocate of first a federation of the British Isles alone and then of the Empire as a whole, he reminded Toronto schoolboys in 1909 that Empire Day was a festival on which "every British subject should reverently remember that the British Empire stands out before the whole world as the fearless champion of freedom, fair play and equal rights." Almost impecunious himself, Grey combined his conviction in imperial federation with a scheme that would have erected in London a grandiose "building in which room ... be found for the housing in a manner befitting the dignity of the Dominions, of the London Offices of the various High Commissioners and Agents General," as well as an imperial trade centre, emigration societies, banks, insurance companies and other institutions of the Empire.[65] It would also be part of a glorious rebuilding of London, with space for imperial ritual, especially along the Strand, Aldwych, and Kingsway, all in some way to Grey's personal profit.

The building was to be higher than St Paul's Cathedral and, in Grey's words, would "rival in grandeur the Houses of Parliament." The London press was generally enthusiastic, but Australia had already begun its own splendid building and Strathcona was opposed to the Canadian offices being located with those of other Dominions, believing that in any case it was both inappropriate and too costly. Canada, he was reported to have said, would wish to be "the only pebble on the beach." However, the gloomy and overcrowded offices on Victoria Street were now so inadequate that the visiting Sir George Foster and Sir Edmund Osler undertook to assist the high commissioner in choosing a site for a Canada House and ascertaining whether the provincial agents general would want to share it. The need for new quarters was pressing. Total correspondence had risen from 19,614 pieces in 1905 to 28,850 in 1910. Growing inquiries about addresses of emigrant relatives and a busy *post restante* service added to the daily workload.

Throughout 1912, however, sites had been identified, one on the east side of Trafalgar Square and the other across the Thames from Parliament, but no decision was taken.* Early in the year, George Perley, minister without portfolio, upon returning from a visit to Britain on behalf of the prime minister, had written to him about newspaper articles as well as a letter from Strathcona describing the inadequacy of the Victoria Street offices. Perley recommended "a modern up-to-date building in as central a locality as possible where all Canadians would be well looked after and feel at home and where all the branches of our service could be accommodated."[66] Perley understood that Strathcona intended to report shortly about "a suitable site at a reasonable price." However, upon Strathcona's death, the Canadian offices were still at 19 Victoria Street, and there they remained until the mid-1920s.

Strathcona's relations with the proliferating agents general of the provinces were at least as unhappy as his relations with both the emigration and commercial agents. The high commissioner never made provincial agents feel welcome and relations with them continued to be strained. Near the beginning of his tenure, Strathcona had proclaimed that he "was the sole representative of the Dominion, including all the Provinces."[67] It followed that "no official recognition should be given to any person as a separate representative of any of the Provinces." What exactly Strathcona thought was the work of provincial agents whom he dismissed as "Advertising Agents and Canvassers" remained clear, but he adamantly opposed any quasi-consular or other official status. To leave no doubt in the minds of either the Colonial Office or the agents general themselves about who ranked where, Strathcona had paraded all the agents from the Empire before the new colonial secretary, ostensibly to extol its growing unity.

---

* Edmund Osler (1845–1924) may not have been entirely disinterested in offering to help identify the best site for Canada House; his name was widely mentioned as a successor to Strathcona. An eminent financier, he sat as the Conservative member of Parliament for West Toronto from 1896 to 1917.

The agents general could have had no illusions about how the high commissioner regarded them, certainly not the agent general of British Columbia. Richard McBride, the redoubtable Conservative premier of British Columbia, was convinced that his province was not receiving the full benefit of its new office because of the hostility of the high commissioner and his emphasis on emigration to the recently created prairie provinces.* When in 1908 McBride attempted to obtain recognition of the right of an agent general to deal direct with the Colonial Office on questions under provincial jurisdiction, Strathcona protested to Laurier about the premier's pretensions and made a lofty appeal to the constitution: "any such action as that recommended by Mr. McBride would be a retrograde movement and opposed to the spirit of the federation ... which if acceded to, might readily lead to confusion and even to embarrassment."[68]

Strathcona had succeeded yet again in calling upon Laurier to do what he wanted. In the case of immigration, trade promotion, and provincial representation, Laurier acceded to his wishes, but in the case of the commissioner general in Paris, who was "to conform to any directions he might receive from the Canadian High Commission," Strathcona was content to let sleeping dogs lie. That the commissioner general was setting extraordinary records of dormancy with regard to Ottawa was not unwelcome to Strathcona. When the Department of External Affairs was established in 1909, reporting to the prime minister, Strathcona had no desire to create problems for himself by getting between it and the autonomous-minded Paris office.

When Commissioner Hector Fabre died in office in 1910, he had completed almost three decades of dual representation of Quebec and of the Dominion in France. Fabre, a former senator, had been appointed agent general of Quebec in Paris in 1882, only two years after Galt had been appointed to London. Additionally, "The Government of Canada availed themselves of Mr. Fabre's presence in Paris to utilize his services." Those services, however, appear to have been both few in number and slight in substance. With the appointment in May 1911 of Philippe Roy, another former senator, as Fabre's successor, Strathcona sent to Ottawa a rather perfunctory statement, calling attention to the continuing responsibility

---

* Richard McBride (1870–1917), born in New Westminster before British Columbia entered Confederation, was a convinced imperialist. He had first met his fellow Conservative Robert Borden in 1902 when, in the aftermath of the South African War, he had advocated an "Assembly of the Empire" to address questions of imperial defence and foreign relations.

of the high commissioner for the supervision of the new Commissaire
général du Canada. In Roy, however, Borden knew that he had a commissioner general who would not emulate Fabre's remarkable record of inactivity. Following a visit to France in 1912, Borden placed the office directly
under himself, thereby terminating London's nominal supervision. The
government also acted indirectly to augment representation abroad, both
by increasing the numbers of trade commissioners and by coupling them,
where appropriate, with British consuls, or relying directly upon British
consuls themselves in the many countries where Canadian trade commissioners had not been appointed.

Shortly after the 1911 imperial conference, Laurier's government was
defeated in the hotly contested election over tariff reciprocity. Unrestricted
free trade with the United States had long been seen by many Canadians
as a threat to the very survival of their country, a view substantiated by
annexationist talk in the United States. Whether the high commissioner
played any direct role in the defeat of Laurier is unknown, but he had
always been a vigorous opponent of free trade with the United States.
Early in February 1911, the long-serving finance minister, W.S. Fielding,
telegraphed to Strathcona in some exasperation. Aware of allegations that
the high commissioner had worked covertly against the free-trade Liberals
of Campbell-Bannerman in the British general election six years before,
Fielding suspected that Strathcona, or at least the CPR, was now working
directly or indirectly against the Liberals in the pending general election.
Someone had been giving both British journalists and "public men ...
erroneous impressions" that the tariff rates agreed upon between Ottawa
and Washington "discriminate in favour of the United States and against
Great Britain." Fielding added pointedly that tariff reciprocity with the
United States had been as much a policy of Macdonald as of Laurier.
Laurier, however, had underestimated the commitment to imperial unity
of many English-speaking Canadians suspicious of the true motives of the
United States and somewhat to his own surprise, Robert Borden won the
election handily.

   The new Conservative government was more inclined to include impe-
rial interests in its policy formulation, but it soon became evident that
Borden was not the advocate of an imperial tariff preference that Tupper,
Strathcona, and the Conservatives in opposition in Westminster hoped.
He was wary of any tariff change that might threaten manufacturing.
In his 1911 advocacy of closer imperial cooperation (but not necessarily a
tariff preference), Borden took a position that was consistent with the line

that he subsequently pursued throughout the First World War. This put him at odds with Mackenzie King who was developing the sterile stance that he was to take for the next three decades. King's convoluted rhetorical commitment to the Empire, however, never carried conviction with those of his fellow Canadians who esteemed more evident imperial links and who found opaque his self-described pragmatism. King was aware of this, contending that it was better to be governed by events than pursue any creative thinking:

Unless one is prepared to follow an imperial programme as fashioned by one school of Imperialists, one is credited with being indifferent to, if not opposed, to the Empire. With me it is because I believe that the Empire can only last by establishing new centres of strength [e.g., Canada] and building on that basis, rather than waiting for centralization in organization, that I could wish for the sake of what we hold in common, men would allow themselves to be governed rather by events and circumstances as they immediately arise than seek to create situations with an ulterior purpose, however worthy that may be.[69]

Upon coming to office, Borden did offer the prospect of an increase in the already substantial Canadian preferential tariff for imports from Britain, recognizing that the United States was already supplying more than 60 per cent of Canada's total imports. However, against the background of British electoral debate, he did not unilaterally implement his offer, explaining somewhat disingenuously to the imperial enthusiast Leopold Amery, the recently elected Conservative member in Chamberlain's home city of Birmingham, that "since the question of food taxes has become a question of such fierce controversy in the United Kingdom, I have endeavored to abstain from any action which might be regarded as undesirable or obtrusive interference."[70] Borden had in mind allegations that Strathcona had involved himself in the British election of seven years earlier. Additionally, new to office, he wanted to avoid stirring up a divisive debate in Canada about imperial commitments.

Borden's basic thinking about the Empire was that if Britain sought help in consolidating it, then the Dominions should have a hand in decision-making. The immediate catalyst for Borden's entry into the longstanding debate was Max Aitken who, throughout his life, was to spend much of his formidable political energies advocating an imperial tariff preference and later imperial free trade. Aitken's first major sally as a neophyte member of Parliament into the contentious world of tariff reform was in 1912 when he encouraged Bonar Law to advocate an imperial tariff preference, recognizing that it would entail placing tariffs on imports from outside the Empire, including food. To many of Law's fellow Conservatives, weary of years in opposition, such a policy was seen as political suicide.

As the divisions within the Conservative party ominously deepened, Aitken worked to induce the new world to redress the balance of the old, apparently without reference to Strathcona, although Aitken was aware that the high commissioner at least privately endorsed his manoeuvres. Aitken encouraged Borden to visit London in June 1912 to explore the whole idea of economic unity of the Empire. He wrote triumphantly to Kipling: "Borden agreed with Bonar Law ... that in [his] next Budget he would refer to the offer emanating not only from the United States but from Germany for Preferential Trade relations with Canada and that he would indicate that the policy of the present administration in Canada is to patiently wait for the present policy of Preferential Trade relations with Great Britain. I cannot overstate the satisfaction which Bonar Law got from his discussion with Borden."[71]

All Aitken's enthusiasms were, however, to come to naught. In the end, the threat to the unity of the British Conservative party by those opposed to "stomach taxes" was such that Law would need either to suspend his support for an imperial tariff preference or resign as leader. His first ploy was to declare that he would not impose tariffs on extra-Empire food unless such were demanded by the Dominion premiers at the pending colonial conference of 1912. But that was not enough to quell the uproar in his own party. The press baron, Lord Northcliffe, successfully aroused public opinion against Law's policy of "tariff reform" (it was he who coined the devastating phrase "stomach taxes"). That "the press had beaten the politicians" was a lesson not lost on Aitken. Reversing himself, he helped Law to wriggle out of his tariff musings, recognizing that Law was more useful to him as leader than as a former leader, whatever the cost in terms of policy inconsistency. No doubt Aitken consoled himself with the comforting thought that he was young, very young, and would live to fight another day.

Upon assuming office, Borden had attempted to address two related questions: what role could Canada hope to play in the formulation of imperial foreign policy, and what contribution should it finally make, if any, to an imperial navy? In July-August 1912 Borden sought to move Canada closer to participation in imperial decision-making. Following discussions with Prime Minister Asquith, his foreign secretary, Lord Grey, and his colonial secretary, Lewis Harcourt,* he wrote to the governor general, "It may be that one of our Ministers without Portfolio will become a member of the Imperial Defence Committee [CID] and will live in London part of the year in close touch with the Foreign Office and with the Colonial Secretary. This of course would only be a temporary expedient until a more carefully prepared system of Empire organization could be discussed."[72]

Three months later, George Perley, minister without portfolio, wrote Borden from London, suggesting that the prime minister, as his own secretary of state for external affairs, represent Canada on the CID. He added that he himself "or someone else" be appointed assistant secretary of state for external affairs to attend, as necessary, in the place of the prime minister. As a first step in strengthening imperial consultation, Borden told Parliament that he welcomed the offer of Asquith to have a Canadian minister participate: "Such Minister would be regularly summoned to all meetings of the Committee ... and would be regarded as one of its permanent members. No important step in foreign policy would be undertaken without consultation with such a representative of Canada."[73] In making such a claim, Borden knew very well that the CID alone could not provide the more comprehensive foreign policy consultation that he sought, but it was an improvement over the void that had existed. The well-informed German ambassador in London reported to Berlin, "Membership in the Committee of Imperial Defence ... no longer satisfies him [Borden]. He wants the Dominion to have a decisive voice in the deliberations which decide peace and war. It is not certain whether an imperial parliament or some other arrangement is contemplated. To such terms the British Government will hardly agree."[74]

Borden induced his cabinet to support Canadian participation in the CID in the person of a minister. Periodic imperial conferences, supported by a secretariat, would, in the bald words of a contemporary British advocate, "check the inevitable impression in the Dominions that the old, militarist Imperialism, with its schemes of cash contribution, centralized administration and British ascendancy ... is again paramount in England." The initiative, now that Joseph Chamberlain was gone, was largely Borden's. Certainly there is no evidence that Strathcona was any more involved in furthering Borden's imperial thinking than he had been in

---

* Lewis ("Loulou") Harcourt (1863–1922) was the son of William Harcourt, Gladstone's formidable chancellor of the exchequer.

influencing Laurier's, even on the central question of who should represent Canada in the CID. Asquith proposed that high commissioners, if possible concurrently ministers, attend the CID, but no one in Ottawa reacted. The cabinet instead agreed that "a Canadian minister, probably without portfolio, should as a rule be in London from February to August ... [with] constant though informal access to the Prime Minister, the Secretary of State for Foreign Affairs and the Colonial Secretary." Lewis Harcourt noted, "The Canadian Government, having changed in the autumn of 1911, it was necessary ... to put these proposals before them ... Mr. Borden ... stated that he saw no difficulty in one of his Ministers either with or without portfolio spending some months of every year in London." Perley was a minister without portfolio when Borden had sent him to London, but this substantiation of Borden's commitment was almost immediately overtaken by the requirement for additional forms of consultation consequent upon the beginning of the First World War. Imperial consultations would, like so much else, never be the same again as a result of the war.

By the end of 1912 the colonial secretary wired the governor general that all basic decisions regarding the security of the Empire and of Britain itself must remain with Westminster. Prompted by the Foreign Office, Harcourt stated that the CID (with Dominion participation) "is purely an advisory body and is not and cannot under any circumstances become a body deciding upon policy." Drawing upon an earlier public speech, he added, possibly recalling Laurier, that such an understanding would avoid opening "up those difficult problems of Imperial Federation which seem to entail questions of taxation and representation which have made that policy for many years a dead issue."[75] Borden did, however, raise with Asquith the apparently flat rejection by Harcourt of imperial consultations on foreign policy, but his response was equivocal. Asquith began positively enough in explanation to the House of Commons (with Borden in the distinguished visitors' gallery): "There rests with us undoubtedly the duty of making such a response as we can to their obviously reasonable appeal that they should be entitled to be heard in the determination of the policy and direction of foreign affairs." But, he added, the basic British position remained that the CID could not "become a body deciding on policy."

The few years immediately before the First World War were nevertheless the peacetime high watermark both of an united Empire and of emigration from Britain and the United States to Canada. An incipient imperial federation of sorts appeared to some to be emerging. The Dominion premiers would meet at least once every four years with the British prime minister. Dominion ministers, resident in or visiting London, could participate in weekly meetings of the Committee of Imperial Defence. A royal commission was charged with preparing an inventory of the resources and commercial legislation of the Empire, a preparatory step towards a possible imperial tariff preference. Here, finally, appeared to be tangible progress towards the goals for which imperial federalists – Galt, Tupper, and Strathcona among them – had laboured.

No tangible progress was, however, made in the long and sometimes bitter debate over what, if any, contribution Canada should make to the Royal Navy. On 29 January 1912 Winston Churchill, the new First Lord of the Admiralty, informed Harcourt that Sir Richard McBride, the premier of British Columbia, had been

brought here specially by Lord Strathcona, and introduced to me by him as being charged with an informal and secret, but duly authorized, mission. Sir [Richard] told me that the Canadian Government propose to seek the advice of the British Admiralty in regard to their Navy policy; that they were earnestly desirous of doing something really effective to help the British Navy; that anything in the shape of a local Navy would fail to carry any enthusiasm in Canada; that even a Canadian Squadron would be abhorrent to the Government now in power. Their only interest was in the Imperial Navy to which they desired to contribute two or perhaps three of the finest vessels in the world. These vessels should be named after Canadian provinces, built out of Canadian money in Great Britain, manned, maintained and controlled by the British Admiralty ... To safeguard the principle of Canadian autonomy, it would be necessary that Canada should have the power to withdraw these vessels at any time on giving sufficient notice to enable them to be replaced. In practice this would never happen. Ultimately it was hoped enough ships might be added to enable each Province to be represented.

The above I gathered was the policy which the Canadian Government, when they ask for advice, would like to be told authoritatively by the Admiralty they could adopt, and on this they believe they could appeal to the country at a special general election with good prospects of success.[76]

McBride's soundings reflected a foray by Borden towards an emergency contribution of three dreadnoughts to the Royal Navy and away from an early Canadian navy.* In London in mid-1912, Borden himself pursued

* When Richard McBride went to London to oppose Laurier's request for entrenched fiscal arrangements, he urged the merits of the Naval Service Act which both Conserva-

McBride's soundings by exploring with Churchill what naval policy his new government should best pursue. Borden had in principle, it seems, already made up his mind, despite the risk of alienating his Quebec supporters. At his request, Churchill helpfully summed up Admiralty needs by stating: "if it is the intention of Canada to render assistance to the naval forces of the British Empire, now is the time when that aid would be most welcome and timely."[77] (Churchill was fully aware of the lead time necessary to build a battleship; those laid down in 1913 would be unavailable until 1915.)

Churchill had, however, another motive in welcoming a Canadian offer of three dreadnoughts. A Canadian contribution might help to delude the Germans into thinking that the Royal Navy was not itself being enlarged. Borden, ready to cooperate in this unlikely subterfuge, sought from Churchill in several private meetings definite substantiation for the argument that he was developing at home: that Britain's maritime supremacy was threatened as never before. Accordingly, an immediate cash contribution by Canada was imperative, given that a "separate Canadian naval organization [could] probably not be made effective inside of twenty-five or fifty years." Borden was, however, unsuccessful in obtaining from Asquith a clear statement that a contribution to the Royal Navy would bring in return the opportunity to share with Britain in the formulation of imperial foreign policy. That consideration was unwelcome at Westminster. For example, nine Liberal members wrote to Asquith in December 1912 that the strings attached to the Canadian offer of three capital ships led them to conclude that Laurier's proposal to create a Canadian navy was to be preferred. In Canada, a direct contribution to the Royal Navy was seen by some as a derogation of fiscal responsibility; in Britain it was seen by others as a derogation of foreign policy responsibility. Six Liberal members of parliament wrote to Asquith:

tives and Liberals had endorsed, but added that "an immediate and unconditional gift to the Royal Navy" should be made. McBride himself purchased from a Seattle yard in August 1914 two submarines being built there for Chile; for a brief period British Columbia had a more effective navy than Canada (before turning the two small boats over to the Royal Navy). Borden is thought to have McBride in mind as a possible successor when in 1910 and again in 1911 he contemplated resignation. McBride visited Britain at least annually. Upon completion of the new British Columbia House in London, he in effect appointed himself agent general in January 1916, resigning as premier to take up the coveted post. He died in London in August 1917, at the age of forty-seven.

If this proposal entails the admission of anyone outside the Cabinet to a position giving control over foreign policy we view it with great alarm ... It does not appear that the demand of Mr. Borden can be satisfied by giving Canada representation on an advisory board such as the Committee of Imperial Defence ... in Canada there is a great body of citizens who take another view, namely ... [that] the Dominions should aim at the gradual creation of a Canadian Fleet, built, manned and maintained at Canada's expense ... Such independent action would show a sense of Imperial responsibility equal to the proposals of Mr. Borden ... Nor is any demand made to interfere with foreign policy.[78]

There were to be no visits by British ministers, Churchill included, but Borden nevertheless confirmed in November that it was his government's policy to introduce a Naval Aid bill to provide as many as three dreadnoughts to the Royal Navy, to be built in British yards (recognizing that no Canadian yard could possibly build such great ships), adding, however, that his government would be gratified if the British yards were to offer to Canada what a later generation would call "industrial offsets." As for the disposition of the dreadnoughts, he publicly welcomed Churchill's "inspiring proposal to form the three Canadian ships with other ships mentioned, all of unsurpassed strength and speed, into a great imperial cruising squadron, based on Gibraltar."[79]

Borden's policy was what Strathcona had hoped to hear for more than a decade, but in the event he appears to have had little to do with his prime minister's commitment to a direct imperial naval contribution nor does he appear to have offered him advice useful in the subsequent and prolonged debate over his Naval Aid bill. It was as Borden had anticipated in a letter to Tupper: "We are calling Parliament about the middle of November and doubtless there will be a keen debate on this grave question. Undoubtedly the conditions confronting the Empire are very grave ... [and] might lead to such an issue that the British Empire would in effect be maneuvered out of existence without the firing of a gun."

His parliamentary forebodings were well justified; the contentious debate dragged on from December 1912 to May 1913. McBride explained to his friend Churchill that the political manoeuvrings of the Liberals had prevented decisive action on Borden's part: "Sir Wilfrid has been making some extraordinary speeches of late in the direction of what might be termed an independent Canada, but of course he is always careful to protect any position of this sort by strong and clever protestations of his affection for British institutions ... Sir Wilfrid is always dwelling on our National autonomy as something that may be jeopardized by a policy of [naval] contribution and he invariably tries to appeal especially to Quebec." In Ottawa on a visit, Asquith's daughter Violet described to her diary the Liberal opposition's policy: it "is a more picturesque one from a *national* point of view – a Canadian built Canadian-manned fleet guarding their own shores and placed at our disposal in moments of stress, etc – but as they have neither ports to build [the fleet] nor men to man it looks a little impracticable. I don't think Sir W. is much of an Imperialist."[80]

Borden's advocacy of an immediate financial contribution for three dreadnoughts was, in the end, to no avail. He did finally force his Naval Aid bill through the House of Commons in May 1913, but its subsequent defeat in the Senate ("a group of eighty-seven elderly gentleman smashed their walking sticks through the windows of the Canadian confederation") decided Borden to proceed no further for the time being. Questions of high policy had deteriorated to a simple calculation of mortality rates. If the mortality rate in the Senate proceeded along normal lines, a Conservative majority would emerge in 1914.* The following month war was declared, leaving Canada with neither a navy nor a contribution to the Royal Navy. And Borden was without that particular bargaining chip for "a greater voice in the councils of the Empire."

Why two successive prime ministers left in office the increasingly inactive Strathcona is uncertain. Rose, Galt, and Tupper before and Perley following him were all relative dynamos in advancing Canada's evolving role, vigorously pursuing trade and investment interests, asserting the right to negotiate commercial treaties, promoting emigration, in effect attempting to think through the place in the Empire of a self-governing Dominion.

When, as leader of the opposition, Borden visited London during the summer of 1909, he discussed with Strathcona both the problems of coordination among various Dominion representatives and provincial agents general. From the secretary of the high commission he received in return a four-page memorandum. W.L. Griffith took care to ensure that his memorandum was "entirely of an impersonal character," referring to Strathcona in the most laudatory terms.† He argued the obvious case for all Canadian government employees to be under the supervision

---

* Senate appointments were then for life and male only.

† W.L. Griffith, the Welsh-speaking successor to Joseph Colmer, returned to his native north Wales from Manitoba in 1897 to become an immigration agent. From there he joined the staff of Canada House where he served until 1938.

of the high commissioner, "decentralization being most offensive to Lord Strathcona."[81] In both Britain and on the continent there were now several trade, agriculture, and emigration agents, but sometimes two in the same city were underemployed while other cities lacked any representation. Also unsatisfactory was the way in which even official visitors sometimes ignored the high commission or attempted to bypass it. The obvious solution was to move towards having a single "Canadian Government Agent" in Europe (i.e., the high commissioner) responsible for all Canadian matters.

Strathcona, by contrast, worked more indirectly to further his own concept of the relationship between what he consistently called the "Mother Country" and the colonies. As late as 1913, he advocated putting the Empire on popular display, a proposal which, after the disruption of the First World War, pointed to the great 1924 Wembley Exhibition and eventually the Glasgow Exhibition of 1938. Additionally, he continued to pursue his business interests, a practice which he, a deaf, nonagenarian widower, followed to the edge of his elaborate grave in Highgate cemetery. There is, however, no extant correspondence of either Laurier or Borden that suggests Strathcona's own views were either offered or sought by Ottawa on the great issues of the day. Admittedly he had never been a minister. The easy exchanges that can mark relations among former cabinet colleagues were not his, contributing to the fact that he, unlike Tupper, was never at the centre of policy debate during his record eighteen years as high commissioner. Yet despite his limited participation in domestic or even imperial policy during the final decade of his long life, two successive prime ministers retained him in London.

Tupper had not been prime minister long enough even to begin to work with his old antagonist (although later they collaborated closely in, for example, establishing the Canadian Chamber of Commerce in Britain). Why Tupper appointed him at all is unclear: he certainly must have been aware that Strathcona held him in something of the same low esteem in which he himself had once held Strathcona. There is no extant record of direct financial contribution to either the Conservative or Liberal parties as such, although several corporations controlled by Strathcona certainly did contribute. Had Strathcona, or more likely the CPR, given substantially to the faltering Conservative party as the election of 1896 approached? All that is certain is that Strathcona cancelled in his will the sizable personal debts owed to him by the estates of the Liberal minister of finance and later minister of trade and commerce, Sir Richard Cartwright, and by the Conservative minister of finance and later minister of trade and commerce, Sir George Foster, both of whom had proven during later years to be wonderfully sympathetic to the railway.*

If it remains uncertain why Tupper appointed Strathcona, it is equally unclear why Laurier reappointed him and why, many years later, Borden continued the practice. In Laurier's case, he may have regarded Strathcona as someone whom it was better to have without the country than within, a high commissioner who could be relied upon to satisfy imperial Canadians that their voice was heard at the centre of an evolving Empire, federated or otherwise. Perhaps also the corporations that Strathcona controlled continued with their largesse, this time to the Liberals. In any event, Rodolphe Lemieux, minister of marine and fisheries, assured a London audience that Strathcona could "stay as long as there was breath in him."

Certainly if Laurier had wanted at any time to replace the high commissioner, he had in his own cabinet an eager candidate. Before and during his notable fifteen years as minister of militia and defence, Sir Frederick Borden had frequently crossed to London to promote there his various business interests in Nova Scotia and New Brunswick as well as to pursue military matters. He was so eager to have "the highest office" in Laurier's gift that he had twice declined his offer of the lieutenant-governorship of Nova Scotia. Laurier certainly intended that he should be high commissioner, but would do nothing to force the issue, writing to Strathcona to withhold his resignation until after the next imperial conference in 1911.

Laurier, when in London for the conference, publicly announced that Frederick Borden and not as rumoured either Sir Montagu Allan or Sir Hugh Graham would be Strathcona's successor. But Strathcona did nothing, apparently still eager to hold on to his beloved office and the imperial life of London. The high commissioner, as aware as anyone in Ottawa that an election was pending, knew that if he delayed his formal resignation, he might not need to resign at all. Frederick Borden and Strathcona were collaborators in the large "Strathcona Trust Fund for the Encouragement of Physical and Military Training in Public Schools," but one could never be quite certain about where Strathcona's allegiances lay, beyond himself. The result of his procrastination – as presumably he had intended – was to block the appointment of his friend and to remain himself in office

---

* On Dominion Day 1912, Foster described Strathcona as "a man who, in the real building up of Canada as she exists to-day, has done as much and more in a Canadian, a national and an Imperial sense, than any other subject of the King who to-day lives under the British flag" (*Country Life*, 15 August 1912).

Although over ninety years old, Lord Strathcona was on the platform at King's Cross station in London in July 1912 to greet the Conservative prime minister, Sir Robert Borden, and Lady Borden. Strathcona had spoken vaguely of retiring from his post as high commissioner, but Laurier and Borden both urged him to continue, which he willingly did until he died in office in June 1914, aged ninety-four.

until after the election of the Conservative government of Frederick Borden's cousin, Robert (in which election Frederick Borden was defeated). The suggestion that he had delayed his resignation to hold the London appointment for his old friend, Sir Edward Clouston, the former president of the Bank of Montreal, or another of several self-appointed candidates to succeed him, remains hearsay.*

* Sir Edward Clouston (1849–1912) the protégé of Strathcona, was the son of a chief trader of the Hudson's Bay Company and the "mixed blood" daughter of a chief factor. Clouston rose to be general manager of the Bank of Montreal where he represented Strathcona's financial and philanthropic interests in Canada "like a son."

Beginning with an appeal in October 1911 to Strathcona to remain at his post (one month before the Canadian-born Bonar Law became leader of the British Conservatives), Borden declined to accept his resignation when he was in London during the summer of 1912 and again when Strathcona was in Ottawa "During the autumn [of 1913] ... I strongly urged him to continue the discharge of his duties," despite the fact that "the infirmities of old age had begun quite visibly to tell upon him at last."[82] The decision of Borden to invite the now infirm Strathcona to remain is puzzling; Borden was thirty-four years younger, with his own developing ideas about where Canada fitted into an evolving Empire. Strathcona himself had felt it necessary to protest yet again his total innocence of intervening in questions of "domestic concern" in Britain, specifically denying that he had entered into "some understanding, arrangement, or agreement" with the British Conservative party "respecting the policy of food taxes." Moreover, Borden, with his strong commitment to a dynamic Empire, was fully aware of the less than efficient arrangements for the representation of Canadian interests. Tupper from London told Borden that Canada was paying a heavy price for having Strathcona continue as its representative. Even the *primus inter pares* status of the Canadian high commissioner had been sacrificed; the Australian had "usurped completely the leadership of the Dominions in this country, and Canada is nowhere."[83]

As Strathcona's death appeared increasingly imminent, Borden planned with his old friend and cabinet colleague, George Perley, what should be done. In February 1912, four months into office and upon his return from Britain, Perley had written Borden about "the not very satisfactory way" in which Canadian business was conducted, while making the now well-entrenched genuflexion in the direction of the "High Commissioner who has been of the greatest service to Canada and who commands the respect and admiration of everyone." Perley endorsed the comments of Griffith of three years before, recommending that "it would be greatly to our interest if everything in Great Britain was done under one head through whom the correspondence and instructions from the different departments would come ... [but] it will be necessary for you as Prime Minister to take some action ... as there are different departments interested." From Tupper came again the advice that a cabinet minister should be high commissioner (Tupper was nothing if not persistent in his convictions) to which Borden replied on New Year's Eve, 1913, "I do not fail to remember your own view that the High Commissioner for Canada ought to be a member of the Canadian Government ... the influence which, as High Commissioner, you were able to exert to the marked advantage of

Canada in matters of high Imperial concern, is a strong argument in support of your views."[84]

Lord Strathcona, aged ninety-four, died at his home on Grosvenor Square on 21 January 1914. He had declined an offer of burial in Westminster Abbey so that he could buried in Highgate cemetery next to his wife who had predeceased him by a few months (a stained-glass window to his memory is, however, in the abbey). Immediately following his death, Griffith reported to Borden that at the end the high commissioner had been "in a greatly perturbed state of mind." He had recently received yet another importuning letter from "Jamesie" Smith, claiming greater consideration as the son of Bella Hardisty's first marriage (he had prudently changed his name to Smith after his mother had "remarried"). Strathcona left instructions that the sixty-two-year-old supplicant was to be dealt with "liberally," but his last days had been rendered "uneasy" by Jamesie's agitation.[85]

Speculation proliferated in the press and questions were asked in the House of Commons about who would succeed Strathcona. The most unlikely volunteer was the impecunious Lord Grey, the governor general, whose term in Ottawa was ending with no gainful employment in sight. Earlier, Tupper had thought of a high commissioner becoming governor general; now a governor general thought of himself as high commissioner. Gradually it became evident that, as *The Times* reported on 5 May, "The Prime Minister has very definite ideals of Imperial policy and probably is convinced that they can best be expressed in London by colleagues with whom he has close and confidential relations in the Cabinet and in Parliament."[86]

CHAPTER FIVE

Sir George Perley, 1914–1922

Within days of Lord Strathcona's death, the choice of high commissioner had narrowed to Robert Rogers, the controversial minister of the interior, and the decidedly more conventional George Perley, minister without portfolio. John Willison wrote in the Toronto *Globe,*

It is no reflection upon whoever may be chosen to succeed Lord Strathcona ... to say that Sir Edmund Osler would be appointed if he would accept. He has wealth and high social position. He has sat in Parliament since 1896, but he would not enter the Cabinet, nor will he entertain the proposal to be High Commissioner. Few Canadians set higher value upon the Imperial connection, but his whole disposition is averse from official service and official distinction ... Mr. Perley, whose appointment is therefore the more likely in all the circumstances, does not hold a portfolio. This is not because he was not entitled by service and ability to control a Department. It is because he stood aside when the Prime Minister was embarrassed by pressure of rival claims and interests, in order that the Cabinet could be formed with the minimum of friction and grievance.[1]

The *Toronto Star* was even more certain that Perley would be appointed: "few are better equipped. He is a student of Imperial affairs. He knows conditions in Canada from Yarmouth to Prince Rupert. He has wide political and administrative experience. He is closer, and more in sympathy, perhaps, with Premier Borden than any other man mentioned for the position. He has great business insight, culture and a standing in the business and financial world."[2] The Conservative *Canadian Magazine* of March 1914 was no less enthusiastic. "At times he added to the labours of the [Acting] Prime Minister the headship of four or five other Departments, and he evinced a capacity for work which kept the secretaries and higher officials much busier than they cared for in the parliamentary recess. Unworried, unhurried, unresting, he kept the machinery of government moving smoothly ... and for all this he drew no more from the public exchequer than if he were a private Member of Parliament."

Perley was certainly an old friend and close confidant of the prime minister. Robert Borden had first been elected in 1896. George Perley, three years his junior, began his political career four years later as an unsuccessful candidate in Russell (Ontario). In 1902 he was again defeated in a by-election in the half-French, half-English constituency of Argenteuil, Quebec, where he had large timberlands. On his third attempt he was elected there in the general election of 1904, by which time his friend Borden had been eight years in the House of Commons and was already leader of the opposition. In 1910, with an election in the offing, Borden appointed the shrewd and cautious Perley chief opposition whip, a role in which he was notably successful, despite the fact that "with the rise of nationalism in Quebec ... and acute dissension over naval policy he had a hard task to reconcile restless and discordant elements."[3] Following the Conservative victory in the election of 1911, Perley was spoken of as minister of finance, but Borden named him minister without portfolio. Although a poor public speaker, he was always at hand as a troubleshooter and as a reformer, attempting to resolve administrative problems facing the new government that were not of a narrowly departmental character and acting as prime minister whenever Borden was absent from Ottawa. In February 1912 Perley was in London to attend CID meetings (a result of Borden's assessment of Canada's place in the Empire) and to examine, among other things, both the form and the content of the High Commission. No reform had been possible as long as Strathcona presided, but what Perley had learned in 1912 helped him two years later in his post-Strathcona decisions of what should be done to rejuvenate the High Commission.

Perley, much more than merely a politician, was well equipped to assess the efficiency of government offices. Born in New Hampshire, he attended school there and in Ottawa before going to Harvard University. His father, William Perley, a prominent Ottawa Valley lumberman, was the Conservative member of Parliament for Ottawa in Macdonald's first government. His son inherited the business, became a director of the Bank of Ottawa and of the Canadian Atlantic Railway, and in time a noted public benefactor, financing a hospital for incurables and another for tuberculosis patients. By 1914, Perley had been married for only a year to his second wife, his first having died in 1911. Emily (Milly) White was the daughter of the journalist Thomas White, minister of the interior in Macdonald's government, where he had served with Perley's father. Perley and his second wife were notably different in temperament. Twenty years later, Lester Pearson described Perley as "a very serious, almost a dour man ... He was as insistent on an ordered routine as he was rigid in his views, by no means an extrovert, but conscientious and persistent in his work ... Lady Perley was the exact opposite of Sir George in temperament, warm, sociable, bubbling over with good will and good humour."[4] When Perley's appointment was still only rumoured, *The Times* had reported from Toronto, "There is no greater social favourite in Ottawa than Mrs. Perley. Nor is her popularity peculiar to the more exclusive social circle. She is known and liked by all classes. If her husband is to be High Commissioner, he could not have made a more fortunate marriage."

Before sailing for Britain in May 1914, Perley had discussed with Borden how best to assess the lagging state of the High Commission in light of his findings in 1912. They had agreed that Perley should assume the additional title of acting high commissioner during his visit. Following a rapid review of what Strathcona had left behind – and some indulgence in the abundant delights of the London season – Perley would return to Ottawa to recommend who might best take charge of the now rudderless mission. Borden could not have made a better choice. Perley's notable administrative and political skills should in short order put the High Commission aright. Speculation having mounted that Perley would be high commissioner, Willison in *The Times* explained why his nature uniquely qualified him:

He is shrewd, cautious, deliberate, and resolute. He is not an orator, but he can make any necessary statement in Parliament or from the platform with force, simplicity, and dignity ... with the wisdom to attempt nothing to which he is unequal. His whole bearing and character suggest trustworthiness. No other man is more highly regarded in Ottawa or in the House of Commons. If he should go to London as High Commissioner, he will illustrate in the discharge of his responsible duties the qualities and characteristics for which Canadians should most desire to be distinguished.[5]

One problem that still needed resolution was relations between the High Commission and the agents general of the provinces. Promptly upon the death of Strathcona (and in the absence of a new high commissioner), the agent general of Ontario had written to Borden questioning why he and his provincial colleagues should not address the British gov-

Canadian government emigration offices in London in the early years of the twentieth century were more visible than ever before: the offices pictured were at 11-12 Charing Cross Road. Galt, Tupper, and Strathcona had urged in vain that extensive emigration promotion be undertaken in several British cities. In the last years of Laurier's government (the photograph is from July 1911) such offices were finally opened or expanded, only to close again with the coming of the First World War.

ernment directly on issues of provincial concern. Ontario House in the Strand had twenty-one people, plus offices in both Glasgow and Belfast; the High Commission in Victoria Street had a staff of only seven. How could Ottawa in all good conscience hinder the work of the Ontario representative by insisting that his contact with the British government be exclusively through the high commission? But Ottawa continued so to insist, both in its response to Ontario and to a later joint statement made on behalf of all provincial governments by the premier of Quebec.

Perley was not, however, going to London only to diagnose the several ills of the High Commission, including the obvious lack of coordination with representatives of several departments and provinces. The order-in-council of 2 June 1914 which sent him across the Atlantic refers to "important matters ... which require the attention of a Minister in London during the present summer, among others, discussion with His Majesty's

Government of proposed amendments to the British North America Act, 1867, and ... the selection of a site for a suitable building to accommodate the Canadian offices in London." In a letter to Harcourt, the colonial secretary, four days later, transmitting the order-in-council, Borden was more specific about what Perley was to do; he was to "discharge the duties of Acting High Commissioner. He will also discuss so far as may be necessary the question of defence with you and with Mr. Churchill, and particularly the question of Canada's participation in the naval defence of the Empire. If it should be thought desirable by His Majesty's Government, Mr. Perley should be summoned to attend any meetings of the Imperial Defence Committee which might be held during his visit ... His good judgment and discretion may be absolutely relied upon and he has my complete confidence as to the policy which we shall pursue in the future." With his deep commitment to the Empire, Borden clearly regarded Perley as having an active role to play in imperial relations, a sharp contrast with both his and Laurier's attitude toward Strathcona.

As the prorogation of Parliament approached, George Perley and his wife sailed for Britain, supposedly for a visit of a few months. Amidst the varied diversions of a flawless English summer, he set about his assignment with characteristic energy and concision, booking his return passage for 11 September, three months hence. At the Committee for Imperial Defence in July, he responded adversely to an Australian proposal for an imperial naval conference in Vancouver, contending that such a controversial subject might best be left to the next quadrennial imperial conference (foreseen for 1915). And he quickly made up his mind about what was needed at the High Commission, having already seen in 1912 what its broad problems were. In any case, Perley had by then become decidedly interested in being appointed high commissioner. Both he and his wife already knew something of life in the higher echelons of British society; they wanted to know more. He had also become intrigued by the work; he would, for example, be at the centre of the continuing debate about the role of the Dominion in the Empire. He recommended to Borden in July two immediate steps to consolidate the office: all activities of any Canadian government department or agency represented in London must be brought under the direct authority of the high commissioner who, second, must be a cabinet minister.

In less than forty years since Confederation, the governor general had been largely eclipsed as interlocutor between the two governments. Perley, building partly on Tupper's advice, was persistent in his conviction that to be a truly effective representative of his government, the high commissioner must be concurrently a cabinet minister, a permanent dual status that Tupper and he would consistently, and always vainly, advocate. Tupper had confirmed to Perley that during the thirteen years that he had been high commissioner, "this office [had] exercised real control over every civil servant and branch of the service in Europe and really represented Canada in all ways, great and small." Perley reminded Borden that Tupper "is and always has been strongly in favour of giving this office as much power and authority as can be done and having a Cabinet Minister here for that purpose." Immediately following the outbreak of war, Perley wrote to Borden, "The next few years are going to be full of problems connected with the Empire and its future relationship and the difficult question of cooperation between its component parts. I cannot but think it will help very much with the solution of these problems if Canada had a Minister in this office who would be in continual touch with the Government of Great Britain."

From August 1914, Britain, France, Russia, Germany, and the Austro-Hungarian Empire were all belligerents as a result of that "damn'd system of alliances" that had enmeshed Europe. Perley knew immediately what the war meant for him personally. "When I left home at your request," he wrote eleven days later to Borden, "it was for the purpose of spending a few months here, to try and administer the office in the meantime and in that way to get an insight into conditions here so that on my return I might report to you ... I had no discussion as to who would be eventually appointed to this office after I returned ... I took it for granted it would depend somewhat upon the report I might make." The sudden outbreak of war determined that it was Perley himself who had to face the challenge of restoring order and morale in what by 1914 had become a ramshackle quasi-diplomatic post, a post, moreover, that was about to be deluged by the unknown demands of wartime. "It is, of course, absolutely imperative that some one should be here to represent us under the present trying circumstances, so that I have simply cancelled my passage until I know your wishes." The oral report that he had planned to make to Borden in Ottawa had instead now to be made hurriedly in writing from London. And the question of who was to be appointed high commissioner – and whether the high commissioner should always be a minister – was resolved by the simple but necessary expedient of Borden designating Perley acting high commissioner while continuing as minister without portfolio. Four months later, Borden confirmed that Perley should remain in London "during continuance of war."

The outbreak of war made Perley's retention in London inevitable, whether or not there was soon to be a general election in Canada. It was, however, awkward for him to take up the appointment so suddenly. He had made no preparatory arrangements at home, having believed that his assignment would be brief: "Some of my matters were not left in exactly as good condition as I should like for any long absence," but he was convinced that a cabinet minister was required if the High Commission was to speak with authority to Asquith's government. Only a minister could revive fully the faltering mission which Strathcona had bequeathed to his successor. "I realize the difficulty that a Member of Parliament would have in filling this office as it would be very hard for him to keep in touch with his constituents, which might endanger his re-election ... it could be arranged that a Senator should fill this office who was also a member of the cabinet."[6] Borden did not act on his recommendation, but in Montreal in December he did extol Perley's industry. "The presence of a Member of the Government as Acting High Commissioner in London during the past four months has been of inestimable value ... It is my duty and privilege to bear testimony to his splendid services to his country during these trying months."

As the war began to place unparalleled demands on the High Commission, Perley's immediate concern was its ability to cope, but he addressed his new tasks with his habitual precision and dour commitment. An acerbic Liberal journalist writing in *Maclean's* magazine in March 1915 disagreed. "Outside of one or two undertakers, I know of no man in Canada who combines chronic reserve and abiding gloom in such just proportions ... so far [Perley] has done nothing out of the routine, except to move the High Commissioner's office from the middle of the block to the corner of Victoria Street."[7] The mess left by Strathcona was not easily cleared as wartime demands mounted. As late as May 1915, Perley reported to Borden that "Canadian methods of administration are rather being laughed at over here."

That Canada, Newfoundland, the other Dominions, India, and the colonies would all be at war on the same day that Britain declared war had never been in doubt. Indeed, any such question would have been regarded as bizarre. As leader of the opposition, Laurier was vocal in his support when Britain itself was threatened. "When the call comes our answer goes at once ... Ready, aye, ready," adding the proposal of a wartime political truce in Ottawa. The government's immediate offer of an unspecified number of troops and its two near-useless warships was routed through the governor general, but it was Perley who consulted with the secretary of state for war about the more exact nature of the Canadian offer. Kitchener's response, that Britain could "use all [troops] you think best to send," was markedly different from the half-hearted reply of Britain to the half-hearted offer of Canada fifteen years before, at the beginning of the South African War.[8] The Canadian proposal of an initial forty thousand volunteers (followed almost immediately by another twenty-two thousand) was promptly welcomed. Perley confirmed to Borden that "as soon as the Canadian troops arrive here they will be entirely under the authority of the War Office and become part of the Imperial army in every sense of the word." But who should command the Canadian Expeditionary Force remained a question. Kitchener recommended to Perley any one of three Canadians serving in the Indian Army (the destination of many graduates of the Royal Military College of Canada). Perley recommended one, Brigadier-General Sir George Kirkpatrick, whose father and grandfather had both been Conservative members of Parliament, but Hughes considering him weak, a Canadian would not be appointed for more than a year. It was widely held that Major-General E.A.H. Alderson, whom the Canadian voyageurs had known on the Nile in 1885 and under whom the Royal Canadian Regiment had served under in South Africa, had the necessary experience to lead the first contingent through its additional training in southern England before taking it to the front. When Kitchener designated Alderson, Perley reported confidently that "we are going to have very satisfactory relations."

Perley was immediately involved in questions of military organization and deployment, not because it was thought that he knew so early in the war much about such matters, but because there was, in a real sense, no other Canadian in London with his authority to take decisions. In early November 1914 he accompanied the King and Queen and Field Marshals Lords Kitchener and Roberts and Sir Richard McBride, the visiting premier of British Columbia, on an inspection of the Canadians under canvas on Salisbury Plain. The troops, having arrived only a fortnight or so before from Valcartier, were still generally in good health. The illnesses that were soon to beset them amidst the mud and the flooding of Salisbury Plain during that terrible winter of 1914–15 were still a few weeks ahead. Three months later, Perley crossed to France "to look after arrangements for the Canadian forces, who will shortly go to the front," despite their now debilitated state.

From the first heady days of the war, Perley and his small staff were plunged into a variety of issues that were to remain with them for the next four years: issuance of passports to stranded Canadians; British contracts for manufactures and foodstuffs; wartime representation in the United States; the acute shortage of shipping on the Atlantic; financial arrangements with the Treasury; the establishment of the Canadian War Contingent charity; the safe storage in Canada of gold owed to the Bank of England by the United States; and, underlying it all, the nature of the relationship between Canada and Britain in a now rapidly evolving Empire.

As the Canadian Expeditionary Force expanded, Perley, upon instructions from the minister of finance, began discussions with the Treasury about war financing. In consultation with other high commissioners and colonial agents, problems of financing purchases of *matériel* in Canada by Britain soon became one of Perley's most pressing challenges. In a cable of April 1915, Ottawa informed Perley of its decision "to bear the whole cost of the Canadian contingents sent for service in the war," although the details of how exactly the expenses were to be met plagued Perley during much of his eight years as high commissioner. Unlike in the South African War, the Canadian Expeditionary Force was to be no "C.O.D. contingent"; all expenses, with only limited exceptions, were to be met by Ottawa. In the background, there already lurked another financial question for Perley to help address: the faltering debt repayment by two of the transcontinental railways, a problem that was to plague Perley and later Arthur Meighen, the minister of the interior.

Perley was left in no doubt by Borden of his immediate priorities. The equanimity with which many Canadians had greeted the outbreak of war (Borden himself had bizarrely noted on 31 July "had delightful evening. Everyone anticipates war") had been prompted partly by the eager anticipation among Tory supporters of patronage and lucrative war contracts. The domestic demand for British orders of all kinds to be placed in Canada soon became a leit-motif in Borden's messages to Perley. Four months into the war, he cabled him:

Not only the people of Canada as a whole but individuals are making sacrifices hitherto undreamed of to support Empire in this War. A very painful and bitter feeling is being aroused throughout the Dominion. Men are going without bread in Canada while those across the line [i.e., in the United States] are receiving good wages for work that could be done as efficiently and as cheaply in this country. You cannot emphasize too strongly the considerations set forth in this message. Public opinion is being so seriously aroused as to most gravely affect our future action.[9]

Borden did not need to make explicit to Perley that "public opinion" over the absence of commercial benefits from the war could also gravely affect his own government's prospects in any early election. He repeatedly pressed Perley to win British contracts for blankets, uniforms, and harnesses in particular, but the products in several instances were so shoddy – as in the South African War – that the British and French refused to accept them or even to take them at reduced prices. A "Shell Committee" had been established by Sam Hughes, but it was soon in difficulties over its questionable practices and had to be replaced by the more effective Imperial Munitions Board, acting under the direction of the British Ministry of Munitions, for all purchases of matériel in Canada. A strong whiff of corruption pervaded a Russian contract negotiated by a close associate of Sam Hughes. Borden, evidently believing that he could not run the domestic political risk of confronting Hughes directly, instead instructed Perley in October 1914 to request the colonial secretary to inform the Allies that Hughes's friend had no official status and did not represent Canada. By Christmas 1915 British patience had run out; Perley had to report that "it has been decided to place no further orders in Canada for the present.[10] Almost simultaneously, Canada perforce resorted to New York for federal and provincial borrowing, given the unprecedented domestic demands on London money markets, the traditional source of development financing for Canada.

Early in the war, ambitious Canadian shipyards had optimistically contemplated a flood of British orders for destroyers, submarines, and even cruisers. Although Vickers in Montreal did eventually complete a few small submarines brought partly constructed from the neutral United States, Canada's prewar political turmoil over naval policy had left it without any significant warship-building capacity. Winston Churchill, First Lord of the Admiralty, who had endured several years of Canadian indecision, was quite clear about what now should be done: "Canada had better concentrate her energy on the Army ... there was no way in which Canada could give naval aid during the war."[11] Ships took too long to build for a war which was seen as lasting for no more than two years or so. Orders for major warships were never placed and it was to be a long time before Canada could produce even merchant ships in any numbers. Ottawa had done nothing to prepare for what was increasingly recognized, in Perley's words, as "really the most serious difficulty we have to face in connection with this war": the shortage of merchant shipping.[12] Immediately following the declaration of war, the Admiralty had instituted its planned requisition of most Canadian as well as British merchant vessels, leaving a deep concern in Perley's mind. In 1916 he could report Admiralty agreement that new ships constructed in Canada would not be requisitioned so long as they were employed in trade with Allied countries, but there were few new freighters constructed in Canada. Only when Lloyd George came to office at the end of 1916 were a Ministry of Shipping and convoys introduced, finally reducing the supreme menace that had faced Britain.

The new war in the air added to the challenges facing an unprepared Canada. From the first days of the war, a myriad of schemes for the creation of a Canadian flying corps, or at least for training schools to qualify volunteers for service with the rapidly expanding Royal Flying Corps, began to descend on the High Commission as well as directly on Ottawa. Prompted by a range of patriotic or self-seeking aviation enthusiasts, Borden and his government blew hot and cold. Perley, necessarily involved in almost daily contact with the War Office about Canadian military plans, had become increasingly bewildered by the contradictory messages that had begun to arrive from Ottawa. R.B. Bennett, the Conservative member for Calgary East, had even proposed the creation of an "Alberta Aviation Corps," but more of the High Commission's time was taken in dealing with various proponents who had contacted directly the Imperial Munitions Board, the War Office, or the Royal Flying Corps about the potential for training in the empty skies of Canada. Perley conveyed without comment one such idea – for the purchase of twelve aircraft complete with pilots from the United States – to the War Office, adding Borden's observation that Canada has "no aviation service and do not think it desirable [to] attempt organization such service during progress [of] war."[13]

The advent of war had increased the manifold need for enhanced imperial consultation. Practical considerations alone were compelling, as military cooperation came to dominate the relationship. But what was regarded as voluntary cooperation on one side of the Atlantic was looked upon by some on the other side as simply the natural contribution of a colony to the urgent needs of the mother country. Upon his return to Ottawa from a visit to Britain, Charles Cahan, the Conservative member for Maissoneuve and long-time collaborator of Max Aitken, urged upon Borden that in making the Canadian voice heard, "you will have to state your case again and again ... before you make any appreciable impression upon the ruling classes in England ... who appear to be ... quite disinclined to devote time and consideration to the question of more efficient imperial organization, except in so far as such an organization may assure larger contributions of men and money to meet the military and naval necessities of the British Government." Cahan's assessment of Asquith's Liberal government was substantiated on the one hand by its seeming indifference to imperial consultation and, on the other, by its requests for more and more troops. Much to Borden's mounting chagrin, these demands were not matched by any apparent willingness to call Canada to the councils of the Empire. Perhaps recalling Asquith's statement about the wholly consultative role of the CID, Cahan was convinced "that the present Liberal Government would never consent that the self-governing Colonies should share in the control of foreign policies in the making of war and peace."[14] Nevertheless, as early as December 1914, Borden had begun to call publicly for their participation "in the councils of the Empire," adding in that connection, "that the presence of a member of the Government as Acting High Commissioner in London during the past four months has been of inestimable advantage to Canada. As a Minister of the Crown, he [Perley] occupies a unique position among those who represent in London the great Dominions."

Fully aware of the direction of Borden's thinking, Perley worked constantly to give some substance to that continuing and elusive will-o'-the-wisp, imperial consultation. In January 1915 he attended a meeting of the CID (it was to be superseded by the Imperial War Cabinet in May), but he also pressed Sir Maurice Hankey, its secretary, to devise a more consistent channel of communication and consultation. Concurrently Perley took public Borden's campaign for a role in imperial policy-making. In a speech to the Royal Colonial Institute, he stated flatly that Canada "could not be expected to do as she is doing now for all time ... without knowing beforehand and being consulted regarding the questions at issue which make such war necessary. We all look forward in the not too distant future to some altered arrangements by which we shall be called to the councils of the Empire regarding really Imperial questions." For his part, Borden had queried Perley as early as October 1914 whether he should soon visit Britain and whether the next quadrennial imperial conference would be held as scheduled in 1915. It soon became clear that amidst the press of war little thought had been given to convening the conference, and Harcourt simply told the House of Commons that "everybody was too busy" to contemplate a visit from the Canadian premier ("there can be nothing in the nature of public entertainments"). Perley recognized that since the British government viewed Borden's proposed visit as "inopportune," it would be difficult to generate publicity around it that might help to win votes in what was still regarded as a pending election. No visit could have the desired "spectacular effect" on the Canadian electorate without the full co-operation of the British. Perley, in telegraphese, added tactfully that "papers full war news everyone exceedingly busy working at full pressure they would be pleased to see you but know of nothing specially requiring attention."

So much for Borden's desire to be seen as contributing more than soldiers and money to the total war effort of the Empire. There remained in his mind the pressing need for more information about what the British general staff was doing or not doing and, more fundamentally, how the British government envisaged the total imperial effort to win the war. Ten months of trench warfare had convinced him that the strategy of attrition meant endless bloodshed. In the wake of the loss of six thousand men of the First Canadian Division at the Second Battle of Ypres, Borden, with R.B. Bennett, visited Britain and France during the parliamentary summer recess of 1915.* For the living, Bennett, chairman of the National Service Board, attempted to gauge at first hand what future demands for reinforcements would be. For the dead, Perley helped to organize a memorial service at St Paul's Cathedral. For the wounded, Borden set himself the impossible goal of visiting every Canadian casualty, but he did visit a remarkable total of fifty-two military hospitals in Britain and France (generally accompanied by Perley). To the Canada Club, he declared:

Not for a single moment shall we be discouraged by any reverse, and not for a moment shall we relax our determination to bring the war to a triumphant and honourable conclusion ... The unity of the Empire has never been more manifest than it is to-day ... There may come a time in the future when we may have to consider a better organization between these Islands and the Overseas Dominions. To those who think such a task impossible, I would commend the example of the men who founded the Dominion of Canada. Any difficulties can be overcome by wise counsel and co-operation of the statesmen of these Islands and of the Dominions.

* There can be no doubt about Bennett's imperial enthusiasm. The year before his visit to the front, he had declared (Bennett did not speak; he declared) to the Empire Club in Toronto, "under the Providence of God we are a Christian people that have given to the world the only decent kind of government they have ever known ... What a splendid trust it is, to think that you and I ... will one day be measured by the manner in which we have discharged our obligations to those subject races ... If that sinks into our minds, how can you and I think of independence, how can we be concerned about an independent Canada? ... if we believe the British Empire is no accident ... how can we talk of an independent Canada? An independent Canada means this, that we Canadians are afraid to accept the responsibilities of our race and breed; afraid to think we are Britons, afraid to face the future in the eye."

In an attempt to help the increasingly frustrated Borden ascertain more exactly what it was that the new Liberal-Conservative coalition government headed by Asquith now intended to do to win the war, Perley had arranged for him an audience with the King and meetings with Asquith, Grey, Churchill, Balfour, Lloyd George, Kitchener, Carson, Law and a variety of officials, as well as with Aitken. The prime minister was even invited to attend a British cabinet meeting – a most unusual proceeding – but Borden felt little more certain at the end of his month-long visit than he had at the beginning about how Canada and the other Dominions might help to advance imperial war policy, if indeed any such policy existed in a coherent form. "I had gone from pillar to post, from one member of the British Government to another, for the purpose of obtaining definite information as to when the British Empire would be in a position to throw its whole strength into the War."[15] For his trouble, he was told by members of Asquith's government that it would be another eighteen months before the full weight of the Empire could be joined in battle. Lloyd George, the minister of munitions, who shared his frustrations, provided Borden with a "damning indictment of departmental negligence." Meanwhile, the stalemate on the western front, with all its attendant slaughter, became more entrenched.

In Max Aitken, Borden had an eager interlocutor and Canadian advocate and, with Perley, one of his few sources of regular information in London. From the first weeks of the war, Aitken had pulled every one of his many levers to be appointed to a staff role in the Canadian Expeditionary Force. To that end, he embarked for Canada, telling Perley of his intention to call upon his many friends in the Conservative government. Aitken's appointment in January 1915 was "Canadian Eye Witness" on the western front, a curious title carrying with it the honorary rank of lieutenant-colonel, "to take charge of the work connected with records generally appertaining to the Canadian Overseas Expeditionary Force, and particularly the reporting of casualties." Hughes regarded the organization of the chaotic records of the Canadian Expeditionary Force as Aitken's principal task; needless to say, Aitken himself had more ambitious plans. From an office in the City (for which he paid the rent), he would not only frequently visit Flanders but would publicly comment on the course of the war, utilizing his extensive connections with Fleet Street to ensure that coverage was given to Canada's growing contribution, recognition that could be useful to Borden in his search for a voice in imperial policy, as well as in an election.

In May 1915 Aitken assumed the additional appointment of Canadian Records Officer, a combination of archivist and publicist. Following Borden's visit a few months later, he had yet another unusual title added: "Canadian Military Representative at the Front." Aitken then turned his extraordinary energy to glorifying what Hughes had once called "the great heart, ability and capability of a dear little Canadian boy." In stressing to Borden that "publicity for Canada during the war is inseparably bound up with Canada's credit" in Britain, he had in mind the postwar role that a heroic Canada could play in leading the Empire to greater unity. Perley must sometimes have wondered at the loose cannon that had been unleashed by injecting Aitken into the confusion of overseas headquarters arrangements and the controversies over the limited information available about what was happening in either Whitehall or Flanders. Aitken attempted on an almost daily basis to pass confidential information and opinion to Borden. Using a rudimentary code – which he soon rightly suspected that the British were reading – he sent frequent cables mixing fact, rumour, and gossip, occasionally even contradicting Perley. What Borden intended by the several appointments of Aitken beyond holding him in his sights is unclear, but Aitken, now an honorary colonel, never flagged in proclaiming his linkages to Canada, even contemplating briefly resigning his seat in the British Parliament to become a member of the Canadian.

During Borden's visit to London, King George v had assured him "that the Dominions should have a voice in the determination of foreign policy." Borden had in turn told Lord Bryce, the former British ambassador in Washington, and anyone else who would listen, "that the Dominions must have a voice in foreign policy. I told him they would either have such a voice or each ... would have a foreign policy of its own."[16] However, his fellow Maritimer, Bonar Law, who, as colonial secretary in 1915–16, might have been expected to be supportive, was instead unhelpful, contending both gratuitously and anachronistically, in light of the already substantial military commitments by the Dominions, that "having a voice in foreign affairs might commit the Dominions to a larger naval and military expenditure than they would care to undertake." Deeply frustrated, Borden responded bluntly that "unless I get precise information, I shall return to Canada with no definite intention of urging my countrymen to continue in the war work they have already begun."[17]

These were strong words. Borden returned to Ottawa in mounting turmoil, both about the British direction of the total imperial war effort and about the indifference that he had generally encountered toward enhanced and systematic consultation with the Dominions in the formulation of policy. Upon arrival home, his worst misgivings were confirmed when Perley reported that Bonar Law had blandly informed the House of Commons: "I am in continual communication with the Governments of the self-governing Dominions on matters relating to the War. Sir Robert Borden has recently been in this country and His Majesty's Government have gladly taken advantage of his presence to have full and confidential discussion with him."[18] Borden and Perley knew that this was nonsense, aware as they were of just how intermittent and insubstantial the "continual communication" was.

From Ottawa, Borden continued his advocacy of a greater role for the Dominions in policy-making. In parallel, Perley pursued his probing and prodding. On 28 October 1915, the month after Borden's return to Canada, Perley cabled to him: "Expect that small war council having special powers will soon be named from [British] Cabinet ... If it were possible for Dominions [to] agree on one man to represent them would like to see him appointed on this Council ... you could be very useful in such a position and it would seem good opportunity [to] make beginning [in] changed Imperial ideas and relations." In a second message of the same day, Perley sought Borden's "views regarding possibility and advisability some way being found for consulting more with you and other Dominions regarding general policy of war operations."[19] The response of the prime minister to Perley's two messages was immediate:

Please inform Bonar Law that we would appreciate fuller and more exact information from time to time respecting conduct of war and proposed military operations as to which little or no information vouchsafed. We thoroughly realize necessity central control of Empire's armies but Governments of Overseas Dominions have large responsibilities to their people for conduct of war and we deem ourselves entitled to fuller information and consultation respecting general policy in war operations. The great difficulty of obtaining information during my recent visit to London seemed partially occasioned by lack [of] proper coordination between several departments responsible for conduct war. Perhaps new Council or Committee can arrange for information and consultation suggested.[20]

Perley set out tactfully Borden's misgivings in a letter to Law of 3 November 1915: "The Canadian Government would appreciate very much if they could be given fuller and more exact information from time to time respecting the conduct of the war and proposed military operations."*[21]

---

* Throughout this prolonged discussion of the role of the self-governing colonies in imperial decision-making, Perley was momentarily distracted by the need to make arrangements with Winston Churchill at the Admiralty for the return to Halifax of the remains

For his trouble, he received a dusty reply the same day. Law pleaded undefined practical difficulties: "I fully recognize the right of the Canadian Government to have some share of the control in a war in which Canada is playing so big a part. I am, however, not able to see any way in which this could be practically done ... if no scheme is practicable then it is very undesirable that the question should be raised."[*22]

Bonar Law was clear enough in his flat refusal to propose a channel for the improved consultation that Borden had consistently sought. In the face of his refusal, Perley returned to the idea that Tupper and he had long urged: the formal confirmation of the office of high commissioner as being of cabinet rank, a "national step in the development of imperial relations." In a personal letter to Aitken, Perley outlined how the title of "acting high commissioner" might replace the cumbersome but more accurate "Member of the Canadian Government in charge of the Office of the High Commissioner in London"; in other words, a cabinet minister as high commissioner.[23] He suggested to Borden that the combination of appointments as acting high commissioner and a minister without portfolio was a status peculiar to him and not entrenched in the office itself. Legislation was needed to make the high commissionership a permanent cabinet post.

Two years earlier, Borden had agreed with Tupper that "the High Commissioner for Canada ought to be a member of the Canadian Government," but on this occasion he sought the opinion of the colonial secretary whether it was not preferable for Perley to continue as acting high commissioner and a minister without portfolio rather than resigning from the government to become high commissioner. "[I] asked him to tell me whether Perley as a member of the Government, did not occupy a more important and distinguished position than if he were appointed High Commissioner [instead of Acting High Commissioner]. Without hesitation, Bonar Law told me that Perley's position as a member of the Government was far higher in the estimation of the British Government and

of Sir Charles Tupper, the last surviving Father of Confederation, who had died at his house at Bexley Heath, near London, on 30 October 1915. Another Canadian politician whose death in London caused Perley some additional distraction was Joseph Martin, who had been premier of two Canadian provinces, Manitoba and British Columbia, and who was the member for East Pancras in the British Parliament from 1910 to 1918.

* Law was inflexible on constitutional questions, a leading Unionist who was deeply opposed to Home Rule in Ireland, declaring in July 1912, "I can imagine no length of resistance to which Ulster can go in which I shall not be prepared to support them."

its officials than if he would actually be appointed High Commissioner. It was a marked advantage in wartime to have a minister as high commissioner, but he [Law] was unable to anticipate what might be best in peacetime when a much more advanced step would be necessary." Borden does not say whether Law speculated upon what that "much more advanced step" might be (presumably some type of council upon which Dominion ministers would sit with a newly created secretary of state for the Dominions as chairman).

Within a year, Perley's own status would be further enhanced by being appointed minister of overseas forces, but Borden took no steps to link permanently minister and high commissioner, despite receiving Tupper's advice during a visit to him at Bexley Heath that "the High Commissioner should be member of the Government ... [although] in discussing Perley, he did less than justice to his ability, resourcefulness and tact." Nevertheless, Borden assured the House of Commons that Perley "has satisfactorily discharged the duties of High Commissioner ... and has had to do with a great many affairs, which, strictly speaking, might not come within the purview of the duties of High Commissioner."[24] Borden later recalled Perley's preoccupation:

Sir George was troubled by Press references designating him "Acting High Commissioner". Frequently he wrote to me with regard to this designation which he greatly disliked, and he sent me Press clippings for the purpose of impressing me with the embarrassing nature of this designation. Apparently he desired to be appointed High Commissioner which would have required legislation that I could not think of introducing.[25]

He also ensured that the Canadian military kept the high commissioner better informed of their activities involving the British – which was just about everything. Anything more to increase his status might only, among other things, trigger a fresh outburst from the suspicious and resentful minister of militia, Sam Hughes.

Borden had been deeply frustrated by Law's flaccid reply, as he was more generally by the Asquith's government's equally flaccid conduct of the war itself. He pondered his options for two months. Having secured parliamentary authority for an increase of the Canadian Expeditionary Force, he exploded to Perley on 4 January 1916:

Mr. Bonar Law's letter ... leaves the matter [of consultation] precisely where it was before my letter was sent.

Vimy Ridge, five months after the Canadian victory there, was dry and quiet. Clad in his obligatory tin hat, Sir George Perley in his dual capacity as minister of overseas military forces and acting high commissioner made several visits to Canadian units and field hospitals near the front.

During the past four months since my return from Great Britain, the Canadian Government (except for an occasional telegram from you or Sir Max Aitken) have had just what information could be gleaned from the daily press and no more. As to consultation, plans of campaign have been made and unmade, measures adopted and apparently abandoned and generally speaking steps of the most important and even vital character have been taken, postponed or rejected without the slightest consultation with the authorities of this Dominion.

It can hardly be expected that we shall put 400,000 or 500,000 men in the field and willingly accept the position of having no more voice and receiving no more consideration than if we were toy automata. Any person cherishing such an expectation harbours an unfortunate and even dangerous delusion. Is this war being waged by the United Kingdom alone or is it a war waged by the whole Empire? If I am correct in supposing that the second hypothesis must be accepted then why do the statesmen of the British Isles arrogate to themselves solely the methods by which it shall be carried on in the various spheres of war-like activity and the steps which shall be taken to assure victory and a lasting peace?

It is for them to suggest the method and not for us. If there is no available method and if we are expected to continue in the role of automata the whole situation must be reconsidered.

Procrastination, indecision, inertia, doubt, hesitation and many other undesirable qualities have made themselves entirely too conspicuous in this war. During my recent visit to England a very prominent Cabinet Minister [Lloyd George] in speaking of the officers of another Department said that he did not call them traitors but he asserted that they could not have acted differently if they had been traitors. They are still doing duty and five months have elapsed. Another very able Cabinet Minister spoke of the shortage of guns, rifles, munitions, etc., but declared that the chief shortage was of brains.[26]

The weak point in Borden's outburst was his reluctance "to suggest the method" for imperial policy consultation and collaboration. On reflection, Borden wired Perley to withhold his letter. Perley did so, although he likely drew upon it in his subsequent discussions with Law and other ministers.

Borden began to ponder a concerted effort with Australia which might possibly encourage even the feckless Asquith government itself to propose a better way to conduct the total imperial war effort. To that end, he asked Perley to see the redoubtable and cantankerous Australian prime minister who was visiting London. "Billy" Hughes had sailed from Australia to Vancouver to visit Borden in Ottawa before he had embarked in New York for Britain. Borden told Perley that "We had very intimate discussions as to matters touching the conduct of the war and the future relations of the Empire ... His opinion as to the future necessity of the Overseas nations having an adequate voice in the Empire's foreign policy coincides entirely with my own."[27] Perley needed no prompting: within a week of seeing the Australian prime minister, he declared to the Associated Chambers of Commerce of Britain his conviction that a postwar Empire could be self-contained and self-sustaining, adding five weeks later to the National Liberal Club that "Our people are proud to be doing their share, but it is evident that ... we should at the same time have a voice in all decisions regarding matters of common concern."[28]

Little resulted. Borden did induce Law to give Perley copies of all correspondence between the governor general and the Colonial Office, thereby ensuring that the High Commission was kept informed of everything that passed between Ottawa and London. Law also sent to Borden on two occasions a few more confidential documents from the Committee of Imperial Defence than he might have received if he had not protested. More to the point, in May 1916 Law did seek Ottawa's reaction to the idea of a conference of representatives of the United Kingdom, the Dominions, and India to consider "what commercial policy should be adopted after the war." Arthur Balfour, the former prime minister, who had seen his government destroyed by Chamberlain's advocacy of an imperial tariff preference, chaired an all-British preparatory committee which had finally and faintly recommended in February 1917 that an imperial tariff preference be instituted. The conference duly adopted a resolution recognizing "the principle that each part of the Empire ... shall give specially favourable treatment and facilities to the produce and manufacturers of other parts of the Empire."

So far so good, but the proposed conference itself would take a longer view of the future of the Empire, dealing with questions of leading importance: "commercial and industrial policy after the war including tariff ... constitution of Empire ... emigration." In the event, further consideration of the agreement in principle reached on these questions was held over until a postwar conference could assess them in light of circumstances. Lloyd George hoped that he had, with Borden's support, finessed the whole matter of an imperial trade preference, with its hazardous implications of a tax on food. His assistant and mistress recorded in her diary "that he had come to an agreement with the Imperial Cabinet on the subject of Preference for the Colonies. He suggested his scheme which he had put forward as far back as 1907, a scheme whereby the colonies are assisted by shipping subsidies, which avoids taxation and therefore does not increase the price of the commodities. D[avid]. put this forward and Borden, to the surprise of everyone, backed it up and spoke convincingly in favour of it."[29]

Borden's procrastination in expelling the erratic and egocentric Hughes from his cabinet is the least credible episode in his long and distinguished public career.* The problem was not that the prime minister had finally

---

* Borden may have felt loyalty beyond the normal to his colleague. Upon Borden being defeated in Halifax in the general election of 1904, Hughes, who had been first elected in February 1892, promptly offered his friend his seat of Victoria Haliburton in Ontario (Borden declined, accepting instead Carleton).

demanded the resignation of his minister of militia, but that, in the midst of a world war, he had allowed himself to be paralysed by perceived domestic political repercussions. Perley in London was as well aware as Borden in Ottawa of the temperamental and egotistical nature of the member for Victoria North – and prominent member of the Loyal Orange Lodge. The mercurial Hughes, from the age of thirteen both a militia soldier and an ardent imperial unity advocate, had shown monumental lack of judgment as well as deep prejudice against French Canadians throughout his twenty-two prewar years in Parliament. He had failed to add to the distinctive French–speaking battalions, instead dispersing French-speaking volunteers to English-speaking units and neglecting the merits of French-speaking officers for promotion. More fundamentally, the governor general had concluded that "Hughes is mentally off his base." Borden later concurred: "his mind was unbalanced." In peacetime, unbalanced cabinet ministers are common and harmless enough, but in wartime they can cost lives.

Perley, who had long deeply distrusted Hughes – "a very dangerous passenger" – helped to screw the prime minister's resolve to the sticking point, but it took an immense amount of his time and effort to get him there. War had hardly been declared before the uneasy Borden had begun to search for some dodge to rid himself of his troublesome colleague who had already made the mobilization of volunteers a much more contentious and complicated undertaking than it had needed to be. Borden's first idea was simply to get him out of Canada. During an early visit by Hughes to Britain, Borden had cabled to Perley that if there were any sign that Hughes would be willing to resign as minister of militia to command instead the Canadian Expeditionary Force, he should have the appointment. "It would be advisable from political considerations to give him the opportunity as he has unfortunately aroused great antagonism by his peculiar methods and manners ... If therefore he is so included [inclined?] and the British Government would cooperate the situation would be considerably relieved." Having taken the measure of Hughes beginning two decades before when he had vainly pressed Laurier to send Canadian volunteers to Khartoum, the British government would most decidedly not cooperate. Kitchener knew his man, telling Perley that Hughes "should return home to attend to work there."[30] The CEF was spared at least that infliction.

Borden's bizarre ploy of attempting to appoint Hughes overseas having failed, he again procrastinated, while Hughes continued to rule over the Department of the Militia as his personal fiefdom, causing deep resent-

ment among Canadian and British military staff, both at home and overseas. Perley was deeply disturbed by Borden's continuing vacillation: he
simply could not understand "why you put up with his ways for so long."
He impressed upon Borden his growing concerns about the chaotic state
of the administration of Canadian forces both in Britain and at the front,
Hughes having excluded his colleagues from any real understanding of
what was happening in his jealously guarded department. Perley relayed
to Borden the reaction of one observer of the mess. "When I hear a man
say that he understands 'There are two Governments in Canada, one of
which is represented here by various people sent over by Hughes and is
apparently not under the control of the other', it makes me squirm."[31]

By mid-1916 even the seemingly ever-indulgent Borden could no longer
tolerate the confusion and waste that Hughes's incompetence and unbri-
dled ego caused, including the misappropriation of munitions contracts.
Lives were being endangered as an indirect result of the futile rivalries
and personal jealousies that he had generated. Early in July 1916, following a brief visit to France to receive President Poincaré at a French-
Canadian field hospital, Perley returned to Ottawa for his first visit in two
years, Borden having assigned the High Commission in his absence to
Sir George Foster, the minister of trade and commerce, who was visiting
London.

In Ottawa, Borden and Perley discussed the problems which had long
since surfaced in the command structure overseas. With Perley and others
pressing the issue, Borden cabled Hughes in London to recommend once
and for all what the command and administrative structure of the CEF
should be. Hughes did not respond to Borden's instructions; instead he
had put in place a "sub-Militia Council" directly under his control. At
this, Borden's extraordinary patience finally ended. An order-in-council
of 28 October 1916 created a Ministry of Overseas Military Forces. The
stage was now set for Perley's shift from minister without portfolio to minister of overseas military forces. Hughes, having convinced himself that
he was surrounded by conspirators and suspecting what was brewing in
Ottawa with Perley there, had protested a fortnight before. As Borden
recorded, he "strongly argued against [the ministry] saying that there
would be nothing left for him, that he would be humiliated ... he gave a
tirade against Perley and decried his ability."[32]

As a last desperate stratagem, Hughes urged Borden to appoint Aitken
minister of overseas military forces and he would continue in Ottawa as
minister of militia. In a letter to Borden of 1 November 1916 – the day
after an order-in-council appointed Perley – Hughes charged that he and

the prime minister, together in Ottawa, had plotted his removal. His ploy of urging that Aitken instead of his enemy Perley be appointed minister was based upon the remarkable assumption that somehow he could control Aitken from Ottawa, but Aitken was too shrewd to entangle himself in what he recognized as a lost cause. Borden took Hughes's letter as the occasion to dismiss him. On 9 November 1916 the prime minister finally acted: "I take strong exception not only to the statements which it contains but to the general character and tone. You must surely realize that I cannot retain in the government a colleague who has addressed me such a communication."[33] A Canadian officer wrote home from the western front, "The mad mullah of Canada has been deposed. We walk with sprightlier step."

Perley's three months in Canada during the summer of 1916 were occupied mainly with the future of Sam Hughes and the transition in the overseas command, but the demands of his neglected constituents in Argenteuil also had to be addressed. When visiting his constituency, he sought volunteers for the army. In doing so, Perley saw for himself the deepening opposition among many French-speaking Canadians to compulsory military service. He knew very well how difficult it was becoming to find reinforcements for the increasingly stretched CEF. He knew equally well, however, what the response would be in Quebec to any departure from a voluntary army. In Ottawa and Montreal, Perley's attention was also taken by his business interests which he had necessarily neglected for two years. Having reviewed with Borden his own future during their discussions of problems that Hughes had created, Perley returned to London from Halifax in late September. Somewhere in mid-Atlantic his ship must have passed the returning Sam Hughes.

The essence of Borden's decision was that Perley should be minister of overseas military forces resident in London while remaining acting (and unpaid) high commissioner. When first appointed minister without portfolio in 1911, Perley had not needed to undergo the statutory requirement to submit himself for re-election upon taking a paid appointment, since ministers without portfolio were unpaid. Upon becoming acting high commissioner in 1914, he had again declined any salary, partly because he did not need it but also because he would not then be required to seek re-election. Two years later, Perley arranged that the order-in-council appointing him minister of overseas military forces would specify that the post was unpaid, thereby for a third time avoiding the necessity to seek re-election in his increasingly uncertain constituency.

With 256,000 men in Britain and on the Western Front and with "large forces in training in Canada," the ordinance for the constitution of the ministry of overseas military forces stated:

There shall be ... a Minister of Overseas Military Forces of Canada, who shall be charged with the control of and shall be responsible for the administration of the affairs of the military forces of Canada in the United Kingdom and on the Continent of Europe; the ordnance, arms, ammunition, armouries, stores, munitions and habiliments of war ... appropriated for the use of the Overseas Military Forces of Canada and all expenditure incurred in the United Kingdom or elsewhere in Europe for or in respect of the Overseas military forces of Canada; ... heretofore exercised by or charged upon the Minister of Militia and Defence.[34]

It was evident from the ordinance that Perley would become deeply involved in the politically hazardous question of reinforcements for the CEF. To be certain that every able man was sent to the increasingly hard-pressed units at the front, Perley instituted a combing out of the 3,500 men who were on clerical duty, 19,500 others who were supposedly undergoing additional training, and 20,000 men of the Fifth Division who had been virtually untouchable, given that they were commanded by Sam Hughes's son.

An added complication awaiting Perley was a highly controversial condemnation of the overseas medical services by a senior surgeon officer. His damning report gave Perley any amount of trouble, not least because Lady Perley had taken a lead among Canadian women in Britain in promoting support for the hospitals of the Canadian Red Cross and of the Voluntary Aid Detachment. Perley constituted a small advisory council who had served at the front (Hughes having preferred reliable cronies of advanced years). Perley and his new council set about reforming the overblown and haphazard army command left by Hughes, rooting out the political patronage and favouritism that had frequently determined who was to be promoted. With Sir William White, the minister of finance, Perley crossed to France in mid-November 1916, returning with the recommendation that General Arthur Currie should command at the front and General Sir Richard Turner (who had won the Victoria Cross in the South African War) command in Britain, a recommendation endorsed by the newly appointed minister of militia, Sir Edward Kemp. Turner and his staff were at work within a fortnight. For his part, Perley resumed visits to the western front, conferring about casualties, reinforcements, and equipment with Byng and, from June 1917, with Currie (whose appointment as corps commander he had supported).

Perley viewed with misgiving his additional administrative responsibilities as minister of overseas military forces. As he told Borden, he would "try for a while and do my best," but it was his role as high commissioner that Perley especially valued. If he had to choose between his two hats, his own preference was clear enough. When Borden offered to send another cabinet minister to take charge of the High Commission for four or five months while Perley grappled with the problems of the CEF, Perley replied: "Much prefer work High Commissioner to being Minister Overseas Forces. If it should transpire later that I cannot do both will advise you so that you can send over another Minister to take charge of Overseas Forces."[35] Subsequently Perley informed Borden that if he had known what was involved in his dual capacity, he would never have accepted his appointment as minister of overseas military forces. What Borden's reaction was to his minister's apparent lack of enthusiasm is not recorded.

As was his wont, Perley was as methodical in his new appointment as he had been in everything that he had touched as minister without portfolio, but in so doing he added to his reputation as a cold and remote administrator. He drew Borden's attention ever more persistently to the question of how, as casualties continued to mount, units at the front were to be reinforced. He knew personally something of the casualty rate, both from his visits to hospitals in the field and in England, and its likely political and practical impact.* He was as conscious as Borden that if the Canadian war effort faltered, the demand for a voice in the direction of the total imperial effort would be even less heard. On a more personal level, Perley also had the difficult task of responding to pleas from desperately worried parents about the dangers facing their soldier sons. In June-July 1917 he replied bleakly to Ed Pearson, a Methodist minister, who had asked that Lester, the third of his sons overseas, be returned to Canada: "The need of men is so urgent that we have had to reduce to the minimum the number returned to Canada, and the circumstances in which a man can be permitted to return must be very grave indeed. I am very sorry not to be able to accede to the request of a family which has given so generously

---

* Including one at Orpington, Kent, financed largely by the province of Ontario, and the Queen's Canadian Military Hospital at Shorncliffe, financed by the Canadian War Contingent Association. In February 1916 Perley attended the opening of the Orpington Hospital by Bonar Law – who lost two sons in the war – and visited it again upon its being doubled in size in July 1917.

to the Cause, and whose sons have done so splendidly, but unfortunately my personal feelings in the matter cannot be allowed to interfere with any duty."[36] Perley was, however, asked to send home from the CEF several Conservative members of Parliament – but no Liberals – to participate in the increasingly acrimonious debates about how to meet the challenge of the appalling casualty rates.

Canada's role in the direction of the war and as a source of troops were pre-eminent questions for the high commissioner, but while striving to contribute to their resolution, he continued to deal also with more mundane questions, including the appointment of a new governor general. In light of Canada's commitments, Borden told Perley that "the time has come, or at least is fast approaching, when a Canadian might with advantage be selected."[37] Borden contemplated proposing Laurier, but before he could discuss his imaginative idea with him, London had acted unilaterally: it simply confirmed to the Canadian government its appointment of the Duke of Devonshire to succeed the Duke of Connaught (who liked to remind Canadians that he was a veteran of the Fenian Raids). The prime minister had to content himself with asking Perley to convey his strong objections not to the ducal surfeit but to the lack of consultation.

On a quite different matter, the high commissioner was repeatedly required to refute allegations that Canadian nickel, of great value in the hardening of steel, was reaching Germany via the neutral United States, having been shipped there for refining by the International Nickel Company (in which the German munitions manufacturer Krupp was a shareholder). Howard Ferguson, the Ontario minister of lands, forests and mines, attempted to reassure the British government, through Perley, that in fact no such shipments were being made (and specifically that 240 tons of nickel had not crossed the Atlantic in a large submarine during the summer of 1916). The efforts of Perley and Ferguson at reassurance were only partially successful. Canadian copper had certainly reached Germany through the United States, eventually to be incorporated into munitions fired at Canadian troops, among others. The controversy continued until the United States itself finally entered the war in April 1917 and Inco transferred some of its nickel refining from the United States to Canada.

Yet more importantly, both Perley and Turner continued to be centrally involved in various proposals to form a Canadian Flying Corps. It having been accepted that to create a Canadian navy was a long-term project, Canadian sailors would accordingly serve mainly in the Royal Navy Canadian Volunteer Reserve. The creation of a distinct Canadian Flying Corps could, it was believed, be more readily achieved. Ottawa had responded positively to queries from the colonial secretary about its readiness to receive a British officer to recruit and help train suitable young Canadians volunteers – there were to be many – for the burgeoning Royal Flying Corps. Following a query from Perley in May 1916 about the possibility of establishing training schools for the RFC and the Royal Naval Air Service and the construction of aircraft factories in Canada, training fields were built. Before long graduate pilots and observers of "RFC Canada" were on their way overseas, but they went to join British squadrons, not Canadian. "It was in this fashion," the official historian of the RCAF has concluded, "that the Canadian government arrived at its posture of colonial dependency in the field of aviation."[38]

Borden was content with this arrangement in the short term, confirming to Perley the strong opposition of cabinet to the distraction of attempting to create a separate Canadian air service. However, he soon reversed himself, incensed by reports of lack of promotion among the many Canadians serving in the RFC. He wrote angrily, "Canadians in flying service are not receiving reasonably fair play or adequate recognition ... The question of establishing a Canadian Flying Corps demands immediate and attentive consideration ... the time for organization of an independent Canadian Air Service has come."[39] Perley responded that Turner and he had concluded that there was "no serious foundation" for allegations of discrimination in promotion but, at their urging, the War Office had offered to help create exclusively Canadian squadrons for service with the Royal Flying Corps, so that the nucleus of a Canadian service, especially for postwar duties, would exist. Borden was receptive, commenting to his minister of militia that the absence of a Canadian flying corps "seems unfortunate ... when so much splendid work is being done by Canadians [in the RFC and RNAS] that they should have no distinctive part."[40] The chief of the Canadian general staff, however, continued to urge that it would be less disruptive to the total military effort if the establishment of an air force were undertaken only following the war. There the question rested until a week after the Armistice when two all-Canadian RFC squadrons were finally formed the nucleus, in April 1920, of the initially small but seasoned Royal Canadian Air Force.

Borden's repeated delays in replacing Hughes had been costly and various subsequent appointments long overdue, but at least they were in place when the British government finally reorganized itself, following the disastrous campaigns on the Somme in 1916. Lloyd George, the minister of munitions, who was pledged to a more dynamic pursuit of Britain's war effort and to full consultation with the Dominions, exploited the widespread discontent at Asquith's detached leadership in order to replace him as prime minister of the Liberal-Conservative coalition on 6 December 1916. Churchill later wrote of Asquith, his former chief, "The phrase 'Wait and see', which he had used in Peace, not indeed in a dilatory but in a minatory sense, reflected with injustice, but with just enough truth to be dangerous, upon his name and policy. Although he took every critical decision without hesitation at the moment when he judged it ripe, the agonised nation was not content ... The vehement, contriving, resourceful, nimble-leaping Lloyd George seemed to offer a brighter hope, or at any rate a more savage effort."[41] Beaverbrook in the second volume of his *Politicians and the War* offers a more extended if incomplete account of the entry of Lloyd George into the premiership, but another, more trenchant summation of Lloyd George has come closer to capturing his essence: "He was the most inspired and creative British statesman of the twentieth century. But he had fatal flaws. He was devious and unscrupulous in his methods. He aroused every feeling except trust."[42]

Ruthless and resolute, persuasive and fertile, a born orator and man of action, the new prime minister, upon taking office, immediately reshuffled the government. Aitken was not invited to join it, instead accepting, to his later regret, a peerage as Lord Beaverbrook. More important, Lloyd George created an inner cabinet of five to conduct the total war effort, with Bonar Law, as chancellor of the exchequer, his closest collaborator. Lloyd George's second priority was an "Invitation to the Dominions and India to send representatives to London to discuss direction of the war. They were fighting not for us but with us." He told his new cabinet flatly, "we should take the Dominions into our counsel in a much larger measure than we have hitherto done ... We want more men from them. We can hardly ask them to make another great recruiting effort unless it is accompanied by an invitation to come over to discuss the situation with us."[43]

Perley attempted to ensure that the British public was made aware of what Canada sought. He advocated in the *Manchester Guardian* on 20 March "a change in the present British system, so that the Dominions have a real voice in peace and war and all matters of common concern. One can justify our sacrifices in this struggle, but it would be impossible to argue that we can regularly and permanently assist in the Empire's wars unless we have something to say as to their declaration and management." True to form, Bonar Law sourly observed to Lloyd George that when the Dominion premiers "are here you will wish to goodness you could get rid of them." Law's visible lack of enthusiasm was common among other members of the War Cabinet and he was not alone in the Conservative party in harbouring ambivalence, if not opposition, to any real participation by the Dominions in the making of imperial foreign policy. That must, in their view, remain a prerogative of Whitehall alone.

Much to his chagrin, Walter Long, the new colonial secretary and a future candidate for the Conservative leadership, had not been among the five senior ministers selected by Lloyd George for his inner cabinet, but it fell to him to carry out the prime minister's pledge to the Dominion premiers that "fuller information should be given of the progress of events and of war policy." A weekly letter would be provided to governors general, prime ministers, and the high commissioners, but Lloyd George had much more than that in mind. Imperial consultation must be rapidly expanded, not merely by "a session of the ordinary Imperial Conference but a special War Conference of the Empire." The prime ministers of the Dominions were invited "to attend a series of special and continuous meetings of the [Imperial] War Cabinet ... for the purpose of these meetings, [each] Prime Minister would be a member." The participation of Dominion premiers and Indian representatives in the Imperial War Cabinet and in an Imperial War Conference to be held on alternate days was a revolution in imperial relations. Lloyd George's enthusiasm for enhanced consultation with the Dominion premiers – the first time that they would gather in six years – arose partly from his conviction that among them he would find ready allies in his unrelenting struggle with the more purblind of the general staff and of his own wider cabinet.

Equally, the question of how to finance the total war effort of the Empire had to be addressed. The United Kingdom, prewar the leading creditor nation of the world, could no longer be paymaster alone, given the staggering costs of the war. Resort to US money markets confirmed the transition of the hard-pressed Britain from a creditor to a debtor nation, leaving Canada to make its way as best it could at home and in New York. Perley recognized the inevitable: "Personally favour American loan if possible [if it can] take care [of] your requirements instead borrowing here just now." When the novel idea of raising money at home was addressed, Ottawa was astonished by the enthusiastic reception given to its first domestic war loan.

Borden welcomed the advent of Lloyd George's government as the occasion to consult candidly on such fiscal measures, as well as to gain the broader role in the direction of the war that he had long sought for Canada. Certainly he was quick to lend the dynamic and determined "Welsh Wizard" all the help that he could; anything was better than the indecision and lassitude of Asquith's government. The Imperial War

Conference, chaired by the colonial secretary, began on 21 March 1917 (upon the return of Borden and Perley from a visit to the western front and to hospitals in southern England). Canada was represented by Douglas Hazen, minister of marine and fisheries, and by that notorious practitioner of pork-barrel politics from Manitoba, Robert Rogers, minister of public works. Following Borden's arrival at the end of February, they had together attended meetings of the conference through March and April, many of which were taken up with discussions about possible peace terms, sub-committees being struck under the chairmanship either of the imperial federalist Milner or of Curzon to review the economic and territorial demands of the British Empire at the eventual peace conference. Borden fully recognized that something quite remarkable was happening as a result of the orchestration of Lloyd George (who himself characterized the arrangements as "extremely elastic"). To the Empire Parliamentary Association in April 1917 he stated:

For the first time in the Empire's history there are sitting in London two Cabinets ... Over each of them the Prime Minister of the United Kingdom presides. One of them is designated as the [British] "War Cabinet", which chiefly devotes itself to such questions ... as primarily concern the United Kingdom. The other is designated as the "Imperial War Cabinet" which has a wider purpose ... To its deliberations have been summoned representatives of all the Empire's self-governing Dominions [and India]. We meet there on terms of equality under the presidency of the First Minister of the United Kingdom; we meet there as equals, he is *primus inter pares*. Ministers from six nations sit around the Council Board, all of them responsible to their respective Parliaments and to the people of the countries which they represent. Each nation has its voice upon questions of common concern and highest importance as the deliberations proceed; each preserves unimpaired its perfect autonomy, its self-government, and the responsibility of its Ministers to their own electorate. For many years the thought of statesmen ... in every part of the Empire has centred around the question of future constitutional relations; it may be that now, as in the past, the necessity imposed by great events has given the answer.

At Lloyd George's suggestion, it was soon unanimously agreed that, following the return of peace, a permanent imperial cabinet should meet at least annually. Lloyd George's collaborative initiatives, the imperial commitment of Milner, and the drafting skill of Borden and Smuts resulted in the famous Resolution IX of the Imperial War Conference of 16 April 1917 – one week after the Canadian victory on Vimy Ridge. Galt, Strathcona,

The imperial war cabinet on the terrace at No. 10 Downing Street, with White-hall in the background. Sir Robert Borden, the Canadian prime minister, is on the left. Next to him in uniform is Jan Christian Smuts, minister of defence of South Africa. Behind Smuts is Bonar Law, chancellor of the exchequer and Conservative leader; on Smuts' left is the Liberal prime minister, Lloyd George. Third from the right is Arthur Balfour, the former prime minister; fourth from the right is Sir George Perley and behind him is Lord Curzon, the foreign sec-retary. Barely visible over Curzon's left shoulder is Leopold Amery, the assistant secretary of both the war cabinet and the imperial war cabinet.

and Tupper had not lived long enough to see it, but the resolution stated, albeit in general terms, what they, in varying ways and over many decades had striven to produce. During the years ahead, frequent reference would be made to Resolution IX, but like much else produced by committees, it was a clever compromise between those who urged imperial federation and those who sought greater autonomy within the Empire.

while thoroughly preserving all existing powers of self-government and complete control of domestic affairs, [relations] should be based upon a full recognition of the Dominions as autonomous nations of an Imperial Commonwealth, and of India as an important portion of the same, should recognize the right of the Dominions and India to an adequate voice in foreign policy and in foreign relations, and should provide effective arrangements for continuous consultation in all important matters of common Imperial concern, and for such necessary concerted action, founded on consultation, as the several Governments may determine.[44]

A postwar imperial conference would be especially convened to put flesh on Resolution IX, to square somehow the concept of autonomous nations with a coherent Empire. It was further agreed that the Imperial War Cabinet would gather again within a year and, following the end of the war, an Imperial Cabinet would meet annually.

In the midst of these high policy discussions, Borden, supported by Perley, did not fail to raise a question familiar to Tupper in particular. Arthur Meighen, the solicitor general, had already protested to Lloyd George about the embargo on the import of live cattle from Canada. Borden's oral protests received a satisfactory, if a shade temporizing, response from the president of the board of agriculture. He assured Borden – in words that Tupper might have used – that "We do not believe that there is now or has been, for a good many years past, the slightest ground to exclude Canadian cattle on the score of disease." Unfortunately, wartime demands precluded shipping being assigned to the cattle trade, so the embargo could be lifted only following the war. In September 1917, the Canadian government issued a white paper on the matter, carefully recording the commitment for postwar change made at the Imperial War Conference.

Borden returned to Ottawa in May 1917, recognizing that Canada's extraordinary war effort would falter if the hitherto unthinkable option of conscription were not soon addressed. The United States had finally entered the war, but its still small and partly conscripted army was ill-prepared for the horrors of trench warfare. The long-suffering French army was shaken by mutiny. On the eastern front, the success of the Bolsheviks in overthrowing the tsarist regime and reaching a separate peace with Germany were deeply worrying, opening the way for the transfer of German divisions from the eastern to the western front. In Canada, the volunteer rate had so declined that reinforcements had dropped below the casualty rate, raising the profoundly disturbing prospect that the CEF could not be maintained at strength. An army of a half million was all that could possibly be raised by volunteering, but even that astounding total was increasingly seen as inadequate, given the casualties in the seemingly endless war of attrition, of futile attack and counter-attack over a few yards of mud. Simple extrapolation as well as the evidence that Borden had gathered from several Canadian officers and British leaders as well as from Perley during his visit to London in March–May 1917 had led him to the conclusion that, strain as it might to encourage volunteers, Ottawa would be forced to impose conscription. Borden had declared in 1914 that "there will not be compulsion or conscription," but as early as the second day of 1916, he had written to his former law partner, Charles Hibbert Tupper:

We have more than two and a half millions of French Canadians ... and I realize that the feeling between them and the English-speaking people is intensely bitter at present. The vision of the French Canadian is very limited. He is not well informed and he is in a condition of extreme exasperation by reason of fancied wrongs supposed to be inflicted upon the compatriots in other provinces, especially Ontario. It may be necessary to resort to compulsion. I hope not, but if the necessity arises, I shall not hesitate to act accordingly.[45]

A system of manpower registration devised by R.B. Bennett, as director of the National Service Board, was no more successful than various public campaigns and incessant local exhortations in generating volunteers. Borden soon found that the debate about compulsory military service would be increasingly marked by emotion, misgiving, and strife:

In all my experience I never encountered so extraordinary a political atmosphere as that which prevailed ... The varying phases of patriotic sentiment and fervour, of racial prejudice and animosity, the rumours and counter-rumours often finding credence although wholly absurd, the alternation of hesitation and distrust with frankness and confidence, the advances and recessions in the loosening or rending of party affiliations, the lack of balance and comprehension and the fluctuating moods affecting the attitude of outstanding figures, created a political kaleidoscope which even one who was in the midst of all the turmoil finds it difficult to recall in some of its constantly changing features.[46]

One specific prospect was only too evident: the imposition of compulsory military service could tear apart the very fabric of Confederation, destroying the work of all those who during the past fifty years had fostered concord between French and English Canadians.

Borden, as convinced as Perley that compulsory service was unavoidable if the CEF were to have essential reinforcements, introduced the Military Service bill on 11 June 1917, more than a year after Asquith had reluctantly introduced his controversial Military Service Act (the first in Britain). Borden had earlier asked Perley to consult urgently constitutional authorities in London about the acceptability of an extended parliamentary term in wartime, but in the end he decided instead upon an Unionist government of Conservatives and pro-conscription Liberals which would adopt the necessary legislation and then seek its popular endorsement in a wartime general election. Perley was dismayed: "It seems to me unthinkable as the energies of everyone are needed to assist in winning it [the war], and spending a lot of time on Party strife would be most unfortunate."[47] He questioned the wisdom of an election that would deeply divide Canada, advice that could not have been welcome to Borden who, beset as he continued to be by a myriad of conflicting pressures, had already determined upon his perilous electoral course.* The Union government would put through its Military Service Act and immediately thereafter call a general election to win endorsement for its action.

Quite unrealistically, the prime minister hoped that somehow even the leader of the opposition might be induced to join a coalition government.† When Laurier declined (Borden believing that he feared being outflanked in Quebec by the implacable Bourassa and his nationalists), the prime minister turned to western Liberals, some of whom, however, also proved to be stubbornly unenthusiastic about a pro-conscriptionist government. With Australia also in continuing turmoil over proposals for conscription, having rejected compulsory service in a referendum in October 1916, rumours appeared in the press that, during recent meetings of the imperial war cabinet, Canada and Australia had been urged to impose conscription, unfounded rumours which Perley asked Long, the colonial secretary, to join Ottawa in denying. Eventually an exhausted and frequently ill Borden concluded that someone else might do better as prime minister to win support for what he now regarded as unavoidable: compulsory

---

* In a 1917 Christmas message, issued a week after the election, Perley included a passage that reflected his concerns: "There is no racial division in the army. May there be none in Canada itself. Major Papineau, while leading his battalion at Passchendaele, was a splendid example, one of many of what French-Canada can do."

† The Ottawa journalist Grattan O'Leary, in *Recollections of People, Press and Politics* (Toronto, 1977), was convinced that Mackenzie King "offered himself for Sir Robert Borden's Union Government in 1917 and was turned down. The story infuriated King all through his political life, and he went to great lengths to lay it by the heels, probably on account of its absolute truth. I had the story from Meighen himself and there is no doubt whatever that King offered his services to Borden in 1917" (aee also MacFarlane, *Lapointe*, 22–3.)

military service. However, since Foster declined Borden's soundings to succeed him, the prime minister soldiered on through one of the most difficult passages in Canadian parliamentary history. The bitterness of the debate over the Military Service Act was greater than even that of the naval bills, but it finally received royal assent on 29 August 1917. A Union government of pro-conscriptionist Conservatives and Liberals was formed in October. The writ was issued for a general election in December.

Borden, having pledged to the CEF that it would receive the reinforcements that it would require, was determined to pull out all stops to win the election. The vote of the overseas soldiers was regarded as central to the government's policy. The Military Voters Act contributed to decidedly unorthodox if not fraudulent electoral practices, including directing votes of soldiers ignorant of their home constituencies to those where Conservative candidates especially needed them. Certainly the overseas soldiers' vote itself was not in doubt, with Lester Pearson writing home about opponents of conscription as treasonous, "detestable ... [giving Canada] a bad name."[48] The Liberal overseas campaign was to have received a much-needed contribution of $25,000 from Peter Larkin, the Toronto tea merchant, but with the inclusion of pro-conscriptionist Liberals in Borden's pre-election Unionist government, the offer faded away.

As the electoral campaign overseas gathered momentum, however, that arch-Liberal and Strathcona's nemesis, W.T.R. Preston, surfaced yet again, this time as the official and highly vocal Liberal scrutineer of the soldiers' vote in Britain (an appointment provided for in the Military Voters' Act), alleging that "In the office of the High Commissioner ... the constituencies were carefully gone over. Instructions came by letter and cable from the Cabinet ... telling the number of fraudulent votes which must be allotted to ensure the return of the Government candidates in their respective constituencies."[49] Perley remained uneasy about several methods to win the overseas vote, telling the prime minister that he hoped that "we can manage in such a way as to avoid serious criticism," a cautious approach that probably did not much recommend itself to the hard-pressed Borden.[50]

The election of 17 December 1917 was a victory for Borden in English-speaking Canada, but a massive rejection in Quebec. By his own decision, Perley had not been a candidate. Foster had reported to Borden during the summer of 1916, when he was briefly in charge of the High Commission, that he had found that their long-time colleague had become "so immersed in the details of his office [that] he lacked the common touch needed in times of emotion and stress." Borden, in his *Memoirs*, picked up

Foster's criticisms (sounding also a little like the *Maclean's* correspondent of 1915):

From time to time during my sojourn in England I listened to complaints as to Sir George Perley who was described as cold, immersed in the details of his office, and lacking in the human touch, which is so essential in periods when people are stirred with a deep emotion. No one could doubt his fine ability, his high ideals, and his intense earnestness, but undoubtedly he was somewhat mechanical and did not do himself justice. On many occasions I urged him to secure at least two diplomatic and resourceful assistants who would meet callers; I urged him also to occupy some of his time in visiting hospitals and thus to correct the unfortunate impression that he was cold and unapproachable and not in touch with conditions.[*] Further, I urged him to engage an active, confidential man who would keep him acquainted with the outlook of the general public, gain valuable information as to possible defects in administration and keep him more closely in touch with actual conditions as they presented themselves to onlookers. My advice, however, did not produce any marked effect; and during this visit and that in the following year, I was forced to listen to criticism which did scant justice to the fine service which he was rendering to our country and to the Empire.[51]

Written a score or more years after the event, Borden's strictures portray Perley as naive. What prompted the prime minister to be quite so condign in his judgment is unclear. Certainly his attitude had changed from his enthusiasms of 1914–15 to coolness and even criticism.

Several facts of Perley's unhappy situation in 1917 can be simply stated. He would not be a candidate in Argenteuil in the 1917 khaki election, knowing that he would almost certainly be defeated, given that a clear

---

* Some would have regarded Borden's strictures of Perley as an example of the pot calling the kettle black. "Stiff," "withdrawn" are but two of the more familiar adjectives applied to Borden himself even by some of his admirers. In any case, Borden's criticism of Perley certainly did not apply to Lady Perley, who worked tirelessly for various charities and for the welfare of Canadian soldiers. With her husband, she continued to entertain visiting Canadians even during the worst periods of the war, including such notable eccentrics as Joe Boyle "of Yukon fame" upon his return to London from succouring the delighted Queen Marie of Romania, Victoria's granddaughter. A notable contributor to Lady Perley's charities along with Beaverbrook was James Rothschild, a French citizen whom Perley arranged to be commissioned in the Canadian army. One of Perley's kindnesses was to seek help for a destitute niece of Tupper who was barely surviving on thirty-five shillings a week, working in the Canadian army pay office in London.

majority of his constituents were strongly opposed to compulsory service. Having concluded, quite realistically, that he could not hold his constituency, he discussed his dilemma with Borden during his mid-1916 visit to Ottawa and later confirmed to him that he would not carry the Unionist banner in his Quebec constituency.

Borden, in the greatest crisis of his political life and deeply motivated by what he regarded as the justness of the war, may have seen Perley's decision as abandonment when he needed all the support that he could muster, especially in Quebec. However, in forming his Union government, he had many more place-seekers, both Liberal and Conservative, than he had cabinet places. In fact, so many were the regional and partisan demands that in August the prime minister had invited the resignation of Foster by offering him the high commissionership. It is unrecorded what the prime minister may have had in mind – if anything – for Perley if Foster had accepted, but it is clear that relations between the two old friends were no longer what they had once been.

By the end of 1917, Perley was no longer a cabinet minister. Much later Borden wrote, "When I formed the Union Government in 1917, Perley was not included in its membership and was appointed High Commissioner. He realized then that he had been under complete misapprehension as to the importance of his former position." Nevertheless Perley continued to recommend that the office of high commissioner should be a cabinet post. Cabinet minister or not, he also urged upon Borden that, despite the British preference to have Dominion ministers sitting in the imperial war cabinet, he could, as high commissioner, be the Canadian representative.* In Perley's mind, the decision to have Dominion participation in the imperial war cabinet should lead naturally to an invitation to the Dominions to designate a minister to join in meetings of the smaller British war cabinet itself. For Perley, wartime pressures had created an opportunity

* In 1926 Borden managed to deliver a long lecture on "Canada in the War" without once mentioning his first minister of overseas military forces (text in *Canada in the Commonwealth*, Oxford, 1929). Perley did not stand in the election of 1921, but he was re-elected in Argenteuil in 1925, 1930 and 1935. He was acting minister of public works and acting secretary of state in Meighen's short-lived government of 1926. In R.B. Bennett's government of 1930–5 he was again a minister without portfolio, frequently acting for the prime minister in his absences and attending, with Brigadier-General A.G.L. McNaughton and Colonel H.D.G. Crerar, the 1932–4 Disarmament Conference and sessions of the League of Nations in Geneva. Perley died on 3 January 1938 and Lady Perley ten years later, on 8 February 1948. Bennett, wanting to keep the Department of External Affairs under his direct control, decided to retain the portfolio himself.

for Canada. "We might have gone on for a generation without such an important development ... [which now] may become permanent." Again he recalled for Borden that he had several times urged a cabinet minister should be

at the head of the High Commissioner's Office and all other Canadian activities over here in peacetime ... The intention of Sir John Macdonald and Sir Charles Tupper in establishing the High Commissionership was undoubtedly that the holder of the office should be in effect the Canadian Government's Plenipotentiary in all matters ... In any case the Minister authorized to attend Imperial Cabinet meetings regularly and the High Commissioner should be one and the same person ... my experience has shown me that it would strengthen the position of the Dominions ... if each of them always had a member of the Government over here. The best way to bring this about would be to change the status of the High Commissioner for this purpose.[52]

Before Borden could have received Perley's letter (although he did receive a brief cable from Perley urging delay until his letter arrived), the prime minister had designated Sir Edward Kemp, who had been Hughes's successor as minister of militia and was now Perley's successor as minister of overseas military forces; he and not Perley would represent Canada in meetings of the British War Cabinet. In so doing, Borden had in effect rejected Perley's proposal to have as high commissioner a member of the Canadian cabinet sitting in the British cabinet. It was not much consolation, but Perley at least remained in Bonar Law's mind the central Canadian in Britain. He told the House of Commons on 16 November 1917, "Sir George Perley's powers included everything connected with the ... Canadians, and also consultation with His Majesty's Government regarding the best methods of employing the Canadian Forces." Borden, however, remained convinced that if Perley had been so eager to continue as a minister and high commissioner concurrently, he should first have fought the good fight for conscription by standing for re-election, however forlorn the prospect.

Borden became convinced a high commissioner was needed not only in London but in Washington. In mid-October 1917, six months after the entry of the United States into the war, Borden cabled Perley, "a special Canadian representative at Washington should be immediately appointed ... The multiplicity of departments and commissions at Washington leads to a disastrous delay if negotiations are conducted through the [British] Embassy which is overwhelmed with a multitude of important matters not directly concerning Canada. I propose therefore to appoint Hazen and to give him the designation of High Commissioner. I shall be glad to receive immediately any observations of the Colonial Secretary."[53]

Long countered Borden's idea with a proposal that a minister (i.e., a diplomatic minister) should instead be attached to the British Embassy: "any political unit can have only one Embassy ... at a foreign capital ... The Prime Minister's proposal ... seemed to me to be incompatible with the unity of the British Empire in its relations with a foreign State. If such a step were taken in respect of Canada, it would almost certainly be followed in regard to other Dominions and the resultant position would ... be equivalent to a breakup of the Empire as a present constituted."[54] He added confidently to Perley that he was "convinced that Borden would scout any action likely to produce such a result." Long had so worked himself up over the possible appointment that he had also cabled the governor general, asking him to inform Borden that the idea appeared "to raise a grave constitutional issues ... it will call for the most serious consideration by the [British] Cabinet."[55]

Rather than delay the appointment in order to settle first the constitutional niceties which Long found so unsettling, Borden simply adopted the precedent of the British themselves and appointed a Canadian "War Mission" independent of the British embassy, yet from its very title it was clear that it was for the duration of the war only. Lloyd Harris of the affluent farm machinery family of Brantford (where he had been a Conservative member of Parliament and a fellow director of Massey-Harris with Vincent Massey) opened the office in February 1918, an appointment "not in any way incompatible with the unity of the British Commonwealth in its relations with a foreign state," Borden adding privately that it was "in effect though not in form a diplomatic mission."[56] Appearances had certainly been saved, with the designation of Harris not unlike the informal assignment of Sir John Rose to London fifty years before.

An earlier Canadian presence in Washington might have been achieved if Borden in early 1919 had accepted Lloyd George's invitation to be British ambassador to the United States (the same appointment that John A. Macdonald had been offered three decades before). Upon declining, Borden did accept the formula whereby the minister (i.e., the second-in-command) at the British embassy would be a Canadian, but even this flexible response to British misgivings about more direct representation came to grief over a dispute about precedence (a subject dear to professional diplomatists). The question remained suspended throughout the terms of Borden and his successor, Arthur Meighen, and was only resolved by

Mackenzie King in 1927 with the appointment of Vincent Massey as the first Canadian minister to the United States.

Borden made a third wartime crossing to Britain and France at the end of May 1918, in part to attend meetings of the imperial war cabinet. The deeply divisive compulsory military service act now in place, the first conscripts had been called up in January. The resultant fissures in Canadian society were to persist for decades to come, but in the short term the Unionist government was firmly in office. Borden arrived in London when the Germans, as feared, were transferring divisions from the eastern to the western front, freed by their separate peace with the Bolsheviks. In addition to ensuring that Borden saw Beaverbrook (recently named minister of information), Perley arranged meetings with Lloyd George at which they shared their frustrations after almost four years of carnage, 1917 having been even worse than 1916.

From 11 June 1918 Borden attended the frequent meetings of the deeply troubled Imperial War Cabinet. Having listened carefully to Perley and Currie (in London from the front), and being determined that the futile slaughter of 1917 would not be repeated, he did "not mince matters" in his initial statement to the Imperial War Cabinet about the continuing "lack of organization, lack of system, lack of preparation, lack of foresight and incompetent leadership."[57] Borden's invective about "the incompetency, disorganization and confusion at the Front," repeated almost daily, reflected his anger and frustration which he had first vented three years before: "We came over to fight in earnest; and Canada will fight it out to the end. But earnestness must be expressed in organization, foresight and preparation. Let the past bury its dead, but for God's sake let us get down to earnest endeavour."[58] But neither Lloyd George nor he seemed able to make much headway against obdurate generals who, lacking any better idea, had convinced themselves that the unspeakable war of attrition must continue unabated until Germany had finally been bludgeoned into unconditional surrender.

In mid-July Borden reported to his colleagues in Ottawa about how Lloyd George had

for eight months ... been "boiling with impotent rage" against them [the high command]. He explained at great length their constant mistakes, their failure to fulfill expectations, and the unnecessary losses which their lack of foresight has occasioned. I asked him why he had not dismissed those responsible during the previous autumn; and he replied that he had endeavoured to do so but did not succeed in carrying the Cabinet; the high command had their affiliations and roots everywhere; and it was for the purpose of strengthening his hand in dealing with the situation that he had summoned the Dominion Ministers to the Imperial War Cabinet.[59]

To Lloyd George, Borden stated bluntly, "if ever there is a repetition of the battle of Passchendaele, not a Canadian soldier will leave the shores of Canada so long as the Canadian people entrust the government of their country to my hands."[60]

Opportunities for the Dominion premiers to concert together rapidly expanded, becoming much more than would have been conceivable even to the most progressive prewar imperialist. During the spring of 1917, Dominion premiers or ministers had attended variously meetings of the Imperial War Conference, the Imperial War Cabinet and even the British War Cabinet. At Lloyd George's own devising, there was added in 1918 a fourth opportunity: with the full agreement of the Dominions and of India, a premiers-only sub-committee of the Imperial War Cabinet was struck. Here under an innocuous-sounding name emerged what some imperialists had long sought: a true imperial council. This sub-committee of premiers, chaired by the secretary of state for war, was an incipient executive that would pronounce itself in ways that, at least in the press of wartime, resembled decisions. Here was a new entity moving beyond information and consultation into the novel world of imperial decision-making. If the war had not ended in November 1918 (the general staff had forecast its continuation to 1920), the practice would presumably have become entrenched, which, if chaired by the British prime minister and coupled with an imperial tariff preference, might in time have expressed a loose form of imperial federation.

Borden was gratified at this evolution in Dominion and Indian participation in the councils of Empire, but he recognized that a fundamental question remained of how consultation and coordination might best be conducted when the Dominion premiers were not themselves in London. On 23 July Billy Hughes, the Australian prime minister, vigorously reminded his colleagues that whenever the Imperial War Cabinet was not in session the Dominions would be left to "meander again through the indirect channels of the Colonial Office." Borden promptly weighed in:

the Dominions had come into the war voluntarily, as free nations of the Empire, because they believed it to be their duty. But the British Government could not call upon Canada to come into another war with regard to the causes of which she had had no voice ... Unless she could have that voice in the foreign relations of the Empire as a whole, she would before long have an independent voice in her own foreign affairs outside the Empire. At present the Imperial War Cabinet met for only two months of the year. It was essential there should be means of constant consultation.[61]

Two days later, Hughes noted that there were critics in Australia of imperial "entanglements" arising from consultation. Borden responded that "a similar view was also held in certain sections in Canada. Sir W. Laurier had always taken up that attitude. He himself had disagreed. He would himself sooner go out of the Empire altogether than adopt this attitude. If he stayed in the Empire it was on condition that he had a voice in the conduct of its affairs."

The imperial war cabinet thereupon concluded that "each Dominion [and India] would have the right to nominate a visiting or resident Minister in London to be a member of the Imperial War Cabinet." Borden continued to ponder the yet larger question of what permanent process there should be for imperial consultation in the postwar world. He speculated to Lloyd George that the British prime minister should double as "a Secretary of State for Inter-Imperial Affairs (Dominions)." Leopold Amery, the assistant secretary to the Imperial War Cabinet, subsequently placed Borden's specific suggestion in the context of a much broader proposal for postwar imperial relations. Amery knew well that the British prime minister, hard pressed as he was, could not also assume ministerial responsibility for relations with the Dominions. There would need to be a separate secretary of state for imperial affairs (an "Imperial Secretary" distinct from the foreign secretary). However, the Imperial War Cabinet noted only vaguely and inconclusively that, in light of the developments which had taken place in the relations between the United Kingdom and the Dominions, new machinery would need to be created for postwar imperial consultation and cooperation.

Pending postwar conclusions, Borden made his dispositions for continuing Canadian representation in the Imperial War Cabinet, but he did it in a curiously offhand way. Three months before the end of the war he wrote to Lloyd George that "At present I do not propose to appoint a resident [cabinet] minister [in London] empowered to act as a regular member of the Imperial War Cabinet [but] Sir Edward Kemp ... will be glad to attend." In a second telegram he added inconsequentially that Perley also "would be prepared to attend."[62]

Perley's involvement in the prime minister's evolving imperial thinking included opposition to Borden's wartime conviction that the "opportunity of bringing these [West Indies] Islands into Confederation is [today] more favourable than it ever will be in the future."[63] Borden cabled Perley in June 1916 asking him to explore with Foster, then in London, how the political union of Canada and the British West Indies, Bermuda, the Bahamas, British Guiana, and British Honduras (joining a total of 2.3 million people with Canada's 11.5 million) might best be accomplished and to seek from Bonar Law, then colonial secretary, Britain's reaction (there was no suggestion that anyone in the Caribbean itself should be consulted). In Borden's view, the benefits for Canada would be several. "The responsibilities of governing subject races would probably exercise a broadening influence upon our people as the Dominion thus constituted would closely resemble in its problems and its duties the Empire as a whole."[64] Commercial benefits for both Canada and the British West Indies would also flow from the expanded confederation, as would recognition that, once and for all, Canada needed a navy. Even more bizarrely, Borden "urged the British Government to consider whether it would not, by the surrender [to the United States] of territories elsewhere, e.g., British Honduras or some other [sic] West Indian possession, persuade the United States to surrender to Canada part or the whole of the Alaska panhandle." Law's typically trenchant reaction to Borden's thinking was not encouraging: "this time of war is hardly propitious for a matter of that kind."

Perley, in transmitting Law's dismissive reaction, was himself muted, anticipating that what Borden had called "subject races" would, as part of Canada, seek more rights than they had under British colonial rule, specifically the right to vote (which Borden had not even contemplated). Clearly sceptical of the whole idea, Perley said, "I see serious difficulties in connection with the franchise," tactfully adding, "Certainly this is a most important matter, and one which will need great consideration – probably more than you can find time to give it under the present press of work."[65] In preparing for the Imperial War Cabinet and the Imperial War Conference in early 1917, Borden nevertheless listed Confederation with Newfoundland and the West Indies as one of his agenda priorities. Accordingly, in Curzon's sub-committee dealing with the territorial demands that Britain and the Dominions might make as part of a peace settlement, Hazen, always with the interests of Atlantic Canada at heart, proposed that Canada should assume control of the British West Indies, a suggestion that was coolly received by officials of the Colonial Office, although warmly endorsed by Milner, the colonial secretary, who saw it as another way of pulling the Dominions together through a sharing of British responsibility for an over-stretched Empire.

More than a year later, in June 1918, as the final German advance on the western front ground to a halt, the question of the British West Indies entering Confederation was raised again, this time by the British. Amery was charged with preparing a memorandum on "The Future of the Imperial Cabinet System." Given his prewar enthusiasm for imperial federation as a member of the Round Table movement of progressive imperialists, he not surprisingly interpreted his mandate so broadly that he offered a blueprint for a commonwealth of nations that, *inter alia*, would, "as has often been suggested," see Canada take "responsibility for the administration of the West Indies," a move simultaneously urged by an anonymous correspondent in *The Times* (possibly Amery himself, a former *Times* journalist). In sending Borden a copy of his lengthy memorandum, Amery knew his man. He urged him to consider how the various components of the enlarged confederation would benefit: "Canada would find capital and energy for the development of the West Indies much more readily if they were federated with herself." Further, if Canada and the West Indies were to merge, Newfoundland might also be brought more readily in "and even, if you liked to have them thrown in, the Falkland Islands."[66] Borden responded promptly but briefly that "The matter is one deserving of much consideration ... it has already been discussed with the Prime Minister of the United Kingdom." Borden's reference here is to a conversation with Lloyd George in August 1918 about which he had noted succinctly in his diary: "He suggested that we should take over the West Indies and I acquiesced."[67]

At the Paris peace conference itself, the British West Indies were to surface yet again. Francis Keefer, member of Parliament for Port Arthur-Kenora and Borden's parliamentary under-secretary of state for external affairs, wrote to him from Ottawa on 30 November 1918, as the conference preparations were gathering their uncertain momentum. He advocated that Canada urgently consider incorporating the British West Indies, partly to head off what was perceived as a growing movement among American imperialists to annex the remainder of the Caribbean (having already seized Puerto Rico and retained a naval base in Cuba following the Spanish-American War, purchased the Virgin Islands from Denmark and effectively acquired Panama from Colombia). Borden responded enthusiastically on New Year's Day 1919 that Lloyd George was sympathetic, having proposed that Canada should thereby "share in the direct responsibility for the Empire." Keefer had noted that "there seems to be only one serious problem for careful consideration, and that is, the negro question as regards representation in the Canadian Confederacy."[68] Borden acknowledged "The difficulty of dealing with the coloured population who would probably be more restless under Canadian than under British control and would desire and perhaps insist upon representation in Parliament. As Canadian negroes are entitled to the franchise, West Indian negroes would consider themselves equally entitled." He concluded, nevertheless, that "I am favourable to the proposal."[69]

Perley, on the other hand, remained sceptical. Perhaps in part to meet the prime minister's acquisitive mood, he proposed instead that Canada "acquire" Greenland from Denmark. Greenland would make an admirable wireless relay station and, more imaginably, in time a useful refuelling station for transatlantic flights. Nothing, however, came from the high commissioner's suggestion, given Denmark's known opposition. The several proposals for acquisition of the whole of the British West Indies, Bermuda, the Bahamas, British Honduras, British Guiana, and the Falkland Islands also gradually faded away. Amidst the myriad priorities of the peace conference, such an imperial fantasy had no real priority. Certainly Perley had no intention of pushing it. Possibly Borden was in the end deterred more by President Wilson's declared opposition to territorial acquisition as part of the peace terms or even by the opposition of the United Fruit Company to the introduction of free-market disciplines into the Caribbean. Certainly Lloyd George erroneously believed that the United States had decisively influenced Borden's thinking. "Sir Robert Borden was deeply imbued with the American prejudice against the government of extraneous possessions and peoples which did not form an integral part of their union. He therefore gave no encouragement to my suggestion, and I dropped it." All that remained was a renewed quest in 1920 for a revised commercial agreement with the British West Indies, an improved steamer service, and a sentimental memory in the minds of some of what might possibly have been.

Arthur Meighen, minister of the interior, was among those accompanying Borden to London in June 1918. His presence, however, was not directly related to issues of war or peace. He was to tackle the contentious question of what was to become of the Grand Trunk Pacific Railway, a subsidiary of the British-controlled Grand Trunk. During the first decade of the century, railway building had reached a wholly unrealistic pace. In addition to the CPR, both the transcontinental Grand Trunk Pacific and the Canadian Northern had by 1914 reached Vancouver, giving Canada three lines where one or at the most two would have sufficed. Borden, having watched Laurier provide expensive concessions to the two newer lines, concluded that no government formed by him would provide additional funds for railways. The chronic financial problems of the Grand Trunk and its Grand Trunk Pacific project were, however, worsened by the wartime closure of the money markets of Europe, the necessary concentration of Canadian finances on the demands of war, and the freezing of freight rates. Nationalization of both the Grand Trunk Pacific and the Canadian Northern had become, in Borden's mind, the only solution. As early as November 1915, he had written to Perley,

it is evident that the Grand Trunk management are thoroughly sick of the Grand Trunk Pacific and are intensely desirous of being rid of the whole enterprise upon the condition that their liabilities will be assumed by the Government ... We are also confronted with an even more difficult situation with regard to the Canadian Northern Railway. It has been a nightmare for several weeks passed, not so much by reason of the fate of the Canadian Northern itself as on account of our concern for the stability and reputation of a large financial institution [the Canadian Bank of Commerce] ... In view of all this it is important to have it appear that we were willing to stand by the Grand Trunk Pacific in the same way as we propose to stand by the Canadian Northern Railway and of course you understand that our desire in that regard is chiefly concerned with the financial stability to which I have alluded, the loss of which would be attended with the gravest consequences.[70]

The bankrupt Canadian Northern was soon nationalized but given the hostility of its directors, the problem of the Grand Trunk Pacific remained. In January 1918 Perley explored with the GTR chairman, who had ill-advisedly declined Borden's initial offer, how best the government could take over the line. Perley was acting upon a request from Borden to confirm that "Public opinion greatly exercised by proposed increase of railway rates ... it seems highly probable that circumstances will compel us to take active steps towards nationalization of Canadian railways in the immediate future. Please take into consideration the terms upon which ... the Grand Trunk and Grand Trunk Pacific might be acquired by Government. Suggested basis of compensation is payment of annual sum to be distributed by Directors or some other authority constituted by shareholders."[71]

The following month Borden offered yet more detailed terms to the Grand Trunk, but the chairman again rejected the proposals, gratuitously adding that he did not want to embarrass the hard-pressed Canadian government in wartime. Through Perley, Meighen put a final offer to him. Again it was rejected. Perley, conscious of the likely adverse reaction in Britain to what some at least among the railway's many shareholders regarded as inadequate compensation for virtual confiscation, was cautious in his subsequent advice to Borden: "It will be wise to give some consideration to the position of the Grand Trunk shareholders and the feelings of financial institutions over here ... I favour trying to arrive at some compromise between your offer and theirs."[72]

The impasse dragged on for more than a year, well after the end of the war, Perley informing Borden in February 1919 that the CPR and the Grand Trunk were together examining a possible cooperative arrangement. In the end, however, no more came of that hoary idea than it had in Tupper's day. The government then stopped supporting the over-extended and unprofitable line, waiting until the Grand Trunk board finally recognized that it must accept Ottawa's offer, however inadequate it appeared to its unhappy shareholders. The sorry tale of the Grand Trunk, dating back seventy years to the involvement of Rose, Galt, Tupper, and Strathcona, finally ended in November 1919 when Borden and Meighen forced nationalization through Parliament. A majority on a subsequent arbitration board recommended in vain that holders of preferred shares should receive compensation, creating thereby a host of disgruntled British investors. One result was that during the postwar years Canadian offerings in the depleted London money market received a cool, if any, welcome.

With the sudden reversal of the German advance in the summer of 1918, there began the final victorious Allied offensive which was to become known as the "one hundred days." Soon the complex question of how best to repatriate restless Canadian soldiers would arise. At a camp near Liverpool they eventually rioted and inconsequentially murdered five of their comrades, presumably as a mindlessly violent expression of their frustration at not being repatriated more rapidly. Perley was petitioned by discontented soldiers and was in turn involved in the attempts to reassure the increasingly alienated British military about Canadian indiscipline some of which had racial overtones, centred on the Second (Coloured) Canadian Construction Company.

As the armistice approached, Perley's time was even more taken by the seemingly endless questions of what Canada should pay for the maintenance of its army in Britain and at the front: in short, how Canada should make good its statement at the beginning of the war that it would pay "the entire cost in every particular." Perley's financial negotiations with the War Office dragged on through 1918 and into 1919, complicated by the additional costs of sending more than four thousand Canadian soldiers to join in the Allied intervention in the Russian civil war during the winter of 1918–19. Borden's basic stance was that if Canada were to be fully consulted by the Allies, especially Britain, it would be in a position to decide whether to join in supporting the White Russian forces against the Bolshevik. Having decided that it should, Kemp, Perley's successor as minister of overseas military forces, joined in the arrangements for both infantry and gunners to sail to north Russia from Britain and to Siberia from Victoria, but again there arose the question of who should pay for what, lingering on into the term of Perley's successor.

With the end of the war nearing, Ottawa puzzled over where postwar markets would be found for its greatly expanded manufacturing as well as its farm industries. Three provincial premiers arrived in London to seek postwar customers both in Britain and on the continent (whose wartime purchases from Canada had been largely made by agencies in Britain). Their recommendation was for an expanded trade mission in London as well as trade commissioners in Liverpool, Bristol, Manchester, and Glasgow. Lloyd Harris, who for eight months had successfully headed the Canadian War Mission in Washington, was transferred to London in November 1918 to direct enhanced promotional activities. He was authorized to communicate direct with the prime minister as necessary, but was advised to "cooperate with, and request the assistance of, the High Commission." Backed by substantial credits, Harris and Perley worked well together for almost three years until the commission was terminated at the end of May 1921, less than a year before Perley himself returned to Canada.

Far less harmonious was the differing approach of Borden and his ministers temporarily in Europe and those who had remained in Ottawa regarding most matters of postwar trade policy and promotion. That governments would henceforth play a more active role was evident. In February 1919 Borden wired the cabinet from London that he and the ministers accompanying him had discussed the "advisability of offering complete reciprocal free trade to Australia, South Africa, New Zealand and Newfoundland ... I pointed out that we should be faced with the charge of discriminating against the United Kingdom, but it was urged in reply that already we gave [from 1897] a considerable preference to British products without any preference in return and that Great Britain could not reasonably expect our comparatively undeveloped [manufacturing] industries to compete with her own."[73] The ministers in Ottawa were not so sure. They rejected the idea of reciprocal free trade if it did not formally include Britain, believing that "we could not discriminate against United

Kingdom. If we did there would be continuous tariff agitation here in favour of extending arrangement to United Kingdom."[74]

Less successful in their postwar export promotion efforts were those who, including Perley, again pushed for Britain to lift its embargo on the import of Canadian live cattle. From February to August 1919 Perley supported officials from Ottawa in making representations to Lloyd George as well as every minister, senior official, or journalist who might possibly be induced to take an interest in the matter. All their efforts, however, were in vain. The undertaking made by Britain in 1917 to remove its ban following the end of the war was now withdrawn on the grounds that postwar farming conditions would prevent any such move. No longer did anyone contend that Canadian cattle were diseased. Now the reason for their continuing exclusion was the uncertain state of the domestic economy. Lord Lee, the president of the Board of Agriculture (soon to be the Ministry of Agriculture), went out of his way in November 1919 to be sympathetic, stating unequivocally in the House of Lords that "I doubt if there is any country in the world which has a more blameless record with regard to cattle disease [than Canada] ... we recognize that the embargo could not be justified on the ground that Canadian cattle if imported were likely to inject our herds in this country ... Sir Robert Borden was fully justified in stating at the Imperial Conference that there would be far more reason to exclude British cattle from Canada ... than there would be to exclude Canadian cattle from this country."[75] Nevertheless, the embargo would continue for all live cattle, whatever their source since it would be "difficult" to lift the embargo from one country and not from another. In any case, economic circumstances did not warrant change. Stanley Baldwin, then financial secretary of the Treasury, also attempted to explain the decision to Ottawa but, as in the case of Lee, without much success.

On New Year's Eve 1920, Perley wrote to Lee, seeking yet again the removal of the ban.* For his trouble, he was told simply that it would continue to be applied to all countries, although it was again recognized that

---

* Lord Lee of Farnham (1868–1947), who had become president of the Board of Agriculture in August 1919, was an artillery officer who had taught history, strategy, and tactics at the Royal Military College in Kingston, Ontario, before marrying an American heiress. In 1900, he was elected member of Parliament for Farnham and served as parliamentary secretary to the minister of munitions, David Lloyd George. Lee and his wife bequeathed their outstanding collection of English silver to the Royal Ontario Museum (and their house at Chequers as the country residence of the British prime minister).

Canadian cattle were free of disease. Perley concerted with Beaverbrook to have a statement that had been made in the House of Commons in Ottawa to be given prominence in the *Daily Express*. Concurrently, Perley confirmed to the clerk of the City of London that he had "repeatedly pressed and will continue to press upon the British Government" the inequity of the embargo. Although he could not accept the clerk's invitation to attend a public meeting at the Guildhall – it was, after all, British "domestic policy" – Perley did send a statement. Despite the British wartime assurances "that the embargo ... would be raised at the end of the war ... this has ... not yet been done." If Canadian cattle were allowed free entry, "the nearer we will get to the very desirable goal of making the Empire self-sustaining." However, none of this changed the government's decision. A frustrated Perley had to acknowledge at the end of his term that this perennial problem, dating back to Galt, would remain for his successor.

With debate about the nature of the postwar world intensifying and the recognition growing that governments would play a larger part in the economy and society than hitherto, there remained unanswered the urgent question of the role of the Dominions at the peace conference. Four years before, the colonial secretary had sent a message to Borden (through the governor general) "that it is the intention of His Majesty's Government to consult him most fully ... when the time to discuss possible terms of peace arrives."[76] British support for participation by the Dominions and India in the eventual peace negotiations solidified as the war wore on, partly to gain a greater voice for Britain, but the basic question had remained of what attitude the Allies, particularly the United States, would take to such enlarged British Empire participation.

A fortnight before the armistice, Lloyd George had urged Borden to embark at once "in order to participate in the deliberations which will determine the line to be taken at these conferences by the British Delegates."[77] Before embarking, Borden replied that "there is need of serious consideration as to representation of the Dominions in the peace negotiations ... Press and people take it for granted Canada will be represented at Peace Conference. I appreciate possible difficulties as to representation of Dominions, but I hope you will keep in mind that certainly a very unfortunate impression would be created and possible a dangerous feeling might be aroused if these difficulties are not overcome by some solution which will meet the national spirit of the Canadian people."[78] He would not cross the Atlantic "to take part in light comedy." Lloyd George, for his part, called a general election before travelling to Paris. His coalition government won a major victory, but only at the price of the Liberal prime minister becoming yet more dependent upon Conservative support.

Into the new year of 1919 the debate within the Imperial War Cabinet (which had moved to Paris intact, having transformed itself into the British Empire delegation) about representation of the Dominions and India spread into the larger meetings of the Allies themselves when the United States questioned the proposed numbers of Dominion representatives (despite the fact that Canada and Australia had each suffered more war dead than the United States). Amery knew well that something more than merely a question of representation was at play.

The extent to which the Dominions are given a really effective voice in the Peace settlement will determine their whole outlook on Imperial questions in future. If they consider that they have been treated in the full sense of the word as partners and have had an equal voice in the decision not merely of such questions as affect them locally but in the whole Peace settlement, they will be prepared to accept the idea of a single foreign policy for the British Commonwealth directed by the machinery of an Imperial Cabinet. If they feel that they have only been brought in as ornamental accessories ... a serious, possibly an irremediable blow will have been struck at the idea of Imperial Unity. There will be no breaking off. But there will be no attempt to treat the Imperial Cabinet as a serious instrument of Imperial policy; each Dominion will begin developing its own independent foreign policy; the centrifugal tendencies will, in fact, definitely get the upper hand ... The only really effective [policy] is to insist upon the direct representation of the Dominions and India in the British delegation at the Peace Conference.[79]

Eventually individual representation for the Dominions and India in plenary sessions was provided, thereby conferring upon them a greater degree of international recognition. Borden was gratified that the Dominions were eligible for the councils of the League of Nations and the International Labour Organization, but they also remained full partners in the single British Empire delegation, where the British shared with them information about sessions restricted to the Great Powers. Further, each of the "British Dominions beyond the Seas" signed for itself the harsh final treaty with Germany. While Perley was in London through most of 1919 attending, among other postwar commitments, meetings of the Imperial War Graves Commission, Borden, Foster, Doherty (minister of justice), and Sifton (minister of customs) formed the delegation at the Paris peace conference.

In June 1919 Doherty and Sifton signed the Treaty of Versailles (Borden having returned to Ottawa to mind the increasingly uncertain domestic political shop). Kemp signed the treaty with Austria, but every month between November 1919 and August 1920 (save January and March) Perley crossed from London to Paris to sign peace treaties with Bulgaria, Hungary, and Turkey or to attend a variety of other international meetings arising from the war (e.g., a conference on international air navigation). He was simultaneously the Canadian member of a committee "considering all claims ... to be submitted to the Reparation Committee at Paris" and was appointed to yet another agency intended to resolve one especially bothersome dislocation of the war: the Imperial Investigation Board on Shipping which attempted, without notable success, to decide how merchant shipping might be registered and allocated to benefit imperial trade. In Geneva he represented Canada in the International Labour Organization, "fixing the minimum age for admission of children to industrial employment" and attempting to limit the use of forced labour.

When all Dominions save Newfoundland became members of the League of Nations, all correspondence and documents were to be channelled through the High Commission. Borden was clear about what should be done:

It is most important that the status which has been secured for Canada ... should be maintained and that any proposal whether made through design, inattention or misconception, which might detract therefrom, should be resisted and rejected. It will be recalled that the effort to win this position has been prolonged, insistent and continuous ... In all this insistence upon due recognition of the nation-hood of the Dominions, Canada has led the way; and in most cases her representatives have made the fight without the active assistance from, although with the passive support of, the other Dominions. The decisions thus reached should make the course comparatively simple for the future; but it is necessary to bear in mind an inevitable tendency on the part of officials and sometimes Ministers to forget that the United Kingdom is not the only nation in the British Empire.[80]

In time, the commitment of the Conservative prime ministers, Borden, Meighen, and Bennett, to the League would be seen as greater than that of Mackenzie King, but in November 1920 Perley had reluctantly to inform the League that Canada declined to participate in a proposed collective effort intended "to put an end in shortest possible time to horrors of Armenian tragedy" instigated by the Turks. This led Perley to see an additional opening for his incessant advocacy of the high commissioner to be a cabinet minister: "while you wish [to] guard jealously Canada's separate status as in League, we must also find such plan by which nations [of the] Empire will as far as possible act together, present united front to rest world and consult together regarding important matters."[81] High commissioners, if cabinet ministers, were incomparably well equipped to do this.

The legal adviser to the Department of External Affairs, Loring Christie, concurred. He had been able to observe at first hand the workings of the High Commission, having accompanied Borden to the Imperial War Conferences in 1917 and 1918, to Versailles in 1919, and the first session of the League of Nations in 1920. He was with Borden in London in March-April 1920, following which he offered his observations about how the High Commission could help to overcome the deficiencies of a Department of External Affairs inadequately placed to do the job expected of it by a prime minister committed to Canada playing an enhanced international role. Christie urged that the high commissioner should be the representative to the League of Nations, with all communications channelled through him. Not only would this make Canada's participation more effective and imperial coordination more practicable, but "anything which increases the High Commissioner's responsibilities and influence in London is of distinct advantage to the Dominion Government." The colonial secretary, possibly prompted by Perley, was supportive to the legal adviser: "the Dominion Government should have some responsible [cabinet] minister or representative resident in London with whom the Government there might consult continuously on foreign affairs and who might keep his own Government informed." Borden did not respond.

In a long memorandum of 11 May 1920, Christie acknowledged at the outset that "It was no part of my mission to London to examine or report upon the High Commissioner's Office," but he then proceeded to review various factors inhibiting the high commissioner.

The High Commissioner is shown the greater part of the correspondence [between the two governments], but except rarely he is not brought into active participation in the matters dealt with ...

Another factor which perhaps militates against the effectiveness of the Office is the practice of conducting the most important discussions through visits of members of the Government to London.

Another condition limiting the High Commissioner is surely the existence in London of a number of separate offices representing Departments in Ottawa and having no very direct or definite relations to the High Commissioner. It would seem that these offices have been allowed to grow up in past years in response to the needs of the different Departments, but without much attention to the needs of the Government as a whole or to the principles which should govern a properly organized system of representation in London. The existence of these separate offices must result in a good deal of confusion in the minds of people who have dealings with them; it must often create difficulties in settling questions; and there must be considerable overlapping of work. It must also have the effect of weakening the position of the High Commissioner in London, and this must mean for practical purposes the weakening of the whole Canadian machinery there; for what is subtracted from the High Commissioner is really not in practice added to the others ... no occupant of the office, whatever his ability or personality, could possibly measure up to the demands implied in the various criticism that one hears. Indeed ... given the conditions, the Office is doing about as well as could be reasonably expected of it.[82]

Perley was at least as aware of these problems as Christie. His solution to what Christie had called "the constitutional aspect" was to continue to press, always in vain, that a cabinet minister fill the office. Perley had reviewed with Borden the problem of the coordination of government departments and agencies as early as July 1914, recommending a consolidation of authority. But wartime demands and expansion of representation had coupled to ensure that he had to pass on to his successor some of the same administrative confusion which he himself had inherited from Strathcona.

Throughout his eight years in Britain, Perley had been at or near the centre of most major decisions about the size, nature, and command of the Canadian Expeditionary Force. In the case of a Canadian air force, he had been instrumental in helping to set the stage for its immediate postwar creation. It was a Canadian navy which remained the most intractable problem. In the summer of 1918, as the end of the war approached, the Admiralty, responding to a request of the 1917 Imperial War Conference, recommended in vain to the Dominion premiers assembled in London contributions to a single postwar navy under a single command. Before the war, Borden had embraced the idea as an emergency measure, but with the end of the war he had come to see it as incompatible with Canada's postwar status. Instead, he advocated a Canadian navy, created from surplus ships of the Royal Navy. But even Borden's bargain-basement proposal was rejected by his own caucus. Preoccupied with postwar fiscal problems, real or imaginary, it would not sanction anything but the smallest expenditure on a navy. To realize any substance with that small expenditure, Perley had to ask the Admiralty to give to Canada two destroyers and a light cruiser. However, in the face of the refusal of Meighen when he came to office in mid-1920 to contemplate anything but the smallest naval expenditure and later still in light of King's deep-rooted suspicion of any imperial naval cooperation, the new Royal Canadian Navy soon relapsed into near oblivion.

In 1920 when Meighen succeeded Borden as prime minister, he sought to avoid doing anything that would be seen as disadvantageous to the Empire to which rhetorically at least he was so devoted. He was, however, even more determined to avoid any obligation for imperial naval defence, partly because that would involve expenditure which he knew that his caucus, fearful of postwar economic recession, would almost unanimously continue to oppose. Largely as a result of his convoluted opposition, four years of study by the Admiralty were ignored. So too was the fundamental question of the Australian Billy Hughes: "By what right would the Dominions discuss questions of foreign policy if they did not contribute to seapower, which was the basis of Empire?"

What was reflected in the approach of both postwar Ottawa and London to foreign affairs was ultimately an unwillingness to surrender any degree of national sovereignty to some sort of imperial entity. The Conservatives in Britain, who had come to dominate Lloyd George's coalition government, and the Conservatives in Canada who under Meighen had formed a fragile minority government, had both reached roughly the same conclusion, although for different reasons. For Curzon, the foreign secretary, there could be no imperial limitations on the freedom of the United Kingdom to pursue whatever foreign policy appeared to be in its interest. For Meighen, his own secretary of state for external affairs, the danger was that his minority government might be undermined by a combination of French-speaking Canadians opposed to what they might see as imperial commitments and those English-speaking Canadians who believed, at least in retrospect, that Canada had somehow been sucked into an essentially European war by anachronistic imperial entanglements. Additionally, Meighen was painfully aware that his vigorous support for conscription in 1917 had cost the Conservatives heavily in Quebec. If his party were to regain any ground there in the foreseeable future, it would certainly not be through a commitment to a common imperial foreign policy.

In November 1919 Perley had recommended to Borden that the special constitutional conference, mandated by Resolution IX, should be held in Ottawa in 1921 to "bring home to everyone the reality of our Empire."

Lloyd George endorsed the idea in principle, but suggested that it be a regular imperial conference, questioning whether it would yet be timely to hold the special constitutional conference given the press of postwar problems in national capitals. Unspoken was the real reason. Lloyd George was under pressure from his Conservative cabinet colleagues, including Curzon, to do nothing that would dilute the ultimate control of Britain over its foreign policy. Only the British Parliament could determine Britain's foreign policy, not the Dominions. For Meighen, however, there remained the legacy of his predecessor's leadership in the formulation of Resolution IX and his endorsement of Perley's recommendation that the constitutional conference be held in Ottawa. There then ensued an elaborate correspondence between Meighen and the colonial secretary, Milner, an arabesque reminiscent of two dogs warily circling each other, neither willing to make the first move, but both determined that, for quite different reasons, the constitutional conference should be postponed *sine die*.

Milner cautiously but unmistakably fired the first broadside, discouraging the idea of an early meeting. With a show of great reasonableness, his letter represents the definitive British retreat from Lloyd George's wartime support for a revised constitutional relationship among Britain, the Dominions and India and a major step toward the tacit rejection of Resolution IX and an imperial foreign policy, however defined (the degree to which Lloyd George, under Conservative pressure, had retreated was reflected in his statement: "The instrument of the foreign policy of the Empire is the British Foreign Office"). On a more positive note, Milner, recalling his experience in the Imperial War Cabinet, asked whether

something like the same machinery ... might not with advantage be resorted to, in order to keep up harmonious cooperation in more normal times? If so, then I think that a fairly early meeting of the "Imperial Cabinet", or whatever we like to call it, is urgently required, in order to give that system of cooperation a fair start.

What is urgently needed is a proper system of communication between Governments, not, as at present, between the Governments of the Dominions and a mere Department of the British Government. And such a system can only be set up by mutual agreement, after very thorough discussion between the heads of the several States.[83]

Borden, fearing in retirement that matters were drifting towards inaction, was decidedly unhappy at Milner's extrication of Britain from its wartime commitment to an early constitutional conference, declaring in a speech at the University of Toronto in October 1921, "The foreign policy of the Empire remains under the same direction and influence as before the War ... that is not what we intended ... when we took our stand in 1917; it is imperative that old conditions should not go on." On the other hand, Meighen, for his own domestic electoral reasons, including his great unpopularity in Quebec, fell into line with Milner's suggestion that the constitutional conference should be postponed to an indefinite date so as to allow a "greater opportunity for public discussion both in parliament and in the press." Only a regular imperial conference, not a special constitutional conference, was accordingly scheduled for June 1921, and it was to be held in London, not Ottawa.

Meighen, at the conference, delivered, in his prolix way, his understanding of the principles that should determine how an imperial council might define and monitor any concerted foreign policy. Having observed that "there exists no council or body responsible to the Dominions ... which can advise our common Sovereign in relation to foreign affairs," including the all-important League of Nations, Meighen proposed a three-point approach:

1. There should be regular, and so far as possible, continuous conferences between the responsible representatives of Britain and the self-governing Dominions and India with a view, among other things, of determining and clarifying the governing principles of our relations with foreign countries, and of seeking common counsel and advancing common interests thereupon.

2. That while in general final responsibility rests with the Ministry advising the King, such Ministry should, in formulating the principles upon which such advice is founded and in the application of those principles, have regard to the views of His Majesty's Privy Council in other Dominions and of the Representatives of India.

3. That as respects the determination of the Empire's foreign policy in spheres in which any Dominion is peculiarly concerned the view of that Dominion must be given a weight commensurate with the importance of the decision to that Dominion.

There ... is no body authorised as such to advise His Majesty in relation to foreign affairs except the United Kingdom Government ... the importance of His

Majesty's Government taking into account, and at times indeed depending upon, the special interest of the Dominion concerned, giving effect to the views of such Dominion, can scarcely be overstated.[84]

Three weeks later, Meighen, still at the imperial conference, was clearer about his opposition to an early constitutional conference: "I do not like the idea of advertising ahead that we contemplate constitutional changes. It has an unsettling effect in Canada ... The fact is that the British Empire is fundamentally a good thing; its people, on the whole, are of a more than ordinary measure of intelligence; they rise above the average of human intelligence ... The only thing ... that is of any practical urgency is that the right to have resident representation here be reasserted and agreed to."[85]

Charles Ballantyne, minister of marine and fisheries and of naval service, and now representative of Canada at the conference (Meighen having returned to Ottawa), urged that all high commissioners be cabinet ministers. Perley had strongly recommended to a receptive Meighen that he match his acceptance of postponement of the constitutional conference with support for the cabinet minister proposal. A formal debate about who was constitutionally responsible for what might thereby be avoided, but high commissioners could provide what Milner had identified as the need for "a proper system of communication between governments" and not between the Dominions and one department of the government of the United Kingdom. Perley was no doubt highly gratified when, beginning with words wonderfully reminiscent of Laurier,

Mr. Ballantyne said that he had very little to say except that the Canadians were a happy and contented people, proud of their own Dominion and proud of the British Empire. They did not desire any material change. Consequently he was not in favour of the proposed special Conference to discuss the Constitutional question. Canada already possessed full autonomous rights. Canada could ask for nothing more unless the silken cord that bound the Empire together was cut, and this was by no means to the will of Canada. In fact, Canada was perfectly satisfied with her autonomous rights ... He was, however, in favour of the establishment of a resident Minister ... He thought both the Canadian Parliament and the public would desire this, and if this were decided on he thought that the Dominions would have every right they could wish for at the present time. As regards foreign affairs, he himself had only been a Minister for about four years, and he felt the Government of the United Kingdom had done the right thing in consulting the Dominions. Often at the Cabinet he had heard read some telegram about Turkey, or perhaps some European matter, and he had always felt that it was very difficult for Canadians, so far removed from these matters, to offer any useful advice. Hence, his only definite suggestion was for a resident Minister.[86]

The conference carefully declared that "the policy of the British Empire could not be adequately representative of democratic opinion ... unless representatives of the Dominions and India were frequently associated with those of the United Kingdom in considering and determining the course to be pursued." But the framework to do so was no longer there. Lloyd George had abolished the British War Cabinet and reverted to the traditional cabinet structure, leaving no nucleus to develop the wartime collaboration of the Imperial War Cabinet (which Milner wanted to restore). The Colonial Office resumed its prewar responsibilities for communication with the Dominions as if nothing much had happened. The Foreign Office continued to take full responsibility for foreign policy as if it had never heard of Resolution IX. There emerged only the innovation of the provision to the Dominions of Foreign Office "prints" of notable diplomatic despatches (sent regularly to prime ministers with copies to high commissioners) and other policy related material. But for Perley, the conference had at least been gratifying in its endorsement of "the existing practice of direct communication between the Prime Ministers of the United Kingdom and the Dominions, as well as the right of the latter to nominate cabinet ministers to represent them in consultation with the Prime Minister of the United Kingdom."

In most other subjects before the conference, the concord was limited. Australia had pressed for an early conference to review the security of the Suez Canal in light of mounting Egyptian nationalism, but no real agreement was reached. What to do about the Anglo-Japanese alliance in face of United States hostility remained unresolved. Direct representation of the Dominions in foreign capitals was still controversial, although Meighen clearly proclaimed his intention to appoint a Canadian representative in the United States. The role of the Dominions in naval construction was to be considered only after the proposed conference on naval limitations in Washington. Reparations from Germany were reviewed without enthusiasm. In postwar emigration promotion, imperial cooperation was enthusiastically embraced by Australia, but again Canada was at best lukewarm. For the first time, Britain was willing to spend substantial funds for officially sponsored migration, including assisted passage to, and settlement in, the Dominions. These were not to be shared-cost schemes merely for ex-servicemen or destitute children: they would be open to all, but organized systematically. Perley, however, had been instructed by Meighen to proceed cautiously. Urban unemployment was worrisome; the prairie provinces did not want emigrants; the costs of assistance could be substantial. At the imperial conference itself, Meighen had been no more forthcoming. He viewed the proposed British programme with misgiving, but suggested nothing in its place. The Dominions finally agreed that the proposals of the State-Aided Empire Settlement Conference were "sound in principle," but only if they did not cost them anything.

One of Perley's final questions in London concerned Canada's sovereignty in the high Arctic, never fully accepted internationally. Strathcona in 1912–13 had recommended to a receptive Borden support for an expedition north of the Alaska-Canada border by the Manitoba-born Vilhjalmur Stefansson (by contrast, Strathcona had been unhelpful to Sir Robert Scott, refusing to intervene with the Hudson's Bay Company to release his first expedition ship *Discovery* for his second expedition to Antarctica). During the summer of 1920 Sir Ernest Shackleton, aware of Strathcona's financial support for Stefansson, had called upon Perley to discuss the idea for an expedition to the Beaufort Sea, "the last unknown sea of the world." According to Shackleton's notes, Perley assured him "of his sympathy with the plans of the Expedition and is communicating with his Government with a view to the Canadian Government giving a certain amount of financial assistance to the Expedition."[87] Eighteen months later, Shackleton was dead, his great venture into the Arctic no more than an unfulfilled dream. Meighen had informed Perley that the establishment of RCMP posts by the proposed expedition would become known to Denmark and the United States which did not recognize Canadian sovereignty in the high Arctic so that it might be better if the expedition were not mounted at all. He declined concurrently yet another request for funds from the ubiquitous Stefansson, again eager to travel through the Arctic.

Perley knew that, if press reports of a Liberal resurgence were to be believed, his eventful eight years in Britain were drawing to a close. The defeat on 6 December 1921 of Meighen's Conservatives by Mackenzie King's newly reunited Liberals brought into office a minority government based largely upon Quebec and dependent upon the support of T.A. Crerar's Progressive party from the west. Perley's long term in Britain had ended. During the following two months, the Perleys were guests of honour at farewell events across Britain, the indelibly Conservative high commissioner having submitted his resignation to the new Liberal government, effective 1 March 1922. With Meighen gone, Perley feared that the commitment to appoint cabinet ministers as high commissioners went with him. His years of advocacy had in principle finally achieved success, not with Borden but with Meighen. Victory was, however, brief. King was to reverse Meighen's undertaking. Still convinced that a cabinet minister should represent Canada, Perley sent a memorandum of 17 January 1922 to King, redolent of his July 1914 memorandum to Borden, adding that "to obtain the best results it can scarcely be denied that all official activities in the United Kingdom should be placed under one control ... that of the High Commissioner ... Canada would have more influence and ... there would be more probability of her wishes being carried out if all her activities come under the aegis of the High Commissioner."

In a final interview published in *The Times* of 20 January 1922, Perley repeated his dynamic concept of the British Commonwealth, ending with a peroration about the increasing influence of the United States in Canada and a plea for more British investment and more British emigrants: "we would rather see British people coming in than those from other countries. Every British settler who comes to the Dominion strengthens not only Canada, but the Empire as well."[88] A week later, on 27 January, *The Times* responded, extolling the great contribution that Perley had made during his eight years in Britain. Upon his arrival home, however, he was greeted by a rather more backhanded compliment in a *Toronto Star* editorial:

He has been too modest. In a private citizen, modesty is a virtue ... There is such a thing, however, as a man's personal modesty, his dislike of notoriety and the limelight, reacting unfavourably upon the cause or country he represents ... At public gatherings, for example, when high commissioners representing various dominions had seats on the platform, Perley never showed himself forward ... Australians and New Zealanders were not so reticent. They saw that they were in a spotlight. Taken on the whole, however, Perley's career in London has been an admirable one, and he returns to Canada with a reputation, already high, distinctly heightened.[89]

However reticent and self-effacing Perley may have been seen by some, in Canada he doggedly persisted in his public advocacy of ministerial status for the high commissioner. Joining with the colonial secretary who had been pressing since 1920 "the desirability of having a responsible Dominion representative resident in London [i.e., a cabinet minister]," Perley continued to recommend the step as a means of providing the essential underpinning for closer imperial consultation and co-ordination.

Undeterred by the well-known hostility of Mackenzie King to the suspected machinations of imperial centralists, Perley stated to the *Toronto Star* five months into the King's first government,

I feel strongly that some plan should be devised for more frequent and regular consultations between the prime ministers' conferences; otherwise we may have misunderstandings which could have been easily avoided. Is it possible to find a way by which each country can govern itself and yet they can all act together as regards foreign affairs? ... He did not believe that public opinion would approve or support the establishment of a Council of Empire. It was better to move slowly and let time and experience show us the wisest solution ... a resolution of the Imperial War Cabinet of 1918 which recommended the nomination of a dominion cabinet minister, either as a resident or visitor in London, to represent the prime minister of each dominion at meetings of the war cabinet. ... it would be satisfactory to have someone clothed with the authority of a cabinet minister ... the question of a high commissioner being a minister is only one of method. The main point was that there must be closer touch between the governments of the Empire if the Empire was to be made to work. He personally did not see how high commissioners could be given the greater authority which they needed, unless they are made members of governments they represent.[90]

King was having none of it.

CHAPTER SIX

Peter Larkin, 1922–1930

Mackenzie King was fully aware of how Laurier had manipulated Strathcona. He had himself dealt with the elderly high commissioner in a decidedly cavalier way. When King became both prime minister and secretary of state for external affairs in December 1921, he was determined to appoint to "the Old Land" (one of his favourite phrases) a personal friend who was malleable, someone who would give him no trouble. In Peter Charles Larkin, King had just the person. And in confirming the appointment, King was also able to reward a principal financial supporter of Laurier and himself, as well as of the national and provincial Liberal parties. George Wrong, the distinguished head of the Department of History at the University of Toronto, was, however, incredulous at what was in the offing. He wrote to the prime minister, "Larkin is a good citizen and a good fellow, but he is about as fit to represent Canada in London as he is to hold my post in the University. Do, do send to London a man of education who can hold his own in any circle there."[1]

But from King's peculiar point of view, the aging Larkin was an ideal choice, whatever his shortcomings in formal education or understanding of public policy. Larkin could not assist in the shaping of policy; he had never done so during his long years of support for the Liberal party and would not begin at the age of sixty-eight. An able businessman, an ardent partisan, and an effective fundraiser, Larkin had sat neither in a cabinet nor even in Parliament. He could not readily imagine from London what was in the minds of those in Ottawa; he had never worked or even lived there. He had long been close to partisan politics, but he had no personal experience of how public policy is eventually defined in the Prime Minister's Office or occasionally in cabinet or even in Parliament. He knew something of Britain, but mainly the imperial tea trade. He had visited London almost annually from 1896 and had served for two months as Canadian representative on the Imperial Trade Commission, but there is no evidence that on his frequent trips to Britain he had ever aspired to an interview with Tupper or Strathcona. That was all to the good in King's mind; certainly the prime minister did not want a strong-willed high commissioner making problems, especially any that might conceivably have adverse domestic political impact in Quebec.

Larkin was intimidated by the prime minister's invitation, having real doubts about his qualifications for what King had described to him as "the first and the highest position within the gift of the Government of our country." He lamented, "I was sixty-seven then [in fact, sixty-eight] and, instead of retiring gracefully to an easy life, I had taken on a job which I was both afraid of and perhaps incapable of performing."[2] In his candid self-doubt, Larkin was unique; no such misgivings assailed any other high commissioner. He was certainly incapable of offering policy analyses in light of either Canadian interests or the actions of the British government. He rarely made recommendations to the prime minister about imperial, foreign or domestic policy, generally sending him anodyne messages that were largely impressionistic or simply repetitive of King's own suspicions about perfidious Albion (especially a perfidious Conservative Albion). And King wanted nothing from him, including foreign policy advice. Under King, Canada largely disappeared from whatever presence it had on the immediate postwar imperial or even world stage, wallowing in much of the same unrealistic isolationism that had seized the United States. From his first months in office, "King began to take steps to dissociate his government from collective imperial responsibilities, and began also to make a critical distinction between imperial diplomacy as a whole and Canada's own particular external affairs, for which alone the Dominion would be accountable."[3]

Imperial relations were in a state of flux, with Resolution IX set aside by Milner and Meighen and with the idea of collective security in the League of Nations facing several challenges. In these circumstances, King had come to office convinced that Canadian unity demanded that the "centralists" – especially if Conservative – had to be watched with unceasing vigilance. Hardly less worrisome was the League, about which he could conceive nothing creative. In his view it was essentially an European institution, the United States Senate having rejected membership in November 1919. Article X of the League's covenant might, in the name of collective security, draw an unwary Canada into distant, incomprehensible conflicts, small or large, any of which could be deleterious to concord between French- and English-speaking Canadians. Larkin played back the prime minister's own thinking when he wrote to him in the aftermath of the Chanak imbroglio of September 1922, "When I see the miserable little struggles for petty personal triumph and [adding tactfully], except on the [part of the] British, the lack of ideals, I don't wonder the U.S. keeps out of the European menagerie."[4] For King, however, the most pressing challenge was, as always, domestic: to rebuild the Liberal party following the divisions left by the conscription debate of 1917, not to worry about a deeply unsettled Europe. Opposition to imperial cooperation and isolation from Europe's travails would play well in Quebec and to a degree in the west, where the Progressive party had temporarily usurped what King regarded as a rightful Liberal constituency.

King knew his high commissioner intimately, from the days when Larkin had been a major financial benefactor of Laurier and latterly of himself. In 1901 Larkin had taken a leading part in funding an annuity for Laurier, "which may relieve his mind from all anxieties ... [offered by] persons having no favours to expect from the Government."[5] In the elections of 1908, 1911, and 1917 he had contributed heavily to King's campaigns. Upon the defeat of the Liberals in the election of 1911, he had arranged for King to be offered the leadership of the Liberal party in Ontario at a "handsome salary" (which Larkin himself would have largely provided). In early 1919 he had written to Laurier urging the necessity of finding a safe seat for King, following his defeat in the "khaki election" of 1917. So well did King know Larkin that he had even idly contemplated in 1919 proposing marriage to his only daughter Aileen, on one of those recurring occasions when he assured himself that he must marry a rich young woman and then invariably so contrived matters that he never married anyone.*

Like many businessmen before and since, Larkin could not bring himself to be a parliamentary candidate (including in the 1917 election when the hard-pressed Laurier asked him to stand), pleading that he had to attend to his business, especially after his only son had enlisted in the army. Nevertheless, he remained throughout his life fascinated by politics. As late as 1925 he wrote King, "I do wish I were younger and had the ability, for I would certainly like nothing better in the world than to have a seat in Parliament and do my share."[6] Instead, Larkin, as the long-serving treasurer of the Reform Association of Ontario (later renamed the Ontario Liberal Association), lived politics vicariously, employing his

---

* Like Mackenzie King, Aileen Larkin (d. 1967) never married. In time she converted to Roman Catholicism and entered a convent for six weeks before discovering that she had no vocation. Earlier, King had considered as a possible wife Frances Howard, Strathcona's granddaughter, but nothing came of that fantasy either.

ample funds to open the way to personal association with Liberal leaders. Larkin had adored Laurier. Nothing had pleased him more than to have the leader of the opposition as his house guest in Rosedale in Toronto and never being more flattered than when told that he resembled his hero (which he did not). He did not have quite the same dog-like devotion to King, but King did at least represent himself as Laurier's anointed heir and that was enough for Larkin.

Following Lady Laurier's bequest of Laurier House in Ottawa as a residence for the leader of the Liberal party, Larkin met the new prime minister on 10 December 1921, four days after the narrow Liberal victory. Larkin confirmed that $40,0000 had been deposited in a bank account in Boston to restore and refurnish the now somewhat dilapidated house. The prime minister equally promptly offered Larkin the high commissioner-ship, stating in a letter of 2 February 1922 that in so doing he was imple-menting Laurier's pronouncement that "there is nothing too good for our friend Larkin."[7] Sir Lomer Gouin, recently premier of Quebec and soon-to-be federal minister of justice, had urged the merits of another candi-date, Sir Charles Gordon, vice-president of the Bank of Montreal, but King remained wary of Montreal Tory money; as always, he knew where his own interests lay. The order-in-council appointing Larkin was dated 10 February 1922. Two months later, the Hon. P.C. Larkin, P.C., his wife Jean, and their daughter embarked for Britain, following farewell dinners at the Reform Club in Montreal and at the Ontario Club in Toronto at which even the leader of the opposition in the legislature, the Conserva-tive Howard Ferguson, had praised Larkin's many public benefactions.

During Larkin's eight years in London, there passed many long let-ters between him and King (the salutations were invariably "Dear Mr. Larkin" and "Dear Mr. Mackenzie King"). The prime minister wrote to Larkin either personal or partisan letters, commenting in detail on the prospects of the Liberal party and the folly of its opponents. Otherwise their correspondence was largely about the domestic problems of the intensely lonely prime minister. From 1923 until his death in 1930, Larkin received detailed descriptions of how handsome were the various pieces of furniture which he had presented to Laurier House: a dining room screen; lamp shades from Paris; brass scones and a curio table. The prime minister reported happily that the effect of a new dining-room carpet was "too lovely for words." Larkin was no less diligent in assisting King in his constant need for domestic staff. They exchanged long letters about the cook, butler, two maids, and handyman/driver, noting how tiresome it was that the servants were frequently "at outs" with each other and how silly they were to give up – as they frequently did – such good jobs. Larkin was tireless in despatching new butlers from Britain and in writing at length about their merits, real or supposed. Even King, despite his endless preoccupation with that singularly boring subject, domestics, was eventually himself struck by the incongruity of his correspondence with Larkin: "It is really rather ludicrous for a Prime Minister to be writing to a High Commissioner on such a topic as this ... but somehow you have assumed the role of a fairy godfather."[8] Yet ludicrous or not, King continued to write page upon page to his fairy godfather about his domestic tribulations: "The new cook showed me where from the refrigerator alone she had taken literally baskets of filth."[9]

Larkin was never displeased or disconcerted to receive yet another letter about King's domestic demands, possibly because he did not have much else to do. Certainly King welcomed in return such reassurances as "Now please don't worry about finances in or out of power. They will be all attended to." In 1925, during his third year as high commissioner, Larkin and a few others contributed the then substantial amount of $225,000 to a fund to free King from any further financial concerns (as Larkin had earlier done for Laurier and recently, with a lesser amount, for King's Quebec lieutenant, Ernest Lapointe). The prime minister was grateful: "Larkin has been goodness itself. He has secured me financially for the rest of my life." King's gratitude was real enough, but was tempered with a continuing concern that all should remain confidential: "about the fund which you have so generously provided for me ... I was perhaps unduly sensitive ... at possible publicity."[10]

King's gratitude was oft-repeated. On New Year's Eve 1926 he wrote, "I seem to have to go on accepting every fresh token of your generosity and goodwill but doing little or nothing by way of having you know all that they mean to me ... You know, I think that I have no living friend for whom I have a greater or truer regard than for yourself."[11] On New Year's Eve 1928 he repeated his gratitude for Larkin's annual goodness: "your benevolence finding expression in some additional means of relieving altogether the possibility of financial strain" was simply beyond his powers to describe.[12] Larkin's personal services to King did not end with his death in London in 1930.* Three years later, King was still consulting his spirit

* Until 1933, investment income of Canadian officials serving abroad was exempt from income tax, a major boon for Larkin and his wife. Like Strathcona, Perley, and Massey, Larkin accepted no salary.

about his real estate transactions, asking it specifically whether he thought that he was acquiring too much land at Kingsmere near Ottawa.*

When Larkin, his wife, and their daughter arrived in London in early April 1922, he was a highly successful tea merchant. Of Irish ancestry, born in Montreal on 14 May 1855 of a stone mason and a charwoman, Larkin had little schooling.† At age thirteen, he had become a traveller for grocery companies, before himself founding the Salada Tea Company, eventually with offices in major cities in Canada and the United States and in London, Colombo, and Calcutta. Partly as a result of his vigorous and innovative marketing, he came to dominate the India tea trade in Canada as well as winning one-tenth of the United States market, making Salada the third-largest tea company in the world. His most profitable innovation was to have his tea packed in small watertight packets lined with foil rather than in large, bulk chests. His tea, as a result, was fresher and sold better. When King appointed Larkin to London, it was estimated that his company was importing tea to the value of £40 million annually, mostly from Ceylon.

A constant and innovative advertiser in newspapers, Larkin joined other leading Toronto businessmen in acquiring the *Toronto Star* in 1899. Eight years later, he was also a director of the *Globe* (which King later hoped that he would buy since "the control of its columns would have given the Party what is most needed in Ontario to-day"). In addition to being a noted Liberal amidst Canada's largely Conservative business community, Larkin was recognized as a model employer, offering a high standard of working conditions, including such innovations as profit-sharing and pensions, and as a philanthropist supporting especially the Toronto General Hospital and the League for the Prevention of Tuberculosis.

Eighteen months after his arrival in Britain, Larkin was saluted with a long, anonymous panegyric in the popular journal *Saturday Night*. Entitled

---

* The late high commissioner was a frequent interlocutor during the prime minister's *séances*, although King's parents, his grandfather and Laurier were present more often. Larkin's voice was, however, to be heard more frequently than that of Gladstone, Leonardo da Vinci, Saints Luke and John and later Asquith, Lord Grey of Fallodon, a hitherto unknown ancient "Hindoo" priest, Koramura, and later still of Borden, King George v and "Frank" Roosevelt.

† Larkin's birth date is frequently given as 1856; the entry of his birth in the records of Notre Dame de Grace parish in Montreal is, however, one year earlier.

"Cleaning up the Shop," it suggested that only such an eminent business-man as Larkin could hope to eradicate the mess left by the incompetent Strathcona and Perley.

Strathcona was a picturesque figurehead ... and the office degenerated into a social affair with more attention paid to garden parties at Buckingham Palace than to alert representation of Canada in the Empire's capital. The stopgap regime of Sir George Perley did not result in much change. Sir George happened to be in England when the office fell vacant and he was instructed to take it over temporarily.[*] A few weeks after ... war broke out and the government had too much on its hands to bother with the selection of a permanent appointee. So the thing was permitted to drift. By and by ... he was pitch forked into a brand new position, that of Minister of Militia Overseas ... These facts are mentioned in order that the conditions which confronted Mr. Larkin when he took over ... may be understood. He found the institution about as dead as Tutankhamen, and wrapped in the mouldy cerements of antiquated methods.

The problem was again the premises on Victoria Street. "One had to engage a guide and an interpreter in order to find it ... [there] he would find a crowd of sad-eyed compatriots eagerly scanning the well thumbed files of ancient newspapers ... It was all very dreary and gloomy ... Oh my, but it was a depressing place."[13]

During three decades or more, the question of where the office should be located was an issue that Larkin's two predecessors had been unable to resolve. Strathcona had rejected the grandiose proposal of his fellow peer, Lord Grey, for a Dominions' House; he had favoured a separate Canada House. Upon Strathcona's death, Perley, who had been commissioned by an order-in-council to resolve the question, had been prevented by demands of the First World War from escaping the "invading traffic roar of Victoria Street."

The order-in-council appointing Larkin repeated almost word for word the language that Perley had employed in recommending to the newly elected Mackenzie King in January 1922 "that all official activities in the United Kingdom should be placed under one control – that of the High Commissioner." His recommendation, embracing in turn the considered analysis of Loring Christie, was reflected in the order:

---

* Perley was in fact in Canada when "the office fell vacant" and did not arrive in London until five months after Strathcona's death.

there are in London ... independent and separate offices, of the Departments of Immigration, Trade and Commerce, Soldiers' Civil Re-establishment and Board of Pension Commissioners [over fifteen thousand soldiers had elected to take their discharge in the United Kingdom], also other departmental representatives carrying on their work outside the control of the High Commissioner ... all the official activities of the various agencies ... should be placed under the supervision of the High Commissioner [who] should ... communicate direct with the Prime Minister.*

In carrying out his duties, Larkin would be assisted by the former Liberal member of Parliament for Megantic, Lucien Pacaud, a journalist by profession whose father, co-founder and editor of *Le Soleil*, had been especially helpful to Laurier as Liberal party organizer in Quebec City. Upon Pacaud's defeat in the election of December 1921, he was appointed secretary of the High Commission in succession to W.L. Griffith (who had completed twenty-seven years of service), but the idea that he would be concurrently agent general of Quebec was firmly rejected by King.

Less ready of resolution than that of Dominion representation abroad was a question that was becoming something of a perennial: the status of provincial agents general in London. In 1919 F.C. Wade, the irrepressible agent general for British Columbia, had deplored in the *Empire Review* how under Strathcona the interests of the provinces had been ignored. In January 1922, upon the occasion of the office of the high commissioner being vacant between Perley's departure and Larkin's arrival, Wade had sensed his opportunity, writing direct to the prime minister "respecting the status of Canadian Agents General" and repeating some of the arguments of his predecessor of eight years before.[14] King, having already discussed the matter with Larkin in Ottawa, replied, "Mr. Larkin [is] most desirous of co-operating with the Agents General ... in a manner best calculated to advance the interests of their respective Provinces," a pledge that Larkin repeated at a welcoming dinner that the agents general held in his honour in May.[15] But when Larkin in fact did nothing, they rightly concluded that he regarded their complaints as a constitutional matter not for him but

---

* In addition to those from the Department of External Affairs, there were six staff from Agriculture, eight from Public Archives, two from National Revenue, a Royal Canadian Air Force liaison officer in the Air Ministry, two from the Postmaster General, five from Trade and Commerce, seventy-nine from the Immigration branch of Agriculture, fifteen from Soldiers' Civil Re-establishment, and three from the Department of Health.

for the prime minister to decide. As a result, according to Wade, they felt that they were "in a helpless position of a shuttlecock." Their status, they said, had been correctly observed by Galt and Tupper, but Strathcona "had succeeded in cutting off communication between the Agents General and the Imperial Government even on all those matters which under the constitution come within the sole jurisdiction of the Province[s] and their representatives."[16]

In continuing uncertainty about how to respond to Wade's broadside, Larkin wrote to King about "another infliction": Wade was obviously "determined to carry on all business between the British Columbia and the Imperial Governments without the intervention of the Dominion Government or its representative ... The other Provincial representatives here ... naturally join with him ... in striving to enhance the importance of their offices."[17] With his recent conversations with King in mind, Larkin replied to Wade:

You would have ... each Provincial Government ... make its own representations direct, quite independent and without intervention or even knowledge of the Dominion Government ... the course now pursued is the ideal one ... [However,] I am expressing an opinion on a matter of State with great diffidence and only because you force me, as I have had only a few months' experience in public life ... I hardly expect that you will see eye-to-eye with me in this and therefore leave it with you to take it up as you suggest, if you see fit, with the Prime Minister at Ottawa.[18]

Wade did so, but to no avail, King replying in December 1922 that Larkin's letter of 2 November expressed the government's view and stating flatly "that this matter will not be reopened for further consideration,"[19] despite the fact that both Ontario and Quebec had joined British Columbia in pressing the question.

Soon thereafter, Larkin, conscious that the Australian states were causing difficulties with Canberra over the status of their agents general, adopted the notably imaginative but ultimately futile Australian response of integrating the several agents into the total representation of the Dominion. The agent general of Quebec would represent Canada on the board of the Imperial Institute, Ontario on the Imperial War Museum, Nova Scotia on the Imperial War Graves Commission, and British Columbia on the British Empire Exhibition committee and the Imperial Air Congress. "The Agents General welcomed the innovation, hoping that it might prove a stepping stone to the restoration of their constitutional right to direct access to the Crown in relation to Provincial Affairs which the Dominion had refused to acknowledge since Lord Strathcona's time."[20] The experiment was not, however, a success. The agents general were hampered by their dual capacities; they soon proved incapable of representing concurrently both a national and a provincial view whenever it did not coincide. The pretensions of the provinces – or their legitimate aspirations depending how one looked at the question – did not disappear. They were to resurface a decade later.

In 1923, the year following Larkin's arrival, the lease on the office on Victoria Street expired. The affluent high commissioner and his wife were themselves well and fashionably lodged in 94 Lancaster Gate, a few doors from where Galt and his large family had lived less securely almost fifty years before. Now something had finally to be done about the wholly inadequate chancery. Soundings had been made about the possibility of transforming the elaborate British Columbia House on Lower Regent Street into Canada House, but Wade, the antagonistic agent general, had successfully urged the provincial government not to sell. As a stopgap, the High Commission was moved temporarily to Kinnaird House at 1 Pall Mall East, while negotiations to acquire the yet more imposing Union Club on the west side of Trafalgar Square were undertaken.

The Union Club, so named to bring together Liberals and Conservatives as originally supported by the Duke of Wellington, had been a favourite of King George IV and, a century later, of Edward VII. Laurier had spent many convivial hours there during his visits to Britain. By the end of the First World War, however, the club was in no financial shape to continue. It was probably with relief that its trustees sold its leasehold which, with the inevitable costs of renovation, brought the total bill to $1.3 million, an amount that appeared extravagant to some members of Parliament. King himself, never a big spender, reported ruefully to Larkin that the debate over the purchase of the Union Club "seemed to present a really critical situation in our House of Commons."[21] To others, however, including Larkin, the price was reasonable for the "best site in London" (and less than the cost of the new Australia House on the Strand). To convert the club into Canada House required major revisions and additions to the original design of a century before of Sir Robert Smirke (the principal architect of the British Museum). Finally, in June 1925, the maple-leaf-festooned bronze doors, flanked for the occasion by two rigid Mounties, were opened by King George V in the presence of the British prime minister, Stanley Baldwin, two of his predecessors, Lloyd George and Herbert

The opening of Canada House by King George V and Queen Mary in June 1925 finally resolved the decade-old question of a suitable chancery for the High Commission. The affluent Peter Larkin, appointed high commissioner by King in 1922, pressed the purchase and renovation of the Union Club on Trafalgar Square to a happy conclusion, bringing together the representatives of a range of government departments and the popular focus for Canadian visitors to London under one splendid roof. From left, Queen Mary, Peter Larkin, King George V, and the secretary of state for the colonies, Leopold Amery.

Asquith, and his successor, Ramsay MacDonald. However, the Canadian prime minister, who had supported his friend's project, found himself unable to cross from Canada, although his minister of public works was there with the imperial-minded Howard Ferguson, premier of Ontario.

The enlarged office space afforded by Canada House had by then become desperately needed. During the previous year in the dark and cramped rooms on Victoria Street, sixty-three thousand letters and eleven thousand visitors (mainly Canadian) had somehow been dealt with, but the efficiency of the mission with its several scattered offices had long been adversely affected by its unsuitable and inadequate space. Despite his misgivings about its cost, King was pleased with the new chancery: "There is something very noble about it all. It is a wonderful symbol of our Dominion to have at the heart of the Empire."[22] It was also something of a showcase (although not a match for the million-dollar Canadian building at the 220-acre British Empire Exhibition at Wembley). Mail despatched from the high commissioner increased to sixty-seven thousand pieces during its first year and its well-stocked library and information services were in constant usage. Next door on Cockspur Street, Larkin encouraged Sun Life to build an imposing colonnaded office. Both Canadian Pacific and Canadian National Railways had their European offices across the street, the latter in the handsome old Grand Trunk offices.

Largely as a result of being able to appeal directly to the prime minister, Larkin could overrule the senior trade commissioner who had opposed the move of his offices from Basinghall Street in the City to Canada House in Trafalgar Square. In the end, Larkin again had his way, following a letter to the prime minister who now undertook to have all representatives of government departments under one roof: "there is no difficulty likely to arise if the administration of the Trade Commissioner's office is conducted from [Canada House]. Concentration of effort will follow; confusion of offices disappear; and economies should be effected in staff and overhead expenses. The Trade Commissioner becomes an advisor to, and executive official of, the High Commissioner on all trade matters affecting the Dominion." Eventually, the commercial activities were augmented by the transfer from Ottawa of the director of the Exhibition Commission, joining the director of Trade Publicity already there. With the trade commissioners more clearly defined as integrated members of the High Commission, the minister of trade and commerce felt able to press the British government to rectify "the status occupied by Canadian Trade Commissioners in foreign countries [which] has been the source of grievous embarrassment." The minister had his wish. The governor general promptly responded that the Foreign Office would arrange through its missions in countries where there were Canadian trade commissioners that they would be accorded all rights, privileges, and recognition.

However time-consuming and interesting Larkin may have found the development of Canada House – and he certainly did – he could not avoid problems of Anglo-Canadian and imperial relations, especially given the postwar turmoil in British politics. When he arrived in April 1922, Lloyd George's coalition government was still in office, but it dissolved in October, to be followed by the ailing Bonar Law's Conservative government.

To the astonishment of many, the lesser-known Stanley Baldwin rather than the controversial Lord Curzon succeeded Law in May 1923. In the election, which Baldwin unexpectedly called in December over tariff policy, his government was defeated. He was in turn replaced by Britain's first Labour government, led by Ramsay MacDonald, dependent upon the support of a still substantial number of free-trade Liberals. An election in October 1924 brought in Baldwin's second government, partly as a result of the Bolshevik scare of the day.* An election in May 1929 (the year before Larkin's death) returned Ramsay MacDonald's second Labour government: in all, four general elections and six governments in eight years.

Despite this bewildering background of political uncertainty, Larkin's role was clear with regard at least to matters arising from the war: he toured battlefields in France and Belgium with King George V and Rudyard Kipling and in London he presided at the Armistice Day luncheon at the Canada Club for the Prince of Wales. Six months after his arrival, he went to Geneva as a member of the Canadian delegation to the third assembly of the League of Nations, although, as King intended, he played no part there. He was absent with influenza from the fourth assembly in September 1923. However, two major problems arising from the war he did help to settle.

During the early 1920s, British fears of bovine disease had ostensibly prompted the postwar continuation of the embargo on the importation of all live cattle, including Canadian, a prohibition first introduced three decades before. Given the postwar availability of shipping and the fact that Canadian cattle were demonstrably free of disease, the embargo was in fact a form of protectionism. Perley had protested in *The Times* on 28 December 1920 that the Canadians at the imperial conference of 1917 had "distinctly understood" that a promise had been given that the embargo would be removed without delay, once the war had ended. The visiting Ontario minister of agriculture campaigned against the ban in a by-election (somehow without incurring the official opprobrium that Tupper had earlier encountered). In 1922, Ottawa, following the doubling

---

* The general election of 1924 saw seventeen Canadians elected (and six defeated), including Hamilton Gault of Montreal who in 1914 had raised, largely at his own expense, the Princess Patricia's Canadian Light Infantry. During a century from Confederation, there was no British Parliament without at least several Canadian members (as well as peers). The high commissioners, however, appear not to have had much contact with them.

of the US tariff on cattle imports and after consultation with supporting British interests, determined to push Westminster to honour its pledge of 1917. It was soon evident at Westminster that both the government and the opposition were divided on the question: Churchill, Lloyd George, and Asquith were in favour of lifting the embargo – Larkin identified Churchill as the principal advocate – and Baldwin and his foreign secretary, Austen Chamberlain, of continuing it. Beaverbrook and Borden and two veteran Canadian ministers visiting Britain lent formidable support to Perley's recollection and Larkin's subsequent advocacy. The result was that Westminster finally redeemed its 1917 pledge, opening the way, at least partially, for free entry of cattle to be fattened for slaughter. Despite misgivings about the reaction of the United States, whose cattle would remain excluded from the British market, Canadian exports were optimistically expected to increase from thirty-two thousand head in 1921 to an estimated two hundred thousand in 1924. Larkin could claim a first triumph, but the negotiation left a decidedly unhappy impression on him. On 16 May, only four months after his arrival, he wrote to King, "When I have had the pleasure of meeting the different Ministers on the [cattle] embargo question ... I leave them with the conviction that in their hearts they have the same feeling towards me that they would have towards a child."[23] George Wrong would have understood their feeling, having predicted it when Larkin's appointment was first mooted.

The High Commission and officials from Ottawa also resolved a yet more complex problem. As in families, money differences among governments are never happy occasions, especially in the wake of nationalization of the Grand Trunk and Grand Trunk Pacific, but Larkin's assignment to help settle war debts was especially contentious. Baldwin's unexpected agreement on a settlement with the United States (when he was Bonar Law's chancellor of the exchequer) linked British repayment to German reparations and to repayment by the Allies of their debts to Britain. Thereafter, Britain and Canada undertook to settle accounts, to attempt again to determine who owed what to whom for wartime expenditures, including munitions, rolling stock, shipping, and training. The initiative was taken against the background of the broader problem of Allied indebtedness to Britain, in turn part of the larger problem of German reparations (upon which a one-year moratorium had been placed in 1922). At the end of the war, it had been estimated that Britain's allies owed it about $7 billion. Britain in turn owed the United States $3.6 billion. The question of Allied indebtedness to Britain was alone difficult enough, but fortunately for Larkin, the British government did not choose to consult the Dominions, instead acting unilaterally in seeking repayment from its wartime Allies.*

As far as Canadian indebtedness to Britain was concerned, King had convinced himself during the electoral campaign of 1921 that Britain had cheated Canada regarding the estimated value of armaments returned at the end of the war. In November 1922, he wrote to Larkin, "Nothing will convince me that behind the shiploads of ammunitions which have come to this country since the War there are not payments chargeable to Canada which there has been every effort to conceal ... [However,] part of [any] inquiry [would be] in Britain and [require] interrogating offi- cers of the British Government which would probably have been strongly resented ... I thought it wise therefore not to press the matter further ... [But] on every shipment profits have been realized."[24]

Both before the meetings of the Inter-Allied Conference on Reparations in London and of the Allied finance ministers in Paris in 1924 and 1925, Larkin struggled manfully with the vexed question of reparations. It was a complex subject about which he gave little evidence of understanding and about which Ottawa sent him few and largely negative instructions – if they could be called instructions at all. He made several attempts to ascer- tain from ministers and officials in Ottawa exactly how much Canada expected in reparations and to obtain a seat for the minister of finance at the ensuing Paris conference. In both initiatives he failed, fuelling a belief among some in Ottawa that Britain was deviously siphoning off for itself the reparations intended for the whole Empire. The correspon- dence between Ottawa and London leaves the impression, at one level, of bewilderment on the part of Larkin and, on another, of outrage, feigned or genuine, on the part of King.

Britain, having bled itself almost white during more than four years of war and having had to sell much of its lucrative overseas investment, fre- quently to Americans, proposed to meet its debts to Canada by paying in sterling at current rates. Finally, in early 1924, an agreement was reached that payment would be in Canadian dollars, but on the recommendation of the agreed arbitrator, former prime minister Asquith, the "normal" exchange rate rather than the "artificial rates of the immediate post-war years" would be applied. Accordingly, the net award to Canada was $8 million instead of the $33 million claimed. Larkin was sarcastic about

* The debts of Greece and Romania to Canada were later converted to government bonds. "Adjustments" to the indebtedness of France and Belgium were made via the High Commission.

his triumphant British interlocutor: "I see that Mr. Otto Niemeyer of the Treasury has been raised to the dignity of a knighthood. That title has been earned by a cost to Canada of twenty-three million dollars." It was not just that the British were hard bargainers. "There is no sentiment in Government ... If you were living over here as I have been for the past two years, you would fall, as I have, from the clouds ... [There is a] great deal of waving of flags and talk of Imperial sentiment and all the rest of it, but when it comes down to business, the sentiment, if any existed, vanishes quickly ... Any courtesies or concessions made to Canada and others here will have to be drawn from them by forceps."[25]

If imperial consultation and coordination had reached a high-water mark in 1917, largely at the initiative of Lloyd George, Borden, and Smuts, it had dropped to a low point within five years, partly at Meighen's reluctance to carry it forward, partly in the face of Mackenzie King's intransigence. Larkin's essentially sterile tenure as high commissioner is understandable only against King's own sterile postwar attitude towards Britain and the Empire. Intensely disliking Tories, whether of the overseas or domestic variety, his partisan prejudices were reflected in his persistent tilting at imperial windmills in the hope of reinforcing his standing in Quebec. Having no creative impulses towards the Empire or Canada's evolving place in it, King followed Laurier in his passive attitude to imperial collaboration (although there is evidence that he had been, for example, at some variance with his mentor over the degree of Canadian participation in the South African War and even over conscription in the First World War).

Other Dominion and most British leaders recognized that the postwar Empire could not be the same as the prewar one. There could be no going back; too much had been suffered to permit such simplistic rhetoric as that of either King on the one hand or Meighen on the other. Australia and New Zealand, geographically isolated, remained ready to give broad, if occasionally differing, substance to a cooperative postwar Empire, but King would have none of it, concluding that Borden's concept of a consultative Commonwealth was "a direct reversal of the whole of Dominion development in the past half century." He sedulously and successfully sought to convince Quebecois that he was their one sure foundation against Tory imperial machinations which would suck them into dire overseas hazards.

What was at the base of King's life-long suspicions was the conviction that French-speaking Canada would automatically oppose collaboration, thereby threatening both the Liberal power base and the unity of the country, he himself having no more positive ideas of how to foster it. Locked in his negativism, he was able to think of little to promote in a positive and dynamic way Anglo-French concord in Canada. A major part of the problem was "Francophone rights remained a low priority for King." In the words of J.W. Pickersgill, his long-time secretary, "he had no affinity with the French culture, a sketchy and superficial knowledge of the language and all the Protestant intolerance of Catholicism."[26] The Manitoba school question of the 1890s and the Ottawa school controversy of 1917 closed off any possibility – if that was ever in his mind – of the Dominion encouraging the provinces in separate language schools or bilingual teaching or higher education. Other possibilities he equally eschewed. There is no evidence that he contemplated additional French-speaking units in the three armed forces or more French-speaking senior officers; more francophone diplomats; bilingualism in the public service generally; more fiscal assistance to ameliorate the economic strains of sustained unity; or even the symbols of bilingual currency and postage stamps. He was clear in his mind that it was a "mistake to press this bilingual business too far."[27] Yet all these things and others would in time be done. It is not an answer to say that they could not have been attempted between the 1920s and the 1940s if strong and imaginative leadership had been present.

A debate emerged over whether King during the 1920s was so preoccupied with pushing Britain out the front door that intentionally or unintentionally he ignored the fact that the United States was much more massively entering through the back door. That Canada went "From colony to nation to colony again, in a few short years" and from "being a British satellite to an American in less than a generation" were allegations that began to be heard.[28] Secure in North America and devoid of any constructive ideas about Empire cooperation, King was equally consistent in his suspicions of the proposals of others. Throughout his life, he remained the devoted disciple of Laurier, who had counselled tactful passivity toward any proposals for change. King had reaffirmed as early as 1911 that it was best for Canada to let "events and circumstances" determine its policy and to take no initiative nor attempt anything creative with regard to the Empire.

Unfortunately for those whom the eminently insecure King regarded as imperial centralists, the bungled and, worse, unnecessary Chanak affair of 1922 had a major adverse impact on him. It fuelled his already overheated suspicions about what the British government – especially a Conservative-dominated government – might have up its imperial sleeve and what that might mean for Liberal support in Quebec.

Lloyd George had first gained political eminence if not notoriety as a radical Liberal, but by early 1922, when Larkin arrived, his shaky Unionist government had become heavily dependent upon Conservatives to remain in office. And on the left, the emergent Labour party was busily outflanking the Liberals, leaving them reduced, dispirited and increasingly isolated. In mid-September 1922, six months after Larkin had disembarked, a sudden crisis appeared to arise in Turkey: "appeared" for no-one ever seemed quite certain what vital British interest was at stake and, if indeed there was one, why armed force was necessarily the most efficacious reaction to Turkey's determination to regain territory that it had been forced to demilitarize by the Treaty of Sévres (which Perley had signed for Canada). France and Italy withdrew their troops, but Lloyd George, urged on by Churchill, the secretary of state for the colonies, and Birkenhead, the lord chancellor, rashly queried whether the several Dominions "would desire to be represented by a contingent" in order to exclude the advancing forces of Turkey from the Dardanelles, "soil which [was] hallowed by the immortal memories of the Anzacs" during Churchill's imaginative but ill-conducted Gallipoli enterprise of 1915. "The announcement that all or any of the Dominions were prepared to send contingents even of moderate size ... might conceivably be a potent factor in preventing actual hostilities."[29] King, who had occasionally acknowledged Canada's commitment to joint action with Britain if any major threat to the Empire itself arose, certainly did not regard the confused situation in Turkey and the apparent plight of the British garrison in Chanak as any such threat.

Beaverbrook later described Lloyd George as "being by this time a weak man, he had decided to be strong."[30] King suspected as much, subsequently recording with great approval that the seemingly guileless Baldwin (despite labouring under the disadvantage of being a Conservative) had told him that at the time of Chanak "England and the Empire were in the hands of three dangerous men [Lloyd George, Churchill, and Birkenhead], all intoxicated with their own cleverness and love of power, and prepared to sacrifice everything to it; foolish ... to the point of believing they could win an election by bringing on another war" (Baldwin himself had been on vacation when the ultimatum had been issued). King was equally gratified by the more austere comment of Lord Curzon, the foreign secretary, at the 1923 imperial conference that the Chanak "manifesto ... was issued without the knowledge or approval of the Cabinet."[31] Twenty-two years later King was consoled by the colourful but inaccurate account passed to him by Hamar Greenwood: "Churchill, Lord Birkenhead and Lloyd George had all been out dining pretty well ... the decision to fight the Turks and to send out the appeal to the Dominions to aid ... was [made] under ... the effect that alcohol had on men." They had sent the message to the Dominions out of office hours so that officials could not cavil.

In his diary, the under-secretary for external affairs, the ailing Sir Joseph Pope, recorded the general consternation in Ottawa. "Tonight the astounding announcement is made that H.M. Government has called upon the Dominions to send troops to fight the Turks in Asia Minor. A regular bolt from the blue, and one calculated horribly to embarrass the Dominion Government." Two days later, even Pope, that "thrice-dipped" Tory, was still confounded: "The fact that Lloyd George should have sent out such an amazing call for assistance to the Dominions is more of a mystery than ever. No doubt that there has been a leak, but why he should have ever considered it necessary to send such a message remains inexplicable and indicates very little consideration for the various Dominion Governments."[32]

Hughes of Australia was hardly less perplexed. That the British request had been made public was "not only embarrassing but deeply humiliating ... Had the position been communicated through confidential channels, we should at least have been able to express our feelings freely, and possibly even to insist that the situation should be handled by the representatives of the Dominions [i.e., the high commissioners] acting with those of Britain."[33] King interpreted this sloppiness or worse as a sure sign of duplicity: the request was "drafted designedly to play the imperial game, to test out centralization vs. autonomy as regards European wars."[34] The Conservative Churchill – whom King was not alone in regarding as unreliable and reckless – and even the Liberal Lloyd George were attempting to employ the press as a means of forcing Canada into acquiescence. The Toronto *Globe* headline had duly proclaimed, the "British Lion calls [its] Cubs to Face the Beast of Asia."

The temporising King, his own secretary of state for external affairs, responded to the British request, when it was finally deciphered, by resorting to that most effective of prime ministerial ploys: procrastination. He was never in any doubt what his answer would be but, as he repeated to Neville Chamberlain on his initial visit to Canada, Parliament would first be summoned. It never seemed to occur to King simply to say no, as Borden had done. That would remove the opportunity to make a great show of withstanding imperial centralists. He was in any case well aware that the House of Commons could not be assembled until long after the

British themselves would have decided whether to go it alone. Neville Chamberlain was not impressed. He noted on a train between Moose Jaw and Medicine Hat that "Loud and deep are the curses on Mackenzie King for his miserable and shameful hedging, but he is a weak man depending for his continuance in office upon the French Canadian vote from Quebec."[35]

King's quest for what he regarded as autonomy in foreign as well as domestic policy and the supremacy of Parliament in deciding all such questions were given added impetus by the unnecessary Chanak request. It also provided a welcome occasion to display the differences between Liberals and Conservatives, the leader of the opposition having affirmed different policy: "There are those who write and talk as though Britain were not our good partner and friend but our chief antagonist, an imperious, designing mistress, seeking to lead us to our ruin." There was no doubt whom Meighen had in mind: he described King's reactions as "a selfish, halting exhibition of procrastination and impotency. Let there be no dispute as to where I stand. When Britain's message came [requesting a contingent] then Canada should have said: 'Ready, aye ready; we stand by you'," a melodramatic pronouncement that compounded Meighen's pro-conscriptionist reputation in Quebec for years to come (despite his intentional parallel with Laurier's declaration of 1914).[36] In Britain, Bonar Law led the Conservatives out of the coalition government and into a victorious election.*

During Chanak and again at the imperial conference of 1923, King continued to demonstrate a wariness of any who sought prior commitments, whether in terms of soldiers for some distant imperial folly or of naval and air units equipped and trained in close coordination with British forces. His various suspicions were increasingly fuelled by the dean of arts at Queen's University, Oscar Skelton, who had years before sounded him about joining the university if he were defeated in the 1908 election. When minister of labour in 1909–11, King had twice employed Skelton as a consultant and was immediately impressed by his apparent understanding and learning. They shared a low level of interest in francophone rights or in opening the way to the greater employment of the French language

---

* Bonar Law was prime minister for only the next few months before cancer forced his resignation; Lloyd George lingered on in Parliament but in the two decades remaining to him, never regained office, although his old colleague Churchill offered him cabinet office or the embassy in Washington at the beginning of the Second World War.

in the civil service, Skelton having once asserted that "the widest possible knowledge of English" was essential for a "common Canadian consciousness" since "this is and will be overwhelmingly an English-speaking country." Further, Skelton had the rare merit of having read King's eminently unreadable *Industry and Humanity*, praising it fulsomely in a speech in Ottawa which he knew that the prime minister would attend ("preaching for a call" as one of his acolytes at Queen's observed). To King's satisfaction, the professor had demonstrated in his long biographies of Galt and of the revered Laurier how they had cleverly exposed schemes of British politicians – especially Tory – to dominate the Dominions. Skelton "never stopped believing that behind almost every British Government scheme – constitutional, economic, military – lay a dark desire to introduce a consolidation of empire." Although none of his writings explain the origins of Skelton's hostility, "There can be little doubt that Skelton was almost pathological on the subject of English Tory imperialism in a manner that smacks of the rejected and the irrational."[37] He denounced to King the basic thesis of Borden that Commonwealth consultation and cooperation would enhance and not hinder Canada's ability to participate internationally and to decide upon its own policies, yet when Bennett was prime minister in the 1930s, Skelton readily endorsed his pro-Empire policies and in concert with Borden.

In the Ottawa speech with King present, Skelton roundly proclaimed, "we have assumed ... control over the greater part of this field of foreign policy through our own government, and that the path of security, the path of safety, the path of responsibility, the path of honour and duty toward other nations ... lies ... in following that course to the logical end." This was welcome rhetoric to King who had convinced himself that the most effective way of keeping the Empire together was to reject consultation. If the Dominions felt at ease with their autonomy, they would in turn more readily come together voluntarily. In attempting to give substance to his commitment to the simple equation of greater autonomy with greater unity, King parted company not only with Meighen but with Skelton. Meighen was, at least in theory, in favour of strong Commonwealth institutions in which Britain would naturally be *primus inter pares*; Skelton would countenance no imperial links or even King's own romantic ties with Britain. He had mistrusted Borden's consultative and cooperative policy, but eagerly supported the prime minister in his suspicions about centralists, although he was ultimately kept in check by King if he expressed himself in favour of no formal linkages with Britain. King would not go whole hog as Skelton yearned to do.

For King, Chanak became, in the view of one historian, "the most important single event in [his] career."[38] Skelton, shortly before becoming counsellor in the Department of External Affairs in 1925, reflected King's own thinking in his conviction that the British government had sought to create a situation in which "the Dominions are committed to action by blank cheques given to the [British] Foreign Secretary by their Prime Ministers." King modestly agreed that his stance over Chanak, in Skelton's gratifying words, had "made history. Never again will a government be stampeded against its better judgement into giving blank cheques to British diplomacy." The adverse impact of Chanak on King, an historian later noted, was pervasive:

When Canada and South Africa failed to support Britain's declared policy ... a breach was made in imperial diplomatic unity that need never have occurred. With regard to British-Canadian relations, however, the crisis had a far more important result, leading O.D. Skelton to mistake the very basis of the imperial association. Rather than assume that the crisis was an aberration, Skelton came to decide that the overseas governments [including Meighen's Conservative government] had written "blank cheques" at the 1921 Imperial Conference in support of imperial foreign policy – that in other words through consultation, and perhaps even mere information, they had been materially committed at Britain's sole discretion to enforcing a collective policy.[39]

In the wake of Chanak, Beaverbrook, Baldwin, and Amery among others laboured mightily and ultimately successfully to replace Lloyd George with Bonar Law. Lloyd George, Birkenhead, and Churchill were to King's great satisfaction excluded from Law's new government, but Tories remained Tories. They were no more to be trusted on one side of the Atlantic than on the other. Law himself, fatally ill, resigned only seven months after assuming office, leaving that master intriguer Beaverbrook for once nonplussed. Law's unexpected and occasionally enigmatic successor, Baldwin, was, in King's view, an improvement on most Tories, but in the end he was still a Tory. It was in any event becoming increasingly difficult to be certain who stood for what as the fortunes of the British Liberal party waxed and waned – mainly waned – and Labour filled the field that the internecine turmoil of the Liberals had left vacant.

During the 1922 election campaign Law repeated his earlier conviction, echoing Borden, that the Dominions should have a voice in shaping imperial foreign policy. To King's consternation, the Montreal *Gazette* reported on 22 November that "Bonar Law's pre-election statement ... has been quickly implemented ... The High Commissioners of the Dominions, including the Hon. P.C. Larkin ... attended a meeting with the Board of Trade yesterday to present their [*sic*] views on the Near East settlement which Britain with her allies is now negotiating at Lausanne." King, dismayed at Larkin's attendance, was prompt in his response: "Any request made to you ... which may be construed as amounting to consultation or representation ... in matters of foreign policy, [must] be immediately referred to our Government for consideration before action taken."[40] Larkin knew again exactly what to reply: "*Gazette's* correspondent under misapprehension. Meeting called to discuss trade relations with Turkey ... Lausanne and Dardanelles never mentioned ... Am always very careful [to] refrain from committing Canadian Government either directly or by implication to foreign policy."[41]

King told Larkin nothing about his vexation at the question of whether the new British government regarded itself as representing the whole Empire or only itself at the Lausanne conference called to clean up the diplomatic mess in Turkey. Entrenched as he was in his conviction that the high commissioner had no role to play in policy questions between Britain and Canada, Larkin could be relied upon to take no initiative. The Chanak affair had coincided with his statement to the agent general for British Columbia that "I have had only a few months experience in public life" and, as he reaffirmed to the prime minister, he had "no powers other than to convey messages between the two governments." King did later stir himself sufficiently to send him a few "copies of the despatches which passed between the British Government and our own," but they were of course sent well after the fact, having travelled from London to Ottawa and then back to London. No comments were invited. His indifference to what Larkin thought about policy can be judged from his comment: "I wish ... that I were a little freer ... so as to be able to write you more fully on these all-important matters."[42] By being left uninformed, Larkin was even less likely to embroil himself in policy.

Philip Kerr, a long-time Round Table advocate of imperial federation, a collaborator of Amery, and, as Lord Lothian, a future British ambassador to the United States, set forth the frustration in London about King's entrenched suspicions. Visiting Canada at the time of Chanak, he had written to his friend, Vincent Massey:

The Dominions should equip themselves with the best possible information about foreign affairs, either by having ambassadors or High Commissioners of their own, or by having a better system of consultation & information in London, or both, so that they have an intelligent policy on its merits about international questions as they arise ... Mackenzie King's policy, which was Laurier's, of pleading ignorance, i.e., the ostrich policy, is the most fatal of all ... The only way is that Canada should have a mind of its own about every issue.[43]

King, in his endless opposition to imperial consultation, had opposed the revival at the 1921 imperial conference of the familiar idea that the interests of the Dominions would be better served if cabinet ministers were to represent them in London. With the 1923 conference pending, the proposal was again raised by New Zealand: "the Dominions had acquired a voice in Imperial foreign policy, the means of making that voice heard were defective." The New Zealand minister advocated "the establishment of an Empire consultative body, broadly on the lines of the [Imperial] War Cabinet to comprise representatives of the different units of the Empire. These men would reside in England and would be able to confer without delay upon important movements in foreign policy." Perley, on a private visit to London, immediately gave his support in a statement to *The Times*, the proposal being what Tupper and he had repeatedly urged:

At first sight, the problem of co-operation within the Empire would appear to be insoluble. On the one hand, there is the wish of the Dominions to preserve their self-governing status, on the other; there is the need for a common foreign policy ... the only possible solution of the problem is by means of more frequent and continuous consultation. In order to make this possible between the meetings of the several Imperial Conferences ... the best method would be to have some understanding so that the representatives of the Dominions would meet with members of the British Government whenever any question of general concern to the Empire arose. This would enable the Canadian representative, for instance, to keep his Government more fully advised regarding all matters affecting our foreign relations. The representatives together could form a consulting body without the authority of, but on somewhat similar lines to, the Imperial War Conference, of which I had the privilege of being a member. My experience is that, difficult as the problems of Imperial relationship may be, they disappear to a great extent when representatives of different parts of the Empire meet around the same table. That was my impression [of the League of Nations] at Geneva, as well as here in London ... a resident [cabinet] minister could carry out these duties more easily than a High Commissioner. My experience in London convinced me of the desirability of appointing a resident minister.[44]

King ignored the advice, as did his advisors at the 1923 imperial conference, Skelton and J.W. Dafoe, editor of the *Manitoba Free Press.** Despite Dafoe's earlier allegiance to the imperialist Round Table movement, both were, if anything, even more mistrustful of the British government than King himself, convinced as they were that the Empire remained locked in the grip of centralists intent upon undermining hard-won but vulnerable Canadian autonomy. Before the conference, King confessed, "I am far from prepared ... I am filled with terror." He told Skelton that "he had never dreaded any task so much and was aging under the strain." He wrote to Amery, now First Lord of the Admiralty, "I dread somewhat my own lack of experience in gatherings of the kind." Then followed a passage of pure Skelton: "So far as I have been able to gauge the effects of the war upon Canadian sentiment, it is that centralization, as regards all matters of imperial policy, is something to be critically viewed, and that the hope of the future lies rather in the recognition of an effective co-operation between self-governing and self-controlling units than in any merging or blending of control."[45] The fact that no one very much in Britain was thinking of "any merging or blending of control" did not deter King and Skelton in their several fantasies. Certainly Larkin would offer no correction. With the anglophobe Skelton urging him on, King made it clear during the six-week conference that he wanted no real consultation and no obligations for implementing policy. As an Australian historian has noted, "It cost him no effort to turn inwards upon Canada. For thus he could avoid the complications of Empire, of the League of Nations, and of foreign affairs outside North America, whilst taking advantage of the shield provided by the United States."[46]

Skelton prepared for King a paper on what to say at the conference, "Canada and the Control of Foreign Policy." The prime minister was

---

* Also aboard King's ship was the Oxford-bound Norman Robertson, the future undersecretary of state for external affairs and high commissioner, who, upon meeting Skelton, found him "extremely dull and if he isn't saturated clean through with dullness then he was also rather discourteous." King, Robertson noted, was simply "hopelessly undistinguished." At the University of Toronto, Professor A.J. Glazebrook sounded like George Wrong on Larkin's appointment when he noted that Skelton "who is going with King ... is a narrow-minded, extreme autonomist, whose time has been spent in hack writing and who is nervously jealous of what he suspects as English 'superiority'. I don't think that King could have made a ... worse selection" (Glazebrook to Dove, 24 August 1923; Bodleian Library, Oxford, MSS, English History, c. 819, folio 177).

impressed by Canadian history according to Skelton, but later C.P. Stacey, the eminent historian, was decidedly not.

This was an ... extraordinarily partisan production. Its most curious feature is the fact that it represents the plan for a unified foreign policy as entirely a British scheme – a British plot, though it does not use that word – and says no word of the Canadian share in it. There is absolutely no reference to Sir Robert Borden's long campaign for a "voice" for Canada in the formation of Imperial policy. Nothing is said even of Resolution IX of the Imperial War Conference of 1917, which Borden originated and moved, with its proclamation of the right of the Dominions "to an adequate voice in foreign policy" and of the desirability of "effective arrangements for continuous consultation in all important matters of common Imperial concern". A whole decade of determined Canadian effort in the field of external policy is wiped from the record. Skelton represents the common-foreign-policy idea as "a direct reversal of the whole trend of Dominion development in the past half-century," and nowhere recognizes the fact that he is urging King to reverse a policy developed by Canadian governments to meet the challenges of the most eventful years in the Dominion's history.

There is no evidence as to Skelton's motives ... One wonders whether he can have refrained from describing Borden's policies from apprehension that King, if fully informed of the extent to which the country had been committed to them over many years, might have taken alarm and hesitated to commit himself to the very different policies that Skelton favoured. Skelton's paper may have been good politics, but it was very bad history. In effect, if not in intent, it was mendacious.[47]

At the conference King, buttressed by Skelton's paper, explained at excruciating length how he viewed the Empire. In an attempt to substantiate his barely disguised allegations of centralism, he drew attention to a statement of Lloyd George of December 1921 "to the effect that the position of the Dominions in reference to foreign affairs had been revolutionised since 1917, that the Dominions had been given equal rights with Great Britain in the control of the foreign policy of the Empire, that the instrument of this policy was, and must remain, the British Foreign Office, and that the advantage to Britain was that such joint control involved joint responsibility." Although this was not what Lloyd George had said, King was gratified with his creation of a straw man which he could then attempt to knock down by quoting approvingly Sir Clifford Sifton who "organized the campaign against the Laurier Government on Reciprocity in 1911 and the campaign for conscription in 1917" (i.e., he could not be dismissed as

Liberal lickspittle): "We now find the Prime Minister of Great Britain making the statement that we have entered into an arrangement by which we assume responsibility for the wars of Great Britain all over the world in return for being consulted ... Premiers drift into London ... no one very sure what is decided ... and the Dominions become jointly responsible for everything the British Foreign Office does in every part of the world." King then proceeded to demolish whatever there had been left by Milner and Meighen of the ideal behind Resolution IX of Borden and Smuts:

No scheme has been worked out, no scheme ... can be worked out, by which each part of the Empire can be not only informed but consulted as to all the relations of every other part of the Empire with foreign countries, and a really joint policy worked out. The range is too vast, the situation too kaleidoscopic, the interests too diverse, and the preoccupation of each government with its own affairs or its own existence too absorbing, to make this possible ... It is possible to consult on matters of overwhelming and enduring common interest; it is not possible to consult on the great range of matters of individual and shifting concern.[48]

But even that broadside did not satisfy King. He delivered himself of a detailed personal account of how the Chanak query had come to him. Small wonder that Maurice Hankey, the perplexed cabinet secretary, later told Skelton that Britain "could not find out where Canada stood. Borden some years ago had asked for a share in foreign policy and [at the] last conference [of 1921] Canada had agreed to uniform policy and common responsibility. Now Canada repudiated this policy."[49]

King treated his long-suffering colleagues to tedious dissertations on questions as diverse as water levels in the Great Lakes and why it would be impossible to give Indian immigrants the vote.* But the most tiresome of all was King's version of Canadian history, a classic exposition of Clear Grit historiography of the Skelton school. He began by denouncing the New Zealand view that "the Dominions had been sponging too much on the mother country in the past ... I desire to take strong exception to it, so far as Canada is concerned. I do not think Canada in any particular has

---

* King's statement was by no means the final word on discrimination against Indians in Canada's immigration policy. For example, H.S. Bassu, the Indian delegate to the League of Nations in 1935, protested to the Colonial Office about the continuing discrimination, noting that "the Japanese community in British Columbia was accorded superior status to that of Indian residents." The Congress Party in India repeatedly protested.

been sponging. The history of the relationship of Canada with the mother country will show that, far from sponging, Canada has been more than ready to assume obligations, and has assumed obligations, in a chivalrous and large way."[50] King evidently did not regard as a free ride the protection that the Royal Navy had long provided Canadian export trade.

In his discursive speeches, King even introduced the oft-debated question of the status of high commissioners, but to no apparent end. He implied that they should be redesignated as representatives of "free nations," having "at least the same standing and rights and privileges as the representatives of countries that are entitled to have [diplomatic] Ministers here." His circumlocutious declaration was received with some puzzlement by the prime ministers of Britain, New Zealand, and South Africa, Smuts in particular inquiring what additional privileges or access high commissioners could possibly need: "I thought our High Commissioner had complete freedom in approaching not only Ministers, but the Prime Minister."[51] Larkin had informed King some months before that he was dissatisfied with his precedence (in other words, he was ranked with and not before representatives of non-Commonwealth nations). King, however, did not appear certain of his ground when he raised the subject, allowing it to trail off inconclusively.

Throughout the conference, the interventions of King were negative, according with what Skelton urged him to say. He summarized his stance with what was for him a classic comment: "Our attitude is not one of unconditional isolation nor is it one of unconditional intervention." The immediate cause of King's typically rotund pronouncement was his recollection of the Chanak imbroglio and the confusions at least in his own mind about whom exactly the British had represented at the subsequent Lausanne conference. He was, however, labouring points on which all had long been in agreement and saying little or nothing about areas of Commonwealth cooperation which the prime ministers gathered to discuss. "What King had to say about Dominion autonomy, about the Imperial Conference not having executive powers, and the right of the Parliaments to be consulted, had all been said by Prime Ministers in their own Parliaments – by Bruce [of Australia] and Smuts [of South Africa] as emphatically as King. Baldwin had also said it upon opening the Conference. 'We stand here on an equal footing and no Government present can bind the next'."[52] With reason, Meighen observed that King was simply attempting to burst heroically through an open door. He had already directed his scorn towards his negativism: "I am not worried by the ghosts that seem always before some people; I do not think, with them, that we have been waging a terrific battle against a reluctant Downing Street in order to gain our rights."[53]

King's repeated opposition to a coordinated foreign policy ran directly counter to the dynamic advocacy of the new Australian prime minister, Stanley Bruce. In doing so, King attracted the disdain of a young Australian, R.G. Casey, liaison officer in the Cabinet Office who was later to become a cabinet minister, a peer, and governor general). "Surely no man can claim credit for having done so much as Mackenzie King to damage what remains ... of the fabric of the British Empire. His efforts to make capital out of his domestic nationalism are analogous to a vandal who pulls down a castle in order to build a cottage."

King was equally the target for the fine-honed contempt – "obstinate, tiresome and stupid" – of Curzon, the foreign secretary, before he turned his majestic mind to weightier matters. Yet Curzon, who made King "shudder," had himself little time for schemes of collective policy-making with the Dominions. If they did not wish to accept a greater degree of consultation combined with recognition of the ultimate primacy of the Foreign Office, they were free to pursue their own foreign policies, but they would then do so without the support of Britain. Sounding similar to Asquith in 1911, Curzon rejected any direct involvement of the Dominions in the formulation of British foreign policy. Accordingly, there would be no additional consultation through "the appointment of Dominion Ministers in London, or an alteration in the status of the High Commissioners." One close student of postwar imperial relations has written:

Mackenzie King's conviction, that by late 1923 he had successfully disengaged Canada from stringent and embarrassing imperial obligations, must be judged against the awkward fact that at no point had his predecessors committed the country to imperial policies beyond the immediate sanction of the dominion government ... problems of communication had already jeopardized the efforts to involve the overseas governments in a reciprocal system of consultation and commitment regarding questions of foreign policy. More importantly, the British government's own approach to policy making in collaboration with the dominions after 1917 was itself the subject of severe and protracted internal confrontations between the colonial and foreign offices. At several critical points, in fact, it was the refusal of the [Foreign Office] to be shackled in its operations by what it deemed dominion interference that constituted the principal threat to the Empire's diplomatic unity.[54]

Paradoxically, Curzon and King, coming from opposite directions, had arrived at much the same place.

The conference effectively settled the question of whether the Dominions would attempt to give meaning to the consultation and cooperation foreseen in Resolution IX or would instead proceed in greater independence of each other. Australia worked hard for more collaboration, but in the end King's intransigent negativism won the day. His reputation for negativism, gained at the 1921 conference, was reinforced in 1923 when again he offered nothing as an alternative concept for an evolving British Commonwealth of Nations. As Amery later commented, "while all the other Commonwealth Prime Ministers were keen and constructive and anxious to get things done, I formed the impression that King's chief aim was to avoid committing himself to anything." Continuous consultation was effectively buried and the right of the Dominions to conclude their own international agreements was formally recognized. The minimalist Skelton was delighted. His hyperbolic congratulations must have been as gratifying to King in 1923 as they had been the year before during Chanak. In his polarized thinking, the prime minister had convinced himself that paradoxically it was the Liberals, and not the rigid Tories, who were holding the Empire together by their flexibility and voluntary commitment. King and Skelton assured themselves that by their intrepid opposition they had defeated the centralists, but Borden was trenchant in his summation of the vacuity of their imaginings: "Mr. King was continually looking over his shoulder at Quebec, and sought evasion of responsibility in a futile and nebulous verbosity which must have been most exasperating to British statesmen."[55]

Nothing much came of the 1923 conference. Constitutional discussions continued to be shelved. Economic collaboration was raised, but little more than platitudes emerged. At King's insistence, military collaboration was shunted aside. Recent revision of the Admiralty's sensible prescriptions for what assistance would be most helpful if Canada intended to give any substance to its own navy, as Laurier had pledged as early as 1902, came to nothing. Larkin had warned King what to expect: "there will be trouble, for I am told that Australia has been very 'ugly' of late and most determined to have an arrangement come to by which the [Royal] Navy will be contributed to by all Dominions."[56] Larkin had grossly oversimplified the Australian position, but King remained deeply suspicious of Admiralty proposals, although he had been relieved to a degree by a pre-conference letter from Amery: "The conception of a centralized navy ... is now completely extinct."[57] Centralization in naval affairs – or in air affairs for that matter – was no more acceptable to King than in foreign affairs, a point that he subsequently made at great length to the conference:

I was a member of Sir Wilfrid Laurier's Government at the time the naval policy was introduced, and ... the reason we held so strongly to the view of Dominion naval services was that we felt that if anything in the nature of contributions were requested, if anything in the nature of centralisation of organisation was expected, we could never expect the Dominion to respond, as we felt sure it would were [*sic*] the people to feel that the naval service of the Dominion was the natural outgrowth of their national standing and national status.[58]

Even a visit with other prime ministers and Amery to the Home Fleet at Spithead did nothing to change King's thinking, possibly because Amery took the occasion, upon their viewing the long lines of grey warships, to observe, "That is why you are Prime Minister of Canada and not, at best, one of the senators for the American State of Ontario."[59]

On the subject of emigration, little also resulted, despite the urgings of Amery that Britain was "terribly congested" while Canada lacked "the human material to give it the fullness, richness and variety which the national life of such a wonderful country as Canada should have."[60] Even in the case of immigration, Larkin, himself the son of an indigent immigrant, remained suspicious of British motives. "Personally I am not at all in favour of doing great things towards helping [emigrants] to go out [to Canada], for in that way we get a poor class as was shown by the vast majority of those who were brought out years ago ... by the Salvation Army."[61] While opposing what it saw as a not too subtle attempt by Britain to foist its unemployed on Canada through its 1922 Empire Settlement Act, Ottawa nevertheless continued to accept – although not to assist – orphans and other destitute children, presumably yet more of the "wrong type" in Larkin's eyes. The British minister of labour, however, concluded on a visit to Canada that the incidence of local abuse of "home children" was such that no more should be sent (the estimated total had increased to one hundred thousand by 1930). In opposing immigrants from Japan and China (the Chinese Immigration Act of 1923 effectively ended even the trickle), King described to the conference how he was working to keep them out: "These Orientals have the capacity for increasing their numbers once they get into the country. The children of Japanese and Chinese families ... are much more numerous in British Columbia than are children of white families."[62]

King, Skelton, and Larkin were no less certain that centralists were as hard at work in the economic sphere as they were in the political. In parallel with the conference of 1923, the British government had convened an imperial economic conference, meeting on alternate days. Although it largely overshadowed the conference itself, it made no more progress in advancing imperial cooperation. At first, the prospects for an imperial tariff preference seemed to be improving. The British Conservative party had begun to move toward protectionism. For the first time in a century, duties on a wide range of imports, even selected foodstuffs, were being actively considered, which could open the route to an imperial tariff preference. Interest in a preference had increased, broadly from a consciousness of unity in the face of shared dangers during the First World War and more specifically from the unanimous recommendation of the Balfour Committee of 1917. In 1919 and again in 1921 Britain had instituted tariffs which, although modest in themselves, would have been unthinkable before the war. In June 1923 Amery had suggested to Larkin, "Why don't you ask for a preference on your flour and other manufactured articles?" But Larkin was immediately suspicious of his motives. He reported to King that "other members of the cabinet do not see eye to eye with him ... it might be that Amery wants you to force [his own] Government's hand."[63]

Australia and the other Dominions had gone to the 1923 conference eager to see an imperial tariff preference constituted for foodstuffs. King had not. Increased sales of Canadian grain were of course a good thing, but not at the price of a negotiated imperial preference. King eschewed the very idea of tariff bargaining with Britain; as in Fielding's budget of 1897, Canada would make tariff concessions only unilaterally; otherwise, Canada's fiscal autonomy might somehow be eroded if it were to negotiate tariff levels with "the Mother Country."* Fiscal responsibility required that each member nation decide itself whether to participate.

Always clear at least to himself about what he did not want, especially in imperial relations, he equally rejected the proposal for an imperial economic committee to meet between imperial conferences. The alarm bells also rang in the mind of Skelton who advised, "This proposal is

---

* Larkin appears to have deviated once from the prime minister's policy. He took the initiative to encourage the British government to keep its tariffs on motor vehicles so that Canada would continue to enjoy a preferential tariff in the British market for "our large export motor trade." King was uneasy, believing that between Canada and Britain preferences should be granted unilaterally (although in the case of the United States they should be negotiated).

simply another variant of the endless schemes for establishing a central government here [in London] ... It would commit us to a central review of every important economic activity of our government."[64] *The Times* on this occasion agreed with King, but for an entirely different reason. It reflected Curzon's conviction that imperial economic unity would reduce British freedom of action and even sovereignty. "Various speeches by the Dominions obviously imply that the Imperial Conference has power to impose taxes [by raising tariffs] upon the people of Great Britain ... It is satisfactory to see that no such false conception of the power of this Imperial Conference has entered into the mind of Mr. Mackenzie King."[65]

Economic uncertainties everywhere gave impetus to the idea of imperial economic collaboration. Pressed by Amery and by the chancellor of the exchequer, Neville Chamberlain, Baldwin finally decided to do what no other British prime minister had yet been prepared to do: go to the electorate with a policy of extending the few existing modest imperial tariff preferences so as to expand markets for British manufacturers while at the same time strengthening imperial bonds. The election of December 1923 was the only election in British history fought mainly over tariffs. The year before, the dying Bonar Law, acutely aware of the mounting divisions within his own party, had promised that "this Parliament will not make any fundamental changes in the fiscal system of this country" (in other words, his government would not abandon free trade). This legacy was widely interpreted as pledging a Conservative government not to institute tariff protection as the necessary basis for an imperial preference. Nevertheless, Baldwin reversed his predecessor's pledge, convinced that mounting unemployment could only be stemmed by tariff walls against imports. There was little real enthusiasm among most of his cabinet colleagues for his *volte face* and, as his hasty and ill-prepared election campaign would soon prove, even less amongst the British electorate.

Baldwin's central challenge was to convert the British people themselves from free traders to protectionists. Only after that could serious discussion begin with the Dominions of collective policies intended to promote greater imperial unity. That occasion in fact never emerged: in the general election at the end of 1923 he lost the Conservative plurality, opening the way to the formation in January 1924 of Britain's first Labour government under Ramsay MacDonald (supported by surviving Liberal free traders). The prospect of "dear food" had appealed to almost no one, but even after the election in which his policy had been so decisively rejected, Baldwin remained unrepentant. "Rightly or wrongly, I was convinced you could not deal with unemployment without a tariff."

The new government disagreed. MacDonald's chancellor of the exchequer informed the House of Commons that

though not for a single moment admit[ting] that we are one whit behind those on the other side in our determination to do all in our power to promote the best interests of the Empire, we have never believed that those interests will in the long run be well served by a system of tariff preference and this view we [the Labour Party] have expressed by our vote in this House on many occasions. In these circumstances, the Government are unable to endorse proposals of their predecessors and we greatly regret any disappointment that this may cause Dominions and Colonies, but for that disappointment not this Government but our predecessors are responsible.[66]

Larkin had been privy to little of Baldwin's inchoate and ill-fated electoral thinking. Preoccupied with acquiring Canada House and, more importantly, forbidden by his own prime minister to engage in or even be present at any policy conversations that might conceivably encourage the always threatening forces of centralism, he lived through one of the climacterics in imperial history without apparently ever realizing it.

The concept of an imperial *Zollverein*, for which Galt, Tupper, Strathcona, and Perley had all striven in their various ways, had effectively perished in the British election of 1923. Their dearest wish had paradoxically arrived at a time when the Canadian prime minister had a deep-seated suspicion of all such proposals. Additionally, King's electoral support turned in part on those who opposed any tariff reductions (including those of an imperial preference), believing that nascent Canadian manufacturing would prove vulnerable to British imports. At the same time, almost unremarked, the United States was replacing Britain as Canada's principal trading partner. To bypass Canadian tariffs, its corporations were establishing branch plants or acquiring Canadian assets to an unprecedented degree.

Wade, the indefatigable agent general of British Columbia, would not, however, give up. He wrote to *The Times* on 16 January 1924, urging the government of Ramsay MacDonald to honour Baldwin's imperial tariff proposals. A horrified Mackenzie King appealed to the premier of British Columbia to silence his outspoken agent general, but he need not have concerned himself. The decisive rejection by the British electorate of what was regarded as the narrow wedge of food taxes meant the end of any real prospect of a broadly based imperial tariff preference. When Baldwin returned to office in late 1924, following the collapse of MacDonald's government, he floated the vague idea of a "guaranteed market under license" as a way of redeeming the pledge to the Dominions at the 1923 imperial conference. Larkin assured King that on this, as on all imperial proposals, "my policy here is to express no opinions." Even the modest idea of an imperial economic committee to consult from time to time on trade policy Larkin suspected "might be a beginning of an endeavour to manoeuvre us into a position which in principle you do not support."

Upon returning to office in November 1924, Baldwin, prompted by Amery, the new colonial secretary, implemented immediately his long-held conviction that the Dominions would have a more effective voice in international relations if he were to share weekly with their high commissioners Foreign Office policy thinking and to receive their comments in return. King, however, recorded his conviction that all such meetings (which, blowing them out of all proportion, he persisted in calling "conferences") were clearly "one of Amery's schemes to set up a Round Table council in London, and may create embarrassments. An effort to pull us into European affairs, Egypt [a matter of first importance to Australia and New Zealand], etc."[67]

It had all begun at No. 10 with a cup of tea (on that at least Larkin could offer an expert opinion) with Baldwin, his foreign secretary Austen Chamberlain, Amery, and the other high commissioners. The prime minister had stated simply that he proposed "to continue calling the High Commissioners together and keeping them informed of everything affecting Foreign policy that might be causing His Majesty's Government any anxiety."[68] This was ominous, but what followed was even more disturbing to King. Amery wrote (through the governor general, not Larkin) that the British government had concluded that not only was a constitutional conference "untimely" but even the mere "preliminary enquiry" agreed upon at the conference of 1923 "would [not] lead to any practical result." That was welcome news to King; he could not have agreed more. On the other hand, what followed was quite unacceptable. To the suggestion that the British government desired to avail itself "of every opportunity that may present itself for personal consultation between [cabinet] ministers· or with such other representatives as the Dominion Governments may at any time wish to entrust with the task of representing their own views or ascertaining those of the British Government," King responded briskly, that "his ministers [i.e., himself] are ... very strongly of the opinion that no change involving a departure from the methods at present accepted should be made."[69] Any change could only be for the worse. He shared with Larkin his suspicion that that the tea party at No. 10 was anything but a tea party; it was probably, a prelude to regular meetings of High Commissioners collectively with the Prime Minister or Foreign Secretary to discuss foreign policy. Such group meetings ... involve approach to proposals of an imperial council in London steadily rejected by Laurier and the country generally, and which bring with them more of responsibility than control ... This whole matter we regard as of more concern and importance than any before us at the present moment.[70]

In a private letter to Larkin of the same day, King added:

The Members of the Government ... express the hope that collective conferences between the High Commissioners of the several dominions themselves would not become an established practice but be discontinued in as tactful manner as might be possible ... The circumstances of the recent meeting of the High Commissioners with the Members of the British Government has given a quite new significance to the whole matter, and it is for this reason that my colleagues felt that I should recall to your mind what our view was before anything of the kind in any possible way had entered your thoughts.[71]

King followed with a similar, if a yet more florid, message to Amery: "Ministers of the Crown in Great Britain and Canada of themselves [must decide] upon the questions that may demand consultation, most appropriate methods of consultation, and upon the extent of their interest and obligation in all such matters."[72] Larkin assured King that he understood perfectly his position. He described how at the first meeting he had said nothing, but had merely listened. However, in case the high commissioner remained uncertain about any aspect of his opposition, King repeated,

Our position, in a word, is that negotiations within the Empire, where they cannot be made a matter of direct and immediate communication between responsible Ministers themselves, should be carried on in a manner wholly similar to that adopted by different nations between themselves, namely through the agency of someone having diplomatic standing and recognition who will act on instructions from his Government and be responsible to his Government ... Your letter expresses exactly what our view is: namely, that the powers of our representative in London should be restricted to conveying messages between the two Governments with freedom to advise his own Government in any way at any time with respect to the wisdom of any particular course.[73]

Larkin replied, "There has been a good deal of talk in the papers of late ... regarding the status of the High Commissioner, many suggesting that he should be a Cabinet Minister ... this would be a very serious mistake. There might at some time be a man appointed as High Commissioner who might place yourself or any succeeding Government in an embarrassing position ... it would be far more prudent to keep your High Commissioner as he is now ... with no powers other than to convey messages between the two Governments."[74] Larkin's mealy-mouthed message was precisely what King wanted to hear, and Larkin knew it. He declared himself quite content merely to convey messages from one government to the other. Echoing to himself Skelton's flattery following Chanak, King happily declared to his diary (with questionable syntax): "I am helping to make History in the lines along which I am defining relations between different parts of the Empire."[75]

The irrepressible Amery was, however, soon stirring the pot again. In June 1925 – the same month that Canada House opened its doors – Baldwin announced that having the Colonial Office deal with the Dominions no longer accorded with constitutional realities. Accordingly, a Dominions Office would be created with its own secretary of state, although for the time being the colonial secretary would fill both posts. Amery confirmed to his old friend Geoffrey Dawson, the editor of *The Times*, that one of his motives in pressing Baldwin for the new ministry was to eliminate "the legend of Colonial Office officials writing to a nigger one minute and then turning around and writing in the same strain to Dominion Prime Ministers." Frequent meetings with high commissioners were at the same time affirmed, whatever the opposition of the Canadian prime minister. Amery invited them to meet with him every Tuesday morning "for a talk." In fact, he added mischievously, the idea originated with the Canadian high commissioner.

I readily took up a suggestion of Mr. Peter Larkin's, the Canadian High Commissioner, that I should be "at home" one morning every week for all the High Commissioners. This ... [gave] me an opportunity of telling them collectively of ... affairs in which they were generally interested ... Unfortunately, when Mackenzie King heard of this ... he at once suspected a sinister design on my part of gradually working towards some sort of Imperial policy council situated in London ... so poor Larkin had to come and tell me, very apologetically, that he was not allowed to see me except by himself. The rest of us continued our friendly and useful talks.[76]

In carefully avoiding any acknowledgment to Ottawa that he himself had proposed the regular meetings, Larkin hesitantly added to King,

I know you do not look on meetings of the kind suggested with favour ... but I cannot see how the High Commissioners can decline to meet the Colonial Secretary when he requests us to do so ... I can hardly see how we can object because we are always describing ourselves as of one family and quite unlike other nations, who would probably object to seeing the Foreign Secretary with the representatives of other nations. In any case, you can rely upon my being most careful and not assenting to anything before consulting you. Immediately after the meetings I will make a memorandum of everything that has taken place and report to you by mail if I think it unimportant, and by cable if I think the slightest importance attaches to it. In this way I shall, I am sure, be acting according to your wishes, and very much in the same way as any Ambassador or Minister would under similar circumstances, i.e., as a conveyer of messages between his own Government and the Government he is accredited to, and in this I think there will be safety.[77]

In his protestations Larkin may have been a little disingenuous, but Philip Kerr of the Foreign Office knew very well what King's reaction to such weekly briefings would be. He advised substituting individual briefings for collective meetings, more time-consuming although they would be, so that King could not characterize them as imperial consultations, but Austen Chamberlain, the foreign secretary, rejected the idea out of hand: "the British Empire is one and indivisible." Separate briefings would be "a denial of unity."[78] King's subsequent negative reaction to the collective gatherings was exactly what Kerr had anticipated.

When the Canadian election of October 1925 reduced the Liberals to a minority government, they had to rely upon the Progressive party to remain in office. In June 1926 fraud in the Customs Department suddenly brought down King's minority government. The governor general, Lord Byng of Vimy, refused the request of the chagrined prime minister for dissolution. King urged him in an anachronistic way to seek the guidance of the dominions secretary. Instead, Byng, on advice, gave Meighen's Conservatives the opportunity to form a government. When Meighen's minority government was soon defeated, King was triumphant in the subsequent election in which he had made, in his mind at least, nationalism versus imperialism the central issue. Certainly King, Valiant for Truth, was in no doubt of the righteousness of his cause: "I go forward in the strength of God and his Might and Right to battle as my forefathers battled for the rights of the people and God's will on earth."[79]

Larkin survived the three months of Meighen's Conservative government, the new prime minister having far more pressing matters at hand
than worrying about the do-nothing Liberal high commissioner. Even
with the resumption of office by the Liberals, the elderly Larkin never
regained even that minuscule degree of momentum that he had prior to
King's defeat. He became even more passive as King, upon returning to
office, resumed his suspicions of what he regarded as British centralists,
primarily as a means of reassuring Quebec against what he habitually
portrayed as Meighen's uncompromising imperialism.

Between the 1923 and 1926 imperial conferences, the uncertain and
clearly disparate reactions of the Dominions to the negotiation of both
the Lausanne and Locarno treaties had raised yet again the question of
imperial consultation and cooperation in foreign affairs. The foreign secretary had signed for Britain alone the Lausanne accord, explicitly stating
that no Dominion need feel bound by it and leaving Britain a free hand
in foreign policy-making. The Dominions, having rejected the Geneva
protocol of 1924 intended to strengthen collective security through the
League of Nations, were absent from the Treaty of Locarno of 1925. The
Dominions had been kept fully informed and were free to join if they had
chosen to do so. That they did not underlined the agreed principle of
1923 that no British commitment would involve Dominions without their
explicit accord. Britain was left to deal with Europe alone, although it was
impossible to envisage the Dominions, other than Ireland, standing aside
in any major conflict. Further, by not being at the negotiating table and
leaving it to Britain to conclude international agreements, Canada, one
historian has argued, "had willingly dropped back into the position under
which high policy was made in London."

Borden did not like that. The abandonment of consultation meant the
abandonment of efforts to achieve imperial coordination. Nevertheless,
"I am wholly confident," he wrote to Austen Chamberlain, "that in the
Resolution [IX] of 1917 the true basis and sure hope of Imperial unity
are [still] to be found."[80] He remained cautiously hopeful that in time
Canada might yet seek "an adequate voice in foreign policy and in foreign
relations" within the Empire: "Continuous consultation seems to have
broken down for the time being, it does not necessarily follow ... that it has
wholly broken down or that its failure is due to inherent defects ... unfortunately, political conditions in the Dominions [i.e., including the election
of Mackenzie King] failed to give such initiative and leadership as might
have contributed to carrying out the original project."[81]

Since diversity in foreign policy had now in effect been acknowledged (driven in large measure by Ireland and South Africa, but not opposed by King), the "equal in status" school of imperial thinking had taken a major step forward. The stage was now set for what would eventually become the Statute of Westminster. Nevertheless, upon his departure for the 1926 imperial conference, there remained in King, as one student of the gatherings has put it,

a powerful feeling that to maintain dominion freedom required continued watchfulness on his part, in all his dealings with the British authorities. His whole approach to Canada's empire relations, in fact, was marked by a fundamental suspicion, which by this time was virtually an element of his public personality, that the British government (more precisely the permanent British establishment ensconced in Whitehall) had not and would never give up their hopes for a centralized imperial structure, with the dominions committed to collective policies on all fronts – diplomatic, strategic, economic ... For King there was this contrasting nightmare of empire, which he found impossible to relinquish. Assiduously reinforced by the warnings of Skelton, Clifford Sifton and other Canadian nationalists, and from London by High Commissioner Peter Larkin, it would haunt him virtually to the end of his political life.[82]

King took with him to the imperial conference Ernest Lapointe, minister of justice; Oscar Skelton, who went, he wrote to his wife, to "stiffen King's backbone"; and Vincent Massey. King had Massey in mind to be Canada's first minister to the United States; unlike the impecunious Arthur Currie but like Larkin, he could readily meet the many expenses which the pittance of a salary and allowances could not possibly equal. King had contemplated sending him to Washington in 1925, but Meighen had briefly come into office before he could do so.

Along with his intention to proclaim the Washington legation, King went to the conference with his recent constitutional disagreement with the governor general and his subsequent electoral triumph over Meighen very much in mind. The role of the governor general must now be stated clearly. Both the Australian prime minister and he agreed that in terms of inter-governmental communication, the governor general had become "merely a post office." When it was eventually acknowledged that the governor general stood "in all essential respects the same position in relation to the administration of public affairs in the Dominion as is held by His Majesty the King in Great Britain," the need was thereby recognized for the appointment of British high commissioners to the Dominions. King was ready with his advice to the British government: "At present Canada had a High Commissioner who lived in the British Government atmosphere and could reproduce that atmosphere in his communications to the Canadian Government ... it would similarly be an advantage to the British Government if they had an English [sic] High Commissioner who could reproduce the Canadian atmosphere to them."[83] King could then communicate directly with the British government without having to do so through the Canadian high commissioner in London, at the centre of the Empire. A high commissioner arrived in Ottawa in April 1928.

King's second goal – aside from instructing Lapointe on what to say to Churchill about the exclusion of Canadian cattle from the British market – was to replace the designation high commissioner; "He had in mind the establishment in the Empire of a sort of diplomatic representation such as existed in the case of the rest of the world."[84] In again advocating an alteration in the designation of representatives of Commonwealth countries, however, King spoke alone. He did not press the point, instead acceding to the related conclusion of the conference that the Dominions would benefit from regular information and comment on foreign affairs from the British government: "the representatives of the Dominions welcome the offer of His Majesty's Government in Great Britain to give full information in regard to foreign affairs, and to discuss foreign affairs with any person representing a Dominion (whether a [cabinet] Minister, High Commissioner, Liaison Officer or other official)."* King did not dissent, but he rendered the provision of "full information" to Canada decidedly more difficult than it was to the other Dominions by insisting that rather than have Canada House act as the medium,

he would much prefer to get information from a British official in Canada. He would rather that [the foreign secretary] should communicate with his officer in Canada, than that [he] should communicate with a Canadian officer here [i.e., the high commissioner], whether as regards the communication of information by the British Government to the Dominion Government or as regards the method by which the Foreign Secretary in London could ascertain the views of the Dominion Governments on any particular matter of foreign affairs.[85]

---

* What use Larkin made of the "full information," principally copies of telegrams and "prints" which the Foreign Office voluntarily supplied, is unrecorded (in 1925 alone, copies of 190 telegrams and 576 despatches from British missions abroad were supplied to Canada House).

He also made clear his opposition to the appointment of a cabinet minister as high commissioner. At the end of March 1926, shortly before his departure for the imperial conference, King had roundly rejected Perley's proposal in the House of Commons that a cabinet minister be appointed to help reverse what Perley described as his neglect of relations with the United Kingdom.

King had long believed that he himself was the only person who could possibly be entrusted with the conduct of relations with "the Old Land." Anyone else might do things that could threaten national unity. Canadians representatives could be subtly seduced, at least metaphorically, by duchesses (King had been reliably assured that even the Labour leader Ramsay MacDonald had in fact been) and the profusion of other douceurs of London life. If communications from the British government were to come to him via the British high commissioner, there would then be no danger of the Canadian high commissioner becoming ensnared in imperial consultations or "conferences." Even then, King was not entirely satisfied. Amery had matched his undertaking to appoint a high commissioner to Ottawa with reconfirmation of the weekly meetings with the high commissioners in London. King had immediately become alarmed. Amery was not surprised. He wrote to Austen Chamberlain that King "wanted to do the least consultation possible ... What I think he is most timid about is the idea of the High Commissioners meeting you or me collectively, lest out of that there should in some way or other grow up some sort of Imperial Council." Later Amery added that King "suspected a sinister design on my part of gradually working toward some sort of Imperial policy council, situated in London – the great bugbear which he always dreaded."[86] Larkin, on the other hand, was reassuring to King. He complacently and wholly unrealistically assured him that the matter of consultation through the high commissioners "is settled now once and for all with the present Minister [Amery] and any other who may succeed him" (presumably he had in mind the arrangement whereby the other high commissioners met collectively with the dominions secretary but he met with him separately).[87]

King summarized his thinking about high commissioners in a long exchange with R.B. Bennett in the House of Commons in which he declared that, on the one hand, the office was unquestionably Canada's highest overseas post with, on the other hand, a flat statement that "the last thing I should wish to see was a cabinet minister filling it."[88] King retained his dark suspicions of British motives, despite the fact that, as a Canadian journalist later observed,

Prime minister Mackenzie King (second from left), minister of justice Ernest Lapointe (first left) and high commissioner Peter Larkin (fourth left) all in *de rigeur* top hats, arrive at Canada House on Trafalgar Square prior to the October 1926 imperial conference in London. Vincent Massey (third left), soon to be appointed Canada's first minister in Washington, was in his bowler. King came away from the conference convinced that he had prevented a British "sinister design ... of gradually working toward some sort of Imperial policy council, situated in London – the great bugbear which he always dreaded."

Equality of status within the Empire was settled, once and for all, prior to the Peace Conference of 1919. It was definitely settled again ... by the Imperial Conference which Mr. Meighen attended during his first brief sojourn among us as Premier. Mr. King, not to be outdone, secured equality of status for us all over again when he went to London during his first tour in the political front line, returning to boast that the discussions anent the Halibut Treaty made it obvious that at last Canada had achieved full nationhood ... The Imperial foregathering of 1926 again tapped the Empire tree ... enabling the Government ... to point out, for the fourth time in seven years, that the goal of even-stephen had been reached at last.[89]

Following the 1926 conference, King made no contribution to the Committee on Inter-Imperial Relations, chaired by Balfour, the former prime minister, which eventually formulated the conclusions of the 1926 conference for the approval of the 1930 conference. Before it began, Balfour, echoing both Resolution IX and Baldwin, had declared that "The rapid evolution of the Overseas Dominions during the last fifty years has involved many complicated adjustments of old political machinery to changing conditions. The tendency towards equality of status was both right and inevitable. Geographical and other conditions made this impossible of attainment by way of federation. The only alternative was by way of autonomy; and along this road it has been steadily sought. Every self-governing member of the Empire is now master of its destiny."[90] After a certain degree of haggling, the Dominions agreed with Balfour's formulation: "They are autonomous Communities within the British Empire, equal in status, in no way subordinate one to another in any aspect of their domestic or external affairs, though united by a common allegiance to the Crown, and freely associated as members of the British Commonwealth of Nations." The premiers were more or less content, but King George V was not: "Poor old Balfour has given away my Empire."

The conclusions of the 1926 conference represented what broadly speaking Mackenzie King had long sought. He congratulated himself with the thought that "the Imperial Conference has helped to give me a place in history." Nevertheless, he told Larkin to be eternally vigilant: "The proceedings ... convinced me more than ever that, as a Dominion, we must preserve an individuality that is distinctly our own, and not become one of a type in inter-imperial affairs. There is no more reason, on an equality of states basis, why you should go and sit with half a dozen others each week than that Amery should come each week with half a dozen to your office to listen to you talk."[91] The hand of Skelton was equally evident in King's subsequent statement, "We must develop within the Empire a system of communication between its Governments, identical on all four, with that now existing between countries that have their own diplomatic services." And in case there was any lingering misunderstanding, King wrote to Amery in March 1927, reaffirming that no meetings of high commissioners could be countenanced. He then proceeded to establish a legation to the United States.

On 18 February 1927 Vincent Massey presented his credentials to President Coolidge as Canada's first minister in Washington. King appears to have valued the symbolism of the appointment since, as C.P. Stacey has noted, "Neither the High Commissioner in London [Larkin] nor the

Minister in Washington [Massey] were very vital functionaries in King's eyes, and gave them little significant work to do ... When he had important business [in London] ... he sent a Prime Minister-to-Prime Minister cable; when he had important business in Washington, he got on the overnight train and went to see the Secretary of State, or preferably the President."[92] But the principle of having a separate Canadian representative in Washington troubled many Tories and even some Liberals, including Fielding. For R.B. Bennett, the opposition leader, Massey's appointment represented nothing less than "the end of our connection with the Empire."[93] Australia later contented itself with having a minister (diplomatic) in the British embassy in Washington.

King had made it courteously but firmly clear to Larkin that any opinion on matters imperial was for the prime minister alone to express. Nevertheless, the dreaded wraith of centralism had almost enveloped the high commissioner in mid-1924 on the question of whether Britain should represent Canada at the inter-allied conference called to endorse the Dawes Plan for the resolution of German reparations. King belatedly stated that Canada would have separate representation, with full powers to sign. Larkin was instructed to "maintain our position strongly and permit no departure therefrom."[94] Larkin subsequently helped to represent Canada at the reparations conference at The Hague in August 1929 where the Young Plan, sponsored by the United States, would, it was hoped, succeed where three years before the Dawes Plan had failed. The elusive goal of putting an end to the continuing question of how Germany's payments were to be proportioned and how subsequently debtor countries were to pay their creditors was primarily a matter for Britain, France, the United States and Germany, but Larkin did fill a minor role by agreeing on behalf of Canada to the reduction of reparations from Germany and by undertaking to return seized German property. A few weeks before Larkin's death, King confirmed to him acceptance of Canada's share of the reparation bonds, payable by 1988.

Six months before his death, Larkin played no role in the concentrated campaign for imperial free trade that was launched by Beaverbrook – his "Empire Crusade." The Conservative party, defeated by Ramsay MacDonald in the 1929 election, was suffering in opposition from the uncertain leadership of Baldwin. "To Beaverbrook the remedy for the Conservative sickness was obvious: to end the party argument about Tariff Reform that had threatened party unity since 1903 by the adoption of 'whole-hog' protectionism ... Baldwin must swallow food taxes ... This was the idea that scared Baldwin most: a revival of the old Tory nightmare that support for any tax on food, when 'cheap food' was the strongest Labour and Liberal card, would bring the party down in ruins."[95] Baldwin's misgivings were understandable, given his defeat in the snap election of 1923. Beaverbrook, undeterred, launched his Empire Crusade:

We declared that the Empire, including Britain, the Dominions, Crown Colonies and Protectorates, possessed a potential supply of all food requirements and nearly all raw materials which the Empire consumed. Our ideal was the welding together of the British Empire in an economic group outstripping in purchasing power, food production and raw materials even the United States. We emphasised in our campaign our ties of race, loyalty and outlook. This plan brought us into conflict with Baldwin. He would not support a British import tax on foreign food with free entry of Empire foodstuffs (then Britain's principal imports from the Dominions and Colonies). He believed that a tax on food, even foreign food, would bring his party down in ruins. 'Stomach tax' the free-food Tories called it – and Baldwin was among the free-food Tories.[96]

Beaverbrook's determination to drag the Conservative party, however unwilling, to Empire free trade arose not from "vanity or boredom," as Churchill lightly suspected, but partly from long-held conviction. His biographers have recorded how

His first mentor, John F. Stairs [of Halifax], had strongly supported the Imperial Preference ideas of Joseph Chamberlain. New Brunswick was the home of a very special kind of imperial enthusiasm. Sir George Parkin from New Brunswick ... was in his day ... the most persuasive, rational and respected of all advocates of Empire unity; a source of Churchill's boyhood inspiration; a friend of Alfred Milner, the mentor of the younger English imperialists ... The Maritimes were full of Loyalist families whose ancestors has left the United States in order to remain under the British flag ... Protection, in Beaverbrook's thinking, was the only way to defend Canadian independence – political as well as economic – against its mighty neighbour.[97]

Beaverbrook in his subsequent advocacy happily seized on any evidence of support from Canada – the *Alberta Farmer* was not surprisingly an early ally – but from Bennett and later King and Larkin he received none. The Canadian high commissioner looked every day at Beaverbrook's campaign headquarters across Trafalgar Square which was under the aegis of a committee which included the New Zealand high commissioner. Beaverbrook's crusade "to visualise the Empire, the Dominions and the Colonies alike, as one eternal and indestructible unit for production, for consumption, for distribution" prompted the leader of the opposition, R.B. Bennett, to record helpfully that he had found "greater interest in Empire Trade in Britain today than even in the time of [Joseph] Chamberlain."* If so, Larkin, in his dying days, could do or did nothing to exploit it.

Macdonald formed his second Labour government in June 1929, to be greeted with Larkin's private analysis that "From now on no one can shut his eyes to the fact that, for good or evil, Socialism backed up by Communism, is gaining ground steadily all over Great Britain, and I think it will continue to do so."[98] This rare political prediction from Larkin may have been taken by King as additional evidence of his friend's gradual decline. Certainly he appears to have sensed a failing in his old benefactor's powers, especially evident following the high commissioner's return from the funeral of Marshal Foch in Paris, his arrangements for Ramsay MacDonald's visit to Canada, and his continuing concern about the level of Canadian duties on tea (about which he had grumbled to the prime minister from time to time). King responded kindly: "More and more, you must feel that you are entitled to delegate many of your duties to others and that whatever you may require in the way of additional staff or assistance toward that end, must be found ... feel free to spend your months and days so as to give yourself plenty of time for travel, plenty of time for rest and change, and plenty of time for friends."[99] In a few months, on 3 February 1930, at the age of seventy-four, Peter Larkin, like Strathcona and Tupper, died in Britain.

* Beaverbrook attempted in vain to interest Hamar Greenwood, now Lord Greenwood, his fellow Canadian, to take the chairmanship. A few years earlier, Clementine Churchill had written her husband warning him off Greenwood: "It makes me blush to think that men of the calibre of you and the P.M. [Lloyd George] should have listened to a man of the stamp of Hamar who is nothing but a blaspheming, hearty, vulgar, brave knockabout Colonial" (Roy Jenkins, *Churchill* [London, 2001], 362). She was no more enamoured of Beaverbrook: "Try ridding yourself of this microbe" (Chisholm and Davies, *Beaverbrook*, 439).

CHAPTER SEVEN

Howard Ferguson, 1930–1935

Three months after Larkin's death, King offered the high commissioner-ship to Vincent Massey, Canadian minister in Washington. King later recalled that "I had a long distance telephone conversation with the Hon. G. Howard Ferguson, the then Premier of Ontario, in which he said, 'I would like to make one suggestion, that you appoint Mr. Massey to London as High Commissioner. No better appointment could be made.'"[1] Colonel Ralston, the minister of national defence, concurred. He wrote to the prime minister from London, "Obviously if Massey can be spared from Washington and wants this position, I feel to choose him would be ideal. He is the sort of man who would comfort our British friends by making them feel that we are not out of sympathy with this perplexed country and at the same time, he is clear-headed and practical and would avoid the jingo Imperialist attitude which dies hard."[2] Whether King agreed with this balanced judgment is doubtful, but on 24 July 1930, four days before the general election, the order-in-council appointing Massey was issued.

A fortnight later on 7 August 1930, R.B. Bennett became prime minister, three years after becoming leader of the opposition in the buoyant days of the late 1920s. He arrived in office with a markedly different approach towards the Empire than that of King and Skelton, with their conviction that full autonomy in foreign policy – as they defined it – was Canada's only future. In any case, in the wake of the market crash of the year before, Bennett's priorities were necessarily economic, not constitutional. The Liberal Massey soon found himself out of the London office before he was in it.

With the Canadian election of 1930, Beaverbrook's imperial crusade, joined with the mounting economic depression, forced the issue of where Britain and Canada each stood in the long debate about Empire trade and unity. Problems began immediately with Beaverbrook's understanding of what Bennett's electoral victory meant. He saw it as having been greatly if unintentionally assisted by the Liberal movement for closer trade relations with the United States. Bennett declared his campaign platform on the floor of the House of Commons on the eve of the dissolution. He said – "I am for the British Empire next to Canada, the only difference being that some gentlemen [Mackenzie King and his ministers] are for the United States before Canada. I am for the British Empire after Canada". He offered ... as an alternative Imperial Preference and Unemployment Relief. He won. The news of his victory gave us joy and gladness. Bennett at last Prime Minister, as I had often foretold. Bennett the mighty man of Empire! Faith in seat of authority and power! I could hardly grasp the reality. Everything, yes everything, would be possible and probable, and indeed quite certain. Glory Hallelujah! Our Empire Free Trade ship was this day launched and safely in the calm waters of a sheltered harbour.[3]

In fact, Bennett won the election advocating not Beaverbrook's imperial free trade but an imperial tariff preference.*

Tariff increases and an associated imperial preference were to be part of Bennett's answer to the depression, requiring that he have his own person in London, and that person would be most decidedly a Conservative. Ever forceful and direct, he acted promptly to reverse King's appointment of Massey, not believing that three years of diplomatic service in Washington had washed away his Liberal hue. Bennett had joined the former Liberal finance minister Fielding in questioning even the need for a Canadian legation in Washington when King had appointed Massey. As leader of

---

* In his flamboyant press and political campaign for Empire free trade, Beaverbrook had the support of many Conservative members of Parliament and peers, including the following Canadians. Sir Arthur Morrison Bell was a veteran of the Royal Canadian Regiment in the South African War and member of Parliament for Honiton from 1910 to 1930. Brigadier-General Alfred Critchley of Calgary was the member of Parliament for Twickenham in 1934–5 and Sir Beverly Baxter of Toronto was the member for Woodgreen and later Southgate from 1935 to 1955. Colonel Walter Grant Morden of Ontario who had vigorously promoted a Canadian air force during the First World War was the member for Brantford and Chiswick from 1918 to 1931, as well as owner of the independent conservative newspaper, *The People*. Baxter, who was for many years employed by Beaverbrook on his newspapers, described his part in the "Empire Crusade" in *Strange Street* (London, 1935). In a flight of pseudo-Churchillian rhetoric, Baxter warned the House of Commons in 1946 that "If the [Labour] Government tries to eliminate Empire Preference a number of us will conduct such a nationwide campaign ... as will light the very beacons on the hills. We will attack them in the market place, in the towns and the cities, we will rouse this whole country against them in such a crusade as will overcome this Government, because we will not have it" (House of Commons Debates, 19 July 1946).

the opposition, Bennett had declared: "If we are a sovereign state [with a legation in Washington separate from the British Embassy] we cannot belong to the British Empire ... what we ought to establish is ... a high commissioner's office" (i.e., in his view an emanation of the government of the day rather than of Canada itself).[4]

On the day that the new Conservative government was sworn in, Massey wrote to Bennett: "I have been in the Canadian service abroad since its extension in 1927, having served as Minister at Washington until recently, when I was transferred to the High Commissionership in London. I am at present ... to proceed to my post early in September. I shall be very grateful for an expression of your wishes in the matter."[5] The new prime minister lost no time in expressing his wishes. He was determined not to have a Grit in London, notwithstanding the well-intentioned advice of Newton Rowell, the distinguished Liberal who had served in Borden's wartime Union government. Rowell urged that Massey's appointment should not be countermanded for partisan reasons. Massey was the person who could resolve "one of the weaknesses in the High Commissionership in recent years ... the diplomatic side (by which I mean consultation with respect to imperial and foreign affairs) has not been developed as it should have been" under Larkin.

Bennett did not heed Rowell's advice. In Massey's recollection of his two meetings with Bennett in mid-August, his "manner at the outset was truculent and surly." The meeting left Massey in no doubt of Bennett's intentions; on 14 August he reluctantly resigned his short-lived London appointment. After consulting King, who as always sensed that some political hay might be made, Massey added to his letter of resignation that he viewed London as "an integral part of our service abroad, differing, of course, in its procedure from our foreign diplomatic offices [then only in Tokyo, Washington, and Paris], but akin to these in the qualifications of its personnel and in the relation of that personnel to the government which it serves."[6] Bennett, convinced that King had drafted Massey's letter of resignation, disagreed. A month later, on 16 September, he replied in his rotund way: "The present Conservative Government considered it proper to adhere to the spirit of the statute creating the office of the High Commissioner ... and to affirm the policy ... by appointing as its representative [i.e., not *Canada's* representative] one who through conviction could fully subscribe to the declared views of the Government relating to the conduct of the affairs of this country in Great Britain."[7]

On 20 September, four days after his cancellation of Massey's appointment, Bennett made a statement to the House of Commons differentiating fundamentally between London and the three "diplomatic" posts:

The Ministers to France, Japan and the United States are permanent and are not to be subject to changes of administration ... With regard to the position of High Commissioner, ... it is a statutory office ... the position has been of a political nature, using the word in the large and proper sense. The High Commissioner should not only reflect the policies that are originated and initiated by the Government of Canada, but enjoy to the fullest degree the confidence of the administration and reflect the spirit and attitude of mind of the administration towards the problems with which they have to deal ... that office is practically a member of the administration [i.e., a minister] ... He is not a diplomat, for under the convention of [the imperial conference of] 1926 communications are from prime minister to prime minister.

Bennett's statement publicly ended any lingering hopes that Massey may have had. As Lester Pearson subsequently noted:

Vincent Massey, who was about to be transferred to London by Mr. King, would have been quite happy if that transfer had been carried out by Mr. Bennett, thus confirming Massey's view that, as minister to Washington since 1927, he was a diplomatic and not a political officer of the government. The tradition, however, that the appointment was solely political and was to be held by a friend of the government in office was too strong. Added to this was the fact that Mr. Massey had for a short time been a member of Mr. King's government in 1926 and was certainly no favourite of Mr. Bennett. The result was Mr. Massey's resignation and the appointment of the Honourable G. Howard Ferguson, a former Conservative premier of Ontario, as High Commissioner to the United Kingdom.[8]

Howard Ferguson's father, Dr Charles Ferguson of Kemptville, Ontario, had been the long-serving Conservative member of Parliament for North Leeds and Grenville and a staunch supporter of Sir John A. Macdonald even during the worst days of the Pacific Scandal, siding with Tupper in his denunciation of Donald Smith. Howard Ferguson's maternal grandfather, Robert Bell, a Conservative member of the legislature of Canada West and editor of the *Ottawa Citizen*, was defeated in the election of 1867.

Howard Ferguson was born in 1870 into the secure world of Pax Britannica, with Canada the leading colony in the world's greatest Empire. When, as a graduate of the University of Toronto and as a young lawyer, he became reeve of Kemptville, he

organized – in a snowstorm – the welcome home for its single veteran of the South African War. "During the past year you and your brothers in arms have done heroic service for the good old British Empire and have covered yourselves with honour and glory ... Those who have had the good fortune to escape the bullet of the treacherous Boer have reason to thank God ..." the band played "British Grenadiers" and "Soldiers of the Queen" ... In little Kemptville the citizens had gathered together to do homage to their warriors and to sing the Empire's patriotic hymns. Events such as these nurtured in Ferguson and his generation in Ontario the spirit of British patriotism that remained characteristic of many of them.[9]

When Ferguson was first elected to the Ontario legislature in 1905, he held a deep suspicion of what he and others perceived as the insidious spread of the French language in Ontario, especially in its school system. Later, in his bigoted advocacy of the infamous Regulation 17, limiting severely the teaching of French, Ferguson gave full vent to his imperial commitment and his ardent opposition to the nationalism of Henri Bourassa and his ilk.

For Ferguson and millions of other English Canadians in 1911, the British Empire and its values were part of their daily experience. The Empire gave meaning to their Canadian nationality, it provided assurance that their country would resist the pull of the great but threatening Republic to the south, and it brought a sense of identity ... To such people, Bourassian ideals of dualism were utterly foreign, while Bourassa's opposition to imperialism could only be regarded as an attack on much of what they held dear.*[10]

Fifteen years a member of the Ontario legislature and, during the First World War, minister of lands, forests and mines, "Foxie" Ferguson reversed the fortunes of the Ontario Conservative party following his confirmation as leader in December 1920. He defeated the government of the United Farmers in 1923, having triumphed over its efforts to destroy him politically by an investigation into alleged partisan corruption in timber licensing, "one of the most sensational incidents in Ontario's political history."[11]

As premier during two consecutive terms through the prosperous 1920s, Ferguson carefully avoided the contentious issue of prohibition of alcohol and concentrated instead on government frugality and management of Ontario's natural resources, while increasingly uneasy at the unprec-

---

* Later Ferguson was prudently to modify his opposition to French language schools in Ontario beyond the elementary level when in the 1920s he successfully sought the support of Quebec in his quarrel with Mackenzie King over provincial claims to water rights.

edented degree of investment flowing into the province from the United States (partly to surmount Fielding's tariff preference for Britain). He was relentless in his campaign for recognition of enhanced provincial rights, including in his unlikely alliance with Premier Taschereau of Quebec, against what he saw as the centralists in Mackenzie King's Ottawa. He was equally unrelenting in his advocacy of closer imperial ties. Throughout his life he remained a consistent, ardent, and vocal exponent of imperial unity, hardly surprising in one who could declare: "We are going to change the course of the Canadian ship of state, we are going to turn toward the east instead of toward the south; and we are going to see that Canada not only leans upon the British Empire, but that she clings to the British Empire."

The international status of Canada and its place in the Empire was, constitutionally speaking, beyond the Ontario premier's purview, but in his dual capacity as minister of education he could at least ensure that each Empire Day was marked by the publication of extravagantly pro-Empire booklets for distribution throughout the schools of Ontario, the texts emblazoned with "One Flag, One Fleet, One Throne." Acutely conscious of the seemingly inexorable inroads that imports and investment from the United States were making, especially in Ontario, Ferguson was a vigorous exponent of an imperial tariff preference. To one who opposed both the appointment of a Canadian as governor general and the abolition of appeals to the Judicial Committee of the Privy Council in London, it was not a big jump to advocate an imperial tariff preference as a means of helping to unify what he regretfully perceived as an increasingly nebulous Empire. In May 1924 he wrote to Stanley Baldwin, the leader of the opposition at Westminster: "We in Canada, and particularly in this province, are staunch imperialists, and are anxious that no opportunity be lost to disseminate and promote greater British sentiment in this country."[12] He had loudly endorsed Meighen's "ready, aye ready" stance at the time of Chanak. But he equally loudly split with him when in November 1925 Meighen, fatally burdened in Quebec by his pro-conscriptionist past, made an ill-fated attempt at reconciliation by going beyond even King's Parliament-must-decide by pledging that a "decision of the Government [to go to war] should be submitted to the judgement of the people at a general election before troops should leave our shores." When Meighen had consulted him privately in advance, Ferguson's opposition was immediate. Now he made it public. Anything that might possibly be gained in Quebec by such a commitment would be more than offset by the sacrifice of support in Tory Ontario. A later vanity press biography set Ferguson apart from what he regarded as pusillanimous leadership:

At the great ... convention held in Winnipeg in 1927, he took an out and out stand as to Canada's course in case of another war. Angrily interrupting the proceedings, he refused to countenance what he considered the paramount issue of imperial defence. Rather than yield any ground he attacked a former prime minister [Meighen] who, he thought, had advocated a too hesitant course. He was right, and Canada knows that he was right ... [As for] Mr. Mackenzie King and the other status mongers ... He described ... as travelling over to London every few months with the object of breaking down the constitution and weakening the imperial ties.[13]

Ferguson was so alienated by Meighen's novel commitment to a general election before a declaration of war that, having rejected suggestions that he himself be a candidate (as Perley had already done), he strongly endorsed Bennett and effectively scuppered any lingering thoughts of a Meighen draft. Ferguson was even-handed in his vigorous condemnations. In Bennett's highly successful 1930 national election campaign, Ferguson denounced Mackenzie King as simply unworthy to hold the office of prime minister. King in turn feigned great surprise: "I have felt hurt today at Ferguson's endeavour to have the campaign made one of personal attack and bitterness towards myself. I am through with Ferguson. He is by nature a skunk."[14]

Ferguson had long stated his intention to retire as premier of Ontario when he reached the age of sixty, following twenty-five years in the legislature. He did so, however, only when he was certain that he was going to the most important Canadian post abroad, where he intended to give greater substance to his imperial convictions. First, however, while still premier, he accompanied the new prime minister to the imperial conference in October 1930. In the presence of Bennett, Ramsay MacDonald and his secretary of state for the Dominions, J.H. Thomas, Ferguson opened the new Ontario House at 163, The Strand. He was also intent upon attempting to patch up the continuing differences between Bennett and Beaverbrook, two old friends who should in his view be natural allies in the struggle to increase intra-Empire trade. He did not, however, suspect that he would himself within a few months become high commissioner. Major-General Alexander McRae of Vancouver was, he knew, intended for the post.*

---

* Alexander McRae had several qualifications for the post, not the least being that he had become well acquainted with Britain during the First World War. Born in 1874 in Winnipeg, McRae and Bennett had known each other when McRae was involved in the sale of CPR lands in the North West. McRae was appointed by Perley to his Overseas

As premier of Ontario accompanying the prime minister, Ferguson lost no time in repeating publicly his imperial thinking. In a long letter to *The Times*, he called for a true imperial economic partnership. At the opening ceremony of the new and much enlarged Ontario House, Ferguson urged Britain to impose tariffs against foreign imports so as to create a preference for goods from the Empire. To the Royal Empire Society, he was more explicit about the growing threat to Canada from United States investment and protectionism. By 1930 two-thirds of Canadian imports were from the United States and half of Canadian exports went there. The response should be an imperial preference. Presumably with Beaverbrook in mind, Ferguson was especially candid in speaking to the Canada Club: "Canada could not have Empire Free Trade. They in Canada must have tariffs if they were to have industrial development. The idea of reciprocal tariffs was one that appealed to them; it was a policy that Canada understood ... They were prepared to change the height of their tariff wall to permit other sections of the Empire to come in and trade with them on equal terms."

The positions of Beaverbrook and Bennett, supposedly like-minded New Brunswickers, were in fact basically irreconcilable. Beaverbrook continued to advocate imperial free trade – that is, no tariffs among members of the Empire (there would then be no difficulties in Britain over food taxes). Bennett, on the other hand, was convinced that what he saw as Canada's infant and vulnerable manufacturing industries could not withstand free trade and continued to require protective tariffs. A preference could certainly be given for imports from the Empire, but a high degree of tariff protection must be retained. In short, Empire free trade was "neither desirable nor possible."

With no high commissioner in place and given the mistrust by Bennett's new government of the Ottawa public service – Liberal as it surely must be after King's term in office – Ferguson was a major influence on Bennett at the imperial conference of 1930 in attempting to win British support for some sort of imperial *Zollverein*. The British electorate had decisively rejected food taxes in Baldwin's "tariff election" seven years before.

Military Council. He played a role in the establishment in 1918 of the British Ministry of Information where he and Beaverbrook knew each other well. He was the Conservative member of Parliament for Vancouver North from 1926 to 1930 and with Perley was a principal organizer and fund-raiser for the 1930 election (in which R.B. Bennett's Conservatives were victorious but in which paradoxically McRae was himself defeated). When he declined the London appointment, the prime minister sent him to the Senate. McRae died in Vancouver in 1946.

Bedrock Tories both, Howard Ferguson (left), the premier of Ontario, and R.B. Bennett, the Canadian prime minister, at the October 1930 imperial conference; the following month Bennett appointed Ferguson high commissioner and, later, concurrently a representative to the League of Nations.

Imperial free trade was a theoretical alternative, but in practice the idea could go nowhere when the Dominions, including Canada, were eager to shelter their own infant manufacturing industries from the full challenge of more sophisticated and efficient British competition. Bennett arrived advocating a 10 per cent increase in tariffs to foreign countries while holding tariffs for the Empire at existing levels, thereby creating an imperial preference. His stance was consistent with his solution to the depression, having continued the recent Liberal practice of increasing tariffs to record levels in retaliation for record US protectionism. There remained, however, confusion about what in fact he intended at the conference. The British high commissioner in Ottawa wrote to the dominions secretary that he had called on Sir George Perley, then deputy prime minister, to discuss the "possible outcome of the Imperial conference. Perley did not seem to know much of what Bennett had in mind; indeed the Government appears to be very much a one-man show."[15]

At the conference itself, the rhetoric of the newly-elected Canadian prime minister was evangelical in tone: "We dare not fail ... the time is now at hand when the doctrine of closer Empire economic association must be embraced, if we would not have it slip forever beyond our powers of recall." In his opening statement, Bennett was at his bullying best: "we must approve or reject the principle [of an imperial tariff preference]. I put the question definitely to you, and definitely it should be answered. There here is no room for compromise and there is no possibility of avoiding the issue ... Delay is hazardous ... The time for action has come." By 1930, almost a century after the British government had first committed itself to free trade, Bennett had decided, upon coming to office, that unemployment in a deepening global depression required higher tariffs which would in turn offer room for an imperial preference. He elaborated his position. "I offer to the Mother Country, and to all the other parts of Empire, a preference in the Canadian market in exchange for a like preference in theirs, based upon the addition of a ten percentum increase in prevailing general tariff, or upon tariffs yet to be created, and in like proposals and acceptances by all other parts of Empire, we attain to the ideal of Empire preference.' Ominously for Beaverbrook, Bennett added, "this proposed preference should not be considered as a step towards Empire free trade ... [which] is neither desirable nor possible."[16]

What Bennett was offering was an elaboration of what he had advocated upon coming to office: all countries of the Empire would increase their general tariffs by ten percentage points, but retain their existing tariffs to each other so as to create an imperial preference. For the British, the problem was that, in the end, their manufacturers and consumers would pay much of the bill, with the rest of the Empire conceding little.

Not surprisingly, the reaction among his fellow prime ministers, Bennett noted, was a "unity of opinion [in favour of an imperial tariff preference] ... except on the part of Her Majesty's Ministers in the United Kingdom." Ramsay MacDonald appears to have been taken aback by Bennett's self-centred proposal. Any bridging initiative on MacDonald's part was, however, partly doomed by the reaction of his chancellor of the exchequer, Philip Snowden, who declared that "The policy of the United Kingdom has always been free trade, and the United Kingdom Government must reckon with public opinion ... and take account of the declared policies of the responsible political parties. The present serious situation in trade made everyone jumpy, and the effects would be very serious if a big change in the fiscal system were carried out and resulted in no substantial improvement."

Snowden was in no doubt about the nature of Bennett's proposal: "Preferential tariffs in the Dominions were, in fact, imposed for purposes of protection, and it was the policy of the Dominions to encourage local production. Canada already had very high duties and had recently raised them. Mr. Bennett proposed no reduction in any of the existing tariffs, although these were designed to keep out British goods. Therefore, he [Snowden] did not see that the proposal would help British manufacturers." To Snowden's scepticism, Bennett revealingly replied, "such a widening of the margin of preference would be of help to our manufacturers. Canada was the fifth most important trading country in the world. She now imported 1,500 million dollars merchandise, of which two-thirds now came from the United States. There was much room here for diversion to the United Kingdom ... It was important to realise the magnitude of Canada's trade, and he thought that an increase in the general tariff rates of ten per cent should divert trade from the United States." Snowden remained unconvinced:

The effect of the ten percent increase in the Canadian general rate would not be to divert trade to the United Kingdom manufacturer. The result would more probably be, firstly, that the United States tariff against Canada would be still further raised, and secondly, that United States firms would establish more branches in Canada ... contiguity would always make Canada and the United States one economic unit. (Mr. Bennett dissented.) The higher Canada raised her tariffs against the United States, the more United States capital would come into Canada.

In his summation, Snowden could hardly have been clearer about the opposition of many in the British government to Bennett's self-serving proposition:

All [Dominions] were agreed on the desirability of increasing trade. The question was how to do it. Mr. Bennett had said that he was not wedded to the method of preferential tariffs, but was prepared to consider other arrangements. He could hold out no hope of any departure from the established fiscal policy of the United Kingdom, especially in respect of taxes on foodstuffs and raw materials. There was no political party in this country pledged to such taxes ... The solution of our difficulties and encouragement of our trade must be found in other directions.[17]

The final communiqué of the 1930 imperial conference was more circumspect, but it needed no more than an elementary understanding of the debate to see that Canada and Britain were on divergent courses; "The United Kingdom [had] declared that the interests of the United Kingdom preclude any international economic policy, like tariffs, which would injure its foreign trade or would impose duties upon food or raw material; the Dominion Governments have declared that the interests of the Dominions necessitate a tariff policy intended to encourage the growth of [their] manufacturing industry." *The Times* correspondent reported that Bennett's stance had evoked deep misgivings even in Ottawa:

I find Conservative opinion of the intelligent sort very dissatisfied with Bennett's performances at the [Imperial] Conference. They particularly dislike the threat of economic separatism ... and ask if he is going to make a reciprocity treaty with the U.S. [A leading journalist] for instance is very critical and says, "He began with an ultimatum and ended with a 'declaration of war.'" What many people also hate is the revelation to the U.S. of quarrels within the Empire.[18]

The reply of Geoffrey Dawson, the editor of *The Times* and sometime Round Table activist, reflected his conviction that the conference might not have ended on quite such a sour note if Massey had been high commissioner: "I regret more and more that Party feeling did not allow the Prime Minister to go on with Vincent Massey, who would certainly have created a new and better tradition in London."[19]

Bennett was in principle as negative about the possibility of imperial defence cooperation as he was about imperial free trade. While in London, he attended a meeting of the Committee for Imperial Defence, but he remained convinced that Canada simply could not afford to spend anything more on its already starved and minuscule armed forces. Equally, he was unwilling to employ them in imperial tasks. When, for example, the proposal was made by Britain that the Dominions might want to assume defence responsibilities for adjacent imperial territories, Bennett responded that "no Canadian Prime Minister could ask for expenditure on the defence of the West Indies without political control."[20] There was, apparently, on this occasion no British response to the implied Canadian interest in somehow absorbing the British West Indies into Confederation (which was presumably what Bennett meant by "political control").

Jan Smuts of South Africa later accurately described the 1930 imperial conference as "what might have been the most brilliant, the most successful and greatest of all the Imperial Conferences has ended in disillusion and disappointment for every part of the British Commonwealth."[21] The basic problem was the growing diversity and special interests of the Dominions. At Westminster, J.H. Thomas, the secretary of state for the dominions, "took the gloves off," denouncing Bennett's proposal for an imperial preference: "there never was such humbug."* In that case, responded an angry Bennett, "I have little hope that any agreement which Canada may reach with the overseas dominions will include the United Kingdom."

In these unpromising circumstances, the prime minister took up an earlier idea of Mackenzie King by proposing – and the British government somewhat reluctantly agreeing – that, following further consideration by committees, an imperial economic conference should be held in Ottawa within six months to consider all ideas of imperial economic cooperation. (In fact, it was delayed for almost two years, partly by elections in New Zealand and Australia.) In the meantime, tariff margins would be frozen. Bennett declared roundly that the Ottawa conference would lay "the foundation of a new economic Empire in which Canada is destined to play a part of ever-increasing importance." Before he embarked for home, Ferguson endorsed enthusiastically the invitation to Ottawa in a letter to *The Times*. The "Old Thunderer" duly declared itself enchanted with the imperialism of the premier of Ontario, as well as with that of the new prime minister of Canada.

One of the few tangible results for Canada of the 1930 imperial conference had not been economic but constitutional: the promotion of provincial against Dominion powers in the formulation of what would become the following year the landmark Statute of Westminster. Largely at Ferguson's prompting, Bennett, upon his return to Ottawa, convened a dominion-provincial conference to review the provisions of the draft British legislation as it pertained to provincial powers. This eventually resulted in the injection of article seven into the Statute of Westminster, asserting a greater authority for the provinces in constitutional change, a gratifying addition that was made during Ferguson's appointment as high commis-

---

* Thomas was not alone in describing an imperial tariff preference as "humbug" (in the British House of Commons on 27 November 1930). Asquith had once denounced the idea as a "squalid imposture." Ferguson himself had the year before described the Liberal tariff and specifically the imperial preference as "the greatest piece of hypocrisy and humbug ever pulled in this country."

sioner. The statute itself, however ambiguous overall, was given second reading at Westminster in 1931, confirming broad formulations of imperial ties, practices, and status that had been canvassed at the imperial conferences from 1917. By 1931, with people throughout the Empire understandably preoccupied with hardships resulting from the depression, little attention was given to the details of the statute, codifying the autonomy of the Dominions. Baldwin, in leading for the Conservatives, explained that the Empire of 1931 was not the Empire of 1914. "After the War, and even more at the Imperial Conference in 1926, it had been a shock to find that politically the Dominions had grown up." Clement Attlee, from his encounters with the Dominions when in MacDonald's government, later observed that the statute "really added statutory effect to what was already accepted in practice, the equality of all the Dominions."

The imperial Ferguson may in fact have considered the Statute of Westminster, as a whole, unnecessary; when it was adopted, he had little to say about it, despite its recognition of provincial powers. More gratifying to his mind was the reintroduction of weekly meetings, instituted soon after Larkin's death, of all high commissioners with the dominions secretary. The avowed Liberal Skelton – who surprisingly had not been removed from office by the arch Tory Bennett – had no choice but to accept what he had long worked so assiduously to prevent.

Before returning with Bennett to Canada in late November 1930, Ferguson unexpectedly informed the press that he was considering accepting the prime minister's recent offer of the high commissionership, following McRae's withdrawal. The Toronto *Globe* welcomed the news: "his place is with the public among the people, acquainting them with the potentialities of the overseas Dominions ... At no time has it been so important that Canada be represented in Britain by a man burning with zeal for the welfare of the Empire." The Montreal *Gazette* was even more rapturous:

Mr. Ferguson's appointment means, to some extent, a new departure in the High Commissioner's service, and his work should be more beneficial to the Dominion and to the Empire than any performed under normal conditions by any of his predecessors in this generation. A striking personality, a fluent and effective speaker, courageous and aggressive and yet tactful and considerate, Mr. Ferguson will fill the role of High Commissioner in a new way, and as an apostle of Imperial unity he will put his natural talents to their fullest and most effective use. Indeed his appointment bids fair to rank as one of the most noteworthy events in Anglo-Canadian history in many years.[22]

The Liberals in Ottawa were not so sure that Ferguson's appointment was such a noteworthy historical event. John Dafoe, editor of the Liberal *Winnipeg Free Press*, was convinced that Ferguson would carry "his vulgar incompetence and cheap smart-aleckism into a position in which he will reflect discredit upon the whole country."[23] In a letter to the principal of Upper Canada College, Dafoe added, "I squirm when I think of what they say in England about Ferguson, the amused contempt, the resolve to treat him with mock politeness as an oaf, a freak from the outer marches."[24] Mackenzie King, the leader of the opposition, certainly did whatever he could to help ensure that Ferguson was so viewed. Having convinced himself that as high commissioner Ferguson "would be a very bitter partisan and very crude in many ways," he wrote privately to Ramsay MacDonald, Lloyd George, and Sir John Simon in an attempt to undermine him. He alleged that Bennett was conspiring with the British Conservatives to bring down the Labour government: "Before Mr. Ferguson has been very long in London, he will be espousing in public, as well as in secret, the cause of the Conservative Party in Britain."[25] King's action was surprising, but hardly more so than that of Robert Borden in writing to Baldwin in October 1930 about his two fellow Conservatives: "Bennett and Ferguson are great masters of bluff and ballyhoo, not too well informed or sincere."[26]

Back in the Ontario legislature in mid-November, Ferguson informed his caucus of his decision to resign as premier to become high commissioner. According to a story from a well-informed but decidedly Liberal journalist in Ottawa, Ferguson claimed that, having at first declined Bennett's offer when in London, King George V promptly sent for him. The King made

a pathetic personal appeal ... the Motherland was going to pot, the socialist government was ruining the country, destroying the morale of the people. Unless something was done, and that quickly, England's greatness would be but a memory. It was a time ... when big men ... were needed to bring Britain back to her senses, awaken the dormant, drugged, genius of the people. Ferguson was such a man ... and [the King] pleaded with him to reconsider and accept ... Ferguson ... [said] that when he listened to his Sovereign ... there could be no refusal ... [He] meant to go to London and do his best to revive the ancient vigour of the Empire.[27]

On 28 November 1930, Ferguson's appointment was formally announced by Bennett. A fortnight before, *The Times* had trumpeted:

Every well-informed Canadian must agree that Mr. Ferguson's avowed aims in accepting the high commissionership are worthy aims, and that in their accomplishment he will render "a very real service, not only to this Dominion, but to every part of the Empire, and especially to the Mother Country." It can surely be suggested without offence to the British people – the finest race on earth – that heavy war burdens and world responsibilities may have temporarily clouded or somewhat obscured their Imperial vision. It may be that a persuasive voice from one of the daughter nations will have an electrical effect in stimulating Empire sentiment ... If any man can fulfil that assignment, that man is the retiring Premier of Ontario. A consummate politician, a wise statesmen, a striking personality, a persuasive speaker, a gladiator of courage and aggressive spirit, he should do a great work in the United Kingdom.[28]

The Conservative *Saturday Night* was no less delighted. On 6 December it informed its readers:

The speed with which the Federal cabinet acted in appointing Hon. George Howard Ferguson ... after he had obtained the consent of his followers in the Ontario Legislature to his retirement from the Premiership, illustrates the keenness of the Bennett cabinet's desire to send him to London at the present juncture. Evidently Mr. Bennett's experiences during his stay in Great Britain have convinced him of the necessity of establishing at Canada House a representative of compelling magnetism, in addition to proven ability ... No other man is better qualified to serve as a good-will ambassador than Mr. Ferguson; none would more heartily enter into all measures for the cementing of Imperial economic unity.

In the hagiographic "hurried biography" published to mark Ferguson's departure, his own convictions are boldly stated: "As citizens of a self-governing state within the Empire, our interests are world-wide, our viewpoint cosmopolitan. Identified with Great Britain and other parts of the Empire, Canadians can do their part in extending the benefits of civilization, in elevating the child peoples of the earth towards self-government, as is being done with India to-day, and in championing the cause of liberty and right wherever it is found in weakness."[29] Ferguson predicted to Toronto newspapers an early British election, which would result in the welcome defeat of the Labour government and its free trade policies. In response, an enraged "Jem" Thomas, the secretary of state for the dominions, coldly told Bennett through the British high commissioner that he would inform Ferguson on arrival of the need "to refrain from anything which could be interpreted as intervention in the politics of the United Kingdom."* Ferguson the Conservative and Thomas the socialist were to have frequent clashes, but Ferguson remained undeterred in his reforming enthusiasms. In a speech to the Technical Service Council in Toronto on 4 December, he declared, "I am not going over there to sell wheat ... [but] I may do something to remould and revive the spirit of the British people. The old Empire ... has not struck bottom yet."[30]

The British high commissioner reported that Perley and his cabinet colleagues were much disturbed by Ferguson's outbursts. The liberally inclined governor general, Lord Willingdon, reported to London on "Ferguson's amazing utterances. [His fellow Conservatives] Robert Borden, Meighen and others have expressed themselves to me in the strongest terms." Journalists put it down to Ferguson's heavy drinking, although Dafoe added that the people would now see Ferguson "for the boor and the boob he is."[31] The Ottawa correspondent of *The Times* provided a private summary of the *opera buffa* which was yet more explicit.

The popular interpretation of it is that he [Ferguson] was drunk but the question is how often is he going to get drunk. He used to get drunk quite frequently, but had abandoned the practice until recently; it is said that the abundant hospitalities, which he enjoyed in England, have brought about a reversion to his old habits. Yesterday afternoon and today I have talked with Willingdon, Willie Clark [the British high commissioner], Perley and they are all aghast at Ferguson's performance.

Between us, Willingdon says he feels like resigning at once and going home. Imprimis he knew nothing about the appointment [of Ferguson as high commissioner] until Ferguson gave an interview on arrival at Quebec in which he said that he had been offered the appointment and would take two weeks to think it over. It is Willingdon who as the executive head [*sic*] of the Canadian nation

---

* In the election of 1905, James Henry Thomas (1874–1949) had been an ardent opponent of Joseph Chamberlain's tariff "reform" which would have led to an imperial preference; twenty-five years later, he was a cabinet colleague of Chamberlain's son, Neville. Thomas, born in poverty in 1874, began work at age nine. He eventually rose to head the National Union of Railwaymen and to be a member of Parliament from 1910 to 1936, filling a variety of ministerial posts. "He had also no common endowment of eloquence, insight, humour, joviality and an engaging common sense – qualities which were emphasized in his speech by a peculiarly pungent working-class accent, a deviant avoidance of the aspirate, and an occasional Rabelaisian turn." Thomas knew Canada well, having travelled there with Balfour's mission in mid-1917 and several times during the 1920s. One of his two married sons lived in Canada.

must sign the order-in-council making the appointment and he protested strongly to Perley at the cavalier treatment accorded him. Perley came and apologised on behalf of the Government; he said he had known nothing about the appointment ... Willingdon I think feels that Bennett and Company regard him as a partisan of the Liberals ... Ferguson when he came back made a speech predicting the early downfall of the [Ramsay] MacDonald Government. Clark thereupon went to Perley and asked him to stop Ferguson making such speeches, which Perley promised to do.

The truth is that he should never have been appointed. He is a likeable fellow who has been a pretty good Premier of Ontario – I have always voted for him – but at heart he a cheapjack country lawyer. He was once Minister of Lands and Forests and there is extant a report ... [which] investigated some scandal charges against his department which shows him in a most unfavourable light. Luckily he got into power before the report was published officially and got it partially suppressed. But it is a very damning document.

Ferguson has also been telling people that many prominent Englishmen besought him to come over and save Britain ... Bennett will be nearly crazy when he lands and finds what his High Commissioner has done.[32]

The saga of Ferguson's appointment was far from over. Bennett did not withdraw it, but he cautioned him to behave himself and commit no more of the *bêtises* which had so convulsed Ottawa. *The Times* correspondent duly reported privately to London:

Ferguson is now a much-chastened person and is singing very low in his speeches. Few public men have ever had such a dressing down as he got for his speech. I understand that Bennett made him face a sort of court-martial before the whole Cabinet and take a vow that he would keep out of British politics. Dafoe writes me that Ferguson is just running true to form, that he has neither intellectual capacity, character nor manners and that he is simply "a village cut-up of whom the Ontario Titania has been unaccountably enamoured for seven years." This is a Liberal view but Ferguson is a most unfortunate choice as High Commissioner. He will get drunk at some City banquet and make other fool speeches. I am not very fond of Massey and dislike his consort [Alice Massey] strongly but I freely admit that it would have been much better if Bennett had allowed them to stay in London. However, the Conservative party simply would not stand for it.[33]

Boob or no boob, Ferguson received little assistance in preparing himself for his difficult assignment – and in saving himself from himself. In Ottawa in late December 1930 and again in early January 1931 he met

briefly with Skelton and an official or two about the staffing and administration of Canada House. He was then sworn in as a privy councillor,
and that was about all that he received in way of introduction to the challenges that awaited him. For his part, Mackenzie King gleefully sensed
that there might be additional political capital to be had from reviewing
how his appointment of Massey had been cancelled and how Ferguson
had been appointed and, more generally, how the office of the high commissioner was being retained as a partisan platform by the duplicitous
Conservatives. Four months after Ferguson had assumed his appointment, King took the occasion of the parliamentary vote of total salaries
and expenses (of $132,260) for the High Commission to launch what he
considered a devastating broadside, but which must have wearied even
ardent readers of *Hansard* (if such exist). King put his basic position succinctly enough. Recalling the debate seven months before, he stated, "I
differ with [Bennett's] view that the position of High Commissioner for
Canada is a political office ... [it] is the highest of all diplomatic offices."
However, in attempting to bestow a non-partisan character upon it, historical accuracy failed the leader of the opposition. In an effort to demonstrate Laurier's non-partisan approach when retaining Strathcona, he
characterized him as "a Conservative who sat in this house as such; he
was appointed by Sir John A. Macdonald's Government." In fact, whatever others may have regarded him, Donald Smith had repeatedly proclaimed himself a non-partisan member. Moreover, he was appointed not
by Macdonald but by Tupper, five years after Macdonald's death.

Undeterred by his errors – which surprisingly went unchallenged,
including the fact that his own appointment of Larkin had been both bla-
tantly partisan and personal – King defined the high commissioner as
"the representative of his country in another country." This was a definition far from the minds of those who recognized the common monarchy
of the two countries. As Bennett responded, a high commissioner represented one government to the other, not one head of state to another. "To
all intents and purposes the High Commissioner for Canada is [a cabinet]
minister in London ... it is in the interests of this country and of Great
Britain as well that the incumbent of that office should be a member of
the government ... Sir George Perley [who may have been present in the
House] entertained that opinion and still does, and there are many who
share the view." King made a great show of measuring Ferguson against
Bennett's criteria of the high commissioner as someone directly reflecting
the views of the government of the day. He happily quoted back Fergu-

son's speech of 4 December 1930 in which he had so vigorously attacked the debilitating doctrines of the socialist government at Westminster. "Has my right hon. friend instructed the High Commissioner to embark upon a regenerating service? ... [did he] think this expression with regard to the British people ... will gain for him any confidence on the part of the government or people of Great Britain?"

Although the House was momentarily diverted by an ardent Orange member from Ontario querying darkly whether a recent audience of Ferguson (who was of Ulster ancestry) with the Pope signified that "he had gone over to Rome," Bennett attempted to answer King's ridicule. But the most that he could lamely reply was that Ferguson had assured him "that he thought all he was doing was talking to a small number of people and there was to be no publicity." As for Ferguson's first speeches in Britain, they represented "great and useful service. The Englishmen with whom I speak have no criticism to make of his observations ... They regard him as an admirable incumbent ... and one whom they are delighted to honour and for whom they have the warmest regard. I have seen [none] who have not spoken in the highest terms of our high commissioner." Bennett's reply was somewhat surprising, given the understandably adverse British reaction to Ferguson's blunt threat to a London audience: "unless you are very careful how you treat us it will only be another generation before we take your place as leaders in industry and as economic leaders of the world."[34]

King was not finished with "the skunk." Later in November, referring to a cable that the high commissioner sent to his successor as premier of Ontario congratulating him on his resounding victory in the provincial election, King had great fun ridiculing Ferguson's jocular salute to the Conservative triumph: "When us Britishers has a job to do, we does it." The conclusion to be drawn was evident to King: "In the mind of Canada's High Commissioner in London, the Conservative Parties of the two countries are allied and they alone are entitled to a monopoly of the term 'Britishers'. The High Commissioner should be promptly withdrawn."[35]

Upon his arrival in London in January 1931 with his wife Ella, a full year after Larkin's death, Ferguson's ambitions had appeared boundless, but his resources at Canada House were decidedly not. Lucien Pacaud, the former journalist and Liberal member of Parliament who had been secretary since November 1922, had been appointed acting high commissioner on 11 February 1930, almost a year before Ferguson's arrival. He had been dealing with such problems as barriers to the import of live cattle; an especially malodorous fraud involving silver fox fur farming in Prince Edward Island; the redemption of Grand Trunk Pacific bonds; and the appointment of Lord Bessborough as governor general.

Following Ferguson's designation, Pacaud rejected an offer of transfer to the staff of the legation in Tokyo and resigned from public service. His replacement, Georges Vanier, arrived in May 1931 from Geneva where he had been advisor to the delegation to the League of Nations. It was intended that Lester Pearson should join Vanier, but various demands in Ottawa delayed his arrival. Vanier was soon acting high commissioner, since Ferguson went to Rome in March 1931 as Canadian representative to the preparatory committee of the second World Wheat Conference and later to Geneva to attend meetings of both the International Labour Organization and the League (Ferguson was to be Canada's representative in Geneva frequently during the next five years). At the League, Pearson, on temporary duty from Ottawa, found Ferguson anything but a boob; he was "a kind and unpretentious chief. He spoke his views frankly and clearly, without verbal camouflage, but his friendly personality usually made it possible for him to express disagreement without giving offence. Moreover ... his political prestige in the Conservative Party gave him direct access to the Prime Minister and ensured that his views would be listened to with respect."[36]

In late 1931 Bennett instructed Skelton to review the whole question of how the British and Canadian governments communicated with each other and to seek the views of the high commissioner, including the revolutionary idea "of sending direct to [him] copies of all despatches ... sent to the Dominions Office, thereby relieving [it] of the responsibility of forwarding them to Canada House." From there, Georges Vanier sought a more active role in the consultation and coordination of foreign policy with the British government. He made a range of more specific recommendations regarding consultation and coordination, but as Massey later ruefully recalled, "apparently it was decided that no action should be taken," the dead hand of Skelton effectively preventing innovation. Vanier on his own initiative told the Dominions Office that he was himself "gravely concerned" that there was no imperial secretariat (along the lines of the League secretariat). He offered several proposals for greater consultation between Canada House and the British government – no doubt to the astonishment of officials of the Dominions Office – including regular meetings among the secretaries of the high commissions and British officials. Skelton recalled very well that when Larkin had raised the prospect of collective meetings of high commissioners, King, at his prompting, had been much agitated. Skelton was not about to change course, unless explicitly so ordered by Bennett. The prime minister, preoccupied by the mounting domestic problems of economic depression, let Skelton have his way.* And the debilitating understaffing of Canada House continued.

Several years later, near the end of Ferguson's term, the Foreign Office informally and candidly assessed the effectiveness of Canada House, whose understaffing had not been rectified. In the wake of an especially tiresome instance of Skelton misunderstanding – or misinterpreting – a British offer of information, a senior Foreign Office official noted to a colleague at the Dominions Office, "Canada House as at present organized is not really equipped for sending to Ottawa accounts of the kind suggested by the Foreign Office."[37] Even more condemnatory was a later observation from the British High Commission in Ottawa, following Ferguson's departure from London and Massey's arrival: "if the High Commissioner is generally regarded as capable and intelligent, as in the case of Massey, or if he is thought to be rather uninformed, as in the case of Ferguson, the effect in each case is to minimize his importance; in the first place because he might aspire to direct Canadian foreign policy from London [a suspicion which King would come to harbour about Massey], and, in the latter, lest he should be unwittingly led into some commitment by the more capable and astute British Ministers ... [it] certainly seems to be rather a thankless task for a capable man!"[38]

If it was thankless, it was partly the result of the persistent lack of co-ordination among the twelve Canadian departments and agencies represented in Britain. A decade before, the order-in-council appointing Larkin and subsequent events had presumably made clear that all their activities "should be placed under the high commissioner," a desideratum that Tupper, Strathcona, and Perley had advocated in their several ways. When Ferguson was in Canada upon his first annual leave, Vanier, sounding like Loring Christie ten years before, wrote to Skelton (without the high commissioner's knowledge):

No organisation can be a success without a head. It is very much as if a large business enterprise with an important branch in a distant city, allowed each depart-

---

* That Bennett did not remove the Liberal Skelton was attributed by the prime minister to being too busy with domestic demands during his first months in office. Eventually, having found Skelton useful, he offered him a knighthood. With what wry humour he did so is unrecorded. Skelton accepted the CMG.

ment in that particular branch to deal direct with the corresponding department (such as advertising, sales, etc.) of the head office, without going through the General Manager of the Branch. At the present time there is no General Manager in London.

In order to know what was being done in the way of co-ordination under the High Commissioners of the other Dominions, I have made it a point to go to each one of the High Commissioners' offices to find out how matters stand there; generally speaking in all cases there is complete co-ordination under the High Commissioner.[39]

Vanier had addressed his letter to Skelton, but it was Bennett who responded most effectively by obtaining a prompt commitment from his minister of trade and commerce that henceforth his department would fully recognize the primacy of the high commissioner. More importantly, Bennett also caused to be adopted an order-in-council of 14 October 1931 (following Ferguson's summer visit to Ottawa) stipulating that the high commissioner should have "charge, supervision and control" over the officials of all government departments represented in London. Ferguson, however, remained unconvinced that in practice all such officials were fully observing it. Five years later, when Massey succeeded him, the question of coordination and supervision had to be set out again in yet another order-in-council.*

Ferguson was to need all the help that he could get from his minute staff and an unresponsive Ottawa, particularly in attempting to tackle the challenging economic policy questions facing the Empire. Everywhere investment had declined and tariffs had been raised as governments struggled in vain to balance their increasingly unbalanced books, creating social and political upheaval and causing in turn yet greater government intervention. During the early autumn of 1931, Britain's financial situation had so deteriorated and unemployment so increased that Churchill, then chancellor of the exchequer, forsook the gold standard. (When Australia, New Zealand, and South Africa followed, there emerged the beginnings of a sterling bloc.) Baldwin agreed to join a national government as lord

---

* Ferguson had less difficulty with provincial pretensions partly because the continuing economic depression led New Brunswick and Nova Scotia to close their offices in London by mid-1931. Ferguson was spared the unhappiness of seeing his beloved Ontario House close during his term as high commissioner, but soon after his departure, Ontario, Alberta, and Quebec recalled their agents general; only British Columbia House continued in a reduced state.

president under Ramsay MacDonald as prime minister. Its subsequent election in October 1931 gave Bennett and Ferguson some hope; MacDonald had brought with him from the Labour party two "traitors" (in the eyes of many Labourites), Snowden and Thomas, but Conservatives would clearly dominate the National government. Neville Chamberlain, serving a second term as chancellor of the exchequer, was rightly convinced that international economic recovery depended upon the cancellation of both German reparations and Allied war debts. Coupled with that, Britain should, in Chamberlain's understanding, abandon free trade to increase the consumption of domestically produced food and manufacturers, but in the meantime it remained unclear what the new government hoped to achieve by its various placebos of tariffs, grain quotas, import boards, imperial trade promotion, and bulk purchases, all at a time of the unsettling re-emergence of Russian lumber and grain on world markets.

Ferguson was determined that, despite the handicaps of inadequate staff and wasteful federal–provincial duplication, he would do all in his power to increase Canadian exports, part of the answer to the alarming unemployment at home. Obstacles to imports of Canadian cattle remained, despite his efforts and those of Perley and Beaverbrook. High tariffs in the United States had virtually excluded Canadian lumber; somehow this loss of market must be offset by increased sales to Britain. Canadian exports to Britain had, however, been declining since the end of the First World War, a decline that was accelerated by the arrival of decidedly less expensive and generally higher quality timber from the Soviet Union, Finland, and the three new Baltic republics. Ferguson was convinced that such competition was unfair, but the basic problem was that Canadian timber was higher priced and transport costs greater than from the Baltic. Ferguson, beginning in January 1932, sought to prove that the Soviet Union, now eager to return to world markets, was dumping timber, produced by slave or forced labour while at the same time striving to export revolution.

The fundamental goal of the Soviet Union, in Ferguson's view, "was to destroy the whole economic structure of the world." Its reprehensible trade policies could threaten the success of the pending Commonwealth economic conference in Ottawa, but receptive British importers nevertheless increasingly purchased the Soviet product, despite Ferguson's imaginative charge that to do so was most "un-Empire." In addition to sending a stiff protest to his erstwhile critic Jem Thomas, the dominions secretary, Ferguson reported to Bennett, "I have secured a number of timber men who sympathize with the Empire idea to write letters to *The Times*. I succeeded in having the subject brought up many times on the floor of the

House of Commons and in the Lords ... We have been able to secure a great deal of publicity in the provincial press that has helped to stir up opinion."[40] At the Ottawa conference of 1932, Soviet trading practices would re-emerge as an irritant in Anglo-Canadian economic relations, but imperial rhetoric on that occasion was little more effective in countering British commercial interests in the re-entry of low-cost Soviet products on world markets than Ferguson's protests were two years before. Until his departure in 1935, Ferguson toiled on, but in the end Canada's share of the slowly recovering British market remained laggard.

Possibly salvation would be found in an imperial tariff preference, especially if underpinned by an agreement to support merchant shipping (the high commissioner was Canada's representative on the Imperial Shipping Committee). Encouraged by Ferguson's reports, Bennett visited London soon after the British election to gauge the prospects for his cherished Ottawa conference, now scheduled for six months hence in July-August 1932. What Bennett found was not at all encouraging: the National government was in a state of disagreement about how to increase exports so as to reduce soaring unemployment as part of the total response to the financial crisis facing Britain and the industrialized world generally. As the depression deepened, the Weimar Republic in Germany was in disarray; Britain, with German reparations suspended and in effect cancelled, could no longer pay in full its war debts to the United States.

The high commissioner bluntly warned the dominions secretary that the proposed introduction of a British tariff of ten percentage points across the board with one-third off for the Empire would not do the trick: if that was all that was on offer, the British "must take responsibility for Empire disintegration." He was scarcely behind his desk in Canada House before he threatened to resign as high commissioner and conduct his own campaign across Britain, as Joseph Chamberlain had once done, for an imperial tariff, "our last chance for the Empire." With reason, British ministers remained suspicious of Canadian motives. As in the 1930 conference, "The tariff discussions were always oddly one-sided. Dominion ministers felt free to attack Britain's agricultural free trade. But British ministers could not attack the growing protectionism of the Dominions ... To British manufacturers and politicians this protectionism was very worrying ... when sterling was overvalued and unemployment was severe."[41]

As Britain and the Dominions continued to flounder over what to do at the approaching Ottawa conference – the options were in fact severely limited – an increasingly beleaguered British government introduced in early 1932 the Import Duties Act, a protectionist tariff of 10 per cent that would apply to all countries, in part as a result of disappointment "at the slowness of the progress made [in arranging imperial discussions] upon the possibility of increasing United Kingdom exports."[42] Thomas was convinced that this pre-conference initiative would prove a useful tool at the conference itself to exact concessions from the Dominions.

Ferguson was outraged. He immediately embarked upon a campaign to win exemption for the Empire at least until the conference decided otherwise, correctly selecting the Conservative chancellor of the exchequer as his most likely ally in the British cabinet. Ferguson assured the sympathetic Neville Chamberlain that the imposition of the tariff on Commonwealth countries would undoubtedly jeopardize the conference. "In the British cabinet Chamberlain reported that Ferguson had confirmed his worst fears. The High Commissioner was being bombarded by [Canadian] Chambers of Commerce, etc. He had also received a telephone message from the Prime Minister of the Dominion, who was much perturbed and had gone so far as to suggest that ... it would be no use to hold a Conference at Ottawa at all."[43]

Ferguson's role in securing temporary exemption for the Dominions from the new import duties, despite the original intent of Thomas, drew high praise from Beaverbrook, who saw the exemption as opening a route to eventual Empire free trade. He wired to Bennett: "The remission of duty in favour of Dominions entirely due to Ferguson's intervention. His influence here is bigger than any High Commissioner of any Dominion at any time."[44] Bennett agreed, adding to Beaverbrook his "sincere gratitude for your [own] untiring and successful efforts." Beaverbrook in turn assured Ferguson that Bennett had been "loud in praise of the service that you are rendering ... Canada has never had a High Commissioner in London before." And Bennett, recalling his debate with King, added gratuitously, "where would we have been if Mr. Vincent Massey had been over there?"[45]

Ferguson was pleased with his success in helping to postpone the application of Britain's new tariffs to the Dominions but, less happily, he also claimed credit for teaching the free-trade British how to engage in the unhealthy practice of applying tariffs. "The question of tariffs is entirely new in this country ... I had a number of interesting talks ... and furnished them with the Canadian legislation and regulations. Their whole organization is set up on the same lines as ours." Ferguson's self-congratulatory hyperbole about teaching the British about tariffs was, however, tempered by a shrewd understanding of the balance of forces at work in the run-up to the Ottawa conference. He counselled moderation and compromise, but Bennett did not listen. In vain Ferguson urged that

nothing so important has happened for a century within the Empire. We cannot sit still as we are. We will either get closer together on a basis of mutual trade or failing that a process of disintegration will set in ... I sincerely hope that Canada will meet the representatives of this country and of the other Dominions in a very generous attitude. Let us start off well. If we make any sort of progress, this will not be the last Conference, and from time to time we can extend the sphere of reciprocal trade ... If we try, however, to create in our first effort a perfect working arrangement dealing with the whole category and variety of products we will make a mess of it.[46]

"Bonfire" Bennett did make a mess of it, partly because he went to the conference heavily influenced by the protectionist-minded Canadian Manufacturers' Association. A leading British Tory, Lord Irwin (later, as Lord Halifax, the foreign secretary), following a four-week visit to Canada, put his finger on what was wrong: "Bennett ... cannot make a very effective offer to Great Britain unless he is able to compel his manufacturing supporters 'to give a bit'."[47]

As the Ottawa conference approached, Ferguson's misgivings deepened. Bennett had proclaimed that "the closer economic association of the British Empire will herald the dawn of a new and greater era of prosperity."[48] Ferguson, however, was aware of the dangers inherent in such high-flown rhetoric. Again he urged moderation, writing to the minister of trade and commerce that "it would be a great pity" if imperial cooperation "were to get a setback because of our bargaining too closely."[49] The omens were not propitious. On the eve of the conference, both Britain and Canada in their own ways remained baffled about what to do. The British high commissioner reported his growing bewilderment: "I frankly find it extremely difficult to say where we stand ... Similarly, I find it very difficult to make up my mind as to what Bennett is really after."[50] Of Bennett, one British minister wrote, "He was the most dictatorial Prime Minister I have known in peacetime ... Bennett entrusted little or nothing to his Cabinet colleagues and kept most of the negotiations and problems in his own hands."[51] Ferguson in London was equally unable to make sense of what was likely to emerge.

The nadir in this pre-conference farce was reached at the end of February at a dinner offered by Hamar Greenwood. With several of his cabinet colleagues, including Baldwin and Neville Chamberlain, present, Thomas attacked Ferguson over Canadian tariff policy. "Jem was pretty skin full and he got across with Ferguson and he said exceedingly rude things about Canada and at last Ferguson said he would report him to his government. Austen [Chamberlain] then apparently did the heavy father, told Jem to remember he was a minister of the Crown and reminded Ferguson that such unofficial talks are never repeated. But it was all very unfortunate and bodes none too well for Ottawa."[52] Leopold Amery, Greenwood's brother-in-law, who was present, recorded that Ferguson's comments "let loose Thomas on a perfectly incredible display of his essentially vulgar and rancorous attitude toward the Dominions ... It is perfectly appalling that a man of Thomas's outlook and vulgarity should be allowed to represent this country at the most critical conference there has ever been. It was clear to me that Ferguson and Thomas hate each other violently."[53] Not surprisingly, Ferguson's apocalyptic version to Bennett was quite different – and decidedly more self-serving. "I did not hesitate to tell [Thomas] that his attitude would ruin the possibility of achieving anything at the Conference. I added that if this Conference fails, disintegration of the Empire would begin, and his would be the responsibility ... I think it opened the eyes of the others present"[54]

Occasionally, but always erratically, Ferguson was provided with a minimal guidance about specific points on the likely agenda of the conference, but ominously no prior understandings with the British were achieved. Disarray on both sides of the Atlantic persisted. The final agenda was available only eight days before the conference began, partly as a result of continuing uncertainties about what to do about German reparations and Allied war debt in the face of the global depression. The preparations were in the hands of the host country and Bennett's government did not find them easy to make, despite the fact that the Sunday before the conference was declared a national day of prayer for its success. Nine Commonwealth delegations totalling 280 persons, together with 190 journalists and 200 business people were to arrive in July 1932, stretching the meagre resources of Ottawa in general and of the departments of external affairs and of trade and commerce in particular to the limit.* Highly skilled although several of the individual officials were, they were

---

* Included among those pressed into the conference secretariat were two future high commissioners, Norman Robertson and Dana Wilgress; Lester Pearson, a future secretary at Canada House, ran the press office.

notable exceptions: the conference was never able to free itself entirely "from the incompetence of the Canadian bureaucracy, as supervised by O.D. Skelton" who "smelt the dreadful odour of imperial federation in every proposal for co-operation."[55]

Beaverbrook, on the other hand, was unrealistically enthusiastic at the prospects, Ferguson having prompted him with material suggesting that Bennett and Beaverbrook saw eye-to-eye (which they did not). Beaverbrook wanted to believe that

Bennett, a devoted Empire leader throughout his political career, had convened the Imperial Conference of 1932, for the sole purpose of promoting his ideal – an Economic Empire. The site was his own capital, Ottawa, and he would be the chairman. Bennett, first among equals of all delegates gathered together! The Canadian Parliament, with a decisive Conservative majority which had been elected on this very issue of Empire trade, gave him authority to act. He was supported in his policy by the majority of the Tory Members of the British Parliament. They looked upon him as the successor of Joe Chamberlain and Bonar Law, prophets of Empire. The British delegation, though led by Baldwin, would be dominated by Neville Chamberlain, hereditary high priest of the Empire faith. Bruce of Australia would uphold the banners of our marching Empire army. He had been a constant supporter of Empire Economic Union.[56]

After his post-prandial confrontation with Thomas, Ferguson feared that the dominions secretary would be the chief British delegate. He worked in whatever ways he could against his appointment, hoping that it would be Neville Chamberlain, but when it was Baldwin he at least regarded him as better than Thomas. Upon departure for Ottawa, however, Baldwin, always well disposed toward Canada (having travelled extensively in eastern Canada as early as 1890 and across the country as recently as 1927 with the Prince of Wales), was uneasy whether he, Chamberlain, Snowden, and four other British ministers could agree among themselves, let alone with the Dominions. Baldwin's misgivings were justified. Snowden, a vocal veteran of the 1930 imperial conference, was, in Churchill's later comment, committed to "free imports, no matter what the foreigner may do to us ... [and to] the 'Free Breakfast Table' even if it is entirely supplied from outside British jurisdiction." On the other hand, Chamberlain was willing to contemplate duties on non-imperial imported food.[57] "The delegation sailed with full power to negotiate – and in full confusion about the terms it might or might not accept." However divided and ill-prepared the British delegation was, it was not as uncertain as the Canadian. An Ottawa journalist summarized the Canadian offer as "next-to-nothing in a limited, highly-protected Canadian market, in exchange for a great deal in a huge and low-tariff Old Country market."[58]

The widespread puzzlement and even despair about what to do in the face of the depression had doomed the conference before it had begun.

The reasons for their [the delegates'] subsequent disillusion and disappointment are not obscure: the nature of the Empire had changed much more than the formal title of Dominion or the Statute of Westminster suggested ... 1923 was probably the last moment at which a genuine economic settlement could have been reached, and in 1932, the atmosphere of hard-headed horsetrading between the delegates discouraged idealism; finally, the Conference was stamped irremediably by the personality of J.B. [sic] Bennett, the Canadian Prime Minister, caustically described as "being possessed of the manners of a Chicago policeman and the temperament of a Hollywood film star."[59]

Another observer dismissed Bennett as "impetuous and quick-tempered, uncivilized rather than uneducated" or, as another put it even more succinctly, "partially educated and wholly uncivilized."

The Ottawa conference failed to address successfully any major problem that had been identified when it was first convened. It soon became a series of bilateral meetings among the nine participating countries. That it would fail to produce a general agreement was inherent in the unresolved debate between imperial free traders and imperial protectionists, aggravated by traditional "tariff reformers," some still believing in the mercantilist concept of a mother country exchanging with an essentially agrarian empire food and raw materials for manufactured products. In addition to its continuing opposition to duties on imported foodstuffs, the British government, through a variety of quotas, minimal prices, and marketing boards, was attempting to ensure the protection of its own farmers, threatened in part by imports from countries which had greatly expanded their production during the war (Australian beef, for example, continued to be a problem to the end). Third, the absence of any clear, consistent or forthcoming attitude on the part of the host country helped to condemn the conference to the oblivion of would-be palliatives to the depression – and to a setback of Commonwealth unity. Cunliffe-Lister, the colonial secretary (later Lord Swinton), wrote in regret:

We had expected that our discussions would be on the basis that we all wanted to make Commonwealth trade as wide as possible ... that was not at all the spirit in which Bennett approached the matter ... Bennett wished to maintain high protection for practically all Canadian industry while producing long but specious schedules of the modest concessions he was willing to make. For example, the Secretary of the Board of Trade discovered that a Mickey Mouse toy figured six times under different nomenclatures. The other [Commonwealth] countries were more forthcoming, but ... Canada was the key; or rather the other countries found it difficult to go faster than Bennett.[60]

A fortnight before the conference reached its few and uncertain conclusions, Walter Runciman, the president of the board of trade, had taken it upon himself to expostulate with Bennett over his continuing tactlessness and even discourtesy as well as his inconsistency between his "enthusiasm for Imperial policy" and his incoherent economic proposals. "I left, carrying with me, I fear, a very indefinite impression of what his views were on individual problems ... that would spring from this shallow restless mind."[61] For his part, Baldwin noted wearily that Bennett "had a brainstorm every day which wiped out what he had agreed to the day before."[62] And Neville Chamberlain stated that the Canadian prime minister had acted in a most un-prime ministerial way: "He had lied like a trooper, and alternately bullied, sobbed, prevaricated, sobbed, delayed and obstructed." In short, he "behaved to me like a pig."[63] The British ministers soon despaired of it all, one at least being convinced that Bennett had arranged for their telephones to be tapped. Another recalled how Walter Runciman had "spent most of his time writing a take-over bid speech for the amalgamation of the Methodists and Wesleyans which was to be consummated in the autumn" (partly inspired by what he learned in Ottawa of creation of the United Church of Canada seven years before).[64]

The time of Runciman may have been at least as well spent on reducing ecclesiastical barriers as it was on attempting to reduce trade barriers. The haggling at the conference, in that exceptionally hot and humid Ottawa summer, came to almost naught. Britain granted more concessions than the Dominions in the twelve modest bilateral agreements concluded, including the indefinite suspension for the Empire of most import surcharges (they continued on foreign wheat, primarily to protect the British farmer). Britain retained the right to cancel even this small duty on non-Empire wheat any time that the price of Empire wheat exceeded the world price. New openings for Dominion products in the British market remained problematic. Although the terms for live cattle imports from Canada were liberalized, cheap Russian lumber continued to find its way

into the British market at the expense of Canadian, despite Bennett's ful-
minations.

At the conclusion of the conference, public proclamations of success
were, of course, many, Bennett hailing it as the result of "almost a half
century of hopes and fears and vain endeavours ... in all the history of the
Empire, nothing has before been achieved comparable in present benefit
or in future promise to that which the Ottawa Conference may claim
lasting credit." Its results were in fact modest, compared to expectations.
What the conference had revealed yet again was the difficulty of welding
the Empire into an effective economic unit.

Mackenzie King characterized the Ottawa agreements as having "increased restrictions; they have raised barriers; they have made trade more
difficult ... as between different parts of the British Empire." Vincent
Massey wrote optimistically but unrealistically:

The outcome ... has strengthened the determination of the Liberal Party ... to
make Imperial trade a reality whenever it comes into power ... In return for
vague promises we have extracted from Great Britain definite concessions which
may prove an embarrassment to the present British Government – those concessions having been courageously granted out of a laudable determination not to
let the Conference fail. It will be a great satisfaction, when the day comes, to be
able to advance Imperial trade so as to help the British producer and Canadian
consumer at one stroke.

That day was never to arrive. Massey misread the enthusiasm of his
own party leader and the prospects for imperial trade, given the longstanding opposition of Canadian manufacturers. As King was wont to
remind anyone who would listen, Laurier's tariff preference for Britain
– and other Dominions – had been a voluntary, unilateral act, not a negotiated, mutual obligation. If at any time Britain wanted to respond with
preferred access for Canadian or imperial exports, that was all to the
good, but if it did not, Canada would nevertheless continue to pursue its
own specific tariff concessions, having in each instance concluded unilaterally that it was in its own commercial interests to do so. In King's mind,
as in Laurier's, there could be no question of negotiating a comprehensive reciprocal tariff preference to provide greater cohesion to the Empire.
That could be interpreted as a reduction in Canada's fiscal autonomy.
Massey did, however, succeed in convening a meeting with King and Liberal spokesmen who, in declaring their acceptance of the Ottawa agree-

ments, committed a future Liberal government to reduce the tariff to 1930 levels, to offer a British (not imperial) preference of 50 per cent and to negotiate reciprocal trade agreements with any who might be interested (i.e., the United States).

As in the case of the Ottawa conference, little or nothing came of the wider World Monetary and Economic Conference, held in London the following year. Ferguson and Norman Robertson were principal advisors to Bennett, while Pearson remained at home as secretary of a royal commission on grain futures (he later served with Ferguson as a Canadian delegate to the International Sugar Conference). Some blamed the failure on complications of the Ottawa agreements, others the opposition of the newly elected Democratic administration in Washington to discussions of exchange rates and currency stabilization. A far greater obstacle emerged, however, from the intention of the United States, in the aftermath of the Ottawa conference, to confront Britain over imperial tariff preferences, especially for manufactured goods. The preferences had immediately caused concern in Roosevelt's Washington where any idea of an imperial *Zollverein* was an anathema. The US secretary of state wrote: "We were obligated to commence with some of the Dominions like Canada, and by a trade agreement with her, to begin chipping off the structure of imperial preference." It was a policy that the United States was to pursue relentlessly for the next three decades or more.

Thanks in part to the Ottawa agreements, however modest, the efforts of the Empire Marketing Board, and Ferguson's own persistent promotion as British economic recovery finally gained momentum, Anglo-Canadian trade did grow substantially during the remainder of his term, although overall the United States soon overtook Britain as the principal source of both imports and direct investment. Ferguson completed his term deeply conscious that his original great expectations would now never be fulfilled. His biographer has caught well his mood during his final years in the capital of the Empire that he so revered. "How slight by 1935 were the remaining fragments of the great dream; yet he clung to those fragments for they expressed not only his past hopes but they continued to represent the values he held dear and to give meaning to his life. Disappointment after [the] Ottawa [Conference] he knew in full measure but the total disillusionment of the realists he could never share. He had been an imperialist all the years of his life and his faith in the Empire would not die."[65]

Absent though Ferguson had been from the Ottawa conference itself, he spent the remaining three years of his appointment attempting to pick up

The ebullient Ferguson worked tirelessly to strengthen trade and other economic ties between Canada and Britain. Given the meagre results of the 1932 imperial conference in Ottawa, the possibility of an imperial customs union had faded but, as in the case of this London shop front, Howard and Ella Ferguson took every opportunity to promote Canadian products

the pieces – or to build upon them. It was neither an easy nor an agreeable task. The limited agreements and the unilateral actions of Britain and the Dominions had created a tangle of misunderstandings and even antagonisms that made the high commissioner's remaining years in London notably more difficult. Despite the paucity of real agreement, Ferguson, as chairman of the largely ineffective Imperial Economic Committee and a member of the Imperial Shipping Committee, worked with British ministers and officials, attempting to make sense of the bewildering tangle of quotas, tariffs, marketing boards, cargo rates, and a range of regulatory measures intended to channel, promote or direct trade (especially in food-stuffs) that had emerged directly or indirectly from the conference. Little came of these efforts, with Australia and New Zealand, generally supported by India and the colonies, advocating greater collaboration, but with Canada "resolutely opposed to the constitution of any single body no matter how closely defined."

Never having lost his intense interest in Ontario politics and in no way deterred by holding public office, Ferguson spent his autumnal holiday of 1933 visiting county fairs across Ontario, taking the political pulse and describing to his successor as premier his deep concern at the widespread despair that he had found in the face of continuing economic depression. Upon his return to Britain, Ferguson turned with renewed vigour to his familiar promotional tasks, although he was often a one-man band. Whenever Bennett was in Britain – and he was frequently – Ferguson joined him in his calls on ministers, despite their evident lack of enthusiasm for their visitor, but given the understaffing of Canada House, Ferguson was frequently alone in his dealings with ministers and senior officials. The high commissioner had little more than his instincts to rely upon; sometimes the results were nevertheless gratifying. He was soon involved in plans to establish a "cis-Atlantic" airmail and even passenger service and in organizing a "Maple Leaf Tour" of Canada for 150 British food importers. He supervised a small advertising budget for Canadian products, but sought free coverage in British newspapers for articles about Canada, and promoted a visit to Ontario by the Lord Mayor of London as "a splendid stroke to stir imperial feeling."

In March 1934 Ferguson departed from the normal activities of even a quasi-diplomatic mission by making Canada House available to the Metropolitan Police for their roof-top surveillance of a Trafalgar Square hunger march. In broader policy terms, both Ferguson and Vanier repeatedly urged that Canada participate in the Committee of Imperial Defence as Australia and South Africa did; if Ferguson's advice had been followed, Canada might have entered the Second World War more competently. Ferguson even took his case public in an article in *MacLean's* magazine, but to no avail.[66] He did at least have the consolation of assisting in the acquisition of two new destroyers for the minute Royal Canadian Navy, although that did little to re-equip Canada's severely depleted armed forces.

At the imperial conference in April–May 1935 (coinciding with the silver jubilee of King George v), Ferguson participated alongside Bennett as a result of an initial decision of the conference that "if a Dominion

Prime Minister wished to bring his High Commissioner with him that would be acceptable."[67] The substance of the discussions was, however, limited, Ramsay MacDonald concentrating upon what he rightly saw as a deteriorating international situation rather than stillborn question of imperial economic unity. "It was necessary for the United Kingdom to take steps to secure the defence of this country; it was impossible to stand by and do nothing while those dangers were threatening. At the same time, the United Kingdom must not allow itself to be pushed into a position of entering [again] into a system of military alliances for the defence of Europe."[68] To a secret meeting, Bennett described his fears that Britain had disarmed almost to the point of danger, although he did not offer on behalf of Canada to do anything militarily to help right the balance. At home, the leader of the opposition, Mackenzie King, increasingly confident that in the pending election the Conservatives would be swept from office, forecast no initiatives to counter the perilous military deficiencies that Bennett was coming to recognize.

From 1932 to 1935 Ferguson had been involved in efforts to promote or to keep the peace, principally at the Geneva Disarmament Conference (as part of a delegation led by Perley) and at the League of Nations. From there Lester Pearson had as early as April 1932 praised to Skelton "the directness and clarity" of Perley's speeches about disarmament. In time, Pearson, again in Geneva, was to be no less pleased about Ferguson's enthusiasm for collective security. In both London and Geneva, the impulsive Ferguson, assisted by Pearson, joined in Commonwealth consultations (frequently initiated by the dominions secretary, Anthony Eden) about League matters, a practice that was as unwelcome to King as it was to Skelton. In way of contrast, an admiring Pearson recorded that Ferguson had "twice cut across rambling apologies and withdrawings and has made it clear that the Canadians are determined to see the collective system put in motion."* All this and much else Pearson respected in his "kind and unpretentious chief": he had never, he later wrote, "worked

---

* When King came to office, he instructed the Canadian representative at the League to reverse Bennett's earlier support for sanctions against the aggressor, Italy. Giorgia Borra de Cousandier, an Italian citizen whom King had met in the early 1930s and who claimed he would have married her if it had not been for the inconvenient fact that she was already married, stated in the early 1950s that it was she who had persuaded him to adopt a more accommodating attitude toward her homeland. In the late 1940s, King had required the reluctant ambassador in Rome to employ her at the embassy.

with any man prominent in public life so natural, unaffected, human and friendly in his contacts."[69]

In the meantime, Liberal attacks on the government (answered during Bennett's absence by Sir George Perley) were, according to *The Times* correspondent, "very mild as the Liberals like ... Perley [and] will not harass him, especially as he is an old man of nearly eighty." The election campaign of 1935 changed all that. Bennett's government was decisively defeated by the Liberals with their campaign slogan of "King or Chaos." Ferguson was probably not surprised, given the impact of the economic depression and the widespread dissatisfaction with Bennett's bombastic but largely empty response, including his last-minute and unconvincing conversion to policies inspired by Roosevelt's New Deal and by William Beveridge's proposals for unemployment insurance which Ferguson had sent to him. Upon Ferguson's hurried return to London from Geneva, the new prime minister, Mackenzie King, requested him to remain as high commissioner for several weeks until Vincent Massey would be free to fill the post.

The editor of *The Times* had heard a bathetic account of Ferguson's final days in London. On 4 December 1935 Geoffrey Dawson wrote to his Ottawa correspondent,

Howard Ferguson has never been a particular friend of mine and indeed I have seen little or nothing of him during his period as High Commissioner, though I have heard increasingly well of his work. But it seems to me incredible that he should have heard of Vincent Massey's appointment (as [Lord] Bessborough [the Governor General] tells me) from the columns of the newspapers, and that his first official intimation of the change should have been a note from the Bank to the effect that his salary was stopped. On the top of this, he and Mrs. Fergie go to meet their successors in a taxi, while the car (which indeed belongs to Canada House but is maintained and run at the personal expense of the High Commissioner) takes the Masseys from the station to their hotel. Finally, I hear from the most unimpeachable source (sitting next to me at dinner) tonight that the King proposed a K.C.M.G. [for Ferguson] on retirement, but that this was vetoed by his namesake Mackenzie [King].[70]

John Stevenson agreed with his editor's description, except that

In one particular the account given by your informant is inaccurate. It happens that the official [Norman Robertson] in the Department of External Affairs who deals with most of the correspondence with the High Commissioners is a close friend of mine; he is an ex-Rhodes scholar and lives near me. I spoke to him about the matter confidentially and he assures me that in regard to Ferguson's retirement, all the amenities were fully observed; he saw to this personally as he knows and likes Ferguson, having been at a conference in Rome with him. He says that quite friendly cables were exchanged after Ferguson tendered his resignation, that a date was fixed on for the change-over and that Ferguson's salary was continued to the end of the month in which he left office so that he got actually more than his nominal due.[71]

There was to be no KCMG for Ferguson, as there had been knighthoods for eminent Canadians during Bennett's restoration of the honours system (which had been set aside following a resolution of the House of Commons in 1919). Ferguson sailed for Canada not as Sir Howard but at least as one whose term had been regarded with admiration by Pearson and Robertson and, like Perley's, had received a warm accolade from *The Times*, despite his notably bumptious beginnings.*[72]

* Eleven years later, Ferguson died in Toronto, age 76, on 21 February 1946. He was buried not far from Peter Larkin in Toronto's Mount Pleasant Cemetery (where Mackenzie King would follow four years later).

CHAPTER EIGHT

Vincent Massey, 1935–1946

Mackenzie King appointed Vincent Massey high commissioner in April 1930, on transfer from the legation in Washington. The following month, the new prime minister, R.B. Bennett, withdrew the offer. Massey waited five years for its renewal. On 30 October 1935, a fortnight after the Liberals' massive victory over the Conservatives, he enthusiastically accepted King's second invitation. The new prime minister, however, was uneasy in his mind with his appointment, suspecting Massey of being a covert – or not so covert – imperial centralist.

Massey had undeniably been associated with the imperial proselytising as early as 1911. Upon his return to Canada from Oxford, "it fell to me to play an active part in the organization of the Round Table movement," joining George Wrong and others at the University of Toronto in the search for greater understanding of what the British Empire had become. "This work was from the outset complicated by a certain ambiguity in the purposes of the movement. Was it (and I and most of our Canadian members came to wish it to be) a purely disinterested study of what we then called 'the Imperial problem', to which those of greatly differing points of view would be ... welcomed? Or was it ... an effort to persuade, to convince, as many as would listen that its solution lay in Imperial Federation?"[1]

In time, Massey demonstrated his commitment to the first and more moderate approach "to examine the problem of Empire," but nevertheless his activities on behalf of the Round Table made King uneasy, even as he wooed him. In August 1925 King had successfully induced him to be a Liberal candidate in the forthcoming election (King having suddenly recalled that the revered Laurier had advised him "to get Vincent Massey to go into public life"). Before the election, Massey had also accepted King's offer of a cabinet appointment without portfolio. King was immensely pleased at landing Massey as a member of his government. This "is a great stroke. Will be a body blow to the Tories – will help to rally the

Unionist Liberals and wavering [manufacturers]."[2] Soon, however, when the Liberals were defeated and replaced by Meighen's short-lived Conservative government, Massey was out of political office. He was never to return. Before the election the following year, he had failed to win a nomination, thereby depriving himself of the office of minister of trade and commerce which King had in mind for him. He had, however, been invited to accompany the prime minister to the 1926 imperial conference before taking up King's offer of appointment as Canada's first minister to the United States in 1927.

Following Bennett's withdrawal of King's offer of London, Massey travelled extensively during the next five years: to London where he was received by King George V; to Rome where an unshaven Mussolini extolled his own achievements; to Madrid upon the eve of the bloody fratricide of the civil war; to China, where he called upon Chiang Kai-Chek; and to Japan at the time of the ominous Mukden crisis. Massey's international interests were reflected not only in his extensive travels; he was president of the Canadian Institute of International Affairs. He was also offered several major appointments. Friends in London, including Leopold Amery, proposed a British diplomatic posting, possibly as ambassador to China. Ferguson's erstwhile antagonist, the irrepressible Thomas, the dominions secretary, offered him the governorship of Western Australia. "I would be automatically knighted and ... this would be the first instance of a person from one Dominion being appointed to a governorship in another."[*3] A more challenging proposal was to be high commissioner of the League of Nations in Danzig which was increasingly coveted by a resurgent Germany. Massey declined all such appointments and any suggestion that he should again be a Liberal candidate for Parliament. He did, however, accept during the summer of 1931 King's invitation to head the new National Liberal Federation, an urgently needed apparatus if the Liberals were to organize and finance the next campaign and win the election, eventually held in October 1935.

Upon Bennett's electoral victory of 1930, King had recognized that, in both financial and organizational terms, the Liberal party was in a perilous condition. He further recognized that Vincent Massey, that *rara avis*,

* From one Dominion to another, perhaps, although not from one colony to another: Sir Ambrose Shea of Newfoundland was governor of the Bahamas in 1887–90; Sir Percy Girouard of Montreal was governor of Northern Nigeria in 1905–06 and of Kenya in 1909–12; Sir Gordon Guggisberg of Preston, Ontario, was governor of the Gold Coast (later Ghana) in 1919–27.

a Liberal millionaire, was the person most likely to pull the party out of the hole. King was convinced that he was not receiving the party support that was his due as leader. By mid-summer of 1931, King and Massey had reached their uneasy agreement about what should be done. The immediate problem facing the Liberal party was financial. It was deeply in debt. King was also fully aware of Massey's undiminished ambition; here was leverage of a direct sort. He readily employed it to do a deal with Massey: be president of the National Liberal Federation for four years, raise the funds to pay off the debt and meet the costs of the next campaign, and the high commissionership is yours. King had told Massey, who was contemplating the governorship of Western Australia, that he must remain where he was if he hoped eventually to have London: "those who left the Party in time of need would get no recognition ... if he were away, it would be impossible to appoint him to London later on." Massey did, nevertheless, depart for a tour of Asia for several months, a Liberal senator commenting to King that "He leaves us behind to do the work of preparing a place for him, if not in Heaven, at least in London."[4]

Upon his return, Massey worked diligently to restore the fortunes of the party. King was at first delighted. "Vincent and Alice Massey have thrown themselves wholeheartedly into the work of party organization ... It is something that I have striven to effect ever since I became leader of the party, but until Massey put his shoulder to the wheel in earnest, and lent his quite exceptional organizational abilities, as well as financial aid ... it was impossible to bring about."[5] King, however, never fully trusted Massey, resenting his interest in public policy which he regarded as his own preserve. At the unwelcome policy conference which Massey organized (and largely paid for) at the appropriately named Port Hope in 1933, a reluctant King stayed with the Masseys at their nearby country house. A timely dream, however, had alerted him to "one snake in the grass ... and a little later a larger one ... it was a warning to be careful ... my hosts ... were not to be trusted." He determined that there should be no more policy conferences.

On behalf of King, the party secretary "told him [Massey] and Mrs. Massey that ... King expected him to attend to the business end of things and in effect this was to be the price of the London appointment. Mrs. Massey said she had been urging this on V.M."[6] As King bluntly told a colleague, "he didn't want V. to speak publicly; let him organize or not as he pleased; London was the stake."[7] As the election year of 1935 approached, the chances of a Liberal victory brightened, although during his four years as president of the National Liberal Federation Massey had so many painful encounters with King that the prospect of London must have at times looked doubtful. For King, Massey was almost too much: "He talked of his own health, but had not a considerate word about myself. Is purely selfish and self-seeking and I find it difficult to be patient with him." Worse was to come. "I feel a resentment beyond words at the manner in which Massey has crowded me in the last year or two. I shall always feel that not a little of my ill health has been due to the 'pressure' he has exerted."[8] During the 1935 election campaign, King recorded,

When [Massey] began telling me what to do, etc. I let out at him very hard. Told him he had caused me more pain and concern than anyone or all else in the Party besides, that I had never had my privacy invaded as he had ... it was always Rex must do this, etc. also his talk about helping me and 'the cause' was all nonsense, it was himself and London that alone kept him to the Party, that I had to tell him, it was only in this way he could hope to get appointed ... It was a scathing review of his selfish actions including telling him frankly he had been quite wrong in his views on most things. He was quite crushed – perhaps I went too far but it was the 'last straw'. I told him when he [too] was 60 [Massey was age 48] he would come to see I was right – that I thought I knew something about political leadership or would not be where I have been for so long a time.[9]

Not surprisingly, Massey had a different recollection. More than twenty years later he recorded how "I had accepted, at his [King's] earnest invitation, the presidency of the new National Liberal Federation. My visits to the leader to report to him and hear his views he quite clearly regarded as intrusions; but I had little doubt that, had I stayed away, he would have complained that he was not being properly consulted. I often failed to receive his complete confidence, and to me he was often quite incomprehensible."[10]

Despite their continuing mutual dislike and distrust, King did appoint Massey to London following the Liberal victory of 1935. On 7 November 1935, as John Buchan, the popular novelist, now the recently minted Lord Tweedsmuir, the Round Table exponent and long-time friend of King disembarked in Quebec as the new governor general, the Masseys embarked for Britain.*

---

* King had been especially impressed with Buchan during the latter's private visit to Canada in 1924, forgiving him even his Round Table enthusiasms. King had pressed hard for the appointment of a commoner as governor general, but Buchan was made a peer before taking office, citing as a reason that it would "revive" his ailing mother. His

Massey's intellectual attainments and interests were likely to make him an active, even an uncomfortable, high commissioner and never merely the passive messenger that King had found in Larkin. Massey was aware of this: "I had known, before taking up the High Commissioner's post, of Mackenzie King's extreme apprehension lest his representative at London should fall too much under the influence of an 'imperial' point of view ... during the 1920s he had actually gone so far as to forbid P.C. Larkin ... to attend any collective meetings of the High Commissioners, but had instructed him always to visit the Prime Minister, the Foreign Secretary or the Dominions Secretary on his own!"[11]

The Masseys arrival in Britain evoked a sardonic reaction from *The Times* correspondent in Ottawa:

I hope they will do well, but the longer they are kept on the other side of the Atlantic the better will most of their acquaintances in Canada be pleased, as I know no couple of people who can raise such clouds of the dust of dislike behind them. They were in high disfavour with King at the end [of the campaign] as he resented the advice which Mrs. Massey insisted upon showering upon him by wire, telephone and personal interview about the conduct of the campaign. The manager of the Liberal campaign [Norman Lambert] gave me an account of a moving interview when King turned upon Massey and told him that he was sick and tired of being hounded with advice by him and his wife. I admit that Massey is a very useful public citizen and has made generous use of his money for the public benefit and he should do all right as High Commissioner, but most of my circle are not fond of him as a private individual.[12]

The Masseys arrived in London on 13 November 1935, the day before Ferguson's departure for Toronto. Although Massey may not have fully realized it at the time, the signature in Washington two days later of a Canadian-American trade agreement was partly the result of Washington's determination to chip away at imperial tariff preferences. Negotiated mainly by Robertson and Wilgress at Bennett's behest and hastily concluded at King's command, the agreement was to mark a major change in Canada's economic and political priorities. C.P. Stacey, that trenchant judge of King's governments, has defined it as the turning point in Canadian relations with both Britain and the United States alike:

1915 novel, *The Thirty-Nine Steps*, was made into a 1935 film in which the hero, transformed into a Canadian, seeks help from the Canadian high commission when he is wrongfully arrested. The film was released as Buchan arrived in Canada.

On 8 November 1935 Vincent and Alice Massey were met on their
arrival in London by Howard and Ella Ferguson. With the defeat of
R.B. Bennett's Conservative government by Mackenzie King's Liberals in October 1935, Ferguson hastened back to London from the
League of Nations in Geneva. The editor of *The Times* reported that
the departing Fergusons had had to go to the rail station in a taxi
while the Masseys had the official car take them to their hotel.

To put it briefly and bluntly, from 1935 onwards Canada's relationship to Britain became less important and her relationship to the United States much more
important in her scheme of things ... Canadians who experience a certain emotional rebellion against this development ... frequently tend to blame the whole
thing on the Liberal party and, more specifically, on Mackenzie King. And it
must be said that in 1935 King gave these critics a lot of ammunition to use against
him. In [an] interview with Armour [the US Minister to Canada] ... he talked
as though his American connections – which were undoubtedly very important
to him – had been the mainspring of his life. He said that people called him 'the

American' ... that he wanted to choose 'the American road' for his country if the United States would make it possible for him; he wanted the United States and Canada brought closer together in every way, politically as well as economically ... O.D. Skelton had talked much the same way to Armour the day after the election ... [On the other hand] the written records of his numerous séances ... reveal a man who was certainly not an American at heart ... He reveres the Crown, has deep respect for British statesmen (though only for Liberals), and is anxious for British approval. On his sixtieth birthday (December 17, 1934) King received good wishes (his word was "love") from a galaxy of dead British Liberal politicians ... Canadian Liberal leaders also came. But it is surely a notable fact that no Americans came to this anniversary observance (of course, there is no Liberal Party in the United States). Theodore Roosevelt, whom King had known in life, did not come; nor did Lincoln, whom he much admired, though Lincoln did speak to King (along with Gladstone) on another occasion.[13]

Like most heads of diplomatic missions upon arrival, Massey was convinced that his predecessor had left a mess for him to clean up. Part of the trouble was once again the autonomous-minded provincial agents general (of which there were four when Massey arrived) and the representatives of several federal departments who went their own ways with little or no reference to the High Commission. Massey himself was clear what had to be done:

It is the duty of anyone holding the post of High Commissioner ... to harmonize as best he can two principles. The first of these is that, as the High Commissioner is the representative of a nation, it is his duty to promote Canadian interests and protect Canadian rights. He has to stand on his own feet in London. The second is that the function of a Canadian representative must always be performed in the closest possible co-operation with the government of Great Britain. He must never forget that we are members of one family of nations.[14]

Massey's reconciliation of these two principles was to "run Canada House as a non-political office." In this, Massey was ably assisted by Georges Vanier and Lester Pearson (whom Massey had known at the University of Toronto when Pearson taught history there in 1924–8), as well as the long-serving chief trade commissioner (later secretary) of Canada House, Frederic Hudd.

Upon arrival, Massey wrote to the prime minister, "I am now taking all the time that I can to study the operations of Canada House ... there is considerable overlapping and adjustments undoubtedly can be made."

Massey knew that King's suspicions and even hostility would be aroused by an activist high commissioner. He was, however, undeterred. His presence, as he set about what he called "this amazing job," was soon everywhere evident, but he did prudently add to King a reassuring if nuanced initial pledge not to fall into the supposed trap of the centralists: "as you said so rightly ... one has to be on one's guard all the time against embarrassing commitments of all kinds."[15] It is unlikely that the prime minister believed Massey's bland assurance any more than the high commissioner meant it in the way that King would have understood it.

That Vincent Massey was both an ardent Canadian and a pronounced anglophile is incontrovertible. The oft-repeated observation ascribed to Lord Salisbury that Massey "always makes one feel like a bloody savage" is familiar to all who have contemplated his remarkably varied life. Charles Ritchie, a future high commissioner himself who joined the Canada House staff from the legation in Washington in 1938, came to know well the potential inherent in Massey's complex nature that the prime minister, who had appointed him, could not or would not recognize.

What a curious and fascinating character Mr. Massey has – that blend of acuteness and superficiality. He has enormous susceptibility to more phoney forms of charm. What he loves in life is delicatezza – the pleasant surface style. He is a puzzling person because behind his London *Times* leading article official views and his carefully polished manner there lurks an ironic appreciation of things as they are and of himself as he is. When he has a decision to make – disappointingly – he always decides in favour of the conventional. His charm is remarkable. It springs, as charm so often does, from his own insecurity. He is painfully easy to hurt or ruffle and full of *prévenances* for the feelings of others if he happens to like them. If not, he is ruthless. Sometimes I have been stifled by the too strong atmosphere of the Masseys' love of power, but I am very fond of them and diverted by them. Their relationship to each other is the most admirable thing about them. I never expect to have another chief who is so personally sympathetic – after all, I share so many of his weaknesses. His critics may have a great deal on their side, but he is so much more interesting as a personality than they are.[16]

Mackenzie King's brooding suspicions about Massey were unfortunate, since during the first four years of his tenure as high commissioner, the world accelerated towards its second global conflict in two decades, with Hitler seizing Austria and the Sudetenland of Czechoslovakia as bitter civil war continued to rage in Spain. Canada could only have benefited from the information so freely proffered in London, possibly even leading to recognition that a degree of rearmament would be prudent instead of waiting until war had almost begun. But King persisted in regarding "Massey's function ... [as] a sherry affair."[17] If so, he could only blame himself; he consistently chose to deal directly with British ministers or with the British high commissioner in Ottawa, bypassing his own high commissioner in London. He did acknowledge the gifts which the affluent Massey sent him, but that was of a piece with his view of the role of the high commissioner from the days of Larkin. Upon receiving from Massey a piece of carved stone from the Palace of Westminster, the prime minister gushed in reply: "Really I have been in raptures about it. By one of those strange coincidences, which have more behind them than appear upon the surface, this British lion arrived at Kingsmere on the day on which an effort was made to frighten King Edward [VIII] by the throwing of a pistol. I do not know whether or not you noticed the extraordinary resemblance between the expression on the face of this lion and that of King George [V]."[18]

Vincent Massey was neither Strathcona nor Larkin, someone to be manipulated by King. And King knew it. Throughout Massey's ten-year term, his relations with King were frequently difficult, always unpredictable, and a continuing source of unease and unhappiness. If their differences had been on a purely personal level, Massey might have found the relationship more tolerable; it was at the official level that he found the alienation most troublesome. The problem was not simply that on some personal level the two men distrusted each other; the difficulties arose over King's notably limited and mutable view of what the high commissionership really was. When Bennett had appointed Ferguson, King had been quick to reject his "view that the position of High Commissioner for Canada is a political office ... [it is] not; it was the highest of all diplomatic offices."[19] Once Massey was in London, however, he changed his mind: there is "no diplomatic service within the Empire."[20] Whatever it was, Canada House was not a diplomatic post charged with reporting on the policies of the host government and conveying Canada's policy thinking to it.

Perhaps King soon repented of his decision to appoint Massey, but in any event he moved promptly to strip any real meaning from the office. He telegraphed bluntly to the new high commissioner, "any important conversation between British Government and Canadian Government should be direct in form of communication from Prime Minister to Prime Minister ... and should not be through the High Commissioner."[21] What was there left for Massey to do? His enjoyment of ceremony and protocol, noted when he had been minister in Washington, could fill an agreeable hour, but Massey was much too interested in international affairs in general and in Anglo-Canadian relations in particular to remain content for long with the flummery of his high office, however elevated the order of flummery in London was. During the late 1930s, a troubling and increasingly perilous time, Massey's occasional correspondence with King and Skelton is shot through with profound differences about what the High Commission should be. With his three years in Washington behind him, Massey was determined to render Canada House into something that the prime minister certainly did not want: a post where the exchange of diplomatic and commercial information would be a daily occurrence, where Canada could benefit from unparalleled sources of information.

Massey took the opportunity of King's visit to London in 1937 to attend both the coronation and the accompanying imperial conference

to find out why I was not being used more as a representative of Canada *vis-à-vis* the U.K. Government as my colleagues the other High Commissioners [in London] were. Why the restrictions on my functions? ... Why so much direct communication between Ottawa and Whitehall? King said this was necessary because G.B. and Canada were not foreign countries to each other and the relations were such as to make it necessary for him to carry on important negotiations himself. "I know this British crowd," he said to me, and then went on to point out how in his opinion they wanted watching. His point of view in this matter seemed to reflect an anti-British bias (one of the most powerful factors in his make-up), extreme egoism and a very definite lack of confidence in my own ability to withstand what he would regard as sinister British influences.[22]

Some years after completing his decade-long appointment, Massey added ruefully:

Our conceptions of the high commissionership ... soon came to differ radically. It was in part because our approach to Anglo-Canadian relations could never be reconciled. I tried to carry out my instructions with scrupulous care, however I might disagree with them at times – and however I might regret the tone of the communications that it was some times my unpleasant duty to convey to the government of the United Kingdom ... My personal relations with Mackenzie King

... were marked at times by conversations that I can only describe as painful. In these there was not only a sharp repudiation of my views ... but a wilful misunderstanding of my motives.[23]

A principal vehicle at hand for a wide range of information, if Massey had been allowed regular access to it, was the periodic meetings between the dominions secretary (and his senior officials) and the high commissioners. During the prewar years Australia remained consistently better informed than Canada, as a result of the participation of its high commissioner (Stanley Bruce, the former prime minister) in both the Committee for Imperial Defence and in regular meetings with the dominions secretary and the assignment of a liaison official to the Foreign Office.* Pearson recorded that despite the obstacles put in his way, Massey "has apparently established quite a position for himself here and seems to have very ready access to most of the people who matter. There is no doubt that he is much better informed of what is actually going on in the Foreign Office than we at Canada House, because he spends at least two hours every day talking to officials there and in the other Government departments. He sees incoming and outgoing despatches and telegrams almost immediately."

King had repeatedly forbidden Larkin to participate in meetings at either the Dominions or Foreign Offices since, in his view, such meetings might somehow become a foreign affairs council of the Empire in which Britain would impose itself on the Dominions. In 1930 R.B. Bennett had welcomed participation, but upon coming to office in 1935, King was again adamantly opposed. Pearson shared his high commissioner's frustration: he had been advised by Skelton to be wary of accepting any information "that the British might want us to know merely for their own purposes ... My independent sturdy Canadian attitude could be weakened, presumably, and I might be lured into the Whitehall net." Specifically, Skelton had strongly warned him against "undertaking any responsibility of communicating to Ottawa anything that the British Government wants communicated."[24] The basic problem was that Skelton "never stopped believing that behind almost every British Government scheme

---

* As Amery wrote to King on 13 March 1925, the Australian liaison officer, R.G. Casey, "has been given a room at the Committee of Imperial Defence, and has the run of this Office [the Dominions Office] and of the Foreign Office" (NA, RG 25, vol. 3419). The fact that Howard Ferguson continued to advocate active Canadian participation in the Committee for Imperial Defence confirmed King in his view that he was another adherent of Conservative centralist imperialism.

– constitutional, economic, military – lay a dark desire to introduce a consolidation of empire or, at the very least, to compromise Canadian freedom of action."[25]

Within two months of his arrival, Massey wrote to King about what was necessary to make Canada House more effective. The priority would be to augment the small political section. "Because of lack of personnel this work has not been attempted in the past," Massey tactfully noted, "but it would be of value to the Canadian Government to receive reports from this Office based on the observations of men who are presumably specifically trained for that purpose, who possess a knowledge of Canadian conditions and policy and who have, or should have, special facilities for securing information not always available to the press." However, Massey, looking warily over his shoulder, hastily added that of course such contact would "be conducted in such a way that there will be no interference with the ordinary channels of communication between the two Governments" (in other words, prime minister to prime minister). And certainly it would be understood that "the mere giving of such information [by the Foreign or the Dominions Office] does not in itself discharge any obligation which the Government here might have to transmit that information [directly and] officially to Ottawa."

Having given these comforting reassurances, Massey proceeded to urge that "this Office should be informed immediately of all official communications exchanged ... Important decisions are often made in Ottawa directly relating to the work of the Office of the High Commissioner, but of which this Office is not informed ... It has been even more embarrassing to secure that knowledge not from my own Government but from the Government of the United Kingdom."[26] Massey offered detailed suggestions about how Foreign Office information might be more expeditiously obtained and transmitted to Ottawa and offered even the novel proposal that the Canadian missions in Paris and Geneva should copy to London any communications of interest to the high commission, but he never received a direct answer to his long and thoughtful review of how Anglo-Canadian relations might be fostered. His recommendations disappeared into a black hole. On New Year's Eve of 1936 Pearson noted wearily in his diary: "It appears that [trade] negotiations have been conducted by the Canadian Government on the one hand and the British High Commissioner on the other ... The British are willing to trust their High Commissioner in a matter of such importance in a way which the Canadian Government will not trust its High Commissioner."[27] Pearson, who was "high in his praises of Mr. Massey," deplored the fact that Ottawa did not use "Canada House ... as a real channel of communication between the Canadian and United Kingdom Governments and not merely as a subsidiary information office which Ottawa tends to consider it." When, for example, the Dominions Office had informed Massey about Germany's renunciation of the Treaty of Locarno and its reoccupation of the demilitarized Rhineland, King had left Massey in no doubt that such communications from the Dominions Office to Canada House were unwelcome; if there were any important information to transmit, it must be done directly between prime ministers. King had then added inconsequentially, "This is the only way in which we can possibly have opportunity required collectively to consider and state attitude and policy and which will ... avoid all possibility of misunderstanding as to what has been said or meant in any verbal communication."[28]

Despite King's circumlocutions, Massey, beginning in April, did attend a series of meetings of high commissioners with the foreign and dominions secretaries to be informed about the troubling German reoccupation of the Rhineland. Malcolm Macdonald, the dominions secretary, later observed: "The High Commissioners ... had been receiving information which was not available even to members of the United Kingdom cabinet, other than those who were actually taking part in the negotiations," but not surprisingly, Massey's contribution to the meetings was limited by the absence of instructions or even any expression of interest from Ottawa.*[29] When the South African high commissioner urged appeasement of Germany by tacit acquiescence in its reoccupation of the Rhineland, Massey agreed, but his attendance at the meetings soon thereafter ended.

King, upon learning of Massey's participation, repeated what he had told Larkin on more than one occasion: "Consultation between Foreign Secretary and the High Commissioners together is ... liable to implication of collective decision. We could not agree to the development of an imperial council on foreign affairs, sitting in London."[30] The high commissioner was, he repeated, to decline to attend the meetings with both the foreign and the dominions secretaries. To gain access to the information that was being shared so candidly with his colleagues, Massey was reduced to the humiliating dodge of sneaking in the back door of

---

* Malcolm MacDonald (1901–81), son of Ramsay MacDonald, entered the House of Commons in 1929, was colonial secretary in 1935 before becoming secretary of state for dominion affairs in the same year. He combined both offices in 1938 before becoming minister of health in 1940. In April 1941 he became high commissioner in Canada. While in Ottawa he married the widow of a Canadian officer killed at Dieppe.

the Foreign Office in the hope of being unobserved while receiving his own private briefings: "a ridiculous application of nationalistic theory – incomprehensible to sensible people and often very embarrassing to me. It was also very unfair to overworked ministers with whom I had to have a special solitary appointment to hear what the other High Commissioners had heard as a group."[31] Eventually, as the Munich crisis foretold the approach of the Second World War, Massey himself ended these ludicrous practices, again joining his colleagues at the regular weekly and soon daily meetings, whether King liked it or not.

Massey, if he had had his way, would also have contributed to a more active policy at the faltering League of Nations in Geneva, as Ferguson had notably done. He was a delegate to its sessions in 1936 and 1937, but had to limit himself in what he said to whatever Skelton and the other isolationists in Ottawa had prepared and on which most decidedly no comment was invited. When Bennett was still in office King had condemned support for the League as "living dangerously." For his part, Massey deplored how "We under the present administration [King's] have decided to maintain an absolutely negative attitude in international affairs even when an opportunity offers itself to help in an important piece of international conciliation."[32] He was not surprised when, upon accompanying King to Geneva in September 1936, the prime minister warned Malcolm MacDonald that isolationism was abroad in the land to the point where, echoing the isolationist Skelton, Canada might decide to stay out of another European war. Massey had to watch King using the League of Nations as a platform to address pompously not the Assembly directly but rather the British government indirectly:

The nations of the British Commonwealth are held together by ties of friendship, by similar political institutions, and by common attachment to democratic ideals, rather than by commitments to join together in war. The Canadian Parliament reserves to itself the right to declare, in the light of the circumstances existing at the time, to what extent, if at all, Canada will participate in conflicts in which other members of the Commonwealth [i.e., Britain] may be engaged.[33]

King had become increasingly unenthusiastic about the League of Nations – he was given to calling it the "League of Notions" – and especially the universal guarantee of territorial integrity and political independence that underpinned it. At the sessions of the League Assembly in 1921 and 1922 and again in 1923, Canada had accordingly attempted to remove or alter Article x of the League Covenant, opposed the election of a Canadian as president of the Assembly and the election of Canada to the council (a Canadian was elected as president in 1925 and Canada elected to the council in 1927). In informing Massey in February 1936 of his decision not to support proposed military sanctions by the League against Italy over its invasion of Abyssinia, King added, "our participation in a European-African war would ... have a serious effect upon the unity of Canada." He cautioned a Liberal backbencher, "As little discussion as possible should be raised in our House of Commons with respect to the present European situation" – so much for Parliament will decide.

The degree to which King had written off the League became yet more evident at the imperial conference in May 1937, chaired by Neville Chamberlain, when King advanced the wholly unrealistic proposal for a new world organization to replace the League that would include "every nation" (that is, the United States) joining together to prevent war "by means of world-wide publicity." King even threatened withdrawal: "With this latest failure [in Abyssinia] and the United States remaining outside, it would be very difficult, if sanctions were insisted upon, to keep Canada in the League ... In Canada, people were saying that membership in the League constituted a real risk of their becoming involved in a war."[34]

If the League could not help to keep Canada out of another European war, the best hope was, in King's view, for Britain itself – and hence Canada – to eschew any alliance of the 1914 variety. In April 1937, King was again in London, en route to Geneva where he lamented: "I wish the League of Nations could be gotten out of the way altogether. Every feeling I had about the mischief being wrought through the intrigues of that institution has been intensified by what I have seen and heard." The League becoming a spent force, Britain laboured to keep the peace in Europe, but access to its thinking which Massey had been offered had been rejected by King and Skelton, ever fearful of becoming enmeshed by the British in some obscure European dispute. As an editor of *Documents on Canadian External Relations* has observed,

Canadian policy often seemed deliberately cloaked in confusion and decidedly negative in substance. Confrontation in international policies was an evil; collective security, an anathema. International appeasement and conciliation, if not vigorously pursued, were at least to be applauded and encouraged. No commitments, the avoidance of consultation (of course, we were offended when we were not consulted on questions that affected us) and a minimum of public examination and debate were the means adopted in achieving the "safety" of a backseat position in international affairs. At all costs, Canada must avoid encouraging Britain in any course that might lead to war and thus expose the Anglo-Canadian relationship and threaten the partisan balance of domestic politics.

Nowhere does there appear ... any appreciation of the greater issues involved in the crises that led to World War II. A crocodile tear or two might be shed at the passing of Loyalist Spain or Czechoslovakia but not even that was risked until they were well and truly dead. When war came, the Mackenzie King government quietly, if despairingly, accepted it for all the *wrong* reasons.[35]

Massey, soon after his arrival in London, noted the variety in his work: the London "Naval Conference one minute, and then the problem of wheat marketing the next, endless interviews and correspondence on the operation of Sanctions [by the League], the sale of Canadian bacon, publicity for Canada in Great Britain, Customs problems, Trans-Atlantic aviation [including a possible role for the new Trans-Canada Airlines] and Trans-Pacific shipping as well as individual questions of all kinds, and so on *ad infinitum*."[36] For Massey the *ad infinitum* included such diversions as presenting to the King, Queen, and the two princesses that amiable impostor Grey Owl while he was on a four-month tour of Britain. Less felicitous was the tea which Massey arranged for the Canadian team in the world ice hockey championships. "The team naturally did not react to the hospitality offered like the Hart House String Quartet would. Their conversation was more forthright than cultivated, the Mayfair doodads that were offered as food were eaten ten at a time and worst of all, they didn't all turn up." On a decidedly less agreeable plane was Ottawa's flat rejection of the High Commission's humanitarian plea to be allowed to arrange repatriation from Spain of the survivors of the twelve hundred Canadian citizens who had volunteered to fight on the Republican side in the civil war. They were left to make their own way home – if they could.

Massey did not participate actively in the negotiation between Britain and Canada of the trade agreement signed in 1937 which to a degree consolidated the confused conclusions of the 1932 Ottawa conference, Ottawa apparently believing that this was exclusively a task for trade experts, led by the ministers of finance and of trade and commerce. The item-by-item hard bargaining of reciprocal tariff preferences was a long way from the ostensibly high-minded unilateral grant of preferences by Laurier and King. By the end of 1936, Pearson confided to his diary, "So far as trade discussions are concerned, Canada House remains as usual completely in the dark or was completely in the dark until the arrival of a despatch this week which told us what had been going on during the last few months."

Trade promotion (as distinct from trade negotiation) was, however, something Massey was left to do on his own initiative. In the pursuit of Ferguson's initiatives, "Canada Calling" became the slogan of a concerted promotional campaign across Britain, with Massey speaking in Belfast, London, and Birmingham. Pearson was hyperbolic in his gratification with the results: "The city is covered now with our posters and our signs and no London housewife buys anything but Canadian food products these days."

An opportunity for Canada to develop trade and to help address economic problems of the British West Indies recurred in 1938, but the dilatoriness of Ottawa was such that no nomination was made in time to respond to a British invitation, conveyed by Massey, to include a Canadian in a royal commission of inquiry. The question of Canada's role in the British West Indies, canvassed during the peace negotiations of 1919, had resurfaced in 1930. The governor general, Lord Willingdon, had stated upon his return from a winter visit to the Caribbean that "it would be a fine thing if Canada relieved Great Britain of the responsibility for the future of the West Indies."[37] King had been prompt in the House of Commons to describe Willingdon's suggestion as entirely personal, but nonetheless it was for him yet one more example of "centralists" attempting to manipulate Canada – and the reason why Skelton and he had in 1938 been so unresponsive to Massey about the invitation to provide a Canadian member to the royal commission on the British West Indies.

In trade promotion and cultural questions, Massey demonstrated notable leadership during the four years between his arrival and the beginning of the Second World War. A role in the successful arrangement of the royal visit to Canada during the summer of 1939 was a gratifying diversion from the waning discussions of imperial tariffs; he knew only too well the prime minister's deep-rooted opposition. In his efforts to enhance the economic links between Canada and Britain as the world pulled itself out of its devastating economic depression, he had first to listen to yet another protest against the financial arrangements that had followed the nationalization of the Grand Trunk Railway. Upon meeting a representative of the bondholders still sore fifteen years after Meighen's nationalization, Massey assured Ottawa that, "I was careful to give him no possible grounds for saying that I expressed any opinion on the issue even by the remotest implication." It did not help in his investment promotion that the curse of the Grand Trunk Pacific lingered until the Second World War finally removed it from among the City's several misgivings about investment in Canada.

Massey also achieved recognition for Canada and its products by his enthusiastic promotion of artists, actors, writers, and scholars to a degree that none of his predecessors had even attempted. As a director of the combined National Gallery and the Tate, Massey arranged with the National Gallery in Ottawa a highly successful exhibition in London, "A Century of Canadian Art." At the same time he purchased systematically outstanding examples of modern British painting which after the war he donated to the National Gallery in Ottawa. King, however, was unimpressed by Massey's efforts to give tangible expression to his conviction that the linkages between Canada and Britain were not limited to political and economic relations. He was predictably astonished at the contemporary taste of the Masseys; he wrote to an English friend, "You cannot possibly like those dreadful pictures Vincent and Alice buy."[*]

From the commodious No. 12 Hyde Park Gardens (which Massey rented at his own expense and filled from his own collection of Canadian paintings), the Masseys moved easily through the *haute monde*, entertaining both British and Canadian visitors, including large numbers of federal and provincial legislators.[†] Ten years older than her husband, Alice Massey had spent her childhood in the Oxfordshire house of her father, the thoughtful imperialist Sir George Parkin, who was of New Brunswick Loyalist stock, former principal of Upper Canada College, and later secretary of the Rhodes Scholarship Trust at his alma mater. Both Alice and her Oxford-educated husband were entirely at home in the salons of London and the concomitant country houses. Their easy entrée to the establishment was especially important in his gathering of information about what was happening in a Britain in turmoil over the abdication of King Edward VIII and in a Europe in more profound turmoil over a resurgent Germany.

Massey, although kept informed by friends, played no role in the machinations surrounding the abdication of Edward VIII in 1936 – the same year that a newly rearmed Germany reoccupied the Rhineland. He did repeat to Prime Minister Stanley Baldwin that in the view of Mackenzie King, while agreeing with the British government's approach to what was a difficult and, for many, an emotional question, the monarch's popularity

* King had rejected Massey's offers of 1932 and 1934 to contribute to the construction of a much-needed National Gallery on government land in Ottawa.

† One who was especially grateful for the high commissioner's welcome was himself to become forty years later high commissioner: the Cambridge-educated Paul Martin, then the rising Liberal member for Windsor.

suggested that "the whole matter should be handled with great delicacy and care."[38] Twelve years before, Massey had described in his diary the then Prince of Wales as "a decent slightly underdeveloped boy [the Prince was then age thirty, seven years younger than Massey] with a natural bent for rather low society."[39] Massey was privately not sorry to see him go. His subsequent satisfaction in the coronation of King George VI only partly offset his incidental misgivings, formed during the abdication crisis, about the "irresponsible, free-booting disposition" of Churchill and the wayward enthusiasms of Beaverbrook.

In their correspondence, Massey and Skelton generally addressed each other as "My dear Skelton" or "My dear Massey"; in the privacy of his diary Massey referred to Skelton scathingly as "Herr Doktor Professor." The under-secretary always knew which way King's mind was moving – and in which way to direct it. *The Times* correspondent in Ottawa went further, reporting to his editor, "The common opinion here is that for nearly two years past, Skelton ... has been the *de facto* premier of Canada. All sorts of questions are turned over to him by King and [he] has more influence on policy than any minister."[40] King had confidence in Skelton, although he recognized that he was "at heart against the Empire." It was the high commissioner about whom he was apprehensive. With him, King had several abrasive exchanges, culminating in a meeting when the prime minister attended the 1937 coronation of George VI and the concurrent imperial conference. Massey had taken another run at the question of how the role of Canada House could be enhanced in furthering Anglo-Canadian understanding and cooperation. His despatch of 15 January 1937 was rightly regarded by Pearson (who had a major hand in its drafting) as "not a very shattering document ... However, it had ... some very useful suggestions for increasing the efficiency without adding to the expenditure of the office, suggestions which will be received with complete indifference so far as Ottawa is concerned." In a private meeting, King accused Massey of aspiring to usurp the direction of Canadian foreign policy. Worse, it was clear that he was succumbing to "malign British influences." Massey, who was generally restrained in his diary entries, on this occasion exploded: "I was struck throughout ... by the unpleasant – almost sinister – expression which was created. It was almost as if he was possessed by something evil. He referred to everything in terms of disparagement. Everybody's motives were given the most unfavourable interpretation ... I am certain there is a pathological interpretation of this appalling mood."[41]

At the imperial conference itself, King's themes were all too familiar to his Commonwealth listeners: again no centralization, including an imperial council; only Dominion autonomy, reflected in all decisions being made by national parliaments. And for Canada there would be no more than a modest increase in defence expenditure. Australia and New Zealand, isolated as they were in the Pacific, could urge what they liked about defence cooperation, but for King there must be no impression of a prior commitment to involvement in war. King's logic, having led him to conclude yet again that there could be no imperial consultation even about the deteriorating situation in Europe, resulted in him rejecting out of hand the suggestions of Australia and New Zealand for a coordinated system of defence for the Commonwealth. The minister of national defence added that the Canadian people supported the government's policy of little or no additional defence appropriations, although privately King appears to have repeated his extra-conference pledge of 1923 and 1926 that Canada would be at Britain's side in the event of a major European war.

Directly before the conference, Neville Chamberlain had succeeded Stanley Baldwin as prime minister. No doubt King's continuing advocacy of lower trade barriers among the United States, Canada, and Britain would have had a certain resonance to a Chamberlain, although it begged the question of what would then be available to other participants in the imperial *Zollverein*. In fact the conference achieved little, Ireland, Canada and South Africa remaining wary of foreign policy discussions and King in effect preventing the adoption of a notably positive statement on Commonwealth unity drafted by Australia. Neville Chamberlain was disillusioned with King whom he had first met fifteen years before; he "seems to me to get more timid as he gets older, and timidity is not the quality most required in Canada today."[42] King, by contrast, was enchanted with Chamberlain, Conservative though he was. To King's gratification, Chamberlain, as chairman of the conference, had recognized "that no useful purpose would be served by publishing anything on which delegations disagreed," thereby providing King with a virtual veto.[43] More significantly, King wrote to his old friend from Toronto, Hamar Greenwood, that Chamberlain "has my best of wishes and most sympathetic understanding in all that he undertakes ... tell him at all costs to keep the Empire out of war."[44]

King, Skelton, Massey, Beaverbrook, and Chamberlain (but not Churchill) agreed upon one thing: what came to be denigrated as appeasement. All were desperately hopeful that Hitler's madness would not drag the world into a second war in twenty years. The very thought of another world conflict involving a second generation drove them all to support a settlement with Hitler (one of the few "imperial" policies which King

enthusiastically supported). Conversely, Churchill was held in deep suspicion, a wild man who had proven to be unreliable on the Dardenelles,
Chanak, the gold standard, India, and the abdication, and was now intent
upon policies which would surely result in war with Germany, not avoid it
as Chamberlain was so reassuringly determined to do.

It is perhaps a distinction without a difference to say that King was
among the more naive of the Canadians favouring appeasement. Confident that his 1928 meeting with Mussolini had been productive of some
ill-defined good, he readily accepted an invitation from Joachim von Ribbentrop, the German ambassador in London, to visit Berlin in June 1937.
As a prewar wine salesman in Canada, Ribbentrop was well aware of the
Massey family; he also invited the high commissioner, but King declined
to have Massey accompany him. Horrified at the thought of another
world war and convinced that the League of Nations had become powerless to prevent one, he saw a meeting with Hitler as "the day for which
I was born."*[45] He told Anthony Eden and Malcolm MacDonald of his
acceptance of the invitation, adding to MacDonald that, "After expressing sympathy with Hitler's constructive work and telling him of the sympathy which was felt with Germany in England [*sic*], he intended to add
that if Germany should ever turn her mind from constructive to destruc-
tive efforts against the United Kingdom, all the Dominions would come
to her aid, and there would be great numbers of Canadians anxious to
swim the Atlantic."

Whether King actually employed his nautical metaphor as a warning
to Hitler is unrecorded, but "I felt in talking to Malcolm [MacDonald] a
sort of feeling as though this whole country [Britain] was looking to me
to help it." He had convinced himself that Hitler was "a fellow mystic,"
an impression which his visit confirmed. Hitler's eyes had "a liquid quality about them which indicate keen perception and profound sympathy."
King's diary entries about his visit glow with self-satisfaction, augmented
by his sudden recognition that "His bible reading the day of the meeting
was by chance just that chapter" that he had read to his mother prior to
her death.[46]

---

* W.D. Euler (1875–1961), the minister of trade and commerce who was of German ancestry, had called upon Hitler in 1936. Four months after King's visit came the notorious visit
of the Duke of Windsor who was at least as impressed by Hitler as King was. (For more
about King's Berlin visit, see C.P. Stacey, "The Divine Mission: Mackenzie King and
Hitler," *Canadian Historical Review*, December 1980).

In April 1938 King again praised to Malcolm MacDonald the forays of Neville Chamberlain into the uncertain world of appeasement. Massey was less naive than King and Skelton; he was closer to understanding what was becoming the seemingly irreversible approach of a second world war. But Massey was hardly less a supporter of appeasement for all that, accepting as King did that the reoccupation of the Rhineland and the *Anschluss* with Austria were somehow inevitable and should be accepted as such. "Massey was in favour of each successive concession to Hitler: 'so long as there is no real surrender of principle, it is worth taking every sharp corner to get past the crisis and save civilization as we know it' – a sentence that embodies the confusion and self-contradiction of the Munich spirit."[47] That was acceptable to King the appeaser, but at the same time he wanted it to be clear that Canada's support for appeasement carried no commitments. When King spoke in Parliament about the threatening situation in Europe, he did not refer to the German occupation of the Sudetenland, but he did make clear that he expected the high commissioner to toe the line: "We have expressed no opinions ... and no one in London [i.e., Massey] is authorized or warranted in interpreting us as doing so."[48]

The diary accounts of both Massey and his wife (reproduced in part in his autobiography, *What's Past Is Prologue*) reflect the desperation of Chamberlain and his colleagues to secure peace. With the Flanders holocaust of twenty years past still clearly in their minds – Massey had participated in the unveiling of the Canadian memorial at Vimy Ridge only two years before – the Munich settlement of September 1938 came as a profound relief. He knew well enough, however, with whom the British government had to deal: "It is a ghastly thing that our fate rests in the hands of a demented paperhanger,"[49] thanks in part to the almost daily briefings by MacDonald and occasionally by Chamberlain. Pearson, who from his arrival at Canada House had made a steady progression from a sort of isolationism to opposition to any further appeasement, was even more condign in his judgment: Hitler was undoubtedly "a pathological case."

From 14 September 1938 – the same day that King sent a message to Hitler welcoming his Munich meeting with Chamberlain – Massey regularly attended the now daily briefings with the other high commissioners, whether Ottawa liked it or not. There was no doubt where the high commissioners stood: they were all appeasers, even more in favour of appeasement than Chamberlain's government. "We are all prepared to pay a higher price for peace ... The difference is because the Dominions are removed further away from Europe, not because our sense of honour

Vincent Massey, Mackenzie King, and O.D. Skelton, the under-secretary of
state for external affairs, all supported Neville Chamberlain's policy of appeasement toward Hitler in the desperate hope of avoiding a second world war with
Germany. In September 1938 Massey (far right) joined other high commissioners and British ministers and officials in wishing the prime minister success on
his departure for a meeting with Hitler which resulted in the infamous Munich
agreement. On Massey's right is Lord Irwin, later Lord Halifax, the foreign secretary, and subsequently ambassador to the United States.

is less acute. [The Australian] Bruce, whose Government uses him (unlike
mine in relation to their H.C.) feels very strongly the German proposals
can't be allowed to be a *causa belli*."[50] Three days later, on 27 September, as
the crisis reached its climax, "We all made it clear for ourselves (and some
spoke for their governments ... that there might be a dangerous reaction
in the Dominions to a decision to plunge the Empire into war on the issue
of how Hitler was to take possession of territory already ceded to him
in principle ... surely the world can't be plunged into the horrors of universal war for a difference of opinion over a few miles of territory ... that
thank God is I believe Chamberlain's view." Not surprisingly, Massey is
to be seen in photographs alongside a beaming Chamberlain embarking
for Munich. The result "was almost unbelievable: without a miracle war

seemed certain and a miracle had happened! We had been only a few hours from a war that would have ended civilization."[51]

In his first communication to Massey in six months, King hailed the Munich agreement as "emphatically the right choice." In what was for him a rare accolade to a British statesman, Skelton saluted Chamberlain for "having worked for peace and achieved it." Convinced that a deal had been done and that peace was now assured, King was even more ecstatic in a telegram of 29 September to Chamberlain in which he expressed his "unbounded admiration at the service you have rendered mankind ... On the very brink of chaos with passions flaming and armies marching, the voice of Reason has found a way out of the conflict which no people in their heart desired, but none seemed able to avert."[52] To the Duchess of Athol – King enjoyed writing to female members of the British aristocracy, especially a granddaughter of Queen Victoria who was politically a pronounced Liberal – he described enthusiastically Chamberlain's "splendid act" (the sceptical Duchess, however, did not agree: she was as opposed to appeasement as she had been to the fascists in the Spanish Civil War). With a show of modesty, King concluded privately that his own visit to Hitler the year before had played a part in making the Munich agreement possible.

Appeasement being in fact to no avail against Hitler's vaulting ambitions, the slide towards war continued inexorably, with Chamberlain becoming disillusioned with Hitler – and Massey along with him. In March 1938, following Germany's *Anschluss* with Austria, King could still write of Hitler, "he is a spiritualist ... his devotion to his mother – that mother's spirit is I am certain his guide ... the world will yet come to see a very great man – [and a] mystic, in Hitler."[53] Massey was travelling in the opposite direction. Germany's occupation of the remainder of Czechoslovakia twelve months later was for him the turning point; the policy of appeasement was now clearly in ruins. How was Hitler to be stopped except by force? Massey thereafter supported Chamberlain's increasingly hard line of rearmament, including conscription. King, however, never wavered in his commitment to appeasement, whatever the aggression, writing to Hitler on 1 February 1939, "an expression of the faith I have in the purpose you have at heart, and some of the friendship with yourself which you have been so kind as to permit me to share."[54]

During 1938 King began to tell Skelton that if a major war were to involve Britain, "we would have to accept the view that Canada was also at war ... [but] the nature and extent of our participation would be for Canada's Parliament to decide." King having concluded that "as part of the British Empire ... [we] should co-operate [in] lending every assistance possible, in no way asserting neutrality, but carefully defining in what ways and how far she would participate." But as late as March 1939, Skelton, clinging doggedly to his neutralist convictions, vented his mounting frustration in a bitter letter to Canada's representative in Geneva, including a passage that revealed his continuing opposition to British offers of consultation, still believing that they were essentially hypocritical in masking centralist ambitions. Further, Skelton assured King that even preliminary planning for an expeditionary force might still be avoided. Australia and South Africa, he was confident, would not send troops overseas. As late as July 1939, Pearson, back briefly in Ottawa, wrote to Massey: "Dr. Skelton tells me that King is not in sympathy with recent British policies, and prefers Chamberlain the appeaser to Chamberlain the avenger,"[55] an attitude that Skelton even more obviously embraced. A month later, one month before war, King was still considering the idea of another visit to Hitler and had accepted an invitation for Canadian students and "officers" to visit Germany for three weeks.* On 25 August, King, with Lapointe's strong support, sent Hitler (and Mussolini and the president of Poland) an appeal "that your great power and authority will be used to prevent impending catastrophe." Only one week before the declaration of war, undeterred on this occasion by constitutional niceties, he wired Chamberlain "to strongly urge" King George to appeal to Hitler to give more time for negotiation.

For all the momentary euphoria at the Munich agreement, Massey had not been convinced that peace had suddenly come to stay – and so began to advise King. Even the prime minister had reluctantly come to recognize that some modest additional expenditure on military equipment and training would be prudent. To his credit, Peter Larkin, when summoned by King from beyond the grave for advice, urged – in one word – "preparedness." King had begun to accept that the Canadian armed forces could hardly be left with only a few effective ships and aircraft and a minute army still largely equipped from the First World War. The Canadian forces had been run down to almost nothing, under Meighen, Bennett, and himself. If Canadian units were to serve again alongside British

---

* Several groups of Canadian young people had already visited Nazi Germany. In 1938, for example, schoolboys were sent by the Overseas Education League of Canada (which had as its principal purpose to promote "a better understanding between the young people of the Dominions and the Old Country").

forces, their augmented equipment must necessarily accord with theirs.* In 1937 a Royal Canadian Ordnance Corps officer had finally been posted to the High Commission and in July 1939 a second RCAF liaison officer had been sent to the Air Ministry, gathering information and recommending purchases. It was at best, however, a slow business compared with that of their colleagues from Australia, New Zealand, and South Africa who had shared in the information supplied to the Committee of Imperial Defence and its sub-committees (on all of which King had banned Canadian participation). In 1936 and again in 1939 a delegation of the Canadian Manufacturers' Association visited Britain, convinced that large orders were just around the corner. However, as in the First World War, few orders had been confirmed when war began. The dreaded prospect of eventual conscription was set aside by the emerging understanding between King and Lapointe that if Lapointe would endorse the need for Canada to stand by Britain in a major war King would rule out in advance compulsory service overseas.

In Britain, the sense grew that time had been bought by Munich, but if so it was time which had to be used to accelerate rearmament and to provide for civil defence: "keep calm and dig." Skelton, however, declined to sanction expenditure on even the protective measures which Massey recommended for the safety of the staff of Canada House, contending that there was no money allocated in the External Affairs budget for protection from air raids. In the face of his refusal, Massey himself paid for the basement shelter, fire equipment, and other safeguards, paralleling those being hurriedly added to public buildings throughout Britain. At the same time, Skelton wrote to Pearson, the secretary at Canada House, instructing him to have the second high commission automobile placed in storage since "no authority exists for the Secretary at Canada House to use it."

Even in the face of mounting evidence that war was coming (Massey, for example, was soon involved in secret arrangements for the safekeeping

---

* In the case of light machine (Bren) guns, King had asked Massey to assist a potential Canadian manufacturer in his contacts in London, but then he procrastinated for two years over an advantageous order from the British government that would have assured a volume of production sufficient for guns to have been supplied to the Canadian army at a reduced price. When he finally screwed up his courage to place the order with the Toronto firm, he was attacked by George Drew, the Conservative leader in Ontario, for corrupt practices. Drew's attack, later withdrawn, was somewhat surprising in light of his long-standing conviction that Canada's military preparedness was best embodied in close cooperation with Britain.

in Canada of more than two thousand tonnes of British gold), King and Skelton continued to reject information proffered by the Foreign Office. King cabled to Massey in March 1939 that, the press having reported that he "and other Dominion representatives [had] conferred with Dominions' Secretary and received latest information on developments in Europe," he must explain himself. Massey replied guardedly:

I attended [two] meetings of High Commissioners ... with Dominions' Secretary called by the latter on Saturday March 18th and Monday March 20th. These were for the purpose of giving information on the latest developments in European situation. In accordance with verbal instructions which I received from you when you were last in London I ceased to attend such meetings and followed practice of requesting an interview with Dominions' Secretary alone after High Commissioners' meetings for the purpose of receiving information which had been given to the other High Commissioners at such meetings. From my conversation with you I trust that on occasions when special circumstances seemed to justify it I was not to be precluded from meetings with Dominions' Secretary along with other High Commissioners. The grave emergency which exists at the present moment appeared to me to justify fully my taking this course. The circumstances of present critical situation make it difficult for me to ask for special conferences with Dominions' Secretary as the latter working under great pressure ... In the absence of further instructions presume I may carry on as indicated above. Dominions' Secretary has invited High Commissioners to meet Foreign Secretary this afternoon. Unless instructed to the contrary I plan to attend this meeting after which I will telegraph any information received which has not been cabled direct.[56]

Chamberlain's guarantee to Poland, however horrifying to King and Skelton, left Massey in no doubt where Europe was going. Amidst the gathering gloom, the royal visit to Canada in the summer of 1939 was a gratifying success. The correspondent of *The Times* was enthusiastic about the visit, but less so about King's motives: "King regards this royal tour as the crowning glory of his career and thinks of nothing else. He is personally supervising all the arrangements down to the last detail and doing the sort of work that a butler should. He has his entourage almost crazy and Government House is in despair ... [at his] trying to make political capital out of the royal visit."[57]

By August 1939 anyone in London could sense that war was imminent. Not so in Ottawa. Skelton sent King a sterile note about the Soviet-German non-aggression pact of that month, describing it as "a crushing condemnation of the handling of British foreign policy. Not only Chamberlain and his Government, but even more so, Churchill and Eden ... must share the responsibility for the greatest fiasco in British history."[58] Given the number of fiascos sustained by the United Kingdom throughout its long history, Skelton was asserting a large claim (especially since both King and he had earlier enthusiastically welcomed appeasement). On 25 August, nine days before Germany invaded Poland and war began, he grumbled to the prime minister:

The first casualty in this [imminent] war has been Canada's claim to independent control of her own destinies. In spite of a quarter century of proclamation and achievement of equal and independent status, we have thus far been relegated to the role of a Crown colony. We are drifting into a war resulting, so far as the United Kingdom's part is concerned, from policies and diplomatic actions initiated months ago without our knowledge or expectation ... If war comes in Poland and we take part, that war comes as the consequence of commitments made by the Government of Great Britain, about which we were not in one iota consulted, and about which we were given not the slightest inkling of information in advance. The British Government with bland arrogance has assumed that whatever its policy, whether it be appeasement or challenge, pro-Russian or anti-Russian, pro-Italian or anti-Italian, a Western European policy or an Eastern European policy, we could be counted on to trot behind, blindly and dumbly, to chaos ... My objection is to our fate being determined without any participation or agreement on the part of the Government of Canada in the commitments made, being determined by policies and decisions of other governments without even the polite formality of consultation.[59]

Quite how Skelton could, presumably with a straight face, accuse the British of "the blind arrogance" of not having offered "even the polite formality of consultation" must have passed all understanding. It was Skelton himself who had consistently recommended to King to reject repeated offers of consultation. It was he who had ensured that Massey had been admonished against consultation; now, days before the war, Skelton suddenly complained that there had been none. One historian has trenchantly summarized the attitude of King and Skelton:

Nothing was more distinctive about Mackenzie King's external policies than their insistence that the Commonwealth should not collectively do anything which might detract from the individual responsibilities of its members; and that, to be on the safe side, it had better not do any thing at all. To Canada's "everlasting no" there were two exceptions. One was its membership of the Imperial War Graves Commission; the other was its endorsement, at the Imperial Conference of 1937, of the policy of appeasement of Nazi Germany. The historian may record, leaving others to moralize upon, the melancholy fact that only in burying the dead of the First World War, and causing more dead to be buried in a Second, would Canada combine with other members of the inter-war Commonwealth in any sort of purposeful activity.[60]

In London, Charles Ritchie had it about right, lamenting on 26 August, less than a fortnight before the German invasion of Poland and the declaration of war,

Still not a word of enquiry or guidance from the Canadian Government. They refuse to take any responsibility in this crisis which endangers the future of Canada. Mackenzie King is condemned in my eyes as unworthy to hold office as Prime Minister. Mrs. Massey and I sat up until eleven p.m. drinking whisky and water in the High Commissioner's big Mussoliniesque office awaiting his return from his meeting with Halifax. London seems very calm – everyone appears resigned to war if it comes. They have lost any positive will to peace. The last year of peace has been too insufferable. If Russia was on our side I think people would not be sorry that war had come at last.[61]

Upon the declaration of war, Skelton wrote, "this is not our war ... the British Government which blundered into it, should have been allowed to blunder out of it."* Skelton duly offered his resignation, and King duly refused it.

With Germany's invasion of Poland, Britain declared war on 3 September 1939. One week later, on 10 September 1939, Canada declared war, King having summoned Parliament to sanction his decision and to hear him declare that his government would not introduce "conscription of men for overseas service ... No such measure will be introduced by the present administration." He added that with the members of the Commonwealth at war, high commissions were to be established in Australia, New Zealand, Ireland, and South Africa. Massey, a fortnight after the declaration by Britain, formally delivered Canada's declaration to King

---

* Skelton's phrase, "this is not our war," apparently remained in King's mind. He suddenly blurted it out during the negotiations in Ottawa of the British Commonwealth Air Training Plan, leaving an unfortunate impression on his prospective partners in the Plan.

George VI on 18 September, his son Hart having driven him to Windsor Castle in his roadster from their nearby country house.

As Perley had found twenty-five years before, war brought with it a myriad of immediate problems for the High Commission. To assist him, Massey fortunately had several of the best and the brightest: Pearson, Ritchie, and soon George Ignatieff. They dealt with everything: questions relating to Canadian citizens now interned in enemy territory; transatlantic passenger priorities; the repatriation of students (those who did not volunteer for British forces); and the hurried evacuation of children and later enemy aliens to Canada. A very different initiative was Massey's recommendation that, following the precedent of the First World War, the Canadian War Memorials Fund should be revived to commission war artists.

Before the Canadian military headquarters was established in London in October 1939, Lieutenant-Colonel E.L.M. Burns from the Imperial Defence College joined Massey's staff temporarily, dealing with 1,800 Canadian volunteers in Britain, acting as liaison with the War Office, and planning for the arrival of the First Canadian Division. Unlike Perley in the First World War, Massey had no ministerial responsibility for Canadian forces overseas. However, he soon found senior officers "quite ready to turn to the high commissioner for such counsel and guidance as he might be able to offer. To them I was a sort of governmental nanny."

To no one's surprise, certainly not to Massey's, the British, in reviewing how their own war effort and that of the Dominions might best be coordinated, recalled the precedent of the First World War. As early as 21 September 1939, when the war was less than three weeks old, Chamberlain had inquired of the prime ministers whether they each wished to designate a minister to travel to London to discuss all aspects of wartime consultation (additional to information regularly provided to the high commissioners and their staffs). This was welcome to Australia, whose high commissioner was a former prime minister, but King was immediately suspicious. He replied cautiously that while his minister of mines and resources, T.A. Crerar, would shortly arrive in London, neither he nor the senior officials accompanying him would remain there indefinitely. To the press, he carefully stated that a report "that an Empire War Cabinet or Conference was being set up is without foundation."

Nevertheless, Massey did, as the senior Canadian representative, play a central role in relating the activities of the new Canadian military headquarters both to the government in Ottawa and to the British. The headquarters under Brigadier H.D.G. Crerar was housed in the Sun Life building adjoining Canada House. When his namesake but no relation,

T.A. Crerar, arrived, the two Crerars concerted together, the senior recommending to King that no ministry of overseas forces was necessary:

I have become impressed with urgency of utilizing Canada House and Brigadier Crerar as sole channel of communication for messages between the Department of National Defence and Department of External Affairs in Ottawa and Dominions Office and War Office ... Above suggestion would not of course prejudice in any way existing system of direct communication between Governments in examination of prospective military policies but consider that when implementation of agreed policy is decided upon it is most important that Canada House and army staff here should be sole agency through which action is obtained.[72]

The last thing that the prime minister wanted was a cabinet minister resident in London, as Tupper and Perley had been. The historian Charles Stacey, who later served at the headquarters in London, surmised:

A cabinet minister permanently domiciled in London might have proved difficult to control, and the position of a minister separated from his cabinet colleagues is constitutionally peculiar. At any rate, no new Ministry of Overseas Military Forces was set up. The senior Canadian civil representative in London continued to the be High Commissioner ... but although Canadian Military Headquarters was a very near neighbour of Canada House and maintained close contact with the High Commissioner and his staff, it was a quite separate organization, responsible to the Minister of National Defence (through the Chief of the General Staff), and not, like the High Commissioner, to the Secretary of State for External Affairs. The High Commissioner was nevertheless (more particularly, in the early days, perhaps) the channel for communications on high policy between the Canadian government and the Canadian field commander; and his relations with the successive field commanders and heads of C.M.H.Q. were always friendly if hardly intimate.[73]

After consulting Massey, T.A. Crerar wired King, recommending what soon proved to be a durable arrangement. Pearson reported what Stacey was later to find, "So far as relations between ourselves, Aldershot [Canadian divisional headquarters] and Military Headquarters [in London] are concerned, I think everything will work smoothly. We are on good terms with them and have evolved a satisfactory system of keeping each other informed on matters of mutual interest. I don't think there will be anything like the difficulty experienced in the last war in the triangular relationship of Argyll House, Canada House [*sic*] and command in the field." The Sam Hughes fiasco had not been forgotten.

Following the outbreak of war in September 1939, the high commissioners met almost daily with the secretary of state for the dominions, Anthony Eden (third from right). Vincent Massey is on Eden's right. By 1938 Massey had begun to ignore Mackenzie King's injunction against attendance at the then weekly gatherings of the five high commissioners.

Massey joined in planning for the arrival of the Canadian First Division. When in early October 1939 Major-General Andrew McNaughton was recalled from the presidency of the National Research Council to command it, a meeting of the prime minister, the minister of finance (J.L. Ralston), and the minister of national defence (Norman Rogers), revealed the first evidence of an eventual problem. At its simplest, it was that Ralston (who was to succeed Rogers as minister of defence within a year) would become willing to contemplate the dispersal of Canadian units among British if operational requirements so demanded, while McNaughton was not. In a meeting in April 1940 with the visiting minister of national defence, Massey learned from McNaughton of the expected formation of a Canadian Corps, an eventuality that Rogers had also contemplated, although he did recall King's statement that support for aircrew training in Canada "was bound to affect other aspects of Canada's potential war effort." McNaughton worked consistently to keep Canada's army together, even if this meant seemingly endless training for restless troops garrisoned mainly in the south of England. His advocacy of a self-contained army, similar to Currie's, prevailed at least temporarily, but it was a question that had been postponed rather than resolved.

More immediate in its impact was Massey's role in launching what was to become a vast training programme for Commonwealth aircrew. With the precedent of the First World War in mind when twenty-one thousand Canadians were trained for service with the Royal Flying Corps and the Royal Naval Air Service, King had vaguely offered at the 1926 imperial conference to consider how a "reserve of airmen" might be created in Canada. Eight years later, there having been nothing done, the Air Ministry had sought to explore with the Canadian government how best to respond to the "considerable number of enquiries [which] have been received from young men in Canada with a view to their obtaining short service commissions in the Royal Air Force." In March 1936 Massey had relayed to Ottawa an informal inquiry which he had received from the secretary of state for air, suggesting that "in addition to the Canadian officers who are being admitted to the R.A.F. under arrangements which call for their training in England, an additional number might be provided with their preliminary training in Canada and taken on the strength of the R.A.F."[62] The British high commissioner in Ottawa had accurately reported in June that, "It was going to be extraordinarily difficult to persuade Canada to do anything" in the way of military preparedness; the best hope "lay in such directions as the supply of pilots in the time of war."

Later that same year, following a conversation between Baldwin and King, the Air Ministry hoped to resume training of RAF pilots in Canada as part of its urgent expansion plans. Despite the fact that a decade earlier King had himself raised the possibility, however vaguely, of Canada-British cooperation in creating a reserve of airmen, he had remained suspicious of all subsequent British inquiries: "It would be inadvisable to have Canadian territory used by the British Government for training school purposes," offering the lame explanation that "It is the intention of the Canadian Government to establish training schools of its own. The situation might give rise to competition between the two governments in the matter of fields, pilots, equipment and the like."[63]

Nevertheless, as part of its broader thinking about aircraft and training requirements, including manufacture, the Air Ministry persisted, returning to the charge several times between 1936 and 1939. Each time King's opposition proved impenetrable, whether in response to requests to train Canadians for the RAF or to train British pilots themselves in the empty skies over Canada. The despatch of a high-level mission to Ottawa in July 1939 finally moved matters forward, but King's ban on Massey attending meetings of the high commissioners had meant that he had been absent from discussions of a possible Commonwealth air-training plan. A modest agreement to train a mere fifty RAF pilots annually was finally reached in September 1939, the same month in which war was declared. Fifty, it was now obvious, was but a drop in the bucket.

Massey was fully aware that such belated and meagre measures would meet neither country's wartime requirements. Only a massive effort, involving Australia and New Zealand as well, could possibly fill the demand. He also knew his prime minister. He was aware of King's rejection of earlier British requests and of his desperate desire to avoid the prospect of a large Canadian army going into action which might in time create a demand for reinforcements that only the dreaded conscription for overseas service could meet. King recalled the adverse impact of conscription on national unity in 1917; he was determined that what had happened to Laurier would not happen to him. In the first week of the war, he incautiously assured the House of Commons, the province of Quebec and perhaps himself that "One strategic fact is clear: the days of great expeditionary forces of infantry crossing the oceans are not likely to recur."[64]

Massey acted decisively to bring about the air training agreement without unduly arousing the prime minister. On 4 September 1939, he reported the likelihood that "Britain will be proposing recruitment and training in Canada of large number of pilots, possibly two thousand per year."[65] The British so proposed two days later. King responded not to Massey but to the British high commissioner in preliminary terms on 12 September. The following day, at Canada House, Massey convened a meeting of Stanley Bruce, the Australian high commissioner, two RAAF officers, one RAF officer, and his own senior air advisor as preparation for meetings at the Dominions Office with Anthony Eden and later with the foreign secretary, the chancellor of the exchequer and a host of officials. At the Dominions Office, "Mr. Massey and Mr. Bruce suggested that consideration should be given to a scheme whereby Canadian, Australian and New Zealand air forces should be trained in Canada on 'planes to be specially built in Canada or the United States and should then be sent to the front as distinctive Canadian, Australian and New Zealand air forces."[66]

As a result, ten days later a telegram was prepared for Chamberlain to his Dominion colleagues proposing what was to become the British

Commonwealth Air Training Plan (BCATP). Having been consulted on the draft, Massey had volunteered an additional paragraph, knowing that any implied British willingness to regard air training as a principal wartime contribution by Canada would appeal to King, especially if couched as a personal request from the British prime minister. It did. "My instinct in suggesting these placatory phrases was not mistaken ... The Air Training Plan was indeed advantageous to him in a political sense. When the Canadian war effort was concentrated to a considerable extent on air training, there would be less pressure for a large army and less risk of a demand for conscription to reinforce it."[67] The high commissioner had manipulated King in something of the same way that King himself had manipulated an earlier high commissioner. "Mr. Massey took the considerable responsibility of sponsoring a plan which was likely to have a major effect upon the structure and balance of the Canadian war effort without telling his government what he was doing."[68]

More than six weeks of intense negotiation in Ottawa followed, with the astonishing British target now being twenty thousand pilots and thirty thousand other aircrew annually, involving Australia and New Zealand as well as Canada and Britain. King's continuing niggardliness helped to ensure that there was no early conclusion, suspecting the British purpose as being "like the Chanak incident," but he finally sanctioned the plan in a message to Chamberlain on 28 September. The announcement was made on 10 October, but not before Skelton had sent to King a mock paragraph which he evidently considered humorous, depicting the accord as neo-imperialist. For his part, King characterized the plan as "a positive inducement for French Canada to admire the Government's wise management of affairs." The BCATP was finally signed on 18 December 1939, the same day that the dominions secretary, Anthony Eden, travelled to Glasgow to welcome the First Canadian Division and, much more to King's personal gratification, on his own sixty-fifth birthday.

The BCATP was a great success. Eventually it trained one hundred and thirty-one thousand aircrew (of whom seventy-two thousand were Canadian). King, however, had always regarded the programme as a British rather than Commonwealth initiative. Accordingly, the British should pay for it. Those trained, including Canadians, should be "placed at the disposal of the Government of the United Kingdom," a strange attitude for a prime minister who only a few years before had enthusiastically endorsed the Statute of Westminster. King's approach was contrary to Massey's recommendation of a distinctive Canadian air force and consequently the RCAF never achieved its full potential, there being so many trained Canadian volunteers serving in the RAF (the judgment of the RCAF historian about air policy in the First World War has a bizarre application to the second as well: "It was in this fashion that the Canadian government arrived at its posture of colonial dependency in the field of aviation"). The large number of Canadians in RAF squadrons and in RCAF squadrons incorporated into larger RAF commands was, however, welcome to Churchill: it "would be not only a winner of the war but a cement of Empire, for the friendship and the comradeship formed by the young men would carry on their beneficent influence long after the war was finished."[69]

King hoped against hope that the combination of the BCATP and financial assistance would somehow avoid the necessity for a large Canadian army overseas. The chiefs of staff knew better. The British army was already in France; Canadian infantry soon joined them. Even if the unthinkable happened and France fell, Britain, fighting on alone, would as in 1915 welcome every soldier from the Dominions to supplement her own hard-pressed forces. Canadian soldiers in large numbers were urgently needed and a second division was soon raised. The "limited liability" war effort was still in place, but Canada's commitment to winning the war had become more tangible and, despite Tory grumblings about its inadequacy and belatedness, a little more persuasive; the Liberals won the suddenly announced March 1940 election with a yet greater majority.

Massey had received first-hand knowledge of the precarious state of France when in April 1940 he had joined Georges Vanier, the former secretary at Canada House and now minister to France, for a visit to the British headquarters near Arras. Two months later, when France had capitulated, he had been at Paddington Station to greet the Vaniers on their arrival from their escape through Bordeaux. But Canada retained relations with Vichy France. With his eye on Quebec, King confided hyperbolically to his diary that "a break would be ... disastrous for Canada."[70] The real reason was the lingering British hope that Vichy might yet prove to be at least occasionally neutral, especially if the United States were to enter the war. King readily agreed with the suggestion of Halifax, the foreign secretary, to Massey that it "might be useful" to have Pierre Dupuy, the former first secretary at the legation in Paris, visit Vichy France. Massey facilitated three such visits by Dupuy before relations were finally terminated when the Allies landed in North Africa in November 1942. He thereupon arranged for Vanier to be accredited to General de Gaulle's Free French

National Committee in London (later Vanier would move to Algiers and eventually return to liberated France with de Gaulle).

As France collapsed, British intelligence and Foreign Office briefings helped Ottawa to recognize that it would soon become Britain's largest ally. The fall of France cost Chamberlain the premiership. Churchill, whom King had long regarded as an unprincipled adventurer, came to office on 10 May 1940, fully aware, as George Orwell observed, that "wars are not won without fighting." Churchill's first messages to King, including a description of his offer to the all-but-defeated France to join in a full Franco-British union, had alerted Ottawa to what to expect in the way of forceful leadership. Chamberlain, now the ailing president of the council, informed the high commissioners on 27 May "that even if France went out of the war there was no prospect of our giving in. We had good reason to believe we could withstand attack from Germany and were resolved to fight on." In response, Massey conveyed to a grateful British government the offer of No. 1 Squadron, RCAF, and the still modest production of Hurricane fighters at Fort William, Ontario, as well as substantial dollar advances for purchases of matériel.

Although King remained unaware of the indispensable intelligence from deciphered German codes, the entry of Italy into the war was at least foreshadowed for him via Massey. Upon Mussolini declaring war on Britain in June 1940, the high commissioner simply substituted the name of Italy for Germany in a submission to the King. More than a year later, Massey would adapt again the basic submission when Canada declared war on Hungary, Romania, and Finland on 7 December 1941 – the same day that Japan and the United States joined the belligerents – and delivered yet another declaration to the monarch for signature. Having drawn upon British intelligence to keep Ottawa informed daily as Denmark, Norway, Luxembourg, Belgium, and the Netherlands were all overrun, Massey was soon asked to establish relations with the London governments-in-exile of Poland, Czechoslovakia, Yugoslavia, Greece, and Norway (and later to arrange with them the terms for the recruitment of their nationals in Canada into their own armed forces in exile). In helping to arrange the opening of Canadian legations in Brazil, Argentina, and Chile, Massey sought the assistance of British missions to pave their way. And it fell to him to work out with the Foreign Office who would replace the United States in representing in Berlin and in several occupied countries the interests of Commonwealth members if Washington eventually decided to enter the war, following upon its massive defence appropriations and its prompt introduction of conscription.

Massey confirmed to the dominions secretary that Canada would soon open a high commission in Newfoundland, but relations with India were to prove a problem throughout the war. The difficulty began with a question in the House of Commons in March 1940: would Canada and India exchange high commissioners? King's reply was noncommittal, but it did not escape Amery's notice. Massey wrote to King describing Amery's enthusiasm for such an exchange since it "would demonstrate to the Indian mind the true nature of the modern British Commonwealth of Nations." His letter went unanswered for three months, King noting for Skelton, "Let sleeping dogs lie. Don't rouse agitation in B.C. in order to keep down one in India." Skelton rehearsed for King all the difficulties that stood in the way "so long as Canada refuses to permit East Indians living in Canada to exercise the franchise."[71] King duly informed Massey that the idea was not "timely" since it "would be certain to reopen the difficult question of the enfranchisement in British Columbia ... [and] also [of] the much larger groups of Chinese and Japanese origin."

T.A. Crerar, the minister of mines and resources, visited Britain for six weeks to encourage purchases, especially of wheat but also of matériel, and to agree upon financial arrangements between the two countries (including payment for the BCATP). Massey, who knew Crerar well, accompanied him on his calls on British ministers. He had arranged for his delegation, which included the deputy minister of trade and commerce, Dana Wilgress, to meet the chancellor of the exchequer who initiated the financial discussions that were to continue throughout the war: how to deploy the scarce dollar resources of both countries to the best effect. How imports, including munitions, were to be financed was also examined, both with the chancellor and with Churchill, then first lord of the Admiralty. As had long been foreseen by the British Treasury, strict foreign exchange controls had been immediately introduced and sterling was declared incontrovertible. Sterling could be freely used within the Commonwealth, but not everywhere (including Canada which continued to trade primarily in dollars).

The decision to protect sterling against speculators and dollar enthusiasts was unavoidable, but it carried within it the seeds of years of postwar disagreement with the United States. For Canada the problem in its essence was simple enough. Canada had long exported much more to Britain that it had imported from it; Canada had imported much more from the United States than it exported to it. In effect, Canada had paid for its trade deficit with the United States by its trade surplus with Britain. That worked well enough in peacetime with full sterling convertibility, but in wartime with sterling inconvertibility the challenge of helping the United Kingdom find dollars to pay for its essential imports from North America moved to the forefront of discussion in Ottawa. As Norman Robertson defined for King: "Our merchandise exports to the United States are keeping up quite satisfactorily, but they do not come close to paying for the great expansion of imports from the United States required by our war industries." Two massive dollar loans, $700 million in 1941 and $1 billion in 1942, were made to assist Britain in increasing its essential purchases from North America.

Crerar's discussions with the British were complex, but at least for Wilgress the visit to wartime London had an unexpected dividend: "We saw a great deal of our colleagues from the other Dominions during the briefings and demonstrations put on for our benefit, and the Commonwealth took on a new meaning for me. Gone were my doubts about its validity, dating back to the Ottawa Conference of 1932."[74] Crerar showed signs of sharing something of the new-found convictions of Wilgress, but King made certain that his minister did not remain in Britain for any sort of Commonwealth consultation or conference. That might smack of centralism. The question of Commonwealth consultation, however, would not go away. When Norman Rogers, the minister of national defence, was in London in April 1940, in part to obtain orders for Canadian manufactures, Chamberlain proposed a London meeting of prime ministers in July or early August. King rejected the proposal out of hand, having just won an overwhelming majority in the election of March 1940 on the platform that "conscription of men for overseas service would not be a necessary or effective step." He cited the necessity to remain at home to keep "Canada itself united ... [and] relations between the United Kingdom and the United States as cordial as possible."[75] Further, King informed Chamberlain that there was really no need for a conference, given the highly satisfactory "means of consultation with yourself and the other members of the Commonwealth afforded by direct communication ... supplemented as they have been by direct communication to and from the Secretary of State for the Dominions and by the immediate and personal consultation maintained through the High Commissioners in London and in Ottawa."[76]

Evidently consultation by high commissioners of which King had consistently fought shy in peacetime was now to be extolled as a virtue in wartime. As transatlantic discussions about a conference of prime ministers continued, he redoubled his efforts to proclaim his newly discovered conviction in the efficacy of existing arrangements. What had been wrong in the past was the absence of rapid communication: "today there are means of immediate and effective communication and consultation between the British government and the governments of the several Dominions which did not exist a quarter of a century ago."[77]

Canada paid a price for its prime minister's refusal either to have a minister or high commissioner participate in an imperial war cabinet. The Australian high commissioner had regular access to more privileged information and Canberra had in turn the opportunity to comment upon it. Attlee soon concluded that "the Canadians weren't worried about the higher direction of the war in the way that the Australians were." King's predictable refusal to participate himself in an imperial war cabinet or to have a minister or the high commissioner participate meant that paradoxically Canada reverted to a near colonial status. King had managed to recreate the very situation which Borden had struggled against twenty-five years before. As an historian of the Commonwealth has noted, "Laurier and King were afraid of consultation on the ground that it might lead to centralization which they both feared. They were always on the lookout for an imperialist plot. Laurier carried the fear to the point where he seemed ready to accept for Canada a subordinate relationship to Great Britain, rather than engage in consultation on foreign policy."[78] Decades later, King remained true to his master. The impatient question of General McNaughton, "Are we a partner or a provider of men and materials only?" answered itself. Canada supplied arms, men, and money, but it had no real voice in their disposition. "Personally," Pearson observed, "I dislike this role of unpaid Hessians." He was fully aware of the price of King's anachronistic fears. At the end of April 1940, he wrote:

Our constitutional position has been recognized. We can participate or refuse to participate in this war. We can send a Division to England; refuse to send it to Norway; or recall it to Canada, in theory. In fact, however, we have no such powers and, so far as policy and planning in this war are concerned, our status is little better than that of a colony. We have practically no influence on decisions and little prior information concerning them. We have no Service representatives on Planning and Operations Boards; we have no representatives on the War Cabinet or on Cabinet Secretariats, for the purpose of securing firsthand information. The Allied War Council meets with Norwegian and Polish representatives; but not Canadian. A very important meeting of that Council took place last Saturday but we have not yet received any information as to what took place at that meeting; neither has North Borneo ... But we do not seem to have been concerned at our exclusion from the Councils of our Allies in a war in which our whole future is at stake.[79]

Pearson recognized that King, not the British government, was largely responsible. By isolating Canada, King and Skelton had achieved the virtually impossible. Canada was providing trained airmen to the Royal Air Force, ships to North Atlantic commands of the Royal Navy and army units under British control – even in Hong Kong – but refused to sit at the same table as British ministers to discuss policy. The choice for Canada was clear enough: either sit at the table or be dealt out of the game. With Quebec in mind, the bogey of centralism was for King more frightful than either the danger of being marginalized or of becoming dominated in time by the United States.

King had rejected Chamberlain's invitation; now he declined Churchill's. Following a largely ineffective discussion between Ottawa and London of war aims, Leopold Amery, again dominions secretary, suggested in November 1940, during the darkest days of the war, "a meeting in London of representatives of the Allied Governments which could be described as a revival of the Supreme War Council."[80] What he and others had in mind was a show of unity when there was little else to show to the world, but the reference to a Supreme War Council set the alarm bells aringing in King's mind. What in fact London was proposing was a meeting of Allied (and not just Commonwealth representatives), but King again replied sternly, "we doubt the necessity or effectiveness of setting up any central body for determining war policy," thereupon in effect surrendering policy direction to Britain.[81] King dressed up his refusal to participate in either Commonwealth or Allied gatherings with elaborate explanations, modestly declaring in May 1940 that it was "in the interest of the Allied Powers for me to be at the seat of government here," and again in June 1941, "I would have to be very outspoken against any such step [as a Supreme War Council] ... As I see it, my place, until the war is over, is on this continent," confident as he now was that the defence of Canada had been guaranteed by Roosevelt the previous August at Ogdensburg, New York, as part of the United States' search for its own security.

That meeting between King and Roosevelt created the Permanent Joint Board on Defence which King welcomed in a way he had never exhibited toward the Committee of Imperial Defence. Privately, he recorded that if he were to absent himself, the pro-conscriptionists might attempt to force the issue. Lapointe would become their target, with disastrous effect on Quebec, resulting in the resignation of Quebec ministers and the collapse of his government (when Lapointe died in November 1941 that particular excuse passed with him). The British prime minister might even raise with him the possible need for conscription, ergo, better not go at all. By default, the British War Cabinet was left to become the central body of King's imaginings.

Although no one could move the prime minister from Skelton's conviction that consultation meant subordination, his critics could not be dismissed as merely mindless Tories bent upon returning Canada to a vassal state. On 6 December 1941, the day before Canada joined the United States, Britain, Australia, and New Zealand in declaring war on Japan, *Saturday Night* decried the contradiction in King's unmistakable refusal to consult:

The passion for avoiding "commitments", which has long been noticeable in Canadian foreign policy ... may have been tolerable ... so long as Canada had no troops anywhere. But from the moment when we begin sending troops to fight for us abroad, we should begin backing them up by diplomatic representations in the quarters where those representations are needed. We cannot be interventionists in the Defence Departments and isolationists in the Department of External Affairs.

In light of growing public pressure, King was especially circumspect in offering reasons for rejecting consultation. In the House of Commons on 17 February 1941 he participated in a debate about Canada's war efforts, during which he confirmed the despatch to Britain of a third Canadian division to form part of a self-contained Canadian Corps. King again emphasized the rapidity of wireless communication with London and the need for him to remain in Canada as an unsolicited interlocutor between London and Washington: "The possibility of immediate personal contact between the Prime Minister of Canada and the President of the United States, in critical situations affecting the relations between the United States and the British Commonwealth, may easily be more important to the common cause than any service which a prime minister of Canada could render at the council table in London." King's long and meandering discussion rejecting consultation, even during the year when Canada was Britain's largest ally, eventually led him to a hypocritical panegyric about Massey that must have astonished all who knew anything about their long-vexed relationship.

It has also been suggested that the Canadian cabinet should be enlarged to include a minister ... who would reside in London and have immediate charge of all Canadian war activities in the United Kingdom and elsewhere overseas. This suggestion is based on the practice in the last war when, for special reasons then existing, such a minister was found necessary by the government of the day. There are several reasons why the present government has felt that no such appointment is now desirable. In the first place, the office of the high commissioner in London is well organized and well staffed. The high commissioner himself has had a long experience in dealing with the various departments of the British government. A new appointee, without Mr. Massey's experience, could not possibly discharge these functions so well. Moreover, in view of the wholly satisfactory, indeed, the splendid services Mr. Massey has been rendering in his present position, the appointment of an overseas minister could scarcely be regarded as other than a reflection upon the high commissioner. Mr. Massey himself is a member of the Canadian Privy Council. His membership in the cabinet could add little to his authority.

Charles Ritchie, however, was not impressed with what he considered King's self-serving posturing in declining to participate in a conference of prime ministers or, more broadly, to share in any responsibility for the direction of the war.

Mackenzie King has been putting on the most remarkable display of panic – was invited to come to the get-together of Commonwealth Prime Ministers. He has cabled the longest apologies to Churchill. 1. He cannot leave the country because of the problem of unity. 2. Labour difficulties. 3. Conscription. 4. External Affairs. 5. Possibility of the United States coming into the war. 6. Needed to campaign the country. 7. Knows nothing about strategy. I do not know why he does not add that he cannot leave because he is having his front parlour repapered and is needed to choose the design. When he says that anyway he does not think the meeting would serve much purpose he is on surer ground – in fact he may be quite right on the whole position. But what maddens one is that it is such a demonstration of cowardice, personal and political. If the cables were published surely he would be dished politically.

As someone has said (General McNaughton) he must be a very brave man to refuse to take the risk of coming. He cuts such a figure. It has put Mr. Massey in a spot – although he thinks that King should come, he does not want to put himself on record as opposing or supporting or confirming King's line – lest he should be made the public scapegoat – and at the same time the ball has been thrown to him, and he is in trouble if he will not play. Personally I would feel very tempted to try to put King on the spot, but that would be short-sighted. 1. The issue is not important enough – it does not involve anything really essential to winning the war. 2. Much as one would enjoy putting a spoke in the old hypocrite's wheel.[*82]

Probably Churchill was in no way displeased by King's rejection of conferences of prime ministers. Desperately hard-pressed as he was, he was unenthusiastic about sharing his wartime powers more widely, despite urgings to recreate an imperial war cabinet (a proposal warmly and vocally supported by, among others, the Conservatives in Ottawa, thereby confirming the invitation in King's mind as a Tory subterfuge). Canadian military and financial support was being provided without demands for a voice in strategy or even regular consultations. All the better, Churchill must have concluded, the Australians being tiresome in their demands. King was not, however, to escape the unwelcome subject of prime ministerial conferences. No sooner had he rejected Churchill's proposal than there arrived on the Ottawa scene the ebullient Australian prime minister, Robert Menzies, for whom patriotism and Empire loyalty were one and the same. By King's own admission, he "took this city more or less by storm." Menzies was on his return journey to Australia from Britain. His government had been severely attacked for the mauling that Australian forces had received in Crete and Libya and, more generally, for the lowly status of distant Australia in British military priorities. "Churchill had evidently told him to discuss with me ... the desire for a Conference of Prime Ministers – some kind of an Imperial Cabinet."[83] Menzies departed empty-handed, King having reacted in exactly the way that Churchill was confident he would do. Nevertheless, in May 1941 Churchill did suggest not an imperial war cabinet meeting but a more nebulous

* The tenth Duke of Devonshire was more cryptic in his condemnation of Mackenzie King's hesitations. "When France fell in 1940, he was Under-Secretary of State in the Dominions Office. 'Minister, your father was Governor General of Canada', said a senior civil servant. 'Yes', he replied. 'And you have two young daughters.' 'Yes.' 'In view of the situation being so grave, are you considering sending them to Canada for the duration where you must have many connections?' 'Send my daughters to Canada?' said the Duke. 'Yes, Minister.' The Duke paused, then said, 'I would rather my daughters were brought up under Hitler than Mackenzie King!'" (*Daily Express*, 11 December 2000).

imperial conference of a month or six weeks' duration, beginning in July. This King found in every way most inconvenient and was greatly relieved when Smuts of South Africa said that he could not attend (a fact of which Churchill may have been aware in advance).

King, echoing Laurier, proclaimed himself fully satisfied with existing channels of communication. He rejected out of hand the idea, advanced first by the Conservative opposition in April 1940, of appointing a resident cabinet minister in London, since he perceived "a real but invisible Imperial Council" (he being especially adept at identifying the invisible). Clearly the Tories had not forgotten the late Sir George Perley's consistent advocacy of the benefits of such an appointment. The under-secretary for external affairs informed Massey by telegram that the prime minister,

after enumerating a number of practical and political objections to suggestion that Imperial War Cabinet might be set up, went on to examine suggestion that a resident minister might be appointed in London in the immediate charge of all Canadian activities overseas. He thought in view of splendid work which you and your staff have been doing, that there were no grounds for any change in present arrangements. Canadian interests in London and cooperation with the United Kingdom were better served by the present system of consultation between Governments and by the arrangement of having a high commissioner permanently resident in London.

The cable concluded by quoting from the prime minister's remarkable peroration about Massey and his colleagues: "Their devotion in difficult and often dangerous circumstances is beyond praise. Mr. Massey himself has discharged his manifold and exacting duties while quite exceptional skill, discretion and patience. He is a representative of whom all Canadians have reason to be proud."[84]

What Massey made of all this in light of King's earlier unedifying efforts to frustrate consultation and to exclude him from any real role must be left to conjecture. Even more damning of King was the 1942 fulmination in *Canada in World Affairs 1939–1941* (published in 1943):

Dominion Ministers have been making occasional trips to Britain, but they have a status at these times which in the nature of things can be little more than that of a distinguished visitor in the confidence of the British Cabinet. They are allowed full information; they inspect troops and ammunition plants, and watch manoeuvres; they are given occasional interviews with British Ministers; they attend, as a supreme favour, meetings of the British Cabinet where they may even be permitted at times to raise awkward questions. But they are, nevertheless, guests (usually of brief acquaintance) who are uncomfortably aware of their unfamiliarity with their environment and are subject to all the limitations which such an atmosphere is likely to produce ... In 1918 Sir Robert Borden and his colleagues from the other Dominions demanded and obtained a comprehensive investigation on the direction of the war; although they had in this endeavour the support of no less a person than Mr. Lloyd George. It seems likely that Dominion Ministers in 1940, no less than in 1918, could have made a real contribution through such a body, and their right to participate in its deliberations was far more obvious than in the last war. This right rested not only on a recently acquired Dominion status, but also on their prominent position as allied powers. It is apt to be forgotten that from the time of the fall of France to the entrance of Russia – a period of some twelve months – the strongest ally that Great Britain had was Canada, and the next in size and consequence was Australia. Canada was raising men by the hundreds of thousands, and Canadian money was being poured out by billions; Australia's contributions and those of the other Dominions and India were proportionately as great; .., Decisions were being taken which might lose the war or might affect the future of Canada for all time to come, but Ottawa remained aloof, unperturbed, and, so it almost seemed, uninterested in the vital decisions which were daily being made. Yet Canada had the same Prime Minister who some years before had battled courageously for the Dominion's right to control its own halibut and, on another occasion, to send a thousand or so men to fight the Turk. Mr. Mackenzie King had strained at the gnat, but had swallowed the camel; and more than that, had swallowed it not under protest, but with every sign of enjoyment.[85]

In the midst of King's arabesque, O.D. Skelton suddenly died in January 1941. From the senior ranks of the Department of External Affairs, King appointed the young Norman Robertson as acting under-secretary. He was confirmed in June 1941, to the consternation of the more senior Pearson and Hume Wrong. In vain Massey had urged upon King the claims of Pearson, but once Robertson had been confirmed, the high commissioner gradually came to see him as more cooperative, flexible and understanding than Skelton had been, a first class brain replacing a second class.

For all King's preoccupation about the inadvisability of his absence from Ottawa, it did gradually dawn upon him, following a tour of western Canada, that domestic pressures alone would sooner or later propel him across the Atlantic. Many Canadians believed that their country could make its most effective contribution only if their leader were in at least occasional personal contact with the beleaguered Churchill and his ministers. In June 1941, King noted ruefully in his diary, "No doubt the Tory press will begin their [sic] attacks on me for not going to London and put it down to some difference re war effort, etc. It might come to result in a pretty serious cleavage."[86] King, in offering to French Canadians his continuing refusal to go to London as further evidence of his life-long success in countering the ambitions of the British to ensnare them in imperial commitments, in effect surrendered the direction of the war to Churchill. *The Times* correspondent in Ottawa was in no doubt about what was behind King's repeated rejection of any role in decision-making, even during the year when Canada was Britain's principal ally. Privately he wrote scathingly to his editor, "King [is] my beau ideal of the successful political charlatan. He has a masterly skill in the arts of political manipulation and evasion of issues ... rarely has there been such a blend in human form of incompetence, chicanery, and moral cowardice. He lives on other people's brains ... he is temperamentally unfit to be a war leader ... his primary concern is not winning the war but the fortunes of the Liberal Party."[87]

In early August 1941, more than a year after King's repeated protests that he could not possibly leave Canada to consult on broad strategy questions, Churchill in a battleship and the still neutral Roosevelt in a cruiser met off Newfoundland to do just that and to proclaim the Atlantic Charter. When confirmation of the meeting arrived in Ottawa, King was nonplussed. Canada was Britain's principal ally and Canada had a joint defence board with the United States, yet the two former naval persons had not invited him. When it became evident that their prime minister had been excluded, English Canadians became more discontent with his continuing absence from the councils of the great. Quebec isolationists might thereby be reassured, but "serious cleavages" could indeed occur if English Canada became convinced that the pendulum had swung too far in Quebec's direction. An uneasy King finally reversed himself, deciding in the aftermath of the Atlantic Charter that the longevity of his government, beset by incessant Tory demands to know where Canada stood in Allied and transatlantic councils, now required him to see Churchill in Britain even if he were unable to think of much to say to him. There was no avoiding the domestic political imperative. The risk that Churchill might raise the need for conscription – which in the event he did not – would simply have to be accepted. On 20 August 1941, with Norman Robertson and Georges Vanier in tow, King boarded an aircraft for the first time, flying to Prestwick, Scotland, where Massey, Ritchie, and Ignatieff awaited him on the tarmac.

On King's initial day in London, he attended a meeting of the War Cabinet (in the same room in which Borden had sat during the First World War). He hastily assured Churchill and his colleagues that he had not crossed the Atlantic to seek any greater voice for Canada in wartime policy. He repeated that "He could not conceive of more effective means of communication than those which existed at present ... they had as their representatives in the United Kingdom Mr. Vincent Massey, a former colleague and a very old friend, who knew his [King's] mind as well as he knew it himself. They understood each other perfectly [*sic*]. Mr. Massey met periodically with the Secretary of States for the Dominions and was given a personal account of what took place in Cabinet discussions. He was able to express the views of Canada."[88] The reality was quite different, as George Ignatieff, a Canadian at Oxford who had been recently been recruited for the Department of External Affairs by his fellow Oxonian, Pearson, soon observed: "During his entire stay in Britain, the prime minister paid only one brief visit to Canada House and it was obvious even to a junior secretary like myself that he didn't want to see any more of Vincent Massey than was absolutely necessary."[*89]

While King was in Britain, Robert Menzies resigned as Australian prime minister. Rumours arrived in London that he wanted to be made a peer and appointed, like Beaverbrook, a member of the British War Cabinet. Churchill, however, had no wish to have the highly vocal former prime minister making trouble in his small war cabinet. If the new Australian government so decided, Menzies could replace Bruce as high commissioner, but only a prime minister in office would be welcomed to the War Cabinet itself. King told Churchill this was entirely what he himself believed, confiding to Lord Halifax that "there was an old school that believed that the Dominions should be kept united by ... [a] central organization in London. That they were wrong ... that the only way to proceed was laid down by the Statute of Westminster."[90] In his meetings in London, King was gratified that Halifax (soon to be ambassador in Washington) had, by agreeing with him, demonstrated that at least he was not of the "old school."

King was decidedly less happy at the end of two days of visiting Canadian army units in the south of England, following a nocturnal visit with Massey to the headquarters of RAF Fighter Command. His welcome by his fellow Canadians on Salisbury Plain was marked by cheers from a few,

---

* Pearson had the disagreeable task of asking the British government, amidst all the pressures of wartime, whether it would ship stone fragments from the bombed House of Commons to enhance King's romantic prewar ruins at Kingsmere.

but by catcalls from many when they were paraded to be inspected by "the old woman" amidst rain and mud. When told that he was expected to address the troops, he later recorded candidly, "I felt what was like a dart pass through my bowels. It made me quite sick and faint, and to break out into a cold perspiration."[91]

Despite such afflictions, King soon convinced himself that his visit to wartime Britain had been a notable success, believing that it had helped to satisfy the instinctive demands of Canadians for consultation and collaboration with Britain. Upon his return to Ottawa in time to receive a visit from the British deputy prime minister and dominions secretary, Clement Attlee, he repeated blandly to the House of Commons that it would be difficult, if not impossible, to improve upon the present system of Commonwealth consultation. The Australians strongly disagreed. They continued to seek a seat in the British War Cabinet, if no imperial war cabinet were to be constituted. In this they were in time successful: their high commissioner became a member of the British War Cabinet, an easy enough transition from his long prewar participation in the Committee for Imperial Defence.

Massey, whom King had pointedly not invited to join him in his calls on Churchill or in his audience at the Palace, was left to content himself with what the high commissioners facetiously described as the "Junior War Cabinet ... not quite ministers but more than diplomats": in other words, the regular meetings of the high commissioners with the dominions secretary.[92] He also had to deal with a backlog of official visitors, released by King's visit, including by Richard Hanson, the leader of the opposition, an all-party delegation under the aegis of the Empire Parliamentary Association, and several ministers (with whose reticence in the presence of British ministers Massey became increasingly wearied, believing that they were cowed by Mackenzie King). On the other hand, George Drew, the visiting Conservative premier of Ontario, was certainly not intimidated by King. Massey found him "a delightful fellow."

Unlike the defeatist and fearful United States ambassador, Joseph Kennedy, the Masseys remained in London throughout the worst of the Blitz. Early in the war they had moved from Hyde Park Gardens to the greater safety of the reinforced concrete of the Dorchester Hotel on Park Lane. They could readily afford "the luxury liner on which remnants of London society have embarked in the midst of the storm,"[93] but the Blitz was no tropical cruise, what with air raid sirens constantly sounding, anti-aircraft batteries in Hyde Park thumping away in the night at bombers overhead, the raging fires, the explosions and everywhere the sounds of destruction, the smell of smoke and the unspoken sense of fear (including at Canada House which escaped several near misses). Massey's two sons were in uniform; the elder had already been captured with a British regiment in the débâcle at Crete and was to spend much of the war in a prisoner-of-war camp.

Throughout all the uncertainties, however, Massey never surrendered his personal standards. Ignatieff was bewildered by what awaited him when he succeeded Ritchie as Massey's assistant.

Of all these responsibilities, the one which I found the most demanding by far was the drafting of Massey's correspondence and speeches. In the midst of round-the-clock air raids and disastrous losses at sea, at a time when the survival of Britain was in serious doubt and negotiations were under way for the possible transfer of the government to Canada, Mr. Massey insisted on absolute perfection of style and tone in all his utterances. Letters would be returned to me five or six times for rewrites, to the extent that it seemed to me that he polished his speeches until they glistened like his shoes. Even banalities ended up sounding like words of wisdom. There were times when this relentless pursuit of the right word or nuance almost drove me to distraction. Here we were with bombs falling all around us, and I was working on my umpteenth draft of a letter to lord such-and-such, thanking him for a gift of antlers he had seen fit to bestow on the high commissioner.

Yet, as time went on I learned to appreciate the tough apprenticeship to which I was being subjected. Nobody could have been better qualified than Vincent Massey to introduce me to the formal and ceremonial aspects of diplomacy. From him I learned that protocol is really a language, a set of rules and conventions which enable people of different nationalities, social backgrounds, and political persuasions to feel comfortable with each other, to avoid embarrassing situations, even to enjoy each other's company. He was a perfectionist, a stickler for detail who would spare no effort in planning every aspect of social functions ... Nobody working for Massey was in danger of developing sloppy habits, no matter how incongruous our activities might seem in the context of an all-out war. Hume Wrong didn't like Vincent Massey any more than Massey liked Wrong; but Hume used to say that every new recruit to External Affairs should spend at least a year being trained by the Masseys – Vincent and his wife, Alice – in the fundamentals of diplomatic procedure and protocol.[94]

In addition to helping to arrange for the continuing arrival of various Canadian forces, including forestry and railway units, Massey was involved in British requests to Canada to provide small garrisons for Newfoundland, Bermuda, Jamaica, the Netherlands Antilles, Martinique, Iceland, and even the kyrolite mines in Greenland (an act which Washington imaginatively described as a possible infringement of the Monroe Doctrine). The occupation of St Pierre and Miquelon by Free French forces was more problematic, a subject for several discussions between Massey and de Gaulle. Even more problematic was a War Office request in September 1941 for two infantry battalions for Hong Kong (possibly somewhere in an oubliette of the War Office collective mind it was recalled that a half-century before, Canada had unexpectedly offered troops for the garrison in Hong Kong). Few in Ottawa appeared to foresee that they were being sent to a crown colony which could not possibly be held once the Japanese forces already surrounding it chose to seize it. The result was that, six weeks after their arrival, two battalions of scarce infantrymen were lost, the survivors being consigned to three and a half years of bestial slave labour.

Massey saw at first hand other results of military and political blundering. Alice Massey and he visited more than two hundred Canadian survivors of the naive raid on Dieppe in April 1942 (which had evoked Pétain's congratulations to Hitler). Ignatieff, who accompanied them, recorded, "This was where that remarkable woman, Alice Massey, was at her best. I was full of admiration as I watched her talking individually to the men, finding words of comfort for those in pain, reassuring the ones going into surgery, promising to write to their wives and parents."[95] The effect of the Dieppe fiasco on Ignatieff and Ritchie was their request to Massey to release them for service in Canadian forces, but in return they eventually received "letters from the prime minister [in his capacity as secretary of state for external affairs] to the effect that we were serving our country more effectively at Canada House than by being at the front, and that we were therefore to remain at our posts in London."[96]

The sense of deep concern which both King and Massey shared at the shambles at Dieppe was compounded by a British proposal to shackle the few prisoners taken. Canadian prisoners, it was understood, had been manacled by Germans who claimed that they had learned from captured British orders that any German prisoners taken were to be fettered. Churchill was exuberantly in favour of shackling the Germans; Howe and Ralston joined Massey in disagreeing "on principle with the whole policy of mutual reprisals." With his elder son in a German camp, Massey may have been especially sensitive to the plight of prisoners of war, but the impression remains that he saw more clearly than most the futility

On 14 March 1940 at Aldershot, where Canadians trained in two world wars, Massey accompanied Anthony Eden on a visit in unusual snow to the Royal Montreal Regiment. Massey is in a black coat and Eden in grey; Major-General A.G.L. McNaughton is second from right. The regiment had arrived in Britain only three months before, but the First Division already formed an important part of the hard-pressed defence of the United Kingdom.

of retaliation as it continued through November into December. Only in mid-December 1942 did the Canadian government finally force the end of shackling in the expectation that the Germans would also stop the practice – which they eventually did. Massey's advice had placed him at loggerheads with Churchill, but he had been in the right.

Once the United States finally entered the war, more than two years after Canada, some Canadians flattered themselves that their country would now form one side, however small, of an isosceles triangle (the advent of "the North Atlantic triangle" theory with which some Canadian policy-makers and academics were to mislead themselves for decades to come). In fact, with the United States' declaration of war and its introduction of conscription for overseas service, Canada became more isolated than ever, Churchill eagerly embracing an exclusive London-Washington axis. Having earlier declined to participate in the only game in town, King left officials to do little else but watch in mounting frustration as the two great powers decided upon global strategy and postwar settlements. From Washington, Hume Wrong wrote to Pearson underlining where the fault lay:

What [little] has happened so far with regard to Canadian participation does not seem to me at variance with the position taken hitherto by the Canadian Government. You and I know of a hundred instances since the war began in which Canada has refused to take responsibility for decisions of policy with which we were not immediately concerned. One difference now is that these decisions tend to be joint decisions of the United Kingdom and the United States in place of decisions by the United Kingdom alone. If Canada has been satisfied before, and if the means of consultation have been as effective as the Prime Minister maintains, should this change cause dissatisfaction now? ... Mainly for reasons of internal political balance the Government has hitherto adopted in these matters what may unkindly be called a semi-colonial position. With the entry of the United States into the war we are not as well placed to influence the conduct of the war as we were when the United States was neutral ... If we had sought earlier to undertake more extensive political responsibilities, it would be easier now to maintain our status.[97]

Also from Washington where he had been visiting, the baseball-loving Pearson described for Massey the Allied conference which flowed from the Atlantic Charter. In the drafting of an United Nations declaration, "The Americans insisted on breaking them [the twenty-eight signatory countries] into a major league and a minor league. Canada was put in the minor league alongside Costa Rica."[98] Through Massey's wartime diaries there runs a similar sorry theme: "This is a question with which I am very familiar – I mean the question of how to bring Canada into the picture and I haven't found the answer."[99] In a diary entry of September 1942, less than a year after the United States had entered the War, Massey recorded regretfully the perception of the dynamic C.D. Howe, the minister of munitions and supply, on a visit: "Howe is greatly perturbed over the virtual exclusion of Canada from a reasonable participation in the joint war effort ... The real trouble of course is that Churchill and Roosevelt have set up a war machinery in the form of a Washington-London axis and no allowance has been made for the effective representation of [others] when circumstances demand it."[100]

Given likely postwar financial uncertainties, Ottawa sought in 1943 to win "functional representation" on certain Allied combined boards, principally those intended to foster European relief and rehabilitation and postwar economic collaboration. The prime minister having early rejected Canadian participation in the direction of the war, officials developed the functional approach which was to become a centrepiece in wartime and immediate postwar relations with Britain and the United States. In Allied activities where Canada played a significant role, it sought to have a commensurate voice: "Representation should be determined on a functional basis which will admit to full membership those countries, large or small, which have the greatest contribution to make to the particular object in question." In Washington this ambition was given a cool reception whether it pertained to wheat, postwar relief, education or civil aviation. Hardly less happy was Massey's brief participation in discussions of what should become of the International Labour Organization and the League of Nations following the war. An effort to provide a comprehensive international regime for the North Atlantic cod fisheries came to little in the face of United States opposition. During the spring and summer of 1942, Massey had played a role in arranging Mutual Aid to the Soviet Union, but Allied coordination was increasingly focused upon a Washington largely indifferent to Canadian aspirations.

To early thinking about the postwar world Massey could have contributed much, but he continued to be deliberately sidelined by his own prime minister. To Hume Wrong, he wrote: "I find myself dealing more and more with problems of far-reaching importance in connection with Canada's position in the postwar world, and it would be of the greatest help not only to be kept in touch with the official point of view at home but also to exchange ideas informally and personally with people like yourself."[101] Although excluded from the Ottawa inner sanctum by King, he paradoxically received direct accounts of the progress of the war and postwar planning from Churchill himself:

the High Commissioners had one of their periodic meetings with Churchill, this time in his bedroom ... The P.M., clad in canary coloured pyjamas and a marvellous flowered dressing-gown, was ensconced in bed smoking a cigar of prodigious proportions and beaming with cherubic pinkness from among his despatch boxes and papers. He gave us a résumé of the war and emphasised throughout the three-quarters of an hour talk the importance of taking a realistic view of the length of the war, the end of which could hardly now come before next spring [1945]. Everything was going well and gains would be made all through the winter. A large scale German counter-offensive was out of the question, but the organized resistance of the enemy could hardly be broken until the weather made possible extensive operations.[102]

This was consultation and information from the highest if notably informal level, but Massey could neither contribute to it nor elaborate upon it for the benefit of either the British or Canadian governments. Ritchie, with his unerring eye for the absurd, summarized well the continuing impact of King's suspicions:

Mr. King was obsessed through these years by the suspicion that Whitehall was plotting designs against Canada's independent nationhood and trying to draw us back into the old imperial framework. Unfortunately for us at Canada House, the Prime Minister came to believe that ... Vincent Massey had succumbed to these sinister British influences. Even Mr. Massey's successes in London were held against him. He had during his time there consolidated his personal and official position in the inner bastions of pre-war London. Cabinet ministers, editors of newspapers, directors of art galleries, the higher ranges of the peerage, not to mention Royalty itself, enjoyed his company and respected his views. This did him no good in the eyes of his own Prime Minister, who reacted with intense irritation to the Masseys' familiarity with the Great. To mutual resentment was added a difference of political views. Vincent Massey was a stout defender of Canada's interests, but he believed in Canada as an actively participating member of the British Commonwealth. Mr. King emphatically did not. Whatever the rights and wrongs of their respective opinions, the resulting estrangement between them put the staff of Canada House in a difficult position. The disembodied presence of the Prime Minister brooded over us. It was not a benevolent influence. In the flesh he was thousands of miles away, but he needed no modern bugging devices to detect the slightest quiver of disloyalty to his person or his policies. Perhaps through his favoured spiritualist mediums he was in touch with sources of information beyond Time and Space.[103]

After the war, John Holmes, reflecting on his wartime experience on the staff at Canada House, wrote about the search for influence that Massey would have entirely endorsed. Canada's history was, in a sense,

an extended exploration of the difficulties of reconciling freedom of action with shared policy-making in an association which we wanted to maintain in our own interests. Regardless of constitutional niceties, Canadian governments themselves made every decision on Canadian foreign policy that they considered important after at least 1867. Nevertheless, a good deal of energy was wasted in the thirties and forties on battling fondly imagined British schemes to drag us into their wars. This phoney war of liberation prevented the public from seeing the problems of large and small powers as inescapable in any context ... By the middle of the war ... this struggle with the "imperial overlord" to get a voice in the conduct of the war was clarified as the persistent and inevitable problem of relating power to influence, which is and always will be the basic challenge of international organization.[104]

The new British high commissioner was an addition to the limited Ottawa scene. Malcolm MacDonald, the lively and intelligent son of the former prime minister, Ramsay MacDonald, was well known to King, who warmly welcomed him to Ottawa in the spring of 1941, recalling that he had "met his father and mother when they were on their wedding trip [to North America in 1896]." MacDonald, both a former dominions secretary and a knowledgeable student of Canada (who had the additional merit of not being a Tory), offered to King a welcome opportunity to exclude Massey altogether as a channel of communication with the British government.* MacDonald drew upon his ministerial and parliamentary experience in attempting to make sense of King's recurring suspicions of what Churchill and his government really intended. There continued to be a need for Commonwealth consultation aplenty, but in Canada's case it remained largely one way, Ottawa being wary of telling its own high commissioner anything very much. "All that I hear comes from the British H.C. in Ottawa via the D.O. [Dominions Office] and the Ministry of Information News Service," Massey lamented.[105] He confided to his diary that a long despatch that he had prepared (based on material supplied by the Dominions Office) might have been ignored: "They never give me any feeling that they want any news on foreign affairs. I haven't heard any word from the Prime Minister since last July. That may be due to a lack of interest or a refusal to use my post as a source of information. Probably a little of both."[106]

As early as July 1939, Lester Pearson, on a visit to Ottawa from London, had put his finger on part of the total problem. He had found the Department of External Affairs "a mess" under Skelton; in a second visit in May 1941 he had written to Massey that under Robertson it was still a mess. "When the Prime Minister's approval has to be secured before a telephone extension can be installed and when the channel for securing that approval must always ... be the Under-Secretary, you will appreciate that any effective reform of Departmental organization and methods is diffi-

---

* Churchill sent as high commissioners to Ottawa and Canberra sitting members of Parliament and former ministers.

cult, if not impossible."[107] The administrative mess was one more reason, although not the major one, why the high commissioner received little or no encouragement from Ottawa. Massey nevertheless persisted in his consultations with both the Foreign and the Dominions Offices and with his Commonwealth colleagues, whether King liked it or not. The flow of information varied throughout the war, given the widely differing nature of those with whom he had to deal and the frequency with which they were rotated. Anthony Eden, briefly dominions secretary before moving eagerly to the War Office, seemed constantly distracted (although later he became a close friend of Massey). His successor, Viscount Caldecote, was simply incompetent, a constant source of frustration to the high commissioners. In their view, Lord Cranborne, the future Marquess of Salisbury, a personal friend of Massey since their days together at Oxford and later a prominent minister in Harold Macmillan's government, was the best of the wartime dominions secretaries. He was, however, himself deeply frustrated: "I do not know what is going on," he wrote to Churchill.

Many of the most important discussions and decisions of the Government are taken at meetings, at which I am not present. Moreover, most of the important telegrams are exchanged by you personally either with Heads of State or with Dominion P.M.s and these I am not empowered to show or even mention to the High Commissioners ... if the High Commissioners want secret information, they tend more and more to go, not to me, but to other sources which apparently talk more freely ... In such circumstances the position of the Dominions Secretary becomes a farce.[108]

In February 1942, Clement Attlee, the taciturn Labour leader became dominions secretary. "Meetings with him were a little like a conversation with a bronze Buddha."[109] He was, however, undeniably intelligent and, more important, as leader of the Labour party, he was deputy prime minister in the coalition government. Attlee would, Massey noted happily but perhaps over optimistically, "give importance to our meetings and to the office of the H.C." (until he became lord president of the council in September 1943).[110]

Britain, even with the Commonwealth, was foreseen as playing at best a secondary international role in the postwar world. Whatever the burgeoning strength and influence of the United States, however, Massey remained true to his early Round Table allegiance. He was never in any doubt of the unique value of the Commonwealth, whether in war or peace.

In June 1943 he wrote: "We need [the Commonwealth] more than ever as a stabilising, humanising influence in world affairs ... if it can be proved ... that it is in Canada's national interest that we should continue as an active partner in an actively functioning British Commonwealth, that belief can be shared by Canadians whatever their racial background and however indifferent they may be to the sentimental and emotional aspect of the question."[111] He was dismissive of American critics of the Commonwealth, extolling it *inter alia* as providing a valuable context in which the further evolution of India and of the colonies to autonomy within the Commonwealth could best take place. At a meeting of high commissioners, "after the reports on the subject of the American attitude towards the British Colonial Empire ... [there was] a useful statement on the subject from the Foreign Office. There is no doubt that a legend of British exploitation and incompetence has developed and will become increasingly hard to eradicate unless something is done to remove American illusions and promise co-operation with her in dealing with colonial problems after the war."[112]

King seemed unable to make up his mind about India. On the one hand he vaguely favoured its evolution to self-governing Dominion status (especially if that would help to placate anti-colonial sentiment in the United States), but on the other hand he had long known of the resentment in India at the second-class status, including disenfranchisement, accorded by British Columbia to those of Indian background. As he had done in November 1940, Massey in 1942 again recommended to King to adopt the suggestion of Amery, now secretary of state for India, that it would be helpful to the Indian war effort if a Canadian high commissioner were appointed to New Delhi. Robertson and Pearson proposed the enfranchisement of those of Indian descent living in British Columbia (Japanese and Chinese would need to await the end of the war). King rejected the idea out of hand. Accordingly, in Ottawa in February 1942 the secretary of the Indians' Overseas Association was informed by the Department of External Affairs that "there is nothing very much that we can do to endeavour to obtain a favourable decision in regard to the proposed appointment of a Canadian High Commissioner to India."[113] A week later, King suddenly and inexplicably reversed himself, cabling Churchill that he "would be glad to make an early appointment of a High Commissioner for Canada in India."[114] Within another week, King had wired Churchill again: "an exchange of High Commissioners between the Dominions and India might be immediately arranged."[115]

Nothing, however, came of King's sudden acquiescence while a mission led by the Labourite Sir Stafford Cripps, the leader in the British

House of Commons, was in India attempting to determine what its post-war status might best be. Thereafter, with the provincial secretary in British Columbia proclaiming that "There is no body in the Province as unreliable, dishonest and deceitful as the Hindus [i.e., Sikhs]," King contented himself with repeating to London that he was "unable to find a suitable candidate" to be high commissioner. Amery, following the prime ministers' conference of 1944, described for the viceroy how King "did nothing at the Conference, or will ever do anything at anytime on any subject, which might risk losing a single vote [in British Columbia]." No high commissioner was appointed until the end of 1946 when a Canadian of pronounced Irish background was finally sent.

In the transfer by Britain of sites for United States bases in Bermuda, the British West Indies, British Guinea, and Newfoundland in return for fifty obsolete destroyers, Massey had been involved in a peripheral way. In the specific case of bases in Newfoundland and Labrador in which Ottawa took a particular interest, Massey had intervened with both the British government and the US ambassador to create tripartite discussions in March 1941 on where and how American units would be stationed. The results were, in the end, more or less satisfactory to Canada, intent as it was upon ensuring that a colony that had been an early prospect for Confederation did not in effect pass to the United States, which had a disconcerting tendency to treat any territory where its soldiers were stationed as if it were its own (as was to happen in the Yukon and Northwest Territories).

With regard to the British West Indies, Massey played no direct part, but he had discussed their future when Hume Wrong visited London in late 1942. Wrong recorded that Harold Macmillan, parliamentary under-secretary for the colonies, "who is one of the ablest young ministers, developed a scheme for devolving Colonial responsibility in certain cases from the United Kingdom to Dominion Governments. I told him ... that I doubted whether the inhabitants of the British West Indies would welcome government from Ottawa instead from London."[116] In mid-1943 the idea, almost a century old, resurfaced yet again. John Holmes from Canada House provided Wrong in Washington with a comment on

the suggestions from Mr. Eden and *The Times* that Canada and other adult [*sic*] nations of the Commonwealth might assume some responsibility for the colonial areas ... It will be recalled that the question of political union of Canada and the West Indies has been raised at intervals in the past and that at the Paris Peace Conference ... Lloyd George suggested to Sir Robert Borden that Canada might "take over" the West Indies. Although there has been some loose talk recently about Canada's "taking over" the British West Indies, it is doubtful if Canadian (or West Indian) opinion would approve of political suzerainty on the part of Canada ... Union could not be on the basis of equality; and the future of a white country and of a black country might far better be worked out independently.[117]

Holmes's words accurately reflected the prevailing attitude in Ottawa. Union or federation with the British West Indies was out, but trade was again emphasized and assistance of various forms was preferred. (Although it was modest, it proved in time to be the embryo of Canada's later global development assistance programme.)

More urgent was the need of Britain for financial assistance, additional to what it was beginning to receive from United States Lend-Lease. Direct Canadian financial assistance was gift-wrapped as "Mutual Aid," helping to pay for the two-thirds of Canada's military production that went to its allies, particularly Britain, reflecting in part the fact that "Canada has an important stake in the future prosperity and sound financial position of the United Kingdom." Canada's own immediate economic difficulties with the United States had been partly resolved by the Hyde Park Declaration of April 1941, but it was not lost on Ottawa officials that this involved additional dependency on the United States and its greater influence in Canada.

In the Battle of the Atlantic, Canadian escort vessels were eventually of significance, but the rapid expansion of the small prewar navy had naturally revealed the price of neglect and the near-overwhelming need for more training and better equipment. With Massey acting as handmaiden, the proposed gift by Britain of larger ships, when joined with the hard-serving corvettes and frigates of the North Atlantic convoys, effectively ended the decade-long debate about whether Canada should have more than a token navy. For the army overseas, the prospect of action remained frustratingly uncertain. From the early months of 1943 there spread increasing unease about the adverse impact of continuing inaction upon morale. Some units had seen no action since their arrival in Britain at the end of 1939, with the exception of those who had spent a few pointless weeks in France in 1940 and those who had survived several bloody hours helplessly pinned down on the beaches of Dieppe in 1942. With the Allied invasion of Sicily in mind, Massey was asked to seek the reaction of his government to a draft memorandum of understanding about the operational control of proposed Canadian units under a British commander-in-chief. Ottawa, including King, was surprisingly prompt to agree, but Massey and McNaughton together were able to persuade Ottawa to retain for the senior Canadian commander an autonomy *de jure* that Currie had asserted *de facto* in 1918. Partly as a result of Massey's discussions with Churchill, Attlee, and Ismay, the First Canadian Division landed in Sicily with British and American units and saw its first action. Its participation was eventually publicly acknowledged, although only after Pearson's additional interventions in a Washington apparently reluctant to distract public attention from the participation of US units.

By late 1943, McNaughton was clearly exhausted and increasingly seen as unlikely to be able to lead the Canadian forces in the pending invasion of France. The chief of the British general staff had told Massey that he was deeply worried that McNaughton no longer had the capacity to command effectively an army in the field. McNaughton, for his part, had long assumed that the Canadian army would fight together under his command and not be broken up as smaller units integrated into larger British formations (as was the RCAF). The late minister of national defence, Norman Rogers, had appeared sound enough on the question of Canadian command of the Canadian army, but about his successor, J.L. Ralston, McNaughton had growing doubts. Ralston had successfully urged upon King the formation of a Canadian Corps, but Massey later came to believe that the minister was "quite prepared to see the Canadian forces serving where they can best be used, although this would probably mean their being divided." Finally, in November, the minister told the general that he could not expect to command the army in the field. With King fearing as always that there might somehow be implications for conscription, the confrontation between general and minister developed in such a way that the resignation of one or other became unavoidable. Massey played a role in facilitating the departure of McNaughton, his replacement by Lieutenant-General Crerar and the survival of Ralston. But it was primarily British willingness to accept ultimate responsibility for what should have been a Canadian decision that finally led to the resolution of a potentially explosive issue.

Although Massey's role during the Second World War did not closely parallel that of Perley during the First, he did undertake an initiative similar to that of Beaverbrook. His lifetime enthusiasm for the arts, expressed in part in munificent financial support, had also found expression in the assignment of Canadian war artists to all three services and in arranging a visit by Karsh of Ottawa to photograph British leaders.

In their extensive support for the troops in Britain, the activities of the Masseys took many forms, but principally the provision, at their own expense, of a country house (Garnons in Herefordshire) for convalescent officers, and in London an officers' club and a large Beaver Club for all ranks. Pearson's biographer has recorded how Massey

greeted visiting Canadian politicians with exceptional grace and trotted them through the appropriate clubs and displayed them at court when occasion permitted. His thespian skills served him well in the myriad ceremonials wartime presented; and one supposes that this most aristocratic Canadian was a useful counterpoint to the Canadian soldiers who were acquiring a rather beastly reputation as they socialized in their own way in the English countryside. Alice Massey, too, became less an irritant and more an asset. She finally quelled the rebellion against her authority in women's war work, and bravely worked herself to death, helping the wounded in war. Her faults were forgotten as her good deeds mounted.[118]

In taking a lead in "women's war work," Alice Massey had soon clashed with Viscount Bennett, who from his restless retirement near Guildford had been making patriotic speeches and seeking to provide leadership for the Canadian Red Cross in Britain.* The relations of Alice Massey with Beaverbrook, understandably preoccupied with his demanding role as minister of aircraft production and later as minister of supply, were smoother. From him, and from several other Canadians and the YMCA, she had received substantial financial help to underpin her own. During the course of the war, tens of thousands of Canadian soldiers passed through the doors of the three centres supported by the Masseys and to a greater or less degree organized and directed by Alice Massey. Her remarkable successes were not, however, achieved without some friction. Massey recorded wistfully, "The Canadian community here is full of complexes, jealousies, and ambitions, fantastically hard to please. Most diplomats regard their local colony as a perennial problem, and I wonder if any of them have difficulties comparable to those created by the Cana-

---

* Bennett had resigned from Parliament in January 1939, confirming that he would retire in England near his old friend, Lord Beaverbrook. He declined the offer of a safe Conservative seat in the British House of Commons, continuing to press for a peerage which he finally received in June 1941. He died in June 1947 and, as he had requested, is buried in the churchyard at Mickleham, Surrey, the only prime minister interred outside Canada.

dian colony here – the more you try to do the more you incur rancour and jealousy." Early in the war, Pearson had written to Skelton,

One of the tribulations here ... arises out of the hopes and fears and ambitions and desires of local Canadians, some male but for the most part female, to indulge in war work. The High Commissioner has taken the view that all this voluntary effort must be supervised and closely connected with Canada House. One of these days he will be sorry. At the present time he is devoting a tremendous amount of time himself to this phase of the work. I, personally, am trying to keep thousands of miles away from it. I would far rather battle the whole of the Treasury over the financing of the [British Commonwealth] Air Training Scheme than try to co-operate with embattled hosts of Canadian war women.

Part of the difficulty for Pearson arose from the early and tiresome meddling by Alice Massey in the work of the High Commission itself, but wartime pressures eventually overcame even that problem. Ignatieff later noted, "It would be hard to exaggerate the humanizing influence that Mrs. Massey had on the life of Canadians in wartime Britain ... She always seemed to know the right thing to do or say to make people feel better."*[119] And Ritchie's recollection of her abides: "She wore herself down in the war by hard work for Canadian servicemen in England ... I see her plodding along Cockspur Street laden with provisions for the Beaver Club [known familiarly as "Mother Massey's Hash House"] ... or at her desk writing hundreds of letters to the relatives of Canadians serving abroad."[120] Of all letters written and received at Canada House, however, the one that gave Massey the greatest amusement was from a woman near Aldershot where so many Canadians trained in both the world wars. She wrote that "A Canadian soldier on leave has visited my house. As a result, both my daughter and I are pregnant. Not that we hold that against your soldier, but the last time he was here he took my daughter's bicycle which she needs to go to work."[121]

In May 1943, upon returning to Ottawa from a brief visit to Washington which coincided with a visit by Churchill, King had told his cabinet colleagues that he was convinced that the British prime minister was determined "to centralize the direction of Empire affairs." Given this

---

* A plaque to the memory of Alice Massey, placed by her husband, is in the south aisle of Grosvenor Chapel in South Audley Street, near the Dorchester Hotel where they resided during the war.

immovable conviction, he had not welcomed Churchill's proposal on 4 April "that some time this year we should have an Imperial Conference in order to show the whole world the strength and union of what we should call in the future the British Commonwealth and Empire."[122] In the event, King to his relief was able to avoid giving a final answer to Churchill's proposal for a 1943 meeting since the Quebec Conference in August of that year superseded the idea, a conference decided upon by Churchill and Roosevelt without prior reference to him. "Far from being resentful at his subordinate position on his own soil, King was proud and elated,"[123] especially at photographs with Churchill and Roosevelt so useful for domestic consumption. Massey was fully aware of King's decidedly limited role, but he appealed for information about what stand, if any, Canada had conveyed to the United States and Britain. He wrote to Ralston for any insight, only to receive the dusty answer that "While I can talk to you very personally and face to face about these matters, don't you think the PM would feel that information regarding decisions made from time to time here had better go forward from him? ... We might all feel unhappy if attempts were made to short circuit."[124]

In August 1943, John Curtin, who had succeeded Menzies as prime minister of Australia, proposed a "new approach to Empire government" after the war, including a "standing consultative body" meeting in London, composed of resident cabinet ministers or high commissioners and supported by a permanent secretariat to help in the formulation of "a concerted Empire policy." In Ottawa, Curtin's thinking was analysed for the under-secretary by his assistant, John Holmes. "In Canada the chief spokesman for this trend has been Premier Drew [of Ontario] whose speeches have been quoted by 'advocates of solidarity'. The United Kingdom is particularly anxious to strengthen its position alongside the immense and populous land powers of the United States and the Soviet Union ... Canada might propose as a compromise solution certain changes in the present daily meetings of High Commissioners in London intended to make them more in the nature of informal discussions of policy."[125] What King thought of such heresy, if he ever saw Holmes's memorandum, is not recorded. Robertson intended to "cut up" a copy – presumably deleting the more heretical passages – to send to him, but there is no evidence that he ever did so, presumably having concluded that there was nothing to be gained by stirring him up.

As thinking about the shape and nature of the postwar Commonwealth went forward in London, Massey recorded that "All manner of ideas received serious attention: a Commonwealth-wide Cabinet; a unified

Commonwealth Defence Service; a Commonwealth Economic Board; more practically, Dominion representation in the United Kingdom Cabinet for questions of foreign policy, exchanges of officials between foreign services of the Commonwealth, amalgamation of the Foreign Office and the Dominions Office, better coordination of publicity, and much else in the same vein." Before Anthony Eden, now foreign secretary, visited Ottawa in April 1943, Hume Wrong noted for Norman Robertson that Eden had spoken in Washington of "his hope that the fourth leg of the stool [on which the United Nations would rest] might be not so much the United Kingdom as the British Commonwealth and [participation] might on occasions be from the Dominions." Wrong foresaw difficulties if "this amounts to a revival of the old concept of the diplomatic unity of the Commonwealth and is an unexpected consequence of our attempts to secure a proper place for Canada in the [United Nations] Relief Administration ... If in one context we were to agree to speak for the whole Commonwealth, undoubtedly in other contexts the assumption would be made that the United Kingdom would speak for us when we were not present."[126]

Massey agreed with Wrong's musings. His conclusions were, however, different: "It would surely be equally undesirable from our standpoint to drift towards the view which lies at the other extreme and to find ourselves regarding our relations with Great Britain as being no different from those with any other friendly country. In this direction lies a gradual weakening of those remaining ties which still bind our two nations, to the mutual benefit of both." Massey sensed clearly where British thinking was going as London contemplated its reduced place in a postwar world:

There is a growing realisation here that after this war Great Britain will find herself standing in greater need than ever of the British Commonwealth. It is felt increasingly that this country may be able to retain her position as a first-class Power only by stressing her membership of the Commonwealth, which as a group would represent a factor in international affairs as important as each of the other two great Powers – the United States and Russia ... The tendency on the part of Great Britain to set greater store by her Commonwealth ties is by no means, in my opinion, to our disadvantage. For the position of Canada too, is surely likewise enhanced by our association with the other nations of the Commonwealth in a great world-wide alliance.[127]

Unknown to King, Malcolm MacDonald had urged more starkly as early as February 1943 that, "If Britain stands alone after the war, she will gradually sink to the position of a second-class Power in world affairs. But there is a means by which she can retain a position of equal authority with America and Russia. That is if she makes herself the central member of a group of nations who are collectively as important as each of those two others. Such a group already exists. It is the British Commonwealth of Nations."[128]

What King did learn to his feigned or real consternation was that as late as January 1944, when it was evident to everyone that the United States and to a lesser extent the Soviet Union – and decidedly not Britain – would dominate the postwar world, Lord Halifax, the British ambassador in Washington, had made a speech advocating postwar Commonwealth cooperation. What Halifax said to the Toronto Board of Trade about the desirability of the Commonwealth acting together to become one of the three great powers of the postwar world seemed to many innocuous enough; similar statements had been made by Lord Cranborne, the dominions secretary, Brooke Claxton, the Canadian minister of national health and welfare, and various Australian spokesmen. King, however, proclaimed himself astonished at Halifax's speech, asserting that it was no less than "a conspiracy on the part of Imperialists to win their own victory in the middle of the war ... If Hitler himself wanted to divide the Empire ... he could not have chosen a more effective way."[129] It was clearly "part of a deliberate design by the United Kingdom Government ... to revive an Imperialism which left the Dominions something less than national sovereignty."

Malcolm MacDonald was fully aware of King's apparent anger, but he astutely suspected that he was also coolly turning over in his mind whether Halifax's speech might be the hook on which to hang an election campaign based upon the edifying anachronism of the Liberals saving Canadians from "reactionary imperialism," a theme that might go down particularly well in Quebec (one cabinet member from there happily characterized Halifax's speech as ensuring the return of the Liberal party at the next election). King soon confirmed his similar thinking to the governor general: "If it were not for the war, I would this evening be asking ... for a dissolution of Parliament to appeal to the people." Despite denials in London that anyone in the government – including Churchill – had known in advance what Halifax had intended to say, King recorded darkly in his diary: "I could not but feel that Halifax's work was all part of a plan which had been worked out with Churchill to take advantage of the war to try and bring about this development of centralisation, of makings of policies in London."[130]

Massey had the hopeless task of attempting to explain to the dominions secretary what all the fuss was about, why King had reacted with what Massey described as "paranoiac fury." He rightly sensed that King saw it all not only as a subterfuge by imperialists to pull Canada into their toils but also as a transatlantic plot between Tories. "The very fact that his [Halifax's] thesis was applauded by Conservative newspapers and given public approval by the Conservative Prime Minister of Ontario [George Drew] ... has served to project the subject of the Empire into the realm of party controversy, which is very unfortunate."[131] To the House of Com-mons, King spoke of the adequacy of existing means of consultation, but John Holmes from Canada House read the prime minister's codewords clearly, concluding wearily that "Mackenzie King could not resist the temptation to posture as the defender of Canada against another imperial plot."[132] And Holmes's colleague, Ritchie, saw it all as sadly anachronistic and a fruitless waste of time:

Our minds much occupied with the incident of Lord Halifax's speech in Toronto. It was not a speech calculated in terms which could appeal in Canada. It was ineptly put and showed no understanding of our psychology. It ought to have been argued in terms of Canadian self-interest. Mr. Massey says that the Prime Minister told him, 'In peace-time I would have gone to the country on it.' Yet Halifax's general argument is hard to answer ... Mr. King says that Empire con-ferences should be for consultation and co-operation but not for the formulation or preparation of policies. Presumably he means that you have a talk but commit yourselves to nothing. While one can agree with him about the dangers of formal machinery, surely that does not mean a totally negative attitude, and how in hell can you co-operate unless you have something to co-operate about, and what can you co-operate in except in plans and policies? The question really is the spirit in which you approach Commonwealth problems. The proper approach it seems to me would be to try to arrive at common objectives towards which we can all work in our separate ways. Where some or all of us can co-operate closely and in detail over plans let us do so without trying to enforce policies on mem-bers to whom they do not appeal. Let us have in mind how best these Empire plans can be merged in the wider objectives which the U.N. will have set before them, but Mr. King does not want to work through the Empire towards broader affiliations. He mistrusts the whole thing.[133]

Departmental thinking about the Commonwealth had become decid-edly more constructive despite King's outrage, real or contrived, at Hali-fax's public musings. From London, Holmes commented approvingly:

"There are good idealistic reasons for thinking of the British Commonwealth as a great congeries of countries some of which have achieved self-government and some of which are in various stages on the way. This, however, has never been a conception which appealed greatly to Canadians and we have preferred not to be classed with niggers."[134] He later described a dinner party that Massey had organized for visiting Canadians to discuss the future of the Commonwealth with senior British ministers. In the presence of the editors of both *The Economist* and *The Times*, Lord Cranborne took the lead in declaring that the advocacy by Australia of a Commonwealth federation, including proposals for a Commonwealth secretariat, was logical, but it was not practical politics:

The present machinery of consultation ... he seemed to consider eminently satisfactory. What was important ... was that there should be as much consultation as possible ... but we should not insist upon unanimity. Cranborne's statement was warmly endorsed by Attlee – what else could he do, given Britain's altered role in the world? – and there the matter rested until the following year when preparations began for a Conference of Commonwealth Prime Ministers in London."[135]

Amidst his broodings about British motives, King suddenly revealed to Massey a glimmer of genuine insight into Canada's real postwar dilemma. By early 1944, the prime minister had become concerned about the control that the United States was asserting in the Northwest Territories. He "held strongly ... that we ought to get the Americans out of the further development there, and keep complete control in our own hands ... with the United States so powerful and her investments becoming greater in Canada we will have great difficulty to hold our own against [its] pressure."[136] During a visit home by Massey in February–March 1944 (his first in seven years), King began by describing to him his apprehension about the suspected reluctance of the United States to withdraw its troops from Canada following the end of the war. Massey recorded that the prime minister

spoke apprehensively of the process of disentanglement which must follow the war when the Americans must withdraw and leave us in full control of our own bases and their wartime installations. The P.M. showed that he had grave doubts as to whether international agreements on this which Canada had secured from the United States provide any practical guarantee against the United States' claims and pretensions. When I suggested that the Americans, although undoubtedly friendly, did not take us seriously enough as a nation, King said that Canadians were looked upon by Americans as a lot of Eskimos. This was a striking observation made by a man who had been so often accused of being subservient to American policy. When I suggested that a spirited attitude towards Washington was essential he warmly concurred. I mentioned the problem which constantly arises in connection with proposals for meetings of the member states of the British Commonwealth in relation to American opinion and the official views of Washington. When I suggested that we should be free to meet as a family when we wished to do so, King concurred. I mentioned ... correspondence I had had ... on the subject of the proposed British Commonwealth Relations Conference next summer in London and [the] feeling that unless American observers were invited to be present it would be regarded as provocative in Washington. King laughed at the idea which he said was ridiculous. I cannot say that the very reassuring attitude that my host took on the subject of the Commonwealth *vis-à-vis* the United States has invariably been shown in recent years in Canadian policy. But it was nevertheless encouraging to hear him speak as he did. I only hope that he will *act* accordingly.[137]

King's unexpected understanding of Canada's postwar dilemma in achieving an equilibrium in its relations with the United States did not, however, alter his continuing rejection of British overtures to promote greater Commonwealth cohesion. In Ottawa, Massey found King still fretting about Halifax's speech:

K. felt that discussion in the abstract of Imperial relationships was very dangerous. He said that the Tories had been very frightened of an exploitation of the issue raised in Halifax's speech and that was why they were so moderate in their references to it. (This I greatly doubt. I think the principal motive was their desire not to drag the Empire into an unhelpful controversy.) The P.M. knew that [Leighton] McCarthy [Canadian ambassador and a prominent Toronto Liberal] had urged Halifax to accept the invitation to speak and had suggested the Empire as the subject.[138]

By 1944 it was evident to all but the purblind that if the Commonwealth was to play a significant role in the postwar world, more consultation would be essential. Attlee repeated the thought in June in words that many Canadians would have welcomed: "If we are to carry our full weight in the postwar world with the United States and U.S.S.R., it can only be as a united British Commonwealth. At the same time, it will be necessary to satisfy the legitimate claim of each of the Dominions to rank in the world as an independent nation."[139] The debate about what the

Norman Robertson, under-secretary of state for external affairs, and Mackenzie King in May 1944 on the second of their two wartime visits to London, this time to attend the sole wartime meeting of Commonwealth prime ministers. Although appearing more confident than during his reluctant visit in August 1941, King nevertheless excluded Massey from most of his official programme.

postwar Commonwealth would be surged back and forth as the end of the war in Europe approached. Would the wartime military, industrial, and financial cooperation of the Dominions translate into new forms of consultation and collaboration in peacetime? A yet more fundamental question – what would the impact be on the Commonwealth of India as a self-governing Dominion? – was not addressed, pending decisions about the future of that brightest jewel in the imperial crown. Although a new Commonwealth would soon emerge from the British decision to grant full independence to India, King's participation in the prime ministers' conference in May 1944 instead looked backwards, an anachronistic exercise coloured by his posturing over the Toronto speech of Lord Halifax.

For three weeks in May 1944, King, again with Robertson, was in London to attend the sole wartime conference of Commonwealth prime ministers. Now more confident of himself and of his likely reception given the relatively weakened state of Britain, King, as he had done repeatedly for two decades or more, arrived cautioning against any "kind of new machinery." Before the meeting, he saw Churchill, who suggested that "there should be at least an annual Conference of Prime Ministers, in England for the most part, at other times in other parts, Australia, New Zealand, South Africa or Canada, mentioning Vancouver ... [and] Chiefs of Staff meeting together for keeping in touch with the needs of defence ... As to the first I said that I hoped nothing too definite as to time would be arranged ... I said nothing about the second."[140] Curtin of Australia repeated his earlier proposals for a standing consultative body with a secretariat and with Dominion representatives in the Foreign Office to exchange information. But against all such proposals, King again warned his fellow prime ministers to "leave well enough alone, not to create some facade that would only raise suspicion as to commitments and also quite emphatically urging [them] not to attempt anything in the nature of com-mitments for annual meetings of Prime Ministers in London."[141] That he should have feared such meetings as late as 1944 reflects either an unre-alistic estimate of the recuperative powers of war-exhausted Britain or a desire to retain his familiar prewar straw man for domestic, especially Quebec, electoral purposes.

The drafting of the communiqué of the conference of prime ministers was redolent of the imperial conferences of 1923, 1926, and 1937 in that King ensured that it spoke of "the principles which determine our foreign policies," a plural usage which, at least in his mind, implicitly rejected any idea of a single, coordinated foreign policy for the Commonwealth. No less resolute was his rejection of any reference to Commonwealth defence cooperation. King left London well satisfied with his performance. "It makes me tremble to think what Canada might be let in for if a different type of person were in office."[142] However, King's performance impressed no one else, including advisors: "He did not speak up until goaded, and he always sounded petty – even to one of his humble servants who had no doubt that the centralized concept should be shot down."[143] Massey knew very well what King would say at the conference and he had dreaded it. That was bad enough, but the High Commission had also to help arrange King's séances for him. Holmes was one day delighted to be assigned by the high commissioner to accompany the prime minister on an "impor-tant call," only to discover that it was to a favoured spiritualist. Holmes waited in the car.

Norman Robertson recalled to a colleague that as the 1944 confer-ence was ending, "he was standing with his back to the wall in the Cabi-net Room at Downing Street to let the Prime Ministers file out, when

Churchill stopped in front of him and remarked without pretext or sequel: 'You seem to have been taking a very cynical interest in these proceedings, young man'."[144] King's participation in the prime ministers' conference had not impressed Robertson or the staff at Canada House. The Conservative opposition in Ottawa was even less impressed. In July, two months after his return from Britain, the Tories were at it again. King recorded wearily in his diary, "all reverted back [*sic*] to an Imperial Council for war; centralized secretariat and one voice for the Empire. Effort also to have it appear that I was not loyal. I did not use enough expressions of loyalty; also that I was against centralization of the Empire, etc."[145]

The one imperial innovation that King did contemplate was to end the practice of British governors general (a change first bruited almost fifty years before). In September 1944 he pondered, like Borden before him, the merits of having "a Canadian Governor General ... I have been thinking over Massey and his wife, Vanier and his wife, and last night quite a bit about McNaughton and his wife. Of the three I really believe McNaughton would be the best and it would be a fine recognition of his services ... Churchill has said to me he would be prepared ... to offer him a Peerage."[146] McNaughton, however, was to be neither a peer nor governor general. For some reason, King soon abandoned the idea of a Canadian appointee. Instead, Massey was asked to sound out the great Cambridge historian G.M. Trevelyan (who declined), before turning to a grateful Field Marshal Lord Alexander who, it was believed, needed a postwar job.

Massey was spared any direct involvement in the termination of the British Commonwealth Air Training Plan which he had done much to launch. The discussions with the Air Ministry about how best to wind it down were conducted largely by Charles "Chubby" Power, minister of national defence for air, who in October 1944 was convinced that perfidious Albion had failed "to indicate that its requirements will be reduced to a mere trickle ... I suggest in all sincerity that even after making allowances for the exigencies of war operations, it would have been an act of elementary courtesy to a partner, which has fulfilled all its obligations, for Air Ministry to have formally notified the Department of National Defence for Air."[147] But Massey did not scold the Air Ministry for its alleged discourtesy. He knew Power and his several weaknesses and erratic nature as well as his strengths; so did the British.

More worrisome to the high commissioner was Ottawa's reaction to the gift by the Royal Navy of two new cruisers and two destroyers in January 1944. Ottawa expressed no gratitude, going out of its way to state that it was accepting them not to benefit Canada but only to "assist in meeting the grave shortage of British naval personnel." Massey wired at once, "May I suggest that an expression of thanks should be incorporated?" Hume Wrong, in a personal reply to Massey, explained that

Mr. King ... spent a considerable time revising [the telegram, suggesting] that our draft sounded too grateful ... We should try to keep you privately more closely in touch than is possible in official communications. The trouble is that the volume of work in the Department seems to grow more rapidly than our capacity to deal with it and Norman [Robertson] and I have, I think, never been so hard pressed as in the last few months ... It is not easy to analyse an atmosphere, and this letter is not very illuminating ... The prevailing assumption in high quarters in the U.K. that everyone wants closer Commonwealth union acts as an irritant. I'll try to explain these impalpables at greater length, but they are hard to put on paper and we could get much further if we could talk them over.[148]

Massey never had the benefit of whatever oral explanations could be offered. A year later, the prime minister was at it again. The Royal Navy had offered the Royal Canadian Navy two aircraft carriers and eight destroyers, "all from new construction," a remarkably generous offer, but King saw it only as an effort to suck Canada into the war against Japan. Although one of the two cruisers of the Royal Canadian Navy was eventually to serve briefly as part of the larger British Pacific Fleet (with King's qualified agreement), even that seemed to require sanction of the United States. With the exception of the forgotten but now victorious British army in Burma, the war in Asia had largely become the preserve of the United States, given its vast and increasingly potent forces there.

As the end of the Second World War neared, the range of issues in which Massey was involved became greater. At the same time, however, the degree to which the High Commission, rather than the Embassy in Washington, was at the centre of discussion had diminished. In addition to visiting both Canada and the army in northwest Europe, Massey spent a good part of 1944 thinking about the postwar world. As early as April 1943, he had sensed that Canada would be left out of major postwar arenas as it had been from major wartime councils. "The 'Big Power' complex seems to be unfortunately far too prevalent at present and we will suffer from it ... until we ... have secured full acknowledgement of the right of Canada to sit on international bodies when for functional reasons it is right and proper that she should."[149]

Massey's forebodings were justified by events: only representatives of China, the United States, the Soviet Union, and Britain gathered in Washington during the late summer of 1944 to agree on the shape and mandate of a new global hierarchy to replace the now discredited League of Nations. This was, however, acceptable to King, suspicious as he still was of any idea of collective security embodied in an international organization. Even to join in the shaping of the United Nations might somehow open the door to imperial centralists. At the Quebec conference of September 1944, King revealed his misgivings to Churchill, concluding that Canada had no ambitions to share in world leadership which was better left to the British prime minister and the president of the United States. In King's mind, Canada had not participated in the events leading to the Second World War; it had shunned any role in the formulation of grand strategies during the war; and it would not be entrapped by postwar commitments. To his diary King confided that Churchill had said,

you have been so fine about letting England lead, not making it difficult for us by insisting always on several having direction. I said it had been difficult to maintain my position at times but that as long as I knew we were being consulted and getting informed on new policies and were able to speak about them before they were settled, I thought it was much better before the world to leave the matter of leadership in the hands of the President and himself. He said that had meant everything in the effecting of needed co-operation.[150]

With what good humour Churchill must have congratulated King on being "so fine about letting England lead" can be left to the imagination, but Massey soldiered on regardless in seeking an enhanced postwar status for Canada. He joined enthusiastically in the continuing efforts of the Department of External Affairs to win acceptance of the idea that Canada should at least be a member in those allied entities where it had a functional role to play. Securing a place for Canada in the United Nations Relief and Rehabilitation Agency (UNRRA) and in evolving international organizations – the International Labour Organization, the International Wheat Council, the International Court of Justice – imposed additional demands on the hard-pressed Canada House. Massey himself became especially involved in the design of the United Nations Educational, Scientific and Cultural Organization (UNESCO), eventually becoming the chairman of the Canadian delegation to its first session which met in London in November 1945. In speaking with Cranborne, the dominions secretary, about membership in international organizations, Massey had stressed that Canada should have a distinct voice, "Canada is in a very different position ... from any of the lesser powers. The other Dominions have no direct concern with Europe. The contribution of all the other United Nations except the four Great Powers is far less than ours, Canada being the fifth country in terms of war production and with a long gap between us and the sixth. Our war effort, therefore, and our contribution to postwar needs entitle us to a place quite unlike that of any other state."[151]

Massey might as well have saved his breath, given King's reluctance to engage with the British. Even the limited consultation in which Canada participated only rarely involved him. In April 1945 King, contemplating an imminent election at home, declined to attend or to send a minister to a Commonwealth meeting convened to discuss the monumental Yalta and Dumbarton Oaks proposals. It was left to Massey and Hume Wrong to advocate in vain that member states providing troops for military action by the United Nations should be represented during such discussions in the council of the proposed organization; the high commissioner could only note, "I wish that our willingness to assume obligations ... was as strong as our capacity for taking offence when we feel our prestige has been slighted."[152] A senior member of the Department of External Affairs was equally clear that the prime minister had failed when decision time had arrived to display any real conviction in collective security: "During the War [King] had urged the creation of an effective collective security system, but as soon as the war was over he began to retreat into his postwar isolationism. We ... never knew which way he would jump."[153]

The end of the war was for the Masseys also a matter for personal rejoicing. They were enormously relieved to have one son return safely from a prisoner-of-war camp and the other recover from wounds incurred while serving with the RCAF in Normandy. But beyond the immediate jubilation, Massey knew well that the end of the war marked a sharp decline in Britain's relative power in the world, leaving the United States and the Soviet Union as the only great powers. "Britain, it gradually became evident, had been greatly and permanently weakened. The war brought her glory and admiration, but very little else. The wealth built up through centuries of prosperity, already much reduced, had been further dissipated in her tremendous effort against Hitler, and her population and natural resources were not equal to maintaining a contest with countries more richly endowed." The election defeat — astonishing at least for the rest of the world – of Churchill's Conservatives and the formation of Attlee's Labour government was for some a portent of a renewed and more egalitarian Britain, but economic difficulties allowed little margin for massive social change. US Lend Lease was summarily terminated in August 1945, only a few days after the atomic bomb had suddenly ended the war with Japan. Canada concluded its Mutual Aid hardly less abruptly. In these circumstances, the economic prospects for postwar Britain were decidedly unpromising: it had somehow to service a massive international debt while promoting the recovery of its crippled and now obsolescent economy.

This postwar plight offered in the eyes of some in Washington an opportunity. The price of economic assistance would be a commitment by the United Kingdom to terminate imperial tariff preferences, an irritant to the United States since the Ottawa conference of 1932. It came as no surprise to Whitehall that Washington would press its advantage. Throughout the 1930s, the United States had repeatedly threatened that if imperial preferences were increased, Washington might endeavour to create its own preferential tariff regime in the western hemisphere. As early as New Year's Eve 1941, Robertson had alerted King to the intention of the United States to link its Lend Lease assistance with postwar acceptance of a free trade world in which Britain would forego imperial preferences.

During the three and a half years that it was in the war, the United States continued with single-minded persistence to bring about the abolition of the tariff preferences which Britain, by contrast, regarded as a significant element in its uncertain economic recovery. However, the abrupt termination of Lend Lease left the United Kingdom with no option but to accept US loans with that condition included. Massey participated in the discussions of what assistance Canada might lend to Britain as its postwar financial problems became more acute. His principal economic advisor summarized succinctly the dilemma:

As a result of the War, Britain had suffered very large foreign disinvestments and had accumulated very large foreign indebtedness, almost entirely to other countries in the sterling area. Its export trade had dwindled to hardly more than a trickle, and its productive capacity had been battered and run down. It was idle to think that Britain could join in moving towards a freer multilateral system of trade and payments unless massive assistance were forthcoming from abroad to help in solving these inexorable problems.[154]

Despite a general election in prospect at home, King attended, although with misgivings, the founding conference of the United Nations in San Francisco in April–May and again in June 1945. However, despite the participation of the United States, King departed from the conference holding much the same reservations about collective action that he had held about the League of Nations twenty-five years before. Massey, like Pearson and Robertson, was by contrast an internationalist, urging support for the nascent world organization. He was, however, decidedly less enthusiastic about proposed Canadian participation in the Pan American Union when King was still blocking more active participation in the Commonwealth, an organization in which Canada's interests were far more engaged. From London in February 1945, Massey had learned that some Canadians were beginning to match an interest in a seat on the proposed United Nations Security Council with a revival of the hitherto rejected idea that Canada should fill its vacant seat at the Pan American Union (the United States had effectively blocked Canada's bid to join in both 1941 and 1942). Massey delivered himself of a broadside that ultimately carried the day:

In the Commonwealth Canada has insisted on the equality of status with all members ... Within the [Pan American] Union, Canada might find she had equality of status with Paraguay ... Canada has consistently opposed the establishment of a Commonwealth Secretariat but the Pan American Union *is* a Secretariat ... it may be difficult for the Canadian citizen to understand why Canada rejected Mr. Curtin's proposal for a Commonwealth Secretariat on the grounds that it might endanger her sovereignty, and then proceed to take part in the activities of a Pan-American Secretariat ... [Further,] we should find it very difficult to avoid joining with Latin America in an anti-United States attitude on the one hand or on the other being classed simply as a puppet of Washington.[155]

Canada joined the successor Organization of American States in 1972, only after a Commonwealth secretariat had finally been established.

In August 1945 the new Labour government of Clement Attlee sought the views of the Dominions on a range of foreign policy questions. Churchill's Conservatives were out of office, but the new government sounded disturbingly like them. King's alarm at Atlee's soundings was immediate: "It is clearly an effort to work into one foreign policy" (a conclusion that contributed to his later conviction that "the present [Labour] Government is even worse than the last in recognition of Canada's part as a nation"). The reaction of Canada House under Massey was much more measured:

When the Council of Foreign Ministers of the great powers met in the autumn of 1945 to consider the peace settlements the new Labour government sent out a discreetly worded invitation to Commonwealth capitals for those who might want to send ministers or others to be on hand for discussions with the British who would be taking part in the council. King did not wish to come ... Canadian participation was through the High Commissioner's office ... There was some suspicion in Ottawa that this was an effort by the new government to put Britain in the position of speaking for the Empire. In fact, it was an effort by Attlee ... to organize some kind of input from the importunate Dominions to the peace settlement with Germany in spite of the arbitrary attitude of the other great powers.[156]

Nevertheless King spent the month of October 1945 in Britain when the Masseys were on home leave. Why the prime minister made the Atlantic crossing is unclear. Early in the war, King had crossed only with the greatest reluctance. Now, as both prime minister and secretary of state for external affairs, he went when there was no pressing need for so doing. A case could be made for consultation with Attlee and his officials on the Gouzenko espionage revelations. However, the impression emerges from his diary that he was attracted by the prospect of consultation now being largely on his terms, rather more between equals than hitherto. Certainly he found Britain sadly reduced from what it had once been. What he saw upon arrival came as something of a shock, although it does not appear to have reduced his suspicions of continuing centralist policies. "The whole city has a gloomy bewildering sort of look about it. I see through eyes wholly different from those in which I looked at London when I first came here in 1900 [1899] and indeed at different times since. A certain glory has passed away. One feels that the masses of people are struggling. One wonders how they manage at all. Food is at impossible prices. Clothing hardly obtainable."[157]

King had told de Gaulle in Ottawa that he intended "to assert ... very strongly" the place of Canada among postwar nations, but when an invitation from Attlee to the 1946 Commonwealth prime ministers' conference arrived in late April, he had immediately suspected that "he was to be made use of, Churchill, Roosevelt, and Stalin could have made commitments as to the whole future of Europe as well as other parts of the world 'without ever consulting any government in advance'."[158] King knew that he would need to struggle yet again "against a one-man authority for all I was worth" (presumably the British prime minister was the "one man"). He later added that his long fight against centralism "is a fight that I have had to make ever since the first Conference I attended in London in 1923 ... I am certainly not going to have Canada made a puppet of any official in the Dominions [Office] or any other official of the British Gov't."

With great reluctance, Mackenzie King had finally visited wartime London in August 1941. By the end of the war, however, he appears to have acquired a taste for transatlantic travel or to have gained more confidence in himself, visiting London annually from 1944 to 1948. In May 1946 he was met at Waterloo Station by a wary Alice and Vincent Massey. He found Massey, whom he disliked and mistrusted, "very silent – uncommunicative."

He was again hot on the scent of the centralists: "It annoys me beyond words to have this effort made ... to commit the Dominions if possible in Imperial affairs, to have pressure put on from a Government in Britain as though our Government were in some way subordinate to it."[159]

As the 1946 conference approached, King became increasingly uneasy about British intentions regarding Commonwealth defence and economic matters (it never seems to have occurred to King himself to consult beforehand with other Commonwealth leaders on their thinking; it was in a very real sense only the British who concerned him). He had already told Massey in March that "imperial [*sic*] defence ... is a phrase that we should like to see dropped from the current vocabulary as it leads to unnecessary misunderstandings and irritations and has little value in relation to the strategic realities of to-day." It fell to the uncomfortable under-secretary to inform British officials, as King had instructed him, that Liberal governments of Canada had not, since 1923, engaged in discussions of Commonwealth defence and trade and would not do so now. Discussion of Commonwealth trade would also be inappropriate "in view of the carefully prepared programme leading up to General Conference on International Trade due late this year or early in 1947."[160] Further, King told Attlee in May that he would not in any case "expect any general discussion on defence matters or on commercial policy or imperial preference to be of very much value without the presence of my Ministers of Defence and Finance."[161]

Massey, convinced that Canada's interests were not served by such prevarication, wrote to King a month before the autumn conference about the Labour government's thinking regarding the Commonwealth in the immediate postwar world:

I have described the considerable interest which has been taken in the proposed meeting, both in press and Parliament, and the confident expectation that matters of defence and trade would be primary matters for consideration ... Those in charge of policy in the present [British] Government have not shown any disposition to encourage the belief that the Commonwealth Prime Ministers would, or should, formulate tightly-knit plans for "Imperial defence". There are many Empire-minded elements in the Labour Party, but partly through prejudice, partly through lack of interest, partly through anti-imperialist habits of though, and partly because of internationalist idealism, the Labour Party do not think in terms of an Imperial orientation of policy as readily as do the Conservatives. Even those elements that had been showing great interest in an Imperial economic bloc do so largely because they conceive of it as a socialist bloc opposed to the "reactionary capitalism" of the United States. In matters of defence, economics, and general political direction, they are as much interested in close association with the Social Democratic countries of Western Europe as with the other Commonwealth countries. The Labour Party are ... anxious to make it clear that they are effective guardians of Imperial interests. They have been under heavy pressure from the Opposition to hold an "Imperial Conference" at which the Commonwealth association could be placed on a firmer basis in many spheres. They would probably not oppose mutually agreeable plans for close co-ordination of Commonwealth defences and a general tidying up of the alliance for the gratification of the British people, but this is not the sort of project that is apt to preoccupy their minds ... On the other hand there is a revived interest among the public ... this country is conscious of its material weakness as compared with the other two Great Powers. One of these Powers, the Soviet Union, is proving hostile. While it is widely recognized here that the security of the British Empire depends on friendly collaboration with the United States, there is ... great reticence about an association with the United States which might in fact mean a surrender of initiative to the stronger partner. The British want to stand on their own feet. One should not overlook the resurgent nationalism that is characteristic of this country in its post-war mood. It is a peculiarly internationalist or non-isolationist form of nationalism which is quite as strong among young Socialists as among young Tories. It is recognized that British strength must rest in the leadership of like-thinking peoples ... All except the extreme left want a close association with the Western European democracies, but no one seems to know how this can be achieved. It is inevitable in this mood attention should be turned to the most reliable allies, the other nations of the Commonwealth.[162]

King was not impressed with Massey's arguments, repeating to Attlee that his ministers could not accompany him and accordingly he would himself participate only in an informal gathering without minutes or press communiqués. Quite simply, he could not, without informing Parliament in advance, "commit Canada to any so-called Commonwealth policy either on defence, trade preferences, international treaty obligations, or the like." *The Economist* and the *Sunday Times* were soon reporting that he was refusing to attend, being unwilling to agree to any new forms of Commonwealth consultation or collaboration. He did finally attend, but arrived late, domestic questions having kept him, he said, in Ottawa.

King listened enraptured and even with astonishment to the incisive and wholly candid *tour d'horizon* of the foreign secretary, Ernest Bevin, including his analysis of the mounting communist threat across Western Europe (although he added little to what Massey had already reported about the new government's thinking). King had already been presented with worrisome evidence of Soviet hostility and subterfuge when he had visited Washington the year before – when Lord Halifax rather than the Americans had been especially forthcoming. Sounding like Dana Wilgress from the Embassy in Moscow, King nevertheless urged patience and caution in dealing with the Soviet Union, adding to the surprise of some of his colleagues: "if an impression should get abroad that the democracies were displaying impatience and lack of understanding in their relations with Russia, they might find among their own people sympathy of surprising magnitude with Russian ideals."[163] Yet King remained adamant about his inability to consider either defence or commercial matters, repeating that "it would be quite impossible for him to discuss in any detail questions of defence or finance. His Ministers for Defence and Finance were not with him."

This was new doctrine; hitherto King had taken the line that only he could engage in imperial discussions; ministers were not required. Now he suddenly proclaimed them indispensable. When a memorandum on Commonwealth defence was tabled by the British, Bevin introduced it by noting that before the war the United Kingdom had been able to pay for the security of the Commonwealth "and for that matter much of the rest of the world also" from its overseas investments. With their sale to finance its wartime purchases, especially from the United States, that role was no longer possible. Holmes at Canada House understood where the British were coming from: they were

concerned not just over the dangers of communism but of anarchy and for the time being at least a precipitous breakdown of the imperial structures in Asia was not to be regarded with equanimity ... Attlee put the Commonwealth representatives on the spot by producing statistics illustrating Britain's near bankruptcy and the appalling burden of maintaining the minimal number of forces required to maintain obligations in Europe and other continents. Attlee foresaw ... compulsory military service for two years and a drain on the finance and manpower of the country which would seriously affect its ability to rehabilitate its economy and overseas trade.[164]

King was, however, unmoved. "The [defence] matter was indeed one which required careful study and he was not in a position to make any commitment ... The question of whether it would not be best to have a Commonwealth defence policy with allocation of specific liabilities was a recurrent one. Suggestions on this subject had been made as early as the Imperial Conference of 1923 and again in 1926. There had been strong Dominion opposition [i.e., Canadian] to the proposals." Time having stood still in King's mind, he concluded with the flat statement that he had already told Attlee that it was "quite impossible for him to discuss ... questions of defence or finance."[165]

On other Commonwealth matters, King showed himself similarly unchanged in his decade-long suspicions. At the mere mention of consultation, the prime minister, in the words of Holmes, "acted as he often did, like a teetotaler at a party into which alcohol has been introduced."[166] He did not, however, contest the conference's proposal that the high commissioners meet monthly with the British prime minister. Although he had consistently opposed such meetings since the 1920s, on this occasion his passive acquiescence may have been the combination of a number of reasons: Skelton was dead, Massey would soon be replaced; Attlee was not Churchill; he was himself old and increasingly weary, no longer able to oppose his Australian and New Zealand colleagues as he had done so frequently in the past. His passive acquiescence, however, had arrived when consultation no longer had much meaning. Canada and, to a greater or lesser extent, the other Dominions were pursuing their own foreign interests in ways which left little room to attempt concerted Commonwealth policies. In brief, King was gratified by the conference conclusions: no defence or economic cooperation and existing consultation was declared adequate. The British press (especially that of Beaverbrook) was on the whole unwilling to give up on the idea of Commonwealth defence cooperation, but King returned home confident that he had ended all such talk. Further, any idea of a geographic division of labour in defence he had rejected (including Canada assuming military responsibility for the British West Indies since inevitably that would mean political involvement).

King had reacted with hostility to suggestions that Canadian troops should, as in the First World War, play a role in the Allied occupation of Germany, suspecting that they would simply free British units for imperial duties overseas. At the prime ministers' conference, King at least agreed to a watered-down invitation to have a Canadian military representative in London attend meetings of the British chiefs of staff, but on the condition that "it was understood it was simply for the sake of information and that no commitments were to arise nor were we to be regarded thereby as being consulted, as distinguished from being informed." Describing himself as incensed, King had written in his diary on armistice day 1946, "after all Canada has done ... and the sacrifices of men and materials we have made, that there should come a demand on this country as if it were some Colonial possession of inferior races."[167] King took to the cabinet the question of the appointment of service attachés to replace the wartime Canadian joint staff in London. Upon his insistence, a cabinet decision duly restricted the appointment of a military attaché to the staff of the high commissioner, receiving instructions from him and reporting to him (any joint staff office as such might somehow be interpreted as Canadian willingness to participate in "imperial defence"). It was to be clearly understood that the Canadian Joint Liaison Office was to be just that: a liaison office with no mandate to engage in any joint planning with British military staff or to convey commitments of any sort. King himself was reluctant in even this modest undertaking, having preferred to see the withdrawal of military attachés from all Canadian missions: "the military, air and naval attaché business ought to be done away with altogether and Embassies should be left free to discharge what are obviously their right duties."[168] King was at least consistent in his opposition. Almost twenty years before, he had dismissed Massey's suggestion of military attachés in Washington and London as "damned nonsense." King, in his concluding statement to his fellow prime ministers, described it as "a good conference," but his own secretary later observed trenchantly, "The fact that the conference was inconclusive and that no real commitments had been given or asked for made it a success from Mackenzie King's point of view."[169]

During the autumn of 1945, Massey had decided to bring to an end his decade as high commissioner. He later wrote that he had felt that it was time to return to Canada, although King suspected that he was also influenced by recognition, in the prime minister's words, that the glory had passed from Britain, leaving a Labour government struggling with a sea of economic problems that threatened at any moment to engulf the war-exhausted country and its residual colonial empire. Massey dealt with the uncertainties about his future by first prudently ascertaining from both Attlee and Addison, the secretary of state for dominion affairs, that if, finding little to do at home he came "trotting back" to Britain, something would be found for him.

The high commissioner sent his letter of resignation to the prime minister at the end of February 1946, suggesting the end of May for his departure. King received the letter with complacency, certainly not urging Massey to continue and later adding sourly that he had resigned probably because he wanted "to get out a publication recording what he regards as his own contribution to the winning of the War." King had anticipated Massey's decision. During their return voyage aboard the *Queen Mary* in November 1945, Robertson had responded to the prime minister's query that although he would like to be Massey's successor, "he would not care for public appearances and public speaking which would be expected in London, but even more he would not like to give up the power of the great position which he now held for something that could not equal [it] in influence." The prime minister turned over in his mind who in the senior ranks of the Department of External Affairs should go where. "It might be wise to have Pearson go there [London] except that he is doing very well where he is [Washington]. I would not mind having Wrong go to

London though I feel Robertson is entitled to the preference if he wishes it. It would be hard to refuse him. I am thinking of asking [St Laurent] to take over [as secretary of state for] External Affairs."[170]

Before his departure, there was much still for Massey to do in London and Oxford (where he reluctantly declined the invitation to become the master of his beloved Balliol), but few events gave Massey more gratification than the full restoration of the National Gallery, a neighbour of Canada House on Trafalgar Square. From 1943, Massey had been its chairman. As a director concurrently of the Tate Gallery, Massey was invited to participate in a panel that recommended the separation of the two galleries and to argue the case before the Parliamentary Standing Committee on Museums and Galleries. In 1946 he welcomed the King and Queen to view paintings returned from wartime safekeeping in Welsh caves. In bleak postwar London, the restoration of the total collection at the National Gallery afforded a brief moment of colour, but nevertheless Massey's decade as high commissioner ended with more a whimper than a bang.

King's reluctant and troubled participation in the prime ministers' conference was greatly relieved by the diverting spectacle of an honour for Massey. While protesting that he found the whole matter tiresome and vexatious, his diary suggests that he enjoyed every minute of it, devoting several pages to a minute-by-minute account of how he had cleverly disposed of the high commissioner's ridiculous pretensions. It all began when Massey joined King for his call on Attlee. King noted in his diary that the high commissioner was "very silent – uncommunicative. Looks as though he had the burden of the world on his shoulders. Hardly had a word of greeting or a pleasant word to say to any of us on the way to Downing Street."[171] King believed that he had understood why when Attlee informed him that King George wished "to have some recognition given Massey's services in England during the time that he had been High Commissioner here and especially in connection with the war. He [Attlee] said that he understood that titles were not permissible under a Canadian resolution but wondered whether there would be any objection to a 'Companion of Honour' being bestowed ... I replied that General Crerar had been made a C.H."[172] King added, however, that there had recently been a tempest in cabinet over his nomination of St Laurent and Isley as British privy councillors (and hence Right Honourables, not mere Honourables) and his exclusion of Howe and Mackenzie, who were deeply chagrined at being passed over. King explained to Attlee that "the whole question of honours had become a most embarrassing one to myself" (although he

Mackenzie King, never eager to include Massey in his official calls
during his visits to London, did at least ask him to join him briefly at
the conference of Commonwealth prime ministers at No. 10 Downing
Street in 1946. From left is prime minister Clement Attlee, foreign secretary Ernest Bevin, Massey, and King.

had had no hesitation in vetoing the skunk Ferguson's KCMG). After the
House of Commons had adopted its 1919 resolution advising the monarch
not to award titles to Canadians normally resident in Canada, he had
also opposed the idea of an Order of Canada, believing that it would
only generate silly vying for preferment. That same evening, however,
the long-serving secretary at Canada House, Fredric Hudd, confirmed to
Robertson that Buckingham Palace wanted to afford Massey recognition

for his wartime services. This prompted King to suspect that Massey had encouraged Hudd to put his nose into it: Massey's continuing hangdog appearance was because he "had been told that I was against doing anything." The prime minister decided to telegraph St Laurent to put before the full cabinet the question of the Companion of Honour for Massey ("I did not wish to take the sole responsibility of either approving or disapproving"), but if the message were to be transmitted via Canada House, Massey would automatically see a copy. Accordingly, having added that McNaughton should also be so honoured, King decided to send his message to St Laurent by airmail.

Although King had wanted the full cabinet to be asked about the proposed honour for Massey, he nevertheless gave most of the day to fretting about sending his query by airmail. The bestowal of the CH would somehow enable Massey to spend his last days at court, something which no doubt he would seek to do. "I said to Robertson he [Massey] would rather get a recognition from the British Government than from the Canadian Government. He had become an Imperialist, and would be such from now on."[173] Learning that Attlee had been at Buckingham Palace the evening before, King decided that he must have gone there for no other purpose than to discuss with the King the honour for Massey. In these circumstances, he concluded that his airmail letter would not convey to St Laurent the great importance of the matter. Accordingly, he would telephone him (a rare event transatlantically in 1946) after ruminating at length and speaking twice to Attlee about the matter. The more he thought about it, he despised "Massey more than ever. It shows all of what is back of his public service – vainglory; desire for Royal recognition; preferring another country, as Bennett did, to his own instead of remaining with the country that had honoured him with the position of High Commissioner." His telephone conversation with St Laurent had a prompt result: a telegram arrived briefly confirming that the cabinet had approved Massey's CH. King took the telegram to the Masseys' rooms in the Dorchester Hotel:

I said to him: Vincent, I think you will be interested in reading this telegram, which I then showed him. He read it over and I could see he had great difficulty restraining himself. He said to me: O Rex, this telegram means so much. There is nothing in the world I would rather have than this. I cannot tell you how deeply I feel or how grateful I am to you. I said: You have nothing to thank me for, Vincent. You have had a great record here; done a great work and I am pleased it has been recognized. It has given me pleasure to have to do with its recognition. I said: You will be glad at this, I am sure, as having been approved by the entire Cabinet. You will know from this that they have wished to share in the recognition of your work. I found it pretty hard to restrain my own feelings. It was such a complete overcoming of one's own personal feelings and forgiving very much on both Vincent's part and Alice's but seeking to not let prejudice in my case stand in the way of recognition of another. He was clearly quite deeply moved and walked back with me to my own suite ... I then said ... I thought probably it was desire on the King's part to have some recognition given before he left and, as a result, in the morning, I had telephoned to St. Laurent and had made the suggestion I did. I shall always believe that in every move, I was directed – that in this connection, I had received some direction from Beyond. Having gone in Massey's room at the time I did the night before, his mentioning of their wishing to give a mark, etc. – all led to my communicating with Ottawa, etc. I confess it made me feel very happy to have felt that I had submerged all my own feelings and to see the complete change in Vincent's mind and nature as a consequence. It will mean when he goes back to Canada, he will return with kindly feelings toward myself and the Government whereas during the last year or two, he and Alice have been rather embittered and a relationship between us purely formal.

I have been prepared to make great allowances for Alice in the anxiety and strain she has had. What I do feel about the Masseys is that vainglory helps to destroy the virtue of service, no matter and to what degree it may have been rendered.

Later in the evening, when I got back from being with Churchill, I went down to congratulate Vincent and Alice. The order of the Companion of Honour was on the arm of the chair. Vincent had been looking at it, if not worshipping it. I said I had come in to congratulate him. He then again spoke of how grateful he was. I had learned that in the interval, he and Alice had been at the Palace and that the King had personally bestowed the honour in the presence of the Queen and the Princesses. This was, of course, the apex of Vincent's ambitions and career.[174]

King found it all an unexpectedly satisfying conclusion to Massey's decade in Britain. On the one hand, he could savour his disdain for him as salve to his own covert and longstanding feeling of inferiority. On the other, being certain that Massey was aware of his opposition to honours for Canadians, he could present himself as the most gracious of patrons, having gone out of his way to seek endorsement of the full cabinet. The symmetry of it all was as satisfying as the hands of a clock being in line, always a gratifying phenomenon for King when he had something significant to accomplish. And most comforting of all was that throughout,

Mackenzie King bad farewell to the Masseys in London in May 1946 upon the completion of the high commissioner's eleven-year term. Upon Massey's departure, King described him as being at "the apex of his ambitions and career," having just received the Companion of Honour from King George VI.

it was clear to him that he had again been guided "in every move" from Beyond.

King had arrived in London on 19 May 1946. Four days later, the Masseys embarked, as long arranged, for Canada, he having in the meantime concluded his decade as high commissioner by accompanying King to two of the concluding sessions of the prime ministers' conference that King had been so reluctant to attend.

CHAPTER NINE

Norman Robertson, 1946–1949

In two respects Massey's Vancouver-born successor, Norman Robertson, was an unusual high commissioner. First, he was upon appointment young relative to his predecessors. In September 1946 he was only forty-two years old. Second, unlike all seven predecessors and most of his successors, he was a career public servant, not an overt partisan politician.

Robertson was, like Massey, a Balliol man. Following a false start in academe, he joined the Department of External Affairs as a third secretary in 1929, although his first posting abroad (to London as high commissioner) was not until seventeen years later. When Robertson was appointed to the foreign service, it was still minute, a few dozen people in total, engaged in a limited range of international questions. As a result of temporary assignments at the League of Nations with Borden and later in London with his colleague, Dana Wilgress, to negotiate tariff reductions, as well as during his many years in Ottawa, Robertson learned well his cherished vocation. He was happiest in economic negotiations, although decidedly not in the chaotic Ottawa conference of 1932. That it was so notably ill prepared "is altogether an absurd and rather tragic situation. I've never been much of an imperialist, but do believe that what's left of the Empire is well worth keeping."[1]

Robertson and Wilgress were despatched to Washington in 1935 by R.B. Bennett to negotiate a bilateral trade agreement with Roosevelt's administration, committed in principle to more open, non-discriminatory commerce. Upon Bennett's defeat, Mackenzie King had the gratification of initialing the agreement, which Skelton welcomed as "preventing the United Kingdom from thinking that we had no place else to go and gouging us accordingly." Two years later, in June 1937, Robertson and Wilgress were again in Washington to seek tariff reductions. In an effort to enhance trade among Canada, Britain, and the United States, the focus was increasingly in Washington which, in the name of free trade, determinedly pursued its policy of "chipping off the structure of impe-

rial preference." Eventually trade agreements involving all three countries emerged, Robertson being gratified that the 1937 agreement with the
United Kingdom restored some balance to the flawed 1932 agreements
but imperial preferences, such as they were, were still largely intact when
the Second World War began.

To those few who believed that they understood King it was not surprising that in January 1941 he appointed Robertson acting under-secretary of state for external affairs to succeed the suddenly deceased Skelton.
But to more senior officers, Robertson's appointment at age thirty-seven
after only twelve years in the department was premature. He was in any
case a hopeless administrator. But King had in fact chosen well. Although
Robertson most decidedly did not admire King, the prime minister was
pleased with his deputy's wartime work, including him as the only non-
minister in the Cabinet War Committee, the central entity responsible
for the conduct of the war. "With the exception of Skelton," the prime
minister wrote of his under-secretary on 22 October 1944, "he has the
finest sense of duty of any man I have known. He will not accept the work
of another, but verifies everything himself, if there is the slightest possibility of error." James Eayrs, in reviewing the documentation of the era, has
concluded that

In the exacting service of the most demanding of employers, that was the beginning of wisdom ... "N.A.R.", initialled on papers of state, guaranteed bite and
tartness. He did not write many: his minutes were few, his memoranda fewer
still. He enjoyed Proust, but his style, abominating length and froth, was anything but Proustian. His reluctance to commit his views to paper became notorious among his colleagues. His method could be disconcerting. "Often, when he
studied a question and saw objections," an associate recalls, "he simply heaved
a long, very long, incredibly long, sigh. He had said everything. We understood
that there were a multitude of problems we had not foreseen in our plans. And
we withdrew without further ado." Documents and letters would remain on his
desk for months on end, in the expectation that the problems they proclaimed
would one day go away. Sometimes they did.[2]

Robertson plunged immediately into every facet of wartime international problems and their domestic implications, ranging from the treatment of enemy aliens to the stockpiling of Canadian nickel by a still
neutral Japan. He attempted to deal with the myriad of such problems
through a department grossly understaffed as a result of prewar parsi-
mony. A remarkable spectrum of policy challenges constantly confronted

him, but if one particular subject dominated his long days in the East
Block on Parliament Hill, it was the wartime economy and its postwar
possibilities, with the United States having assumed the dominant position
in the world. During the war, Robertson crossed the Atlantic twice with
the prime minister and was several times in Washington, deeply involved
as he was in discussions of how the mounting Canadian war effort could
best be financed, how assistance could be provided Britain, and related
and complex questions of commercial policy resolved.

As the end of the war approached, Ottawa's efforts to win for Canada a
role in wartime and postwar institutions – other than the Commonwealth
– were belatedly accelerated. In 1944 at Bretton Woods, New Hampshire,
negotiation of the International Bank for Reconstruction and Development (the World Bank) and the International Monetary Fund was successfully concluded. The payments regime of fixed exchange rates there
defined helped to open the way for a parallel United States priority: a
trade regime based upon the most-favoured-nation principle (tariffs to be
identical for all partners in an agreement), thereby eliminating imperial
preferences. "The world cannot have too much trade" became a by-word
in Ottawa, given Canada's dependence upon exports (far exceeding that
of the United States). Ottawa joined Washington in its advocacy of a new
multilateral order to replace the bilateral tangle of trade restrictions from
which a world bewildered by depression and war had not yet freed itself.
Robertson played a major role with the Department of Finance in directing the Canadian preparations for both the World Bank and for the six
months of negotiations in London and Geneva from early 1946 that failed,
in the face of US congressional opposition, to produce the International
Trade Organization, but did eventually lead to the General Agreement
on Tariffs and Trade (GATT).

In the spring of 1945 at the San Francisco conference which established
the United Nations, Robertson, Pearson, Wilgress, and Ritchie strove
to secure a place for Canada commensurate with its wartime sacrifices
and economic development. There Ritchie's admiration for the work of
his colleague was unbounded: "What does Norman not understand? His
mind is as capacious as his great sloping frame. He has displacement, as
they say of ocean liners, displacement physical and intellectual, and he is
wonderful company with his ironic asides, his shafts of wisdom and his
sighs of resignation."[3] Canada's success at the UN conference was limited,
but on a personal level, Robertson's notable participation had an unexpected result a decade later. Basil Robinson, departmental advisor to the
then prime minister, John Diefenbaker, observed that a partial explana-

tion of Diefenbaker's coolness towards Robertson (whom he regarded as an incorrigible Liberal)

may lie in an incident which took place in 1945 when the Canadian delegation was preparing to attend the UN conference in San Francisco. Diefenbaker had arranged to attend ... as an adviser to Gordon Graydon, M.P., the Conservative party's representative on the delegation. When Diefenbaker applied for a diplomatic passport for travel to the conference, Robertson, at the direction of Prime Minister Mackenzie King, signed a letter to Diefenbaker denying his application, presumably on the ground that he had not been appointed as an official member of the delegation. That explained a great deal, Robertson said ... He knew that Diefenbaker was not one to forget such a thing.[4]

From San Francisco, Robertson returned to Ottawa and the seemingly inescapable administrative challenges of a burgeoning foreign service with which he was notably unable to cope. He also returned to deeply unsettling revelations of Soviet espionage throughout the west (the Gouzenko case in which he was to be centrally involved), ending the debate about whether nuclear secrets should be voluntarily shared with the Soviet Union as part of a wider postwar settlement. The evidence was mounting of how an increasingly dangerous cold war was replacing the hot war so recently ended.

Robertson, as early as the autumn of 1944, had begun to ponder how and when he might end his burdensome labours with the coming of peace (Pearson had just been appointed ambassador to the United States, the first career appointment to Washington). When in February 1946 following the first General Assembly of the United Nations, Massey had begun to consider when he might best resign as high commissioner – a fact of which the under-secretary would have been aware – Robertson thought of Canada House for himself. However, when Massey embarked for Montreal on 22 May no successor had been designated. A month later, Robertson offered the prime minister several suggestions. King told Robertson that "Pearson would be the best man for London unless he wished to go there himself." Robertson, responding incongruously that he "would like to go to some small place like Switzerland or Dublin," prepared a memorandum for the prime minister:

If it should be decided to appoint a Minister [of External Affairs], then I think Wrong or I could be assigned abroad, or both of us if it were thought desirable to bring Pearson back from Washington as Under-Secretary. Having in mind the job of work that has to be done in London during the next year or two, I am inclined to think that one of the three of us should be assigned there. I have been thinking about the possibility of Wilgress for London, but feel that his best qualities are not those specially needed there now. He has shown himself in Moscow to be a wise and shrewd observer, and a first-class diplomatic reporter of conditions and attitudes of mind. In general, he is more effective on paper than in conversation. This would, I think, be a draw-back in London, where the urgent need is to have the general Canadian position in relation to the United Kingdom, the rest of the Commonwealth and the United States more clearly understood in policy making circles than it is now.[5]

Robertson evidently knew that King now intended to appoint a career diplomat to London. Following Massey, King was not about to have anyone of an independent character, wanting instead someone sensitive to domestic policy priorities and immune to "centralists." Robertson suggested three possibilities, all civil servants and no politicians (neither Ralston nor Claxton, who were rumoured to be interested).

Robertson having indicated his unexpected and unconvincing choice of Ireland or Switzerland, King discussed the high commissionership with Pearson who was on a visit to Ottawa from Washington at the end of June 1946. Pearson's reply, as recorded by the prime minister, was direct: "London would represent the highest post of all and he would greatly welcome going there. He is concerned, however, about Robertson. He realizes that he [Robertson] is very tired and a little at a loss to know what decision to make respecting himself."[6] Robertson's indecision became yet more evident when King told him about his conversation with Pearson.

To my amazement, he said that he had felt disappointed ... He said that he himself would have liked London. I said immediately to him that I had from the beginning told him that whatever post he wanted, he could have, mentioning London specifically ... I then said to him would he say definitely that he wanted London, and he would have it. He ... mentioned Dublin or Geneva; if he could be there for two or three years. I said that to me it would be an indignity so far as he was concerned; also to the office, his position and Canada. These were trivial posts and he had a great position which should be maintained. In the position that he now held, he exercised a great influence, not only in Canadian affairs and in Continental affairs but also in world affairs. He admitted he liked politics and like to have to do with that side of things and would hate go give it up. I said I thought that probably after he had been in London for a short time, he would realize the power he had exercised had passed into other hands. He would begin perhaps to regret that he had given up the most influential post in the service of the country (excepting possibly that of the Deputy Minister of Finance). I said it was for him to say he wanted London and that would then be decided. I would feel perfect confidence of his handling of situations in London. I notice he is very tired and that there is no doubt he has very decidedly lost his grip on administrative end of departmental affairs.[7]

Robertson remained uneasy about his decision to accept the high commissionership. King and Pearson agreed that "Robertson had really not known his own mind and had changed it at the last." Robertson told King that he did "not feel too sure that he had done the right thing ..." King added, "As other men begin to take on one's place, one realizes what one's particular position means. If I had been Robertson, I would never have changed."[8] Finally Robertson's elaborate indecision ended with him again signalling that in fact he did want London, "his only reason for not saying so was he did not want to appear to be asking for anything himself or to be embarrassing for me." Exhausted though he might be by his wartime exertions, Robertson had agonized over his decision since he could not yet bring himself to relinquish the central role that he had played in the formulation of foreign and economic policy for several years. On 6 July, King finally brought the question to a conclusion by telling him that it must be decided without delay. Three days later, he finally accepted the appointment.

In September 1946 the debilitated Robertson, his Dutch-born wife Jetti, and their two young daughters embarked for Britain. Pearson, about whom King had persistent doubts, returned from Washington to Ottawa to replace Robertson as under-secretary of state for external affairs on the same day that the prime minister finally relinquished to St Laurent the portfolio of secretary of state for external affairs.

London was not an entirely happy appointment for Robertson, in large part because he was essentially a public policy person. Intensely interested in international relations, especially economic, and frequently offering brilliant insights and devising ingenious strategies, he was an incompetent administrator and awkward in his representational duties, including, as he had himself acknowledged, speech-making. There was a certain shyness, if not intellectual reserve, in Robertson's complex character which did not allow him to move as easily through British society as Tupper, for example, had done many decades before or Massey more recently. He described himself as still pursuing the "Trappist vows of silence and anonymity which [were] the principal prerequisites of the civil service." On the other hand, Douglas LePan, a self-confessed hero-worshipper, who from the artillery in Italy had joined the staff of Massey (whom he had known well as a prewar student at Oxford) later wrote of Robertson,

of all that remarkable group of economic experts who were in the service of the Canadian Government during and after the War, he always seemed to me to be the most like [Maynard] Keynes. He had the same mixture of bulk with fun and sprightliness. He had the same almost shambling gait. His interests were almost as wide, although he had never had the opportunity to indulge them so fully. He was as fertile in device, in resource. He had a similar power of being able to enter imaginatively into an economic problem, or an economic situation, or even into a welter of statistics, and give it human shape and perspective. If I am sometimes a little more reluctant than many of my friends to attach a unique value to the imagination of the poet or artist, it is because I have seen imagination working hardly less sovereignly in other minds, in other materials, and to other ends. That demonstration I owed first to Maynard Keynes, and later, over a much longer period time, to Norman Robertson. I loved the man, only this side idolatry.[9]

Certainly King was pleased with his choice of high commissioner. He felt toward Robertson no convoluted social inferiority as he had with Massey. Fifteen years before, the prime minister had piously informed the House of Commons that he regarded London as a place to send professional diplomats and not partisan politicians of the likes of that skunk, Howard Ferguson. In 1946, with the appointment of Robertson, he gave substance to that conviction. King had done all he could to side-track Massey; now in Robertson he had sent a high commissioner who, although a skilled public servant, could not act as comprehensively at Westminster as a capable former minister. Robertson had good friends in the upper ranks of Whitehall, but he had not the easy access at Westminster of his predecessors (with the notable exception of Larkin who had no real access to anyone). He came in time to be admired by the redoubtable Labour foreign secretary, Ernest Bevin, and the more austere chancellor of the exchequer, Stafford Cripps, but it was for his subtle policy thinking rather than his ready political acumen. In time, following King's death, both Conservative and Liberal governments would resume the practice of appointing former ministers of the crown.

Further, during the immediate postwar years, Anglo-Canadian relations lost the dynamic that the elusive quest for an imperial defence policy or tariff preference had long helped to provide. King remained convinced that an imperial tariff preference was unworkable, but he felt

an even greater concern with the efforts being made to hold the Dominions liable for security of the Commonwealth as a whole and to centralize the direction and administration of affairs in London and the manner in which the services are lending themselves consciously and unconsciously to this end ... I could see how carefully planned the whole British programme had been and how deliberately they were seeking to force our hand regardless of any decent feelings ... [I] was quite incensed when I received a despatch from Attlee, written by the War Office, in a tone which would indicate that Canada had to give an accounting to the United Kingdom as to what she was going to do in the Commonwealth policy – a complete reversal of the order of things which has been the kind of relationship toward different governments in Canada over the last forty years [*sic*]. The worst feature of it all is that after all Canada has done, and before we have been able to begin to meet the obligations arising out of the gifts of money, and the sacrifice of men and materials we have made, that there should come a demand on this country as if it were some Colonial possession of inferior races. I have not been far wrong in sensing the kind of situation which is developing under those at present in control of war policy in London. I can see a battle ahead and I may have to speak out pretty plainly. This perhaps will help me to recover some confidence in myself which I have been losing rapidly of late.[10]

So much for consultation on defence policy in the postwar world. Economic unity of the Empire had never, at least in King's view, been much more than a will-o'-the-wisp or a centralist trap, given the varying preoccupations of the British and colonial or Dominion governments. But the idea of imperial economic cooperation, coupled with military cooperation, had provided at least a rhetorical unity. Even if the holy grail had never been found, the search for it had at least induced in some a sense of common endeavour. However, economic upheaval resulting from the Second World War and the consequential creation of the International Monetary Fund, the World Bank and especially the GATT had ended even the imperial rhetoric and eventually the sterling bloc.

Britain in 1946 was in any case no longer a country where the policy brilliance of Robertson could particularly shine, even if Mackenzie King continued to value his advice at least to the degree that time and distance permitted. Almost bankrupted by the war, Britain was neither a happy nor confident country, understandably preoccupied as it was with its dire postwar economic plight. The euphoria of victory had been brief, soon giving way to profound concerns about how to pay one's way in a world transformed by war. Exhausted as Britain was by its extraordinary contribution to victory, sustained for six years, the Labour government was beset by the problem of how to rejuvenate industry in face of massive debt, overwhelming competition of the United States in foreign markets, pressing demands of labour unions at home, and the costs of maintaining armed forces abroad. The cold, hard European winter of 1946 was marked by dingy austerity – complete with extensive rationing and power cuts – and uncertainty in the face of the new government's commitment to fundamental change in public policy, especially social policy and public ownership of major industries. At both home and abroad, the British people, greatly deprived in peace by their victory in war, were being called upon to face an uncertain world. They did so with their habitual sang-froid, but it was not easy.

At Canada House, Norman Robertson was ably supported by his newly appointed deputy, Dana Wilgress, by Charles Ritchie, and by John Holmes and Douglas LePan, two of the brightest officers in the department. Both the diplomatic and local staff were increasingly numerous, as were representatives of various federal government departments and provincial agencies. Robertson, although sickly for much of his first year, nevertheless helped to keep the many Canadian officials moving in more or less the same direction, assisted by the fact that for once a high commissioner needed to have no reservations about the activities of provincial agents general. In February 1947, six months after Robertson's arrival, Pearson wrote to him that Roland Michener, Ontario provincial secretary, had told him of his eagerness to ensure that relations between federal and Ontario representatives "should be on the friendliest possible basis and that Ontario House should not overlap or get in the way of the work which can more effectively and appropriately be done at Canada House."[11] Michener, in inquiring directly of his fellow Oxonian whether there was duplication, demonstrated a cooperative attitude in sharp contrast with the combative and even antagonistic approach to federal-provincial relations of his premier, George Drew. Robertson was entirely reassuring to Pearson: "Without exception, relations with the Provincial Offices have been exceedingly cordial. They are well disposed and most co-operative. I am sometimes a little puzzled about the purpose they serve in the absence of either administrative or representational duties but, as far as the present officers are concerned, their presence here does not constitute any real problem or complication in the representation of Canada in the United Kingdom."[12] Indeed, another Oxonian, Graham Spry, the recently appointed agent general of Saskatchewan, introduced Robertson to Stafford Cripps, the chancellor of the exchequer (for whom he had worked closely in both Britain and India during the war).

During that damp winter of 1946, Robertson again became sick. A lifelong heavy smoker (lung cancer was eventually to kill him) who seldom took exercise, he was anything but robust. His resistance had been further reduced by his strenuous wartime labours to the point that illness was to remove him frequently from Canada House. He could not, however, have played an overt part in policy consultations even if he had been well. Despite his confidence in him, King remained convinced that ultimately no one but he could ensure that Canadian interests were protected in dealings with "this British crowd." Robertson was never constrained to the degree that Massey had been, but even he could not fully escape the effects of King's anti-consultation fiat. He necessarily employed some of the same indirect approaches developed by Massey to get around King's ukaze against more direct methods, including intelligence sharing.

In terms of Robertson's policy advice to Ottawa, King continued to value it. Such advice could, however, only be intermittent or longer term, there being practical constraints on how promptly Robertson could offer it. Cryptic telegrams and occasionally even hurried telephone calls were displacing carefully considered despatches as the principal communications link between Ottawa and London, but time differences remained. Above all, absence from the daily tempo of Ottawa policy discussion meant, as King had rightly anticipated, that "the power he [Robertson] had exercised had passed into other hands."

Canada's part in the further shaping of the United Nations was a case in point. Robertson, the San Francisco veteran, worked quietly with British officials to ensure that Canada contributed positively and constructively, despite King's dislike of the new organization which he saw as "fiddling and fussing and interfering on everything." At Canada House, moreover, John Holmes had identified a dimension to the first session of the United Nations General Assembly (held in London in early 1946) that Robertson subsequently followed in his consultations with Whitehall. "What would be the implications for Canadian policy of greater American involvement in Europe and also the British quest to establish understandings across the Channel?" Ostensibly, Robertson's advice about the United Nations was limited to such matters as whether Canada could successfully seek election to a term on the council (following Australia's success over Canada in the inaugural elections). In fact, he worked assiduously with senior Foreign Office officials in striving to help adapt the organization to the emerging realities of the cold war. Later he was included in the delegation to the second General Assembly held in Paris, but there he spent much of his time with the prime minister at a hotel separate from the delegation, helping to prepare "unsatisfactory drafts for his great swan song to the [General] Assembly."[13]

The agenda of Anglo-Canadian relations in the postwar years was in large part economic: tariff policy and the creation of an international trade organization; trade in commodities; monetary policy and exchange rates, shipping controls, international labour standards and, more generally, adjustment to a new world in which the United States was incomparably the dominant economic as well as military power. In the spring of 1946, to facilitate Britain's painful postwar reconstruction, Canada lent $1.25 billion at a minimal rate of interest, cancelled more than $400 million in debt from the British Commonwealth Air Training Plan, extended the interest-free loan of 1942 to 1951, and delivered wheat at below the international market price, all measures in the interests of Canada as well as Britain; Canada urgently needed the restoration of its export markets. But important though these initiatives were, and substantially greater in per caput terms than assistance from the United States, they remained essentially placebos. What was required was internal reform in Britain and a restructuring of the world economic order in the wake of depression and war. Canada had played a significant part, but once Robertson had become high commissioner, distant and ill as he was, he could no longer fill the pivotal role that he had played so effectively in Ottawa. Nonetheless he did chair meetings of Canadian ministers and officials gathered in London in February 1946 for joint economic policy discussions.

The Economic and Social Council of the United Nations (which was briefly pre-eminent in international economic affairs before becoming hopelessly mired in cold war rhetoric) had constituted a preparatory committee, of which Canada was a member, to organize a conference on trade and employment. Shortly after Robertson's arrival, the preparatory committee completed its task and the conference was duly held in Geneva from April to August 1947. Wilgress, having meanwhile been transferred from London to Switzerland, headed the Canadian delegation which joined in the negotiation of what became in time not the anticipated international trade organization but the General Agreement on Tariffs and Trade (GATT). Although more sceptical than Pearson in what might be expected from the proposed international trade organization, Robertson remained enthusiastic about it, and about the parallel IMF and the World Bank. All were fostered primarily by the United States in its conviction that open world trade was an essential element for its own economic growth and for the restoration of a war-shattered Europe able to withstand communist expansion. Robertson was unaffected by those on the British left who feared a threat from international organizations to Labour commitments to the welfare state and full employment and those on the right who put their faith in the sterling area and imperial tariff preferences. He watched with understanding although with mounting doubt the British quest for economic salvation in a latter-day imperial *Zollverein* of sorts, the sterling bloc. He was convinced that it would be unable to withstand pressures from the United States, committed as it was, in the words of George Woodcock, "to promote the salvation of Britain and at the same time hasten the final destruction of its Empire."

Although imperial preferences became increasingly vulnerable given the opposition by the United States, they nevertheless retained a certain negotiating value. King, their arch sceptic in the 1920s, now wrote to President Truman, "our people attach a great deal of importance to the Imperial preference." If it were to be abandoned as the multilateral regime evolved, there would need to be compensation, including tariff reductions on the part of the United States. As Holmes later recalled,

Canadians might not like the Commonwealth preference system very much but they were not going to hand it over for nothing. Their philosophy was universalist, based on the General Agreement on Tariffs and Trade which envisaged the gradual reduction of quantitative and tariff barriers and the extension of the MFN [most favoured nation] principle. This was Canada's first choice, but they avoided a doctrinaire attitude and agreed to participate in GATT in the first place only if existing Commonwealth preferences could be maintained. Participation in GATT enabled Canada to take advantage of MFN privileges in the United States, and as a result there was a large increase in exports to that country along with a proportional reduction of exports to the Commonwealth area, especially the United Kingdom. This reorientation of Canadian trade certainly helped the balance-of-payments problem, but it increased a dangerous dependence upon what one memorandum referred to as "a historically unstable market [i.e., the United States]." In spite of their relative decline, exports to the Commonwealth remained substantial ... amounting to about one-fifth of total trade. Fear was expressed in Ottawa that the decline in trade to Commonwealth countries had decreased Canada's political and economic bargaining power *vis-à-vis* the United States. To avoid this situation, emphasis continued to be placed on both export and import trade with the Commonwealth.[14]

The ailing Robertson was absent from Canada House during much of this period, although he had been able to act as the alternate to the minister of trade and commerce at the International Wheat Conference in London in 1946. Eventually the unhappy task fell to him to propose the postponement of a wheat agreement, given the lack of accord between Britain and the United States on international prices. He was also involved in the conclusion of peace treaties with various belligerents, the detailed drafting of the mandates for several specialized agencies of the United Nations, and the transport to Canada of tens of thousands of "displaced persons" (concurrent with King's announcement that "any considerable Oriental immigration" would cause unrest). From May to September 1947, Robertson was forced to take an extended leave of absence for treatment. Believing that Robertson might now be terminally ill, King discussed with Pearson in June 1947 the return of Wilgress to Canada House from Berne, this time as high commissioner.

The threat of these changes prompted the prime minister to set out yet again his thinking on the type of person who should be high commissioner. First, the appointment must be made by the prime minister and not by the Department of External Affairs; second, the appointee should be a former minister or "some person who enjoyed very closely the confidence of the Prime Minister" at least to the extent that it would be recognized that a new government would want its own person in office. King was more candid to Pearson and to his diary than he had been during his earlier posturing over Bennett's appointment of Ferguson:

the High Commissioner represented the Government of Canada, not any department of government, and that while the Department of External Affairs carried on the work of communication, etc., the High Commissioner was the appointee of the Prime Minister, not of the Secretary of State for External Affairs ... If another party came into office they might very well wish to have an entirely different representative but must be free to have it so. I might have mentioned how both Ferguson and Perley had tendered their resignations as High Commissioners when we came into office knowing that the Government would wish to make its own appointments in a confidential relationship.[15]

Robertson was, however, sufficiently recovered by October, one year after his arrival, to retain his posting and even to travel to Ottawa to participate in the first gathering of heads of diplomatic missions. It was also the occasion to receive a complete medical examination to attempt determine whether he should continue in Britain over the longer term.

Upon his return to London, Robertson was unable to escape a question to which he knew very well what Mackenzie King's answer would be. He had responded to a request from Ottawa to discuss "the broad issue of how understandings are to be arrived at between the United Kingdom and other nations of the Commonwealth on the handling of questions of foreign policy closely affecting Commonwealth interests."[16] He had speculated that "It is not impossible, particularly in view of the very difficult situations in which this country is finding itself, that the kind of arrangement for consultation and agreement with the Dominions used by Mr. Churchill last spring [1946] might be revived [but] ... the realities of Commonwealth foreign policy are gradually becoming apparent to the people of this country." Robertson, knowing King's mind, attempted to coax him into a less anachronistic, less negative attitude:

The British people have become accustomed to reading of the active and independent roles played by Australia, South Africa and Canada in United Nations conferences and in the Paris Conference. They may welcome or regret such independent activities, but they have come to take them for granted, for the most part without thinking very much about their implications. Few of them have worked out the logic of this behaviour in theories of Commonwealth consultation or joint responsibility, but as their minds become adjusted to a Commonwealth which behaves in this way the old conceptions of Empire do not occur to them so readily. It is perhaps significant that at the time of the recent announcement of the intention to proceed with an Anglo-French Alliance the question as to whether the Dominions had been consulted, or had given their consent, was never raised (except in Canada) or at least not raised sufficiently prominently to attract any attention.[17]

Robertson added that Lord Addison, the Labour secretary of state for the dominions, had offered to meet fortnightly with the high commissioners. The Australian, whose foreign minister had long been unhappy at the lack of consistent Commonwealth consultation, was delighted with Addison's offer, but Robertson, fully aware of King's decades-long aversion, suggested that such gatherings be ad hoc rather than periodic, convened only when a subject arose which needed to be addressed. Robertson knew his prime minister, whose office duly confirmed that, "Mr. King feels strongly that this is a matter in which great caution ought to be exercised, and that 'we must not get into a position where we begin to assume responsibility for shaping "imperial policy" and having "a cabinet of High Commissioners'."[18] Although this was February 1947 and not February 1927, Pearson instructed Robertson to pursue only ad hoc consultation. Accordingly, Robertson informed the next meeting of high commissioners that Australia's conception of its "role in the formulation of United Kingdom policy ... did not apply in the case of Canada." Sounding remarkably like Curzon in the 1920s, Robertson proclaimed that "We conceded to the United Kingdom the right to have a foreign policy of her own, just as we assumed that right for ourselves. We wished to keep each other informed of our intentions, but we did not consider that each country had to secure the consent of all the others before deciding on policies. I was certain that if Mr. King were asked he would express his appreciation of information of United Kingdom diplomatic activities and policies which was received through the usual channels." Robertson himself knew that his intervention might temporarily lay low the idea of regular meetings of high commissioners with the dominions secretary, but he certainly understood that it would not end it.

Like Massey, Robertson was fully aware of what had prompted some in Britain to turn again to the Commonwealth: it was what Malcolm MacDonald had mused about in Ottawa in 1943 and Halifax had expressed in Toronto in 1944. Economically the country, at least in the short term, faced a bleak future, severe austerity measures notwithstanding. If a few began to look to European cooperation for economic stimulus, more believed that Commonwealth collaboration would enable Britain to achieve recovery and accordingly play a significant role in the postwar world. Having attended a dinner of senior Commonwealth enthusiasts, Robertson wrote to Ottawa:

The background of this effort was a feeling that this country's economic and financial position was likely to be a good deal tougher this winter than it is now, with loans running out and exports falling far short of meeting the deficiency. The occasion would require a demonstration of Empire solidarity, proof to the world that if necessary our countries could carry on alone in the postwar period the way they had in 1940–41, etc., etc. They were all decent, disinterested people, full of the friendliest feelings towards all the other countries of the Commonwealth, overflowing with gratitude and appreciation for the aid and succour they had received – and totally unaware of the real bases on which it had been given. I was defeated and discouraged by the whole performance, because I didn't know where to begin to put the record straight. I thought, however, I had better add a dash of Canadian cold water to the Australian wine and South African brandy, and did say that I personally had serious misgivings about the wisdom and timeliness of the whole project. I thought a useful job could be done

in reminding United Kingdom consumers of the efforts which our bacon producers, butter producers, etc., had made during the war years to meet this country's essential needs; that they had foregone other and more profitable markets in
an effort to keep the essential supply lines working; and that they were entitled to
a real measure of consumer preference in the postwar years when supplies were
ample and competition again prevailed. I thought it would be a great mistake
to mix up these sensible, if low level, considerations with the suggestion that the
Commonwealth could be in any sense considered as a bloc with pretensions to
self-sufficiency. I don't think this made sense in economic, financial or political
terms, nor was it a realistic approach for any of the Commonwealth Governments to encourage. In the present climate of opinion, a gesture such as they
had in mind was quite likely to complicate the multilateral trade programme in
which we still had hopes and which would quite possibly be reaching a critical
stage next autumn. In furthering that programme it was in our interest to stress
all the community of interest with the Americans that we could find, rather than
emphasize the issues that divided them from us, etc., etc.

After this homily I left, feeling like a leper, probably having done irreparable
damage to Commonwealth relations. I have been thinking about writing for my
recall for some months now. This may be as good an occasion for action as any.[19]

During discussions in 1947 in Canberra of the Japanese peace settlement, it became evident that Australia, still frustrated at its inability to
make its voice heard among the "great powers," particularly on Asia-
Pacific questions, was reverting to the durable idea of having the Commonwealth represented in international meetings by that Commonwealth
member which was judged to be most directly interested in the matter
under discussion. Not surprisingly, King promptly rejected any idea of a
Commonwealth roster, Robertson so informing the British government.
King was equally opposed at the end of 1947 to Canadian participation in
the proposed United Nations Temporary Commission on Korea intended
to facilitate the establishment of democratic government in, ideally, a reunited country. As he told his diary,

The truth is that Pearson with his youth and inexperience [Pearson was then
aged fifty] ... had been anxious to have Canada's E.A. [Department of External
Affairs] figure prominently in world affairs and has really directed affairs [at the
United Nations] in N.Y. when he should have been in Ottawa, and without any
real control by Ministers of the Crown and proper consideration of these questions. All meant well but very much the inexperience of youth. I am sure that
if Skelton had been alive, he would not have advocated our going afield in that

fashion. Also in England Robertson told me he thought it was a great mistake for E.A. to be touching matters in Korea. I feel the same about Palestine.[20]

A few days later, King added the Balkans to his list of regions of the world where Canada should absent itself, repeating that "so far as E.A. [External Affairs] is concerned, they have been allowed to run far too much on Pearson's sole say so ... He is young, idealistic, etc. but has not responsibility. I am thankful I held responsibility for E.A. as long as I did. At least, I did not get the country into trouble by [injecting it into] things it had no business to interfere with."[21] Robertson in 1947 was age forty-three. Pearson was fifty. The advice of the younger Robertson was responsible. Pearson's was not, being "too young" to offer responsible advice. What the irresponsible Pearson made of all this he does not say in his memoirs, but no under-secretary can have enjoyed seeing the high commissioner have at least occasionally greater policy influence upon the prime minister and secretary of state for external affairs than he had himself.

Amidst the efforts of Pearson and Robertson to counter King's mounting excitements that the Labour government was emulating earlier Conservative governments by plotting to impose upon the hapless Dominions an "imperial policy," there had arrived a message that the wedding of Princess Elizabeth and Prince Philip in 1947 could offer the occasion for "a brief and informal meeting of Prime Ministers." This merely increased King's mounting suspicions of Labour's intentions. Robertson had anticipated his reaction in a letter to Pearson:

I have been worrying about the arrangements for the Prime Ministers meeting in November ever since I learned of them ... but have been diffident about volunteering comments which may or may not be helpful. Though the agreed agenda will be short and the proceedings brief and informal, I fear that in present circumstances a big preliminary press build-up is inevitable and that the consequential let-down afterwards will be equally unavoidable and embarrassing to all the Governments taking part in the meeting. These fears have been fortified by Bevin's Southport speech which had led a large part of the United Kingdom public to look for some escape from their present troubles in closer association between Commonwealth countries and will make them expect large achievements from a meeting of Prime Ministers at this time. Our friends in the Antipodes are lavish with the large words which sound well in communiqués, and even if they accept the limited agenda which has been proposed they can be counted on to make it public that, for their part, they would have been glad to have taken the occasion of this meeting to discuss questions of immigration, defence and commercial policies. Canada will be blamed quite wrongly for the elimination of these questions from the agenda ... In these circumstances, and since no official word of the meetings has yet reached the press, I have been wondering whether the Prime Minister would not prefer that his visit to London should be simply for the Royal Wedding and for such informal discussions with other Commonwealth Prime Ministers as their simultaneous presence in London made possible, i.e., that there should be no meetings of all the Prime Ministers as such, no agenda, no group photograph and no final communiqué. If this is what he would prefer, then, I do not think it is too late to suggest, perhaps to the Palace, in the first instance, that inter-Governmental discussions of policy questions of mutual concern should not be mixed up, even by coincidence of place and time, with the participation of the nations of the Commonwealth in the celebration of the wedding of the heir to the throne.[22]

Not surprisingly, King promptly endorsed the high commissioner's thinking, Robertson having told him what he wanted to hear. The high commissioner was instructed to state that Canada would not support the idea of a full prime ministers' conference. The British tactfully responded that they would be content "to take advantage of the presence in the United Kingdom of the Prime Ministers ... to have informal separate talks with them which might, if agreeable, include also a general discussion on the world position." In these circumstances, largely of their own devising, Robertson and Pearson soothingly reassured King that the gathering would be "a purely informal and friendly discussion of the major issues, in which he will not be called upon to commit himself in any way."

The 1947 conference revealed a Commonwealth much altered and a Britain much weakened. From his post as counsellor at the embassy in Paris, Ritchie urged Ottawa "to give all possible support to the United Kingdom in her desperate effort to maintain her position." A western world, including Canada, dependent upon the United States alone "is neither healthy for the countries concerned nor for the United States." But increasingly Mackenzie King appeared to be too weary and too ill to care, simply taking refuge yet again in opposing consultative innovation and ignoring the major contribution that the Foreign Office made to Canadian understanding of what was happening in the wider world. As Holmes noted, in addition to copies of telegrams and despatches which were freely shared, "British embassies and consulates continued to serve Canadians in all places where the Canadian flag had not been unfurled. For many years the Canadian foreign service remained dependent on British communications, including couriers ... as the problems of Canadians occupied an increasingly larger proportion of the work of the British offices, they pressed Ottawa to do its own work. This happy evolution is somewhat at odds with the myth of Canada's 'struggle' to wrest control of its foreign policy from Westminster."

Holmes realized that in any case meetings of high commissioners were unlikely, in immediate postwar circumstances, to contribute much to international understanding.

The growing maturity of the Canadian attitude – as well as the declining influence of King – might be noted in the changing attitude adopted towards group meetings of the high commissioners ... with British ministers. Before the war King and ... Skelton had become obsessively preoccupied with this question ... After the war it should not have been a serious issue, but the Canadian attitude remained dogmatic ... When, after 1947, the circle of high commissioners in London widened beyond the cosy group of palefaces, joint sessions tended to be less confidential and less rewarding ... By the early 1950s high commissioners meetings as an institution ceased to be of any significance.[23]

By the time that Robertson was well enough to attend the weekly meetings, the high commissioners of India, Pakistan, and Ceylon were also present. The level of candour declined, the British in particular fearing that the foreign ministries of the new Commonwealth members were notably leaky (the British were themselves reading their diplomatic traffic, while several of their own officials were in turn regularly supplying classified information to the Soviet Union). Later, Robertson speculated upon the impact on the Commonwealth of the arrival of new attendees:

The old question of the status and duties of the High Commissioners has been stirred up recently from two new quarters. The new Secretary of State for Commonwealth Relations, with all the ardour of innocence, is anxious to re-institute regular meetings of High Commissioners and generally to make our little mob into a corps ... When I went to call on Mr. Noel-Baker shortly after my return to London, I enquired about these new developments and explained the view that our Government would be likely to take of them. We did not think it desirable to give the High Commissioners any kind of corporate status, and thought it would be foolish and possibly dangerous to try to make a new agency or instrument of Commonwealth consultation out of their meetings in London. Apart from political and constitutional misgivings about the trend of this kind of development, I suspected he would soon find himself grudging the time required for weekly or fortnightly meetings with the High Commissioners collectively. I thought this moral of a year's experience would be reinforced this winter when there would be in London new High Commissioners from India, Pakistan, Burma, and perhaps Ceylon. Direct exchanges of views between Governments of the Commonwealth did not in fact all take place on the same level of confidence and security. The political considerations which under present conditions made some degree of differentiation inevitable would in fact also operate within the meetings of High Commissioners, and would invalidate any argument that such meetings might provide an informal opportunity for supplementing secret communications exchanged direct between Commonwealth Governments, since the Foreign Secretary or the Secretary of State for Commonwealth Relations were unlikely to say things to the High Commissioner for Burma and the High Commissioner for India which they would be reluctant to communicate by telegram to the Governments of Canada and Australia ... at the luncheon given by the Prime Minister ... for [the departing High Commissioner for South Africa] at which the other High Commissioners and a number of Mr. Attlee's senior colleagues were present [the South African High Commissioner] spoke with great earnestness about the status and functions of High Commissioners. He felt that their status and precedence were inadequate, and their responsibilities underestimated. His valedictory was a plea for upgrading the office and its occupants (all of whom should have enjoyed Ministerial position in their own countries before translation to such a post). With the right kind of High Commissioner sent here in the first instance, and given appropriate status and recognition by his own government and by the Government of the United Kingdom, it would then be possible to construct out of their joint deliberations in London a new and effective instrument of Commonwealth cooperation. He wanted to see the meetings given a corporate, institutional character.[24]

It might have been thought that a confirmed old anti-centralist like Mackenzie King would have welcomed dilution of the Commonwealth by the addition of Asian members, but he remained paradoxically unenthusiastic about them, telling his new secretary of state for external affairs that he was horrified at the thought that they would soon form a majority. When in late May 1947 the British proposed, despite having imposed yet more rationing at home, modest development assistance for the countries about to emerge from the old Indian Empire, King was indignant:

India was a dependency of Britain. She should deal with the matter herself. That this was part of an effort on Britain's part to get rid of her burdens and throw them on to the Dominions ... I can see pretty clearly what the British have in the back of their minds is ... to create a Commonwealth policy here which we were all to follow; they found that impossible to do under the name of Empire. They are going to try to do the same thing under the name of Commonwealth. I have fought all through my public life for Canada as a nation. I do not intend, at this stage of my career, to become a mere echo of any department or government in London ... We were not consulted about India's independence.[25]

Pearson had to write to Robertson that even the imaginative ideas of the Department of External Affairs about how India might best be encouraged to remain in the Commonwealth represented for King "an unnecessary, and possibly dangerous, interference in matters which were of no special concern to the Canadian Government; that it seemed to approve a doctrine of participation in Imperial affairs which he had opposed all his life, and which might be exploited by people in London for undesirable purposes."[26]

Throughout his two years plus as high commissioner, Robertson could never escape discussions about Commonwealth consultation. Although he had himself worked for the full membership of India, Pakistan, and Ceylon in the Commonwealth (Burma declined), he was eventually instructed to speak against the British and Australian proposal of January 1949 that periodic meetings of Commonwealth foreign ministers be instituted. The cabinet did at first agree to regular meetings following sessions of the UN General Assembly, but even that limited acquiescence was reduced a week later to the invalorous formulation that "since agreement between [sic] all members of the Commonwealth on arrangements for consultation was not now possible, the subject be left in abeyance." Robertson was also instructed to employ almost the exact words of Laurier in stating that "the Canadian Government is quite satisfied with the existing mechanisms of consultation within the Commonwealth."

In terms of financial assistance to a sadly reduced Britain, Robertson was expert. He had been involved in the discussions in Ottawa which had resulted in the massive 1946 Reconstruction Loan. Within a year, however, during the worst of continuing balance of payments crises, there arose in Ottawa the ill-substantiated fear that Britain might somehow be working to detach Canada from the dollar bloc and push it into the fragile and vulnerable sterling area to which all other members of the Commonwealth belonged. As early as 1945, King had gratuitously warned Churchill against any "form of sterling area isolationism." In 1947 Wilgress in Geneva was informed by Pearson that, "If the United Kingdom feel ... that our dollar difficulties with the United States are making us more receptive to an Empire Customs Union, they are making a great mistake."[27] Having rejected "adherence to anything in the nature of a Commonwealth Customs Union," this was yet again an instance of setting up an imperial straw man. "Mackenzie King enjoyed horrifying himself with the old familiar spectre."[28]

In the new year of 1947, Robertson remained deeply concerned at the ability of Britain to pull itself out of its postwar economic difficulties without additional assistance from Canada and especially from the United States. "I can hardly exaggerate the problem of the dollar deficit. It is a time bomb ticking away in the heart of Whitehall, and awareness that it might yet blow up the Government and ruin this country's hopes of recovery affects consideration of almost every other major problem."[29] That July, Britain, in the face of intense US pressure, made sterling convertible for the first time in eight years. This reluctant response to American insistence proved to be the economic disaster that Maynard Keynes and others had predicted. One month later, sterling was again made inconvertible. By September, despite the prospect of the Marshall Plan, Britain remained in desperate need of dollars to pay for essential imports, including food (meat and petrol rations had been further cut and bread was rationed for the first time).

Some in Whitehall again saw Canada as a promising source for help, being in the dollar rather than sterling zone. Upon his return to London from the heads of mission meeting in Ottawa, Robertson prepared for the visit of the minister of finance and separately of his senior officials who were working to identify ways in which Canada could assist, while at the same time attempting to become again a major source of British imports of foodstuffs. Upon reflection, however, King added four days later a rationalization for not attempting to modify the wheat contract. Almost complacently, King noted that the Russians would then be unable "to say that there is a break between the U.K. and the Dominion, or [more importantly] our political opponents [i.e., the Conservatives would say] that we were turning from Britain to the U.S. to be controlled by the latter country."

At the end of that dreary year, as the discussions with the British continued, Pearson described to Robertson how in a meeting in Ottawa with senior British officials

the Prime Minister stepped in yesterday with decisive force. He talked ... frankly last evening, and said that they were very lucky indeed to get any financial help from us at all; that we had no justification for giving it to them on financial grounds, and that we were taking great risks. He then added that we were will-ing to take such risks in order to avoid the cancellation of a [wheat] contract which might arouse misunderstanding between the two countries and cause a feeling of resentment in the United Kingdom that we were prejudicing the bread ration. Mr. King, as you know, has returned in a very pessimistic frame of mind about political developments in Europe, and that was to him the governing con-sideration in this case ... [however,] he felt that an inability to agree here and a cancellation of the wheat contract would be interpreted as an abandonment of the United Kingdom, would be exploited by unfriendly elements [i.e., the Con-servative Party] and would be generally undesirable.[30]

Canadian exports were increasing, but partly as a result of US and Canadian credits offered to Britain and western European countries whose foreign exchange reserves were again perilously low. Britain, for its part, could not hope to increase its exports rapidly enough to pay in dollars for anything but the most limited imports from beyond the sterling area. The dollar shortage was everywhere felt, including in Canada which could no longer count upon its exports to Britain to pay for its imports from the United States. And British investment, all but eliminated by wartime sales, was out of the question, given the acute shortage of dol-lars. On this occasion, King was decidedly not impressed by Robertson's arguments, confiding to his diary: "I have said repeatedly in the cabinet that I thought we were foolish in extending the credits we were to so many countries ... Also we were making a mistake in expecting that the British Govt. would show any thanks for what has been done" (this despite the fact that the chancellor of the exchequer, Treasury officials and others had recently been fulsome in their gratitude to the visiting minister of finance and other Canadians).[31]

By February 1948 Britain's gold and dollar reserves were again depleted. The Marshall Plan was taking form, but its full benefits were not yet real-ized. With a second dollar crisis approaching, Wrong from Washington and Robertson from London were called to Ottawa. Robertson, unde-terred by Canada's own foreign exchange difficulties and King's nega-tivism, waded in on behalf of additional assistance: "there are circum-stances in which prudential calculations can be carried too far and ... this is one of them."[32] With the recent communist coup in Czechoslovakia in mind, he hoped "that those who are properly anxious about our financial position will feel at this critical moment that it is possible for us to share in this additional but comparatively modest way in the risks involved to safeguard western Europe from further [communist] encroachments and infiltration." In September, however, he was again brought back to Ottawa to assist in preparations for a visit from the chancellor of the exchequer which largely focused on the Canadian demand that in extending additional credits to Britain, commitments be made to buy certain minimal levels of foodstuffs. However, discussion of Canada's role in relation to Marshall Plan assistance was soon concentrated in Washington, leaving Robertson largely out of that policy loop.

The Commonwealth being increasingly seen as of no real assistance in economic revival, the British government began to consider urgently whether western Europe might be. Ernest Bevin, in a memorable speech at Southport on 3 September 1947, had called for "a Customs Union for the Commonwealth ... [nor] could [the Commonwealth] any longer do without common defence and common acceptance of certain economic principles." This was what the Beaverbrook press wanted to hear, especially from a Labour foreign secretary, but it was equally what King did not want to hear, especially from a Labour foreign secretary. Bevin had advanced his Commonwealth thinking as a final offer at the same time that others in the British government were considering what might in time become a customs union of western Europe. It was not, however, this emerging choice that Robertson knew would bother King; he would suspect even now that perfidious Albion was somehow up to its old tricks – and this time by a Labour and not by a Conservative government. From Ottawa, Pearson agreed with the misgivings of the sickly Robertson, but his understanding attitude had little impact. Bevin's speech, he commented to Robertson,

was both overcharged and over-emotional. That speech, as you know, has had a great deal of publicity in this country and, for the life of me, I cannot see what useful result Mr. Bevin expected would follow from it – at least in Canada. It has done no good here, especially in its references to common defence and a customs union. All the old skeletons are rattling furiously in the cupboard.

I realize, of course, that in the present crisis there is an increasing tendency to fall back on the "Empire" and to plug the idea that now is the time for all good Britishers to come to the help of the Mother Country and rally around the flag. However, you can take it from me that, in spite of a very real sympathy here for the United Kingdom in her present predicament, in spite of a genuine desire to help, and in spite of the developing economic difficulties with the U.S., this tactic will produce no useful results in Canada. We are not so impatient with the U.S.A. as all that but, in any event, if we are forced to choose some closer economic and financial alignment, and I hope we won't be, it will have to be with

Washington rather than with London. Surely the British have enough sense to realize that and surely they have enough sense, therefore, not to put Canada in any position where such a choice would have to be made. That is why this new campaign of economic and strategic unity can accomplish nothing but harm here, no matter what it may do in Australia or New Zealand.

I suppose, however, that nothing can be done with men like Mr. Bevin and Mr. Churchill, who are so dazzled by the greater vision that they cannot see the nervous tremors in Ottawa. I suggest, however, that it is a matter of first importance to urge, at every opportunity, that broad general declarations about the Commonwealth, especially in regard to strategic and economic matters, should be avoided like the plague. I know this is a counsel of perfection, but I do not need to labour its importance. There is a real danger of dramatic, perfervid utterances in London making much more difficult here an already difficult situation. Between the dehydration of Mr. Attlee and the geysers of Mr. Bevin. I prefer the former.[33]

King and Pearson took Bevin's speech more or less at face value, but LePan, the economic policy officer at Canada House, astutely detected that it was not simply a latter-day Labourite conversion to centralism, but rather a more subtle opening ploy in what at least some in Whitehall foresaw as the long negotiation of an European customs union that the Marshall Plan was promoting. LePan wrote:

Bevin's reference to a Commonwealth Customs Union ... may not have been entirely the blunt and innocent expression of a purely personal opinion which it appeared. There is no sign that the government here have seriously entertained the project; but, on the other hand, Bevin's reference may have been a deliberate tactical device directed towards the Americans.

the United Kingdom authorities have felt a certain amount of irritation at what they have considered the rather too facile advocacy of a Customs Union for Europe by ... the United States Administration. The American attitude ... is altogether too simple-minded and minimizes unduly the great difficulties in the way. After prolonged discussion in the Cabinet here on the subject of a European Customs Union in which a great deal of scepticism was expressed, the Foreign Secretary concluded the argument by saying that it was necessary for the United Kingdom, if it expected to receive any aid under the Marshall Plan, to take the risks involved in working towards a [European] Customs Union ... This step, which may appear tentative and halting, represented in fact a considerable development in United Kingdom thinking on this subject. Nevertheless, a great deal of reserve remains ... and also considerable uneasiness over what is considered to be the uncritical enthusiasm in the United States for a project which at best could only be realized in the distant future. Bevin may well have thought that there could be no harm in showing that two could play at the game of throwing about facile and vague suggestions for economic integration.

This is exactly the attitude which you would expect if, as I believe, the suggestion was not a firm indication of what the United Kingdom Government's policy would probably be, but nevertheless had some substance as a tactical move made for the purposes I have suggested above.[34]

The subtlety of LePan's understanding was lost on the Canadian cabinet. Without reference to Britain's possible option of Europe, the cabinet, prompted by the prime minister, solemnly, if indirectly, replied to Bevin by declaring on 11 September 1947 that Canada would be unable "to contemplate adherence to anything in the nature of a Commonwealth customs union." In time, during future debates over British membership in a European customs union, a revival of the idea of some sort of Commonwealth alternative would be advanced by the government of John Diefenbaker and his high commissioner, George Drew, but the cabinet's statement of September 1947 remained in effect the final Canadian rejection.

Bevin was in fact no more enthusiastic than Churchill about Britain becoming part of a European federation or union. But the foreign secretary (as distinct from the leader of the opposition) had to deal daily with reality. The reality was that the United States was urging upon Europe a customs union as a precursor of a global free trade regime to be embodied in an international trade organization. Bevin understood the economic arguments for closer European integration, but he opposed anything which might undermine the sterling bloc and the Commonwealth, confirming the demise of Britain as a world power. At a minimum, as LePan had observed, Commonwealth economic cooperation could be a useful ploy in any eventual European negotiation. Robertson, fully agreeing with LePan, also recognized that something of fundamental interest to Canada was now afoot. In June 1947 he wrote to Ottawa:

The United Kingdom and France ... will undoubtedly address themselves to a pretty thorough examination of [the] feasibility [of a western European customs union] ... suggest you study likely short and long term effects of such a development on Canadian export trade ... suggest you consider implications ... not only in terms of its probable direct effect on volume and direction of Canadian exports, but as means of underwriting our general political and economic interest in [Europe's] stability and prosperity ... Canadian interest and encouragement of closer European economic co-operation would add an element absent from U.S. endorsement in that it would come from a country of the Commonwealth and from a beneficiary (nominal) of existing preferential arrangements. Some recognition that the United Kingdom can play its full part in European economic co-operation and still be a member of the Commonwealth in good standing, just as Canada combines Commonwealth membership with the fact that it is also an "American" country.[35]

In Geneva, during Commonwealth consultations at the world trade talks, Wilgress stated that the Canadian government "would not want to place any obstacles in way of European countries promoting their common welfare through closer economic integration."[36]

At the end of March 1948 the United Kingdom formally inquired whether there would be particular products on which Canada would like to retain a tariff preference if the United Kingdom were to enter an European customs union. The Cabinet Committee on External Trade Policy responded blandly that "the Canadian Government looks generally with favour upon the broad purpose of achieving a Western European Customs Union ... our position in negotiations would be sympathetic to the achievement." This was all good Liberal stuff, but in the cabinet of 20 April 1948, "some ministers" supported "strongly the maintenance of both our free entry in the U.K. market and the retention of the preferential arrangements which favour us; ... it would be unwise ... to indicate to the U.K. that we would be prepared to make any sacrifice of the existing preferential arrangements." Following the signature of the Treaty of Brussels by Britain, France, and Benelux, Ottawa wired Robertson: "We would not oppose any plan which would result in a closer integration of the economies of the European countries and which would assist in their recovery." Ottawa then proceeded to contradict itself by adding, wholly unrealistically, that any such integration should be opposed "if the participation ... in a European Customs Union meant that preferential treatment for Canadian products would disappear or European products would receive better treatment [in the British market]."

The cold war was at the same time deepening. In the aftermath of fascism in Europe, communism was gaining in acceptance, including among the intelligentsia, to the point where it became possible that communist parties in France and Italy would dominate their governments. Attlee was deeply concerned about what the United States, the Commonwealth, and western Europe might do together "to stem further encroachment of Soviet tide." St Laurent, supported by Pearson, proposed a North Atlantic alliance, but King continued to fret about whether Attlee – of all people

– had become a neo-Conservative seeking to centralize Commonwealth "powers and resources under a common direction and for a common use."

The Truman Doctrine of March 1947 (three months before the announcement of the Marshall Plan) assisted Turkey and broadened the help available to Greece from that afforded by the British taxpayer alone (King had earlier joined Americans in questioning Churchill's commitment to a postwar democratic regime in Athens). Although it had rapidly run down its military forces, independent of what Britain or other members of the wartime alliance were doing, Canada joined western Europe and the United States in negotiating an agreement calling the North Atlantic Treaty Organization (NATO) into being in April 1949. Anglo-Canadian consultations had played a constructive part, conducted in Ottawa or by Canadian ministers or officials visiting London (all of whom benefited from the advice of the high commissioner), although the essential discussions were again in Washington. From London, Robertson warmly welcomed a new transatlantic alliance. "A situation in which our special relationship with the United Kingdom can be identified with our relationship with other countries in Western Europe and in which the United States will be providing a firm basis, both economically and probably militarily, for this link across the North Atlantic, seems to me such a providential solution for so many of our problems that I feel we should go to great lengths and even incur considerable risks in order to consolidate our good fortune and ensure our proper place in this new partnership."

Pearson and Robertson joined in encouraging King to understand that NATO would be all the more effective if it were to be underpinned by transatlantic free trade. As King confided to his diary,

negotiations were on at Washington for the establishing of an Atlantic Security Pact – negotiations between the U.K., U.S. and Canada. The stage, at the moment, was on exploration only. That I felt trade proposals might be made to fit as it were into the larger Atlantic Pact. That if, for example, the Atlantic Security Pact were agreed upon and were brought before Parliament and be passed as it certainly would be, we might immediately follow thereafter with trade agreement as being something which still further helped to further the object of the pact, namely the removal of restrictions to trade within the area arranged by the Pact.[37]

When Washington unexpectedly began to show interest in bilateral free trade with Canada, largely as a means of ending imperial preferences at least in the Canadian market, King was at first enthusiastic, seeing it

as a step toward transatlantic free trade and instructing his finance minister "to lose no time in furthering it." Unlike others, he envisaged that
any free entry negotiated with the United States should also be offered
to the United Kingdom and the other members of the Commonwealth
(i.e., the old Commonwealth). "The Agreement [would represent] a tremendous advance toward freedom of trade throughout a large part of the
world." King's enthusiasm was, however, short-lived. In a matter of days,
he began to convince himself that the arguments for free trade with the
United States were not, after all, so compelling, being on the Canadian
side mainly a concoction of the unreliable Department of Finance. In any
case,

I doubted myself whether I had the mental energy and physical strength to make
an explanation in the H. of C. ... It would be represented that we were seeking
to separate from Britain. I said I would feel no matter what happened that we
would have to offer Britain the same rights in our market as we were offering the
Americans. It might also be desirable later to add the United Kingdom to such
discussions. If, in fact, the discussions could be somewhat widened in this way,
it would remove one of the political obstacles to bilateral arrangements at the
present time for free trade between the two countries.

King soon began to have yet greater misgivings about what the Conservatives, long opposed to free trade with the United States, would make
of it electorally.

The Tory attack would be that I had wanted annexation, and this could mean
separation from Britain, etc. but that I was really not in any shape to aid a movement of the kind in Canada. That I had not the mental power. Was feeling
fatigued and exhausted, now I was incapable of another general election campaign. That I could not do justice to the situation in the House [of Commons]
and that this was a factor which would have to be taken into account. I said I
was even beginning to doubt my own judgment on many matters. I found myself
much too cautious and conservative in international matters to feel that my views
were shared by some of the younger men around me.
    The Americans in their attitude were carrying out what I felt was really
their policy and had been so over many years of seeking to make this continent
one. That I thought they had long seen that a conflict likely to come would be
between Russia and themselves, and that they had felt that their position would
be strengthened if they controlled all of North America ... If I were an American
I might easily share that point of view ... personally I would rather have Canada

kept within the orbit of the British Commonwealth of Nations than to come within that of the U.S. That all my efforts had been in that direction ... I thought we could keep all of this in mind in anything that was done at this time to see that all British considerations were taken into account.

More than two months after the finance minister had first raised the free trade prospect with him, King finally decided that

the issue was very large. That unquestionably came back to what the future of Canada either in the British Commonwealth or as a part of the U.S. will be ... the long objective of the Americans was to control this Continent. They would want to get Canada under their aegis. If I was [*sic*] an American, I would have the same view, especially considering Russia's position, etc. On the other hand, I did not feel we would be as well off in a State of the Union as we will be possibly as the greatest of the self-governing portions of the British Commonwealth of Nations. At any rate, I would not want myself to take a position contrary to this.[38]

At the request of the prime minister, Pearson had telephoned Robertson on 21 April 1948, instructing him to press the proposal for free trade with the countries of the (white) Commonwealth and of western Europe, but within a week the under-secretary had reluctantly to admit that any such grand strategy was at an end, given the growing weariness of the prime minister.

Pearson and Robertson, certain that King could be only a few months from retirement, managed to contain their impatience. They were nevertheless disconcerted by the prime minister's flaccid response to the blockade of West Berlin by the Soviet Union. When Soviet troops cut off all rail traffic across East Germany to the isolated city in late June 1948, challenging the occupying powers of France, Britain, and the United States, King bizarrely came to regard the Berlin blockade not so much a dangerous manifestation of the aggressive nature of the Soviet Union as another occasion of Britain attempting to impose itself on Canada. On 28 June, at a meeting of high commissioners, Bevin turned to Robertson "and said that the United Kingdom and the United States would be very grateful for any assistance other countries could give in making [available] additional transport aircraft"[39] to supply beleaguered West Berlin. Pearson in turn endorsed to King Robertson's appeal that the foreign secretary's request be given "prompt and serious consideration." Instead of giving such consideration, King indulged himself, for the benefit of his cabinet, in a wholly gratifying recollection of how more than twenty-five years before, he had foiled the dastardly attempt of Churchill *et al.* to embroil Canada in the defence of the Chanak garrison.

I stressed mostly the feeling of indignation I had that on a matter as grave as this, it should be projected into the press of the world by some persons in Britain who ... I believed would prefer Empire and war to no war and separate nations of the Commonwealth ... [it] reveals the view of many centralists in England who want world control and hope to get it through centralization of Commonwealth problems in London. I said the whole position reminded me of the Chanak incident ... Asquith had said that some of the Dominion statesmen [i.e., King himself] were wiser than some of their men [Churchill and Lloyd George] were.[40]

Despite the fact that Australian and New Zealand aircraft were soon participating (the RAAF alone eventually flew over seven thousand tons of supplies and seven thousand passengers), Ottawa procrastinated throughout the remainder of 1948, Robertson having been instructed to inform a puzzled Bevin that "great embarrassment [would be caused] to us if any request were made for transport planes." Later, even when Robertson had returned to Ottawa as secretary of the cabinet, King feared that participation by Canada, not being an occupying power, might upset the Soviet Union. In any case, a request for aircraft should have come from the United Nations Security Council. Accordingly, no RCAF aircraft ever joined in that audacious allied response to Soviet aggression. "Just how this attitude squared with Canadian activity over the North Atlantic Treaty at the same time is hard to determine ... It was a time of confusion and illusion inescapably associated with its [Canada's] new stance in the world and shed the inhibitions of a previous existence."[*41] For King, the basic problem about the Berlin airlift was that the request to participate had come via the British government (or, as he saw it, via the London press). If it had come from all three western occupying powers, he might possibly have reacted differently, but to have the request come via the British was a clear signal that once again they were up to their old cen-

---

* · What Robertson did achieve in 1948 in the way of Canadian aircraft deployment was to help organize consultations between Lionel Chevrier, the minister of transport (and a future high commissioner), and his British homologue over Ottawa's decision to designate Canadian Pacific Airlines rather than Trans-Canada Airlines as the Canadian carrier for Pacific routes involving Fiji.

tralist tricks. In his dark suspicions, he managed to lose sight of who was doing what to whom; the Soviet Union was replaced as miscreant by the British. He never recorded in his diary any indignation at the blockade nor any recognition that its eventual defeat was a major milestone in stopping Soviet expansion.

In early 1948 King finally decided that he should retire in the summer or autumn. A Liberal convention would be convened in August to select his successor. When Attlee proposed in the spring of 1948 a conference of Commonwealth prime ministers in June, King pleaded fatigue and the pressure of domestic politics prior to the convention as reasons for being unavailable. The British countered with the query whether he would find it more convenient for the Commonwealth to meet in Ottawa. King replied petulantly to Robertson that Attlee should simply agree to his counter proposal for a meeting in London in October, adding that "I have done my utmost throughout the years I have been in office ... to assist British Governments in meeting difficult and embarrassing situations, and ... to effect on all matters as large a measure of unity as possible between all parts of the Commonwealth."[42] The other Commonwealth prime ministers duly accommodated King by deferring the conference until October.

When the invitation arrived from Attlee to attend the rescheduled conference in October, St Laurent, the newly elected leader who had not yet taken office as prime minister, urged King to attend both the conference and the third session of the General Assembly of the United Nations in Paris, leaving him in Ottawa as acting prime minister (perhaps St Laurent had in mind the reaction of some in Quebec if he himself were seen as going to London immediately after becoming prime minister). For King, this prompted the satisfying reflection on his own longevity in office:

I put [this] down to having taken just the opposite view to that taken by those of an Imperialistic outlook. I recall during the war strongly refusing to be made a member of an Imperial War Cabinet. I strongly opposed going to Britain, at different times, for conferences, etc., where I felt my real duty was to Canada first ... [the absence of Smuts] will ... make a great difference [to the struggle] ... that whoever represents Canada at the next conference will have to wage in London. There will be again a tremendous drive for centralization, etc. I will be the elder statesman ... what a complete change from the position as it was in my earlier years in office! – with the London *Times* trying to drive me out.[43]

St Laurent, elected leader of the Liberal party on 7 August, had to wait three months before finally becoming prime minister on 15 November,

Mackenzie King, too unwell in London in October 1948 to attend the conference of commonwealth prime ministers, asked Norman Robertson, the high commissioner, to take his place. King George VI is at the centre left; prime minister Clement Attlee is on the king's left; Robertson is on Attlee's left; and Nehru, the Indian prime minister, is on the extreme left of the king.

having received King's anachronistic valediction that "You will probably need to fight all Sir Wilfrid's battles over again."

Before the conference, Stanley Bruce (now Viscount Bruce who in his twelfth year as Australian high commissioner was participating in debates in the House of Lords) had proposed that the prime ministers form a "Council of British Nations." Periodic meetings of ministers would address particular forms of cooperation such as finance and transport. Monthly meetings of high commissioners, to be chaired by the British prime minister, would be supported by a secretariat to keep all major questions under constant review, to furnish information and reports to member governments and to prepare for meetings of the council. An External Affairs memorandum, with an eye on the prime minister, was having little of this: "The present set-up seems, on the whole, to meet more adequately the dual requirements of co-operation and flexibility."

On 15 September 1948, well before the conference of Commonwealth prime ministers, King sailed for France, to be met at Cherbourg by Georges Vanier who joined him for the Paris session of the UN General Assembly. Subsequently, in London, Robertson accompanied King on his calls on Attlee and Addison (as well as giving a dinner for the visiting Masseys, whom King received at their wartime residence, the Dorchester Hotel). Although King was deemed too unwell to attend the actual conference, he was able to see Nehru and later the Indian high commissioner who sought his opinion on whether the role of high commissioners should not be enhanced by the Foreign Office keeping them even more informed through regular consultations. This manifestation of what King regarded as centralist thinking coming from an Indian, of all people, must have disconcerted him. He cautioned the new Indian representative that "there was a danger of High Commissioners becoming a sort of government unto themselves and also developing a secretariat here."[44]

Less easy to deal with was the suggestion from King George VI that high commissioners should be ministers of their respective governments. The King had kindly called at the Dorchester to see his ailing Canadian prime minister who was immensely flattered by this attention from his monarch, but much less happy about what he said. To his consternation, George VI sounded remarkably like Tupper or Perley.

His Majesty thought that what we ought to have here [in London] was a Minister of the Crown from the different Dominions. That they would be able to give the background of situations, etc., to their Governments. I said they had that arrangement when necessary during the First War, but the danger I saw in an arrangement of that kind was that the several Ministers from different parts of the Commonwealth, all residing in London, would begin to form a little government of their own, and imagine they were determining Commonwealth policy and that their whole point of view would be chosen from London.[45]

Robertson, who had been in Ottawa to help prepare for the conference, represented Canada for the first few days until St Laurent could arrive on 14 October to replace the bed-ridden King (Pearson being fully occupied in Ontario in winning the by-election that would see him enter Parliament as the presumptive secretary of state for external affairs). To the assembled prime ministers, Robertson read a message from King:

I wish to express ... my great regret at not being able to be present this morning at the opening meeting of the Conference to which I have been much looking forward for the past few months. I should like, however, through Mr. Robertson, to convey to all present my warmest of greetings. I send a special word of greetings ... to the representatives of India, Pakistan and Ceylon, who for the first time are seated around the table at No. 10 Downing Street.

The first meeting of Prime Ministers and others which I attended was the Imperial Conference of 1923. Since that time I have been present at a number of other conferences and meetings. Each occasion has helped to widen and extend my appreciation not only of Commonwealth but of world affairs, and to confirm more strongly than ever my belief in the great value to be attached to co-operation between the different nations of the Commonwealth, and to the larger co-operation which our unity has made possible with the peoples of other nations. While I shall not be able to be present at the meetings, I am arranging for a member of the Canadian Cabinet to be present in a day or two. Meanwhile, Mr. Robertson, who has been associated with me in the work of government over many years, will, I feel confident, be able to represent my views accurately and adequately.[46]

At the conference, Robertson loyally expounded the conviction that Canada could not participate in both a North Atlantic security pact and Commonwealth defence arrangements. It would not object if other members of the Commonwealth wished to collaborate, but following his arrival, St Laurent would reject inclusion of New Zealand, Australia, and South Africa in NATO, repeating at the same time that Canada could not contemplate sharing in the defence burden within the Commonwealth. Both Canada's defence and economic policies would be integrated with western Europe and especially with the United States: "it would be quite unreal for Canada to regard as effective either general or regional plans of defence which would compromise Commonwealth countries exclusively."[47]

St Laurent also sounded like King in rejecting a British proposal for periodic meetings of Commonwealth ministers of defence, foreign affairs, and economic affairs, but he did agree to a toothless Commonwealth Economic Committee of officials (to be chaired by Frederic Hudd), but remained passive towards Attlee's proposal, supported by India, New Zealand, Australia, and Ceylon, for "closer and more regular personal contacts between Commonwealth High Commissioners in London and the Foreign Secretary. Mr. Bevin had recently invited High Commissioners to approach him directly on matters of foreign policy and he hoped that they would take full advantage of this." Attlee added, perhaps as a result of having himself been once dominions secretary, that "the Secretary of State for Commonwealth Relations would be kept informed of such meetings and would normally be present at them."[48] This St Laurent let pass with little comment. He also remained silent about New Zealand's renewed suggestion that it was time to create a Commonwealth secretariat. The British at least cannot have been surprised. Two months before the conference, King had stated flatly to the visiting British cabinet secretary who had urged accommodation of the views of the newly independent members, that "It would be unwise even to discuss proposals for centralization of the Commonwealth, for any Commonwealth secretariat, or imperial defence mechanisms."[49]

By February 1948, less than eighteen months after his arrival in London, the restless Robertson began to campaign in Ottawa for his return to his old job as under-secretary of state for external affairs. He had not "hesitate[d] to make clear to me his preference to be back in Canada and to hold the position here that he had before." King was acquiescent. "I really think Robertson's judgement is sounder than Pearson's ... less likely to get the Govt. into trouble." Pearson was too energetic, too fond of travelling, too committed to participation in collective security and too much given to advising "both the United Kingdom and the United States as to what it is wisest for them to do."[50] Jetti Robertson reinforced her husband's request by asking to see the prime minister when he was in London in October. King recorded "we had a nice little talk together. I spoke of the name that Norman had made for all of us here [in Britain] and how well he had done ... She said that Norman liked England, but she thought his heart was really in [the] External Affairs Department. I said he was more than a departmental man. That he was a government man – very helpful for policies generally. I said that we had missed him very much."[51]

In France in September, Georges Vanier had been "delighted beyond words" at King's suggestion that he should be high commissioner if Robertson were soon to vacate the post. Robertson remained in London, however, for another year, as Pearson, now minister, indicated that he would prefer Arnold Heeney, the clerk of the Privy Council, as under-secretary. St Laurent, having succeeded King as prime minister in November, decided that Robertson would be clerk of the privy council and secretary to the cabinet. Dana Wilgress later recalled that in January 1949, Robertson, temporarily in Geneva for discussions about a common currency for divided Berlin, had told him "that he was being transferred to become secretary to the cabinet and [that] the Department of External Affairs had asked him to sound me out on the possibility of my succeeding him as High Commissioner in London."[52] St Laurent, during his two years as secretary of state for external affairs, had relied heavily on Pearson's advice,

In 1948 the British government mounted a "Britain Says Thank You" exhibition, one expression of the widespread gratitude for Canadian economic assistance, both wartime and immediate postwar, to a badly battered country. Norman Robertson, on the first of his two tours as high commissioner, escorted the formidable Queen Mary through the exhibition.

especially about senior appointments in the foreign service. The fact that Robertson had been asked by Pearson and not by St Laurent to sound Wilgress on a transfer from Berne to London fitted with the thinking that London had become more of a conventional diplomatic post, although in a way still *primus inter pares*. However, neither the subsequent appointment of Robertson to Ottawa nor Wilgress to London were notably successful, experienced, intelligent, and knowledgeable though they both were.

CHAPTER TEN

Dana Wilgress, 1949–1952

Dana Wilgress was delighted to be appointed to what he later described "as the [post] most sought-after in the service. It was in fact the most interesting government position available to any Canadian, not a member of the cabinet ... the busiest office in the diplomatic service."[1] It is, however, difficult at this distance to understand why Wilgress, whatever his enthusiasms, was appointed. Undeniably he was experienced, having begun his career as Canadian trade commissioner in Omsk in 1916, thirty-three years before. Subsequent service in Vladivostok, Bucharest, London, and Hamburg had equipped him for more senior appointments in the Department of Trade and Commerce, including as deputy minister. Along with Norman Robertson, he was Canada's most experienced trade negotiator, having been involved in almost every major trade negotiation throughout the 1930s. In 1943 he was appointed minister (and later ambassador) to the Soviet Union. During the immediate postwar years, he wore two hats as minister to Switzerland and as Canada's delegate to the preparatory commission which eventually led to the General Agreement on Tariffs and Trade (GATT).

In his disappointing *Memoirs*, published when he was seventy-five years old and suffering from a stroke, Wilgress candidly acknowledged that he had done in London what Norman Robertson had advised him to do: "just to place myself in the hands of the staff and relax," at least with regard to his representational activities. Of his long-serving deputy, Frederic Hudd, the diffident Wilgress wrote that he

understood the eccentricities of life in London. He advised me on what invitations to accept and not to accept, whom to cultivate and whom to avoid, and on a lot of little things which could spell success or failure in the position of High Commissioner ... [there was also] the Social Secretary, without whose expert assistance I could never have managed in London. She advised on whom

I should entertain and in what manner ... those rating an invitation to a cocktail party, to a luncheon or a dinner.[2]

In all this, Wilgress and his Russian-born Swiss wife Olga sound as if they were something of babes in the London woods, but worse perhaps was that "speeches always caused me great difficulty."[3] As Robertson had observed to King in 1946, "he is more effective on paper than in conversation."[4]

It was not that Wilgress lacked representational facilities: he and his wife moved into the newly leased Canadian residence on Upper Brook Street, a few hundred metres from Grosvenor Square, in the spring of 1950.* In part to mark the event, the social secretary evidently advised him to offer an inaugural luncheon in honour of the King and Queen. One of the last official acts of Wilgress was to join the other high commissioners in escorting the coffin of the King from Westminster Hall to Windsor Castle. On that occasion, Wilgress appears to have been more certain of his Commonwealth commitment: "I felt privileged to have been a participant in one of those tributes of emotion and affection that characterize the strength and solidarity of the British family of nations."[5]

That strength and solidarity continued to be severely tested, at least economically, from Wilgress's first day at Canada House. Britain's dollar crisis continued unabated, cutting sharply into Canadian exports, despite the best efforts of a meeting of Commonwealth finance ministers and a tripartite meeting of senior officials in Washington, both attended by Robertson. A massive devaluation of the pound helped temporarily. The demand for resources triggered by war in Korea from mid-1950 restored Canadian exports, but they went to the United States and not to Britain which, in attempting to meet the high costs of rearmament and full participation in the war, experienced yet more debilitating inflation and severe balance-of-payments difficulties. In parallel, US investment, especially in Canadian resource industries, soared.

Wilgress, as high commissioner, was in any event unable to spend much time on bilateral economic relations, that being centred in large part on Robertson in Ottawa. During his three-year term, Wilgress was absent from London for long periods, heading delegations to the multilateral

---

* The Wilgresses would have moved into a more spacious residence in Kensington Palace Gardens if Mackenzie King had not rejected the gift by the estate of Sir Harry Oakes as being too opulent.

GATT and to NATO and travelling to Ottawa to discuss their work. In 1947, two years before his arrival in London, Wilgress had participated at both Geneva and Havana in the abortive attempt to devise an international trade organization acceptable to the United States Congress. Under the terms of the GATT, imperial preferences were allowed to linger on, matched by a commitment by Britain – at an unspecified date – to restore sterling convertibility.

Wilgress's absences from London were partly a reflection of the conviction in Ottawa that his experience of the Soviet Union gave him a unique Canadian understanding of the need for collective security in face of its hostility. His reports from Moscow between 1943 and 1946, urging patience with the obsession of the Soviet Union about its security but also warning that there would be "a reaction against excessive adulation [in the West] when it was discovered that the Soviets were as totalitarian as the Germans," had been read with particular attention in Ottawa. Additionally, when Wilgress was appointed to London, the conviction had grown that Canada House was in fact no longer "the busiest office in the diplomatic service." The high commissioner, if supported, as Wilgress certainly was, by a notably competent staff, would have time for temporary assignments elsewhere in Europe. For Wilgress these assignments were to become more time-consuming than his duties as high commissioner. In the case of trade negotiations, as the much respected chairman of the first five sessions of the Contracting Parties of the GATT, he departed almost immediately after his arrival in London for the third session in Annecy, France, remaining there from April to August 1949 and hence absent from the special conference of Commonwealth prime ministers in April 1949 which resolved the question of how republics could be members. The following year, he was in Geneva from February to April for the fourth session. Later in 1950 he was in Ottawa, in part to brief the cabinet on NATO. He was in Torquay, England for the fifth GATT session for much of the period from September 1951 to April 1952.

What Wilgress did during his prolonged absences was largely determined by an interdepartmental committee on external trade policy chaired by Robertson which, for example, guided him in protesting United States anti-dumping practices and its restrictions on the import of Canadian dairy products in particular. Yet more fundamentally, Wilgress was to recognize, "now that the United States indicated that it would not ratify the Havana Charter for an International Trade Organization, the GATT remains the only multilateral instrument under which negotiations can be arranged to deal with tariffs and related questions ... [Canadian delegates] should ... support measures designed to ensure the stability of the GATT organization and the provision of the necessary financial support."[6]

In April 1949, only a few weeks following his arrival in Britain, Wilgress sent to Pearson a long dissertation about the periodic meetings of high commissioners, based on his attendance at two such meetings held every other Friday. The hand of someone else – likely Hudd – seems implicit in the letter, given the familiarity with which it deals with practices during the terms of Massey and Robertson.

For some time before his departure ... Mr. Robertson was perturbed by the course which the High Commissioners' meetings seemed to be taking, but he was too busy during his last six weeks here to do anything about it. In the course of the last year it appears that the Commonwealth Relations Office has gradually reinstituted the practice of regular meetings of High Commissioners, and the two which I have attended, if they are typical, and I am assured that they are, also lead me to believe that it is a matter which we cannot any longer let drift without an examination of all its implications.

Wilgress declared himself worried by the nature of the meetings, presumably as conscious as Hudd of Mackenzie King's adamant opposition and uncertain of St Laurent's attitude.

While the reasons produced in 1927 against having the meetings of High Commissioners have not quite the same force today, nevertheless there is still ... a possibility that some of my colleagues and/or the United Kingdom Government may wish to interpret the meetings as constituting some sort of inner Cabinet of the Empire ... In addition to having little utility value, they tend to become forums for discussion of controversial points, and often after some of the more violent discussions, those High Commissioners who have been most vocal have to admit that they are talking only for themselves and do not know what their governments' policies are. To my way of thinking, the meetings are actually doing harm by the exacerbation of personal relationships, due largely to the personalities of the Australian, Indian and Ceylonese High Commissioners ... The one really useful reason I can think of for continuing the meetings is that it does give us an opportunity to find out the special approach to world problems of the new Dominions. On many occasions the Indian, Pakistan or Ceylonese High Commissioners have produced refreshing light on some international development, which, for my part at any rate, I would not have thought of. Since our contacts with these three Dominions are not very close, there is perhaps something to be said for the opportunity which these meetings afford us of finding out their points of view. ... a very real question arises as to whether these meetings of High Commissioners serve a useful purpose and should continue to receive our support.[7]

Although Wilgress had been unable to come to any conclusions or recommendations, the laconically positive reply from Ottawa a full six months later was decidedly different than it would have been if King were still in office: "It does not seem advisable for us to stay out of the arrangements if the other countries concerned are anxious to continue it."[8] The response did nod in the direction of King's traditional opposition by adding that of course Canada participated on the understanding that no sort of Commonwealth cabinet was contemplated. The addition of this irrelevancy was apparently felt to be a necessary if anachronistic genuflexion to King's memory as late as September 1949, whatever the realities and benefits to Canada of the contemporary Commonwealth. The fact was that the Commonwealth was changing almost beyond recognition.

A new form of Commonwealth collaboration soon emerged from the first meeting of its foreign ministers in January 1950 in Ceylon. There the means of strengthening the vulnerable economies of Asian members were discussed, including technical assistance. As a result, the Colombo Plan was launched within the year. It was a Commonwealth initiative, but the economic realities of the postwar world meant that the necessary resources to make the plan a reality would only be available if the United States somehow participated. Accordingly, almost as soon as it was launched, the pioneering Colombo Plan lost something of its distinctive Commonwealth character. But it did remain the precedent, along with the United Nations Technical Assistance Programme, for a range of later international development activities.

When in 1951 the British government proposed a meeting of the Commonwealth prime ministers, St Laurent was prompt to accept. In a speech to the Canada Club in London, he declared optimistically that in the polarized world of the cold war, the new Commonwealth offered one of the few places where Asians and westerners could meet candidly and informally. In July, with King gone and Skelton's suspicions all but forgotten, the Department of External Affairs urged that any Canadians who had continued to do so should cease looking at the Commonwealth as if it served primarily British interests and should evaluate it objectively in terms of Canadian interests. A departmental policy paper sent to Wilgress shortly before a visit to Ottawa of the recently re-elected Churchill asserted belatedly, "Canada need no longer fear domination from Whitehall, but we are increasingly aware of the overwhelming influence ... of Washington." This tardy insight led to the timid conclusion – revolutionary although it would have been in King's time – that

the Canadian Government should now be prepared to modify slightly [*sic*] its attitude towards attempts to have the Commonwealth speak with one voice in world affairs ... there may be occasions on which it will serve our purpose to have the Commonwealth take a united stand on an issue ... It may well serve Canada's interest to increase the influence and prestige of the Commonwealth association by active cooperation in foreign affairs ... Our policy should now be that if we agree that concerted action is necessary, we should unhesitantly pursue it along with the rest of the Commonwealth, and not qualify and hedge as we have often done in the past.

This thinking clearly recognized the decline of British power compared to that of the Soviet Union and the United States.

The inability of the United Kingdom to speak on equal terms with these two Great Powers makes it very difficult for her to exercise a moderating influence on the policy of either, as she would undoubtedly be inclined to do.

This is an obviously deplorable situation and one which should be remedied if any remedy can be found. The remedy most advocated at present is that of building up the Commonwealth as a whole into a Great Power which could exercise the influence on world events formerly exercised by the United Kingdom, alias the British Empire. This policy is contrary to that of Canada, which has always felt that it was essential for her independent national status and the understanding of this by foreign countries that she should avoid giving grounds for suspicion that her foreign policy was framed under British influence. In particular, the major consideration of Canadian foreign policy has been the maintenance of friendly and confidential relations with the United States; this has depended in the past, and still largely depends, on leaving no reason for the United States to suppose that Canadian policy is influenced unduly by any country whose interests are less closely allied to those of the United States than Canada's are.

The present question for the Canadian Government to consider is, therefore, how far we can and should go in trying to build up a common front among the nations of the Commonwealth, with a view to making the Commonwealth a strong moderating influence in the world.

The memorandum did not go so far as to suggest that such a moderating influence might be assisted by close and continuing Commonwealth consultation, but it did recognize that Canada, under King, had "distrusted proposals for Commonwealth machinery, as disguised attempts to re-establish imperial control. Granting such extensive powers to high commissioners or individual cabinet ministers might obscure the ultimate responsibility of each Commonwealth government for formulating its own policy." Given its past reluctance to participate in any machinery in the Commonwealth, the paper added wryly that Canada's participation in the machinery of NATO was a contradiction.[9]

The election of Churchill's final government in October 1951 and the accession of Queen Elizabeth II in February 1952 raised questions of how countries of the Commonwealth, especially India and Pakistan, might best describe the new monarch. In Canada's case, "Queen of Canada" was employed, but throughout this rather metaphysical discussion, Wilgress was not much involved, relations with the monarchy being conducted primarily through the office of the governor general. Similarly, the high commissioner's role in the appointment of Massey as the first Canadian-born governor general was slight; it was arranged chiefly between Rideau Hall and the Palace. It was Pearson who had the pleasure of inquiring of his erstwhile head of mission as early as February 1950 whether he would accept the appointment. Massey's response was enthusiastic, but it was not until January 1952 (when Massey was on a private visit to Britain) that he assumed office: Churchill had brought Lord Alexander's term as governor general to a conclusion by appointing him secretary of state for defence, thereby opening the way for Massey's designation.

In the formative period of NATO, Pearson and Robertson had won only lukewarm British support for Article 2 of the draft North Atlantic Treaty – the so-called Canadian clause, conceived in March 1948. Article 2 stated that discussions of additional economic cooperation, however well intended, should not impede the early acceptance of mutual military obligations. As Wilgress later recorded, "it is the feeling of the United Kingdom authorities that this article was included largely at Canada's request" and they wanted to know what exactly had Canada in mind.[10] Ottawa, however, remained divided, replying lamely to Wilgress, "members of the Canadian Government ... have stressed the fact that the Treaty would not be solely a military alliance. It is therefore to be hoped that the Organization ... will include organs for ... economic collaboration, although adding that 'the Canadian Government has no specific suggestion to make ... with respect to the economic machinery which might be established under the Treaty.'"

Here was a classic case of a minister (Pearson) attempting a major policy initiative in the face of the scepticism and even covert opposition of some bureaucrats. "Canadian officials in the Department of Finance and Trade and Commerce, as well as in the Bank of Canada, were opposed on economic grounds and even senior diplomats such as Hume Wrong and Dana Wilgress considered Pearson's aim unrealistic and declined to take it seriously."[11] Some spoke derisively of the "North Atlantic Commonwealth." The real problem was in Washington, where the secretary of state, Dean Acheson, was convinced that any meaningful economic article would raise unnecessary problems with Congress. John Holmes, who was engaged in the discussions with the Foreign Office, recalled later:

It was the ingenious approach of Norman Robertson who realized among other things that a controversy had developed within External Affairs and between External Affairs and its friends abroad which was self-perpetuating and out of touch with reality. For some, this step ended the hope of economic action under Article 2. For others it ended the necessity. It was a good functionalist measure. OEEC, with its own membership, could deal with economics, and NATO consisting of those willing to fight, would be the military organ. Drew [leader of the Conservatives] and Coldwell [leader of the CCF] both endorsed this Canadian association with OEEC when it was announced in the Commons, thereby taking some of the heat off Article 2.[12]

Mutual Aid, the gift of military equipment to NATO allies, and the vexed question of whether Turkey and Greece should be NATO members, occupied much of the time of the high commissioner and of his staff, along with the NATO-related questions of finance, defence research, and flying training in Canada. In addition to being the representative on the NATO Deputies Council in London, Wilgress was a delegate to the first session of the North Atlantic Council, held in Ottawa. There the unrepentant advocates of the economic as well as the military cohesion of NATO still seemed to him to have no definite idea of what they expected. Upon his return to London in October 1951, Wilgress wrote about his continuing bewilderment:

I have long been mystified as to what exactly was the reason why we sponsored Article 2 of the [North Atlantic] Treaty. Ever since I became Canadian Deputy I have not been able to obtain instructions as to what position I should take whenever the question of "implementation of Article 2" came up for discussion ... I have never been able to take seriously the proposal for closer integration with the North Atlantic countries ... The Schuman Plan[*] and the Pleven Plan may be considered to be the first steps in the creation in western Europe of a great new power "comprising roughly the territories of the Empire of Charlemagne." However, this development is one which is fraught with some danger ... This could only be avoided if the United Kingdom could take part in the closer integration ... Since I have been in London, I have seen that this is impossible because the United Kingdom has no more desire of becoming embroiled in close integration with the countries of the Continent than Canadians are likely to have in becoming embroiled in a closer integration of the North Atlantic countries.[13]

The "Canadian article," although finally incorporated in the North Atlantic Treaty, faded away, largely unloved and unwanted, except by Robertson and Pearson. Eventually it was awkwardly subsumed into western European integration, freeing Wilgress from having to puzzle over what it all meant.

During Wilgress's three years in London, Britain continued to move haltingly and for the most part reluctantly toward greater European economic integration as the most promising route to its economic renewal. Western Europe itself was on the move with a proposal in May 1950 to establish an European coal and steel community. To the meeting of Commonwealth Foreign Ministers in Colombo in January 1950, Pearson welcomed "the prospect of closer economic co-operation among the countries of Western Europe," before turning to the particular plight of Britain:

We would not like the United Kingdom to be embarrassed or inhibited in examining these European proposals, some of which originate in the United States, on their merits because of fears that Canada as a member of the Commonwealth would unreasonably object. On a great number of occasions Mr. Bevin has shown high courage and a lively sense that it is often necessary to go forward even though there are a lot of difficulties in the way, some of them obscure ones. We in Canada would not like him to be prevented from making another such act of faith because of the feeling that Canada as a member of the Commonwealth is unreasonably frightened of the unknown.[14]

* The Schuman Plan of 1950 established the European Coal and Steel Community in which Britain declined to participate.

By the summer of 1951, the Department of External Affairs had shifted its attention to the value of Commonwealth economic connections as it contemplated the treaty establishing the European Coal and Steel Community, signed on 18 April 1951.

Apart from the economic disadvantages of being too closely connected with the unstable United States market, the steep decline in our trade with Commonwealth countries and the concomitant increase in our trade with the United States has probably decreased our political and economic bargaining power *vis-à-vis* that country. A continuation of this trend might in the long run compromise our political independence ... we should direct our efforts toward maintaining economic connections with Commonwealth countries as they represent a cohesive political association which can be used to offset United States pressure.[15]

This was again revolutionary stuff, especially when coupled with the department's earlier question of how far Canada should now go in attempting to build a common foreign policy front among the nations of the Commonwealth.

Wilgress was involved in consultations in a more substantial way when he joined the delegation to the first meeting of Commonwealth finance ministers, held in London in mid-January 1952. It was not an easy meeting for Canada, the only member of the Commonwealth outside the sterling bloc, preoccupied as the conference was with "the long-term prospects of the Sterling Area and the possibility of an eventual move to, or substantially towards, convertibility." The somewhat preaching tone of the Canadian delegation was unmistakable, even in the pious report that Wilgress sent to Ottawa:

None of the officials here is too hopeful that the measures which it has been agreed to recommend to Commonwealth Governments either will be implemented or, if implemented, would be effective in preventing a recurrence of crisis ... it seems pretty well agreed that it would be inopportune for Canada, at this stage, to play an active role in suggesting policies to be adopted by the Sterling Area countries which we may think are right for them and which, at the same time, would advance our cherished long-term objectives of multilateral trade, non-discrimination and convertibility ... Such an initiative on our part, if followed through, might have broken the Sterling Area and would hardly have served our long-term interest, quite apart from the damaging effect which it would have had on Canada-United Kingdom relations. There seems to be no doubt that the better policy is to let the pressure of events bring about the kind of atmosphere and policies which the situation in our view appears to demand.[16]

Having begun his career as a trade commissioner in Omsk in Siberia in 1916, Dana Wilgress was wholly at ease with his trade promotion responsibilities when high commissioner in London from 1949 to 1952. He was on hand to welcome King George VI and Queen Elizabeth to the Canadian display at the 1945 British industrial fair. The presence of a Canadian exhibit may appear incongruous at a fair focused on reviving British industrial capacity, but postwar Canada was eager to restore its exports to Britain.

Those pressures of events soon arrived in the form of the third major dollar crisis that confronted Britain and the sterling zone since 1945. Between June 1951 and March 1952 imports from dollar countries were sharply curtailed by Britain, an unhappy response to the short-term challenge to its solvency. With many a grumble in Ottawa, the advice of Wilgress to be patient was followed, there being in fact no other option.

Despite his multilateral distractions, Wilgress repeated from Canada House the familiar bilateral lament regarding the overlapping jurisdictions of the High Commission and the offices of provincial agents general. He wrote to Robertson, worse still, that "The office of one [federal] Department can no longer be considered in isolation from the others and there is room for a much greater degree of co-ordination of the activities of the various Departments ... in the interests of efficiency and economy ... the total personnel of Canadian Government employees in London, excluding those in the offices of the provinces, is approaching the 500 mark. In 1939, only seven Departments were represented here. We now have twelve departmental offices and also a number of Canadian Government agencies."[17] He received no response to his misgivings.

In promoting British emigration to Canada, Wilgress had raised with the director of immigration the question that every high commissioner had addressed since Galt: how to increase the number of British emigrants to Canada. War brides had provided a temporary surge, but when Wilgress arrived in London, the annual total of British emigrants had declined to forty thousand from forty-five thousand. He had, however, no specific suggestions to make about reversing the downward trend, other than believing that a more active Australian promotion campaign was having an adverse impact on emigration to Canada, as it had done almost a century before. He argued that the real problem arose from differences among London representatives of federal departments, although more important was the limited allowance that Britain, desperately short of dollars, would permit an emigrant to transfer to his or her new homeland. Wilgress did, however, succeed in shortening the queue of emigrants by obtaining Ottawa's agreement to subsidize fares on British Overseas Airways Corporation and Trans-Canada Airlines flights to Canada. Such a measure was, however, no panacea: a backlog of about twenty thousand emigrants remained. With some difficulty, agreement was reached at the end of 1951 to have both BOAC and TCA offer weekly charter flights in an additional, although inadequate, effort to reduce the waiting list. No such problems existed with regard to would-be emigrants to Canada from the British West Indies, India, Ceylon, or Pakistan since strict limits continued to apply to them. Caribbean immigrants were not to exceed two hundred family members of Canadian citizens. In the case of south Asia, the annual limits for India were increased to 150, to one hundred for Pakistan, and to fifty for Ceylon.

NATO was a direct expression of the cold war. So too was Korea, where a hot war began in that highly unstable, divided and impoverished country in June 1950, a little more than a year after the signature of the North Atlantic Treaty. The invasion of South Korea by North Korea, backed by both the Soviet Union and China, achieved immediate success as North Korean troops drove southward from the thirty-eighth parallel, raising questions among Europeans whether the United States, having prompted

Mackenzie King's continuing nightmare of an "imperial council" dominated by the British led him to oppose throughout his many years as prime minister consultation among the Dominions, including periodic meetings in London of the high commissioners with the British prime minister or ministers. However, in 1951 Dana Wilgress (centre) joined other high commissioners in meetings held every other Friday with the secretary of state for Commonwealth relations, Patrick Gordon Walker (second from right). By then the meetings were of less significance, given the decline in the international influence of Britain and the increasing disparity among Commonwealth members.

United Nations' intervention against the communist aggressor, would now replace its lingering anti-colonial rhetoric with anti-communist rhetoric and whether it would support action against communist insurgents in Malaya and in Indo-China, as well as "unleashing" Chiang Kai-Chek from Taiwan in his constantly threatened attempt to return to mainland.

Wilgress reported that Britain, a permanent member of the Security Council, would support a UN resolution calling upon member states to provide military support to beleaguered South Korea. In the Canadian House of Commons, George Drew, the opposition leader and long-time militant anti-communist, contended vigorously (he always spoke vigorously) that what was at stake was not only the future of Korea but also the future of the United Nations itself. King did not agree. From the sidelines, he contended vainly that rather than involve itself in a distant conflict, Canada should withdraw from membership in the United Nations. Now only a few weeks from death, his influence, as in the case of all former prime ministers and ministers, had all but vanished on the day that he had left office.

The fierce fighting soon involved British as well as American troops and, not long after, forces from Canada, Australia, and New Zealand (but not India and Pakistan). Attlee's prompt decision to send substantial forces arose partly from pressure from Washington in the wake of the triumphant Berlin airlift, but it increased debilitating defence expenditures, with dire implications for Britain's already severe balance-of-payments difficulties. The nature of a Canadian contribution was discussed at several cabinet meetings, including one on 27 July 1950 held on a special train carrying the corpse of Mackenzie King to burial in Toronto. In light of the prompt US and British action, Canadian involvement was agreed in principle more quickly than the subsequent question of whether Canadian units should be designated as part of a Commonwealth division.

By the end of August, Pearson sent to Wilgress (as representative to NATO) a statement worthy of the late prime minister: "We are not in favour of the constitution of a Commonwealth Division, as such, but we are in favour of troops from the various Commonwealth nations serving in the same divisional formation."[18] On this occasion, the British for once declined to defer to this mealy-mouthed legacy of King. If Canada did not want to participate in a Commonwealth division to be formed otherwise by Australia, Britain, and New Zealand, that was Canada's decision. Urged on by the Toronto *Globe and Mail* and the *Vancouver Sun* among others, Ottawa capitulated, but it was only in the autumn of 1951 that Ottawa finally brought itself to employ with any ease the term "Commonwealth Division." Surprisingly, the long and protracted gestation of what to an outsider was an obvious designation had not involved Wilgress; discussions were almost wholly with and through the British High Commission in Ottawa, with Robertson chairing interdepartmental meetings.

Concurrently, the cabinet had been debating a NATO request for a Canadian brigade in West Germany (additional to the one in Korea). When the cabinet approached its favourable decision in April 1951, the chief of the general staff was ready with a well-argued paper which ranged well beyond the impracticability of Canada attempting to establish its own supply system (or "line of communication") for its proposed brigade.

The question for Canada to decide is whether it is in her best interests to move in a direction which may start a land-slide towards the US camp and assure the complete dominance of the US, or whether her influence should be used as one of the locking stones in building a dam against this strong pressure ... Canadian forces are going to be more and more closely associated with US forces in North American defence. It seems desirable that outside of North America, there should be a counter-balance to integration and absorption.

If Canadian forces are grouped with British forces it represents merely the continuation of an association which has existed in two world wars and which has been profitable and deeply satisfying to both parties. To group with the US forces now means severing a past connection and establishing a new. Both in the UK and among the other Commonwealth countries, this will be interpreted as a drift from that association at a time when it is in greatest need of support. Canadian statesmen have reiterated on numerous occasions that it is Canadian policy to support the Commonwealth. The grouping of Canadian forces in Europe with those of the US will certainly be widely interpreted as a change from such a policy and as implying on Canada's part some loss of confidence in the practical value of the Commonwealth association.[19]

On 6 November 1951 the chief of the general staff stated flatly that "the Supreme Allied Commander in Europe is placing 27th Canadian Infantry Brigade Group under command of the Commander-in-Chief, British Army of the Rhine."[20]

As a reassurance to Europeans, fearful about local Soviet intentions when American forces were increasingly engaged in distant Korea, the United States declared itself supportive of West German rearmament and an unified NATO command. When General Douglas MacArthur displayed in Japan a growing belief in the efficacy of attacks on Manchuria and of threats, including nuclear, on China, consultation between a deeply-worried London and Ottawa accelerated. In these and other exchanges, however, Wilgress acted as an interlocutor rather than as a policy contributor. He was marginally involved in the decision to base both the Canadian army brigade and twelve fighter squadrons in Germany in recognition of the fact that western Europe, not Asia, was "the vital centre of our global defence." For the brigade in Korea, difficult fighting was followed by a long period of only occasional clashes, but much hardship remained even after the end of the war. For the other two sides of what some whimsically described as the North Atlantic triangle, the war and its eventual termination in a divided Korea had yet again underlined the predominant role of the United States in world affairs and the waning ability of an overextended United Kingdom to undertake global military commitments.

The NATO Council of Deputies had long met weekly in a spacious house on Belgrave Square, but at a meeting in Lisbon in the spring of 1952 the necessity for a better-organized, more effective NATO was recognized. A supreme commander for Europe and a secretary-general were appointed and permanent representatives of member states formed a NATO Council in Paris, the headquarters of both NATO and of the Organization for European Economic Co-operation (OEEC). When Arnold Heeney, the under-secretary of state for external affairs, was transferred to the new NATO council in April 1952, Wilgress was relieved of his double-hat function in London, but soon thereafter his term as high commissioner came to an end.

Robertson, deeply unhappy in Ottawa as secretary of the cabinet, had arranged for himself a second tour in London. Wilgress, surprisingly, was in turn given the under-secretaryship of external affairs, an unsatisfactory appointment that was to last for less than a year, as did Heeney's to NATO. In mid-1953, Heeney went to Washington and Wilgress went back to NATO, on this occasion full-time. In his sketchy memoirs, Wilgress seems a little bewildered by all three moves. Speaking of how he had enjoyed the high commissionership, despite the limited time or attention that he had been able to give it, "it came as something of a shock to learn that I was shortly to leave London to be succeeded by Norman Robertson, whom I had myself succeeded more than three years previously. We sailed from Liverpool late in May, 1952, and had been at sea only a few hours when our ship passed the incoming vessel, which I knew was bringing Robertson to the United Kingdom. I hoped that I should enjoy my new assignment as much as I knew he would enjoy his second one in London."[*][21] Quite what all this coming and going was about is difficult today to be certain. Why Pearson, himself an unofficial candidate for secretary-general of the United Nations, was willing to preside over such churning of appointments remains unclear. In any event, one result was that Robertson became the only incumbent to serve twice as high commissioner.

* Dana Wilgress died in Ottawa on 29 July 1969.

CHAPTER ELEVEN

Norman Robertson, 1952–1957

In April 1952 Norman Robertson, having freed himself from the unloved cabinet secretaryship, returned to a Britain in some respects gradually altering for the better. The National Health Service was beginning to improve the general well-being; higher education was opening to more applicants; and industry was being reformed in a world in which computers were beginning to appear, although commercial exploitation of innovation remained laggard. Britain in 1952 was a little more confident, a little more firmly on the road to eventual economic recovery, but the early 1950s remained a dreary time for most. Currency controls continued; twelve years of petrol and food rationing were just ending. The imaginative Festival of Britain in 1951 and the pageantry of the coronation of Elizabeth II two years later did something to reintroduce almost-forgotten colour and romance, but for the most part daily life remained hard slogging. What advances there were, economically and socially, were longer-term in their benefits.

In the short term, Churchill's last government, formed in 1951 with a precarious plurality over Labour, was faced with the all-too-familiar challenges of balance-of-payment difficulties and the uncertain course of the cold war. Neither Britain nor the Commonwealth were what they had been. The independence of Burma, Ceylon, India, and Pakistan had been achieved (although Burma had elected to leave the Commonwealth, following Ireland). A terrible communal price was paid, however, in the division of India and the later fighting in Malaya and Kenya. Eventually apartheid policies of South Africa would underline the fact that the retreat from Empire was not without its bumps and that the postwar Commonwealth would not be free of dissension and dispute. Against this kaleidoscopic background, the United Kingdom began to grope toward some new relationship with western Europe. The rapid consolidation of NATO under United States leadership had successfully incorporated North America in the defence of western Europe against Soviet aggression – a divided Germany offering the most obvious flashpoint – but in so doing had underlined the fact that Britain and France neither separately nor together could play the prime role in the defence of western Europe against the Soviet Union. On the other side of the world, the Korean War had been fought to an uneasy stalemate, but it had left a profound unease about the intentions and might of China which, having intervened militarily in Korea, seemed likely to hazard its arm next in an effort to regain its province of Taiwan.[1]

Secretary to the cabinet had certainly not proven to be a happy appointment for Robertson. His wife later recalled his immediate reaction upon becoming head of the public service: "the new job is a mistake. There is nothing for me to do."[1] Within three months, he had written to Arnold Heeney, the under-secretary of state for external affairs, that he had come to "the conclusion that the best way to clear up an unsatisfactory situation is to move me somewhere else for two or three years."[2] Bizarrely, Robertson had again proposed that he be ambassador to Switzerland or Yugoslavia or even Canada's first representative to the Vatican – all this from someone who in his first London posting had yearned to be again at the centre of policy formulation. "Robertson's time as Clerk of the Privy Council and Secretary to the Cabinet had not been a success. He had realized quickly that he had made a mistake in returning to Ottawa, but had hung on, his unhappiness evident to his close friends and colleagues. By late 1951 ... St. Laurent ... had the impression that Robertson would prefer to return to London. St. Laurent was willing – 'if that is what he wants to do we'll just arrange it.'"[3]

Something more fundamental was also in play, making for a less than happy second posting for Robertson in Britain. *Canada in World Affairs, 1953–1955*, published periodically by the Canadian Institute of International Affairs, reflected the reason. "In this volume ... there is [for the first time] no separate section on Great Britain or the Commonwealth. This omission has been deliberate. In this period, neither Great Britain nor the Commonwealth ... occupied a place of very apparent prominence in Canadian foreign policy."[4] The staff at Canada House, both Canadian-based and locally-engaged, nevertheless remained numerous, totalling more than five hundred. Robertson was again to find their administration both bothersome and difficult. After failing to arrange the appointment of his old friend C.M. Drury, the deputy minister of defence, as his deputy, he was supported by the experienced former ambassador to Brazil who had the additional merit of sharing his passion for bridge.

Robertson was fully familiar with the question that pressed most heavily on postwar Britain and on Anglo-Canadian relations: its continuing inability to export enough to the dollar area to pay for its essential dollar imports and interest on its dollar borrowings. The long-term positive solution was to increase its dollar exports; the short-term negative solution was to make further reductions in imports from dollar countries. In West Germany economic recovery began to accelerate, initially fuelled by the Marshall Plan, but Britain remained debilitated by the seemingly endless confusions of sterling crises, of balance-of-payment difficulties, of inflation and export stagnation, of looking, in Robertson's words, "for a cure to sterling's recurrent crises in external rather than domestic measures." A Commonwealth economic conference of prime ministers was convened in November–December 1952 upon the recommendation of the Commonwealth finance ministers who had met at the beginning of the year. During the preceding months of preparation, Robertson had reported a conversation with R.A. Butler, the chancellor of the exchequer, who had agreed with his observation that given the "light-hearted way in which [his] government had proposed a Commonwealth conference ... it would be difficult ... to make substantial progress."[5] Robertson could suggest little in the way of positive contribution, Canada being the only Commonwealth country outside the sterling bloc.

Ottawa remained unenthusiastic about the whole idea of a Commonwealth economic conference, instructing Robertson to tell Churchill that Canada could not countenance "any impression that the Commonwealth is seeking to create a common front against the United States."[6] He was spared the humiliation of delivering this bizarre lecture by the prime minister's absence from London, but the world-weary Lord Salisbury, the secretary of state for Commonwealth relations, received a muted version, presumably taking it for what it was worth. At preparatory committee meetings, Robertson allowed himself a similar world-weary rejoinder to Ottawa: "There is no particular need at this juncture for any public preaching from Canada about what the United Kingdom should do to be saved."[7]

In the end, little that was immediate or concrete came of the conference beyond the timely expansion of Colombo Plan development assistance, the British government remaining convinced that it could not yet risk either full sterling convertibility or a reduction of quantitative restrictions on imports from beyond the sterling bloc. Thus Canadian exporters, including the growing number of subsidiaries of United States corporations, became even more dependent upon the market to the south.

Robertson worked tirelessly at the conference, attempting to explain sterling diplomacy to Canada and dollar diplomacy to Britain, adding an
occasional pro forma appeal to Britain to commit "as soon as possible" to
full convertibility of sterling and to the reduction or elimination of trade
barriers, policies repeatedly pressed by the United States in both the IMF
and the GATT.

In June 1954, two years after the conference, at a meeting chaired by
Robertson of the United Kingdom–Canada Committee on Trade and
Economic Affairs, a senior British official continued to stress that there
could be no firm timetable for convertibility of sterling. Equally, Commonwealth discussions about the GATT achieved little, with Britain coupling its reluctance to make sterling convertible with its unwillingness
to negotiate away Commonwealth preferences. The 1954 conference of
Commonwealth finance ministers in Sydney proved little more productive than the 1952 conference. Even less productive – at least from a Canadian viewpoint – was the subsequent gathering of the Commonwealth
finance ministers concurrent with the IMF and World Bank meetings in
Washington. Walter Harris had succeeded Douglas Abbott as finance
minister. R.A. Butler was the chancellor of the exchequer. Heeney, now
ambassador in Washington, wrote to Robertson, reporting that the first
encounter between Harris and Butler "was hardly a case of love at first
sight," there being no meeting of minds about what might best be done to
resolve sterling-dollar discord, Harris repeating the unwanted advice that
non-resident sterling convertibility should soon be reintroduced.[8]

From London in early 1955, Robertson injected himself, as he had in
the past, into discussions of how to handle a major trade dispute with the
United States. A blanket waiver for its agricultural protectionism had been
sought by Washington from the other Contracting Parties of the GATT as
the price of congressional endorsement of the GATT's draft revised stat-
utes. Canadian ministers visiting Washington protested, concerned as
they were that the momentum of trade liberalization would suffer a major
blow and set a dangerous precedent for protectionist-minded Europeans
if the United States received a waiver for such a major derogation from its
most-favoured-nation commitment. Ottawa decided to vote against this
early manifestation of US exceptionalism (which, as always, had been justified on the grounds of inescapable demands of domestic politics). Robertson was not so sure. He cautioned Ottawa that "even if we found that
we could muster enough votes to keep the United States from getting the
necessary two-thirds in support of their waiver, I am far from convinced

that it would be wise to defeat the United States on this issue. Have we really examined the implications of driving the United States out of the GATT and presumably destroying the Agreement? ... [Or] Do we intend to leave the GATT when we find that we cannot prevent the United States from getting a waiver?"[9] The high commissioner's somewhat apocalyptic view was not compelling in Ottawa. In the event, Canada joined a minority of GATT members in opposing the waiver; others, including Britain and Australia, held their noses and supported it, fearing the collapse of the GATT itself. For the first time in many years, Robertson's views on a basic trade policy question had not prevailed.

Although NATO, from the autumn of 1952, had a secretary-general and Canada a permanent representative to both NATO and the OEEC, Robertson remained involved in questions of the western alliance, especially during a visit by Pearson to London in September. Anthony Eden and Lord Alexander (home recently from Canada to become secretary of state for defence) and several NATO representatives shared with Pearson and Robertson their misgivings about US pressures on them to mount greater military efforts when their economies, although now recovering, remained fragile. Pearson and Robertson were gratified by the candour of their British interlocutors, but upon returning home Pearson cautioned Robertson against being sucked into a common NATO policy with Britain by the way of consultation. Mackenzie King would have been pleased to read the injunction of Pearson, about whose judgment he had had such doubts, that "it should not be considered that because we receive information from the United Kingdom Government ... the Canadian Government should be required to take the same position as the United Kingdom on questions of interest to NATO."[10] Within a few months, however, Ottawa reversed itself, seeking more information from the Foreign Office on NATO questions and even complaining that the British did not consult Canada sufficiently on NATO.

More straightforward was Robertson's role in arranging, under Canada's mutual aid programme, for the delivery to the RAF of airframes for four hundred jet fighters. At the same time, Robertson continued to be involved in that most elusive of international subjects: disarmament. In recognizing that east-west antagonism was unlikely to generate agreement on even limited monitoring of disarmament, the high commissioner in June 1954 advanced on his own initiative the novel idea that NATO might in effect monitor itself. The merit of the proposal was not only in its practicality; it offered indirectly a way of facilitating West German rearmament – a contentious issue within NATO – in a more reassuring context. It had become clear that proposals for a European Defence Community were going nowhere in the French Assembly; some new way had to be found to contain an urgently-needed and reformed *Wehrmacht* within a NATO framework. Robertson had reluctantly concluded that the idea of an European Defence Community was unlikely to succeed. The British had supported the EDC for others, but in it they would not place their own army. They were no less opposed to any extension to NATO's limited political role. Robertson wrote to Ottawa,

These are the understandable reactions of a great power. The United Kingdom fears to lose its comparative freedom of action in Europe, and its privileged entrée in Washington, by any closer association with the continental countries than appears essential ... The greatest difficulty is likely to arise [with the United States] ... it would appear most unlikely that the United States would be prepared to release information, even to its NATO partners, on the size and distribution of [its] forces other than those specifically committed to NATO commands, and on most aspects of its atomic weapons development and production programme.[11]

When, however, Robertson discussed his thinking with Anthony Eden, the foreign secretary, he ascribed his idea for NATO self-monitoring to Ottawa rather than to himself. He then reported to Ottawa that "the United Kingdom would be extremely interested in studying how you [*sic*] had developed the idea of an armaments control built into NATO. He [Eden] anticipated that difficulties would be made by the United States and probably by his own military advisers, but he thought that ... it might simplify the job of getting [West] Germany in."[12]

From the spring of 1954, Robertson was the chief Canadian representative at the desultory disarmament talks in London between the Soviet Union and the west. Following a deadlock in the larger Disarmament Commission of the United Nations, a London sub-committee composed of the Soviet Union, the United States, Britain, France, and Canada soon became as mired in acrimonious propaganda exchanges as the commission itself had earlier been. Progress was not helped by the fact that the first hydrogen bomb had been exploded by the United States, creating yet more fears about who could do what deadly acts to whom. In Ottawa, Paul Martin Sr, then minister of health and welfare, supervised Canadian disarmament policy, helping to shape it in the direction of mutually agreed arms limitation and control. However, John Holmes was to recall that there was no specifically Canadian interest or approach to be put forward. The paramount Canadian interest was in getting an agreement that would lessen the danger that Russians and Americans would have a nuclear war over their heads. A respectable and useful Canadian contribution was guaranteed by having as participant Norman Robertson who was not only one of the most intellectually gifted but also morally dedicated of senior Canadian external affairs officers. He was an unillusioned idealist. As one of his advisers at the sub-committee later commented: "I think Norman's basic attitude was that the meetings were hopeless, but essential." Neither he nor anyone else would have been naïve enough to imagine that Canada could pose as a mediator in that company or pretend to be neutral. Nevertheless, his ingenuity and imagination made him useful in putting forward suggestions.[13]

When Churchill paid his final visit to Canada at the end of June 1954, Anthony Eden and he were able to report that in Washington an agreement in principle had been reached on how the *Wehrmacht* could best join in the defence of western Europe. Pearson also informed Robertson that Eden and he had done what they could – in the event successfully – to discourage the infirm and aged Churchill, in his single-minded quest for lasting peace, from meeting with the hostile Soviet leadership. Disarmament initiatives were making no progress in a world of deep mutual suspicion.

On an entirely different plane, Robertson was, within a year of his return to London, involved in the planning of Canadian participation in the coronation of Queen Elizabeth II which included, as in 1936, the construction of temporary stands on the Cockspur Street side of Canada House to accommodate some of the thousands of Canadian spectators of the great procession.

The festivities surrounding Elizabeth II's coronation reflected more than a simple loyalty to the Crown, although there was plenty of that. They represented a hope, almost a faith, on the part of millions of Canadians that Britain had recovered from the war and was now back near the top of the international heap. The Commonwealth Conference that coincided with the coronation showed that Canada was still an important member of a functioning international organization, the most important after Britain itself. The Commonwealth, representing Britain and the 'old dominions,' Canada, Australia, New Zealand, and South Africa, as well as the new members, India, Pakistan, and Ceylon, held out the

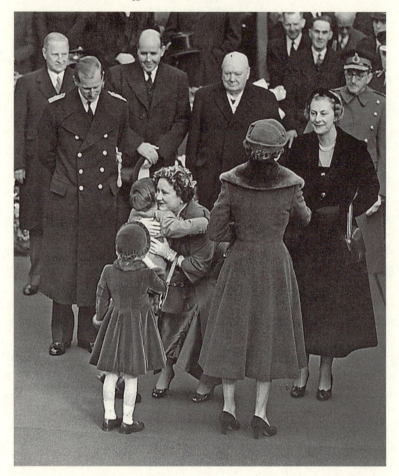

To the amusement of Winston Churchill, Norman Robertson, and
Prince Philip, Prince Charles and Princess Anne break ranks to embrace their grandmother, Elizabeth the Queen Mother, while Queen
Elizabeth greets others (including Field Marshal Lord Alanbrooke to
the right).

promise that it would be a genuine bridge between the underdeveloped world
and the Western powers.

Canadians prided themselves on the fact that the Commonwealth had successfully made the transition from a colonial body to a post-colonial association, from centralized control to decentralized co-operation. But that change
implied another: old Commonwealth institutions lost their significance. Defence

co-operation, for example, gradually unravelled. It was generally admitted that the Commonwealth would never fight again as a single body, because its members could hardly be expected to agree on what would be important enough to fight about; as it later developed, several members of the Commonwealth would war against each other.[14]

During Robertson's first term as high commissioner, the entry into the Commonwealth of those emerging belligerents, Pakistan and India, had profoundly altered it. Now during his second term the impact of the independence of African countries would also be pervasive. That most if not all British colonies would achieve independence in the next years was increasingly acknowledged; it was less clear what this transformation of the Commonwealth would entail. In August 1953 Robertson had drawn Ottawa's attention to the revival in Whitehall of a formula declaring that while the grant of responsible self-government to a colony was a matter for Britain and the colony alone, its membership in the Commonwealth was a question for all members. The increasingly repressive apartheid policies of South Africa had partly prompted this formulation. Robertson noted that the question of defining the terms of membership

brings into relief the dilemma of how the multiracial composition of the Commonwealth can be further extended without irreparable damage being done to the existing structure and fabric ... The United Kingdom authorities appear to have definite misgivings about the wisdom of adding indiscriminately and hastily to the present nucleus of eight full members ... [they] are apprehensive lest the entry of new members [from Africa] should cause the withdrawal of an existing member [South Africa] ... the expansion of the Commonwealth may go far to nullifying the peculiar value of the periodic meetings of Prime Ministers.[15]

For his trouble, the high commissioner finally received a reply from Ottawa fully ten months later. It proved to be a classic on-the-one-hand-but-on-the-other-hand effusion, culminating after five pages in an invitation to Robertson to send "your further views in due course."[16] By that time the 1955 Commonwealth prime ministers' conference had compelled a Canadian response of sorts. With African colonies nearing independence, the British pressed the question on other members whether there should be some sort of interim two-tiered membership or full equality from the beginning. Prompted by Robertson and Pearson, St Laurent joined the majority in opposing concessions to South African sensibilities and opted clearly for complete equality of Commonwealth membership.

Thus was buried, at least temporarily, the latent problem of South African apartheid that was to become acute in three years when John Diefenbaker was prime minister and George Drew high commissioner.

The diary of Pearson, who attended the 1955 conference, records the efforts that Robertson and he made to redraft to the satisfaction of a weary and occasionally depressed St Laurent his various statements and public speeches (in the event they went well, Pearson telling Robertson that "the P.M. could read the London telephone directory and make it sound sincere and moving").[17] On the side, they together discussed with the associate deputy minister of trade and commerce, Mitchell Sharp, in London from Geneva, "the completely negative approach to GATT matters we are taking in Ottawa" as a result of Canada's failure to block the waiver that the United States had demanded for its protectionist agricultural policies. At the Commonwealth meeting itself, Pearson rejoiced in observing Churchill "in really magnificent form – vigorous, imaginative, impressive and picturesque. He also has the same old mischievous glint in his eye ... It is a fascinating cross section of the world which is represented at this conference, with about as many views as there are governments, but everybody very sincerely anxious to benefit from the viewpoints of the others and to find the highest common denominator of agreement."[18] This was Commonwealth consultation with a vengeance. Here everything from the tension over Taiwan, the Middle East, the hydrogen bomb and the cold war was discussed candidly, but even within the Commonwealth, almost every policy had now to be measured against United States attitudes.

Britain and Canada exercised the diplomacy of constraint with their closest ally, but their influence was minimal. Churchill had called for "a place on the bridge within reach of the wheel," but he got no further than a place at the captain's table. The Americans acted in their own interests with no regard for the interests of their allies, and the fact that they came to much the same conclusions about Korea had precious little to do with promptings from London or Ottawa, which were seen as little more than tiresome carping. Korea clearly showed that the United States was a hegemonic power and that the much-vaunted "special relationship" was the fond illusion of a second-rate power.[19]

The conference had covered a range of subjects, revealing as expected a variety of approaches to international tensions, but as the report of the Canadian delegation later stated, "there was no discussion of the constitutional aspects of the Commonwealth or problems of Commonwealth organization. Proposals for greater centralization, the creation of machinery for formal consultation, and suggestions that Commonwealth policy be coordinated and concerted through a permanent secretariat, which have exercised Commonwealth leaders at previous meetings, played no part in the proceedings."[20] There was, however, the consolations of social activities that recalled another era of Commonwealth amity. Pearson recorded, "Tonight a very nice dinner at the Robertson's [residence on Upper Brook Street]; my partner the intelligent and very nice Lady Reading. I've been lucky at these dinners, with Lady Macmillan at Buckingham Palace, and the new Mrs. Herbert Morrison at No. 10."[21]

At the conclusion of the conference, St Laurent spoke words of gratitude to Churchill, who was "deeply moved because he must have known this was the last time he would preside over a Commonwealth meeting – said a few words in reply, and then we just drifted away."[22] What in retrospect was perhaps most notable about the gathering was that it did not concern itself about the future of the Suez Canal, seen as the vital link between Britain and Australia, New Zealand, Hong Kong, and Asian countries of the Commonwealth. A year before, Britain and Egypt had agreed upon the terms governing the withdrawal of the large British garrison from the Canal Zone (British ownership of the canal itself would remain intact). And that, it was widely hoped, was the resolution of that particular post-imperial problem.

Robertson had joined in February 1954 in an unexpected revival of the question of what, if anything, Canada could do to provide substance to Article 2 of the North Atlantic Treaty which had given Dana Wilgress so many misgivings. From his embassy in Bonn, Charles Ritchie had recognized its possible utility as a way of further entrenching West Germany in NATO, but he was no more successful than Wilgress in Paris had been in eliciting a substantive response from Ottawa. In the meantime, however, his reference to Article 2 had at least helped to force Ottawa to think again about transatlantic economic relations. Wilgress, wearing both his NATO and OEEC hats, also waded in, proposing an annual review by the North Atlantic Council of progress made in economic collaboration. Not surprisingly, given his paternity of the idea, Pearson cautioned the department about making a negative response to the recommendations merely on the grounds that some argued that economic collaboration did not belong in NATO. "Some of the Europeans who are quite vocal in supporting the establishment of a discriminatory [tariff] regime for Europe [i.e., the European Economic Community] ... might find it less appropriate to express such views in a NATO Ministerial meeting."[23] However, at the meeting in December 1955, Article 2 became a dead letter. The United States, Britain, and France "were not prepared to intervene" in support of additional transatlantic economic cooperation. What economic discussion there was remained "relatively meagre" compared to that of military questions.

That nothing very much had come of the imaginative Canadian thinking was not the fault of either Robertson or Ritchie. European economic integration gathered momentum (without Britain), but the sense of a North Atlantic free trade area had gathered none at all. The fact was that no major member of NATO wanted transatlantic economic collaboration to impede the early formulation of an European Economic Community. The Canada article finally faded away, never to return. Ironically its demise was concurrent with the beginning of the fourth negotiating round of the GATT in mid-1956 which, in a development not unrelated, increased through tariff reductions the continental links between Canada and the United States.

In June 1955 at Messina, the six members of the European Coal and Steel Community agreed "to work for the establishment of an United Europe by the development of common institutions, the gradual fusion of national economies, the creation of a common market and gradual harmonization of social policies." The long-term significance of the Messina conference leading to the Treaty of Rome was lost on many in Europe and North America alike. One thing, however, became clear; Britain would not join. For the Six it might be all very well, but not for Britain with its Commonwealth, sterling bloc, and a conviction that fundamentally Europe was incorrigibly protectionist. In any case, European economic integration might lead in time to European political federation, an unthinkable prospect for Britain. When Paul-Henri Spaak, the Belgium foreign minister, visited Ottawa, he confirmed what Wilgress and Robertson had reported: Britain had informed the members of the European Coal and Steel Community "that although they [Britain] might participate in a 'freer trade area', they would not be a party to a European common market ... and have continued to oppose all supernationalist trends."[24] At the end of December 1955, Robertson urged caution in the Canadian response:

we should not commit ourselves to a purely negative position which ... which will earn us little sympathy in Europe and which may be blamed for their failure to get together on a common policy. I fully recognize the dangers which the common market proposals imply for Canadian interests, but I have a feeling that these dangers could be neutralized and the common market initiative turned to advantage by correlating it in one way or another with the collective approach to a freer trading world to which we are already committed.[25]

Harold Macmillan, then chancellor of the exchequer, told St Laurent in February 1956 that Britain was still uncertain whether to respond with a proposal for a free trade area embracing both the emerging common market of the Six as well as Britain, Sweden, and Portugal. About possible moves a note of scepticism if not inchoate opposition was beginning to be faintly heard from Ottawa. In time, with a change of government, the volume of hostility would be greatly increased.

Throughout the next twelve months, Ottawa and the missions in London, Paris, and Geneva debated the Canadian response to the emergence of a common market of the six and what would become a free trade area of the seven. In urging a "constructive attitude" towards European unity, Robertson offered an analysis of the challenge facing Britain. "The position of this country in relation to the common market poses a number of difficult problems by no means all of which have been thought through. The basic problem, of course, is how to reconcile the United Kingdom interest in safeguarding its access to the European market on equal terms with the continuation of some form of Commonwealth preference. A free trade arrangement is at least one in which the United Kingdom could conceivably participate without abandoning its preferential commitments altogether."

In September 1956 he reported that, despite the myriad distractions of the Suez crisis, "to all intents and purposes decision has been reached [by Westminster] to associate the United Kingdom with the European common market by way of a free trade arrangement." A response would be required from Canada at the imminent meeting of the Commonwealth finance ministers. The high commissioner again urged a constructive statement:

It is important to recognize that the free trade area association is not 'the easy way out' for this country. It has risks because nobody can say confidentially how the different sectors of the economy will respond to this new challenge. This being so, I should think that our statement would show some recognition of the bold and imaginative nature of the action which the United Kingdom is preparing to take.[26]

In the event, the statement was more sceptical than Robertson had advised, including the observation that "there are many in Canada who take a serious view ... of our alleged economic dependence on the United States. It would be necessary for us, therefore, to give a great deal of thought to proposals for a new and large-scale [European] preferential system which might add to the concern." Robertson, on a visit to Ottawa the following month, pursued his crusade for a balanced approach to European integration which he was to continue during Diefenbaker's hostile government.

Robertson also accompanied St Laurent to the Commonwealth prime ministers' conference of June–July 1956 which decided to welcome the Gold Coast upon its independence in March 1957 as the new state of Ghana. The discussions were wide-ranging, including recurring problems in the Middle East and with China (older Commonwealth members having not recognized *de jure* its communist regime). These and other subjects confirmed that Commonwealth consultation on foreign policy had been achieved – but in a very different Commonwealth. This new-found candour was, however, soon to be put to major strain over the Suez Canal a few months later. That crisis was the final confirmation that the tide of British imperialism was receding across the world in the face of increasing nationalism, that impossible demands were being made on the exchequer to sustain even the remnants of empire and, in the aftermath of the Second World War, that something of a loss of will to set clear international goals and to achieve them had spread through Whitehall and beyond. Perhaps worst of all were differences with Washington. Although an ambivalence existed in US foreign policy as a result of what were considered emerging cold war imperatives, Washington generally remained fixed in its understandable but largely futile efforts to conciliate nationalists in former colonial territories.

The Suez Canal Company was expropriated – or nationalized – in July 1956, placing under exclusive and deeply mistrusted Egyptian control what many British still regarded as the essential link with the east, as well as the short route for oil from the Middle East – what in 1929 Eden had characterized as "the swing door of the Empire." Pearson was increasingly worried about British reaction to Egyptian ambitions, sharing with Robertson his conviction that any unilateral action would fail unless it had the support, both political and economic, of the United States. Robertson in turn told Pearson of his deep misgivings: "I hope that the United Kingdom would not be too quick to gather too many spears to its own bosom." He also shared with Pearson the belief that a peaceful settlement could still be reached; as late as August Pearson assured his cabinet colleagues that the "situation had eased a good deal and he doubted if really serious trouble would occur."[27]

Pearson's optimism was soon undermined. As the crisis deepened, Robertson was in almost daily contact with Alec Douglas-Home, the secretary of state for Commonwealth relations, Selwyn Lloyd, foreign secretary, and their senior officials, urging them to take the matter to the United Nations. Lloyd, Robertson reported, had told him that he "was as ready to bash the Egyptians as anybody, but he had to ask himself where this country and the Commonwealth would stand after the job of bashing had been done."[28] When Lloyd asked Robertson whether Canada would support Britain if it resorted to force, he received a flat "no." In their frequent exchanges, Robertson and Pearson recognized that if force were attempted, Britain would probably need to resume direct control of the Canal Zone, a daunting enough challenge at any time, but one into which the Egyptians rather than Britain would no doubt promptly introduce the United Nations, if not the Soviet Union, in response.

The imbroglio deepened with the coordinated Israeli invasion of Egypt at the end of October and the subsequent Anglo-French military intervention ostensibly to separate the two combatants. Pearson wrote to Robertson about "our feeling of bewilderment and dismay at the decisions which they [the British and French governments] have taken ... decisions which came as a complete surprise to us and which had not been hinted at in any previous discussion."[29] As Robertson reported, meetings of the high commissioners with the foreign secretary had underlined how small was the support in the Commonwealth for the Anglo-French initiative, Australia and New Zealand being the two notable exceptions. The subsequent strain on the United Nations, NATO, and the Commonwealth was profound, as international incredulity grew about the real purpose of the intervention, beyond securing freedom of passage through the waterway, access to Middle East petroleum, and the separation of Israel and Egypt. In Hungary simultaneously, the Soviet Union seized upon the diversion to crush an incipient rebellion against its hegemony, an act of international violence that was largely overlooked as the Suez crisis deepened, "all the more deplorable," in Pearson's words, "in that it prevented the free world from taking a united stand ... against this naked aggression."

Robertson was instructed to seek urgently British reaction (as Heeney was American) to an "adequate UN military force to separate the Egyptians from the Israelis." Anglo-French units had only slowly gathered momentum, hindered by changes of plans, indecision, and muddle, but they were finally ashore in Suez before the United Nations peacekeeping force could be given form and substance. Robertson's role in Canada's contribution to the resolution of the crisis was at first central, given the primacy of Britain's participation in the Suez invasion, placing him in daily contact with ministers and senior officials. It was, however, an acutely difficult time for him. On 31 October he ruefully informed the foreign secretary (who regarded him as ill and depressed):

We had a bad three months in which I had found it difficult to explain to my Government the reasonableness of the policies which his Government had been advocating and acting on since Nasser's seizure of the Canal. I was afraid that some of the foundations of the relationship between Commonwealth countries had been severely shaken. The UK and France had somehow got themselves into a truly tragic position. Neither of them had any closer friend and ally than Canada, but at this pass I could not see what we could do to help.[30]

Charles Ritchie, on a visit to London from his embassy in Bonn, urged, "I hope that in Ottawa they realize the time has come to help save the face of the British over Suez. The British will be there long after Eden has gone and will remain the best bet in a bad world. They should not be humiliated and Canada should be the first to see that."

Israel and France each had its own reasons for conspiring covertly in the armed intervention, as did Britain. But in the end their collusion was victim to the mounting pressure on their vulnerable economies inherent in the eagerness of the United States – with its eye on the Soviet Union – to curb Israel and to conciliate Egypt and its third-world supporters, including India. A crisis of confidence in sterling set in, about which the United States would do nothing, thereby forcing an Israeli withdrawal and an end to British and French intervention. Robertson continued to help shape Canadian involvement in the eventual solution, but the essential focus was now at the United Nations, where the whole depressing story was fraught with deception, exaggeration, misunderstanding, perfidy and, in the eyes of some, a double standard on the part of the United States. From 2 November when Robertson reported that the foreign secretary was "seriously interested" in Canada's proposal for "a UN Police Force ... in the Middle East" and the following day that "they might even be able to vote for it," Pearson worked tirelessly to enable the tripartite forces to withdraw as the United Nations Emergency Force was hastily assembled and despatched, the whole under the command of E.L.M. Burns, the same officer who had worked with Pearson at Canada House in 1939.[31]

In the aftermath, Robertson conveyed to Ottawa the thanks of Anthony Eden for Canada's "steadying influence" at the United Nations, as well as a request for assistance in clearing the canal which the Egyptians had predictably blocked.

The Suez fiasco is imbued with a sense of imperial twilight or of a Britain that, in the later controversial observation of the US secretary of state, Dean Acheson, had lost an empire but had not yet found a role. Not surprisingly, the autumn of 1956 was for Robertson, as he had informed Selwyn Lloyd, "a bad three months." The deep divisions throughout Britain were reflected even in the Foreign Office itself, with the severe illness of Eden only compounding the policy muddle. Robertson lamented, "It is unfortunate ... that at this terribly difficult and indeed decisive moment in British history, the Prime Minister should be one who has lost so much ground politically and physically and has as chief associates two such complicated and unclear personalities as Butler and Macmillan."

Although British uncertainties were a major part of the problem and the remedy to the post-imperial folly was being formulated at the United Nations, Robertson was, nevertheless, a focus of attack, however muted, from some in Britain who had convinced themselves that Nasser of Egypt was a treacherous dictator bent upon the expulsion of the United Kingdom from all territories south or east of Suez. Canada was somehow condoning his nefarious intentions, which were backed by the Soviet Union, although other British regarded their own prime minister's policy as absurd or worse and welcomed Canada's role in helping the three co-belligerents to extricate themselves. The high commissioner more than anyone knew the depth of feeling, silent or articulate, especially among both British and Canadian Conservatives – and the newspapers that supported them – that Canada had abandoned or even betrayed Britain. John Diefenbaker, speaking for many Canadians, railed almost daily at the government: "Canada should not be a mere tail on the American kite but should, as a senior member of the Commonwealth, give to the Government of the United Kingdom moral support and encouragement." Although distant were the days of Meighen's "ready-aye-ready" response to Chanak, Robertson had nonetheless to counter a lingering resentment from some that Canada, unlike Australia and New Zealand, had not lined up with Eden in his ill-conceived Suez venture. Certainly much of the fun had, at least temporarily, gone out of being high commissioner.

In June 1956, shortly before the débâcle of Suez, which demonstrated conclusively the decline of British power, St Laurent had the impression that the high commissioner was again restless. Two years before, the sudden death of the under-secretary of state for external affairs, Hume Wrong, had prompted Robertson to indicate indirectly that, after less than two years in London, he would like to return to his old Ottawa job as under-secretary. After Suez, Robertson, feeling largely sidelined, again thought of moving, although, incongruously, almost two decades later he wrote of his two postings, "my own memories of life in London are probably the happiest I have had." By March 1957, when he did depart London, Macmillan had replaced the ailing Eden as prime minister. Even more significantly, it was the month in which the Treaty of Rome was signed, establishing from 1 January 1958 the European Economic Community. As widely anticipated, Britain did not join.

Following almost five years in Britain, Robertson was transferred to Washington in May 1957. He had readily accepted St Laurent's offer of the embassy, a post for which he was not notably suited (although he had known the city well in prewar years). He remained there only fourteen months. They were not satisfying. What awaited him in Ottawa, as he again became under-secretary in October 1958, was not, given the uncer-tainties of John Diefenbaker's new government and its suspicions of the foreign service, any more promising.

Prospects were not heartening, but at least Robertson had departed London to the accolades of senior British public servants and the press. A few years later, the head of the British diplomatic service hailed him as "a rare spirit and his mind one of the finest. His attitude was that of a phi-losopher and he was not content until he had searched any problem to its depths. His mind was exceptionally well-stocked and it always produced something of wisdom. Above all, he was a man of integrity, tolerance, patience. He was the best type of Canadian who combined with his genu-ine nationalism with a strong sense of internationalism which certainly embraced warmly the concept of Commonwealth and true friendship with Britain."*32

* Robertson retired from the Department of External Affairs in 1965 and died in Ottawa on 16 July 1968, age sixty-four. Pearson and he are buried near each other in the MacLaren Cemetery at Wakefield, Quebec.

CHAPTER TWELVE

George Drew, 1957–1964

John Diefenbaker, long a Conservative candidate in both Saskatchewan and national elections, had finally succeeded the ailing opposition leader George Drew in December 1956. The House of Commons was dissolved by a weary and pessimistic St Laurent in April 1957. In the election of that June, the eager Conservatives, highly critical of the Liberals' stance in the Suez crisis, the degree of US influence in Canada, and a range of domestic issues, came to office as a minority government, following twenty-two long years in opposition. The governor general, Vincent Massey, swore in Diefenbaker's untried ministers on 21 June 1957.

On that momentous day the new prime minister had in mind his predecessor as Conservative leader for two reasons: although not enthusiastic about the prairie populist, George Drew had promptly sent him a remarkably warm congratulatory letter (presumably drafted in anticipation of electoral victory). That afternoon the new government passed an order-in-council appointing him high commissioner, the appointment that he had increasingly indicated that he would welcome. Diefenbaker had, however, lingering doubts about his old antagonist. On the morning of the cabinet swearing-in, he had met with Lester Pearson who, as outgoing secretary of state for external affairs, briefed him about what he might expect at the conference of Commonwealth prime ministers, now only five days away. The new prime minister "asked what I thought of George Drew as High Commissioner. I said I thought the Drews would be admirable [Pearson knew Drew from the University of Toronto], but I got the impression that this was not the kind of reaction that John Diefenbaker desired. He wondered whether Mr. Drew, having been an important public figure in his own right, might not be inclined to take a somewhat independent line in London."[1]

It was soon evident to all at Canada House, including George Ignatieff on his second tour, that

Diefenbaker and Drew had no use for each other. Not that there were any fundamental policy differences between them. Both were totally committed to the British connection; indeed a closer relationship with the mother country had been an important part of Diefenbaker's election platform ... Yet Drew clearly could not forget that, had it not been for his serious illness following the pipeline debate in 1956, he would have led the Conservative Party into the 1957 election and would, presumably, have become prime minister ... watching their personality clash was like reliving Mackenzie King's 1941 visit to London and his icy relationship with Vincent Massey.[2]

When Drew and his wife Fiorenze disembarked in Liverpool in July 1957, the office of the high commissioner had been vacant for four months. Canada House having been led for more than two decades by Mackenzie King's appointees, Drew arrived convinced of partisan leanings among the Canadian staff, notwithstanding their impartial civil service status (Diefenbaker was even more inclined to suspect the worst of the public service, speaking of them with characteristically heavy humour as "Pearsonalities.")* Drew's difficulties with public servants were compounded by the perennial problem that had plagued every high commissioner since Strathcona. "At the time Drew first arrived in London ... he found some seventeen or eighteen Canadian government departments scattered in various high-rent quarters all over the city, with next to no co-ordination between them ... Drew decided to consolidate all these bits and pieces under one roof on Grosvenor Square, where he had persuaded the Diefenbaker government to buy the building formerly occupied by the US Embassy. He was also determined to reduce the number of officials – there were literally hundreds of them – living in London at the taxpayers' expense."[3] Drew's remedy was drastic but largely ineffective: the offices of various government departments were consolidated under two roofs (Canada House on Trafalgar Square and Macdonald House on Grosvenor Square), but somehow the number of public servants continued to grow and, as always, to go their separate ways.

Drew's apprenticeship in politics and imperial affairs (he came only reluctantly to employ the term "Commonwealth") had been long and varied. Born in 1891, he was from a family of United Empire Loyalists who

---

* Diefenbaker was not alone in suspecting partisan inclinations in the Department of External Affairs. In January 1922 King had recorded in his diary that "the Department ... is a Tory hive."

had settled in Upper Canada in the late eighteenth century. In Guelph, Drew's grandfather was an ardent supporter and friend of Sir John A. Macdonald; his lawyer son, Drew's father, had been hardly less active in local Conservative politics. Drew was remembered at Upper Canada College as not "much of a group person, he didn't have any set of friends. Of course, George Drew was always very handsome. No matter what he did, every button, every hair was in place ... He was always respected but never what you would call popular. He was always too right, too perfect, and too proper."[4] It was a stuffy image that was to plague Drew throughout his long political career.

Of all the high commissioners, Drew was the only one who had seen overseas military service (Lieutenant-Colonel Massey had been a musketry instructor and staff officer in Canada in 1914–15). Drew, an enthusiastic prewar gunner in a Guelph militia regiment, was in Flanders for eight months in 1915–16 before being wounded. He continued in the militia after the war, eventually being appointed honorary lieutenant-colonel of his regiment, a distinction in which he rejoiced, being thereafter most happy whenever addressed as colonel. During the 1930s, however, he pursued a two-track, somewhat contradictory approach to questions of war and peace. He was clear that the merchants of death were abroad in the world and, as he was given to saying, "war was too dangerous a business for the generals." He joined such disparate critics as Senator Alexander McRae and Vincent Massey in attacks upon arms manufacturers. However, at the same time as fulminating in *Maclean's* magazine against the Undershafts of this world, Drew somewhat incongruously called for an improvement in Canada's minuscule armed forces, describing the militia as "a bow-and-arrow army" and RCAF aircraft as "hopelessly out of date." To help draw public as well as government attention to the continuing deplorable state of the forces, he played a leading part in the establishment in 1932 of the Conference of Defence Associations, thereafter regularly addressing its annual conferences, as well as employing his presidency of the Empire Club of Toronto to advocate his particular understanding of Canada's evolving role in the Empire.

A graduate of the University of Toronto and Osgoode Law School in 1920, Drew practised in Guelph and served as alderman and mayor. He was chairman of the Ontario Securities Commission before his years as a political partisan were further rewarded by being elected leader of the Conservative party of Ontario in 1938. A year or more before, in supporting a Conservative candidate in a by-election, he had sacrificed any support that he might otherwise have later nourished in Quebec by declaring: "the French are a defeated race and their rights are rights only by tolerance of the English element who ... must be regarded as the dominant race."[5] Drew never lost his suspicion that French-speaking Canadians had somehow come to dominate Canada.

A seat for the new leader of the opposition in the Ontario legislature was hastily opened in a by-election in early 1939, seven months before the Second World War. His ascendancy had, however, been marred by a vigorous if private exchange with the federal Conservative leader, R.B. Bennett. In a bitter internecine dispute in 1938 over whether Drew had supported his predecessor in contemplating a coalition with the Liberal premier Mitch Hepburn, or whether Bennett had abandoned true Tory principles in his last-minute, desperate "New Deal" to avert the defeat of his government in 1935, Drew engaged in an "abusive and offensive" correspondence with him. So vitriolic did it become that Drew finally informed Bennett "that I thought you were suffering from some acute mental disturbance ... you are not a pleasant spectacle."[*6]

Once in the Ontario legislature, Drew's success was immediate. In January 1940, following his frontal assault on King's "do-nothing" wartime leadership, Hepburn concurred and moved "that the Federal Government ... had made so little effort to prosecute Canada's duty in the war in the vigorous manner the people of Canada desired to see." King was enraged by such a bipartisan attack, being convinced that the criticism was motivated not by wartime patriotism on the part of the Tories or his perfidious fellow Liberal but simply by a desire to denigrate him personally. Even late in the war King could convince himself that Conservative allegations about the inadequacy of military hospitals arose from an intention "to spoil as far as possible ... the possible effects of any mention or celebration of my twenty-fifth anniversary as Leader of the Party."[7] Hepburn, his increasingly bitter antagonist, suddenly called an election in August 1943. Drew won, but only with a minority.

Continuing to charge that Ottawa was woefully remiss in its assistance to Britain, Drew remained throughout the Second World War a bête noire for King. His unrelenting attacks from Queen's Park included the allegation that the government knew that Hong Kong could not be held when it took the surprising decision to send two largely untrained battalions there in the autumn of 1941. In his denunciations of King and other

---

* Drew's adverse opinion of Bennett's sanity was not unique. Three decades before, Robert Borden had noted of his Conservative colleague, "Many think his mind is becoming affected."

violent offensives, Drew was seldom able to make much of his mud stick, but at least offered himself as a clear alternative to the Grits. The Tories in Ontario and later in Ottawa were seldom so starkly defined as they were under Drew.

In March 1945, six weeks before the end of the war in Europe, Drew's minority government in Ontario was unexpectedly defeated on a vote of confidence by a combination of Liberals and CCF. In the ensuing provincial election in early June, however, Drew was swept back into office, winning sixty-eight seats against the Liberals' eleven, the CCF's eight, and the Communists' two. By 1948 Drew had become a leading national figure. In foreign as well as in domestic affairs he was known as an anti-communist of the first order, railing against aggression abroad and subversion at home. With his great majority in the Ontario legislature, Drew participated in the August 1946 meetings of the Dominion-Provincial Co-ordinating Committee and the Dominion-Provincial Conference as the most outspoken of the various provincial advocates, publicly contending that postwar economic recovery should be primarily a matter for fiscally autonomous provinces. He privately argued that any recovery programme should not be a vehicle for the redistribution of national income to Quebec. He was no less outspoken against proposals for national health insurance.

During his last year or so as prime minister, King feared the worst about Drew. He saw him under every stone. He even suspected, wholly unfairly, that Drew had surreptitiously engineered the ultimate insult to him as wartime prime minister. In May 1947 he learned that new carillon bells ordered by the Niagara Falls Bridge Commission had been cast with the inscription, "To God's glory and in grateful memory of our nation's leaders, Winston Spencer Churchill and Franklin Delano Roosevelt." King was outraged that even in his own country he was not to be recognized as a wartime leader alongside the prime minister of Britain and the president of the United States. He was convinced that some unnamed culprits "are seeking to change the tone of the nation down through the ages to come."[8] In time, King had to acknowledge that the premier of Ontario had nothing to do with it, feeling "a sense of relief that Drew had not lent himself to anything so extreme," but he remained convinced that Drew was capable of anything, including participation in placing such "a black blot on the escutcheon of chivalry."

Defeated in Toronto by a prohibitionist in an otherwise lacklustre Conservative victory in the provincial election of 1948, Drew took the occasion to move from Queen's Park to national politics. In March 1948, at the Conservative leadership convention, King had been certain of two things: Drew would win but that would "mean the Tory Party will be out of power for good, the chances of a Tory Party being returned or of ever being returned again will be nil. [Drew] has an arrogant manner, worse than either Meighen or Bennett, and has a more bitter tongue than Meighen ... I could not stand having Drew as an opponent. I would find too much of perpetual antagonism."[9] Drew won on the first ballot, defeating John Diefenbaker. King, age seventy-four and in uncertain health, saw Drew's subsequent election as member of Parliament for Carleton as one more reason why he himself should retire: he would then need not face the new vitriolic leader of the opposition. "I should find it very unpleasant to be facing Drew [in his role] as Leader of the Opposition. I have such contempt for the man that I would find his arrogance unbearable. I had my fill of that kind of thing under Meighen and Bennett and do not see why I should voluntarily incur the sort of insulting behaviour to which I would have to submit."[10] King and Drew never faced each other in the House of Commons; Drew became leader of the opposition two months after St Laurent succeeded King.

For all his bluster and invective, Drew's nine years as leader of the opposition were difficult for him, including having to explain away his more extreme partisan and pompous utterances as Ontario premier. He lost two elections to the avuncular St Laurent before resigning amidst the Suez crisis of September 1956, "suffering from physical and nervous exhaustion," and opening the way for Diefenbaker finally to be elected leader. The new leader urged him to remain in Parliament, offering him a cabinet post in any government that he might form, but Drew had had enough, as indeed some Conservative members had had enough of him.

George Drew arrived in Britain only after the arrival of the new prime minister to attend the meeting of Commonwealth prime ministers, which had been scheduled for London from 25 June to 5 July 1957. Before his departure for London, Diefenbaker had admitted that he had no very precise thoughts about what he hoped to achieve at the conference or in the Commonwealth generally, beyond hoping to clear away British *froideur* – as he saw it – left by the Liberals' clumsy intervention in the Suez crisis. Of Diefenbaker's foreign policy upon assuming office, Basil Robinson, his able foreign policy assistant seconded from the deeply suspect Department of External Affairs, later wrote:

In the 1957 election campaign ... he had seen and heard enough to confirm his belief that, notwithstanding Lester Pearson's acclaimed performance at the

A benign-looking George Drew beams over Anthony Eden, who had recently resigned as British prime minister, and the visiting Canadian prime minister, the newly elected John Diefenbaker, who accurately described himself as having "a deep and abiding emotional attachment to the Commonwealth." Try as Diefenbaker and Drew might, they were unable to persuade the British government to stick with the Commonwealth and to forego its application to join the burgeoning European Economic Community.

United Nations, a sizeable number of pro-British and pro-Israeli voters had been uneasy over the Canadian stand in the recent Suez crisis. Diefenbaker had an almost religious devotion to the Crown and to the relationship with the United Kingdom. He could be counted on to move to repair relations between Ottawa and London.

He could also be relied on to maintain, and to try to enhance, Canada's standing in the Commonwealth. If he had a vision in international affairs, it fell within the Commonwealth framework. This relationship not only provided a wider setting for the bonds linking Canada with the United Kingdom and the Crown, but it was an essential counterweight to US influence. It could ... be developed as a commercial association to benefit its members, and as an instrument through which economic and technical aid could be channelled to new members in need. He was, of course, not alone in seeing the Commonwealth as a bridge to the newly independent nations of Asia and Africa, which might help them progress along the constitutional path already followed by Canada, Australia, and New Zealand.[11]

Diefenbaker made his commitment clear: "Throughout my life, I have had a deep and abiding emotional attachment to the Commonwealth ... I saw the Commonwealth as a tremendous force for good in the world: for peace, progress, and stability in a world fraught with tension and on the brink of nuclear cataclysm."[12] He was highly gratified to be the first Conservative prime minister to visit London since Bennett in 1935. Pearson and officials had, however, cautioned him not to expect too much from the depleted Commonwealth as a counter to the overwhelming United States presence in Canadian trade and investment.

The new cabinet endorsed Diefenbaker's decision that he should propose at the meeting a Commonwealth economic conference in Ottawa (shades of 1932). Diefenbaker had a covert if naïve purpose in mind, additional to the more obvious and nebulous one of strengthening Commonwealth links: "If it were agreed to hold discussions in Ottawa in September, the British might not move so fast on the FTA [European Free Trade Agreement] front."[13] In contrast, the opposition Liberals were more relaxed about the British initiative, some contemplating it as a possible step toward a North Atlantic free trade area.

In London, an exhilarated Diefenbaker greatly enjoyed his audience with the young Queen and his calls with Drew on prime minister Harold Macmillan and luncheon with the elderly Churchill. So great was the new prime minister's gratification that, according to Graham Spry, the agent general for Saskatchewan, "to read some of the cheaper newspapers one would think that Canada had not only rejoined the Commonwealth, but was almost going to amalgamate with the United Kingdom."[14] Many Canadian Conservatives had remained convinced that Pearson had been on the wrong track at Suez, subjecting at least "Old Commonwealth" ties to almost intolerable strain. At the conference, Diefenbaker concluded that while

there was a greater spirit of give and take, frank discussions, strong opinions expressed ... All this could not, however, obscure the fact that Britain's relationship with Canada had been seriously affected by the parting of ways over Suez in 1956. No matter how much the two governments might now wish to restore the spirit of the old family partnership, the post-Suez mentality would make reconciliation more difficult, even if Britain, under Macmillan, were not determined to forge stronger links with Europe. Between Canada and Britain, things would not be the same again.[15]

During the conference, which *The Times* characterized as "a friendly but colourless affair," Diefenbaker urged Macmillan to offer assurances that if the United Kingdom did participate in a Europe-wide free trade area, agricultural imports from the Commonwealth should somehow continue to enjoy a preference in the British market. The chancellor of the exchequer confirmed that this was Britain's "firm intention." Thus buoyed, Diefenbaker proclaimed on July 1 to the Canada Club (in a speech subsequently described by *The Economist* "as really rather dreadful"), "the time has come to extend our [Commonwealth] trade on a wider basis than ever before." Nevertheless, British scepticism (joined with that of Australia, New Zealand, and South Africa) greeted Diefenbaker's vague proposal for a meeting of Commonwealth finance ministers in September, to be followed immediately by an economic conference. No one knew what exactly he had in mind; it is quite likely that he did not himself. All that was agreed was that the meeting of the finance ministers in late September (immediately following the annual meetings of the World Bank and International Monetary Fund in Washington) would consider whether, as in 1952, a full Commonwealth economic conference should be convened.

Almost casually, upon his return to Ottawa on 6 July, Diefenbaker, to the consternation of officials, suddenly injected into the continuing uncertainties of Commonwealth economic collaboration a more quantifiable element. As *The Times* reported, "Canada had as a planned objective the diversion of 15 per cent of her present imports from the United States to imports from the United Kingdom. Such a diversion would make a substantial difference to trade with the Mother Country without actually hurting trade with the United States." The minister of finance, at a meeting with officials on 11 July, summed up the government's thinking. "The U.S. was a good neighbour and antipathy towards her was not the reason for prompting the Government to seek a wider diversification of markets. What was sought was a strengthening of Commonwealth ties through an increase in Commonwealth trade."

It was into this new and promising – at least for any anglophile and Commonwealth advocate – environment that the sixty-three-year-old George Drew arrived in London in July 1957. It was already becoming obvious that, despite his wide range of interests, one subject would dominate his years as high commissioner: British relations with western Europe and their impact upon the Commonwealth. The Treaty of Rome of 1 January 1958 brought into existence the European Economic Community (EEC), the members of which were Germany, France, Italy, Belgium, the Netherlands, and Luxembourg. Having finally increased sterling convertibility, the year following was spent by Britain, with Scandinavia and Portugal, in attempting to gain for a European free trade area a parallel agreement for its tariff-free access to the EEC.

Throughout the prolonged British approach to Europe, Drew was ready to join any attempt to confound such a knavish project, drawing upon all the energies that he had habitually displayed in his imperial enthusiasms and sharing Diefenbaker's conviction that the Commonwealth would be severely weakened by the reduction of its economic ties with the United Kingdom. Basil Robinson regretted his influence (thereby confirming Drew's suspicions that most External Affairs officials were closet Grits):

George Drew was an outspoken and passionate critic of British entry into Europe. His appointment in 1957 as high commissioner had been Diefenbaker's first and most striking acknowledgment of the continuing significance in Canada of the "British connection." Now, hardly a day passed in Ottawa without the prime minister receiving a telephone call or a personal telegram or letter from Drew warning of some impending British stratagem, or transmitting an editorial from the Beaverbrook press certain to stoke up the fires of Diefenbaker's disillusion. The *Daily Express* in particular had been conducting an all-out campaign against British entry into the Common Market ... Occasionally Drew, in an effort to keep some item of correspondence out of the hands of the Canadian bureaucracy, would ask me to see that it was routed directly to the prime minister. I presume he did this on the assumption that Diefenbaker would not object if he knew that the message was in my hands and had not otherwise gone astray. Unfortunately this was not always a safe assumption, even after my four years in Diefenbaker's service. Once, after I gave him a telegram that Drew had sent through External Affairs channels with a prefix asking me to give it personally to the prime minister, Diefenbaker told me that his correspondence with Drew on this subject was entirely private. On other days correspondence similarly addressed and on the same subject would be turned over to me to decide what needed to be done. One had to be flexible.[16]

The anomaly of two Canada Houses did not escape the *Globe and Mail*. From London it reported that "In effect there are now two systems by which Canada House reports to Ottawa: the normal one, prepared from the work of the official staff of experts here, and a second one shaped by Mr. Drew's personal view of what is happening and sent personally to particular ministers."[17] Not surprisingly, at least one student of Canada's international relations has concluded, "It was widely believed at the time that Mr. Drew had more influence upon the decisions of the Canadian Government with respect to the UK–EEC negotiations than any other man."[18] Drew's whole instincts were with Diefenbaker's vague but deeply-held pro-Commonwealth sentiments (also shared by the new secretary of state for external affairs, Howard Green) even if officials at Canada House, as well as in Ottawa, wondered whether such sentiments could be successfully transformed into a more unified and dynamic policy. The task of identifying how Canada could divert a substantial part of its imports from the United States to the United Kingdom was, in the minds of officials, a hopeless one.

Undeterred, Drew reported to Diefenbaker at the end of August that "Your suggestion that as much as 15 per cent of our imports from the U.S.A. might be shifted to the U.K. has aroused very great interest." Fully conscious of the marked lack of enthusiasm among its own people for withdrawal east of Suez and "the feeling of disillusionment and second thought about the proposed European Free Trade Area," the British government despatched its secretary of state for agriculture, Derick Heathcoat Amory, to Ottawa in early September to respond positively if somewhat sceptically to Diefenbaker's offhand suggestion. As Britain had done at the 1930 imperial conference and as Beaverbrook had done in his Empire crusade, Whitehall proposed free trade between Canada and Britain. The most-favoured-nation principle of the GATT militated against enhanced Commonwealth tariff preferences and in any case Britain could not surmount existing tariffs to supply the range of competitive products necessary to reach Diefenbaker's goal of diverting to British suppliers 15 per cent of imports from the United States. Free trade was the only possible response.

Britain's bold proposal of free trade was welcomed by Pearson and the Liberal opposition (and public opinion generally), but Diefenbaker, sounding like R.B. Bennett, rejected it. "He recognized the advantages [that] it would provide to U.K. exports, but [he] could not see what advantage there would be in it for Canada," being convinced, as Meighen and Bennett had been, that he must protect domestic manufacturing with tariff walls against British competition. The Liberal *Winnipeg Free Press* regarded it all as an advanced case of hypocrisy: the new Conservative government "will indulge in just that degree of skin-deep friendship with Britain that its nature, which is protectionist, will permit."[19] Not knowing what other response to make, Drew urged upon Diefenbaker the early visit of a Canadian trade delegation to Britain, led by the minister of trade and commerce, as a token of good intentions, but no real increase in trade flowed from its November visit.

That Diefenbaker's capricious idea of trade diversion soon withered in the face of rational analysis and the timidity of Canadian manufacturers did not mean that it left no trace. The conclusions of the Commonwealth finance ministers' meeting had been "obscured by accounts in the press of the United Kingdom proposal for a free trade area with Canada." It was, however, agreed to accept Diefenbaker's invitation to hold a Commonwealth trade and economic conference in Montreal one year hence, in September 1958, a device, in Diefenbaker's mind, to slow the British move towards Europe and away from the Commonwealth. While visiting Ottawa in June, Macmillan was vague about what the British expected from the Montreal conference, except possible agreement to establish a Commonwealth bank. In the event, in the face of US opposition to any derogation from the GATT principle of most-favoured-nation, it adjourned with not much more than the pious hope that there could be "an expanding Commonwealth in an expanding world economy." The sentiment lingered on in the Canadian campaign to protect existing Commonwealth tariff preferences if Britain, in pursuit of its own economic interests, persisted in its goal of attempting to associate an European free trade area with the European Economic Community. As Diefenbaker had urged upon Macmillan during his June visit, if Britain were to be linked to the EEC, the Commonwealth would not be the same – especially to an emotional imperialist like Diefenbaker – and neither would Anglo-Canadian trade. Macmillan had at least given "an assurance that the United Kingdom would continue to pay close attention to the interests of Canadian agricultural producers in the United Kingdom market and would ensure that their interests were not adversely affected."[20] Diefenbaker was gratified, but a later memorandum from the Privy Council Office concluded tersely, "our dependence on the United States market will inevitably be increased."[21]

Within months President de Gaulle of France delivered himself of the first of his vetoes regarding Britain's participation in the economic and ultimately political integration of Europe. There would be no free trade between the EEC and an European free trade area, leaving Britain to choose between joining a free trade area without a tariff-free link to the EEC or attempting to join the EEC itself. Given his own opposition, Drew had been reassured by Diefenbaker's account of his visit to de Gaulle in November 1958, during his round-the-world tour which had included many Commonwealth countries. De Gaulle, still feeling betrayed by the United States opposition as well as by the British withdrawal at Suez, and reluctant to give up France's hegemony of Europe with Germany, had stated that Britain was "not going to get in," either directly or indirectly. Diefenbaker later recorded that when he reported this to Macmillan, he had responded simply that Diefenbaker must have misunderstood the general. Satisfied that he had not, Diefenbaker turned his attention to organizing a tour of Canada for the queen.

Drew was at least as clear in his militant anti-communism as he was in his opposition to any British application to join the EEC; his frequent tirades against the Soviet Union were well known to all who had sat with him in the Ontario legislature or the House of Commons. To the heads of Canadian missions in Europe, assembled in December 1957 to meet the new prime minister while he attended a NATO meeting in Paris, he delivered himself of a particularly thunderous denunciation. George Ignatieff, now ambassador to Yugoslavia, had reviewed Tito's thinking on the nature of the cold war. "George Drew was furious. Not only did he consider himself, as High Commissioner to Britain and former head of the Conservative Party, several notches above the likes of me; he also made it clear that he found my remarks offensive and inappropriate. The Diefenbaker government's first priority, he said, should be a resounding declaration of support for the western alliance. He for one was not interested in the anti-NATO views of communist dictators."[22]

In the midst of Diefenbaker's initial foray into the arcane world of European politics, his government had to decide who should head the Canadian delegation to the first Conference of the Law of the Sea in Geneva in March 1958. No eminent Conservative of experience being available, Drew must fill the post concurrently with his duties in London. As chairman of the delegation, he spent several months in Geneva, building upon the Canadian position at the League of Nations conference in 1930 in support of the traditional three-mile limit (with a contiguous nine-mile zone of fisheries control) and in opposition to any coastal-state jurisdiction beyond that narrow territorial sea. He soon convinced himself that Britain had deceived Canada by advocating a six-mile zone. At a United States delegation gathering intended to reconcile the conflicting positions of western nations, "dinner became steadily more acrimonious and ended with Drew, after considerable provocation, informing Britain's Attorney General [Sir Reginald Manningham-Buller] that he was 'a pompous ass'. The following morning the legal advisor to the British delegation telephoned ... the senior legal advisor of our delegation, to inform him of the crisis: 'Our heads of delegation almost came to blows'. However, Sir Reginald was prepared to drop the matter if Drew apologized to him. [Drew's] vocabulary and his wrath had lost none of their heat overnight. His reply ... left no doubt that there would be no apology – unless Sir Reginald was disposed to make one to Drew."[23] The episode did nothing to improve the already frosty reception that Drew had received in Whitehall and Westminster for his outspoken opposition to any British linkage with the EEC.

If Britain adopted the common tariff of the EEC, duties on a number of Canadian exports to Britain would be increased. Wheat shipments from Diefenbaker's home province of Saskatchewan would, it was believed, particularly suffer. However, the net result, as officials in Ottawa forecast, would not be catastrophic. Only about 10 per cent of total exports to Britain would be adversely affected, with some possible diversion to the United States. During Diefenbaker's two visits to Britain in the spring and autumn of 1960, Drew joined a wary Norman Robertson (again undersecretary of state for external affairs) in setting forth for the prime minister a myriad of trade concerns over British membership in the EEC. At public meetings, he took as his starting point his own dated view of Anglo-Canadian trade, proclaiming that while the resources of the Commonwealth had immense potential, the EEC could offer Britain only limited access to raw materials. It was obvious, at least to Diefenbaker, Drew, and Beaverbrook what the British choice must be. The opposite was obvious to Macmillan: Diefenbaker received notice in September 1960 of the British decision to revive negotiations with the EEC.

Not surprisingly in light of its earlier thinking, the United States had continued to urge Britain to join the EEC, doing so, Macmillan later wrote, "on the general ground that if a United States of America was almost a divine plan for 'God's own country', a similar constitution might revive a decadent Europe." Macmillan met Diefenbaker in Ottawa in April 1961, following a visit to the recently-elected President Kennedy in Washington. The message which he brought with him was unmistakeable, however unpalatable to Diefenbaker. As Macmillan's private secretary stated, "the principal motive for the vigour of American support for United Kingdom entry into Europe was the desire to have the United Kingdom fully engaged in European affairs and available with its influences and ... its reliability to act as a stabilizing factor *vis-à-vis* Germany and France." Further, without EEC membership, Macmillan feared British bankruptcy. He was convinced, and had convinced his cabinet, that chronic balance-of-payment problems and inflation could finally be ended only by free access for British goods into the now-flourishing markets of western Europe and the acceptance of the disciplines of rationalization and modernization that would flow from trade liberalization. Diefenbaker's biographer has summarized the dilemma in which the prime minister and the high commissioner had placed themselves in light of Macmillan's fundamental intentions:

The confused nature of the Canadian campaign was a product of Diefenbaker's unreconciled emotions ... It was also (and not by chance) an echo of Lord Beaverbrook's campaign in the pages of his *Daily Express* against British entry into Europe. Drew and Beaverbrook shared their views on the subject, and Drew provided Diefenbaker with frequent reports from the *Daily Express* ... The Canadian government's campaign was controversial from the beginning, and especially upsetting to the old core of Conservative supporters because it publicly criticized Great Britain. It was disturbing also to others – including many businessmen and the Liberal opposition – who felt that obstruction would undermine rather than benefit Canada's political and commercial links with the United Kingdom.[24]

Duncan Sandys, the self-assured secretary of state for Commonwealth relations (and son-in-law of Churchill), was despatched by Macmillan on a Commonwealth visit in July 1961, only weeks in advance of the formal British application to join the EEC. Canadian officials had dutifully developed an impressive panoply of ultimately futile or simply irrelevant arguments against British entry. From his vantage point in the prime minister's office, Basil Robinson recorded in his diary where things were going:

the government has decided to try and kill U.K. participation in the Common Market and that efforts to point out the advantages of adjusting ourselves [to its membership] have no political appeal. Officials are of course also divided but all agree that collective Commonwealth consultation is not likely to advance Canadian negotiated interests. But the P.M. evidently thinks that if all the other Commonwealth members gang up, the U.K. may be dissuaded.[25]

Two decades later, Robinson added,

I took an opportunity to ask the prime minister about the government's real intention about Britain and the Common Market. Did they mean to scupper it? Diefenbaker denied wanting to prevent British entry but said he did not want to be hurried. He feared that in sending Sandys for bilateral talks, the British were pulling a fast one and might announce plans to enter Europe before there had been a full opportunity for consultation. The United Kingdom was free to enter Europe but his concern was to ensure that Canada would retain the trade benefits it possessed through Commonwealth preferences. He thought that there was a real risk involved to Canadian trade interests, especially as he felt that France would insist on Britain's joining the Common Market treaty without qualifications.[26]

Officials warned ministers that Sandys would probably deploy principally political arguments in favour of membership and cautioned them to be balanced in response. "It would seem wise to press alternative judgments sufficiently to protect Canada's negotiating position [officials assumed whimsically that Canada had some negotiating clout], but not so far as to appear to be aiming at obstructing the United Kingdom from following a course which in their view is in their national interest." In any case, "Latest indications of the French attitude toward the possibility of the United Kingdom joining the Six are that France may set conditions [i.e., full acceptance of the Treaty of Rome] which could well be too rigorous for the United Kingdom to accept." Having offered these admirable cautions, the several memoranda before the prime minister and ministers (all copied to Drew) rehearsed a remarkable range of commercial and political reasons – some highly imaginative – why British membership would not only be detrimental to the basic interests of Canada but also to those of Britain itself. Adherence to the Common Agricultural Policy was seen as a reversal of the century-old policy against stomach taxes. "Ever since the repeal of the Corn Laws more than 100 years ago, the United Kingdom, as a matter of national policy, have obtained their basic foodstuffs from the cheapest sources of supply with little or no tariff in order to keep down costs."[27] Now as a price of membership, Britain was contemplating the acceptance of just such tariffs.

Turning to political questions, officials queried, "Do the United Kingdom think it would be possible to preserve the special type of consultation and co-operation which has been traditional between the United Kingdom and Canada?" Robinson noted in his diary for 13 June that the under-secretary, Norman Robertson, "thinks that undignified public exhibitions between Canada and the U.K. are deplorable not only in Commonwealth terms but in the light of Berlin, Laos, etc. where we shall badly need to stay close to the U.K. whose position is sensible and close to our own. NAR spoke to Green today, blowing off steam. Green completely on the defensive." For the secretary of state to be on the defensive was not, however, enough:

Robertson ... felt so strongly about the barrenness of the government's tactics that just before Sandys's visit he took what was for him the unusual step of attending a meeting of the cabinet committee dealing with questions arising out of Britain's interest in joining the Common Market. He told me that he felt it his duty to speak out against the public line being followed by the government, and preferred to do this in a setting where it would not cause undue embarrassment. He said that he did not want to attend the meeting with Sandys for fear of feeling it necessary to disagree with Canadian ministers ... what he said at that time ... reflected so poignantly the difficulty Robertson had in his role as head of the department during the Diefenbaker years and, at the same time, the spur of conscience which drove him to find a way to make his views known to the government.[28]

Although Diefenbaker and Drew were convinced that Britain had decided to join the European Community on whatever terms it could get, both still believed that louder public protest might help deter Britain. At the meeting, Sandys listened to Canadian economic and political concerns and rehearsed in turn British imperatives, stressing "the overriding ... the virtual certainty that the United Kingdom would suffer a severe economic decline if it stayed out of Europe." His reaction to the Canadian position was decidedly impatient, a fact hardly disguised by the terse official communiqué. Privately,

according to a Canadian reporter in London who saw Sandy's confidential report on his visit, the British minister had not been impressed with Canadian arguments. The Canadians had not yet read the Treaty of Rome, he said, and their objections were made in ignorance and coloured by political considerations ... [this] was paralleled by Canadian editorials that were beginning to denounce Ottawa's "dog in the manger" attitudes to Britain and the Market.[29]

Sandys left Ottawa aware of the conviction of Diefenbaker that British membership in the EEC was incompatible with leadership of the Commonwealth and that such membership would inevitably result in Canada being drawn further into the orbit of the United States. For his part, Drew did not disguise his disdain and even contempt for Sandys and several other British ministers, carrying on the practice that he had first displayed at the Law of the Sea conference in Geneva. "Drew spent much of his own time on the economic side of our work and was a hot and sometimes indiscreet opponent of Britain's entry into the European Economic Community," one of "Pearsonalities" at Canada House later recalled. "The dislike of a major UK policy fuelled Drew's dislike of some British ministers which he illustrated pungently at some of our weekly cabinet meetings – as we called our staff gatherings which the Chairman invested with a more portentous flavour."[30]

During much of 1960 and 1961, relations between the British and Canadian prime ministers had in any event deteriorated, in part as a result of what was seen as the unhelpful stance of Diefenbaker, the long-time civil libertarian, on the question of the continuing membership of South Africa in the Commonwealth, following its declared intention to adopt a republican constitution (somewhat similar to the situation with regard to India in 1948). At the difficult 1960 Commonwealth prime ministers' conference, the subject had become unavoidable, given South Africa's increasingly repressive racial policies that had become something of an issue in the cold war, with the Soviet Union, as always, eager to attempt to portray itself as the champion of the downtrodden everywhere. The presence of Nigeria at the conference only emphasized the growing hostility among both new and pending members, backed by India, toward having amongst them a government proclaiming the hateful apartheid policy.

Diefenbaker, cautioned by Drew, avoided any major role in the 1960 conference's inconclusive consideration of continuing South African membership, a contentious issue skilfully sidelined by Macmillan into "private" discussions pending the referendum in South Africa on a republican constitution. That Diefenbaker remained on this issue largely inconspicuous was partly at Drew's urging, but it was also the result of conflicting advice from Keynes's Cambridge disciple Robert Bryce, the secretary of the cabinet, who opposed the readmission of South Africa if the question would split the other members of the Commonwealth, and of Norman Robertson, the under-secretary, who was not so certain that much purpose would be served by such a policy. "Robertson declared himself against any chastising action by Commonwealth countries. He saw the Commonwealth as a product of history, a family, some of whose numbers went to church, others to jail, but not susceptible as a group to discipline nor a court of morality."[31]

Diefenbaker went to the March 1961 conference with options on South Africa limited by cabinet discussion. His policy attitudes had come to be shaded by his dislike of Mackenzie King's old antagonist, Robert Menzies, and his growing sense of being patronized by Macmillan. However, he persisted in his illusions that in Drew he had a private route to the British prime minister, secure from the inquisitive gaze of his own Department of External Affairs. Drew's parallel practice of bypassing the department was in part his reaction to the fact that, as one official noted,

the different levels in the Department were having as much trouble in agreeing on what to submit to the prime minister as he was in deciding what to do ... While the Department of External Affairs worked away to produce texts of statements for all conceivable contingencies at the [1961] meeting, George Drew maintained a steady flow of letters and telephone calls to the prime minister ... it was easy to see what direction Drew's advice was taking. Essentially, he was ensuring that the prime minister was fully aware of the British arguments against making an issue of the racial question. He was also promoting an idea that consideration of the racial issue could justifiably be postponed ... Drew's persistence ... had intermittent influence on Diefenbaker, as did signs, also conveyed by Drew, that some ... non-white Commonwealth prime ministers would not force the basic issue and were looking for a lead from Canada ... In a letter of 24 February [a week before the conference], the High Commissioner argued strenuously for "finding some device by which a clash with South Africa may be avoided."[32]

Diefenbaker followed the advice of Robertson to support a postponement of the issue to a future conference, pending additional consultation and until actual constitutional change had taken place in South Africa. But when postponement was in effect rejected by non-white members, Diefenbaker finally endorsed their refusal to tolerate apartheid within the Commonwealth. South Africa thereupon withdrew its application for continued membership. Beaverbrook wrote to Drew in a combination of bewilderment and exasperation about why Diefenbaker had "pushed

South Africa out of the Commonwealth, and then places barriers against immigration into Canada."

Following the formal British application to join the European Economic Community on 31 July 1961, the Foreign Office kept Drew informed about the progress, or lack of it, despite the fact that British ministers and officials can only have viewed Canadian attitudes as unhelpful and even obstructionist. At a Commonwealth economic gathering in Accra in mid-September, the Canadian ministers of finance and of trade and commerce bluntly and repeatedly informed other delegates of Canada's "disappointment and grave apprehension," while mobilizing opposition to the British venture. They "made a very strong pitch for the consideration of Canadian interests as a result of Britain going into the EEC – and there were very serious problems at that time ... strangely enough the reaction in Canada was 'Poor little Britain', the very opposite to what you would expect."[33]

Several ministers in Ottawa began to have second thoughts about the degree if not the principle of Canadian opposition, but in London, Drew prompted a visiting Canadian delegation to press for an answer to the question of "what measures the United Kingdom proposed to ensure that damage to essential Canadian interests would be avoided?" Drew was both frustrated and angry – he was readily moved to anger – about what he regarded as a sell-out of the Commonwealth by a British government (a Conservative government at that) which was hell-bent on EEC membership. "What does protection of the position of members of the Commonwealth really mean? Surely it means what it says. Our trade in every field ... must be protected ... The Canadian Government has not sought to tell the British Government how to run its own business. But it has a duty as well as a right to tell the Canadian people what the result would be."[34] At home, however, the entry of Britain was widely expected. Even the cabinet recorded its belief that "Canada should now accept as a *fait accompli* the United Kingdom decision to try to enter the European Economic Community."

When the chief British negotiator and convinced European, Edward Heath, the future prime minister, proposed to consult with all the high commissioners in early November, Drew declined to attend on the grounds of ill-health. However, as Robinson recalled, Beaverbrook's newspapers

left the impression that Drew's failure to attend a meeting of Commonwealth high commissioners on the subject of United Kingdom negotiations with Europe was a deliberate snub to the British. Diefenbaker, worried at the public effect of the report, asked me to prepare a telegram to Drew instructing him to deny that his absence from the meeting had been deliberate. The message went off, and Diefenbaker followed it up with a phone call to make sure that the high commissioner acted on it promptly. The denial must have looked strange to those journalists who had been told by an official on the staff of the high commissioner that Drew's decision not to attend the meeting had indeed been intended as a snub. The incident was minor but, like the Accra affair, it illustrated the difficulty Diefenbaker had in coordinating the public statements of his senior colleagues on matters where his own feelings were mixed and his signal therefore muffled.

As the year ended, the news did not improve. The British negotiator with the EEC [Edward Heath] informed Drew in early December that there would be no progress on the treatment to be accorded to manufactured goods by the Six so long as the United Kingdom insisted on the principle of maintaining existing arrangements for their entry into the United Kingdom.[35]

The British solution to the conundrum of reconciling the free entry accorded to countries of the Commonwealth in the United Kingdom market with the EEC common external tariff was to urge upon the Six that their duties on twenty-five specific items be reduced to zero (thereby largely preserving for Commonwealth countries their duty-free access to the British market). As expected, the proposal was not well received by the Six, but it did at least provide the British government with an alibi; it had attempted to induce the EEC to adopt free trade in products of major interest to the Commonwealth. When the obdurate EEC rejected such a trade-liberalizing measure, no one could say that Britain had not attempted to protect Commonwealth economic interests.

Macmillan tried repeatedly during the spring of 1962 to convince Diefenbaker that British membership was, all in all, a good thing for everyone. On a visit to Ottawa in early January, Heath, backed up the easy-going British high commissioner, Lord Amory, had explained the current state of play and delivered an invitation to the pending Commonwealth conference to discuss Britain's application. In Heath's recollection, Diefenbaker was increasingly conscious of press as well as parliamentary opposition to the sterility of his policy.* Donald Fleming, the minister of finance, with

* Faced with an election in a few months' time, Diefenbaker explained to Heath, "the really important thing is the state of the harvest and that, of course, will depend upon the rainfall. If we are dry in July the crop will be bad, and we shall lose support. If the rainfall is strong we shall get good crops in September and our position will be sound.

the election in view, made "the astonishing request that the British Government refrain from seeking from the Canadian any written judgments on the Brussels negotiations. He explained that all senior [Canadian] officials had been trained by the Liberal Party during its twenty-two years of power, and all of them still had the closest connections with the Liberal leaders ... any written views on the merits of particular British proposals, even at the most confidential ... would be brought to the notice of their [i.e., the government's] political opponents within a matter of minutes."[36]

Pearson found Diefenbaker's continuing opposition as tiresome as the British did Drew's in London. In criticisms of government policy, the leader of the opposition, as Robinson recorded, attacked the government's

"sterile, negative, and complaining" attitude towards Britain's interest in joining the EEC, and its indifference to the benefits to be sought in a freer trade area encompassing both Western Europe and North America [as foreshadowed in Article 2 of the North Atlantic Treaty]. He touched a raw nerve on the government front bench by recalling the "cool and qualified endorsement" given to new multilateral trade proposals presented by the American delegates to a recent joint meeting of economic ministers. Quoting liberally, as it were, from speeches by the prime minister and the minister of finance, Pearson reopened a file of incidents best forgotten from the government's standpoint – the Accra speeches, the Canadian high commissioner's absence from a meeting in London, and other examples of allegedly exaggerated anxiety over British aims and methods of consultation. The government, Pearson said, had gone out of its way to make things difficult for the British, and had overstated the political risks that British entry into Europe would pose for the Commonwealth.[37]

In the House of Commons, Pearson, again reflecting the thinking behind Article 2 of the North Atlantic Treaty, pleaded in vain with Diefenbaker to modify his fruitless pursuit. "If we do not wish to weaken the western coalition and if, in Canada, we do not wish to face the United States alone or become too economically dependent on them, then surely the best policy for us is to seek economic interdependence within the North Atlantic community through freer trade." The response of Diefenbaker was surprisingly muted. He had himself become uneasy at Drew's

So what I have to do is to find out what the rainfall will be. This I have arranged to do by sending a water diviner out to the plains, and he will be able to tell by the twitching of his stick whether it will be rain in July or rain in September" (Heath, *The Course of My Life*, 224).

unrelenting opposition, fearing it might conceivably help Labour against the British Conservatives. Drew, however, was not much inclined to listen to what Diefenbaker said. Efforts to rein him in came to little.

Macmillan persisted in his efforts to reconcile the Commonwealth and especially Canada to British entry to the EEC but, in the end, he would press on regardless. Coupled with a visit to Washington, the unflappable Macmillan returned to Ottawa in late April 1962, his second visit in less than a year and only months after Heath. Drew warned Diefenbaker in advance that Britain was "engaged in the unilateral planning of the fragmentation of the Commonwealth ... all the King's horses and all the King's men may never be able to put it together again." The influence of the United States in Canadian life would only mount by a weakening of the Commonwealth link, a major reason in his mind why the United States was so enthusiastic about British entry to the EEC (but without the extension of Commonwealth preferences to the EEC). Diefenbaker duly emphasized to Macmillan "the importance of Commonwealth prefer- ences to Canada as a means of staving off United States domination ... Canada could not be unconcerned that, if the United Kingdom should join the EEC, the basic buttress of the Commonwealth might go." Mac- millan was seemingly sympathetic, but all Diefenbaker's imperial or anti- continentalist rhetoric did not deflect him from his fixed course.

As negotiations in Brussels dragged on, the British complained of Canadian policy sterility and especially of Drew's speeches, well-pub- licized by Beaverbrook (who himself issued a sharply worded pamphlet against the British application). "Empire not Europe" was typical of the *Standard's* headlines. The exchange of information between the two gov- ernments and press comment through the spring of 1962 culminated in Lord Amory, home from Ottawa, calling upon Drew in late June 1962 to express "regret that the Canadian Government was not taking a more active part in putting forward positive ideas during the present negotia- tions." To this Drew replied blandly that consultations were inadequate. As the high commissioner recalled in a note that he dictated the same day,

I said to Amory that personally I could not understand how the word "consulta- tion" can be correctly applied to the discussions which preceded the British deci- sion to apply for membership in the EEC. The British Government decided to proceed with their application and the Commonwealth Governments were then informed of the way in which the application was to be presented. I said that I understood consultation to mean ... a meeting at which the problem is examined and the course decided following an exchange of opinions. In this case one government had made the decision as to what would be done and then merely asked the other governments to comment on what they proposed to do.

Drew's semantic exchanges followed an agreement to convene the Commonwealth prime ministers in September 1962. Amory was pessimistic about the outcome, believing apparently that the Commonwealth was in any case going nowhere: "we must realize that in ten years at the most, all the new members of the Commonwealth [i.e., the African members] are almost certain to have authoritarian governments ... since the Commonwealth as it now exists would so soon be coming to an end, the period after 1970 is not so important in any event." To this Drew (who expressed no dissent) asked Amory whether this was not an added reason "for assuring the very highest degree of confidence between the four members of the Commonwealth which are still monarchies, and still have precisely the same parliamentary system ... [Amory] said ... we might find it necessary to have some two-tiered system of consultation."[38]

For their part, Macmillan, Heath, and their colleagues believed that they had done their consultative best. Heath later recalled that "We had kept the High Commissioners in London personally informed at regular intervals about all the proceedings, as well as discussing aspects of particular concern to individual countries with their own High Commissioners. We had also sent regular information to every government in the Commonwealth."[39] Officials in Ottawa advised Diefenbaker, before his departure for London,

first, that the decision ... the United Kingdom should enter the E.E.C. was for the U.K. government to make; second, that Canadian and other Commonwealth trade interests were not sufficiently protected by the results of the negotiations so far held between the United Kingdom and the E.E.C.; third, that the occasion of the prime ministers' meeting should be taken to articulate the political and economic apprehensions of the Canadian government; and, fourth, that care should be taken to avoid a position in which Canada would be seen as leading the opposition to U.K. entry into Europe or of allowing Canada to be branded as the principal cause of the failure of the British application.

Diefenbaker was no longer immune to such advice, but he did argue that

United Kingdom entry into Europe might be probable, but "this should not be taken for granted." He told the cabinet [on 30 August 1962] that nine out of every eleven letters he received from the Canadian public were opposed to British entry. Opinion polls in the United Kingdom showed that only 28 per cent of the British population were in favour. He might have added that, at the London end, the Canadian high commissioner was straining every sinew to frustrate the aims of the Macmillan government.

At the conference itself, Heath recorded that "there was a general fear that the relationship between the old Commonwealth countries ... and Britain would be irrevocably damaged if we joined the European Community. To this we had to answer that Britain's only credible choice for economic development was in the EEC, that this would undoubtedly increase our influence both politically and economically in the world and that such a development could, in turn, be of great benefit to the Commonwealth ... I was certain all along that the Commonwealth would survive and that future generations at home would curse us if we allowed nostalgia to blind us to the real needs of our nation."[40] During the meetings, Heath's long expositions did not deter Diefenbaker, egged on by Drew, from continuing to question the British application, speeches which Macmillan considered "false and vicious," delivered by a "mountebank," a "very crooked man ... so self-centred." Several British newspapers dismissed Diefenbaker as a tedious dog-in-the-manger. Worse, the Canadian media were becoming increasingly critical of his performance; Diefenbaker was clearly not carrying a major portion of the Canadian public with him in his continuing opposition to Britain's application.

In the end, to Diefenbaker's relief, Macmillan's initiative to join the EEC came to nought. Diefenbaker proclaimed himself not surprised. At the September 1962 Commonwealth prime ministers' conference, Heath "was flushed with anticipated success, confident that Britain would be admitted to the Common Market within a few weeks. Prime Minister Menzies [of Australia] asked how I could ever have come to such an absurd conclusion [to the contrary]."[41] As Diefenbaker had ponderously forecast, de Gaulle – opposed to any dilution by Britain of Franco-German pre-eminence in the Community and deeply suspicious of Anglo-American nuclear co-operation among other things – vetoed the British application in January 1963. For the time being, the debate over British membership and its effect on the Commonwealth had ended. Diefenbaker and Drew were gratified, especially at their escape from additional charges of assisting in the sabotage of British interests.

In later years, when Diefenbaker wrote his tendentious autobiography, he ingenuously attempted to rebut the charge "of my government's supposedly uncooperative attitude to Britain's attempts to negotiate an entry into the European Economic Community ... To set the record straight, from the beginning in 1957, my government's policy towards all the European regional trade plans was, while recognizing their broad political and strategic implications, to safeguard our own trade and economic interests."[42] Diefenbaker added that in the wake of the British failure to secure EEC entry, Canada had developed a "major initiative on Commonwealth and international economic questions," but before it could be revealed, it had been misplaced in the electoral reverses of 1962.

In April 1963, Pearson's Liberals drove Diefenbaker's Conservatives from office. Drew, however, remained as high commissioner for eight more months, despite hospitalization, long after most observers had expected him to be replaced by a Liberal. Pearson had more pressing issues with which to deal than to concern himself about an early replacement for his classmate from the University of Toronto. In any event, it did no harm to give the appearance of non-partisanship in the office of the high commissioner. When eventually at a press conference on 19 January 1964 he named his cabinet colleague, Lionel Chevrier, as Drew's successor, Pearson was as positive about the term of the Tory incumbent as he had once been about earlier Conservative high commissioners, Sir George Perley and Howard Ferguson. He "took pains to squelch any lingering suspicions that the former Conservative leader had embarrassed Ottawa by hanging on to his London post after the April [1963] election. 'There is no more distinguished public man in Canada than George Drew', said Pearson, adding the personal postscript that Drew 'entered the University of Toronto the same year I did, and we have been friends ever since.'"* Pearson's nemesis, Diefenbaker, could make what he liked of that.

---

* George Drew died ten years later on 4 January 1973 in Toronto.

CHAPTER THIRTEEN

Lionel Chevrier, 1964–1967

Opposing the application of Britain to join the European Economic Community had been the principal occupation of George Drew. During the three years when Lionel Chevrier was high commissioner, the question did not resurface in any formal or immediate way, but it remained only just below the surface as the lagging British economy continued to suffer from chronic balance-of-payments problems. De Gaulle's veto roughly coincided with the arrival in office of Pearson's Liberal government. Fully aware of the rancour left in London by the antics of Drew and Diefenbaker, Pearson wrote to Chevrier: "The question of entry to the Common Market is basically for the British to decide ... I very much hope that we can avoid striking a public attitude on this prematurely."[1] Pearson knew full well that no Canadian interest was served by the continuation of an economically uncertain and vulnerable Britain, whatever the short-term adverse impact on Canadian exports might be of Britain's adoption of the generally higher external tariff of the Six.

Chevrier was the first and remains the sole francophone high commissioner, but he was not by birth a Quebecois. At age sixty-one, when he was appointed high commissioner, he had been in the House of Commons for a total of twenty-five years. A native of Cornwall, Ontario, and, like Drew, a graduate of both the University of Toronto and Osgoode Hall, the affable Chevrier had first entered Parliament as the member for Stormont upon the defeat of Bennett's government in 1935. King appointed him successively parliamentary assistant to C.D. Howe, a delegate to the Bretton Woods conference, and in 1945 minister of transport. He joined King, Robertson, Vanier, and Wilgress at the third session of the United Nations General Assembly in Paris in the autumn of 1948. Later, having overseen legislation creating the St Lawrence Seaway Corporation, Chevrier left Parliament in 1954 for three years to become its first president. He returned to the House of Commons in June 1957, via the safe seat of Montreal-Laurier. He was made president of the Privy

Council by St Laurent, and following Diefenbaker's victory in September he was opposition house leader. Six years later, when Pearson succeeded in forming a government, he appointed Chevrier minister of justice. The new minister was in office for only eight months, however, before resigning to become high commissioner.

Why did Chevrier leave the new government? A Franco-Ontarian, despite holding Montreal-Laurier, he was not seen as representing Quebec or at least the "new" Quebec. His former colleague in the House of Commons, Jean Lesage, now Quebec premier, better reflected the ferment in the province. Chevrier, by contrast, was regarded as uncertain in his ability to deliver the province for a federal Liberal government in need of every seat it could get. The *Windsor Star* was typical of many Canadian newspapers in stating: "Mr. Chevrier is French, [but] he was not accepted as Quebec French by many of the French-speaking people of that Province. It is one of those quirks of nationalism that dwindles down to provincialism."[2] Guy Favreau, the newly elected member for Papineau, had impeccable Quebec credentials and was not seen to be in the hands of the old guard. Further, in the election of 1962 the Liberals in Quebec had won only thirty-five seats instead of the expected fifty. In the election of the following year, the Liberals had done better, but still not well enough. And again Chevrier was regarded in Liberal ranks as part of the problem. Pearson duly designated Favreau as his Quebec lieutenant. Chevrier, having filled that role himself, could hardly be expected to serve under him.

Would Chevrier have preferred to remain in the cabinet rather than to go to London? And why London when the embassy in Paris was also available upon the retirement of Pierre Dupuy? Chevrier was never clear on either point, talking rather vaguely of the importance of having a francophone high commissioner. In fact, when Pearson had offered him a choice between Paris and London, Chevrier had, to no one's surprise, picked his ancestral homeland. But one account has friends in Montreal expostulating with him that he had made the wrong choice: "We hear you're going to Paris. You'll never be happy in Paris ... You know damn well you can't get along with de Gaulle ... you know he's an impossible fellow ... You're the Acting Prime Minister. Go back and tell Pearson you want to go to London."[3] When Chevrier did so, the prime minister protested that he had already spoken "to someone else" about what the *Globe and Mail* called "the prestige-laden post of High Commissioner."[4] Who the "someone else" was is uncertain, but Norman Robertson, again ill and unhappy in Ottawa, had sought a third term as high commissioner.

Pearson, however, decided that Robertson was in no fit condition to go to London a third time, so in January 1964 Chevrier and his wife Lucienne were on their way. His appointment was well received as additional evidence of Pearson's determination to make the foreign service and the public service generally reflect better Canada's bilingual composition.* Following an introductory call on the new British prime minister, Sir Alec Douglas-Home, Chevrier was closely questioned by the press about what was happening in Quebec. "It is my firm belief that ... [co-operative federalism] will develop a new sense of unity in Canada ... and that separatist sentiment in Quebec ... will subside very largely."[5] It did not in fact subside and it was never to be far from Chevrier's mind during his three years in London.

When the Chevriers arrived in London in February 1964, the staff of Canada House had risen to 850, with nineteen federal government departments and agencies represented. A year later, Chevrier wrote in a seven-page letter to the under-secretary of state for external affairs that the composition of the staff almost wholly ignored the existence of the French fact in Canada (as he had protested in vain during the war about the absence of francophones from the more senior ranks of the armed forces). Visitors to Canada House were not accorded services in both official languages. Additionally, the British were misled about the true nature of Canada, especially when a muted welcome had recently awaited the Queen in Quebec – to the humiliation of the governor general, Georges Vanier. Chevrier added his apologies to her for the coolness of her reception (to which the Queen replied that she had felt sorry for Premier Lesage).

At Canada House the root of the problem was the paucity on the diplomatic list of names "à consonance française." The under-secretary discussed Chevrier's letter with his minister, Chevrier's old friend Paul Martin, but Chevrier was dissatisfied with their answer that the ultimate solution lay in righting the overall insufficiency of French-speaking officers in the department as a whole. He wrote directly – in English – to the more receptive prime minister, largely repeating what he had said to Cadieux in French. He had himself arranged for bilingual signage in both Canada and Macdonald Houses and had induced his former colleagues, the ministers of transport and of trade and commerce, to place

---

* The ambassador to France has, however, never been an anglophone, since Quebec "always regarded the Canadian ambassador to Paris as more a representative of Quebec than of Canada."

During Chevrier's three years as high commissioner, two British prime ministers held office, Alec Douglas-Home and Harold Wilson. Chevrier's relations with the amiable Home were especially cordial, as were those later of his successor Charles Ritchie, when Home was foreign secretary in Heath's 1970 government that finally succeeded in negotiating the entry of the United Kingdom into the European Economic Community.

bilingual signs at the nearby offices of Air Canada, Canadian National Railways, and the Canadian Travel Bureau. In a more symbolic way, he had also sought from Treasury Board funds to match a small bronze statue of Wolfe (which Peter Larkin had placed in Canada House) with one of Montcalm.* In his letter to Pearson and again when on leave in Ottawa in May 1965, Chevrier, knowing his commitment to bilingualism and biculturism, recommended that the prime minister:

(A) Approach the Secretary of State for External Affairs so that he would increase the number of French-speaking personnel at Canada House;
(B) Approach your colleagues in the Government who have departmental representation [in London] ... asking them to instruct their officers to set up bilingual signs, notices, letterheads, etc., where required to post bilingual personnel in their respective departments from time to time so as to reflect the true character of our country.[6]

During the annual Commonwealth prime ministers' conference in June 1965, Chevrier raised again with Pearson the question of French-speaking personnel:

In June you were good enough to have this matter placed on the cabinet agenda and I gathered that some action would be taken. As I indicated to you ... on December 20th last, no action has been taken at all and the matter seems to have been entirely forgotten ... There are two points that strike me. The first is that in Paris a large portion of the personnel are English-speaking, perhaps more than 25%. Here in London the position is certainly anomalous – less than 5% in External Affairs and not even 1% in other Departments being bilingual. The other point is that it is all to the good to have French-Canadians come to London. Not only is it good training for them, but the atmosphere and surroundings are such that when they return to Canada their outlook ... is entirely different and certainly not in conformity with the separatist tendencies we hear of from time to time.[7]

As Chevrier was writing, Pearson was appointing the newly-elected Pierre Trudeau both his parliamentary secretary and principal advisor on constitutional and other changes intended to counter the growing separatist movement in Quebec. The deficiencies that Chevrier had found in

* The bronze donated by Peter Larkin was the maquette for the large statue of Wolfe erected near the Greenwich Observatory in 1923.

London, Trudeau found in the federal civil service generally. Bilingualism beyond that advocated in the royal commission report of 1963 now became a government priority. Chevrier could at least content himself with the thought that, although he had made only limited progress, he had added to the cumulative pressures to promote greater unity.

Chevrier's understandable concern at the minimal use of French at the High Commission reflected his continuing focus on domestic Canadian interests. All of his predecessors had been pre-eminently concerned with Canada's evolving relations with Britain, the Commonwealth, and the wider world. Chevrier viewed the relationship between Canada and Britain much as he did that of Canada with any other major country. However nuanced, complex, and of long duration the Anglo-Canadian relationship might be, Chevrier regarded it as being essentially that of two friendly countries. There is little speculation or reflection in his correspondence about the evolving relationship. What comment there was from London about Anglo-Canadian relations came largely from the pen of Geoffrey Murray, the anglophone deputy high commissioner.*

In mid-April 1966 the under-secretary of state for external affairs invited the deputy high commissioner to comment upon "the frictions which seem to be a feature of our present relations with the British ... the deterioration in the atmosphere ... [and how] to set our relations on a more promising course." In his reply, Murray attempted to define Anglo-Canadian relations in the context of the postwar world.

in 1966 Canada does not share the same respect and confidence which may have existed at an earlier time in our relations with the United States and Britain. During the Second World War and immediately afterwards we were in a happy but artificial triangle with the other two. Canada had earned this position through its wartime efforts and co-operation. With the substantial recovery of European countries, and the emergence of new states in Asia and Africa, and the polarization of the world into superpowers, Canada's place in the scheme of things may have appeared to slip, although in my own view it was more a case of our finding our own level.

This observation Murray expanded at the end of the month into seventeen pages, much of it surprisingly superficial in its analysis. Chevrier was aware of his deputy's work, but he did not attempt to influence whatever

---

* Thereafter, the deputy high commissioner was almost invariably a francophone, matching an anglophone high commissioner.

thinking there was behind it. He evidently agreed with it. Murray did at least get right the importance of London as a place of information and consultation: "Notwithstanding the changes which are becoming apparent in Britain's status and role in international affairs, London continues to be one of the most important diplomatic cities in the world ... Whitehall is still the site of one of the most efficient civil services in the world, and especially of a most effective diplomatic service with a global network of missions and agents. As a post for observation and reporting, London may rank second to none." Chevrier later echoed his deputy in his speeches: "Let there be no mistake about one thing ... Britain – and particularly London – continues to lie on a heavily trodden crossroads, frequented by international leaders of politics, business and culture. It still affords a boundless opportunity for seeing, hearing and influencing major world developments." Murray concluded his review with the self-evident observation that

Britain has lost its place and direction in the rapidly changing world of the sixties. In part the questions [of Anglo-Canadian relations] may be a reflection of the shock of Suez or the disappointment of the Diefenbaker years. In part they may be simply symptomatic of a broader dismay about disintegration of old ideas, old values, old relations and an old order of things. Whatever the cause, there is no room for complacency about the need for early answers which can help to set Canadian-British relations on a new course toward the goals of co-operation, confidence and cordiality which history entitles conscientious people on both sides of the Atlantic to expect.[8]

Upon completion of his tour in Britain, Chevrier would conclude his own evaluation of his term by setting it in an international context, not in a bilateral one. "The three years of my stay in London have been a very busy time ... with three conferences of Commonwealth Heads of Governments, a NATO Ministerial Meeting, a change of British Government after thirteen years and an economic crisis of incalculable consequences. Her Majesty the Queen visited eastern Canada ... there was also the fall of Mr. Khrushchev, the landslide election of President Johnson, and the death of Sir Winston Churchill, the deepening crisis on Rhodesia."[9]

However, only in four of these – the economic crisis, the unilateral declaration of independence by Rhodesia, the Commonwealth prime ministers' conferences, and the Queen's visit to Canada – was Chevrier in any sense a player or even a direct observer. During his first year in Britain, the Commonwealth prime ministers decided, after three decades of intermittent discussion, to establish a secretariat in London. The following year, a distinguished Canadian diplomat, Arnold Smith, was elected as first secretary general, but Chevrier played little part in his selection or the design of the secretariat.

The British application to join the European Economic Community remained just below the surface of Chevrier's term. As one astute observer of the British application to join the EEC has noted, Harold Wilson's Labour government was narrowly elected in October 1964, although

without any serious debate about Europe having taken place. The application for entry [had been] Macmillan's last throw, and [de Gaulle's] veto was his last straw ... So the issue was latent ... which his successor, Sir Alec Douglas-Home, was obliged ... to try and defend. But it was not made much of. The Labour manifesto clung to the old world, in which choices could be blurred. 'Though we shall seek to achieve closer limits with our European partners,' it said, 'the Labour Party is convinced that the first responsibility for a British Government is still the Commonwealth.' A National Plan, designed to end the stop-go cycle that had been the curse of the post-war economy, was wheeled enthusiastically into place ... To the enactment of this paean of belief in state economic planning, the Wilson Cabinet turned most of its energies between 1964 and 1966. The European option was relegated to a negligible parenthesis.[10]

Wilson's plurality being eventually reduced to three in a six hundred-plus House, the Labour government was unable to cope with persistent strikes and wildcat action by trade unions which were supposedly the bedrock of its support, a contentious state aggravated by dissension within the party itself. When Wilson, an arch manipulator, sought a new mandate for his fragile government only two years into his first term, he won a plurality of ninety-seven, an endorsement, it was hoped, sufficiently large to enable him to deal with chronic economic difficulties. The "stop-go" cycles, however, continued. A long-term incomes policy to eliminate restrictive labour practices and to promote efficiency and greater productivity failed in the face of union hostility, leaving no option but to impose in July 1966 a mandatory price and wage freeze which reduced the balance-of-payments problem but only at the price of stultifying economic growth.

Before applying such a radical remedy, the British government had naturally assessed the state of its trade with all its major partners, given the fact that Britain's trade with continental Europe had overtaken trade with the Commonwealth. In the case of Canada, the threat of import restrictions seemed to Chevrier so real that he wrote to Pearson in February 1966, underlining the continuing British dissatisfaction with Canadian anti-dumping legislation, government purchasing practices, and the adverse implications for Britain of the Canada-US Automotive Agreement (about which Wilson had protested to Pearson in February 1965). Pearson's reply was broadly sympathetic, but concluded that "the main reason why we run up large surpluses with Britain year after year is that we are the most economic source of many agricultural products and the industrial raw materials that Britain needs to import." In fact, a British observer might have protested, Canadian exports to Britain were increasingly manufactured products and in any case the basic problem was the British difficulty in penetrating the Canadian market to seek some balance in the trade relationship. Not so, said Pearson in anticipation, the difficulty is that British products are largely uncompetitive with American: "their weakness in trade with Canada reflects a broader weakness in the British economy as a whole." The argument had come full circle: British economic performance was weak because it did not export enough; it did not export enough because of "a broader weakness in the British economy." Pearson could think of little that Canada could do, although "this does not imply any unwillingness on our part to be helpful."

His conclusion to Chevrier was not unlike that of Macmillan and Heath: Britain's economic salvation, her release from perennial crises, lay in membership in the European Economic Community, a project which became a significant issue in the British election of that April.[11] Edward Heath, leader of the opposition, warmly supported British entry; Wilson cautiously contented himself with pledging that Britain would join only if the conditions set by the Six were satisfactory. Chevrier, in the wake of Drew's agitation of five years before, admirably observed Pearson's original injunction against "striking a public attitude on this prematurely." The Commonwealth, having proven to be no economic alternative and the economic pressures to join mounting yet again, Wilson announced to the House of Commons on 2 May 1967 that Britain would undertake renewed negotiation. Chevrier had departed from London a few weeks before, but following his return to Canada he did permit himself a public recollection about Britain's dilemma.

Hardly a voice at the present time can be heard arguing against Britain's joining the march toward closer continental co-operation. During the past six months, Britain has moved very much closer to a decision on whether to apply anew to join the European Economic Community. There is widespread recognition for

In 1965 at the Upper Brook Street residence of the high commissioner, Lionel Chevrier, prime minister Harold Wilson (right) was told by Canadian prime minister Lester Pearson that if the United Kingdom decided to renew its French-vetoed application to join the European Economic Community, his government, unlike that of his predecessor, John Diefenbaker, would regard it as a question "basically for the British to decide."

Britain to find a firm footing in the nearby European markets, to throw its political weight on the balance pan of European power, and to bring about technical co-operation with European countries to help prevent virtual monopoly by the United States.[12]

The existence of the Commonwealth had consistently complicated Labour as well as Conservative thinking about joining the European Economic Community. More directly, it also defined, during Chevrier's term, British policy toward the newly independent former colonies in Africa. "Although the evidence of a long-term downward trend away from Commonwealth trade could not be refuted, this special British relationship with a multi-racial Third World was something with great appeal to the Labour soul ... But the middle 1960s saw a rending of both the economic and political ties with the Commonwealth."[13] The question of continuing membership of South Africa had finally been resolved by its withdrawal; now the problem was Rhodesia. Throughout Chevrier's tour and certainly at the prime ministers' conference of 1964, 1965, and the two conferences of 1966, the future of Rhodesia was a major issue. Following the 1964 conference, he delivered a letter from Pearson to Ian Smith, the prime minister of Rhodesia who was in London for talks with the government. Chevrier reported that Smith had not been impressed by Pearson's counsel of caution in his racial policies: "He received me rather coolly and did not encourage me to stay." The 1965 Commonwealth conference made yet clearer the conviction of many African countries that Britain, still dilatory, should head off any unilateral declaration of independence by the use of force if necessary. The powers of Rhodesia's locally elected, all-white government were circumscribed by the residual powers insisted upon by London, although not to the point of using force. Pearson played a notable part as mediator between the restless black Africans and temporizing British.

Rhodesia declared unilaterally its independence on 11 November 1965. The Smith government, elected by the white minority, had rejected all British proposals for transition to eventual majority role. It declared itself free to pursue its own policies, including racial discrimination. Most Commonwealth members contended that Britain and indeed the United Nations were not doing enough to bring the local government to its senses and to end its illegal independence. Britain's answer was economic blockade, especially of petroleum, not wholly effective when Portugal and South Africa continued to supply Rhodesia and when certain other countries were eager to make a quick dollar by publicly endorsing the economic embargo but turning a blind eye to the actions of their own corporations.

Upon Rhodesia's unilateral declaration of independence, Pearson announced that Canada, having not recognized the independence of Rhodesia, would join in the international embargo against it. Although the economic isolation of Rhodesia had no early impact, it did have a major adverse effect on neighbouring Zambia (the former Northern Rhodesia), dependent as it was on Rhodesia for access to the sea and a major portion of its imports. To keep Zambia supplied with petroleum, an airlift was mounted which included RCAF aircraft. As the High Commission reported somewhat ambiguously, "Canadian support of British action has been consistently firm and forthright ... Canada's role has been from time to time to seek middle positions acceptable to both the British and the Africans." At a special conference of Commonwealth prime ministers in Lagos in January 1966, Pearson strove mightily to keep some balance between the demands of the Africans and what he knew that the British, in terms of *realpolitik*, could do. An economic sanctions committee was endorsed, but African expectations of more direct action were again frustrated.

Economic sanctions continued to be seen as the sole means of persuasion. An unexpected result was an additional role for Chevrier: he was elected chairman of the Commonwealth Sanctions Committee. At its first meeting following the Lagos conference, it became evident that British eagerness to chair it was matched by opposition of other members who remained sceptical of the degree of British commitment to an early resolution of what was basically a racial issue. Chevrier had agreed that the secretary of state for Commonwealth affairs should be chairman, but he himself was elected at the committee's second meeting in February 1966. His role was not easy. Wilson's government hoped against hope that economic sanctions alone would bring down Smith's government. Not surprisingly, they did not. Meetings between Wilson and Smith were no more successful. When Chevrier resigned as high commissioner in February 1967, after chairing thirteen meetings of the sanctions committee, Smith was still defiant, leaving Chevrier convinced that it "would rather go down to defeat fighting than conceding a representative share of the government to the [black] majority," although he added optimistically that "the experts seem to think that [its] downfall is only a question of time."[14] Mounting civil war in Nigeria was diverting some international attention, but Rhodesia long remained a problem for Britain, for the Commonwealth, and for the United Nations.

The circumstances of Chevrier's departure from London gave rise to even more speculation than his appointment three years before. As early as January 1965, at the time of Churchill's funeral, he had told a visiting senator that he wanted to return to active politics. In April he asked Pearson to accept his resignation to defend himself against allegations in the *Toronto Star* that he was responsible for unsavoury appointments to the Department of Justice that were threatening the future of Guy Favreau, his successor as Quebec lieutenant. In June 1966 he told Pearson, during a visit to Canada, that he would like to leave by year-end. Pearson declined, reportedly offering him the embassy in Washington upon completion of his tour in London. Chevrier in turn declined. In October, Pearson announced that he had persuaded him to become "Commissioner General for Visits of State" for Canada's centennial year, 1967.

In marking the completion of Chevrier's tour, the *Globe and Mail* described him "as chiefly notable as a social diplomat. The almost daily round of lunches and dinners – often including two or three white-tie affairs a week – finally wore him down and he told Mr. Pearson some months ago that he wanted to retire to private life by the end of this year."[15] Southam Press contented itself with observing that he had found the high commissionership "immensely frustrating" without explaining why. By contrast, Chevrier himself later described his London years as "the most exciting, at the crossroads of the world." The fact that speculation immediately arose over whether he, now age sixty-three, was to return to the House of Commons and, more unlikely, make a bid for the Liberal leadership on the retirement of Pearson is less a comment on Chevrier's thinking than on the likelihood that the member for Mount Royal, Pierre Elliott Trudeau, would succeed Pearson. Chevrier left London in late March 1967, six months after Pearson had announced his appointment as "Commissioner General for Visits of State."* Almost his final official act was to unveil a bilingual plaque recording that in Canada's centennial year, Canada House had, after two years' work, been expanded by the addition of the adjoining building of the Royal College of Physicians (facing Pall Mall). Much of the staff of the High Commission were still scattered over the west end of London; now more of them could be brought together in Canada House.

Although Chevrier's successor was widely rumoured to be Donald Gordon, the dynamic and controversial head of the Canadian National Railway Company, it was the urbane Canada House veteran, Charles Ritchie, who became high commissioner in August 1967, the third career diplomat to do so. It was Ritchie who would oversee the implementation, at the London end, of the acquiescent policy of Pierre Trudeau towards Britain's application to join the European Economic Community, thereby affirming the profound transformation of the Commonwealth.

* Lionel Chevrier died in Montreal on 8 July 1987.

CHAPTER FOURTEEN

Charles Ritchie, 1967–1971

Britain finally and formally became a member of the European Economic Community on 1 January 1973. Although on that day Jake Warren, a Canada House veteran and former deputy minister of industry, trade and commerce, was high commissioner, it was the ineffable Charles Ritchie who from August 1967 to September 1971 monitored to its conclusion the problematic British application, with all its implications for the Commonwealth and Anglo-Canadian relations.

Canada could not have had a more perceptive and experienced observer of this revolutionary shift in British foreign policy and in the transformation of the Commonwealth. In 1967 Ritchie was at least as familiar with and as entertained by Britain as Massey had been more than three decades before. An Oxford man like his predecessors Massey and Robertson, he had spent most of his childhood in Britain when not at school in the still imperial Halifax. With his notable panache, he was as at ease as Massey in the salons and senior common rooms of London and Oxbridge. He knew full well that the London of 1967 would not be the London that he had known intimately from the 1920s and especially during the Second World War. He was nonetheless delighted to be returning for what would be his final posting in a distinguished diplomatic career; he had been successively ambassador to Germany, the United Nations, the United States, and NATO. About his departure for London from Paris – a Paris he loved decidedly more than the Brussels to which the headquarters of NATO was about to move – Ritchie later wrote:

My daily walks in the Bois de Boulogne were a pleasure. But I had my eye on London. The tenure of Lionel Chevrier as High Commissioner was nearing its close. There was a possibility of a political appointment; on the other hand, a professional diplomat might be chosen ... I had very much wanted the London posting. Who would not? It is, to use a detestable adjective, a "prestigious" appointment. The attractions are obvious: to reside in London in a fine house, to be given the entry to varied English social and political worlds. I had reason to be delighted with my good fortune. It was to be my last post before retirement and I looked forward to it in a spirit best expressed by my friend Douglas LePan, who wrote, in congratulation, that my motto should be that of the Renaissance Pope – "God has given us the Papacy, now let us enjoy it." ... The official car was the largest, most indecently ostentatious vehicle to be seen in London. (It has since been sold to an undertaking firm and must add class to any funeral, rivalling the hearse in length and gloomy grandeur.) My office in Canada House was on a scale to match the car. It had been the dining room of the old Union Club from whom the Canadian government had originally purchased the building. I knew the room well from the years when Vincent Massey had been High Commissioner and I, as his private secretary, inhabited the adjacent cubbyhole. How often had I trod the acres of carpet that separated the entrance from the outsize desk behind which the small figure of the High Commissioner was seated. How often had I stood looking over his shoulder while he peered dubiously at the drafts of speeches I had written for him. It was under the great chandelier that hung from the middle of the ceiling that he had stood when, in 1939, he had announced to the staff Canada's declaration of war. Vincent Massey had been a distinguished representative of Canada. He was a well-known and respected figure in political, social, and artistic circles in London. He had dignity without pomposity, intelligence and charm. Here I now was in his place; it remained to be seen what I could make of it.

Once in London, Ritchie was more certain that the traditional intimacy in the relationship was largely unimpaired or at least "the relations between the Canadian and British governments ... were, for the most part, untroubled, or, as they say in official communiqués, 'cordial and friendly'. They offered no challenges or ordeals to a Canadian High Commissioner." He knew, however, from personal experience that in fact

the times had changed, and so had the relationship between Britain and Canada. In the days of Vincent Massey the Canadian Government, under the leadership of Mackenzie King, was obsessed by the suspicion that Whitehall was plotting designs against our nationhood and trying to draw us back into the imperial framework.

Now, in 1967 ... We no longer harboured fears of British dominance. We had finally emerged from the motherhood of the British Empire, only to struggle for breath in the brotherly embrace of Uncle Sam. There were still enduring ties, rooted in history and common institutions, which gave Britain a special place in the affection of Canadians – at any rate of Anglo-Canadians. We were allies in NATO, fellow members of the Commonwealth, owing allegiance to the same Queen. There was extensive trade between us; there were innumerable special links between groups – professional, business, and cultural. Every spring, London was inundated by our fellow countrymen. They came for the historic sights, for the theatre, for the charms of London and the English countryside, sometimes to visit scenes where they had served in the war or for reunions with friends and relatives. The affection for England was there, but British influence was gone. No future Prime Minister was ever likely to call his book *Canada at Britain's Side.*[*][1]

In May 1967, Britain had again applied to join the European Economic Community. At the end of November, three or so months after Ritchie's arrival in London, de Gaulle had delivered himself of a second veto. Unlike 1963, this time it was informal, but there was no mistaking the general's meaning when he laid down that Britain had still to make "a vast and deep mutation" to qualify. And this time there was none of that satisfaction that Diefenbaker and Drew had done so little to conceal on the occasion of de Gaulle's first rejection. Britain, following the General's second broadside, decided to wait him out by the eventually effective expedient of simply not accepting no for an answer.

Pearson, knowing Britain's intention to apply again whenever circumstances were more propitious, praised in a speech in London (arranged by Ritchie), a "strong and united Europe, not isolated from North America" in which Britain would provide the transatlantic bridge as "a central and integral part of the new Europe, politically and economically."[2] The annual report of the Department of External Affairs for 1967 duly defined the Liberal government's position as "not stand[ing] in the way of the British application while seeking, nevertheless, constructive ways to protect Canadian interests involved."[3] And Paul Martin, now secretary of state for external affairs, had on visiting Britain stated flatly, "the decision whether to apply is, of course, one for the British Government to make, in light of all the relevant considerations."

When Pearson stood down as prime minister in April 1968, Ottawa's "hands-off" attitude did not change. His successor, the enigmatic Pierre Trudeau, pondered whether the Commonwealth was simply a latter-day manifestation of British imperialism. Ritchie was aware that in the office of the new prime minister "there is disillusionment too with the failure of the Atlantic community idea and our concept of Article 2 of the [North

---

[*] Early in the Second World War, Mackenzie King had published a collection of his speeches and broadcasts, *Canada at Britain's Side* (Toronto, 1941).

Charles and Sylvia Ritchie (third from right and extreme left) entertained almost non-stop at the residence of Upper Brook Street. In 1970, the year before Ritchie's reluctant retirement from London to Ottawa and his native Nova Scotia, the Queen, Prince Philip, Prince Charles, and Princess Anne dined.

Atlantic] Treaty." But Trudeau had no more intention than Pearson of intervening in what he regarded as a matter for the British alone to decide. Officials in the Department of External Affairs, however, regretted that the mere prospect of British membership in the EEC had already wrought changes in Anglo-Canadian relations. In commenting on a telegram that Ritchie had sent in June 1968 with the unpromising title of "The End of an Era?" a senior official lamented over the "persistent deterioration in the warmth and intimacy of relations ... communication with British Ministers and officials is no longer as easy or as intimate as it once was and with the bitterness which so often erupts in connection with problems of otherwise relatively minor significance." British officialdom was said to be "remote, detached and ungrateful."[4] Such a gloomy analysis of current Anglo-Canadian relations was not, however, to go unchallenged. Another senior official responded,

Take Britain's attitude towards the Commonwealth at the present time. Whatever we think of Mr. Wilson and his Government, it is quite clear ... that officials in Britain are deliberately and conscientiously seeking to find that magic formula which will provide the Commonwealth with a new lease on life.

Britain is at least defining its attitude towards the Commonwealth in terms that have meaning to its population. We in Canada have been part of the Commonwealth for some time but we are not really very sure what our attitude towards it and to its members really ought to be.

To suggest ... that the British appear "remote, detached and ungrateful" is to reduce our entire relations with Britain to economic terms. I fail to see why, if Britain cannot see its way to getting into the Canadian market, it should not try to find the way in which it can get into the European market and do so, furthermore, without causing relations between Britain and Canada, when viewed in political terms, to become strained.[5]

In face of continuing stagnation of its economy and especially given widespread labour unrest, Britain had once again to devalue sterling, a move which many still regarded at best as a panacea. The true remedy for its continuing competitive ills lay in Europe. Domestically public attention was largely taken by the increasingly sordid war in Vietnam and opposition to the contemporary social order which it was seen as exemplifying. Harold Wilson, however, undeterred by de Gaulle's trenchant demand that Britain had to make a "deep mutation" before it could join the EEC, soon had his reward. Unexpectedly, the aging de Gaulle, having lost a constitutional referendum, somewhat quixotically resigned as president in May 1969. The way had suddenly opened for Britain. When details of the British position became public, John Diefenbaker, leader of the opposition, found the absence of any reference to Canada a denial by the British government of its vague undertaking given, he claimed, by Macmillan in 1960, to safeguard Canada's interests. Trudeau's minister of industry, trade and commerce replied blandly that the British "in their own interests ... would be mindful of our interests."[6] A memorandum to the prime minister recommended a continuation of the Liberal approach: "The Canadian Government has in the recent past [i.e., since Diefenbaker] taken the position that the British accession to the EEC is a decision which rests with the British Government and that Canada should not stand in the way."[7]

In attempting to define Whitehall's negotiating stance, particularly with the new French government of Georges Pompidou, Ritchie reported that the British were taking the line that until the EEC responded, there would be little for them to tell us that we don't already know ... We do not believe that an approach which does not take into account, nor accept as a fact of life, the negotiating position which the British have formally adopted can be expected to encourage them to give serious consideration to Canadian interests ... We see risk in an approach that includes a large shopping list in the same way we have done in the past and which denies in effect our acceptance of the reality of their negotiating position. The British still refer to Canadian concerns about exports of church vestments as an illustration of the futility of such consultations ... It is not to suggest that we could not expect ... very much by way of accommodation for Canada, but there may be more scope ... if we deliberately set out to remove the lingering suspicion about Canada's declared benevolent neutrality.[8]

Ritchie's thinking, well known in Whitehall, may in turn have inspired a letter from Wilson to Trudeau. On 8 May 1970 Wilson repeated the commitment to "continuing close consultations" that he had earlier made at the January 1969 conference of Commonwealth heads of government. In forecasting that negotiations with the EEC would resume in the summer, Wilson proposed regular meetings of high commissioners. Ottawa responded with alacrity. Wilson, however, made his offer only one week before he announced the general election of 18 June 1970.

Wilson saw out de Gaulle, but he did not see Britain into the EEC. The election, fought by Labour on the uninspiring theme of "put the economy right" after it had already had five years to do so, resulted in a substantial victory for the Conservatives led by the pro-EEC Edward Heath. Within a week, Ritchie had called on the new foreign secretary, Sir Alec Douglas-Home, whom he regarded as "quite exceptional in his wisdom, tolerance and charm." Once Ottawa's prime questions of Arctic pollution and an European security conference had been disposed of, Ritchie again entered a plea for continuing consultation by both ministers and officials on the British application to join the EEC. His proposal had evidently been accepted by the "somewhat vague affirmative noises" of the foreign secretary. However, to make certain that, whatever the opposition of the past, there was no doubt in Whitehall about the Canadian desire for "continuing consultation," he was asked in September to deliver a letter from Trudeau to Heath, seeking assurances that Britain recognized that "it will be important to maintain ... that close bilateral consultation we have always had."[9]

At first Trudeau was decidedly reluctant to participate in the 1969 conference in London, ostensibly because of pressing demands at home, but chiefly because of his hostility to the colonialism of the past. His days at the London School of Economics in 1947 had not, it was thought, had the impact on him that Oxford had on Massey, Robertson, and Pearson. But upon his return to Ottawa, well satisfied with the openness of the discussions, he reported to the House of Commons: "I assured the London Conference that Canada firmly supports the Commonwealth principle."[10] He told his cabinet that the informal consultations, even about the civil war in Nigeria, had been of "incalculable benefit."

Ottawa's approach to what increasingly looked like the final negotiation of British entry was summarized by departmental officials in that wonderfully anodyne prose that can be spotted by an old Ottawa hand ten miles offshore: "This enlargement, together with the economic and political consolidation of the EEC, should eventually allow Western Europe to play a more positive and outward-looking role in world affairs, to assume more of its defence, to realize its economic potential, and make a full intellectual contribution to western civilization." Following this latter patronizing observation and a pious expression of regret that regional rather than multilateral trade liberalization was being pursued, the department concluded darkly:

Enough has been said above to indicate the problems, economic and political, short and longer term, which British entry to the E.E.C. will pose for Canada. We do not think it would come amiss if you were to state emphatically to Sir Alec that, while the Canadian Government does not wish or intend to interfere with decisions which are properly those of the British Government, nevertheless the course on which they have embarked will have fundamental and possibly damaging implications for Britain's relations with Canada; for example, a part of our existing commercial relationship, the preference, is bound to be abolished. In the face of these portentous changes, Canada will necessarily be deeply preoccupied by the way in which its own interests will be affected. The extent that Britain is able to ensure that Canadian interests are adequately protected will be of great importance in preserving the advantages of the present relationship which is so valuable to both countries.[11]

Ritchie had never been in any doubt that, sooner or later, British patience would pay off in terms of EEC entry. The imperative of economic recovery and reform, implicit in Britain's application, was inescapable. Toward the end of 1970, as British prime minister Heath prepared to visit Canada, Ritchie offered Ottawa a brief comment on Anglo-Canadian relations in light of Heath's stronger commitment to Europe than that of the sometimes ambivalent Wilson. The strength of Heath's commitment had reduced Whitehall's interest in the Commonwealth, fuelled in part by vexatious contemporary disputes about arms sales to South Africa. There was also a sense that Trudeau was so uninterested in NATO that he might not only reduce but even withdraw forces from Europe (possibly encouraging a US reduction) which in turn raised questions about how real Canada's interest in Europe was. In Ritchie's view, the basic answer lay in a new and positive transatlantic policy: "There is tendency in London to be sceptical when we express our concern that possible economic and political polarization between Europe and North America will push us further into the embrace of the United States ... There is a feeling in some quarters that we are trying to have it both ways. If we are to receive more sympathetic accommodation, it is their view that we should show more interest in and commitment to Europe."[12]

Heath was in no more doubt than Ritchie where Britain's economic salvation lay. And it was his great fortune, in his unswerving commitment to taking Britain into the Community, that he had the practical Georges Pompidou with whom to deal. Pompidou talked of Heath as a true European, signalling clearly (from the same room in which de Gaulle had pronounced his first veto) that Britain was now well on its way to membership.

The conference of Commonwealth heads of government in Singapore in January 1971 had as its primary focus African discontents with Britain's continuing defence relations with South Africa, with Trudeau acting as an interlocutor between the Africans and the British (offering the fundamental truth that "racial discrimination is perhaps the epitome of human indignity ... if we tolerate it even privately – in our own hearts – then we have diminished our own stature").[13] In contrast, Britain's application to join the EEC did not much interest most of the newer members, but Heath offered continuing consultation, an offer that Trudeau welcomed, given his growing enthusiasm for a multiracial forum from which the United States was absent and in which he could converse freely with leaders from Africa, Asia and the West Indies. Ritchie soon reported that Geoffrey Rippon, Heath's minister in charge of negotiations, would shortly visit Ottawa, demonstrating "a basic British desire to sustain close consultation during a period when pretty fundamental adjustments in our relationship loom ever closer."

Rippon's visit in March 1971, two months before Britain finally broke through French opposition, would be an occasion to forego the tiresome Canadian preoccupation with short-term economic disruptions consequent upon British entry, a concern which, in the crunch, Britain would in any case be able to do little to allay. Ritchie urged (in a sentence uncharacteristically convoluted): "There seems to be every reason to spell out clearly ... where a more energetic effort on Britain's part to accommodate specific Canadian interests at this time seems called for in the framework of our transatlantic and Commonwealth relationship." According to a departmental memorandum, the conversations with Rippon had been more political than economic.

It was the political aspect that was the over-riding consideration for the British Government in pressing for entry into the E.E.C. ... if the Atlantic alliance was to be really strong, the "European pillar" must be strengthened. Europe could not go on indefinitely relying upon the present level of United States forces for its defence. The "political union of Western Europe" was an objective that he [Rippon] thought Canada should welcome since Canada had sent troops to fight in Europe in two world wars ... Common institutions would evolve, but he saw no "instant federalism.[14]

Rippon having stressed the political goals of membership rather than economic benefits, Heath followed with a letter to Trudeau emphasizing that he had sought at Singapore to reassure his Commonwealth colleagues "that Britain, as a member of a larger European Community, will be able to take a more effective part in the varied work and enterprises of the Commonwealth and that, while our entry will provide a challenge it will also provide great opportunities. The ties of friendship and goodwill will not be weakened and the special value which we attach to the Commonwealth will be in no way diminished."[15] Heath's reassurances arrived, paradoxically, when the Department of External Affairs, in undertaking one of its recurring reorganizations, decided to remove Britain from the decades-old Commonwealth division and place it, with Scandanavia, in a new sub-division of the European Bureau. Ritchie protested that at the very time that the British prime minister was proclaiming that the ties of friendship would not be weakened, the department had concluded that "Britain was considered peripheral to our interests and placed in an 'and others' category."*[16]

Talks between Heath and Pompidou in May 1971 confirmed Whitehall's conviction that while negotiations were far from complete and a major

---

* Ritchie's misgivings about the place to which Britain was being relegated in the priorities of Canadian diplomacy were only increased by the lack of coordination among

challenge of selling EEC membership to a still sceptical British people remained, the final phase had indeed begun. Australia was vocal in its deep misgivings about the adverse impact on its economy (New Zealand continued to hope for special treatment), but the *Financial Times* hailed the absence of complaint on the part of Canada. Diefenbaker's strident opposition was conveniently forgotten, a British white paper noting complacently that Canada's export interests would not be seriously affected, with only 9 per cent of its total exports going to the British market.

The completion of the EEC negotiations came suddenly. Heath informed Trudeau in confidence on 6 July 1971 that he would announce in Parliament the following day that "The United Kingdom would join the European Communities on the terms which we have negotiated," effective 1 January 1973. A reply of sorts – hardly congratulatory – to Heath's message was drafted jointly by representatives of the Department of External Affairs, Finance, Industry, Trade and Commerce, and Agriculture – but not of the High Commission. The sterile draft reply gave every appearance of being the product of a committee, sinking to the lowest common denominator, offering no felicitations and repeating yet again "our particular concerns over possible disruption of our agricultural exports and general deterioration in terms of access for many of our exports." The whole question of the impact of British membership in the EEC upon the future of the Commonwealth was disposed of with a simple reference back to the broad commitment of support which Trudeau had offered Heath in Singapore. Instead, the prime minister's office substituted a much more congratulatory message, in the event the only felicitations that Heath received from a Commonwealth head of government.

The British Parliament endorsed the agreement with the EEC at the end of October. Ritchie had left London the month before, deeply regretting his departure:

I can no more imagine life after retirement than life after death. When I wrote to [the Under-Secretary] and told him that I did not wish to "cling to this job", I meant precisely the opposite. I do wish to cling to this job, and of course he knows that I do.

A letter from the Department: "I regretfully must confirm that you should plan your retirement at the normal date, that is, September 23, 1971." So that's

---

various Canadian government departments in London. A senior External Affairs visitor protested, in words familiar for a century, about "the almost complete lack of any cohesion or purpose among the various government departments."

that. It will take some sharp hustling to get out of this house by that date, with two months of the London Season and continual entertaining coming in between, and then the dead month of August. It is the end of thirty-seven years in the Foreign Service.[17]

Shortly before Ritchie's departure, Trudeau, on a visit to London, called upon Heath. The high commissioner's report on the meeting reflected its largely empty character. Heath had succeeded in taking Britain where Macmillan and Wilson had failed. Trudeau, with other things on his mind – pre-eminently national unity – was not unduly concerned about British membership in the EEC (he did not, in any case, follow willy-nilly the briefing notes of officials). The agreeable but largely vacuous nature of the meeting confirmed Ritchie's regrets. As early as April 1969, he had noted despondently, "there is no interest in Canada in tightening relations with the United Kingdom or in reporting home on British politics. Despatches from Paris are read because French politics affect our future as a nation, whereas Britain has virtually no influence at all. The 'British Connection' seems to be receding out of view." The Commonwealth, in terms of Canadian interests, was becoming equally indistinct, despite the fact that it offers "links in a world where there are not too many," a sentiment with which Trudeau would have very much agreed.*[18]

This was as close as Ritchie came to writing a farewell to Anglo-Canadian relations and the Commonwealth as he had known them. He was not a man to compose a sentimental *nunc dimittis*; for all his rare sense of romance, there was a hard core of reality in him. He did, however, sign a telegram prepared by his staff a month before his departure, surveying the current state of Anglo-Canadian relations: "We have stressed the danger of assuming that our traditional links will continue to sustain a level of relationship consistent with Canadian self-interest while in fact traditional mortar ceases to bind and while British priorities are increasingly directed towards Europe." Ritchie added a valedictory comment of sorts, following a farewell call upon Heath. The conversation had been footling, primarily about Heath's hope for a visit from Trudeau on some indefinite date, although Ritchie modestly noted that the prime minister had added "some civil things about my mission here." Heath contented

---

* In Kuala Lumpur in 1970, Trudeau said of the Commonwealth: "It may well prove to be the most important of all international bodies simply because it has no role and because it emphasizes nothing but the importance of the human relationship."

himself with envisaging Anglo-Canadian relations as "developing with no difficulties (except in the case of divergencies over African questions where he sometimes found our attitude difficult to understand)."[19]

Ritchie's final telegram did help to shape departmental briefing notes prepared for a meeting between Mitchell Sharp, the secretary of state for external affairs, with Douglas-Home, then British foreign secretary: for Trudeau's visit to London; and for an additional return visit to Ottawa by Heath. The notes picked up Ritchie's thinking, even his language. "Essentially Anglo-Canadian relations suffer from an element of drift and lack of focus ... We should not complacently assume that our links of the past will sustain the relationship ... As Canada House has noted, the traditional mortar ceases to bind ... We should try to develop a policy embracing all aspects of our relations with Britain rather than simply taking them piecemeal ... [following British entry to the EEC] most of the running will probably have to be done by Canada in seeking to improve our bilateral relations with the British."[20] However, even the officials who wrote such briefing notes did not believe that much would come of their recommendations. One later added sourly, "Our files show that other such reviews have been launched in the past, but have been largely [disregarded]." In any event, Ottawa was preoccupied with its relations with Washington, a Washington now intent upon implementing a drastic programme to counter its balance-of-payments difficulties, whatever the damage to its trading partners, including its largest, Canada.

Ritchie's final message was, more or less, his official swan song. What he really thought upon his departure from Britain he did not record for Ottawa, but in his candid and highly polished diaries, he offered a brief summation. "There remained the bonds of the past, but our future was no longer any concern of theirs. If our preoccupations were with the United States, theirs were increasingly with Europe." But one thing had not changed: "Throughout the stresses and strains of these years the underlying strength of British character and British institutions remained intact. The English themselves were – as they had always been – kindly, ironic, and stoical. Britain remained one of the most civilized countries in the world, if civilization is to be judged by standards of tolerance and humanity."[21]

NOTES

1. SIR JOHN ROSE

1 Rose to Macdonald, August 1869; National Archives of Canada (NA), MG 26A, vol. 258.
2 Grey to Elgin, 18 May 1849; Morison, *British Supremacy*, 266–7.
3 Tupper interview, *Vancouver Daily Province*, 26 April 1913.
4 Skilling, *Canadian Representation*, 3.
5 *Canada, Sessional Papers*, 1869, no. 8; Report of the Minister of Agriculture.
6 Pope, *Memoirs of the Rt. Hon. Sir John A. Macdonald*, 66.
7 Stevens, *Canadian National*, 1:229.
8 British House of Commons Debates, 26 April 1870.
9 Dufferin to Carnarvon, 2 February 1876; Farr, *Colonial Office*, 304.
10 Macdonald to Rose, 16 November 1869; Pope, *Correspondence*, 104.
11 British House of Commons Debates, 26 April 1870.
12 Granville to Russell, 28 August 1869; Fitzmaurice, *Life of Granville*, II:22.
13 Farr, *Colonial Office*, 166.
14 Rose to Macdonald, 3 April 1873, NA, MG 26A, vol. 258.
15 Macdonald to Rose, 11 January 1872; A.A. Den Otter, "Nationalism and the Pacific Scandal," *Canadian Historical Review (CHR)*, September 1988, 333.
16 Cartwright to Rose, 8 March 1875, NA, MG 26A, vol. 258.
17 Dufferin to Carnarvon, 2 April 1874; C.W. deKiewitt, and F.H. Underhill, *Dufferin-Carnarvon Correspondence 1874–1878* (Toronto, 1955), 23; Skilling, *Canadian Representation*, 85–8; and Farr, *Colonial Office*, 255–6.
18 Canada, Senate Debates, 30 March 1874. See also the protests of Senator Peter Mitchell, minister of marine and fisheries, about Jenkins's advocacy of imperial federation (ibid., 5 May 1873, 75).
19 *The Times*, 6 April 1875.

2. ALEXANDER GALT

1 Gladstone to Lorne, 7 March 1879; MacNutt, *Days of Lorne*, 230–1.
2 *Canada, Sessional Papers*, 1880, no.105; Skelton, *Galt*, 524.
3 Macdonald memorandum, 11 March 1880, NA, MG 26A, vol. 17.

4 Macdonald to Lorne, 5 February 1880, NA, Lorne Papers, vol. 1; Creighton, *Old Chieftain*, 279, and MacNutt, *Days of Lorne*, 55.

5 Lorne to Salisbury, 29 September 1879; MacNutt, *Days of Lorne*, 234–5.

6 Salisbury to Lorne, 5 November 1879; ibid., 235–6.

7 Lorne to Salisbury, 28 November 1879; ibid., 236–7.

8 Skilling, *Canadian Representation*, 94.

9 Rose to Macdonald, 2 November 1879, NA, MG 26A, vol. 216.

10 House of Commons Debates, 1 April 1880.

11 Toronto *Globe*, 9 August 1859.

12 Galt to Young, 15 May 1869; and Galt to Cartier, 14 September 1869; Skelton, *Galt*, 452.

13 Galt to his wife, 14 January 1867; NA, Galt Papers, vol. III; Skelton, *Galt*, 192, and Bodelson, *Studies in Mid-Victorian*, 45.

14 Granville to Young, 14 June 1869, Colonial Office Papers, 42/678.

15 Hammond, *Confederation*, 145.

16 Macdonald to Rose, 23 February 1870; Pope, *Correspondence*, 128.

17 Macdonald to Brydges, 28 January 1870; ibid., 125, and Skelton, *Galt*, 279.

18 Macdonald to Lorne, 17 May 1880; and Galt to Macdonald, 8 May 1880; Creighton, *Old Chieftain*, 290.

19 Campbell to Lorne, 4 July 1880; MacNutt, *Days of Lorne*, 252.

20 Galt to Tilley, 15 April 1880; and Galt to Macdonald, 10 June 1880, NA, MG 26A; and Skelton, *Galt*, 529.

21 Galt to Macdonald, 26 May 1880, NA, MG 26A, vol. 217.

22 Galt to Macdonald, 10 June 1880, ibid.

23 Macdonald to Lorne, 25 May 1880; Creighton, *Old Chieftain*, 290.

24 Draft instructions to Galt, 24 May 1880; NA, Minutes of Council, PC 935.

25 Macdonald to Carnarvon Commission, Stewart, "Sir John A. Macdonald and the Imperial Defence Commission," 94.

26 Galt to Macdonald, 26 May 1880.

27 Ibid., 10 June 1880.

28 Roberts, *Salisbury*, 384.

29 Macdonald to Lorne, 13 March 1882, NA, MG 26A.

30 Macdonald to Galt, 26 February 1882, Pope, *Correspondence*, 285–7.

31 Stephen to Rose, 16 December 1880; Cruise and Griffiths, *Lords of the Line*, 90.

32 Stephen to Macdonald, 16 December 1880, NA, MG 26A.

33 Macdonald to Tupper, 22 November 1883; Saunders, *Tupper*, II:22–3.

34 Stephen to Macdonald, 11 January 1882; Masters, "Financing," *CHR*, December 1943.

35 Kimberly to Lorne, NA, MG 26A, vol. 219.

36 Galt to Macdonald, 16 April 1881, ibid.

37 Lorne to Argyll, 16 July 1881; MacNutt, *Days of Lorne*, 254.

38 Macdonald to Galt, 7 January 1882; Creighton, *Old Chieftain*, 328.

39 Galt to Macdonald, 18 January 1883, NA, MG 26A, vol. 220.

40 Macdonald to Galt, 2 February 1883; Skelton, *Galt*, 540.
41 Macdonald to Galt, 21 February 1883; Pope, *Correspondence*, 298–9.
42 Tupper to Macdonald, 31 March 1881, NA, MG 26F, V.
43 Galt to Tupper, 7 February 1881; Skelton, *Galt*, 547.
44 Macdonald to Galt, 15 May 1883; Pope, *Correspondence*, 301.

3. SIR CHARLES TUPPER

1 Tupper to Macdonald, 12 July 1883, NA, MG 26A, 525.
2 Lorne to Derby, 22 April 1883; Creighton, *Old Chieftain*, 350.
3 Hammond, *Confederation*, 243.
4 Tupper, *Political Reminiscences*, 14.
5 Rosebery to Ripon, 2 December 1894; Waite, *Man from Halifax*, 241.
6 Macdonald to Tupper, 25 July 1883, NA, MG 26A, vol. 525.
7 Macdonald to Tupper, 22 November 1883, ibid., 22.
8 Macdonald to Tupper, 4 December 1883, NA, MG 26F, vol. 267; Pope, *Correspondence*, 308.
9 Stephen to Macdonald, 10 February 1884; Masters, "Financing," *CHR*, December 1943.
10 Canada, *Sessional Papers*, 1891, no. 6E.
11 Tupper to Macdonald, 13 July 1885, NA, MG 26F, vol. 335.
12 Macdonald to Tupper, 4 June 1884; Saunders, *Tupper*, II:33, and Stewart, "Canadian-West Indian," *CHR*, 1950.
13 Tupper to Macdonald, 24 February 1885, NA, MG 26A, vol. 283; Saunders, *Tupper*, II:46, and Pope, *Correspondence*, 337.
14 Macdonald to Tupper, 12 March 1885; Pope, *Correspondence*, 337–8.
15 Rose to Macdonald, 29 May 1884, NA, MG 26A, vol. 259.
16 Tupper to Macdonald, 25 January 1887, ibid., and Saunders, *Tupper*, II:83.
17 Salisbury to Colonial Conference, 4 April 1887; Roberts, *Salisbury*, 464.
18 Memorandum by Bayard, 31 January 1881; Tansill, *Canadian-American Relations*, 74–5.
19 Waite, *Man from Halifax*, 217.
20 Tupper, *Recollections*, 208–9, and *Vancouver Daily Province*, 5 April 1913. Macdonald subsequently declared Tupper his successor at several public meetings (see, for example, Creighton, *Old Chieftain*, 233).
21 Tupper to C.H. Tupper, 17 June 1888; Tupper, *Supplement*, 105.
22 House of Commons Debates, 27 May 1887.
23 Colmer to Macdonald, 21 February 1884, NA, MG 26A, vol. 129610.
24 Macdonald to Tupper, 24 September 1884; Saunders, *Tupper*, II:39.
25 Saunders, *Tupper*, II:217.
26 Shields, "Tupper."
27 Stephen to Tupper, 13 August 1884; Saunders, *Tupper*, II:38.
28 Tupper to Galt, 15 March 1883; Macdonald to Tupper, 13 August 1884, NA, MG 26F, vol. V.

29 Tupper's speech to the Imperial Federation League, 22 June 1889; Tupper, *Recollections*, 247–8; a reworded version is in the *Vancouver Daily Province*, 26 April 1913.

30 Macdonald to Tupper, 14 August 1889, Tupper, *Recollections*, 248–9;

31 Tupper to Macdonald, 13 September 1889, ibid., 249–50.

32 Macdonald to Tupper, 15 January 1888; Creighton, *Old Chieftain*, 494–5.

33 Macdonald to Tupper, 10 July 1886, NA, MG 26F, vol. 384.

34 Thompson to his wife, 10 June 1891, Waite, *Man from Halifax*, 297.

35 Pope, *Public Servant*, 104.

36 *Vancouver Daily Province*, 23 April 1913.

37 Tupper to his son, 29 January 1895; Saunders, *Tupper*, II:182–3.

38 Tupper interview, *Vancouver Daily Province*, 26 April 1913, and Tupper to Borden, 5 December 1913; Tupper, *Supplement*, 102.

39 Borden, *Memoirs*, I:191–2; Pearson, *Words*, 36.

40 Pope, *Public Servant*, 108–9.

41 House of Commons Debates, 7 February 1916.

4. LORD STRATHCONA

1 Griffith to Borden, 7 February 1914, NA, MG 26H, IC, vol. 173.

2 House of Commons Debates, 10 May 1878.

3 Smith Election Statement, February 1887; Willson, *Strathcona*, 421–2.

4 Vaughan, *Van Horne*, 208–9.

5 Willson, *From Quebec*, 49.

6 Preston, *Life and Times*, 217.

7 Preston, *My Generation*, 352.

8 Garvin, *Chamberlain*, II:333–4, and Kendle, *The Colonial and Imperial Conferences*, 20.

9 Chamberlain speech to the Canada Club, London, 25 March 1896; Willison, *Laurier and the Liberal Party*, II:306; Garvin, *Chamberlain*, III:179.

10 Laurier speech to the Canada Club, London, 13 June 1896; Willison, *Laurier and the Liberal Party*, II:287.

11 Willson, *Strathcona*, 8.

12 Ibid., 224.

13 Smith to Chamberlain, ibid., 541.

14 Smith speech to Congress of the Chambers of Commerce of the British Empire, 6 June 1896 and resolution of the Congress of the Chambers of Commerce of the British Empire, 1896; ibid., 228–9.

15 House of Commons Debates, 16 May 1899; Skelton, *Laurier*, II: 73.

16 Chamberlain speech to the colonial conference, 24 June 1897; Wilde, "Chamberlain," 229.

17 Smith to Laurier, 16 August 1896; Willson, *Strathcona*, 476.

18 Smith to Sifton, 16 July 1897, NA, MG 17, II, D15, vol. 33, and Sifton to Smith, 26 July 1897; Hall, *Sifton*, I:260.

19 *Hamburger Nachtrichten*; Willson, *Strathcona*, 496.

20 Creighton, quoted in Berger, *Imperial Relations*, ix.

21 Strathcona rectorial address, 18 December 1900; *Rectorial Addresses delivered in the University of Aberdeen*, ed. J. Anderson (Aberdeen, 1902), 306–10.

22 Chamberlain to Minto, 3 July 1899; Stevens and Saywell, eds., *Minto's Canadian Papers*, 92.

23 Chamberlain to Strathcona, 3 August 1899; Willson, *Strathcona*, 515.

24 Tupper memorandum to Minto, 23 September 1902, NA, MG 27 II, BI.

25 *Vancouver Daily Province*, 26 April 1913.

26 Strathcona to Laurier, 11 October 1899, Stevens and Saywell, eds., *Minto's Canadian Papers*, I:148–9.

27 Laurier to Minto, 26 February 1900, ibid., 302.

28 Chamberlain to Minto, 2 March 1900, NA, MG 27, XIV; Wilde, "Chamberlain," 227–8.

29 Laurier Memorandum to Minto, 9 April 1900, NA, MG 26G.

30 Minto to Chamberlain, 14 April 1900, NA, Minto Letterbook, I.

31 Hutton to Minto, 2 March 1900, Stevens and Saywell, eds., *Minto's Canadian Papers*, 305–6.

32 Laurier to Strathcona, 1 February 1900, Penlington, "General Hutton," Berger, ed., *Imperial Relations*, 56.

33 Laurier to Strathcona, 22 February 1900, ibid., 48.

34 Tupper to Strathcona, 18 March 1900, Willson, *Strathcona*, 528.

35 Minto to his wife, 13 June 1904, Stevens and Saywell, eds., *Minto's Canadian Papers*, II:472.

36 Minto to Elliott, 3 November 1901, ibid., 84.

37 Preston, *Canada and Imperial Defence*, 314.

38 Chamberlain to Colonial Conference 1902; Kendle, *Colonial and Imperial*, 130–2.

39 Hall, *Commonwealth*, 91–2; Preston, *Canada and Imperial Defence*, 287.

40 Strathcona to the Colonial Club, 12 February 1903, *Canadian Annual Review 1903*, 264.

41 Chamberlain to Minto, 28 December 1903, Stevens and Saywell, eds., *Minto's Canadian Papers*, II:402.

42 House of Commons Debates, 30 May 1904.

43 Strathcona message to the Birmingham Celebration of Chamberlain's Seventieth Birthday, *Canadian Annual Review 1906*, 619.

44 Kendle, *Colonial and Imperial*, 219–20.

45 Laurier to Preston, 6 February 1906, NA, MG 26G.

46 Preston, *My Generation*, 220.

47 King Diary, 1 October 1906; Dawson, *Mackenzie King*, I:149.

48 King to Laurier, 31 January 1909; Eayrs, *In Defence*, III:228.

49 Borden to Perley, 17 July 1914; *Documents on Canadian External Relations* (DCER), I:649.

50 Trade and Commerce *Weekly Report*, 23 January 1905; Hall, *Canada's Salesman*, 55.

51 O'Hara to Cartwright, 1 September 1909, NA, MG 26G, vol. 405.

52 Hill, *Canada's Salesman*, 57.

53 MacNaughton, *Strathcona*, 325.

54 Strathcona to Laurier, 15 December 1909, Willson, *Strathcona*, 563.

55 Preston, *Strathcona*, 258–9.

56 Chisholm and Davie, *Beaverbrook*, 69–71.

57 King to Stanhope, 23 July 1909, Kent Archives Office, Stanhope Papers, U 1590/C 649; Dawson, *Mackenzie King*, 215.

58 Borden to Casgrain, 26 March 1909; Brown, *Borden*, I:153.

59 *Canadian Annual Review 1909*, 96;

60 King to Stanhope, 29 May 1910, Stanhope Papers, U 1590/C 649, and NA, MG 27I, A7.

61 Kendle, *Colonial and Imperial*, 203–4.

62 Laurier to Imperial Conference 1911, 25 May 1911, *DCER*, I:253.

63 Asquith to 113th Meeting of the Committee of Imperial Defence, 1911; Hall, *Commonwealth*, 91–2.

64 Larkin to Foster, 5 April 1912, Foster, *Memoirs*, 168–9.

65 Grey to Laurier, 10 January 1910, *DCER*, I:246.

66 Perley to Borden, 7 February 1912, NA, MG 27 II, D12, vol. 198.

67 Skilling, *Canadian Representation*, 109.

68 Strathcona to Laurier, 8 March 1908; Willson, *Strathcona*, 556.

69 King to Stanhope, 8 January 1911, NA, MG 27 I, A7, vol. XV.

70 Borden to Amery, 20 January 1913, Brown, *Borden*, I:234.

71 Aitken to Kipling, n.d., Chisholm and Davie, *Beaverbrook*, 114.

72 Borden to Connaught, 30 July 1912, NA, MG 26A.

73 House of Commons Debates, 5 December 1912.

74 Tucker, *Naval Service*, I:199.

75 British House of Commons Debates, 5 December 1912.

76 *Churchill*, ed. R. Churchill, Companion Volume, Part III, 1911–1914, 1509.

77 Churchill to 118th Meeting of the Committee of Imperial Defence, 11 July 1912; Tucker, *Naval Service*, I:179.

78 Nine members of Parliament to Asquith, 18 December 1912, Bodleian Library, MSS English History, C 659, folio 113-6.

79 Tucker, *Naval Service*, I:197.

80 Violet Asquith diary, 13 January 1913, *Lantern Slides*, 375.

81 Griffith to Borden, 3 October 1911, NA, MG 26H, I C, vol. 173.

82 Willson, *Strathcona*, 442–3.

83 Tupper to Borden, 5 December 1913, C.H. Tupper, *Supplement*, 112.

84 Perley to Borden, 7 February 1912, NA, MG 26H, I C, vol. 173.

85 Griffith to Borden, 7 February 1914, ibid.

86 *The Times*, 5 May 1914.

5. SIR GEORGE PERLEY

1 Toronto *Globe*, 12 February 1914.

2 *Toronto Star*, 16 February 1914.

3 *Canadian Annual Review 1910.*

4 Pearson, *Mike,* 1:88.

5 *The Times,* 26 April 1914.

6 Perley to Borden, 15 August 1914, DCER, 1:18–22.

7 H.F. Gadsby, *Maclean's,* March 1915.

8 Perley to Borden, 8 August 1914, DCER, 1:43.

9 Borden to Perley, 26 November 1914, ibid., 59.

10 Perley memorandum, 2 July 1915, ibid., 86.

11 Perley to Foster, 23 December 1915, NA, Foster Papers, vol. XVIII.

12 Perley to Borden, 4 March 1916, ibid., 118.

13 Perley to Borden, 21 October 1914; Wise, *Canadian Airmen,* 47.

14 Cahan to Borden, 16 January 1915, NA, MG 26H.

15 Borden, *Memoirs,* 1:507.

16 Ibid., 506.

17 Ibid., 508.

18 British House of Commons Debates, 22 September 1915.

19 Perley to Borden, 28 October 1915, DCER, 1:92.

20 Borden to Perley, 30 October 1915, ibid., 93–4.

21 Perley to Law, 3 November 1915, ibid., 95, and Hilliker, *Canada's Department,*
    1:67.

22 Law to Perley, 3 November 1915, DCER, 1:96.

23 Perley to Aitken, 4 January 1916, NA, MG 27 II, D12, vol. IV, file 116.

24 House of Commons Debates, 21 February 1916.

25 Borden, *Memoirs,* II:682.

26 Borden to Perley, 4 January 1916, DCER, 1:104.

27 Borden to Perley, 24 February 1916, ibid., 115.

28 Perley speech to the National Liberal Club, 6 April 1916; *Canadian Annual
    Review 1916,* 449.

29 Stevenson, *Lloyd George,* 156.

30 Borden to Perley, 19 October 1914; Brown, *Borden,* II:15.

31 Perley to Borden, 9 May 1915; Nicholson, *Canadian Expeditionary Force,* 205;
    and Brown, *Borden,* II:31.

32 Borden diary, 19 October 1916, *Memoirs,* II:568.

33 Borden to Hughes, 9 November 1916, Brown, *Borden,* II:57–8.

34 Annex to order-in-council, 28 October 1916, DCER, 1:148.

35 Perley to Borden, 1 and 2 November 1916; Morton, *A Peculiar Kind,* 92–3.

36 English, *Shadow,* 1:41.

37 Borden to Perley, 14 March 1916, NA, RG 9, III, vol. 80.

38 Wise, *Canadian Airmen,* 75.

39 Borden to Perley, 27 May 1917, NA RG 9, III, vol. 80.

40 Borden to Kemp, 14 July 1917, DCER, 1:173.

41 Churchill, *Great Contemporaries,* 149.

42 Taylor, *English History,* 192–3.

43 Middlemas, *Thomas Jones,* 1:12; Thomas Jones, *Whitehall Diary, 1916–1925,*
    London, 1969, 12; and Lloyd George, *War Memoirs,* 1:1026.

44 War Cabinet Report 1917, 8–9; Brown, *Borden*, II:80–1, and Extracts from Minutes of the Proceedings of the Imperial War Conference, 1917, 16 April 1917, *DCER*, 1:308.

45 Borden to C.H. Tupper, 2 January 1916, NA, MG 26H I C, vol. 173.

46 Borden, *Memoirs*, II:697.

47 Perley to Borden, 29 November 1916; Morton, *A Peculiar Kind*, 135.

48 English, *Shadow*, 41.

49 Preston, *My Generation*, 368.

50 Perley to Borden, 18 November 1917, NA, MG 26H, vol. 79, and English, *Decline of Politics*, 183.

51 Borden, *Memoirs*, II:681–2.

52 Perley to Borden, 12 December 1917, *DCER*, 1:319–20.

53 Borden to Perley, 13 October 1917, ibid., 24.

54 Long to Devonshire, 26 October 1917, ibid., 26.

55 Ibid., 25.

56 Devonshire to Long, 6 February 1918, ibid., 35; Skilling, *Canadian Representation*, 198.

57 Borden memorandum, 15 June 1918, *DCER*, 1:202.

58 Borden to the Imperial War Cabinet, 13 June 1918, NA, MG 26H, 2484; Brown, *Borden*, II:137.

59 Borden diary, 14 July 1918; Borden, *Memoirs*, II:827.

60 *Letters to Limbo*, ed. H. Borden, vi, and Brown, *Borden*, II:138.

61 Borden to Imperial War Cabinet, 23 July 1918, NA, MG 26H.

62 Borden to Lloyd George, 15 August 1918, ibid., 354.

63 Borden to Perley, 2 June 1916, ibid., 714.

64 Ibid., 3 June 1916.

65 Perley to Borden, 27 June 1916, *DCER*, 1:716.

66 Amery to Borden, 18 August 1918, ibid., 717.

67 Borden to Amery, 4 September 1918, ibid., 718; Borden, *Memoirs*, II:844.

68 Keefer to Borden, 30 November and 6 December 1918, NA, MG 26H, vol. 319; Eayrs, *Northern Approaches*, 92 (Keefer's estimate of the population of Newfoundland was understated by approximately the power of ten).

69 Borden to Keefer, 1 January 1919, *DCER*, III:758.

70 Borden to Perley, 27 November 1915, Stevens, *Canadian National*, 466–7.

71 Borden to Perley, 24 January 1918, ibid., 489.

72 Perley to Borden, 28 February 1918, ibid., 490.

73 Borden to White, 17 February 1919, *DCER*, III:287.

74 White to Borden, 18 February 1919, ibid.

75 House of Lords Debates, 12 November 1919.

76 Harcourt to Connaught, 21 January 1915, *DCER*, 1:284.

77 Lloyd George to Borden, 27 October 1918, ibid., 218.

78 Borden to Lloyd George, 29 October 1918, ibid.

79 Amery, "Representation of the Dominions at the Peace Negotiations," 14 November 1918; Wigley, *Canada and the Transition*, 70.

80 Borden, "Memorandum with Respect to Further Work of the Peace Conference," 12 May 1917, NA, Foster Papers.

81 Perley to Borden, 4 May 1920, *DCER*, III:411.

82 Memorandum by legal advisor, 11 May 1920, ibid., 21–3.

83 Milner to Meighen, 4 October 1920, ibid., 158–60.

84 "Extracts from Stenographic Notes of Meetings of Representatives of the United Kingdom, the Dominions and India, 1921," 24 June 1921, ibid., 171–3.

85 Ibid., 12 July 1921, 202.

86 Ibid., 27 July 1921, 212.

87 Roland Huntford, *Shackleton* (London, 1985), 679–82.

88 Perley memorandum to King, 17 January 1922, NA, RG 25, D1, vol. 792.

89 *Toronto Star*, 4 February 1922.

90 Ibid., 28 April 1922.

6. PETER LARKIN

1   Wrong to King, 2 February 1922, NA, MG 26, J1, vol. 78.

2   Larkin to King, 18 January 1929, ibid., vol. 183.

3   Wigley, *Canada and the Transition*, 144.

4   Larkin to King, 14 September 1922, ibid.

5   *Canadian Annual Review 1903*, 21.

6   Larkin to King, 22 December 1925, NA, MG 26, J1, vol. 78.

7   King to Larkin, 2 February 1922, ibid.

8   King to Larkin, 23 April 1924, ibid.

9   King to Larkin, 21 April 1928, ibid., vol. 171.

10 Larkin to King, 22 December 1925, ibid., vol. 134.

11 King diary, 31 December 1926; Stacey, *Double Life*, 131.

12 King to Larkin, 31 December 1928, NA, MG 26, J1, vol. 156.

13 *Saturday Night*, 15 September 1923.

14 Wade to King, 23 January 1922, *DCER*, III:34.

15 King to Wade, 22 March 1922, ibid., 34–5.

16 Wade to Larkin, 26 October 1922, ibid., 36–7.

17 Larkin to King, 2 November 1922, ibid.

18 Larkin to Wade, 2 November 1922, ibid.

19 King to Wade, 12 December 1922, ibid., 37.

20 *Canadian Annual Review 1923*, 109.

21 King to Larkin, 23 April 1924, NA, MG 26, J1, vol. 113.

22 King to Larkin, 31 December 1926, ibid., vol. 156.

23 Larkin to King, 16 May 1922; Eayrs, *In Defence*, 1:14; and "The Roots of Irritation," in Lyon, ed., *Britain and Canada*, 43.

24 King to Larkin, 27 November 1922, *DCER*, III:303.

25 Larkin to King, 3 June 1924, ibid., 15.

26 Bliss, *Right Honourable Men*, 175.

27 Pickersgill, "Mackenzie King" in English and Stubbs eds., *Mackenzie King: Widening the Debate*, 34.

28 MacFarlane, *Lapointe*, 132.

29 Lloyd George to King, 15 September 1922, *DCER*, III:74.

30 Beaverbrook, *Decline and Fall*, 162.

31 Curzon to Imperial Conference, 8 October 1923, *DCER*, III:264.

32 Pope diary, 16–17 September 1922, Pope, *Public Servant*, 285–6.

33 Carter, *British Commonwealth*, 86.

34 King diary, 17 September 1922; Stacey, *Canada and the Age*, II:23.

35 Chamberlain to his sister, 24 September 1922.

36 Meighen speech to Toronto Liberal-Conservative Men's Club, 22 September 1922, Graham, *Meighen*, 210.

37 Hillmer, "Anglo-Canadian Neurosis," in Lyon, ed., *Britain and Canada*, 67–75.

38 Thompson with Seager, *Canada 1922–1939*, 43.

39 Wigley, *Canada and the Transition*, 282.

40 King to Larkin, 24 November 1922, ibid., 87.

41 Larkin to King, 27 November 1922, ibid., 88.

42 King to Larkin, 23 April 1924, NA, MG 26, J1, vol. 113.

43 Kerr to Massey, 17 November 1922; Eayrs, *In Defence*, I:21.

44 Perley interview, *The Times*, 18 February 1923.

45 King to Amery, 17 July 1923, *DCER*, III:222.

46 Hall, *Commonwealth*, 509.

47 Stacey, *Canada and Age*, II:67.

48 King to Imperial Conference, 8 October 1923, *DCER*, III:239–44.

49 Hankey to Skelton; Cook, "J.W. Dafoe...," 36–7.

50 King to Imperial Conference, 17 October 1923, *DCER*, III:253–4.

51 King and Smuts to Imperial Conference, 31 October 1923, ibid., 272.

52 Baldwin to Imperial Conference, 3 October 1923, Hall, *Commonwealth*, 522.

53 House of Common Debates, 20 March 1924.

54 Wigley, *Canada and the Transition*, 3.

55 Borden to Christie, 16 April 1926, Eayrs, *In Defence*, I:24.

56 Larkin to King, 19 March 1923, ibid., 173.

57 Amery to King, 4 July 1923, *DCER*, III:221.

58 King to Imperial Conference, 17 October 1923, ibid., 252.

59 Amery, *My Political Life*, II:276.

60 Amery to King, 4 July 1923, *DCER*, III:221.

61 Larkin to King, NA, MG 27 III, E1.

62 King to Imperial Conference, 8 October 1923, *DCER*, III:237.

63 Larkin to King, 16 June 1923, NA, MG 27 III, E1.

64 Skelton memorandum, 2 October 1923, Dawson, *Mackenzie King*, I:471.

65 *The Times*, 23 December 1923.

66 British House of Commons Debates, 31 January 1928.

67 King diary, 19 November 1924, Neatby, *Mackenzie King*, II:41.

68 Larkin to King, 20 November 1924, *DCER*, III:368–9.

69 Devonshire to Amery, 12 December 1924, ibid., 372.

70 King to Larkin, ibid., 373.

71 King to Larkin, ibid., 373–4.

72 King to Amery, 13 December 1924, ibid., 374–5.

73 King to Larkin, 15 December 1924, ibid., 376–7.

74 Larkin to King, 3 December 1924, ibid., 45–6.

75 King diary, 2 April 1924, Neatby, *Mackenzie King*, II:36.

76 Amery, *My Political Life*, II:377.

77 Larkin to King, 15 June 1925, *DCER*, III:379–80.

78 Glazebrook, *Canadian External Relations*, 378.

79 Borden to Austen Chamberlain; 26 October 1925, Borden, *Memoirs*, II:269.

80 Ibid., 159; English, *Shadow*, I:128.

81 Borden to Christie, 8 November 1925, Eayrs, *In Defence*, I:24.

82 Wigley, *Canada and the Transition*, 266.

83 King to Imperial Conference, 4 November 1926, *DCER*, IV:130–1.

84 Ibid., 139.

85 Ibid., 138.

86 Amery, *My Political Life*, II:377.

87 Larkin to King, 16 April 1927, Neatby, *Mackenzie King*, II:43.

88 House of Commons Debates, 31 January 1928.

89 Roberts, *So This Is Ottawa*, 129.

90 House of Lords Debates, 10 July 1926.

91 King to Larkin, 28 February 1927, NA, MG 26, J1, vol. 170.

92 Stacey, *Atlantic Triangle*, 112.

93 House of Commons Debates, 13 April 1927.

94 King to Larkin, 7 July 1924; Wigley, *Canada and the Transition*, 219.

95 Chisholm and Davie, *Beaverbrook*, 278.

96 Beaverbrook, *Friends*, 50–1.

97 Chisholm and Davie, *Beaverbrook*, 279.

98 Larkin to King, 1 June 1929, NA, MG 26, J1, vol. 183.

99 King to Larkin, 31 December 1928, ibid.

7. HOWARD FERGUSON

1 House of Commons Debates, 15 May 1931.

2 Ralston to King, 1930, Bissell, *Imperial Canadian*, 141.

3 Beaverbrook, *Friends*, 24–5.

4 House of Commons Debates, 13 April 1927.

5 Massey to Bennett, 6 August 1930, Massey, *What's Past*, 171.

6 Massey to Bennett, 14 August 1930; text in House of Commons Debates, 15 May 1931.

7 Bennett to Massey, 16 September 1930, Massey, *What's Past*, 176.

8 Pearson, *Mike*, I:75.

9 Oliver, *Ferguson*, 20.

10 Ibid., 45–6.

11 Oliver, *Public and Private*, 47.

12 Ferguson to Baldwin, 12 May 1924, Ferguson Papers, Public Archives of Ontario.

13 Henderson, *Ferguson*, 118.

14 King diary, 17 May 1930; Oliver, *Ferguson*, 365.

15 Clark to Thomas, 2 October 1930, *Times* Archives.

16 Bennett to Imperial Conference, 8 October 1930, *DCER*, IV:228–9.

17 Minutes of Meetings of Prime Ministers, 9–13 October 1930, ibid., 231–6.

18 Stevenson to Dawson, 5 December 1930, *Times* Archives.

19 Dawson to Stevenson, 21 December 1930, ibid.

20 Bennett to Committee of Imperial Defence, 28 November 1930, *DCER*, IV:359.

21 Hall, *Commonwealth*, 323.

22 Toronto *Globe*, 22 November 1930; Montreal *Gazette*, 7 December 1930.

23 Dafoe to Sifton, 26 November 1930, Oliver, *Ferguson*, 378.

24 Dafoe to Grant, 27 December 1930, ibid., 414.

25 King to MacDonald and Lloyd George, 3 December 1930, and to Simon, 5 December 1930, ibid., 378.

26 Borden to Baldwin, 9 October 1930; *Times* Archives.

27 Dexter to Dafoe, 8 December 1930, Oliver, *Ferguson*, 378–9.

28 *The Times*, 12 November 1930, ibid., 142.

29 Henderson, *Ferguson*, 117.

30 Ferguson speech to the Technical Service Council, Toronto, 4 December 1930, Toronto *Globe*, 5 December 1930; Henderson, *Ferguson*, 136.

31 Dafoe to Sifton, 23 December 1930, Oliver, *Ferguson*, 380.

32 Stevenson to Dawson, 5 December 1930, *Times* Archives.

33 Ibid., 10 January 1931.

34 House of Commons Debates, 15 May 1931.

35 House of Commons Debates, 22 November 1931; Toronto *Mail and Empire*, 23 November 1931.

36 Pearson, *Mike*, 1:93.

37 Sargent to Batterbee, 16 April 1935; Oliver, *Ferguson*, 414.

38 Archer to Batterbee, n.d. 1936, ibid.

39 Vanier to Skelton, 21 August 1931, *DCER*, IV:15–16.

40 Ferguson to Bennett, 4 March 1932; Oliver, *Ferguson*, 391.

41 Drummond, *Imperial Economic Policy*, 171.

42 Ibid.

43 Cabinet Minutes, 3 February 1932; Oliver, *Ferguson*. 397.

44 Beaverbrook to Bennett, 4 February 1932, ibid., 398.

45 F.D.L. Smith to Ferguson, 16 February 1932, ibid.

46 Ferguson to Smith, 3 March 1932, ibid.

47 Irwin to Baldwin, 3 February 1932, Middlemas and Barnes, *Baldwin*, 432.

48 Drummond, *Imperial Economic Policy*, 178.

49 Ferguson to Stevens, 5 March 1932, Oliver, *Ferguson*, 399.

50 Drummond, *Imperial Economic Policy*, 183.

51 Swinton, *Sixty Years of Power*, 217.

52 Camrose to Baldwin, 2 March 1932, Middlemas and Barnes, *Baldwin*, 671–2.

53 Amery diary, 30 February 1932, Barnes and Nicholson, eds., *Empire at Bay*, 237.

54 Ferguson to Bennett, 3 March 1932, Oliver, *Ferguson*, 396.

55 Drummond, *Imperial Economic Policy*, 208–9.

56 Beaverbrook, *Friends*, 69.

57 Churchill, *Great Contemporaries*, 293.

58 Roberts, *So This is Ottawa*, 29.

59 Middlemas and Barnes, *Baldwin*, 674–5.

60 Swinton, *Sixty Years of Power*, 218.

61 Runciman memorandum, 5 August 1932, Drummond, *Imperial Economic Policy*, 299.

62 Middlemas and Barnes, *Baldwin*, 680.

63 Chamberlain diary, 20 August 1932; Macleod, *Neville Chamberlain*, 161.

64 Swinton, *Sixty Years of Power*, 218.

65 Oliver, *Ferguson*, 416.

66 *Maclean's* magazine, 15 April 1937.

67 Notes on Meetings of Prime Ministers, 30 April 1935, DCER, V:107.

68 MacDonald to Meeting of Prime Ministers, ibid., 109.

69 Pearson, *Mike*, 1:93, and English, *Shadow*, 1:176–7.

70 Dawson to Stevenson, 4 December 1935, *Times* Archive.

72 Stevenson to Dawson, 9 January 1936, ibid.

73 *The Times*, 6 December 1935.

8. VINCENT MASSEY

1 Massey, *What's Past*, 35.

2 King diary, 14 September 1925, Neatby, *Mackenzie King*, II:67.

3 Massey, *What's Past*, 180.

4 Whitaker, *Governing Party*, 24.

5 Esberey, *Knight of the Holy Spirit*, 174–5.

6 Whitaker, *Governing Party*, 42.

7 Ibid., 40.

8 Esberey, *Knight of the Holy Spirit*, 176.

9 King diary, 5 October 1935, Neatby, *Mackenzie King*, III:121; Bissell, *The Young Vincent*, 233.

10 Massey, *What's Past*, 448.

11 Ibid., 236–7.

12 Stevenson to Dawson, 9 January 1936, *Times* Archives.

13 Stacey, *Canada and the Age*, II:177–9.

14 Massey, *What's Past*, 224.

15 Massey to King, 29 November 1935, ibid., 227–8.

16 Ritchie, *Siren Years*, 137–8.

17 King diary, 8 December 1936, English, *Shadow*, 188.

18 King to Massey, 4 August 1936, ibid.

19 House of Commons Debates, 15 May 1931.

20 King diary, 30 October 1936, Bissell, *Imperial Canadian*, 75.

21 King to Massey, 14 March 1936, Massey, *What's Past*, 231.

22 Massey diary, 17 June 1937, ibid., 242.

23 Ibid., 448–9.

24 Pearson, *Mike*, I:109

25 Hilliker, *Canada's Department*, I:185.

26 Massey to King, 9 January 1936, NA, MG 32, A1.

27 Pearson diary, 31 December 1936, English, *Shadow*, 189.

28 King to Massey, 14 March 1936, DCER, VI:961, Massey, *What's Past*, 231.

29 MacDonald to Meeting of High Commissioners, 13 March 1936, Hall, *Commonwealth*, 739.

30 King to Massey, 1 May 1936, Massey, *What's Past*, 238.

31 Massey memorandum, 19 September 1938, Bissell, *Imperial Canadian*, 78.

32 Massey diary, 21 September 1937, *What's Past*, 234.

33 King speech to League of Nations, September 1936, Stacey, *Canada and the Age*, II:195.

34 King to Imperial Conference, 21 May 1937; DCER, VI:915.

35 Munro introduction to ibid., xiii.

36 Massey to Rundle, 3 February 1936, *What's Past*, 228.

37 Willingdon speech to the Empire Club, Toronto, 28 March 1930.

38 Massey diary, 26 November 1936, *What's Past*, 250.

39 Massey diary, 16 October 1924, Bissell, *The Imperial Canadian*, 8.

40 Stevenson to Dawson, 16 December 1938, *Times* Archives.

41 Massey diary, 17 June 1937, Bissell, *The Imperial Canadian*, 119.

42 Neville Chamberlain to Tweedsmuir, 8 June 1937, NA, Tweedsmuir Papers.

43 King diary, 9 August 1937; Dilks, *Britain and Canada*, 13.

44 King to Greenwood, 6 October 1937, Neatby, *Mackenzie King*, III:224.

45 King diary, 26 June 1937; Bissell, *Imperial Canadian*, 93.

46 King diary, 29 June 1937; Neatby, *Mackenzie King*, III:223; Esberey, *Knight of the Holy Spirit*, 212–13; Stacey, *Double Life*, 186–7.

47 Bissell, *The Imperial Canadian*, 89.

48 House of Commons Debates, 10 September 1938.

49 Massey diary, 12 September 1938, *What's Past*, 257.

50 Massey diary, 24 September 1938.

51 Ibid., 27 September 1938.

52 King to Chamberlain, 29 September 1938; Eayrs, *In Defence*, II:70.

53 King diary, 27 March 1938; Stacey, *Double Life*, 187.

54 King to Hitler, 1 February 1939, *DCER*, VI:1122–3.

55 Pearson to Massey, 16 July 1939, Eayrs, *In Defence*, II:74.

56 King to Massey, 21 March 1939, and Massey to King, 22 March 1939, ibid., 1142–3.

57 Stevenson to Dawson, 28 April 1939, *Times* Archives.

58 Skelton memorandum, 22 August 1939, *DCER*, VI:1233.

59 Skelton Memorandum of 25 August 1939, ibid., 1247–8.

60 Eayrs, *In Defence*, II:25.

61 Ritchie diary, 26 August 1939, *Siren Years*, 42.

62 Massey to Skelton, 27 March 1936, Douglas, *National Air Force*, 195.

63 Pickering Memorandum, 11 September 1936, NA, MG 26, J4, 151.

64 House of Commons Debates, 9 September 1939.

65 Massey to King, 4 September 1939, *DCER*, VI:1290.

66 Dominions Office Memorandum, 16 September 1939; Massey, *What's Past*, 304.

67 Ibid., 305.

68 Stacey, *Arms, Men*, 19. The most comprehensive account of this unnecessarily difficult negotiation is in Douglas, *National Air Force*, 193–342.

69 Eade, ed., *War Speeches*, II:32.

70 King to Massey, 29 August 1940, *DCER*, VIII:560–1.

71 Skelton to King, 20 January 1941, ibid., VII:19.

72 Crerar to King, 4 November 1939, ibid., 381.

73 Stacey, *Arms, Men*, 206–7.

74 Wilgress, *Memoirs*, 113.

75 King to Rogers, 7 May 1940, *DCER*, VII:411.

76 King to Chamberlain, 10 May 1940, ibid., 414.

77 King to Churchill, 22 June 1941, ibid., 427.

78 Hall, *Commonwealth*, 115.

79 Pearson Memorandum, 30 April and 1 May 1940, Stacey, *Arms, Men*, 141.

80 Amery to King, 1 November 1940, ibid., 216–17.

81 King to Amery, 5 November 1940, ibid., 219.

82 Ritchie diary, 16 June 1941, *Siren Years*, 110–11.

83 King diary, 8 May 1940, Pickersgill, *Mackenzie King Record*, 1:213.

84 Robertson to Massey, 20 February 1941, *DCER*, VII:439.

85 Dawson, *Canada and World Affairs*, 209–12.

86 King Diary, 24 June 1941, Pickersgill, *Mackenzie King Record*, 1:217; Eayrs, *In Defence*, III:208.

87 Stevenson to Dawson, 8 September 1941, *Times* Archives

88 King Diary, 21 August 1941, Pickersgill, *Mackenzie King Record*, 1:240.

89 Ignatieff, *Making of a Peacemonger*, 67.

90 King diary, 28 August 1941, Pickersgill, *Mackenzie King Record*, 1:251.

91 King diary, 23 August 1941, ibid., 259.

92 Massey, *What's Past*, 298.

93 Ritchie Diary, 16 October 1940, *Siren Years*, 73.

94 Ignatieff, *Making of a Peacemonger*, 62–3.
95 Ibid., 69; Alice Massey was the aunt of George Ignatieff's wife, Alison Grant.
96 Ibid., 71–2.
97 Wrong to Pearson, 3 February 1942, DCER, IX:125.
98 Pearson to Massey, 9 January 1942; Massey, *What's Past*, 350; Creighton, *Forked Road*, 65–6.
99 Massey diary, 14 May 1942, *What's Past*, 352.
100 Massey diary, 30 September 1942, ibid.
101 Massey to Wrong, 7 January 1944, Eayrs, *In Defence*, III:29.
102 Massey diary, 28 October 1943, *What's Past*, 377–8.
103 Ritchie, *Siren Years*, 11.
104 Holmes, *Shaping of Peace*, I:148.
105 Massey diary, 30 November 1940, *What's Past*, 296.
106 Ibid., 29 September 1939.
107 Pearson to Massey, 27 May 1941, Granatstein, *Man of Influence*, 186.
108 Cranborne to Churchill, 18 November 1941, Bissell, *Imperial Canadian*, II:126.
109 Massey diary, 26 July 1943, ibid., 125.
110 Massey diary, 20 February 1942, *What's Past*, 301.
111 Massey to Macdonnell, 1 June 1943, ibid., 416–17.
112 Massey diary, 29 July 1942, ibid., 361.
113 Keenleyside to Polack, 21 February 1942, DCER, IX:1081.
114 King to Churchill, 6 March 1942, ibid., 989.
115 King to Churchill, 15 March 1942, ibid., 991–2.
116 Wrong to Robertson, 14 December 1942, ibid., 1002.
117 Holmes to Wrong, 25 June 1943, ibid., 1067–8.
118 English, *Shadow*, 227.
119 Ignatieff, *Making of a Peacemonger*, 69.
120 Ritchie, *Siren Years*, 10.
121 Anon., *Canada in London*, 54; "Massey's War," *Globe and Mail*, 10 July 1980. Ignatieff, *Making of a Peacemonger*, 71; and Peter Newman, *Merchant Princes*, 135, have slightly different versions, Ignatieff adding that the High Commission compensated the daughter for her stolen bicycle.
122 King diary, 4 April 1943, Pickersgill, *Mackenzie King Record*, I:507.
123 Stacey, *North Atlantic*, 89.
124 Ralston to Massey, 27 August 1943, Eayrs, *In Defence*, III:29.
125 Holmes to Wrong, n.d., with a covering memorandum from Wrong to Robertson, 28 October 1943, DCER, IX:971–7.
126 Wrong to Robertson, 19 March 1943, ibid., 871.
127 Massey to Robertson; 10 April 1943, ibid., 876.
128 MacDonald to Dominions Office, 2 February 1943, Sanger, *MacDonald*, 213.
129 King diary, 25 January 1944, Pickersgill, *Mackenzie King Record*, I:637–8.
130 Ibid., 637.

131 Massey diary, 26 January 1944, *What's Past*, 394.

132 Holmes, *Shaping of Peace*, 1:148.

133 Ritchie, *Siren Years*, 163–4.

134 Holmes to Wrong, 4 August 1944, DCER, XI, Part II, 1194.

135 Holmes Memorandum, 28 February 1945, Massey, *What's Past*, 421.

136 King diary, 17 February 1944, Pickersgill, *Mackenzie King Record*, 1:644.

137 Massey diary, 17 February 1944, *What's Past*, 396–7.

138 Ibid., 7 March 1944, 401.

139 Attlee Statement, 15 June 1943, Stacey, *Canada and the Age*, II:365.

140 King diary, 28 April 1944, Pickersgill, *Mackenzie King Record*, 1:664.

141 Ibid., 669.

142 King diary, 15 May 1944, ibid., 687.

143 King diary, 6 May 1944, ibid., 664.

144 LePan, "Portrait of Norman Robertson," 5.

145 King Diary, 4 August 1944, Pickersgill and Forster, *Mackenzie King Record*, II:55.

146 King diary, 23 September 1944, ibid., 119.

147 Power to MacDonald, 16 October 1944, DCER, X:285.

148 Wrong to Massey, 18 January 1944, ibid., 320–1.

149 Eayrs, *In Defence*, III:163.

150 King diary, 17 September 1944, Pickersgill and Forster, *Mackenzie King Record*, II:90–1.

151 Massey diary, 4 January 1944, *What's Past*, 427.

152 Ibid., 10 January 1944, 428.

153 Escott Reid, in Eayrs, *In Defence*, III:7.

154 LePan, *Bright Glass*, 67.

155 Massey to Robertson, 22 February 1945, DCER, XI:1155.

156 Holmes, *Shaping of Peace*, 1:152.

157 King diary, 27 April 1946, Pickersgill and Forster, *Mackenzie King Record*, III:216.

158 King diary, 22 April 1946, ibid., 202.

159 King diary, 12 May 1946, ibid.

160 King to Addison, 23 March 1946, DCER, XII:1255.

161 King to Attlee, 10 May 1946, ibid., 1259.

162 Massey to King, 8 April 1946, ibid., 1237–8.

163 King to Conference of Commonwealth Prime Ministers, 22 May 1946, DCER, XII:1271.

164 Holmes, *Shaping of Peace*, 1:152.

165 King to Conference of Commonwealth Prime Ministers, 22 May 1946, DCER, XII:1268.

166 Holmes, *Shaping of Peace*, 1:151;

167 King diary, 11 November 1946, Pickersgill and Forster, *Mackenzie King Record*, III:364.

168 King diary, 20 May 1946, ibid., 223–4.

169 J.W. Pickersgill in ibid., 229.

170 King diary, 21 February 1946, ibid., 177.

171 Ibid., 230.

172 Ibid.

173 King diary, 22 May 1946, ibid., 231.

174 Ibid., 233–4.

9. NORMAN ROBERTSON, 1946–1949

1 Robertson to his parents, July 1932, Granatstein, *Man of Influence*, 42.

2 Earys, *In Defence*, III:31.

3 Ritchie diary, 23 May 1945, *Siren Years*, 195.

4 Robinson, *Diefenbaker's World*, 101.

5 Robertson to King, 14 June 1946, DCER, XII:5.

6 King diary, 5 July 1946, Pickersgill and Forster, *Mackenzie King Record*, III:269.

7 King diary, 5 July 1946, ibid., 270–1.

8 King diary, 4 August 1946, ibid., 295.

9 LePan, *Bright Glass*, 62–3.

10 King diary, 10 November 1946, Pickersgill and Forster, *Mackenzie King Record*, III:364–5.

11 Pearson to Robertson, 26 February, 1947, DCER, XIII:67.

12 Robertson to Pearson, 5 March 1947, ibid., 68.

13 Holmes, *Shaping of Peace*, I:182–3.

14 Ibid., II:182-3.

15 King diary, 25 June 1947, Pickersgill and Forster, *Mackenzie King Record*, IV:55–6.

16 King to Robertson, 29 January 1947, DCER, XIII:1212.

17 Robertson to King, 19 February 1947, ibid., 1212.

18 Gibson to Robertson, 27 February 1947, ibid., 1214.

19 Robertson to Pearson, 8 March 1947, ibid., 1215–16.

20 King diary, 18 December 1947, Pickersgill and Forster, *Mackenzie King Record*, IV:135–6.

21 King diary, 22 December 1947, ibid., 140.

22 Robertson to Pearson, 9 September 1947, ibid., 1229–30.

23 Holmes, *Shaping of Peace*, II:165–6.

24 Robertson to Pearson, 16 December 1948, DCER, XIV:1406–7.

25 King diary, 28 May 1947, Pickersgill and Forster, *Mackenzie King Record*, IV:42–3.

26 Pearson to Robertson, 2 June 1947, DCER, XIII:1373.

27 Pearson to Wilgress, 10 September 1947, ibid., 1537.

28 Holmes, *Shaping of Peace*, I:185.

29 Robertson to Pearson, 8 January 1947, Granatstein, *Man of Influence*, 216.

30 Pearson to Robertson, 24 December 1947, DCER, XIV:1351.

31 King diary, 9 December 1947, Pickersgill and Forster, *Mackenzie King Record*, IV:125.

32 Robertson to Pearson, 16 March 1948, Granatstein, *Man of Influence*, 228.

33 Pearson to Robertson, 8 September 1947, *DCER*, XIV:1240–1.

34 LePan to Pearson, 9 September 1947, ibid., 1241–2.

35 Robertson to St Laurent, 19 June 1947, ibid., 1533.

36 Wilgress to St Laurent, 4 September 1947, ibid., 1535.

37 King diary, 22 March 1948, Pickersgill and Forster, *Mackenzie King Record*, IV:264.

38 King diary, 22 March 1948, *DCER*, XIV:1046.

39 Memorandum from Under-Secretary of State to Secretary of State for External Affairs, 29 June 1948, *DCER*, XIV:787.

40 King diary, 30 June 1948, Pickersgill and Forster, *Mackenzie King Record*, IV:191.

41 Holmes, *Shaping of Peace*, II:103.

42 King to Robertson, 1 June 1948, *DCER*, XIV:1337.

43 King diary, 28 May 1948, *Mackenzie King Record*, IV:305.

44 King diary, 12 October 1948, ibid., 404–5.

45 King diary, 21 October 1948, ibid., 413.

46 Robertson to Conference of Commonwealth Prime Ministers, 11 October 1948, *DCER*, XIV:1357.

47 Extract from Minutes of Conference of Commonwealth Prime Ministers, 21 October 1948, ibid., 1384.

48 Attlee to Conference of Commonwealth Prime Ministers, 18 October 1948, ibid., 1369.

49 Pearson memorandum, 17 August 1948, ibid., 1413.

50 King diary, 20 February 1948, Pickersgill and Forster, *Mackenzie King Record*, IV:161.

51 King diary, 29 October 1948, ibid., 424.

52 Wilgress, *Memoirs*, 160.

10. DANA WILGRESS

1 Wilgress, *Memoirs*, 6.

2 Ibid., 161.

3 Ibid., 168.

4 Robertson to King, 14 June 1946, *DCER*, XII:5.

5 Wilgress, *Memoirs*, 164.

6 Memorandum from Secretary of State to Cabinet, 28 August 1951, *DCER*, XVII:596.

7 Wilgress to Pearson, 6 April 1949, ibid., XV:1296.

8 Heeney to Wilgress, 14 September 1949, ibid., 1299.

9 Department of External Affairs Circular Document no. A.61/51; NA, RG 25, file 6133-6140, vol.4132.

10 Wilgress to Heeney, 25 May 1949, *DCER*, XV:625.

11 Heeney to Wilgress, 27 May 1949, ibid., 628.

12 Holmes, *Shaping of Peace*, II:223–4.

13 Wilgress to C. Ritchie, 30 October 1951, *DCER*, XVIII:942–3.

14 Pearson Statement to the Commonwealth Conference, Colombo, 21 January 1950, ibid., XVI:1199.

15 Department of External Affairs Memorandum, 1951, NA, RG 25, file 6140.

16 Reid to Wrong, 21 February 1952, *DCER*, XVIII:906.

17 Wilgress to Robertson, 6 August 1950, ibid., XVI:110.

18 Pearson to Wilgress, 24 August 1950, ibid., 115.

19 Simonds to Claxton, 16 July 1951, *DCER*, XVII:734–6.

20 Simonds to Commander, 27th Infantry Brigade, 6 November 1951, ibid.

21 Wilgress, *Memoirs*, 168.

11. NORMAN ROBERTSON, 1952–1957

1 Granatstein, *Man of Influence*, 246.

2 Robertson to Heeney, 12 July 1949, ibid., 250.

3 Ibid., 281.

4 Masters, *Canada in World Affairs*, 200.

5 Robertson to Pearson, 22 August 1952, *DCER*, XVIII:928.

6 St Laurent to Robertson, 26 July 1952, ibid., 916.

7 Robertson to Pearson, 22 August 1952, ibid., 928.

8 Heeney to Robertson, 2 October 1954, ibid., XX:796.

9 Robertson to Pearson, 21 January 1955, ibid., XXI:209.

10 Pearson to Robertson, 18 August 1952, ibid., 742.

11 Earys, *In Defence*, V:92.

12 Robertson to Pearson, 10 September 1954, ibid., 650.

13 Holmes, *Shaping of Peace*, II:315.

14 Bothwell, Drummond, and English, *Power, Politics*, 141.

15 Robertson to Pearson, 13 August 1953, *DCER*, XX:779.

16 Pearson to Robertson, 26 May 1954, ibid., 790.

17 Pearson diary, 7 February 1955, ibid., XXI:515.

18 Pearson diary, 30 and 31 January 1955, ibid., 508.

19 McKercher and Aronsen, *North Atlantic Triangle*, 240–1.

20 Memorandum, 1 March 1955, *DCER*, XXI:527.

21 Pearson diary, 4 February 1955, ibid., 514.

22 Pearson diary, 8 February 1955, ibid., 518.

23 Pearson to Harris, 26 September 1955, ibid., 470.

24 Memorandum from Leger to Pearson, 23 September 1955, ibid., 1067.

25 Robertson to Pearson, 30 December 1955, ibid., XXIII, Part II:519.

26 Robertson to Pearson, 14 September 1956, ibid., 553–4.

27 Extract from Cabinet Conclusions, 29 August 1956, ibid., 150.

28 Robertson to Pearson, 28 September 1956, ibid., 174–5.

29 Pearson to Robertson, 30 October 1956, ibid., 180.
30 Robertson to Pearson, 1 November 1956, ibid., 189.
31 Robertson to Pearson, 2 November 1956, ibid., 196.
32 Garner, "Britain and Canada in the 1940s and 1950s," Lyon, ed., *Britain and Canada*, 91.

12. GEORGE DREW

 1 Pearson, *Mike*, III:22.
 2 Ignatieff, *Making of a Peacemonger*, 178.
 3 Ibid., 176.
 4 Bawtinhimer, "Ontario Tory," *Ontario History*, 590.
 5 December 1936, Manthorpe, *Power and Tories*, 25–6.
 6 Drew to Bennett, 12 September 1938; Beaverbrook Papers, House of Lords Records Office, BBK/C/121.
 7 King diary, 7 August 1944, Pickersgill and Forester, *Mackenzie King Record*, II:45.
 8 King diary, 8 May 1947, ibid., IV:37.
 9 King diary, 19 July 1948, ibid., 347–8.
10 King diary, 21 August 1948, ibid., 375–6.
11 Robinson, *Diefenbaker's World*, 4.
12 Diefenbaker, *One Canada*, II:187.
13 Robinson, *Diefenbaker's World*, 10.
14 Spry to Douglas, 3 July 1957, Granatstein, *Canada, 1957–1967*, 43–4.
15 Robinson, *Diefenbaker's World*, 61.
16 Ibid., 211.
17 *Globe and Mail*, 11 November 1961.
18 Lyon, *Canada in World Affairs, 1961–1963*, 68.
19 *Winnipeg Free Press*, 7 October 1957.
20 Memorandum from Secretary of State for External Affairs to Cabinet, 23 June 1958, *DCER*, XXIV:1027.
21 Privy Council memorandum, 28 December 1959, Granatstein, *Canada, 1957–1967*, 46.
22 Ignatieff, *Making of a Peacemonger*, 172.
23 Gordon Robertson, *Very Civil Servant*, 96–7.
24 Smith, *Rogue Tory*, 421–2.
25 Robinson diary, 9 June 1961, *Diefenbaker's World*, 212.
26 Ibid., 212–13.
27 Memorandum of Clerk of the Privy Council to Cabinet, 28 June 1961.
28 Robinson, *Diefenbaker's World*, 213–14.
29 Granatstein, *Canada, 1957–1967*, 48.
30 Reece, *Rich Broth*, 65.
31 Robinson, *Diefenbaker's World*, 126.
32 Ibid., 179–81.

33 Stursberg, *Diefenbaker Leadership*, 165.
34 Drew to Fleming, 8 October 1961, NA, Fleming Papers, vol. 158.
35 *Evening Standard*, 11 November 1961; Robinson, *Diefenbaker's World*, 216–17.
36 Heath, *Course of My Life*, 221–2.
37 Robinson, *Diefenbaker's World*, 266.
38 Memorandum on conversation between Drew and Heathcoat Amory, 26 June 1962, NA, MG 32, C3.
39 Heath, *Course of My Life*, 224–5.
40 Ibid., 279.
41 Diefenbaker, *One Canada*, II:205.
42 Ibid., 187.

13. LIONEL CHEVRIER

1 Pearson to Chevrier, 29 April 1966, NA, MG 32, B16.
2 *Windsor Star*, 30 December 1963.
3 Good, *Chevrier*, 172.
4 *Globe and Mail*, 15 January 1964.
5 Chevrier press conference, London, 13 February 1964, NA, MG 32, B16.
6 Chevrier to Pearson, 17 May 1965, ibid.
7 Chevrier to Martin, 25 March 1966, ibid.
8 Murray to Cadieux, 27 May 1966, ibid.
9 Notes for speeches to the Royal Commonwealth Society, London, August 1966, and to various service clubs in Canada, autumn 1966, NA, MG 36, B16.
10 Young, *This Blessed Plot*, 181–3.
11 Pearson to Chevrier, 29 April 1966, NA, MG 32, B16.
12 Notes for speeches to various service clubs in Canada, autumn 1966, ibid.
13 Young, *This Blessed Plot*, 187.
14 The quotations regarding Rhodesia are from an undated memorandum apparently prepared by Chevrier at the end of his term in the United Kingdom, NA, MG 32, B16.
15 *Globe and Mail*, 21 October 1966.

14. CHARLES RITCHIE

1 Ritchie, Introduction to *Storm Signals*, 86–90.
2 Pearson's speech at Mansion House, London, 27 November 1967.
3 *Department of External Affairs Annual Report, 1967*.
4 Memorandum by Langley, 4 October 1968, NA, RG 25, vol. 8624.
5 Munro to Collins, 8 October 1968, ibid.
6 House of Commons Debates, 4 December 1969.
7 Memorandum to the Prime Minister, 19 January 1970, NA, RG 25, vol. 8624.
8 Ritchie to Under-Secretary of State for External Affairs, 17 March 1970, ibid.

9 Trudeau to Heath, 16 September 1970, ibid.

10 House of Commons Debates, 20 January 1969.

11 Departmental memorandum, 21 September 1970, NA, RG 25, 8624.

12 Ritchie to Under-Secretary of State for External Affairs, 11 December 1970, ibid.

13 Trudeau Statement to Commonwealth Prime Ministers' Conference, Singapore, January 1971; Trudeau, *Conversation*, 6.

14 Departmental memorandum, 5 March 1971, NA, RG 25, 8624.

15 Heath to Trudeau, 6 July 1971, ibid.

16 Ritchie to Under-Secretary of State for External Affairs, 29 March 1971, ibid.

17 Ritchie diary, 29 March and 19 May 1971, *Storm Signals*, 148–9.

18 Ritchie diary, 15 April 1969, ibid., 129.

19 Ritchie to Under-Secretary of State for External Affairs, 21 September 1971, NA, RG 25, vol. 8624.

20 Departmental memorandum, 5 March 1971, ibid.

21 Ritchie, *Storm Signals*, 92–3.

BIBLIOGRAPHY

Adams, D.K., ed. *Britain and Canada in the 1990s*. Aldershot, 1991.

Amery, Leopold, *My Political Life*. 3 vols. London, 1953.

– *The Empire at Bay: The Leo Amery Diaries, 1929–1945*. John Barnes and David Nicholson, eds. London, 1988.

Annett, Douglas Rudyard, *British Preference in Canadian Commercial Policy*. Toronto, 1948.

Anon. *Canada in London*. London, n.d.

Barnett, Correlli. *The Collapse of British Power*. London, 1972.

Bawtinhimer, R.E. "The Development of an Ontario Tory: Young George Drew," *Ontario History*, 1977.

Beaverbrook, Lord. *Friends*. London, 1959.

– *Decline and Fall of Lloyd George*. London, 1963.

Berger, Carl, ed. *Imperial Relations in the Age of Laurier*. Toronto, 1969.

– *The Sense of Power: Studies in the Ideas of Canadian Imperialism*. Toronto, 1970.

Bernard, Kenneth. "Lord Strathcona," *The Wide World Magazine*, March 1907.

Bernier, Serge, and John MacFarlane, eds. *Canada 1900–1950: A Country Comes of Age*. Ottawa, 2003.

Bissell, Claude, *The Young Vincent Massey*, Toronto, 1981.

– *The Imperial Canadian: Vincent Massey in Office*. Toronto, 1986.

Bliss, Michael. *Right Honourable Men: The Descent of Canadian Politics from Macdonald to Mulroney*. Toronto, 1994.

Bodelsen, C.A. *Studies in Mid-Victorian Imperialism*. London, 1924.

Borden, Robert. *Canada in the Commonwealth: From Conflict to Co-operation*. Oxford, 1929.

– *Robert Laird Borden: His Memoirs*. H. Borden, ed. 2 vols. Toronto, 1938.

Bothwell, Robert. "The Failure of Bureaucratic Imperialism," Ph.D. thesis, Harvard University, 1972.

Bothwell, Robert, and Michael S. Cross, eds. *Policy by Other Means*. Toronto, 1972.

Bothwell, Robert, and Norman Hillmer, eds. *The In-Between Time: Canadian External Policy in the 1930s*. Toronto, 1975.

Bothwell, Robert, Ian Drummond, and John English. *Canada since 1945: Power, Politics, and Provincialism*. Toronto, 1981.

Bray, Matthew. "Fighting as an Ally: The English Canadian Response in the Great War," *Canadian Historical Review*, LXI, April 1980.

Brodeur, Nigel D. "L.P. Brodeur and the Origins of the Royal Canadian Navy," in *The RCN in Retrospective, 1910–1968.* James A. Boutilier, ed. Vancouver, 1982.

Brown, Robert Craig. *Canada's National Policy, 1883–1900: A Study in Canadian-American Relations.* Princeton, 1964.

– *Canada, 1896–1921.* Toronto, 1974.

– *Robert Laird Borden.* 2 vols. Toronto, 1975 and 1980.

Brown, Robert Craig, and Ramsay Cook, "Sir Robert Borden, The Great War, and Anglo-Canadian Relations" in John S. Moir, ed. *Character and Circumstance.* Toronto, 1970.

Bryce, Robert B. *Canada and the Cost of World War II: The International Operations of the Department of Finance, 1938–1947.* Montreal, 2005.

Buckley, Suzanne. "Attempts at Imperial Economic Co-operation, 1912–1918: Sir Robert Borden's Role," *Canadian Historical Review*, XXXV, 1974.

Buckner, Phillip, ed. *Canada and the End of Empire.* Vancouver, 2004.

Burgess, Michael. "Sir Charles Tupper and the Dissolution of the Imperial Federation League: The Politics of Unintended Consequences," *Bulletin of Canadian Studies*, Autumn 1968.

Butler, L.J. *Britain And Empire: Adjusting to a Post-Imperial World.* London, 2002.

Carland, John M. "Shadow and Substance: Mackenzie King's Perceptions of British Intentions at the 1923 Imperial Conference," in *Studies in British Imperial History*, Gordon Martel, ed. London, 1986.

Carter, Gwendolen. *The British Commonwealth and International Security: The Role of the Dominions, 1919–1939.* Toronto, 1947.

Cheng, Seymour. *Schemes for the Federation of the British Empire.* New York, 1931.

Chevrier, Bernard. *Lionel Chevrier, Un Homme de Combat.* Montreal, 1997.

Chisholm, Anne, and Michael Davie. *Beaverbrook.* London, 1992.

Clark, Lovell C. "The Conservative Party in the 1890s," *Canadian Historical Association Report*, 1961.

Coates, Colin, ed. *Imperial Canada, 1867–1917.* Edinburgh, 1997.

Colvin, James A. "Sir Wilfrid Laurier and the British Preferential Tariff System," *Canadian Historical Association Report*, 1955.

Constantine, Stephen. "Anglo-Canadian Relations, the Empire Marketing Board and Canadian National Autonomy Between the Wars," *Journal of Imperial and Commonwealth History*, XXI, no. 2, May 1993.

Cook, G.I. "Sir Robert Borden, Lloyd George, and British Military Policy, 1917–1918," *Historical Journal*, 1971.

Cook, Ramsay. "A Canadian Account of the 1926 Imperial Conference," *Journal of Commonwealth Political Studies*, III, March 1965.

Cooke, A.C. "Empire Unity and Colonial Nationalism: 1884–1911," *Canadian Historical Review Report*, 1939.

Cooper, Andrew Fenton, ed. *Canadian Culture: International Dimensions.* Waterloo and Toronto, 1985.

Corbett, P.E. and H.A. Smith. *Canada and World Politics*. London, 1928.

Creighton, D.G. "The Victorians and the Empire," *Canadian Historical Review*, XIX, June 1938.

Creighton, Donald. *John A. Macdonald: The Old Chieftain*. Toronto, 1955.

– *Canada's First Century*. Toronto, 1970.

– *The Forked Road, Canada 1939–1957*. Toronto, 1976.

Cross, M., ed. *Politics By Other Means*. Toronto, 1972.

Crowley, Terry. *Marriage of Minds: Isobel and Oscar Skelton Reinventing Canada*. Toronto, 2003.

Cruise, David, and Alison Griffiths. *Lords of the Line*. Toronto, 1988.

Cuff, Robert, and J.L. Granatstein. "The Rise and Fall of Canadian-American Free Trade, 1947–8," *Canadian Historical Review*, LVIII, 1977.

Currie, A.W. *The Grand Trunk Railway of Canada*. Toronto, 1957.

Dawson, R. MacGregor. *The Development of Dominion Status 1900–1936*. London, 1937.

– *William Lyon Mackenzie King, A Political Biography*, vol. I: 1874–1923. Toronto, 1958.

Denison, George T. *The Struggle for Imperial Unity*. London, 1909.

den Otter, A.A. *Civilizing the West; The Galts and the Development of Western Canada*. Edmonton, 1982.

Dewey, A. Gordon. *The Dominions and Diplomacy: The Canadian Contribution*. 2 vols. London, 1929.

Diefenbaker, John. *One Canada*. 3 vols. Toronto, 1975–1977.

Dilks, David. *Britain and Canada in the Age of Mackenzie King*. London, 1978.

– *A View on Two Squares: John Holmes in London and Moscow, 1944–1948*. London, 1993.

– *Great Britain, the Commonwealth and the Wider World*. Hull, 1998.

– *The Great Dominion: Winston Churchill in Canada, 1900–1954*. Toronto, 2005.

Douglas, W.A.B. *The Creation of a National Air Force*. Toronto, 1986.

Drummond, Ian M. *British Economic Policy and the Empire, 1919–1939*. London, 1972.

– *Imperial Economic Policy*. London, 1974.

Drummond, Ian M., and Norman Hillmer, *Negotiating Free Trade: The United Kingdom, The United States, and Canada and the Trade Agreements of 1938*. Waterloo (Canada), 1989.

Durant, Vincent. *War Horse of Cumberland: The Life and Times of Sir Charles Tupper*. Hantsport, 1985.

Eayrs, James. "The Round Table Movement in Canada, 1909–1920," *Canadian Historical Review*, March 1957.

– *Northern Approaches*. Toronto, 1961.

– *The Commonwealth and Suez*. Oxford, 1964.

– *In Defence of Canada*. vol. I: *From the Great War to the Great Depression*. Toronto, 1964; vol. II: *Appeasement and Rearmament*; vol. III: *Growing up Allied*. Toronto, 1965.

Egremont, Max. *Balfour*. London, 1980.

Elliott, Shirley. *Nova Scotia in London*. London, 1988.

English, John. *Borden: His Life and World*. Toronto, 1977.

– *Shadow of Heaven: The Life of Lester Pearson, 1897–1948*. Toronto, 1989; and *The Worldly Years, 1949–1972*. Toronto, 1992.

English, John, and J.O. Stubbs, eds. *Mackenzie King: Widening the Debate*. Toronto, 1977.

English, John, and Robert Bothwell. "Canadian Trade Policy in the Age of British Decline and American Predominance," *Canadian Review of American Studies*, VIII, Spring 1977.

Esbery, Joy E. *Knight of the Holy Spirit: A Study of William Lyon Mackenzie King*. Toronto, 1980.

Ewart, John S. *The Kingdom of Canada, Imperial Federation, the Colonial Conferences, the Alaska Boundary and Other Essays*. Toronto, 1908.

Farr, D.M.L. "Sir John Rose and Imperial Relations: An Episode in Gladstone's First Administration," *Canadian Historical Review*, March 1952.

Farr, David. *The Colonial Office and Canada, 1867–1887*. Toronto, 1955.

Ferguson, Barry. *Remaking Liberalism*. Montreal, 1993.

Finlay, Karen A. *The Force of Culture: Mr. Massey and Canadian Sovereignty*. Toronto, 2004.

Fitzmaurice, E. *Life of Lord Granville*. London, 1905.

French, Doris. *Ishbel and the Empire*. Toronto, 1988.

Gallagher, J.A. *The Decline, Revival and Fall of the British Empire*. Cambridge, 1982.

Garner, J. *The Commonwealth Office, 1925–1968*. London, 1978.

Garvin, J.L., and Julian Amery. *Life of Chamberlain*, 6 vols. London, 1933–1969.

Gates, Paul W. "Official Encouragement to Immigration by the Province of Canada," *Canadian Historical Review*, March 1934.

Gilbert, Heather. *Awakening Continent: The Life of Lord Mount Stephen*. 2 vols. Aberdeen, 1965.

Girard, Camil. *Questions d'empire; Le Times de Londres, 1908–1922*. Québec, 1988.

Glazebrook, George. *A History of Transportation in Canada*. Toronto, 1938.

– *A History of Canadian External Relations*. 2 vols. Toronto, 1966.

Good, M.T. *Chevrier*. Montreal, 1987.

Gordon, D.C. *The Dominion Partnership in Imperial Defense, 1870–1914*. Toronto, 1967.

Graham, Roger. *Arthur Meighen: A Biography*. 3 vols. Toronto, 1960–5.

Granatstein, J.L. *Canada's War: The Politics of the Mackenzie King Government, 1939–1945*. Toronto, 1975.

– *A Man of Influence: Norman A. Robertson and Canadian Statecraft, 1929–1968*. Toronto, 1981.

– *The Ottawa Men: The Civil Service Mandarins, 1935–1957*. Toronto, 1982.

– *Canada, 1957–1967, The Years of Uncertainty and Innovation*. Toronto, 1986.

– *How Britain's Weakness Forced Canada into the Arms of the United States*. Toronto, 1989.

– *The Generals.* Toronto, 1993.

Granatstein, J., and Robert Bothwell. "A National Self-evident Duty: Canadian Foreign Policy 1936–1938," *Journal of Imperial and Commonwealth History,* III, no. 2, January 1975.

Granatstein, J.L., and Robert Bothwell. *Pirouette: Pierre Trudeau and Canadian Foreign Policy.* Toronto, 1990.

Hall, D.J. *Clifford Sifton.* Vancouver, 1981.

– "Clifford Sifton: Immigration and Settlement Policy," in *The Settlement of the West.* H. Palmer, ed. Calgary, 1977.

Hall, H. Duncan. *Commonwealth.* London, 1971.

Hammond, M.O. *Confederation and Its Leaders.* Toronto, 1927.

Hayes, Frank. "The Evolution of Canada's Commonwealth Relations, 1945–1968," Ph.D. thesis, University of Toronto, 1979.

Heath, Edward. *The Course of My Life.* London, 1998.

Henderson, John. *Howard Ferguson.* Toronto, 1930.

Hill, O. Mary. *Canada's Salesman to the World.* Montreal, 1977.

Hilliker, John F. "No Bread at the Peace Table: Canada and the European Settlement, 1943–7," *Canadian Historical Review,* September 1980.

– "The British Columbia Franchise and Canadian Relations with India in Wartime, 1939–1945," *BC Studies,* Summer 1980.

– "The Politicians and the Pearsonalities: the Diefenbaker Government and the Conduct of Canadian External Relations," *Canadian Historical Association Papers,* 1984.

– *Canada's Department of External Affairs.* vol. I, *The Early Years, 1909–1946.* Montreal, 1990; vol. II, John Hilliker and Donald Barry, *Coming of Age, 1946–1968.* Montreal, 1995.

Hillmer, G.N. "British-Canadian Relations, 1926–1937," Ph.D. thesis, Cambridge University, 1975.

Hillmer, Norman. "The Anglo-Canadian Neurosis: The Case of O.D. Skelton," in Peyton Lyon, ed. *Britain and Canada: Survey of a Changing Relationship.* London, 1976.

– *Britain and Canada in the Age of Mackenzie King.* London, 1978.

– "A British High Commissioner for Canada, 1927–8," *Journal of Imperial and Commonwealth History,* I, no. 3, May 1979.

– "O.D. Skelton and the North American Mind," *International Journal,* Winter 2004–5.

Hillmer, Norman, and J.L. Granatstein. *Empire to Umpire.* Toronto, 1994.

Holland, R.F. *Britain and the Commonwealth Alliance, 1918–1939.* London, 1981.

Holmes, John. "The Anglo-Canadian Neurosis: A Mood of Exasperation," *The Round Table,* July 1966.

– *The Better Part of Valour.* Toronto, 1970.

– *The Shaping of Peace, 1943–1957.* 2 vols. Toronto, 1979 and 1982.

– *Life with Uncle.* Toronto, 1981.

Hutchison, John. *Sir Alexander Tilloch Galt.* Toronto, 1930.

Ignatieff, George. *The Making of a Peacemonger.* Toronto, 1985.

Inglis, Alex. "Loring Christie and the Imperial Idea, 1935–1939," *Journal of Canadian Studies*, May 1972.

Innes, H.A. *A History of the Canadian Pacific Railway.* London, 1923.

James, R. Warren. *Wartime Economic Co-operation.* Toronto, 1949.

Jay, Richard. *Chamberlain.* Oxford, 1981.

Jenkins, Roy. *The Chancellors.* London, 1998.

– *Churchill.* London, 2001.

Johnson, F.A. *Defence by Committee: The British Committee of Imperial Defence.* London, 1960.

Judd, Denis. *Radical Joe: A Life of Joseph Chamberlain.* Cardiff, 1993.

– *Empire.* London, 1996.

Kendle, J.E. *The Colonial and Imperial Conferences 1887–1911.* London, 1967.

– *The Round Table Movement and Imperial Union.* Toronto, 1975.

Keenlyside, Hugh. *Memoirs.* 2 vols. Toronto, 1982.

Knapland, P. *Gladstone and Britain's Imperial Policy.* London, 1927.

Lamb, W. Kaye. *History of the Canadian Pacific Railway Company.* Toronto, 1977.

Langley, R.S. "Cartier and McDougall, Canadian Emissaries to London, 1868–1869," *Canadian Historical Review*, March 1945.

LePan, Douglas. "Portrait of Norman Robertson," *International Perspectives*, July/August 1978.

– *Bright Glass of Memory.* Toronto, 1979.

Lloyd, Lorna. "'What's in a Name': The Curious Tale of the Office of the High Commissioner," *Diplomacy and Statecraft*, XI, no. 1, March 2000.

– "Family Diplomacy: Canada and the Commonwealth Office of High Commissioner," *International Journal*, Winter 2004–5.

Lloyd George, David. *War Memoirs.* 6 vols. London, 1933–1936.

Long, Morden H. "Sir John Rose and the Informal Beginnings of the Canadian High Commissionership," *Canadian Historical Review*, March 1931.

Longley, J.W. *Sir Charles Tupper.* Toronto, 1916.

Lyon, Peter, ed. *Britain and Canada; Survey of a Changing Relationship.* London, 1976.

MacFarlane, John. *Ernest Lapointe and Quebec's Influence on Canadian Foreign Policy.* Toronto, 1999.

MacIntosh, A.W. "The Career of Sir Charles Tupper in Canada, 1864–1900," Ph.D. thesis, University of Toronto, 1960.

Mackenzie, Hector. "The Path to Temptation: the Negotiation of Canada's Reconstruction Loan to Britain in 1946," *Canadian Historical Association Papers*, 1982.

– "An Old Dominion and the New Commonwealth: Canadian Policy on the Question of India's Membership," *The Journal of Imperial and Commonwealth History*, XXVII, no. 3, September 1999.

– "Sinews of War and Peace: The Politics of Economic Aid to Britain, 1939–1945," *International Journal*, Autumn 1999.

Macleod, Iain. *Neville Chamberlain*. London, 1961.

MacMillan, Margaret. *Peacemakers*. London, 2001.

MacNutt, W. Stewart. *Days of Lorne*. Fredericton, 1955.

Marder, Arthur. *From the Dreadnought to Scapa Flow: The Royal Navy in the Fisher Era, 1904–1919*. Oxford, 1967.

Marquand, David. *Ramsay MacDonald*. London, 1977.

Martin, Chester, ed. *Canada in Peace and War*. Toronto, 1941.

Martin, G. "Mackenzie King, The Medium and the Messages," *British Journal of Canadian Studies*, 1989.

Massey, Vincent. *What's Past Is Prologue: The Memoirs of Vincent Massey*. Toronto, 1963.

Massie, Robert K. *Dreadnought: Britain, Germany and the Coming of the Great War*. London, 1992.

Masters, D.C. "A.T. Galt and Canadian Fiscal Autonomy," *Canadian Historical Review*, September 1934.

– "Financing the Canadian Pacific Railway, 1880–1885," *Canadian Historical Review*, December 1943.

Mcdonald, Donna. *Lord Strathcona: A Biography of Donald Alexander Smith*. Toronto, 1996.

McElrea, Patrick. "The Office of the High Commissioner: Canada's Public Links to Gentlemanly Capitalism in the City of London, 1869–1885," MA thesis, McGill University, 1997.

McKenzie, David, ed. *Canada and the First World War*. Toronto, 2004.

McKercher, B.J.C, and L. Aronsen, eds. *The North Atlantic Triangle in a Changing World: Anglo-American-Canadian Relations, 1906–1956*. Toronto, 1996.

McLeod, R.J.M. "The Evolving Role of the Commonwealth in Canadian Foreign Policy, 1956–1965," Ph.D. thesis, University of London, 1994.

McNaughton, John. *Lord Strathcona*. Oxford, 1926.

Middlemas, Keith, and John Barnes. *Baldwin*. London, 1969.

Miller, J.D.B. *Britain and the Old Dominions*. Baltimore, 1966.

Moir, John S., ed. *Character and Circumstance*. Toronto, 1970.

Morton, Desmond. *Ministers and Generals: Politics and the Canadian Militia, 1868–1904*. Toronto, 1970.

– *A Peculiar Kind of Politics*. Toronto, 1982.

Morison, J.L. *British Supremacy and Canadian Self-Government, 1839–1854*. Glasgow, 1919.

Morrison, A.E. "R.B. Bennett and the Imperial Preference Trade Agreements, 1932," MA thesis, University of New Brunswick, 1966.

Muirhead, Bruce. "The Politics of Food and the Disintegration of the Anglo-Canadian Trade Relationship, 1947–1948," *Journal of the Canadian Historical Association*, 1991.

– "Canada and the Collective Approach to Free Trade and Payments, 1952–1957," *Journal of Imperial and Commonwealth History*, XX, no. 1, January 1992.

– "The Development of Canada's Foreign Economic Policy in the 1960s: The Case of the European Union," *Canadian Historical Review*, LXXXII, December 2001.

Muirhead, B.W. *The Development of Postwar Canadian Trade Policy: The Failure of the Anglo-European Option*. Montreal, 1992.

Neatby, Blair. "Laurier and Imperialism," *Canadian Historical Association Report*, 1955.

– *William Lyon Mackenzie King: The Lonely Heights*, vol. II: 1924–32. Toronto, 1963.

– *William Lyon Mackenzie King: The Prism of Unity*, vol III: 1932–39. Toronto, 1976.

Nicholson, G.W.L. *Canadian Expeditionary Force*, Ottawa, 1962.

Oliver, Peter. *Public and Private Persons*. Toronto, 1975.

– *G. Howard Ferguson: Ontario Tory*. Toronto, 1977.

Page, Robert. "The Canadian Response to the Imperial Idea during the Boer War Years," *Journal of Canadian Studies*, February 1970.

– "Tupper's Last Hurrah: The Years as Opposition Leader, 1896–1900," in Carl Berger and Ramsay Cook, eds., *The West and the Nation: Essays in Honour of W.L. Morton*. Toronto, 1976.

Palmer, G.E.H. *Consultation and Co-operation in the British Commonwealth*. London, 1934.

Pearson, L.B. *Words and Occasions*. Toronto, 1970.

– *Mike: The Memoirs of the Rt. Hon. Lester B. Pearson*. 3 vols. Toronto, 1972, 1973 and 1975.

Penlington, Norman. "Canada's Entry into the Boer War," MA thesis, University of Toronto, 1937.

– "General Hutton and the Problem of Military Imperialism in Canada, 1898–1900," *Canadian Historical Review*, June 1943.

– *Canada and Imperialism, 1896–1899*. Toronto, 1965.

Penson, Lillian. "The Origin of the Crown Agency Office," *English Historical Review*, XL, April 1925.

Pickersgill, J.W. *The Mackenzie King Record*, vol. I: 1939–44. Toronto, 1966.

Pickersgill, J.W., and D.F. Forester. *The Mackenzie King Record*. vols. II: 1944–45; III: 1945–46; IV: 1947–48. Toronto, 1968 and 1970.

Pope, Joseph. *Memoirs of the Rt. Hon. Sir John Alexander Macdonald*. London, 1894.

– *Correspondence of the Rt. Hon. Sir John Alexander Macdonald*. Toronto, 1921.

Porritt, Edward. *The Fiscal and Diplomatic Freedom of the British Overseas Dominions*. Oxford, 1922.

Porter, Bernard. *The Absent-Minded Imperialist: What the British Really Thought about Empire*. Oxford, 2004.

Preston, Richard. "Canadian Resident Representation in London; Responsible Government to High Commission," Ph.D. thesis, University of Toronto, 1965.

– *Canada and "Imperial Defence": A Study of the Origins of the British Commonwealth's Defence Organization, 1867–1919*. Toronto, 1967.

Preston, W.T.R. *The Life and Times of Lord Strathcona*. London, 1914.

– *My Generation of Politics and Politicians*. Toronto, 1927.

Rea, J.E. *T.A. Crerar: A Political Life*. Montreal, 1997.

Reece, David. *A Rich Broth: Memoirs of a Canadian Diplomat*. Ottawa, 1993.

Reid, Escott. *Time of Fear and Hope*. Toronto, 1977.

– *Radical Mandarin*. Toronto, 1989.

Ritchie, Charles. *Siren Years*. Toronto, 1974.

– *Diplomatic Passport*. Toronto, 1981.

– *Storm Signals*. Toronto, 1983.

Roberts, A. *Salisbury: Victorian Titan*. London, 1999.

Roberts, Leslie. *So This Is Ottawa*. Toronto, 1933.

Robertson, Gordon. *Memoirs of a Very Civil Servant: Mackenzie King to Pierre Trudeau*. Toronto, 2000.

Robinson, Basil. *Diefenbaker's World*. Toronto, 1989.

Robinson, J.M. "A Canadian at the Court of Queen Victoria: The High Commissionership, 1880–1895," MA thesis, University of Calgary, 1967.

Rooth, Tim. "Britain's Other Dollar Problem: Economic Relations with Canada," *Journal of Imperial and Commonwealth History*, 27, no. 1, January 1999.

Roskill, Stephen. *Naval Policy between the Wars*. 2 vols. London, 1968 and 1976.

Roy, Patricia E. *A White Man's Province: British Columbia, Politicians and Chinese and Japanese Immigrants, 1858–1914*. Vancouver, 1989.

– *The Oriental Question: Consolidating a White Man's Province, 1914–1941*. Vancouver, 2003.

Sack, B.G. *History of the Jews in Canada*. Montreal, 1965.

Sarty, Roger. "Canadian Maritime Defence, 1892–1914," *Canadian Historical Review*, LXXI, December 1990.

Saunders, E.M., ed. *The Life and Letters of the Rt. Hon. Sir Charles Tupper*. 2 vols. London, 1916.

Shields, R.A. "Imperial Reaction to the Fielding Tariff of 1897," *Canadian Journal of Economy and Political Science*, November 1965.

– "The Canadian Treaty Negotiations with France: A Study in Imperial Relations, 1878–1883," *Bulletin of the Institute of Historical Research*, November 1967.

– "Sir Charles Tupper and the Franco-Canadian Treaty of 1895: A Study of Imperial Relations," *Canadian Historical Review*, 1968.

Shortt, G.E. "The House of Barings and Canada," *Queen's Quarterly*, August 1930.

Skelton, O.D. *The Life and Times of Sir Alexander Tilloch Galt*. Toronto, 1920.

– *The Railway Builders*. Toronto, 1920.

– *Life and Letters of Sir Wilfrid Laurier*. 2 vols. Toronto, 1921.

Skilling, H. Gordon. *Canadian Representation Abroad; From Agency to Embassy*. Toronto, 1945.

Sleight, Robert. *Vanier: Soldier, Diplomat and Governor General*. Toronto, 1970.

Smith, Arnold. *Stitches in Time: The Commonwealth in World Politics*. Toronto, 1981.

Smith, Dennis. *Rogue Tory: The Life and Legend of John G. Diefenbaker*. Toronto, 1995.

Smith, W.I. "The Origins and Early Development of the Canadian High Commission, 1869–1896," Ph.D. thesis, University of Minnesota, 1968.

Stacey, C.P. "John A. Macdonald on Raising Troops in Canada for Imperial Service, 1885," *Canadian Historical Review*, June 1957.

– *Canada and the British Army, 1846–1921.* Toronto, 1963.

– *A Very Double Life.* Toronto, 1969.

– "From Meighen to King: The Reversal of Canadian External Policies, 1921–1923," *Transactions of the Royal Society of Canada*, 1969.

– *Arms, Men, and Governments.* Ottawa, 1970.

– "Laurier, King and External Affairs," in John Moir, ed. *Character and Circumstance.* Toronto, 1970.

– *Mackenzie King and the Atlantic Triangle.* Toronto, 1976.

– *Canada and the Age of Conflict.* 2 vols. Toronto, 1977 and 1981.

– "The Divine Mission: Mackenzie King and Hitler," *Canadian Historical Review*, December 1980.

– "Canadian Leaders in the Second World War," *Canadian Historical Review*, LXVI, 1985.

Stevens, G.R. *Canadian National Railway.* 2 vols. Toronto, 1960 and 1962.

Stevens, Paul, and J.T. Saywell. *Lord Minto's Canadian Papers*: A *Selection of the Public and Private Papers of the Fourth Earl of Minto, 1898–1904.* Toronto, 1981 and 1983.

Stevenson, Frances. *Lloyd George: A Diary.* London, 1965.

Stewart, Alice. "Sir John A. Macdonald and the Imperial Defence Commission of 1879," *Canadian Historical Review*, June 1954.

Stewart, A.R. "Canadian-West Indian Union, 1884–1885," *Canadian Historical Review*, 1950.

– "Sir John A. Macdonald and the Imperial Defence Committee of 1879," *Canadian Historical Review*, 1954.

Stursburg, Peter. *Diefenbaker: Leadership Gained, 1956–62.* Toronto, 1975.

Swan, Kenneth. "Reconsidering Canada's War Effort: Mackenzie King, Canada, The North Atlantic Triangle and The Second World War," M.Sc. thesis, University of Edinburgh, 2002.

Swettenham, John. *McNaughton.* 3 vols. Toronto, 1968–70.

Swinton, Earl of. *Sixty Years of Power.* London, 1966.

Tansill, C.C. *Canadian-American Relations, 1875–1911.* Toronto, 1943.

Taylor, A.J.P. *Beaverbrook.* London, 1972.

Tennyson, B.D., ed. *Canada and the Commonwealth Caribbean.* Lanham (USA), 1988.

Thompson, J.H., with Allen Sager. *Canada 1922–1939, Decades of Discord.* Toronto, 1985.

Thornton, A.P. *The Imperial Idea and its Enemies.* London, 1959.

Timothy, H.B. *The Galts: A Canadian Odyssey.* 2 vols. Toronto, 1977.

Troop, William. H. "Canada and the Empire: A Study of Canadian Attitudes to the Empire and Imperial Relations since 1867," Ph.D. thesis, University of Toronto, 1933.

Trudeau, Pierre Elliott. *Conversations with Canadians.* Toronto, 1972.

Tupper, Charles. *Recollections of Sixty Years in Canada.* London, 1914.

– *Political Reminiscences: Supplement to my Life.* ed. W.A. Harkin, London, 1914.

Tupper, Charles Hibbert. *Supplement to the Life and Letters of the Rt. Hon. Sir Charles Tupper.* Toronto, 1926.

Turner, Wesley B. "Colonial Self-Government and the Colonial Office: Changing Concepts of Permanent Canadian Resident Representation in London," Ph.D. thesis, Duke University, 1970.

Tyler, J.E. *The Struggle for Imperial Unity, 1868–1895.* London, 1938.

Vaughan, Walter. *The Life and Work of Sir William Van Horne.* Toronto, 1926.

Venice, D.M.R. "The Acting Overseas Sub-Militia Council and the Resignation of Sir Sam Hughes," *Canadian Historical Review,* 1950.

Vincent, John, ed. *The Diaries of Edward Henry Stanley, Fifteenth Earl of Derby.* Oxford, 2004.

Wade, F.C. "High Commissioners and Agents General," *The Empire Review,* October–November 1919.

Waite, P.B. *Canada 1874–1896, Arduous Destiny.* Toronto, 1971.

– *The Man from Halifax: Sir John Thompson, Prime Minister.* Toronto, 1985.

Walden, David. *The Chanak Affair.* London, 1969.

Wallace, W. Stewart. *The Memoirs of the Rt. Hon. Sir George Foster.* Toronto, 1933.

Wallace, W.S. "The First Canadian Agent in London," *Canadian Magazine,* April 1919.

Whitaker, George. *The Government Party: Organizing and Financing the Liberal Party of Canada, 1930–1958.* Toronto, 1977.

Wigley, P.E. *Canada and the Transition to Commonwealth: British-Canadian Relations, 1917–1926.* Cambridge, 1977.

Wigley, Philip, and Norman Hillmer. "Defining the First British Commonwealth: The Hankey Memoranda on the 1926 Imperial Conference," *Journal of Imperial and Commonwealth History,* VIII, October 1979.

Wilde, Richard. "Joseph Chamberlain's Proposal of an Imperial Conference in March, 1900," *Canadian Historical Review,* September 1956.

Wilgress, Dana. *Memoirs.* Toronto, 1967.

Williams, R. *Defending the Empire.* London, 1991.

Willison, J.S. *Sir Wilfrid Laurier and the Liberal Party, A Political History.* 2 vols. Toronto, 1903.

Wilkes, George, ed. *Britain's Failure to Enter the European Community, 1961–1963.* London, 1977.

Willson, Beckles. *Lord Strathcona, The Story of His Life.* London, 1902.

– *The Life of Lord Strathcona and Mount Royal.* 2 vols. Cambridge, 1915.

– *From Quebec to Piccadilly and Some Other Places.* London, 1929.

Wilson, Harold A. *The Imperial Policy of Sir Robert Borden.* Gainesville, 1966.

Wilson, John. *C.B.* London, 1973.

Winks, Robin W. *Canadian-West Indian Union: A Forty Year Minuet.* London, 1968.

Wise, S.F. *Canadian Airmen and the First World War.* Toronto, 1980.

Woodcock, George. *Who Killed the British Empire? An Inquest.* London, 1974.

Young, Hugo. *This Blessed Plot.* London, 1998.

INDEX